PROCEEDINGS OF THE THIRTY-NINTH COLLOQUIUM ON THE LAW OF OUTER SPACE

INTERNATIONAL INSTITUTE OF SPACE LAW
OF THE
INTERNATIONAL ASTRONAUTICAL FEDERATION

OCTOBER 7-11, 1996
Beijing, China

Published and Distributed by
AMERICAN INSTITUTE OF AERONAUTICS AND ASTRONAUTICS
Alexander Bell Drive, Suite 500
Reston, VA 20191

ISBN 1-56347-251-1

Printed in the U.S.A.

IISL BOARD OF DIRECTORS 1996-1997

Members of the Board

Honorary Directors

INTRODUCTION

by

Nandasiri Jasentuliyana
President, IISL

I am deeply honoured to have been elected President of the International Institute of Space Law (IISL) for a second three-year term. I am touched by this show of confidence and trust. I am privileged to have been chosen to carry the torch of the IISL, the foremost international non-governmental organization in the field of space law, to the beginning of the next millennium.

When I took over the reins of the IISL three years ago, I set for myself two important goals to achieve, during my tenure as the IISL President. The first was to forge a closer relationship between the Institute and the UN COPUOS, in particular its Legal Subcommittee. I am pleased to say that this has been more than successfully accomplished. The IISL has been engaging in a more intensive and broader cooperative relationship with COPUOS. The work of the Institute being highly complementary to that of the United Nations, the IISL has been making a unique contribution to the discussions of both COPUOS and its Legal Subcommittee. For example:

(i) the IISL has submitted legal and policy statements to these bodies, through the International Astronautical Federation, the parent body of the Institute. These statements, which provide timely information on the latest developments in space law and policy, and propose future courses of action in the field of international space law-making, have been warmly welcomed by the delegations attending the UN meetings;

(ii) the Institute began to make a valuable contribution to one of the most important annual review publications of the Committee, "Highlights in Space", in a section describing the space law issues that have arisen during the preceding year;

(iii) the IISL now organizes, on an annual basis, Legal Symposia during the meetings of the COPUOS Legal Subcommittee. Recent symposia have examined commercial and environmental aspects of space law. During the 1996 session of the Legal Subcommittee, the Institute organized a symposium on "Protection of the Space Environment", a topic of particular interest to the international space community. The IISL symposia generally discuss contemporary or future space law issues, thus identifying potential regulatory areas that the Committee may wish to consider. Through these symposia, the IISL also plays a leading role in bringing new space law issues to the forefront of international debate and discussion;

(iv) in 1995, the Institute played a prominent role in the Round Table discussion on space law that was organized at the United Nations Headquarters in New York, as part of the Congress on public international law, during the 50th Anniversary commemoration of the United Nations; and,

(v) in 1996, the Institute joined with the United Nations to bring fourth a publication, "Space Law: A Bibliography", a cumulative author/subject index of all the proceedings of the IISL colloquia up to 1994, thereby making a useful and timely contribution to the work of the Legal Subcommittee. I am happy to report that the bibliography is becoming a "best seller" not only in the United Nations, but among the international space law community, at large!

The second goal that I had set for my tenure as president was to expand the time available for substantive discussions of important issues at IISL colloquia and to expand and improve the interaction among colloquium participants. To my great satisfaction, this, too, has been a tremendous success. Now, each colloquium has a separate session for discussions, allowing participants to get more involved in the exchange of views, leading to a broader and more extensive examination of the issues under discussion. This format has also allowed sufficient time for authors to present their papers at the colloquium.

I am also pleased that during my first term as President, the IISL Statutes were revised and formally adopted by the Institute and the IAF, at Beijing, in October 1996. The new Statutes can be found in the Colloquium Proceedings.

During my second term, I will continue to further implement the important goals I set for myself previously. In addition, I intend to propose new policy guidelines for the IISL for the 21st Century. Space law is rapidly emerging from its cocoon of esotericism. In the next few decades space law will spread its mantle over those areas of human endeavour in space resulting from rapidly proliferating space technology and greater privatization and commercialization of space activities. Our organization would thus need dynamic new guidelines for it to keep up with the world driven by 21st century technologies and new and innovative means of communication.

Some elements that the Institute could consider, within its existing mandate, for a new millennium policy should include the following:

(i) Forging greater cooperation and co-ordination with other international law bodies such as the International Law Association and the International Law Commission. With the increasing commercialization of space activities, the Institute could take on a bigger and more productive role in formulating space law and policy. One area in which law is sure to make dramatic developments in the 21st century is the area of private international space law. This is where the Institute, with its wide-ranging international membership, with its expertise in all the legal systems of the world, could engage in looking at such emerging issues in space law;

(ii) Forming new specialized committees to concentrate on different areas of the newly developing space-law issues, and to coordinate the research work or studies being undertaken by the Institute;

(iii) Making greater use of the Internet, e-mail and other similar innovative technologies to put online publications such as the IISL Newsletter, the Space Law Bibliography and the History of the Institute, to help the Institute keep in regular contact with its membership, and to otherwise promote the goals and work of the Institute;

(iv) Putting into place a more vigorous membership enrollment drive, to attract more individuals and institutions. It is gratifying to note that more young lawyers are taking a greater interest in the activities of the Institute. At the Beijing Colloquium, for example, several rising international lawyers were admitted as new members of the Institute. Recent years have also seen a greater number of members of the younger generation presenting papers, and otherwise participating actively, at the Institute's annual colloquia;

(v) Expanding the Manfred Lachs Space Law Moot Court Competition, covering all continents. Presently, only law schools in North America and Europe are taking part in the competition. Schools from Asia are due to have their own Regional Round, to select a team for the finals in 1997. However, to truly reflect the international character of the competition and, indeed, the Institute, the Moot Court needs be conducted on a much larger scale and level, and include law schools from Africa, Central and Latin America and the Caribbean, as well;

(vi) The forging of even more closer cooperative links with academic space law & policy teaching institutions, for the greater dissemination and exchange of knowledge on international space law and policy. The IISL has long been cooperating closely with the European Centre for Space Law (ECSL). This cooperation ought to also include other institutions in Europe, the Americas, Africa, and the Asia-Pacific region. Being the leading space law Non-Governmental Organizations in the world, it is incumbent on us to bring together educational institutions, either formally or informally, which are interested in space law;

(vii) The need for closer links with space scientists and engineers, so that we space lawyers are kept better informed of the scientific and technical sides of space exploration. This will enable the IISL to engage in more productive space policy-making and promoting space law-making; and,

(viii) Forging greater ties with national and regional space agencies and the space private industry.

There is no doubt that space law has become one of the "hottest" topics for the future. This has been recognized by the International Court of Justice, itself. At its recent unique Colloquium, to Celebrate the 50th Anniversary of the Court, in April 1996, space law and environmental law were chosen as the two subjects for consideration to equip the court to deal with these developing areas of international law. The fact that space law was one of the topics chosen for examination, at the highest judicial level, on this momentous occasion, speaks volumes of the importance of space law.

In formative years of space law, soon after the birth of the space era, the Institute internationalized awareness and knowledge of space law. Now that a basic international space law framework is in place, the legal problems of the new century will allow us to expand the structure of space law. Space law will thus mature. For the Institute to keep up its good work, it needs a new policy for the new century. And that essentially is what I should like to work on during my second term as President.

I. Background

The International Institute of Space Law (IISL) was founded by the International Astronautical Federation (IAF) in 1960. The IISL replaced the Permanent Committee on Space Law which the IAF had created in 1958 under the chairmanship of Andrew G. Haley. Since 1958, the IISL has held annual colloquia on space law in many nations. The IISL presently has some 350 elected members who are distinguished for their contributions to space law development. While a component of the IAF, the IISL is authorized to function autonomously in accordance with its Statutes.

The purposes and objectives of the Institute include the cooperation with appropriate international organizations and national institutions in the field of space law, the carrying out of tasks for fostering the social science aspects of astronautics, space travel and exploration, the organization of meetings and colloquia on juridical and sociological aspects of the space sciences, and the publication of proceedings, reports and other publications.

The IISL recognizes that activities in the new dimension are both earth and space oriented, and that in both domains laws must be formulated for future developments. It is necessary to provide for the coordination and regulation of space activities by law in order to promote international cooperation and avoid conflicting claims and competition which would jeopardize beneficial uses for all mankind. Considering the multidisciplinary nature of problems and situations arising from the exploration and uses of outer space, the Institute plans programs which afford opportunities to analyse national and international legal matters in the total context of developing space science, technology and the social sciences. The IISL may play an important role in rallying distinguished specialists who interpret existing principles and rules of the law of outer space and prepare proposals for states to consider in concluding treaties or accepting other instruments of cooperation or otherwise contribute to the development of the law of outer space.

The financial resources of the Institute are derived from membership dues, research grants, remuneration received from the sale of its publications, and donations received from individuals, associations, institutions, foundations, and other organizations with interests in the development of law governing space activities. The headquarters of the International Institute of Space Law are located at 3-5 rue Mario Nikis, 75015 Paris, France.

II. IISL and the United Nations

IISL members have been appointed by the International Astronautical Federation as Official Observers to annual sessions of the United Nations (UN) Committee on the Peaceful Uses of Outer Space and its Legal Subcommittee.

The 1996 session of COPUOS' Legal Sub-committee and the Plenary session of COPUOS were both held in Vienna. E. Back Impallomeni, E. Fasan, and M. Vivod were appointed as official IAF observers for the COPUOS Legal Subcommittee meeting, which took place from 18 -28 March, whereas E. Back Impallomeni, E. Finch, S. Gorove, B. Smith, and Y. Hashimoto were appointed as official IAF observers for the Plenary COPUOS session which took place from 3-14 June. Only one pre-designated person serves as official spokesman for the IAF, at each session.

During annual sessions of the Legal Subcommittee, the IISL sponsors a program for the COPUOS delegates and staff on non-agenda space legal issues. On 18 March 1996, the IISL organized a symposium in cooperation with the European Centre for Space Law, which also co-hosted the reception, on the topic "Protection of the Space Environment" for the delegates attending the Legal Subcommittee session; the speakers were Dr Perek, Dr Lafferranderie, Mr F. Bryan Cheuvront III of Motorola and Dr Kopal. The Coordinator of the 1996 program was Dr. E. Fasan. Next year, the symposium will celebrate the 30th anniversary of the Outer Space Treaty.

III. 39th IISL Colloquium

The 39th Colloquium on the Law of Outer Space was held in Beijing, China, during the 47th Congress of the International Astronautical Federation (October 7-12, 1996). The Colloquium was attended by some 50 participants who attended the four sessions whose results are published in this volume:

- Session 1: The Legal Status of Property Rights on the Moon and Other Celestial Bodies.

Chairman: Dr. He Qizhi (China).

Rapporteurs: A. Markkanen and S. Heikkilä (Finland)

- Session 2: Cases and Methods of Dispute Settlement in Space Law.

Chairman: Prof. K.-H. Böckstiegel (Germany).

Rapporteur: D. Crowther (France)

- Session 3: Legal Aspects of Sharing Benefits from the Conduct of Space Activities.

Chairman: Dr. S. Doyle (USA).

Rapporteurs: B. Coebergh and J. Richer (USA)

- Session 4: Other Legal Subjects.

Co-Chairmen: Prof. T. Kosuge (Japan), Dr. E. Fasan (Austria).

Rapporteurs: Y. Hashimoto (Japan) and Abu Bakar Munir (Malaysia).

- A Scientific-Legal round table was organized in cooperation with the IAA on "The future of space telecommunications".

The 5th Manfred Lachs Space Law Moot Court Competition was held at the University of Beijing on 10 October 1996. The case concerned Liability for commercial space endeavours (Parlivia vs. Californium et al.), written by Pamela Meredith. The University of Helsinki (Finland) and the University of Wyoming (USA) competed before a bench composed of Judge Chr. Weeramantry, Judge G. Herczegh, and Judge V. Vereshchetin of the International Court of Justice. The team of the University of Helsinki won the competition. A report on the competition, the case and the winning briefs are published in this volume. The competition will be held for the sixth time in Turin.

IV. Awards

An IISL Certificate was awarded in Beijing to Prof. F. Lyall of the University of Aberdeen, Scotland UK, "in recognition of his outstanding contributions to space law, as a distinguished lecturer and author on space law, and for his enthusiastic guidance and leadership provided to the Institute as a member of the Board of Directors".

A special certificate was presented to Dr. He Qizhi of the Department of Treaties and Law of the Chinese Foreign Ministry, "in recognition of his outstanding contributions to space law and policy, as an author and teacher, and diplomat representing the People's Republic of China to the United Nations Committee on the Peaceful Uses of Outer Space, and in special recognition of his invaluable services to the International Institute of Space Law, as a distinguished member of its Board of Directors".

V. 40th IISL Colloquium

The following sessions will be held during the 40th IISL Colloquium, which will take place in Turin, Italy, from 6-10 October 1997:

"Symposium celebrating the 30th Anniversary of the Outer Space Treaty of 1967"

- Session 1: Background and History of the Outer Space Treaty
Chairmen: N. Hosenball and A.A. Cocca

- Session 2: Concepts of Space Law and the Outer Space Treaty
Chairmen: E. Galloway and G. Catalano Sgrosso

- Session 3: Applications & Implementation of the Outer Space Treaty
Chairmen: S. Doyle and G. Lafferranderie

- Session 4: The Future Applications of the Outer Space Treaty
Chairmen: K.-H. Böckstiegel and A. Terekhov.

The Manfred Lachs Space Law Moot Court Competition, as well as a

Scientific/Legal Round table will also be held.

VI. 41st IISL Colloquium

The 41st Colloquium will be held in Melbourne, Australia, from 28 September-2 October 1998. The session topics for this colloquium will be decided in the Spring of 1997.

VII. Elections

Board of Directors

The result of the Board elections was as follows:

Re-election as Board Members:
Dr G. Catalano Sgrosso (Italy)
Dr N. Jasentuliyana (UN/Sri Lanka)
Dr. M. Komar Kantaatmadja (Indonesia)

Election as Board Members:
Dr R. Gonzalez (Amb. of Chile, Romania)
Dr L. Perek (Astronomical Inst., Academy of Sciences, Czech Rep.)
Dr Marcia Smith (Congressional Research Service, Library of Congress, USA)

Re-election as President:
Dr N. Jasentuliyana (UN/Sri Lanka)

Election as Honorary Directors:
Dr A. A. Cocca (Argentina)
Dr G. Gál (Hungary).

Secretariat

IISL Secretary Tanja Masson-Zwaan has moved to Singapore. She remains Secretary of the Board, but several tasks will be maintained at the Paris office, such as the mailing of newsletters, bank matters, etc.

The Paris address will remain the official mailing address of the IISL. Ms Daphné Crowther, the Secretary of ESA's European Centre of Space Law, was appointed by the Board to serve as Assistant to the Board. Her appointment was approved by ESA, and endorsed by the General Assembly.

New IISL Members Elected in April and October 1996:

- Max Planck Institute for Comparative Public Law & Int'l Law, Germany (Institutional Member)
- Ms Daphné Crowther, France (ECSL)
- Mr. Jean de Mourzitch, France
- Mr. E. Julian Hermida, Argentina
- Mr. Boakye Danquah Kofi Henaku, The Netherlands
- Mr. Kazuhiro Nakatani, Japan
- Prof. Rosa Maria Ramirez de Arellano y Haro, Mexico
- Mr. Rafaël Roelandt, The Netherlands
- Prof. Hiroshi Saitoh, Japan
- Dr. Hamid Shadkar, Iran
- Prof. Dr. Soon-Kil Hong, Korea
- Mr. Daniel Stein, France
- Prof. Hozumi Tanaka, Japan
- Mr. Walter Thiebaut, France (ESA)
- Dr. Volker Thiem, Germany
- Mr. Wan Normazlan Bin Che Jaafar, Malaysia

TABLE OF CONTENTS

LEGAL ASPECTS OF SHARING BENEFITS FROM THE CONDUCT OF SPACE ACTIVITIES

OTHER LEGAL MATTERS

ADDENDA

International Institute of Space Law
October 7–11, 1996
Beijing, China

IISL President Mr. Jasentuliyana introduces Moot Court Competition.

Moot Court Judges From the International Court of Justice. Left to Right: Judge G. Iterozegh, Judge Chr. Weeramantry, and Judge V. Vereshchetin.

Finnish team, winner of '96 Finals: Mr. Satu Heikkila and Ms. Anna Markkanen.

Session 1:
THE LEGAL STATUS OF PROPERTY RIGHTS ON THE MOON AND OTHER CELESTIAL BODIES

Chairman: H. Qizhi, China

DOMINIUM LUNAE, PROPRIETAS LUNAE.

Dr. Ernst Fasan
Honorary Director, Interntional Institute of Space Law
Neunkirchen, Austria

Abstract.

Legal History has shown an extensive debate about the question whether the Moon (and other celestial bodies) could be annexed, appropriated, occupied or not, according to *lex lata*.

The *res nullius* theory was of the opinion that the Moon, like an uninhabited newly discovered terrestrial island, could be occupied. This was the opinion of (in alphabetical order) *Bin Cheng, Fasan, Haley, Jenks, Kovalev and Cheprov, Mc. Dougal, Rauchhaupt, Verplaetse*,, etc. and of the *American Bar Association*.

Another position was that of the *res omnium* communis or *res extra commercium* theory. The Moon were free for the use of all, like the high seas. That was the opinion -among others- of *Cocca, Diederiks Verschoor, Keating, Menter, Meyer, Munro, Smirnoff, Tamm, Valladao*. Both schools requested a solution *de lege ferenda*,preferably within the framework of UN.

This solution was found on Dec. 20., 1961 by the unanimously accepted United Nations General Assembly (U.N.G.A.) Resolution 1721/16 which negated the appropriation of any celestial bodies, and requested their use for peaceful purposes only.

These principles were repeated in U.N.G.A. Resolution 1962/18. Finally the „Treaty on Principles Governing the Activities of States in the Exploration and Use of Outer Space including the Moon and other Celestial Bodies“ of Oct 10., 1967 once more repeated these notions. Now, the non appropriability of celestial bodies was treaty law, and the said Space Treaty was signed and ratified by most Nations, including the space faring ones. Consistently, the following manned and unmanned Moon landings brought about no claim of sovereignty.

For eight years, the UNCOPUOS and its Legal Subcommittee (LSC) discussed a draft text for specific regulations regarding the Moon and other celestial bodies. It resulted in the Agreement Governing the Activities of States on the Moon and other Celestial Bodies of Dec. 18.,1979.

This agreement however, was not ratified by more than 9 Nations, and the Space powers were reluctant to do so. Especially the „Common Heritage of Mankind“ principle made States cautious and reluctant.

On Dec 9., 1994 the U.N.G.A. decided not to take action regarding a revision of the Agreement, although the ten year period, foreseen for such a revision, had elapsed.

New deliberations and discussions are necessary in order to reconcile the interests of those States which reach the Moon and want to exploit its natural recources on the one hand, and the common interest of all terrestrial Nations in an appropriate sharing on the other hand. It would be detrimental for all mankind if due to an unclear legal situation the hiatus in expeditions to the Moon and other celestial bodies would be extended too long. It would be illogical to protect natural resources on the Moon more strictly than those on Earth. The Moon should remain free but ist natural resources should serve mankind.

1) A short Legal History

No one shall own the Moon!

This was the final result of a heated scientific debate in the late fifties and the sixties of our century.There were two -or rather three- legal theories about the juridical qualification of the Moon and other (accessible(1)) celestial bodies.

One was the *res nullius* theory, which said in short that the Moon and the planets- like uninhabited islands on Earth - were no mans land, and therefore could be occupied by any state whose expeditions landed there and hoisted that nations flag *animo occupandi*.

The other school was that of the *res omnium communis* theory. The Moon and other celestial bodies were free for the use of all nations, like the High Seas (or-by way of the Treaty-Antarctica). Therefore celestial bodies could not be occupied by any nation.

A third school gave the Moon a special legal status.

How, then, argued these schools? There were many scholars involved. To pay them tribute, a few quotations are in order, arbitrarily starting with the *res nullius* theory:

Haley, one of the creators of the Space Law Sciences, pointed out:
„*The Moon may be alighted upon by human beings within the next five or ten years, and if in the meantime we do not reach an understanding concerning the Moon, the nations achieving this great scientific acquisition may well, under the classical principles of terrestrial international law, claim sovereignty over the Moon.* "(2)

Bin Cheng said very clearly:
„*What of laws for the Moon and the planets? In law, extraterrestrial bodies are not greatly different from territories on the Earth which are not subject to the sovereignty of any State. Accordingly any State may annex such territories through effective occupation.* "*(3)*

Jenks thought about our question convincingly::
„*The ideal Arrangement would indeed appear to be that sovereignty over unoccupied territory in the moon or other planets or satellites should be regarded as vested exclusively in the United Nations. Failing such a solution, title to territory would have to be determined by applying the usual rules concerning discovery and occupation with any necessary adaptations, and problems analogous to those which arose during the partition of Africa, and even more closely analogous to those which have arisen more recently in the Antarctic, might well arise.* "*(4)*

Rauchhaupt pointed out:
„*On the safe (and permitted) arrival at the uninhabited (or inhabited) territory the crew can claim it according to public international law, and they may make use of its national treasures as far as they are accessible. Unsystematic destruction or spoils ought to be illegal.* "*(5)*

McDougal wrote:
„*Most claimants, while asserting their own rights to engage in such sharable activities, will probably acknowledge or at least not deny that others may do the same. Like many traditional claims in public and private international law, these claims will carry a promise of reciprocity, combined wherever possible with latent or expressed*

threats of retaliation or reprisal if the complementary promise is dishonored." (6)

Huss said sharply accentuated:
„*Columbus stuck the Spanish Flag into the sands of a West Indies beach - and we or the Russians would be perfectly within the concept of international law to claim possession of the Moon by shooting our national flag there by rocket.*"(7)

The American Bar Association in 1959 had very carefully and extensively investigated the Legal Problems of Outer Space, and had found as follows:
„*We may look to similar ventures in space. These should not be precluded by claims made on various grounds to 'sovereignty' over such bodies; nor should their acceptability depend on the recognition of any such claims.*"(8)

and had resolved:
„*That in the common interest of mankind outer space should be open to all for exploration, research, development, navigation, and other comparable non-aggressive uses, and that celestial bodies should not be subiect to exclusive appropriation.*"(9)

As for *myself*, I may quote the following sentence:
„*The accessible Celestial Bodies are <u>res nullius</u>, because they have not yet been acquired for the Whole of Humanity.*"(10)

Lipson and Katzbach of the *American Bar Foundation* had done an enormously valuable work by gathering numerous points of view regarding Space Law Problems for NASA. From this very basic investigation I may quote the following sentences:
„*Whoever gets to the moon first can claim it.*"

„*Traditional conditions of acquisition of new territory are. 1)discovery; 2) symbolic annexation; occupation sufficient to insure the status of the claimed territory, will probably be applied to the Moon.*"(11)

Cocca, who was often cited as being against the possible occupation of a Celestial Body, wrote, demonstrating existing International Law:
„*Neither can any terrestrial nation which might be able to carry out the successful occupation of the Moon extend its own sovereignty to cover it. It will have temporary supremacy in the sense that it will reap the benefits derived from the occupation of the Moon, but will not have sovereignty in the strictest sense.*"(12)

Kovalev and Cheprov expressed their points of view as follows:
„*Man's conquest of the celestial bodies may pose the question of state Possession. This question, evidently, will be decided by taking into account the known method of international law in acquiring territory, namely, the law of 'first discovery' and 'occupation'.*"(13)

For the other. the *res omnium communis* theory, we may quote the following opinions:

Sir Leslie Munro stated clearly:
„*that international law as we know it in respect to the acquisition of title by occupation and possession and settlement is not applicable to celestial bodies.*"(14)

The well known words of *Hammarskiold*, „*that outer space, and the celestial bodies therein, are not considered as capable of appropriation by any state.* may be recalled (15).

Rivoire was against the possibility of occupation, writing:
„*it would be an analogy to say that France and Switzerland lay claim to sovereignty over the depths of the ocean as their nationals were the first to penetrate to the bottom of the sea in bathyscaphes. This would be considered to be sheer nonsense, and it is no less ridiculous for a state to lay claim to sovereignty over a planet.*"(16).

Smirnoff stated:

„We think that the classic principle of sovereignty of the State over the space above its territory has no application to outer space."(17).

Meyer reported about the ILA Conference in August, 1960:
„Mrs. Diederiks Verschoor (Netherlands) repeated, that the Celestial Bodies are res omnium communes, incapable of any occupation."(18).

Meyer himself was one of the most famous scholars voting in the same direction. He wrote for instance:
„Celestial Bodies are for me not res nullius, but res omnium communes and therefore not occupable."(19)

A third group gave its opinion that the Moon has a special legal status:

Knauth said:
„The fact that the Moon does not pause permanently in the area of any one sovereign is not material. Like an aircraft in flight, it passes from the space area of one sovereignty to the space area of another. While it is in the space area of a certain sovereign. However temporarily it is subiect to that sovereign at least in the legal sense."(20)

And *Rinck* wrote, being of the same opinion:
„. . . that the sovereignty of any State reaches as far as the attractive power of the Earth. That gives broad consequences. The Moon moves within the gravitational field of the Earth. It passes through different spheres of sovereignty . . . it is . . .no res nullius, because it is within different zones of sovereignty."(21)

Cocca stated correctly, that the Moon is Earth's natural Satellite and that there is a relationship of dependence or of physical subjection. He continued:
„This fact must be taken into account by jurists in order to study its legal position under the aspect of servitudes, and not under the aspect of annexation of territory in Space."(22).

Analogously thought *Tamm:*
„The moon, though, is a natural satellite of Earth attracted to the Earth and its orbit. The moon, then, as a satellite, is within the sphere of influence of the Earth, therefore subject to its control, and, to that extent, a natural possession of Earth os an entirety."(23).

These opinions, practically of three groups of scholars, then, were the starting point for trying to find a solution. The United Nations took over that task (24).

2) Work and its progress within the UN.

On Oct 4., 1957 the then USSR started successfully the first terestrial artificial satellite, namely Sputnik 1. The Space Age had begun.

On Nov. 13. the same year, The USA and other Nations requested at the UN the creation of a new system of control in order to watch over the use of outer space for exclusively peaceful purposes(25). The USSR on the other hand requested on March 15., 1958 the prohibition of the miliotary uses of outer space(26).

On Dec. 13., 1958 the UN General assembly passed a - not unanimous - Resolution, to create an Ad Hoc Committeefor the Peaceful Uses of Outer Space which was requested, *inter alia* to study legal questions in connection with the exploration of outer space.Its report mentioned questions regarding the exploitation of the celestial bodies(27). But discussions continued and brought about the unanimous U.N.G.A. Resolution of Dec. 20., 1961(28), from which I may quote the following passages:

„Outer Space and the celestial bodies are free for the exploration and use for all States in conformity with international law

and are not subject to national appropriation"

With this a principle was generally accepted which solved the dispute: Celestial Bodies (the Moon was not mentioned specifically) should not be appropirated, not be occupied and were thus, *res omnium communes*.

The following U.N.G.A. Resolutions held this principle upright(29).

Quite consistently, the notion of unappropriability of celestial bodies was not sincerely questioned when the Treaty on Principles Governing the Activities of States in the Exploration and Use of Outer Space , Including the Moon and other Celestial Bodies (The Space Treaty) was discussed And its Art. II. thus reads as follows:

„Outer Space, including the moon and other celestial bodies, are not subject to national appropriation by claim of sovereignty, by means of use or occupation, or by any other means".

This was -though the most important one- not the only provision of the Space Treaty, dealing with topics of ownership. The freedom of exploration and use (not of exploitation),the peaceful purposes principle, the notion of cooperation, of noncontamination the authority of states to be maintained over their nongovernmental entities etc was agreed upon for the Moon and other celestial bodies as well as for Outer Space itself(30). Thus, when *Armstrong* and *Aldrin* landed on the Moon on July 20., 1969, they hoisted the US Flag but they did not claim sovereignty, nor was this done by the US government on this occasion or on the occasion of later manned landings.

On Nov. 29, 1971 the U.N.G.A. Resolution 2779(26) requested the UNCOPUOS and its Legal Subcommittee to work on a text for a treaty on the Moon and other Celestial Bodies. In the following discussions (31)the principle of non-appropriation was never questioned. And thus, Art 11(2) of the Agreement Governing the Activities of States on the Moon and other Celestial Bodies of Dec 18., 1979 reads:

„ The Moon is not subject to national appropriation by any claim of sovereignty, by means of use or occupation, or by any other means."

This principle had remained and is valid still although not many Nations have signed and less even ratified the Moon Agrement (32). It is one of those principles which are treaty law since the Space Treaty, and which are not questioned. And it is enforced by a new notion, namely that *„Neither the surface nor the subsurface of the Moon, nor any part thereof or natural resources in place , shall become property of any State, international intergovernmental or non-governmental organisation, national organisation or non-governmental entity or of any natural person*(33).

However, there is another legal notion to be found in the Moon Agreement which has given rise to many disputations. It is the sentence that the Moon and ist natural resources are the „ common heritage of mankind"(34), enforced by the request to establish an „international regime" for the exploitation of the Moons natural resources(35).

On the other hand, there seemed to be no doubt that State Parties should have the right to collect and remove samples of Moon material from our natural satellite, for scientific purposes and to use such materials in quantities necessary to support of their missions(36).

And the installation of stations etc. on or below the surface of the Moon was permitted, even for extended periods(37). Anyway, this should not lead to the acquisition of a kind of ownership(38).

There remained one unclear point: Was exploitation of natural resources of the Moon permitted, even though an „international regime“ had not yet been established, or was such exploitation prohibited?

Hosenball was of the opinion that there was no moratorium intended for using the Moons natural resources before the said establishment.(39). And COPUOS agreed in its report about the draft agreement „*that article 7 is not intended to result in prohibiting the exploitation of natural resources which may be found on celestial bodies other than the Earth, but, rather, that such exploitation will be carried out in such a manner as to minimize any disruption or adverse affect to the existing balance of the environment*“(40).

3) The Basis for a new Start.
Apparently, this was not enough to calm the doubts of the great space powers. And thus, they did not ratify or even sign the Moon Agreement.

Here the matter rests. When at the UN according to Art.18 of the Moon Agreement the question came up whether to renegotiate the Agreement, it was unanimously decided by the General Assembly on Dec. 9., 1994, upon recommendation of the COPUOS and it Legal Subcommittee (LSC), not to take action on such a revision(41).

However, in its Resolution of 5,Feb. 1996, the U.N.G.A.invited „*States that have not yet become parties to the international treaties governing the uses of outer space to give consideration to ratifying or acceding to those treaties;*“ And here, the Moon Agreement is expressedly mentioned (42).

Thus, *Gorove* was right when he pointed out that the Moon Agreement had failed to receive sufficient support from the space faring nations largely due to ist provisions dealing wth the exploitation of lunar resources which were to be regarded as the „ common heritage of mankind“.(43)

The problem seemed to be not very pressing at the moment. But that could change rapidly. For on the one hand we have a Moon Agreement that obviously is not accepted by most states. On the other hand, the U.N.General Assembly invites the states to sign and ratify (among others) this very Agreement. And thirdly, the possible revision of the Agreements text is (at least) postponed. This somehow unclear situation invites scholars to investigate possible solutions. It is therefore quite appropriate that the IISL has put this question on this years agenda, The continued efforts of IAA, and the committee under the chairmanshipt of *Koelle*(44) demonstrates that soon manned or unmanned space missions might reach out to the Moon or even Mars, It might become vital to clarify a situation which seems to be at present detrimental for the progress of space travel to the Moon and other celestial bodies.

It is necessary to come to the heart of the matter. It is necessary to reconcile the interests of those States which would reach (again) the Moon and want to exploit its natural recources on the one hand, and the common interest of all terrestrial Nations in an appropriate sharing of those resources.on the other hand. This reconciliation is necessary and it is not impossible. To exploit what is needed to assist space travel, to create stations on the Moon, even maybe to cover costs of going to our natural Satellite seems unavoidable and should be clearly permitted in an unambiguous language. To exclude other, especially developing Nations from going there later, for doing their own research, and even their own exploitations, should be prohibited at the same time in a language equally clear.

It would be detrimental for all mankind if due to an unclear legal situation the hiatus in expeditions to the Moon and other celestial bodies would be extended too long. And it would be illogical to protect natural recources on the Moon more strictly than those on Earth. The Moon should remain free, free of appropriation. But its natural resources should serve all mankind. And he who can bring them down here, should be assured and rewarded by a clear space legal contractual regulation.

References:

1. There was never an opinion expressed that the Sun or other fixed stars could be occupied or appropriated. *Fasan,* Weltraumrecht, Krausskopf, Mainz, 1965, 107.
2. Survey of Legal Opinion on Extraterrestrial Jurisdiction, Proceedings of the Third Colloquium on the Law of Outer Space, Stockholm, 196o, ed. by the Swedish Interplanetary Society, Stockholm, 1961, 72.
3. Problems of Space Law, The New Scientist, May 19.,1960, London, 1258.
4. International Law and Activities in Space, International and Comparative Law Quarterly, Jan 1956, 110.
5. World Space Law, Second Colloquium on the Law of Outer Space, Springer Verlag, 126f.
6. Perspectives for a Law of Outer Space, Legal Problems of Space Exploration, A Symposium, U.S.Senate, 87th Congress, 1st Session Doc. No 26., March 1961 (Symposium 1961), 417.
7. Lets Claim the Moon- Now!, Mechanics Illustrated, Feb.March 1957, 71
8. Reprinted Symposium 1961, 588f
9. Ibidem, 596
10. Reprinted Symposium 1961, 231f.
11. Souveränität im Weltraum, Raketentechnik und Raumfahrt Heft I Bd.6., 8.
12. Principles for a Declaration with reference to the Legal Nature of the Moon, Proceedings of the First Colloquium on the Law of Outer Space, The Hague, 1958 Springer Verlag, Vienna, 1959, 36
13. Artificial Satellites And International Law, Paper with English summary, Soviet Yearbook of International Law 1958, Moscow, 1959, 149
14. Reprinted Circular No 5 of Working Group 3 of the IISL.
15. Adress before the 12th Session of the U.N.G.A. June 11., 1958, quoted Symposium 1961, 372.
16. Design for a Law of Space, First Colloquium (12), 98.
17. The Need for a new System for Space Law, ibidem, 107
18. Zeitschrift fürLuftrecht und Weltraumrechtsfragen, Köln, (ZLW) 1960, 305
19. Ibidem, 311.
20. If we land there soon, who owns the Moon, American Bar Journal 1958,15.
21. Recht im Weltraum, ZLW 1960, 196.
22. See (12).
23. A Concept for a Space Law, Symposium 1961, 676.
24. A very good overview is given ba *Eilene Galloway* in her Introduction to the Symposium 1961, XIIff., and by *Reijnen,* Legal Aspects of Outer Space, 1976, 133ff. See also *Christol,* The Moon Treaty enters into Force, American Journal of International Law, Vol. 79., Jan. 1985, 163ff.
25. UN Doc. A/C.1PV.821, 6.
26. UN Doc. A 3818.
27. U.N.G.A. Res. 1348 (13)
28. U.N.G.A.Res. 1721 (16).P. 1.b.
29. U.N.G.A.Res. 1962 (18), P. 2.
30. *Dula* , Free Enterprise and the proposed Moon Treaty, Houston Journal of Inzternational Law 2, 1979, No.1.
31. See Agreement Governing the Activities of States on the Moon and other Celestial Bodies, May, 1980, US Senate, Committee Report, 96th Congress, 2d Session , especially 7ff.
32. Status of International Agreements relating to Activities in Outer Space, Committee on the Peaceful Uses of Outer Space, Legal Subcommittee (LSC of COPUOS), UN Doc.

A/AC.105/C.2/1996/CPR.2 (prepared for participants only) of March 15., 1996. There were ratifications listed only by the Nations of Australia, Austria, Chile, Mexico, Morocco, The Netherlands, Pakistan, Philippines, and Uruguay. Signed but not ratified was the Agreement by France, Guatemala, India, Peru and Rumania.

33. Art 11,3.

34. Art 11,1..

35. Art 11,5.

36. Art.6,2.

37. Art 9,1.

38. Art 111,3.

39. *Hosenball,* at Oversight, Hearings before the Subcommittee on Space Sciences and Applications of the House of Commons, 96th Congress, 1st Session, 90-100, 1979on the Activities of the U.N.Committee on the Peaceful Uses of Outer Space.

40. Report of the Legal Subcommittee on the work of ist 18st Session, 1979, UN.Doc. A/AC. 105/240 , Par 65, deeply investigated by *E. Galloway,* Issues in implementing the Agreement Governing the Activities of States on the Moon and other Celestial Bodies, Proceedings of the Colloquium on the Law of Outer Space, Tokyo, 1980.

41. On Dec. 9., 1994, U.N.G.A. Res. 49/34. See Highlights in Space 1994, UN Office for Outer Space Affairs, *N. Jasentuliyana*, Director , Vienna, 1995, 52.

42. U.N. Doc. A/RES/50/27.

43. *Gorove,* Space Law in the Global Community, Report, J. Space L.1995, 201.

44. See International Academy of Astronautics, Annual Report of the President 1995, published by IAA by arrangement with Elsevier, Science Ltd., No 22., 2, citing the studies of *Koelle* and *Morgenthaler.*

PROPERTY RIGHTS ON THE MOON AND CELESTIAL BODIES

ALDO ARMANDO COCCA*

Introduction

To analyse the legal régime in force to govern the Moon, it is necessary to pay attention to the text of two fundamental international instruments: the Space Treaty and the Moon Agreement. The precedents of some principles that have been established in these international instruments can be found in the United Nations Charter.

To a better understanding of the legal régime of the Moon, the common opinion of jurists, the statements of members of the Legal Subcommittee of COPUOS during the elaboration of said texts and other proposals and drafts debated in the United Nations are useful.

Some of the United Nations principles found their definitive enunciation in the law of Outer Space. By other side, Space Law reinforces international law facing the strong development of human rights and of the environmental right as well as the emerging international constitutional law and international civil law.

Doctrine: from 1945 to 1966.

I include within the concept of doctrine the statements of the Conference of San Francisco in order to the reception in the text of the Charter of the concepts of *mankind* and *generations*.

In the Vth International Congress of Astronautics (Innsbruck, 1954) I expressed that the exploration of outer space should be undertaken by humankind for its own benefit. In this regard I proposed the internationalization of space sciences and technologies. To allow that space activities were developed without secrets and exclusively with peaceful purposes.[1]

In the 1st International Colloquium on the Law of Outer Space (The Hague, 1958) I offered some principles with reference to the legal nature of the Moon. I pointed out five prior considerations to be discarded from a legal point of view:

1. The Moon does not constitute either a territory or a zone in space;
2. The Moon cannot be declared independent of the States of the Earth;
3. The Moon cannot be declared autonomous;
4. The Moon cannot be declared a sovereign state; and,
5. There are no rights of ownership on or over the Moon.

The principles recommended in said paper are:

1) The Moon is free for the utilization of the States of the Earth. Consequently an

* Trustee of IAA, Director IISL;

adequate regulation for this purpose and for peaceful purposes, is necessary;

2) Regarding the exploitation of its natural resources, the procedure should be similar as that governing the exploitation of the resources of the high seas;

3) For interplanetary travel, there are liberties of transit and scale on the natural satellite.[2]

In the Vth Colloquium (Varna, 1962) I stated that it is necessary to establish a regulation for the common use of the Moon with peaceful purposes exclusively. In the same sense, a regulation for the common use of the natural resources of the Moon should be agreed upon.[3]

At the same time Ernst Fasan asked to the members of the Committee 3 (Celestial Bodies) of the IISL: What does *national appropriation* means, and which clues have been given by authorities for its definition? Is it the same as *occupation* or *annexion?* In fact, the Soviet Prime Minister Krushchev, used exactly the term *annexion* in his letter to the US President Kennedy.[4]

In opportunity of the Paris Colloquium, I explained the meaning of the expression *res communis humanitatis* that I was using in my chair and in papers. In Space Law the subject is humankind as a whole, and the benefits obtained belong *ab initio* to humankind —which embodies all human beings— hence, a *condominium.*

The agent who does the material work of extracting the wealth can only expect a profitable compensation for his task, not an appropriation of the good obtained.

What we have called the fourth juridical dimension, is humankind, and in this way, Law has surpassed its national and international characters when it is projected towards outer space in order to reach a higher category, comprehensive of all mankind.[5]

Ernst Fasan proposed in this Colloquium, a draft resolution concerning celestial bodies: Part B, par. a) and b) determines: The right to use a celestial body shall include the right to exploit its eventual material resources; b) Any state, which, in the exercise of this right, undertakes the exploitation of such resources, shall notify this fact to the Community of Nations and share with the other nations the benefits, obtained by this activity.[6]

The question of the legal condition of celestial bodies was discussed in 1964, once again. In this opportunity, and after reminding the legal basis to adopt the expression *res communis humanitatis* in connection with the status of celestial bodies, I offered the concept of celestial product: it is an object separated or extracted from a celestial body and transported to Earth. Products may be brought to Earth not only for scientific purposes but for their economical value, as well. In this case the product enters into commercialization, the question rises: What is the status of this product imported to Earth? Is in this moment that the idea of creating an organism to deal with the commercialization of these products, arose. This organism should control both the exploration and the ultimate application of the celestial product on Earth.[7]

In connection with the distribution of benefits derived from the Moon, I understood that any distribution assumes the existence of an organ or machinery for the administration of that resources. In my view, in conformity with art. 55 a) of the United Nations Charter, the interests and needs of developing countries and the rights of those undertaking the activity of extraction of the natural resource of the Moon, are taken into account. It represents a balance which every law is supposed to reach in the light of justice and equity.[8]

In the same opportunity —and linked with the matter— I presented another paper where I gave the scientific fundament of the condition of humankind as subject of international law. The new subject received an increasing personality and patrimony.

The expressions *province of all mankind* and *common heritage of all mankind* have a great juridical sense and mean a deep evolution in the field of law.[9]

It was said that nothing which is found on the Moon could be subject to appropriation; its study and use concern all mankind. In the face of the Space Treaty, appropriation of space resources is fully banned. The establishment of an international organization for space activities becomes essential. A specialized agency —depending of such organization— should be in charge of the administration of space resources.[10]

It has also been said that until the appropriate international machinery is established all states shall use their good offices and mediation in the settlement of disputes, and shall refrain from belligerent action on celestial bodies or in outer space.[11]

A reflection was made by a jurist that resumes the hope of many others: The legal regulations are to be invented, and must assure that the exploration and use of the space, the Moon and other celestial bodies will really serve the common interests of the whole mankind, and the co-operation in this field will contribute to the development of science, to the amelioration of the condition of life, the development of the economical and social circumstances of the present and coming generations, to the improvement of the mutual understanding between the states and peoples and strengthening their amicable connections.[12]

During the elaboration of the Moon Agreement it could be observed that the question of its natural resources belongs to the controversial issues of the draft. In this sense it was proposed the following text:

"Neither state, international intergovernmental or non governmental organization, national organization having the status of juridical person or not, nor natural persons, may claim the surface or subsurface of the Moon as their property".

The provision forbidding any arrangements or transactions between persons, between persons of international or national laws, concerning parts of the surface or subsurface of the Moon, seems to be more suitable.[13]

In connection with the exportation to Earth of Moon resources, it was stated that, "if the states which spend huge sums for the exploration of the Moon will not have the legal possibility to exploit those resources, then they will be confronted with two possibilities:

1) To stop the exploration; or,
2) To continue those exploitations ignoring the non-realistic formulations of the treaties.

I hope however that it will be possible to find out a formulation (for example along the line of Cocca's idea of the utilization of the Moon by the whole 'humanitas') which could be acceptable for all or for the very big majority of states."[14]

The Draft Moon Treaty proposed by the ex-Soviet Union established that the emplacement on the Moon of "vehicles or equipment... including the construction of installations integrally connected with the surface or subsoil of the Moon" i.e. the practical creation of a station on the Moon, does not create "a right of ownership over portions of the surface or subsoil of the Moon". The draft of this article goes even further and underlines that the surface and subsoil of the Moon may not be the property not only of states but also of international intergovernmental or non-governmental organizations having the status of juridical persons or not, including natural persons. Item 2 of article II renders a detailed enumeration of those juridical acts in which portions of the surface or subsoil of the Moon cannot be the object of, namely, concession, exchange, transfer, sale or purchase, lease, hire, gift or any other arrangement or transaction with or without compensation between states and the fore mentioned organizations and persons. These provisions are of no small importance, their seemingly abstract character, notwithstanding. This article must put an end to the unrealistic wishes of separate individuals to somehow acquire portions of the Moon.[15]

The controversy risen in the COPUOS Legal Subcommittee in the 1970 session period of New York, when the Argentine Delegation answered the Soviet Delegation document on common heritage of mankind, put in evidence that the most complex problem to reach the Moon Agreement conclusion, was the interpretation of said principle.

In the XVth of Bakú (1973) I concluded, with reference to the Moon Agreement, that the first question to be solved is not only to announce the principle of the *common heritage of mankind* but to give it a juridical content.[16]

In 1977 the question of human heritage of mankind was still controversial: "It appears that the clarification of the notion *exploration* and *use* of natural resources of celestial bodies, as well as of other notions applied in a new branch of international law, is of great importance. It could prevent misunderstandings which occurred as sometimes authors mean different things using different terms and expressions in international documents. As an example such misunderstanding occurred with the notion *common heritage of all mankind.* The clarification and the common approach to the terms and understanding of these or those notions could undoubtedly promote further progressive development of International Space Law".[17]

It has also been stated that the question of humankind legal personality seems to be one of the main legal points of this problem. The creation o a real community of mankind instead of a community of states, is a task reserved to future generations, based in safeguarding peace, social progress of all nations and the falling of the political barriers between them. The legal contents of the "common heritage of mankind" is the creation of an international régime to govern the exploitation of the natural resources of the Moon with special consideration to the interests and needs of the developing countries as well as the efforts of those countries which has contributed to the exploration of the Moon.[18]

Once aimed the consensus for the definitive text of the Moon Agreement, the point of view of a former Ambassador and expert space jurist offered this conclusion: "The Committee on the Peaceful Uses of Outer Space has already produced by consensus five treaties which have been ratified by the US and which have made exemplary progress in the Law of Outer Space. This treaty seems more appropriate considering the rapidly advancing science for the use and developing of resources from space for the benefit of all mankind. We should encourage informed debate on the interpretation of the proposed treaty. To be avoided are hasty interpretation, inappropriate analogies and unwise political action tending to diminish the role in advancing man's activities in outer space."[19]

By that time it was also expressed: "It is well known what the theory of marxism-leninism says about the fact that the State will die out however it comes from the idea that this process will be long and gradual and can happen only by means of strengthening a state and, which is very important, not any state but a socialist one that reflects the interests of the people. It proves unreal to speak of mankind as a subject of law, i.e. a bearer of rights and obligations since mankind in this meaning is very vague, unconcrete and a politically amorphous notion. The phrases which are met in international agreements on space about "the common interest of all mankind in the progress of the exploration and use of outer space for peaceful purposes" and about "astronauts as envoys of mankind", have no any concrete legal meaning, but they are of emotional and solemn nature. [20]

The question of the possession and industrialization of minerals was pointed out simultaneously: "It would be unrealistic to deny a country its rights of possession of discovered substances, after it has researched or authorized their research according to the laws of that country. The same laws should apply to minerals that are absolutely essential for the maintaining of an established structure or space station. According to our judgement this is in agreement with the principle that prohibits the national appropriation of portions of celestial bodies. The last point concerns the exclusion of sovereignty and not the civil law of possession. On the other hand we agree with the general position of existing literature whereby the present regulations exclude industrial exploitation".[21]

After concluding the negotiation of the Moon Agreement the IISL put as the first item of its agenda the Implications of the Agreement Governing the Activities of States on the Moon and other Celestial Bodies. This question was examined in 16 papers. One of them is referred to the protection of the environment of celestial bodies as a whole that comprises measures both for the preservation and rational utilization. Such a system of measures for protection of the environment of the Moon and other celestial bodies, including their natural resources should precede an elaboration of the exploitation régime to be applied to this resources. What term could be employed to express the juridical nature of the resources of celestial bodies? Maybe common heritage of mankind would do? But this term in conformity with the 1979 Agreement also refers to the celestial bodies of the solar system and their resources. The common heritage of mankind, as a term and a notion, has a broader meaning to be used in a restricted sense, i.e. to express the juridical nature of the resources of the Moon and other celestial bodies.[22]

Ernst Fasan in the same Colloquium referred that several problems remained unsolved. In connection to the international régime, he remarked that the word régime has been carefully selected, because it is identical in English, French and Russian. He also stated that it is necessary to put in clear that states <u>undertake</u> to establish such a régime and that this means that <u>not</u> such a régime would have been established already by the Agreement. To "undertake to establish" may mean that such a task is performed successfully by states in a certain space of time, but it may mean that such an undertaking fails, also. Such a régime might even be the first step toward a Space Agency which has been proposed by several authors.[23]

Concerning the prompt enforcement of the Agreement it has been held that "the potential benefits to the US of ratification of the Moon Treaty significantly outweigh any potential disadvantages. This is particularly true in line of the facts that such potential disadvantages would arise not from this Moon Treaty, but rather from a subsequent accord which would require separate approval or disapproval. Refusal to ratify would simply and devastatingly exclude the US from legal entitlement to the benefits and protections included in the Moon Treaty, and could seriously complicate the prospects of gaining concession from other states in the future régime negotiations. In itself, this would only give rise to investor insecurity and probably make it more difficult for US to shape the results of those future negotiations.[24]

In connection with the future of the Moon Agreement, Eilene Galloway understood that the major issues arising for discussion are the legal status of understanding in COPUOS; the definition and implications of "the common heritage of mankind"; the probable nature of a future international régime; the meaning of equitably sharing of benefits derived from exploitation; and ensuring the development of an harmonious body of space law. At the end of her paper she offers guidelines for the future development of space law.[25]

Her son, Jonathan Galloway demonstrated in his paper that the common heritage of mankind concept is new in international law but it has roots in classical political philosophy, economic thought and religious doctrine. Reference to conservative, liberal and radical thinkers indicate the long history of the terms in the concept which, at a minimum, implies some means of sharing to benefit the whole community and he adds, that the exact nature of régime for the Moon and its natural resources cannot be specified by moral, political or economical theory. He added that the common heritage of mankind concept indicates a commitment to some degree of co-operation, co-ordination and linking of state activities and to some formula for sharing the benefits of ventures on the Moon. The operating institutions for the Moon can expect to benefit from the precedents in place for other organizations in space like INTELSAT and INMARSAT. "However, as Ambassador Cocca of Argentina writes: it is rather dangerous to crystallise in a definition the principle involved in a concept which is just being born in the new domain of space Law, such as the 'common heritage of mankind' as it was established in the Moon Agreement. As the international régime is concerned I dare say it is not a matter of definition; I feel it must be the outcome of the implementation of the guidelines set forth in the Agreement". [26]

In connection with the common heritage of mankind principle, it was stated that "the common heritage of mankind provision in the Moon Treaty is not a hollow phrase, but the expression of an existing and developing legal principle, for which as far as the exploitation of natural resources is concerned, detailed legal rules will have to be worked out pursuant to paragraphs 5 and 7 of article XI".[27]

Martin Menter said with optimism and faith in the future development of Space Law, that "In the interests of avoiding seeds for conflicts encountered through history on Earth, the world community tailored the Outer Space Treaty to a new set of legal principles proclaiming outer space and celestial bodies as the province of all mankind and that its exploration and use shall be carried out for the benefit of all peoples. It is believed that rather than limit private sector opportunities, The Treaty of the Moon will enhance them by opening new vistas with rewards —as in the past— depending upon initiative, ingenuity and industrial capability, with government support tailored to high risk endeavours.[28]

The major references made about the Moon Agreement were made on the common heritage of mankind principle. In other words: "Since the opening of the Treaty for signature much has been written about the exploitations provisions of the Moon Treaty and the meaning of the phrase 'common heritage of mankind' as used therein. These provisions have drawn so much attention that substantial commentary on other provisions of the Treaty is virtually non-existent."[29]

There have been suggested some ways to complete the Moon Agreement. Present and future states parties to the Moon Agreement as well as there institutions and nationals will need a guarantee to be able to commit more extensive activities on the Moon; among them:

- ✓ Establishment of the international régime on a very short term;
- ✓ Instant establishment of a provisional temporary régime;
- ✓ Establishment of an international space agency, to deal with the practical aspect of exploitation of Moon resources.[30]

The legal text in force

The Space Treaty adopted by UNGA on 19 December 1966 —and in force since 10 October 1967— uses in its Preamble the expression "common interests of *all mankind* in the progress of the exploration and use of outer space for peaceful purposes"; and, "the exploration and use of outer space should be carried on for the benefit of *all peoples* irrespective of the degree of their economic or scientific development".

Article I establishes that the "exploration and use of outer space, including the Moon and other celestial bodies, shall be carried out for the *benefit and the interests of all countries* irrespective of their degree of economic or scientific development, and *shall be the province of all mankind.*

Article II states: outer space, including the Moon and other celestial bodies, *is not subject to national appropriation by claim of sovereignty, by means of use or occupation or by any other means.*

Article V: states parties to the Treaty shall regard *astronauts as envoys of mankind in outer space.*

History of the Moon Treaty

The Argentine Delegate used by the first time the expression *common patrimony of mankind* in the United Nations on June 19, 1967.

The phrase *patrimonio común* was translated into French as *patrimoine commun.* and in English as *common property* (UN Doc. AAC 105/C.2/SR 75, p. 15). The paternity of the expression is sometimes attributed to the mission of Malta basing the presumption in a verbal note of 17 August 1967, two months later than the Argentine proposal.[31]

On June 13, 1969 the Argentine Delegation proposed in occasion of the previewed arrival of man to the Moon, a recommendation for the study of the legal condition of materials, resources and products of the Moon (UN AAC.105/C.2/L.54, 13 June 1969).

The antecedents of the Argentine draft Agreement related to the Moon, was the proposal made by Argentina and Poland (A/AC. 105/C.2/L680); which was followed by the proposal of Argentina, France and Poland (A/AC. 105/C.2/L 69).

The draft Agreement on the Principles Governing Activities in the Use of the Natural Resources of the Moon and other Celestial Bodies (A/AC 105/C.2/L.71, 23 June 1970).

The Moon Treaty was adopted in December 1979, entered into force on 11 July 1984. In its article 1 it establishes that the provisions relating to the Moon shall also apply to other celestial bodies within the solar system other than the Earth and the reference to the Moon shall include orbit around or other trajectories to or around it.

In accordance with article 4, the exploration and use of the Moon *shall be the province of all mankind* and shall be carried out *for the benefit and the interest of all countries.*

Article 9 prescribes that state parties may establish manned and unmanned stations on the Moon. A state party establishing a station shall use only that area which is required for the needs of the station.

Article 11 is the most important when it determines that the Moon and its natural resources are *the common heritage of mankind*; the Moon is not subject to national appropriation by any claim of sovereignty, by means of use or occupation, or by any other means. Neither the surface nor the subsurface of the Moon, nor any part thereof or natural resources in place shall become property of any state, international intergovernmental or non-governmental organization, national organization or non-governmental entity or of any natural person. The placement of personnel, space vehicles, equipment, facilities, stations and installation on or below the surface of the Moon, included structures connected with its surface or subsurface shall not create a right of ownership over the surface or the subsurface of the Moon or any areas thereof. The foregoing provisions are without prejudice to the international régime to be established.

In this regard, state parties undertake to establish an international régime, including appropriate procedures, to govern the exploitation of the natural resources of the Moon as such exploitation is about to become feasible. This provision shall be implemented in accordance with the provisions concerning the question of the revision and review of the Agreement.

In the text of the Moon Agreement the following terms are utilized:

- *appropriation,* that means a right concerning possession, which belongs to oneself, to set apart for, or assign to, a particular use in exclusion of all other uses, to make to oneself in exclusion to other, to claim use as by an exclusive right;
- *use* or *occupation*, these expressions are related to prescription, the acquirement of the title or right to something through its continued use or possession for time immemorial or over a long period, it also contemplates the possibility of *usucapion.* The acquisition of the title or right to property by the uninterrupted and undisputed possession of it for a certain term prescribed by law;
- *ownership* the state or the fact of being an owner as synonymous of proprietorship, domain;
- *heritage*, property that is or can be inherited, something handed down from one's ancestors.

- *utilization* to put to profitable account or use, to make useful, as utilize natural resources; to consume, expend, or exhaust by use.

There are other rights that do not appear expressly in the text:

- *real property* from Latin **realis**, **res**, a thing. Relating to permanent immutable things, as real estate land, including the building or its natural assets as mineral water, etc. The owner has the right to control use and dispose of as he wills;
- *usurpation*: the act of occupying a property of another without right; unlawful occupation;
- *patrimony*, from Latin **patrimonium**, property inherit from one's father or ancestor.

It is well known that property rights was a conflict question in the history of humankind, because it is linked with political and economical factors. By other side, any tempted modification to the right of property is always resisted, because there are some associated considerations that spoil the inner essence of law.

Once consensus was aimed among all legal and political systems within COPUOS, it was noticed with surprise that some nations —that endorsed from the beginning the principle of common heritage of mankind— opened a debate that contradict the performance of their own representatives in the elaboration of the Agreement.

In our days we do not discuss property. Humankind is the owner of the whole of the Moon and celestial bodies and of outer space. This means that every member of humankind is owner of an undivided part of the whole as member of the collective owner. Therefore, each part of humankind exercises ownership over its undivided part of the whole good that is owned by humankind. Possession, use, exploitation and utilization are expressions and rights derived from the complex and complete right of property.

Conclusions

The Space Treaty and the Moon Agreement mention and found their principles in institutions taken from Civil Law.

It is correct that the number of real rights is not exhausted, consequently the question poses over Civil Law more than in international law and there are no obstacles for the space jurist, to create new real rights for the space environment and celestial bodies.

In the Moon and celestial bodies there is no sovereignty to guarantee the exercise of any right, nor to organize the simultaneous use and exploitation of the same celestial body.

Therefore it must be created an organ invested of sufficient authority, with jurisdiction and control, to organize and protect the free and full enjoyment of the common patrimony.

It is necessary to recall that when for the first time the expression —now known as common heritage of mankind— was used, the term I utilized was *patrimonio* which was translated into English as *common property* and in French as *patrimoine commun*.

There is a need to harmonize the rights of men with those of who that exploits the resources, bearing in mind that an illegitimate enrichment is not admissible by who did not co-operate in said exploitation. This is the real legal reason for the existence of the principle of international co-operation as legal condition to legitimate space activities. This harmonization only can be made through an international agency.

References

1 A.A. Cocca, ***Die Rechtliche Natur das Weltraums***, Bericht über den V. Internationalen Astronautischen Kongress, Innsbruck, 5 bis 7 August 1954, Springer Verlag in Wien, 1955, page 283-290.

2 A.A. Cocca, Principles for a Declaration with reference to the legal nature of the Moon, ***Proceedings of the Ist Colloquium on the Law of Outer Space*** (The Hague, 1958), Springer Verlag, Wienn, 1959, page 37.

3 A.A. Cocca, Basic Statute for the Moon, ***Proceedings of the Vth Colloquium on the Law of Outer Space*** (Varna, 1962), Washington, 1963, page 37.

4 E. Fasan, Law and Peace for the Celestial Bodies, ***Proceedings of the Vth Colloquium*** (Varna, 1962), Washington, 1963, page 71.

5 A.A. Cocca, Determination of the Meanings of the expression *res communis humanitatis* in Space Law, ***Proceedings of the VIth Colloquium*** (Paris, 1963), Washington 1964, page 67 and 69.

6 E. Fasan, Basic Principles regarding the Celestial Bodies, ***Proceedings of the VIth Colloquium*** (Paris, 1963), Washington, 1964, page 124.

7 A.A. Cocca, Legal status of celestial bodies and economic status of the celestial products, ***Proceedings of VIIth Colloquium*** (Warsaw, 1964), University of Oklahoma, Norman, 1965, page, 21.

8 A.A. Cocca, Legal status of the natural resources of the Moon and other celestial bodies, ***Proceedings of the XIIIth Colloquium*** (Constanze, 1970), University of California, Davies, 1971, page 148.

9 A.A. Cocca, Mankind as a new legal subject: a new juridical dimension recognized by the United Nations, ***Proceedings of the XIIIth Colloquium,*** cit., page 214.

10 S.M. Williams, The principle of non-appropriation concerning resources of the Moon and celestial bodies, ***Proceedings of the XIIIth Colloquium*** , cit., page 157-159.

11 C.E.S. Horsford, Rules of human activity on celestial bodies, ***Proceedings of the XIIIth Colloquium*** cit. page 210.

12 L. Szaléky, The way of the further perfection of the legal regulation concerning the Moon and other celestial bodies especially regarding the exploitation of natural resources of the Moon and other celestial bodies, ***Proceedings of the XVIth Colloquium*** (Bakú, 1973), University of California, Davies, 1974 , page 198-199.

13 V. Kopal, The development of legal arrangements for the peaceful uses of the Moon, ***Proceedings of the XVth Colloquium*** (Vienna, 1972), University of California, Davies, 1973, page 159.

14 M. Smirnoff, The Need for a treaty on the legal status of the Moon, ***Proceedings of the XVth Colloquium***, cit., page 175.

15 E.G. Vassilevskaia, Legal regulation of activities on the Moon for the cause of peace and progress, ***Proceedings of the XVth Colloquium***, cit., page 180.

16 A.A. Cocca, The principle of the common heritage of all mankind as applied to natural resources from outer space and celestial bodies, ***Proceedings of the XVth Colloquium***, cit., page 176.

17 E.G. Vassilevskaia, Notions of "exploration" and "use" of natural resources of celestial bodies, ***Proceedings of the XXth Colloquium*** (Prague, 1977), University of California, Davies, 1978., page 475.

18 R. Arzinger, Legal aspects of the common heritage of mankind, ***Proceedings of the XXIInd Colloquium,*** (Munich, 1979), American Institute of Aeronautics and Astronautics, New York, 1980, page 89-90.

19 E.R. Finch, Jr., 1979 United Nations Moon Treaty encourage lunar mining & space development, ***Proceedings of the XXIInd Colloquium***, (Munich, 1979), American Institute of Aeronautics and Astronautics, New York, 1980, page 124.

20 E. Kamenetskaya, Subjects of international Space Law, ***Proceedings of the XXIInd Colloquium,*** (Munich, 1979), American Institute of Aeronautics and Astronautics, New York, 1980, page 164-165.

21 M. Miklódy, Some remarks on the question of

possession of mineral resources of the celestial bodies, ***Proceedings of the XXIInd Colloquium,*** (Munich, 1979), American Institute of Aeronautics and Astronautics, New York, 1980, page 179-180.

22 R.V. Dekanozov, Juridical nature and status of the resources of the Moon and other celestial bodies, ***Proceedings of the XXIIIrd Colloquium*** (Tokyo, 1980), American Institute of Aeronautics and Astronautics, New York, 1981, page 6-7.

23 E. Fasan, Some legal problems regarding the Moon, ***Proceedings of the XXIIIrd Colloquium*** cit., page 10.

24 E.R. Finch Jr. and A. L. Moore, The 1979 Moon Treaty encourages space development, ***Proceedings of the XXIIIrd Colloquium*** cit., page 17.

25 E. Galloway, Issues in implementing the Agreement Governing the Activities of States on the Moon and other celestial bodies, ***Proceedings of the XXIIIrd Colloquium*** cit., page 19 and 23.

26 J. F. Galloway, Political, philosophy and the common heritage of mankind concept in international law, ***Proceedings of the XXIIIrd Colloquium*** cit., page 25 and 27.

27 P.P.C. Haanappel, Article XI of the Moon Treaty, ***Proceedings of the XXIIIrd Colloquium*** cit., page 30.

28 M. Menter, Commercial space activities under the Moon Treaty, ***Proceedings of the XXIIIrd Colloquium*** cit., page 43.

29 R. W. Norris and R.L. Bridge, Some implications of the Moon Treaty with regard to public order in space, ***Proceedings of the XXIIIrd Colloquium*** cit., page 57.

30 H.L. van Traa-Engelman, The Moon Treaty —Legal consequences and practical aspects, ***Proceedings of the XXIIIrd Colloquium*** cit., page 76.

31 S.M. Williams, The Role of Equity in the Law of Outer Space, ***The Journal of the David Davies Memorial Institute of International Law,*** London, vol. V, N° 1, May 1975, page 702-703.

IISL-96-IISL.1.03

THE LEGAL STATUS OF PROPERTY ON THE MOON AND OTHER CELESTIAL BODIES

SUBMITTED BY DR. HARRY H. ALMOND, JR. Formerly Senior Attorney, International Law and International Relations, Department of Defense; Professor, National Strategy, National War College, and currently Professor, National Security Studies Program, Edmund A. Walsh School of Foreign Service, Georgetown University.

ABSTRACT

Power, in the objective sense, is the value most prized among states and the basis of attaining and protecting all other values. Other values, such as resources, energy, wealth, prestige and so on are directly dependent upon power, and upon states seen to be exercising it to protect or advance their interests. Clarification of the legal status of the property rights claimed among states in outer space discloses the policy link between private and public law. The concern of states extends beyond their inherent stakes in property. Such claims impute influence, power and prestige among states, and ensure those claims by the resources, including energy that is a part of those resources. Bu space presents a separate, overriding challenge: states that make these claims and seek to enforce them must also be the master of the relevant technologies for this purpose. Aside from property as a claim to resources, as a claim to energy, as a challenge to technologies, and as a claim to power and influence, property in the territorial sense becomes a claim for sovereignty, exclusive controls and strategic advantage. Such a claim extends to the supplemental claim to force others out of arenas exclusively held. Most of these claims cannot be explored in depth in this inquiry, and many are clearly speculative in nature. Such widened claims using the vocabulary of the jurists speak of the critical value of power, the subterranean claims of states to exclusive control, jurisdiction and authority over property and territory.

Most importantly, the implications associated in the legal order with the rights to property reach to the perceptions of states concerning their security. Because security is associated with the bases of power, to be invoked or protected, these claims involving and linking property, territory and security march together. Aside from claims of this nature are those associated with the rapidly advancing civil and military technologies: these instruments of power and policy are promoted by property because technologies generally address property rights, tangible or intangible.

DISCUSSION

Exclusive claims to property coupled with a relentless advance in the power-based technologies of exploitation and use necessarily lead to power, and to the claims of states to the exclusive authority they identify with "sovereignty." Property rights in municipal law protecting the interests of the citizen or resident also establish their claims to the governance of the social order: rights to property - both for simple occupancy and for production - and the citizens' rights to govern themselves go hand in hand. And the legal theory of property rights in outer space, encompassing primarily the claims of states, is a theory that is correct only if it embodies the sovereign claims of states. A "revolutionary change" in this perspective would require a new, and revolutionary alignment of states, presumably, and exclusively, under the jurisdiction and control of a global public order. Hence the 1967 Outer Space Principles Treaty anticipates at the first stage of the space age a collective, orderly change swept on under the operational principles of cooperation.

A major problem that we face in participating in the law making processes and in seeking our legal precedents and experience for effective and economical future regulation, is to give law its operational basis. The claims for prestige and power aside, the jurist concerned with global order looks to a standard of reasonableness as a principle balancing opposing claims and counterclaims. At present, we have no reliable set of principles and practices that balances, on an interdisciplinary basis, the status quo among states as to their power against the dynamic features that come in terms of an advancing competition for resources and power and the reach for the technologies that give the claims their support. We cannot predict the direction or velocity of change even if we are given guidance by closer ties to reliable trends.

The legal status of property rights in space is not spelled out in detail or in comprehensive conceptual framework, and much must be invoked from general principles of law applicable to property in terms of terrestrial claims. States necessarily engender an array of responsibilities, and these increase as they engage in increasing numbers of activities. Launching satellites leads to a responsibility and liability to those that might be harmed. Maneuvering satellites create responsibilites for their owners or possessors. They must meet the pervasive standards of the utmost due care as the activities move toward more hazardous levels. Satellites are dangerous objects and liability for their harm is a general principle of law. The activities of satellites, similarly establish an obligation or responsibility for harm consistent again with the standards of due care, so that negligence, accidents, and even unforeseen harmful incidents are subjected to general principles of law. All of these activities are regulated primarily through the shared patterns of expectation of behavior, tolerances in behavior and distinctions of what is permissible, and through the claims and tolerances that enter into this process of claim. The outcome is customary international law a matter that is established only with great difficulty and care.

<u>The Major Treaties of Outer Space.</u>[1] What are the sources of the law of property rights, aside from the customary international law or the principles often adopted as a part of the generation of that law?

The primary treaties relating to outer space are multilateral treaties and are intended to become the law of outer space for all states.[2] The expectation arises that all space active states will become parties to the treaties, and participants in giving them strength and effectiveness. The first of the major treaties, that is those that are constitutive, or constitutional, in nature is the treaty on principles governing activities in outer space, dated January 27, 1967, closely parallelling the resolutions adopted in the General Assembly in 1967. To reduce repetition, reference in this paper to space or outer space is intended to be a reference to the moon and other celestial bodies.

The first of the principles in this treaty raises the question of property. Article I declares declares in pertinent part that the "exploration and use of outer space, including the moon and other celestial bodies, shall be carried out for the benefit and in the interests of all countries." This principle is vague and ambiguous and it is meaningless until we have the state practice to give us the precision and the leval of interactive tolerances in state behavior that we need. For example, claims among states regarding sovereignty become confusing in light of the first two Articles of this Treaty. There is no language that insists with absolute clarity that states are forbidden sovereign rights that do not fall within the notion of "national appropriation." Principles of law, in general, give us a symbolic and economical grasp of general, shared expectations of law, but they need the exercise of authority and control to reach out and apply as law. Put in question: Are the activities mentioned to be regulated by states? Are they to be the subject of reports among the states? Are there activities not covered by the language "exploration and use?"

Follow on principles appear in Article II banning claims of states to "national appropriation by claim of sovereignty, by means of use or occupation, or by any other means." Article III supports the notion that the activities, necessarily including those relating to property, fall in a regime of cooperation, primarily aimed at achieving the objectives of the UN Charter, including in particular "maintaining international peace and security." Article III of this treaty preserves the right of self defense, transferred to customary international law [but not the whole of customary international law]. Article 51 is necessarily included in Article III, so that actions in self defense in space, or for that matter terrestrially are not prohibited assuming that in resorting to force the standards under international law are met.

Article VI introduces the adoption of regulatory standards and principles in terms of function, so that various functions we associate with our claims to property including the possession, ownership and use may be regulated. The fact that such regulations of functions does occur in the various treaties on outer space is evidence of the intended, growing expectations of the reach of property rights. Article VI imposes "international responsibility for national activities in outer space," and the subsequent articles indicate how the responsible participants are to be identified. Article IX referring to the exploration and use of outer space, restates the principle of cooperation and mutual assistance, and the duty to protect the environment, i.e., "to avoid their harmful contamination and also adverse changes in the environment of the earth, resulting from the introduction of extraterrestrial matter.." This provision plants the seeds for developing the appropriate space law for the environment and for maintaining it free of pollution, contamination, and "harmful materials" of all kinds. Environmental law, in turn, is closely associated with how the legal status of property is to be regulated.

It is evident that with the expanding perspectives about the law relating to the environment that this provision will require amendment and refinement in future efforts to regulate the activities that may cause environmental harm. The continuing appearance of more hazardous activities and hazardous substances can be expected, and with this appearance the growing demand among states in outer space to ensure full protection against harm caused by those engaged in using their "property" or space objects in space. Domestic regulation by numerous states furnish the principles to be invoked.

The Agreement on the Rescue of Astronauts does not address property rights except for strengthening the linkages of responsibility to the launching states. Future amendments to this Agreement might look to the problem of liability, linking the Agreement with that problem and its resolution.

Articles A-1, A-2 and A-21 are among the provisions of the Convention on International Liability for Damage Caused by Space Objects, March 29, 1972, that are pertinent to the legal status of property rights. Between them they cover with greater clarification what constitutes a space object, impose important standards of liability upon states launching space objects, and in A.21 provide further content to the law relating to the matter of dangerous activities and space objects. This Convention is a set of procedures intended to ease states through alternative dispute measures that might enable them to improve their cooperative arrangements and fulfill their responsibilities where damage is caused.

The Convention clearly implies that those engaged in space are introducing objects that involve a property interest. They may be acting in behalf of the launching state, or states, or in behalf of individual or joint enterprise involving satellites. The general principles of law that might be adopted for further precision in future treaties or international agreements can be taken from general state practice as the current legal basis for determining and allocating that responsibility and the liability for damage. The implication here is that responsibility for harm and the imposition of liability that flows from the possession or use of property is identified, and that standards for assessing harm are measured by the degree of danger, risk or threat to others, and by the foreseeability of harm arising from the property and its use. This Convention does not create a mandatory, specific set of procedures, but makes alternatives and options available, and includes the option of negotiation.

The Convention on Registration of Objects Launched into Outer

Space, January 14, 1975, provides a regime for identifying objects launched into space, and for setting forth the technical data and details relating to the objects launched. Registrtion presupposes that states have a property interest in their space objects, will maintain them under effective control, and where responsible for harm or damage, will promptly pay compensation or afford other corrective relief as might be imposed through community procedures. It establishes how that interest is to be identified in terms of the technical features of the space object and its launching. In doing these things, it gives us a more precise conception of the nature of space property, i.e., as property that is regulated closely to prevent harm, interference of states in their activities, and so on.

The Agreement Governing the Activities of States on the Moon and other Celestial Bodies, December 5, 1979, has not been widely ratified: major states like the United States and Russia have not become party. The Moon Treaty has a number of provisions addressing property, primarily in the context of the trade, commerce and production associated with property. The Treaty was an attempt to fill some of the gaps relating to activities involving the moon and other celestial bodies, including some involving the property claims and uses of space objects, which are a form of property expressed in terms of property claims. As with the other treaties, the Moon Treaty preserves the application of the Charter of the UN, and its supremacy over other treaties that might be inconsistent with it, and it also includes the more ambiguous Declaration on Principles of International Law Concerning Friendly Relations and Cooperation, adopted by the General Assembly on 24 October 1970. This declaration is ambiguous because it purports to be international law formulated as a grouping of general principles, but because the principles are vague and lack the substance essential for enforcement, the law making effort that would make such principles serve as law await future state practice.

The Moon Treaty has additional ambiguities that call for clarification before it will become a desirable instrument of control or regulation. But some of its detailed provisions indicate the direction states were moving in establishing a regulatory regime and its controls about what the owner or possessor is to be permitted to do with his property on the moon and other celestial bodies. They call for example for greater protections of the environment, clarification of the activities to be regulated under international law with regard to launching and personnel, the right of states to establish manned and unmanned stations on the moon, with the implication that states will thereby have the protections needed for their property in these stations, the spelling out of cooperative measures with regard to common core problems such as those relating to the health and well being of personnel on the moon. This array of provisions and others to be mentioned below suggest that through the details states are gradually telling each other what is property, what they can or cannot do with it, and who makes the decisions about these matters.

The detailed provisions of Article 11 introducing the ambiguous notion of a "common heritage of mankind," is given some precision in the Moon Treaty because this principle is specifically limited to its application to the Moon Treaty. The common heritage notion is described as the notion that "finds its expression in the provisions of this Agreement [i.e., the Moon Treaty] and in particular in paragraph 5 of this article." The directive in Article 11 that simply declares that states are to conduct their property-related activities under "an international regime."

A literal reading of the provisions that set up the international regime indicate clearly that the drafters of the provisions expected to establish collective enterprise, ousting the market control and market forces. The stumbling block arose because this regime with trends bent toward collective exploitation of resources from space will necessarily promote cartels among nations and their productive or industrial entities, and these cartels will control prices, the amount of goods produced, and even the use of the goods. They would reduce, or even eliminate, competition as a major market factor. Article 11 (5) reads:

> 5. States Parties to this Agreement hereby undertake to establish an international regime, including appropriate procedures, to govern the exploitation of the natural resources of the moon as such exploitation is about to become feasible. This provision shall be implemented in accordance with Article 18 of this Agreement.

The anticipated international regime is a regime of cooperation, collective in outlook. This anticipated regime would overturn past practice, turning back the global movement toward a market oriented regime, and away from what is expected with productive property. Paragraph 7 indicates what has been done:

> 7. The main purposes of the international regime to be established shall include: (a) the orderly and safe development of the natural resources of the moon; (b) the rational management of those resources; (c) the expansion of opportunities in the use of those resources; (d) and equitable sharing by all States Parties in the benefits derived from those resources, whereby the interests and needs of the developing countries as well as the efforts of those countries which have contributed either directly or indirectly to the exploration of the moon, shall be given special consideration.

Property rights are also covered in the other provisions of the Moon Treaty. These include the retention of jurisdiction and control by states over property and personnel, the development of the notions of international responsibility, as set forth in Article 14, the provisions for cooperation and compatibility in the conduct of enterprisory activities, and so on. We are now witnessing the gradual strengthening of regulatory powers vested under the outer space treaties, with the relevant participants in the regulatory network extending to space active states, the United Nations and its Secretary-General.

FUTURE WORK. Future work on the treaties relating to outer space can be discerned already. Aside from the treaties discussed here there are numerous treaties applicable to activities terrestrially that can be invoked to reach the wider range of state activities and applied with regard to those activities. These need to be brought together and made accessible for easy retrieval in order to avoid the chaotic conditions that might occur if bilateral or non-constitutive treaties are negotiated without careful alignment with the public law of space. Treaties already in force that can be transferred to regulate activities in space include the UN Charter, along with the countless agreements running the gamut of state activity. Future efforts and study are needed in this area. International organizations and institutions can be scrutinized to determine the possibility of extending their control or jurisdiction or regulatory powers into space even though they were designed with terrestrial regulation in view.

For the immediate period ahead we can anticipate that the major space powers and those most comprehensively in command of the technologies pertinent to outer space are the states that will take the lead in adopting additional treaties, or in providing amendments and refinements to the treaties we have. Nonetheless, we can expect that such efforts like surveys are likely to be launched by the United Nations and its committees concerned with outer space to determine what matters or gaps in the existing law is troubling to states. This would lead to a "small" state "collective" effort, similar to those found some decades ago when the Charter of Economic Duties was put forward. Such surveys will guide the treaties and agreements that may be needed, and even to the urgency of negotiating those instruments. General principles of law to be applied by future treaties or international instruments addressingf outer space can be taken from the municipal legal systems or from other treaties and international agreements. A most important, on-going task might be to consider the possibilites or potential situations and potential crises that might, in the future, lead states to disputes, and to invoking the use of force. If these can be identified, and if measures can be taken to reduce their eruption, a major step will have been taken to avoid the use of military force in space.

RECOMMENDATIONS. Among the specific recommendations that might be made with regard to this subject these should be included:

(a) clarification and the quieting of controversies over ambiguous or contentitious principles such as the "common heritage of mankind," (b) the preparation of an updated research report to bring up to date the Report of Leon Lipson and Nicholas Katzenbach, entitled "Report to the National Aeronautics and Space Administration on the Law of Outer Space" (published by the American Bar Foundation, July 1961); (c) the consideration of amendments to the outer space treaties such as the

Moon Treaty to eliminate its interference with the right of states and of the rights of their citizens freely to enjoy and pursue their activities in outer space in a congenial setting for the market economy; (d) the determination of normative principles and standards and an assessment of whether they can provide useful criteria and guidelines for the future activities in space; (e) the monitoring of developments of agreements and international instruments affecting space to determine whether such instruments need amending or refinements, or even replacement; (f) the identification of areas where rules of the road can be adopted to prevent harm or damage from space activities or inter-state interference; (g) the design of working drafts and supplementary opinions to ease the adoption of alternative dispute measures to resolve differences in a spirit of cooperation among states or their enterprises conducted in space; (h) the increased use of research, development and testing activities that are shared among states as to the work performed and the benefits to be enjoyed in joint or reciprocating tnerprise in space.

CONCLUDING OBSERVATIONS. By way of brief overview, the legal rights to property established among states in the global community are major factors upon which states rely in controlling or extending their claims to control, exercise sovereignty, and influence in general. States defend themselves, their citizens and the property under their jurisdiction and control. The initiation of the use of force is in large measure a matter for each state to determine for itself so that future actions taken to restrict, provide guidelines for determining the initiation of war, or to guide the war-making decisions will be of increasing importance for regimes of deterrence or prevention as we gain further technological control over the weapons of the future.

How does the element of property and property rights apply in this area? Setting aside the competition over property and the ambiguities over proprietary rights treated as property, it is evident that when the competition is over strategic locations of sites or objects in space, or over large deposits of resources and energy easily accessible, or over the more habitable locations in space that competition might lead to disputes as they have in the past, and to warfare. Competition for locations in space by the same token to enhance the strategic position of military forces terrestrially may lead to military conflicts and disputes with regard to terrestrial conflicts, aided or supported by activities in space.

Because states may defend themselves by recourse to military force wherever they are opposing each other, a major recommendation of this paper is to find the means to reduce the opportunities for exclusive claims over property or territorial property that might be the subject of competition. This, apparently, is what the treaties on outer space attempt, even though they are have not be drafted deliberately for this purpose.

The conceptual framework for looking at the rights of states in outer space is currently framed under traditional perspectives, i.e., under the perspectives of states that consider the exclusive claims and rights to activities and property are paramount, We can choose to regulate under this framework with little change to the framework. Or we can examine the more complex task of looking into a public order that we might draft in detail to cover the activities of space in the future. This second alternative calls for the promotion of new perspectives among states about cooperation, sharing rights and benefits, and so on. But the choice between the two, or a mixture of the two, will determine the future law and legal rights of property as part of that law.

It is apparent that the claims of states to property extend to claims that reach natural objects and the resources they contain, including asteroids, planets, and so on, as well as to manmade objects. The claims of states are largely dependent upon their control or mastery of the applicable or relevant technologies and the deference afforded to them and their claims for controls over how outer space is to be regulated in view especially of the major changes in the applicable technologies. Outer space activities are activities that entail great costs. These costs are incurred for achieving controls and mastery over the relevant technologies, but lead to the expectations among the space active states that they will receive major benefits or rewards for their efforts. Not the least of these is control over the regime and regulation of activities in space.

International law, regulating the activities and relations among states, is in many respects a "soft" law, or law that is subject to differences ranging from nuances and subtleties to major and opposing claims among those who interpret and apply it. Only through a continued practice among states will these be problems of uncertainty with regard to the relevant law and its applications be overcome, and a hard law established for the maintenance of international peace and security and the promotion of human rights shaped into force. The primary need, it seems, aside from drawing up the norms and norm guided practices is the assurance that states live up in good faith to their commitments and pursue them to achieve common social goals.[4]

Dr. Harry H. Almond, Jr.

1. Numerous treaties, aside from those cited in this paper, have functional regulation, or legislative impacts, affecting or regulating property rights involved in outer space. See for such documents, Committee Print, 95th Cong. 2d Sess., SPACE LAW, December 1978, U.S. Govt Print. Off., Washington. The page numbers given below are taken from this Print. Among the functional elements that might be mentioned are those concerning the regulation against harmful interference in the telecommunications conventions [p.140; 81; 83; 87; the responsibilities for maintaining rational use with a superficial resemblance to Article 11 of the Moon Treaty [see p.86]; the property allocations in terms of radio frequencies, the advancing control through the sequence of regulations, the problems involving reserved orbits; and the duty to provide for a rational use of space for radio frequencies and communications; other treaties provide similar impacts. Special attention should be given the emphasis in U.S. legislation upon promoting science and technology in the Comsat Legislation, p.541 et seq., and upon the environment, pollution, contamination, health care, peaceful uses of space, and the national security.

2. The treaties referred to in this paper: The UN Charter, entered into force on October 24, 1945, UNTS Vol. 557 p. 143; Treaty on Principles Governing the Activities of States in the Exploration and Use of Outer Space including the Moon and other Celestial Bodies, entered into force on October 10, 1967, UNTS Vol. 610, p.205; Agreement on the Rescue of Astronauts, the Return of Astronauts and the Return of Objects launched into Outer Space, entered into force on December 3, 1968, USNTS Vol. 672, p.119; Convention on International Liability for Damage caused by Space Objects, Entered into force on September 1, 1972, UNGA Res. 2777 (XXVI) Annex, of November 29, 1971; Convention on Registration of Objects launched into Outer Space, entered into force on September 15, 1976, UNGA Res. 3235 (XIXX) Annex, of November 12, 1974; Agreement Governing the Activities of States on the Moon and other Celestial Bodies, entered into force on July 12, 1984, UNGA Res. 34/68 Annex, of December 5, 1979. The paper does not consider the numerous bilateral agreements, and only refers, by implication to the major treaties creating such institutions as INMARSAT, and to the International Telecommunications Convention (entered into force for the United States April 7, 1976. TIAS 8572). This Convention contains provisions for allocating frequencies and radio bands among states, and these provisions involve a property interest. The Convention also regulates such frequencies as property. They are not to be the source of harmful interference - a matter that is of the nature of regulated property.

3. One major future event might bring states together, notwithstanding their differences in wealth and influence. If a major space object - whether manmade, or an object such as a comet, asteroid, or other natural object - were to threaten the earth, the costs and technologies for diverting the space object, or disintegrating it, would be very great. We could anticipate a very

large public support worldwide for immediate action regardless of cost to overcome this threat, for shared and cooperative efforts on a great scale with regard to the technologies and funds involved, and so on. This is the major problem of space debris presently being considered by the members of the IAF.

4. The texts concerning outer space and its conceptual problems are numerous. Among them, with substantial bibliographies, are those of Christol, THE MODERN INTERNATIONAL LAW OF OUTER SPACE, Pergamon: New York, 1982; Lipson and Katzenbach, THE LAW OF OUTER SPACE [Bibliography, up to 1961, needs revision to the present date, to complete the "data bank" at general disposal], American Bar Foundation: Chicago, 1961; Benko, de Graaff and Reijnen, SPACE LAW IN THE UNITED NATIONS, Nijhoff: Dordrecht, 1985; Lay and Taubenfeld, THE LAW RELATING TO ACTIVITIES OF MAN IN SPACE, American Bar Foundation: Chicago, 1970 [contains major bibliography, but not up to date]; McDoungal and Associates, STUDIES IN WORLD PLUBLIC ORDER, Yale Univ. Press: New Haven, Conn. 1960 [contains essay of McDougal and Lipson on outer space]; McDougal et al, THE PUBLIC ORDER OF OUTER SPACE, Yale Univ Press: New Haven 1980.

IISL-96-IISL.1.04

THE COMMON HERITAGE OF MANKIND: IMPLICATIONS FOR THE LEGAL STATUS OF PROPERTY RIGHTS ON THE MOON AND CELESTIAL BODIES

by

V. S. MANI
Professor of International Space Law,
School of International Studies,
Jawaharlal Nehru University,
New Delhi, India, and Member,
IISL

ABSTRACT

The concept of common heritage of mankind (CHM) cannot be understood in terms of the Roman law concepts, as it is of recent origin, a product of confluence of the various cultures of today's world. It stands for community property, for community benefit, and for the benefit of the posterity. Equity is the basis for its understanding. The Antarctica model of resource management pays scant regard for CHM. The UNCLOS 1982 model is perhaps more tolerable, though not the ideal. In view of the increasing commercialisation of outer space, it is time we reiterated the objectives of CHM in outer space and established a community perspective of sharing of common resources of outer space.

I. CHM - A PERCEPTION

The concept of Common Heritage of Mankind (CHM) is of nascent origin in international law. It refers to things that should belong to, be shared and benefited by all mankind, and that should be protected and preserved for the future generations for similar enjoyment. This concept is not necessarily comprehensible or explainable through the `ancient' Roman law concepts such as *res nullius*, and *res communis*, because the community awareness to common problems and of the `heritage' content of commonly sharable resources and amenities (`global commons') is of modern origin on the international plane. This apart, the concept of CHM represents the aspirations and expectations of the overwhelming majority of the contemporary international community. To this majority, comprising mostly the developing countries, resources of the international spaces must be shared equitably taking into account the special needs of these countries. Equality is not necessarily equity, nor is equality of opportunity or access necessarily equity, where such opportunity or access is meaningless without technological and economic capability to utilise it. Furthermore, expansion of international community to encompass the countries of the Third World also brought with it the rich cultural and civilizational heritage of the ancient communities of Asia and Africa where the concept of community property has a special meaning and special connotation in contradistinction to the Roman law variations of *res communis*.[1] This CHM, to the countries of the Third World, connotes a common pool of facilities and benefits owned by the community but managed in such a way that they are distributed equitably to all its members and that they are in essence preserved for the benefit of the future generations as well. The Hindu law, for instance, speaks of the joint family property in this sense, the common pool of property, of life, and of relations, contributed by each member of the extended family building on what was inherited from the past, with each member legally entitled to a floating share in the property (the exact share crystallising only at the time of legal partition), and with the seniormost managing the affairs for "the benefit of the estate", often in consultation with fellow elders of the family. The rights and obligations in respect of the property transcend generations. The concept of CHM in respect of sharable resources and amenities or global commons is here to stay. From the concept of world cultural heritage, to that of common heritage of resources and to that of common environmental heritage, the CHM is still evolving. President Bedjaoui of the International Court even talks about the technological heritage of mankind.[2]

II. THE 1967 SPACE TREATY

The legal aspects of the CHM started taking concrete shape in the context of the Antarctica, in view of its global relevance. Some of the elements of the concept of CHM in the context of outer space began to emerge with the Outer Space Treaty of 1967 through the UN Outer Space Declaration of 1963, represented by the term "province of all mankind", and the transposition of the Antarctica principles. However, conceived as it was against the background of the Cold War, the main concern of the 1963 Declaration and the 1967 Treaty was prevention and elimination of Big Power conflict from the realm of outer space. Also, at the time of adoption of these legal instruments, the awareness of the natural resources content of the `use' of outer space, was unclear. Yet the Third World countries did place on record of what order their expectations of equitable sharing of outer space benefits would be[3] The Big Powers no doubt looked at the treaty mainly as one of the arms control/disarmament measures between the two Blocs - as is clear from the depository clause of the treaty.

With space transportation and space industrialization becoming near-term realities, it is now time to re-examine the problems and prospects for an Outer Space Resource Management Regime.

III. THE UNCLOS III MODEL

Although it was Ambassador Cocca of Argentina who first used the CHM concept in the context of outer space resources, the immediate concern of the international community was the need for insulation of the international sea areas from Big Power conflicts and prevention of `sea-grabbing' by the technologically advanced countries. Hence the Pardo proposal of 1967 to proclaim the international seabed area and its resources "beyond the existing national jurisdiction" to be the CHM, which triggered the Third United Nations negotiations on the law of the sea (UNCLOS III). Pardoes dream, however, floundered at the altar of state sovereignty. As the law of the sea debates progressed, first the CHM's area and resources shrank with the international community recognizing the coastal states' claims for jurisdiction over vast expanses of the adjacent sea areas under the concepts of the Exclusive Economic Zone and the Continental Shelf, making the adjective "existing" preceding "national jurisdiction" redundant. The second, more sustained, onslaught of state sovereignty over the CHM came from the developed countries to whom the CHM meant the institutionalisation of the `menace' of international socialism (read communism), proliferation of international bureaucracy, and threat to their technological superiority - in short it was an anathema to everything the Western capitalist ideology stood for. The more powerful of these countries by their threat of boycott forced substantial compromises on the concept of CHM, as reflected in the 1982 Convention of the Law of the Sea. As if this was not enough, the new Reagan Administration in the United States retracted from a host of `gentleman's agreements', stormed out forcing further watering down of the institutional and operational aspects of the CHM.[4] Even the 1982 version of these aspects in fact amounted to merely a few breadcrums thrown at the Third World;[5] but the 1994 version represents a further sell out with new concepts leading to doing away with transfer of technology, which means little prospects for the great international CHM experiment to materialise into reality.

The UNCLOS III unfolded through three broad phases, namely (1) the adoption of the CHM Declaration in 1970, (2) initial divergence of views on whether an international machinery was necessary to manage the CHM, or whether the attempt at such a machinery was premature, leading finally to a broad agreement in principle on the need for an international machinery; and (3) operational aspects of the international machinery for the international seabed area.

The second phase of the negotiations revealed state positions varying between three standpoints, namely (a) that there was no need for an international machinery or that it was too premature at that point in time; (b) that there was an urgent need for it in order to pre-empt potential conflicts and to ensure equitable distribution of all potential benefits from the CHM, and (c) that it was desirable to implement the idea of international machinery first in response to the actual needs of seabed exploitation. From this flowed a further set of three main questions:[6] (i) Who should explore and exploit the resources of the international seabed area? (ii) What should be the *modus operandi* to control and regulate exploration and exploitation activities in the area? (iii) What resources and activities should be covered by the projected regime? Of these, the first question provoked two extreme views at the outset; one, that the international machinery should not engage in sea-bed exploration and exploitation activities; and the other, that the international machinery should have the exclusive right to engage in such activities representing the CHM. From the first view emerged a projected compromise view that the international machinery participate in sea-bed exploration and exploitation alongside states and their national entities, according to its financial and technical capability. And the second view softened into another compromise position that the international machinery be given an option to participate in the seabed mining activities either directly or "in such other manner as it may from time to time determine" (which phrase opened the door for direct participation by states or state-sponsored entities under licences). Many countries of the Third World forcefully argued against the international machinery to be a mere licence-issuing body. Mexico asserted that there was nothing to justify a "system of operating permits which would assign to the legitimate owner the role of a mere spectator".[7] The Iraqi delegate even argued that "a purely mercantilist *lassez faire* system of licences" could not be reconciled with the concept of the CHM.[8] To Sri Lanka, the "ability" of the international machinery to carry out mining operations on its own represented "the highest expression of its control role as the administrator of the common heritage of mankind".[9] It would appear that the second compromise view (i.e. the fourth view) underlies the UNCLOS Convention 1982.

The divergence of views on the *modus operandi* to control the mining activities closely followed the divergence of positions on who should conduct the mining activities. The developing countries such as India proposed an International Sea-bed Authority with an Assembly of plenary powers and a small executive organ called the Council responsible to the former, and a seabed corporation with a legal personality of its own to operate as a business organisation within the general policies of the Assembly.

The third question, what seabed resources and activities should be covered by the emerging international regime, proved to be equally controversial. Should the international seabed regime concern itself with all the non-living resources of the seabed, or only with the polymetallic manganese nodules? Should it regulate all activities on the international seabed area or only mining-related activities? What was the impact of the principle of non-appropriation on the commercial interests in the recovery and marketing of the resources? It was finally agreed that the regime should only deal with mining-related activities. The principle of non-appropriation led to a distinction between "resources" *in situ* (all non-living resources) and "minerals" (i.e., "resources, when recovered from the Area"). While the resources were not subject to alienation, the minerals could be alienated and rights over them acquired by states or natural or juridical persons according to the regulations laid down under the convention or by the International Seabed Authority.

Differences of views, in the third phase of the UNCLOS III, then focussed on the basic conditions of seabed operations.[10] In other words, if the basic conditions were spelt out in great detail defining clearly the scope of the discretionary power of the Authority and the rights and duties of participants in the seabed activities with a disputes settlement mechanism, doctrinnaire debates would become merely academic. The result was Part XI of the Convention, with Annexes supplemented by the PREPCOM decisions and the 1994 agreement. Despite the onslaughts dealt by these "supplements" on the concept of CHM, there is no doubt that the CHM principles contained in Articles 136 to 149 of the Convention will provide guidance in the interpretation of the whole Part XI.

IV. THE ANTARCTICA MODEL

The draft Antarctica Minerals Treaty of 1988 has proved to be controversial despite the fact that it, like the Antarctica Treaty of 1959, swears by "the interest of all mankind". The questions whether it was legitimate for the Antarctica Treaty parties to institute a mineral exploitation regime in the interest of all mankind, yet ignoring the claims of the United Nations to participate in the negotiations, or whether such a regime was compatible with the Antarctica Treaty of 1959 or the Law of the Sea Convention of 1982, may be relevant *per se,* but they need not arrest us here. The draft treaty, now shelved for 50 years since 1991, mainly envisages a licensing regime for "prospecting", "exploration" and "development" (i.e. exploitation) activities. The draft treaty defines "mineral resources" to mean "all non-living natural non-renewable resources, including fossil fuels, metallic and non-metallic minerals". The draft seeks to provide for policies and standards for environment impact assessment of the Antarctic and associated ecosystems, and atmospheric, terrestrial or marine environment, and of the global or regional climate or weather patterns. The institutional mechanisms envisaged include the Antarctica Mineral Resources Commission to be assisted by a Scientific, Technical and Environmental Advisory Committee, with the Commission empowered to establish an Antarctic Mineral Resources Regulatory Committee for each area identified for purposes of resource management. The draft treaty defines the rights of the operators and the powers of the treaty organs and provides for a disputes settlement mechanism.

V. CHM AND THE MOON TREATY

The drafting history of the Moon Agreement, 1979, has been well documented elsewhere.[11] Suffice it to note here that the treaty as finally adopted represents the consensus that while the moon, other celestial bodies and their resources constitute the CHM, the concept finds expression not only in the provisions of the treaty, but also in the international regime to be established when exploitation of the natural resources of these celestial bodies is about to become feasible. In fact, Article 11 of the Moon Treaty 1979 does three different things: (a) It anticipates the eventual establishment of an international regime for exploitation of the outer space natural resources; (b) It postulates four broad principles to which the new regime shall accord with.

Is the concept of CHM applicable in outer space without a future resource management regime? The answer seems to be in the affirmative for two reasons. First, a principle of international law may exist independent of any linkage with an international organisation.[12] Second, Article 11(1) of the treaty clarifies that the CHM encompasses not only the resources but the celestial bodies themselves and that the future resource management regime would only govern the exploitation of the natural resources of these bodies.

The moon treaty identifies "the natural resources" of the celestial bodies for exploitation. The natural resources *in situ* would be part of CHM and inappropriable. However, the Article 11(5) regime could provide for their recovery and alienability of rights in them. The treaty clarifies that the activities to be dealt with by the future regime to be agreed upon pursuant to Article 11(5) would relate to the exploitation of these natural resources. The future Article 11(5) regime will not deal with other uses of the celestial bodies, as other uses are not "natural resources" of the celestial bodies. Use of one of the celestial bodies as a stop-over or a further launching pad, or use of samples of substances from these bodies for scientific research purposes, will not amount to an activity relating to exploitation of the natural resources.[13]

While it is pragmatic to expect that

conceptually, the Article 11(5) regime will fall in line with the international seabed regime under the UNCLOS 1982, the former must, for its validity and legitimacy, embody provisions for fulfilment of the four CHM objectives laid down in Article 11(7), namely:

a) the orderly and safe development of the outer space resources;

b) their rational management;

c) expansion of opportunities in the use of these resources; and

d) equitable sharing of benefits derived from these resources.

Evidently, both the environmental and safety concerns as well as the equitable sharing of opportunities and benefits are underscored by Article 11(7), on equitable sharing of benefits two points may be noted: One, "benefits" are not necessarily confined to monetary benefits; they encompass all benefits of space resource exploitation, including those of technology. Two, equitable sharing should take into account both the special interests and needs of the developing countries, as well as the efforts of those countries which have contributed to the exploration of the celestial bodies.

In order to ensure these Article 11(7) objectives as against the ever-increasing commercialisation of outer space, a mere licensing body will not do. There is a need for an International Space Resource Management Authority with close linkage with the United Nations. One of the objectives of this agency should be to associate and encourage all interested states in space resource activities. Such a space resource regime would also need simultaneous strengthening of the space liability regime, the Registration Convention, the Rescue and Return of Astronauts convention, the intellectual property regime, exchange of information, transfer of space technology, and so on. Indeed, there is a need for international financing of space resource endeavours as well.

Will the Space Powers rise above their short term, narrow, Shylockian view of profits, and meet the challenge of the next millennium with magnanimity, compassion and camaraderie to the whole of international community?

REFERENCES

1. See P.K. Kartha, "Some Legal Problems Concerning Outer Space", IJIL, vol. 3 (1963), p. 1. He quotes Peru at p. 10.

2. Mohammed Bedjaoui, Towards A New International Economic Order (UNESCO, Paris, 1979), p. 231.

3. See Kartha, note 1, pp. 9 ff.

4. For more on this, see R.P. Anand, "UN Convention on the Law of the Sea and the United States", IJIL, vol. 24 (1984), p. 153.

5. For this view, see V.S. Mani, "The United Nations, Law of the Sea and the Developing Countries", in M.S. Rajan, et al (ed.), The Non-Aligned and the United Nations (New Delhi, 1987), p. 56.

6. See V.S. Mani, "Resources of the Seabed Beyond National Jurisdiction : Who Shall Exploit and How?", IJIL, vol. 14 (1974), p. 245.

7. UN Sea-bed Committee's Working Group Document, U.N. Doc. A/AC. 138/94/Add.), reprinted in Doc. A/9021, vol. II, Article 9(c), cited in Mani, note 6, p. 248, fn. 24.

8. See UN Doc. A/AC.138/SC.1/SR. 40, p. 116.

9. See UN Doc. A/AC.138/SC.1/SR. 43, p. 154.

10. V.S. Mani, "Basic Conditions for Sea-bed Operations", International Studies (New Delhi), vol. 15 (1976), p. 321. The debates had also led to studies of economic implications of seabed products on landbased economies. See Vathsala Mani, "Exploitation of Seabed Minerals : Some Economic Issues", India Quarterly (New Delhi), (1979), p. 54.

11. See, e.g., Carl Q. Christol, The Modern International Law of Outer Space (Elmsford, N.Y., 1982), pp. 246-341.

12. Nicaragua Case, ICJ Reports 1986, p. 14 at p. 105, where the ICJ held that the right of self-defence is a customary law right, despite the organisational linkage provided in Article 51 of the UN Charter and exists independently of the latter.

13. See also Kartha, note 1.

Clearness regarding Property Rights on the Moon and Other Celestial Bodies

H.L. van Traa-Engelman
The Netherlands

Abstract

Human activities in Outer Space have prompted the need to identify and evaluate the rights and risks of those engaged in space activities. Commercialization of space activities has added another impulse to this evaluation, urging the assessment of property rights in the field of space activities against the background of current law systems.
Enlarging the scope of space applications - the main theme of the 1996 IAF Congress - will include space activities in relation to the future exploration and exploitation of the Moon and Other Celestial Bodies. The legal system governing such activities will influence the decision-making process on further research and development. Moreover, it will be of specific importance for the actual involvement of organizations and entrepreneurs in the exploitation of these regions in outer space.
In the light of this evaluation the Outer Space Treaty and the Moon Agreement - as lex specialis - will be examined; with special attention to the provisions concerning the establishment of an international regime to govern the exploitation of the natural resources of the moon and other celestial bodies.
An analysis of these provisions and their status as a part of international space law will set the stage for future international efforts to accommodate the exploitation of these natural resources against the background of present realities.
The execution of property rights and in particular intellectual property rights outside the earth environment will probably challenge existing national systems in order to come to an internationally agreed and acceptable system.

Introduction

Man's presence in outer space yielded the need to establish a legal system for his activities in the outer space environment resulting into the body of international space law, consisting of the five international Space Conventions. The evolution and diversification of space activities, necessitated the international community to create more specific rules for varying space applications and for international cooperation in the different fields.
The next stage, the commercialization of space activities and private enterprise involvement urged to identify the rights and risks of those engaged in space activities, effecting national space legislation. Enlarging the scope of space applications to activities on the Moon and Other Celestial bodies, urges us to examine the existing framework of space law against the background of present realities.
An assessment of the rights and risks connected with space activities performed on the Moon or Other Celestial Bodies will be necessary to judge whether the present regulation will accommodate not only states, but also private entrepreneurs to involve in such activities.
In particular private entrepreneurs and investors will only be motivated to engage in costly space endeavour, when the legal environment accommodates specific rights, such as property rights in general and intellectual property rights in particular.
Current prospects to exploit the Moon and Other Celestial Bodies strengthens this need to assess the rights and obligations connected with a commercial use of the natural resources in these areas.
The legal status of property rights in these areas of outer space will determine the commercial viability of the exploitation of the natural resources present.
Therefore we should examine in the first place the existing legal regime in place, that is to say the Outer Space Treaty and in particular the

Moon Agreement 1), being the *lex specialis*, governing the area of the Moon and Other Celestial bodies.

Reassessment of existing regulation

Assessment of the Moon Agreement has already taken place during a number of IISL Colloquia, the first already 15 years ago in Tokyo 2) under the issue "Implications of the Agreement Governing the Activities of States on the Moon and Other Celestial Bodies". And I like to quote one of the first sentences of my paper presented at that occasion, dealing with the legal Conse quences and Practical aspects, reading "The achievement of the Moon Treaty, no matter how controversial the follow-up will be, seems to be a new step in the development of the Law of Outer Space, reflecting man's progress in astronautics and relating technologies as brought together within and governed by a set of international rules".

And indeed controversy has appeared among space lawyers and politicians as to the contents of the Moon Agreement, in particular regarding rights and obligations connected with the use and exploitation of the natural resources of the Moon and Other Celestial Bodies.

It is evident that the commercialization of space activities in general has shifted the accent from the activities of states towards a progressive involvement of private enterprise.

Therefore, a re-evaluation of the rights and risks connected with the exploitation of natural re sources of the Moon etc. will not only influence the decision-making process on further research and development by governments, but even more so by private enterprise.

Moreover, it will be of specific importance for the actual involvement of organizations and entrepreneurs in the exploitation of the natural resources of these regions in outer space, specifically the Moon, Mars and the asteroids, where natural resources are known or thought to in clude oxygen, silicon, carbon, aluminum, iron, titanium, manganese, magnesium, chrome, water, nitrogen and hydrogen. 3)

To assess the existence and/or possibility of property rights on the Moon and Other Celestial Bodies, we have in the first place the Outer Space Treaty, governing the Activities of States in the Exploration and Use of Outer Space, including the Moon and Other Celestial Bodies 4)

Article I tells us that "The exploration and use of outer space, including the Moon and other celestial bodies, shall be carried out *for the benefit and in the interest of all countries .....*" whilst that region shall be *free for exploration and use by all States* without discrimination of any kind, on the basis of equality and in accordance with international law, and there shall be *free access* to all areas of celestial bodies.

Moreover :There shall be freedom of scientific investigation, and States shall facilitate and encourage international cooperation therein.

Apart from the freedom principle expressed by the just mentioned provisions, Article VIII rules that jurisdiction and control of objects launched into outer space remains with the state of registry.

Property rights

Hence for property rights in relation to these space objects, it refers back to the national law of the relating state. It establishes the conditions for a legal regime based on quasi-territoriality. This is in line with the fact that in general - property rights and intellectual property rights in particular are based on the principle of *territoriality*.

In relation herewith the International Government Agreement on the Space Station (IGA) 5) applies in its Article 21, par 2, the fiction of territoriality over activities taking place in or on a specific space station element.

In order to bring national legislation into conformity with the fiction of territoriality the US, for instance, has added a new section to the existing US Patent Act. 6)

An International Government Agreement after the example of the IGA on the Space Station, may solve the questions on property rights connected with the commercial exploitation of the natural resources of the moon by creating a similar regime based on *quasi-territoriality*.

Regarding Outer Space itself : Article II of the Outer Space Treaty stipulates that Outer Space, including the Moon and Other Celestial Bodies, is not subject to national appropriation by claim of sovereignty, by means of use or occupation, or by any other means. Thus applying the non-appropriation principle.

Regarding the meaning of the non-appropriation

principle 7), the history of the Outer Space Treaty indicates that this term reinforces the principal of freedom and access expressed by Article I. However it should be conceded that free access to all areas of celestial bodies may be limited by the provisions of Article XII, depending on the meaning one attaches to the use of the term reciprocity as stipulated in the rule that "All stations, installations, equipment and space vehicles on the Moon and other celestial bodies shall be open to representatives of other States, Parties to the Treaty, on the basis of reciproc ity........"

In any case imposes this formulation, a slight limitation on the execution of property rights vested in those stations, installations etc.

Subsequently we have to research the position of the Moon Agreement 8) as lex specialis and a more recent instrument of law, governing the activities of States on the moon and other celestial bodies, and compare its provisions with those of the Outer Space Treaty discussed - above.

The freedom principle can be found in Article IV stating that :"The exploration and use of the moon shall be *the province of all mankind...*" a term also found in Article I of the Outer Space Treaty 9).

Article XI, par.2 of the Moon Agreement ex presses the non-appropriation principle using the same wording as the OST.

However the first paragraph of the same Article XI adds that:"The moon and its natural re - sources are the *common heritage of mankind* which find its expression in the provisions of this agreement and in particular in paragraph 5 of this article.

Paragraph 3 provides moreover:"Neither the surface nor the subsurface of the moon, nor any part thereof or natural resources in place, shall become property of any State, international intergovernmental or non-governmental organization, national organization or non-governmental entity or of any natural person.

This regulation seems to provide more clearness than the OST since it specifically prohibits appropriation of natural resources of the moon and other celestial bodies of any kind by anybody.

However, at the same time reveals the use of the wording natural resources "in place" a weakness in the system of complete prohibition.

Leading to the suggestion that natural resources, when removed, are not covered by the non-appropriation principle and thus offering enter prises interested in the exploitation of natural resources a possibility to establish property rights. However this can only be realised when the existing Moon Agreement does not imply a moratorium 10) on the commercial exploitation of the natural resources of the moon for the states, parties involved, a point to which I will return later.

A further strengthening of the non-appropriation principle in relation to the surface and subsurface of the moon and other celestial bodies, appears to be provided by the stipulation :"the placement of personnel, space vehicles, equipment facilities, stations and installations on or below the surface or subsurface, shall not create a right of ownership over the surface or the subsurface of the moon (and other celestial bodies) or any areas thereof.

But this provision leads, in my opinion not automatically to a prohibition of property rights in relation to the exploitation of natural resources.

International regime for the exploitation of natural resources of the moon and other celestial bodies

However, the same provision does make a connection with paragraph 5 of the same Article XI, which reads :" States Parties to this Agreement hereby undertake to establish an international regime, including appropriate procedures, to govern the exploitation of the natural resources of the moon as such exploitation is about to be come feasible",

whilst paragraph 7 describes the main purposes of such an international regime being:

(a)The orderly and safe development of the natural resources of the moon;

(b) The rational management of the natural resources;

(c) The expansion of opportunities in the use of those resources;

(d) An equitable sharing by all States Parties in the benefits derived from those resources, whereby the interests and needs of the developing countries, as well as the efforts of those countries which have contributed either directly or indirectly to the exploration of the moon, shall be given due consideration

The Moon Agreement versus Outer Space Treaty

For property rights vested in objects brought from the earth to the Moon etc we have Article XII par.1 of the Moon Agreement stipulating : "States Parties shall retain jurisdiction and control over their personnel, vehicles, equipment and facilities, stations and installations on the moon. The ownership of space vehicles, equipment, facilities, stations and installations shall not be affected by their presence on the Moon.

This provision is in line with Article VIII OST, applying the principle of state sovereignty and accommodating the application of national law for property rights.

Although, paragraph III of the Moon Agreement contains a slight limitation of property rights by stipulating:"In the event of an emergency involving a threat to human life, States Parties may use equipment , vehicles, installations, facilities or supplies of other States on the moon."

But this seems very reasonable, whilst moreover in such a case prompt notification should be made to the Secretary-General.

Furthermore, in line with the provision of the OST, Article XV, par.1 of the Moon Agreement secures accessibility by stating that "all space vehicles, equipment, facilities, stations, and installations on the moon shall be open to other States Parties. But it has left out the wording "on the basis of reciprocity" as defined in the OST, whilst it connects the provision itself with the right to assure compatibility with the provisions of the Agreement. The paragraph provides further for consultation with reasonable advance notice, like the provision in the OST, but elaborates extensively on procedures worked out in the paragraphs 2 and 3.

The Moon Agreement offers moreover in Article VIII States, Parties the freedom to land space objects on the moon and to launch therefrom as well as to place and move personnel, space vehicles, equipment and facilities, stations and installations anywhere on or below the surface of the moon, although such activities must not interfere with the activities of other States Parties, in which case consultations must be undertaken in accordance with Article XV, par.2 and 3.

Returning to the possibility to establish property rights in relation with the natural resources of the moon etc. we still have to scrutinize the legal regime of these natural resources as provided for by Article XI of the Moon Agreement.

As mentioned before, paragraph 3 of this article stipulates non-appropriation of the natural resources *in place*. This restricts in my opinion the application of the non-appropriation principle to natural resources as long as they are not re moved from their original place.

However this does not necessarily lead to the conclusion that appropriation can take place at random when the natural resources are being moved.

In this respect we have to look at the connection with paragraph 5 regarding the establishment of an international regime. And it is exactly the regulation providing for an international regime, that according to some critics, might inhibit commercial activities on the moon and other celestial bodies by placing a moratorium on the exploitation of the natural resources outside a framework of an international regime as stipulated by the provisions of Article XI (of the Moon Agreement).

As the Moon Agreement stands today Article XI, par.5 reads :"States Parties to this Agreement hereby undertake to establish an international regime, including appropriate procedures, to govern the exploitation of the natural re sources of the moon *as such exploitation is about to become feasible.*

Furthermore, obliges paragraph 6 States to inform the UN General Secretary, the international scientific community and the public of the discovery of any natural resources in order to facilitate the establishment of such an international regime.

Finally paragraph 7 elaborates on the main purposes of such international regime, as mentioned before.

It is evident that the Moon Agreement and in particular the regulation of an international regime for the exploitation of its natural resources refers to States, Parties .

Hence in principal are individuals or private commercial organisations not directly bound by its provisions .

On the other hand it is also true that Article XIV of the Moon Agreement vests States Parties with international responsibility for national activities on the moon whether such activities are carried on by governmental agencies or by non-governmental entities, and for assuring that national activities are carried out in conformity with the provisions set forth in the present Agreement". It obliges them moreover to maintain authority and continuing supervision.

Hence States, Parties are bound not to authorize private entities activities not in compliance with the Moon Agreement as much are they are themselves bound by its provision.

Having said all this the main issue focuses on the question whether Article 11 and in particular the provisions regarding the establishment of an international regime for the exploitation of the natural resources of the moon place a moratorium for commercial exploitation activities in general. The history of the Moon Agreement, including the discussion in UNCOPUOS, confirms the understanding that the Moon Agreement does not derogate from or limits the provisions of the Outer Space Treaty of 1967 11).

Where the OST permits private enterprise to conduct activities in outer space within the rights and obligations provided by Article VI, and in accordance with Article II, the Moon Agreement corresponds with these rules as laid down in Article XIV and Article XI, par.2.

Article II of the Moon Agreement, which de clares that all activities on the moon including its exploration and use shall be carried out in accordance with international law, strengthens the opinion that the Moon Agreement does not derogate from the tenet of the OST.

If an important change of mind had taken place in view of the newly established Moon Agreement this should have been brought about by a clear use of language.

The same argumentation goes for the meaning of the word "use" in the term exploration and use .

It is undisputed that the term "use" in the OST includes commercial use 12), hence covering *exploitation* by private enterprise. The same wording maintained in the Moon Agreement does not leave room for a totally new or restricted meaning of use in relation to the area of the moon.

Nevertheless, the fact that so few states have ratified the Moon Agreement, still expresses dissatisfaction or rather uncertainty regarding the permissibility to exploit the natural re sources, apart from the establishment of an international regime as provided for by Article XI.

In relation herewith I like to quote from a publication in 1980 13), which still appears to be relevant when suggesting" that the anticipation of an international regime to govern the exploitation of the natural resources of the moon leads some persons to argue that future interpretations and negotiations will inevitably work against the interests of certain states (read in stead of certain states: the United States) 14).

A novel kind of property rights

Hence, concluding that there still is a risk for a moratorium on the exploitation of natural re sources on the moon etc, which might hamper commercial exploitation under the existing provisions of the Moon Agreement, this problem might be solved by the attachment of an Understanding to the Moon Agreement. Ensuring, that whatever legal regime ultimately comes into being, the ability and right of states as well as private enterprise to use and exploit the natural resources of the moon will be recognised in so far as this will be done in accordance with the purpose as expressed in paragraph 7, Article XI of the Moon Agreement. This would pave the way for a novel kind of property rights, which take due care of the interests of investors combined with the interests of mankind at large in the exploitation of the natural resources of the moon and other celestial bodies.

The accommodation of these property rights and intellectual property rights in particular could be based on an International Government Agreement after the example of the Space Station, taking due regard to special characteristics in relation to space resources and being subject to specific requirements including the principle "for the benefit of all mankind".

Harmonization

Harmonization amongst different national systems should be reached by imposing specific requirements responding to the provisions of Paragraph 7, Article XI of the Moon Treaty.

In this manner the Moon Treaty supplemented with the Memorandum will provide an incentive for investment in exploitation activities by interested parties as soon as national legislations provide a legal regime where special property rights for national resources on the moon or other celestial bodies can be established.

As soon as an international regime will be established in accordance with Art. 11 of the Moon Treaty, States Parties will have to make provisions to honour specific property rights on natural resources of the moon etc. acquired through national legislation, but to be accomodated within the constraints and requirements of such an international regime .

A mechanism to resolve disputes will have to be included in the rules and regulations of such an international regime.

Notes

1. Agreement Governing the Activities of States on the Moon and Other Celestial Bodies, done at New York on 18 December 1979, entered into force on 11 July 1984 (18 ILM 1434; UN Doc.A/RES34/68 of 14 December 1979 Annex)

2. Proceedings of the 23rd Colloquium on the Law of Outer Space, held in Tokyo, 1980, AIAA, 1981

3. See Raclin, Crier C., From Ice to Ether: The Adoption of a Region to Govern Resource Exploitation in Outer Space, Northwestern Journal of International Law & Business, Fall-Winter 1986, Vol.7 Number 4, p.728 etc., The commission report of the US National Commission on Space, Pioneering the Space Frontier 3 (1986). See also Harris, P.R., A case for permanent lunar development and investment, Space Policy 1994, 10 (3) 187-188, note 1, referring to two recent American and two European studies; and Chicako Iguchi, International Cooperation in lunar and space development: Japan's role, in particular note 1, referring to the Intermediate Survey Report on Lunar Base and Lunar Resources, Future Technology Institute, Tokyo, 1989, pp. 25-26

4. January 27, 1967 (entered into force October 10, 1967 18 UST 2410; TIAS 6447; 610 UNTS 205)

5. Done at Washington D.C., 29 September 1988. See for Text of the IGA, Proceedings of the Colloquium on manned Space Stations - Legal Issues -, Paris, 7-8 November 1989, ESA SP-305, ISBN 92-9092-062-9, January 1990

6. H.R. 2946

7. See Jasentuliyana and Lee, Manual on Space Law, Vol.I, p.11, Oceana Publications Inc., Dobbs Ferry, New York/Sijthoff & Noordhoff, Alphen aan de Rijn, 1979.
See also van Traa-Engelman H.L., Commercial Utilization of Outer Space, Law and Practice, Chapter II, Kluwer Academic Publishers, 1993

8. See supra note 1

9. See Christol, C., The Modern International Law of Outer Space, Chapter 7, esp. P.252, Pergamon Press, 1982

10. See supra note 7, van Traa-Engelman at page 27

11. See supra note 7, van Traa-Engelman at Chapter 7

12. See supra note 7, van Traa-Engelman

13. Smith, Delbert D., The Moon Treaty and Private Enterprise, pp. 62-65, Astronautics and Aeronautics, January 1980

14. See also Reynolds, Glenn Harlan, The Moon Treaty: prospects for the future, Space Policy, May 1995, pp. 115-120, esp. Note 9, The Moon Treaty: Hearings before the Subcommittee on Science, Technology and Space, Committee on Commerce, Science and Transportation, United States Senate, 96th Cong. 2d Sess., 29&31 July 1980, Serial No. 96-115

IISL-96-IISL.1.06

Acquisition of Property in the Legal Regime of Celestial Bodies

Gyula Gál
Budapest University ELTE

In this summer UPI reported that parcels on the Moon were offered for sale by a businessman from California. The seller claimed to be owner of the hither side of the Moon acquired by him under the Homestead Act. The price was very modest: USD 15.- only for one parcel. The news agency also reported that some 1600 persons really bought parcels on various fixed places on the surface of the Moon — allegedly well-known persons among them. The best news in silly season coming just at the right moment, the Hungarian press picked it up.

The next one: a German gentleman is going to launch a process against the American swindler. The Moon namely has been his family wealth since Frederick II ("the Great") King of Prussia had donated it to one of his forefathers. The deed of gift is to be found in the Bundesarchiv — the German Government has to search for it.

Acquisition of property, private ownership on the Moon? This basic questions are hidden in both funny stories.

The answer seems to be simple in an interview for radio listeners: the American businessman could not buy from and can not sell real estates to anybody on the Moon. Otherwise Frederick II conquered Silesia and obtained a part of Poland but never the Moon. Consequently he was not in the position to donate it to one of his worthy subjects. The Moon and other celestial bodies today are "res communis omnium" a certain kind of collective property of all mankind, it can not be occupied.

The space lawyer is right giving this summary explanation in good faith for the mass media. Nevertheless a critical analysis of the legal regime of celestial bodies for real cases does not result in such a clear-cut conclusion. This paper attempts to give voice to some doubts concerning positive law aspects of acquisition of property in this regime.

National appropriation in the Space Treaty

The theory of international law often applies civil (Roman) law notions for simplified labeling of analogous institutions. The original mode of acquisition of property in civil law has been the model for the original mode of acquiring territory. A state extends its sovereignty by the effective occupation of a territory which is not under the jurisdiction of any other subject of international law. (*Res nullius i. e. terra nullius cedit occupanti*) The development of this legal institution had been in close connection with process of colonization. All territories which were not under the sovereignty of a state recognized as belonging to the international community — regardless of the native population — were in view of colonizers terra nullius. Occupation as a unilateral legal act consisted of two elements: establishment of an effective dominion (corpus) and the intention of acquiring sovereignty (animus occupandi).

In the opinion of some authors in the early literature of space law the revival of this concept in the space exploration could not be excluded. This possibility was expressed e. g. by *J. G. Verplaetse*:

> As far as we can go back in history any res which is not under authority can be brought under authority. ...Therefore the obvious conclusion is that individual nations can obtain sovereignty over such parts of a celestial body upon which their power is properly vested. (1)

In the space law theory of the presatellite age, however, the view was predominant, that outer space could not be subject of national appropriation. Science, using the terminology borrowed from civil law, designated this status as *res communis omnium*. This character was underlined also by the term *res extra commercium*. (*B. Cheng, C. W. Jenks, R. Probst*) This theoretical approach in the post-satellite years 1957–1967 was confirmed by unanimously accepted UN.GA resolutions (1721/XVI, 1962/XVIII) and interstate practice. (2)

The Space Treaty was rather declarative in

> Article II.
>
> Outer space, including the Moon and other celestial bodies, is not subject to national appropriation by claim of sovereignty, by means of use occupation or by any other means.

No doubt, outer space, the Moon and other celestial bodies according to positive space law even before the first Moon landings were not "res nullius" as newly discovered territories on Earth in ancient times. The question, however, can not be evaded whether the status of "res communis omnium" does except objects "res corporales" from civil law appropriation. In other words: is the acquisition of property prohibited by Article II in the legal regime of celestial bodies?

The grammatical interpretation of the Treaty does not offer an unequivocal affirmative answer to this question. *National appropriation* does not belong to the traditional terminology of international law. It seems to be a space law term coming from UN resolutions. The phrase "national appropriation by..." demonstrates that the "means" are subordinated to this notion.
It does not cover the occupation as an original mode of acquisition of property in civil law. All the more it can be only interpreted as a unilateral act of states extending their sovereign rights to a "terra nullius". (3)

Commentaries to the Space Treaty generally do not differentiate between two kinds of occupations under Article II. We find attempts to include civil law occupation into national appropriation indirectly e.g.: acquisition of property is only possible in the framework of a state jurisdiction which can not be extended to the celestial bodies. (4) Others refer to the discussions of the Legal Subcommittee of COPUOS. The delegates underlined there that by prohibition of national appropriation also civil law exclusivity will be prohibited. Nobody before and after the Space Treaty represented an opposite view.

On the other hand: The chairman of the Space Law Committee of International Law Association circulated a questionnaire concerning legal nature of natural resources of celestial bodies. The answers were by no means consonant. *S. Gorove* and *A. A. Cocca* represented the view that Article II of the Space Treaty was applicable to natural resources of celestial bodies i. e. national appropriation in sense of civil law should be forbidden. According to the opposite view of *B. Cheng, E. Pépin, C. Horsford, S. M. Williams* the appropriation of natural resources merely formed part of the freedom of exploration and use of outer space. (5)

It is not meaningless to mention some facts of international practice. As a big achievement of *Apollo 11* mission U.S. astronauts collected and transported to earth 22 kg of Moon samples in 1969. The following Moon landings carried out the same task. In the same way the Soviet *Luna* space probes from 1970 on brought back samples from the Moon-surface taken by automatic instruments. These objects were appropriated by U.S. and Soviet authorities respectively and have been owned by them without objection from the international community.

Article II consequently can be interpreted that the prohibition of national appropriation i.e. the "res communis omnium" character of celestial bodies do not involve the same legal status of objects on celestial bodies prohibiting the acquisition of property.

National appropriation and property in the Moon Agreement

The Agreement Governing the Activities of States on the Moon and other celestial bodies under the main principle "the Moon and its natural resources are the common heritage of mankind" has gone further in details of the principle of non-appropriation.

The freedom of scientific investigation involves restricted rights to appropriate certain objects:

> Article VI.
>
> 2. In carrying out scientific investigations and in furtherance of the provisions of this Agreement, the States Parties shall have the right *to collect and remove* from the Moon samples of its mineral and other substances. Such samples shall remain at the disposal of those States Parties which caused them to be collected and may be used by them for scientific purposes.

This wording carefully avoids such terms for objects collected and removed as property, ownership, though above stipulation grants certain rights of an owner to the states concerned.

Property rights are also implied in the rather moral obligation:

> ...States Parties shall have regard to the desirability of making a portion of such samples available to other interested States Parties and the international scientific community for scientific investigation,...

The last sentence of Par. 2 refers finally to right of use only:

> ...States Parties may in the course of scientific investigations also use mineral and other substances of the Moon in quantities appropriate for the support of their missions.

On the other hand the Agreement refers to property in a negative sense concerning materials for non-scientific purposes.

> Article XI.
>
> 3. Neither the surface of the Moon, nor any part thereof or *natural resources* in place shall become property of any state, international intergovernmental or non-governmental organization, national organization or non-governmental entity or of any natural person.

Property rights shall not be created by placement of personnel and installations on or below the surface of the Moon.

Above wording of Par.3 of Article XI *a contrario* could be hardly interpreted otherwise than prohibition of acquiring property does not concern *resources non-in-place*. *C. Q. Christol* concludes to my mind correctly:

> ...by the introduction of the term "in place" the negotiators intended to legalize the removal of natural resources from the surface or the subsurface of the Moon thereby *establishing the right* of ownership and of property in the possessor of such resources. (6)

At the same time Par.3 ends with the reservation: "The foregoing provisions are without prejudice to the international regime referred to in paragraph 5 of this article."

The acquisition of ownership and property rights over natural resources of the Moon is made in this way the subject of a caveat.

The international regime referred to in Par.5 does not exist. The Moon Agreement has been ratified by 8 states only, the most important space powers are not among them. (7)

* * *

All things considered, from above analysis may be concluded that in the legal regime of celestial bodies following principles of appropriation in broader sense can be stated:

1. *National appropriation* i.e. extending sovereign rights to the Moon and other celestial bodies or any parts thereof is prohibited.

2. *Appropriation* i.e. acquisition of property on the Moon and other celestial bodies of removable objects within the limits of general principles of their legal regime is not prohibited.

Such principles are:
a) Exploration and use of outer space with *due regard to the corresponding interests of all other states.* (S.T. Article IX.)

b) Due regard *to the interests of present and future generations* (Moon Agreement Article IV.)

The principles *CHM* and *"province of mankind"* today can give an extremely general orientation in interpreting space law rules of acquisition of property on celestial bodies, though both are connected in treaty law with this problem.

Unfortunately mankind is not a subject of international law. It can not act as a legal person, can not launch a process, can not claim anything in his own name. The same is true also for the principle above under b) Coming generations have not a single "ombudsman" among us to represent their interests, which we can not understand in many respects. For our subject: it would be science fiction to speak about property rights on celestial bodies which some time in the future will be acquired by mankind itself.

Footnotes

1. Proceedings of Fourth Coll. IISL 1961, p. 323. Similar views: *F. Berber*: Lehrbuch des Völkerrechts, Vol. I. München-Berlin 1960, p. 345. *C. E. S. Horsford*: The Law of Space. Journal of British Interplanetary Society, 1955, p.144. *R. K. Woetzel*: Die internationale Kontrolle der höheren Luftschichten un des Weltraums, Bad Godesberg 1960, p. 79., *E. Bornecque-Winandy*: Droit de l'imperialisme spatial, Paris 1962, pp. 30-31. etc.

2. Statements after LUNIK-2 hit the Moon. (September 14, 1969) *G. Gál*: Space Law, Budapest 1961, pp. 188-189.

3. *H. Bittlinger*: Hoheitsgewalt und Kontrolle im Weltraum, Köln etc., 1988, p. 136. (hoheitliche Tätigkeit)

4. *M. Dauses*: Zur Rechtslage des Mondes und anderer Himmelskörper. Zeitschrift für Luft- und Weltraumrecht, 1975. p. 271.

5. See: *S. M. Williams*: The Exploitation and Use of Natural Resources in the New Law of the Sea and the Outer Space. Proceedings of Twenty-Ninth Coll. IISL 1986, p. 201.

6. *C. Q. Christol*: The Modern International Law of Outer Space, New York etc. 1982, pp. 262-263.

7. Space Law. Basic Documents. *K. H. Boeckstiegel–M. Benkő* Vol. 1 — A. V. 2

IISL-96-IISL.1.08

PRELIMINARY JURISPRUDENTIAL OBSERVATIONS CONCERNING PROPERTY RIGHTS ON THE MOON AND OTHER CELESTIAL BODIES IN THE COMMERCIAL SPACE AGE

By Patricia M. Sterns*
LAW OFFICES OF STERNS AND TENNEN☆
Attorneys and Counselors at Law
Phoenix, Arizona USA

G. Harry Stine‡
THE ENTERPRISE INSTITUTE, INC.
Phoenix, Arizona USA

Leslie I. Tennen**
LAW OFFICES OF STERNS AND TENNEN☆
Attorneys and Counselors at Law
Phoenix, Arizona USA

ABSTRACT

The activities of mankind in the early space age proceeded at a remarkable pace. Human and robotic explorers revealed a universe filled with wonder and the promise of unlimited opportunity. However, without the incentive of cold war competition, governments will not continue to commit the resources necessary to be the predominant participants in developing the utilization of space. That role must be assumed by the private sector.

The use of satellites for telecommunications has become a multi-billion dollar market. Yet this application represents

* Corresponding Member IAA
Member IISL, ASIL, ABA, IBA
Senior Member AIAA

‡ Commissioner, Arizona Space Commission

** Commissioner, Arizona Space Commission
Member IAA, IISL, ASIL
Senior Member AIAA

☆ Member IAF

The opinions expressed in this article are those of the authors only and should not be attributed to any organization with which they may be affiliated only a small fraction of the potential space-based economic activities of the next century. Lunar and asteroidal resources appear capable of providing significant economic incentives to enlarge the scope of space applications. However, private investment and development of these diverse space applications will depend upon establishing acceptable rules to encourage private enterprise, prevent conflicts, and resolve disputes in a peaceful manner.

This article explores the present legal status of property rights on the Moon and other celestial bodies *vis-a-vis* the commercial development of space. The existing space treaties are surveyed for specific provisions that either encourage or hinder private activities. Relevant issues are identified that will require timely resolution for the orderly, reliable and predictable recognition and protection of property rights in space into the next millennium.

INTRODUCTION

The activities of mankind in space are at a crossroads. The era of governmental dominance is ending, as political and budgetary restraints act to prevent the commitment of national resources necessary to develop space for purposes other than national prestige and security. The private sector can fill this void, and open the vast reaches of space for commercial opportunities. However, the extant relevant treaties which will be applicable to space commerce were drafted when governments were the major participants in space activities. Thus, these international agreements did not have as their primary purpose the regulation of commercial activities and the relationships among private entities or between states and private entities. The *corpus juris spatialis* must be examined to determine whether it will have a helpful or a harmful effect on prospects for commercial operations in space, and modifications must be proposed where appropriate.

In relation to commercial ventures, the specific articles of existing space treaties may be neutral, favorable, unfavorable, or ambiguous. Most provisions might be considered ambiguous in the literal text, and have both positive as well as negative implications on commercial development. The only certain conclusion is that the treaties reflect a broad spectrum of interests and policies. Nevertheless, the issues concerning the commercialization of space are becoming critical, as extraterrestrial resources are recognized as significant economic incentives for private development.

SURVEY OF SPACE TREATY PROVISIONS WITH POTENTIAL APPLICATION TO COMMERCIAL VENTURES

The *corpus juris spatialis* contains numerous provisions which will be applicable to private development and commercialization of space. Virtually every article of the Outer Space Treaty[1] has relevance to commercial ventures in one context or another. For example:

- Private entities specifically are permitted to conduct activities in space, subject to the authorization and supervision of the appropriate state of nationality (article VI).
- The exploration and use of outer space, including the Moon and other celestial bodies, shall be the province of all mankind, and all states have a right of access to space on the basis of equality (article I).
- Outer space, including the Moon and other celestial bodies, is not subject to national appropriation by claim of sovereignty, by use or occupation, or by any other means (article II).
- States retain jurisdiction over their personnel and objects, even when in outer space (article VIII).

---

1. Treaty on Principles Governing the Activities of States in the Exploration and Use of Outer Space, Including the Moon and Other Celestial Bodies, *opened for signature* January 27, 1967, 18 U.S.T. 2410, T.I.A.S. No. 6347, 610 U.N.T.S. 205 [hereinafter referred to as the "Outer Space Treaty"].

- Astronauts are "envoys of mankind" and shall be given all due aid and assistance in case of emergency (article V).[2]

- Activities in space shall be conducted to prevent the harmful contamination of outer space and celestial bodies, and also to prevent adverse changes to the environment of the Earth through the introduction of extra-terrestrial matter; activities in space or on celestial bodies are to be conducted to prevent the harmful interference with the activities of other states parties (article X).

- The Secretary-General of the United Nations shall be informed, to the greatest extent feasible and practicable, of the nature, conduct, locations and results of activities in space, including the Moon and other celestial bodies, and information concerning these matters is to be made public (article XI).[3]

Article VII of the Outer Space Treaty provides that states which launch or procure the launch of an object into outer space are internationally liable for damage by such object on Earth, in the airspace, or in outer space. This provision has been supplemented and clarified by the Liability Convention,[4] which establishes procedures for the presentation and resolution of claims. Nevertheless, the Liability Convention does not alter the primary international liability of a launching state as expressed by the Outer Space Treaty.

The Moon Treaty reaffirms the non-appropriation doctrine[5] of the Outer Space Treaty. The Moon Treaty, however, goes much further, and expresses specific regulations concerning the use of lunar resources. In addition, the Moon Treaty subjects the exploitation of such resources to an international regime, which states parties have agreed to undertake to establish.[6]

The foregoing survey of the space treaties, while not intended to be exhaustive, is illustrative of the broad range of provisions which could have direct applicability to private commercial ventures in space. It is clear that space law will need to adapt to the change in emphasis from public to private space programs. The primary issues in need of resolution relate to the application of the non-appropriation doctrine, the international legal regime applicable to the use of extraterrestrial resources, and the respective liabilities of the launching state and the private entity conducting commercial space operations. As we look further into the future, the rights of

---

2. *See also* Agreement on the Rescue of Astronauts, the Return of Astronauts, and the Return of Objects Launched Into Outer Space, *opened for signature* April 22, 1968, 19 U.S.T. 7570, T.I.A.S. No. 6599, 672 U.N.T.S. 119.

3. *See also* Convention on Registration of Objects Launched Into Outer Space, *opened for signature* January 14, 1975, art. IV, 28 U.S.T. 695, T.I.A.S. No. 8480, 1023 U.N.T.S. 15, which obligates states to disclose specific but limited information concerning the location, function, and where applicable, basic orbital parameters, of objects launched into space.

4. Convention on International Liability for Damages Caused by Space Objects, *opened for signature* March 29, 1972, 24 U.S.T. 2389, T.I.A.S. No. 7762, 961 U.N.T.S. 187 [hereinafter referred to as the "Liability Convention"]. The Liability Convention distinguishes between damages on Earth or to aircraft in flight, for which strict liability principles are applied (article II), and damages to other space objects, which predicates liability on fault (article III).

5. Agreement Governing the Activities of States on the Moon and Other Celestial Bodies, *entered into force* July 11, 1984, art. 11.2, 1363 U.N.T.S. 3, *text reproduced in* Report, Committee on the Peaceful Uses of Outer Space, 34 U.N. GAOR Supp. (No. 20), U.N. Doc. A/AC.105/L.113 Add 4 (1979); UNITED NATIONS TREATIES ON OUTER SPACE 27 (1984); *and* 18 I.L.M. 1434 (1979)[hereinafter referred to as the "Moon Treaty"].

6. *Id.* at art. 11.5.

space settlers to autonomy in the governance of their daily life must also be considered.

THE NON-APPROPRIATION DOCTRINE IN SPACE LAW

The non-appropriation principle of the Outer Space Treaty and the Moon Treaty is of primary importance. This doctrine prohibits national appropriation of outer space, including the Moon and other celestial bodies. By extension, states could not license private parties, particularly their own nationals, to appropriate privately that which cannot be appropriated publicly.[7] However, the inability to claim exclusive title to specific surface or subsurface areas on the Moon, or to orbits or other locations in space, could be viewed as a severe limitation inhibiting private development of space.

The question may be raised, therefore, whether the prohibition of national appropriation in space should continue to be a viable principle of international law in the commercial space age. The abrogation of the non-appropriation doctrine would enable states to claim sovereignty over various land masses, mineral deposits and other resources, asteroid bodies, orbits, or other "assets" of space, and thereafter to license, grant, permit, recognize, authorize and/or enforce rights of private ownership and development of such assets. Whether the abandonment of the non-appropriation doctrine would promote the commercial development of space, however, is yet to be demonstrated.

Abrogation of the non-appropriation doctrine cannot be justified merely to eliminate a potentially inhibiting circumstance to space commercialization. Rather, the basis on which the non-appropriation doctrine was adopted as a principle of space law must be considered. It is only where the original purposes of the doctrine cease to remain applicable that justification would exist for its removal as a principle from the *corpus juris spatialis*.

The advent of the space age followed historical antecedents for exploration and discovery. Throughout the classical age of exploration, colonial powers claimed discovered lands by a variety of ceremonies, ranging from physical presence, to planting the flag, to other rituals. There were no particular international standards for recognizing which of these ceremonies was legally superior. Some claims were made on the basis of mere sighting, without any physical contact with the area claimed. In the end, these claims were enforced and recognized on the basis of military power.[8]

The launch of Sputnik I by the Soviet Union on October 4, 1957, demonstrated that the presence of satellites in Earth orbit had profound national security implications. The global community was faced with two choices: concede the historical right of the technologically superior nations to lay claim to vast portions of outer space, including the Moon and other celestial bodies, or prohibit the assertion of such claims in the first instance. Clearly, international peace and security would be served by the prevention of conflict over competing terran claims to portions of the cosmos. The resolution of this issue, therefore, was a universal prohibition of national appropriation in space.[9]

---

7. *See* C.W. JENKS, SPACE LAW 201 (1965).

8. *See generally* A. HALEY, SPACE LAW AND GOVERNMENT 118-23 (1963).

9. *See* International Co-operation in the Peaceful Uses of Outer Space, U.N.G.A. Res. 1721(XVI)A, December 20, 1961, U.N. Doc. No. A/4987, at 1(b), declaring that "outer space and celestial bodies . . . are not subject to national appropriation." Thus, general agreement on this issue was reached by the community of nations a mere four years after the launch of the first artificial satellite. *See generally* Haley, *supra* note 8, at 123-34. The non-appropriation doctrine achieved the status of binding international law when it was incorporated into article II of the Outer Space Treaty, *supra* note 1. The consideration of the non-appropriation doctrine also involved examination of other important but distinguishable issues by the global community, such as the right of access to and freedom of

Technology utilized in space activities continues to have national security implications. Such implications have become more profound and subtle as the technology has become increasingly sophisticated.[10] Although the collapse of the Soviet Union reduced international tensions in a variety of contexts, that historic event did not eliminate all possible hostile uses of space and space technology by all nations. Moreover, the historical antecedents of nationalism and colonialism, which resulted in countless wars of conquest and conflicts over competing claims, were developed prior to any ideological competition of the 20th century.

It is up to the international legal community to achieve the maximum exploration and use of outer space by both the public and private sectors while at the same time preventing the spread of armed conflict beyond this planet. At this time, the abandonment of the non-appropriation doctrine does not appear to serve that purpose. The reasons which justified the inclusion of the non-appropriation principle in the Outer Space Treaty and the Moon Treaty continue to apply today. The abrogation of the non-appropriation doctrine, moreover, may in fact be detrimental and antithetical to the interests of free enterprise in space.

Abrogation of the non-appropriation doctrine would permit, and indeed make inevitable, claims of national sovereignty in space by the technologically advanced nations, particularly the United States and Russia (as the successor in interest to the Soviet Union). These claims would include various orbits, the Moon, and other areas where the claimant had any basis for asserting that it had been first to "discover" the subject of the claim, whether by exploration, use, landing, imaging, mapping, or surveying. The Russians, under this state of affairs, would have the historic justification for claiming vast reaches of near-Earth space because they had the undeniable firsts in the initial days of the space age. Other nations could be anticipated to lay claim to space "properties." The Bogota Declaration,[11] for example. expressing claims to the geostationary orbit, could be expected to be re-asserted with vigor.

The various claims likely would overlap and thereby give rise to international tensions and the potential for armed conflict. Wars of conquest also could result, and the assertion of claims ultimately would be based on successful application of military force. Such a circumstance would not be conducive to the activities of private commerce in space. Moreover, to the extent states would be able to claim sovereign rights over natural space resources, there would be nothing to prevent each of the states from imposing substantial taxes, royalties, duties, auction fees or other charges for the acquisition of rights by private entities to utilize such resources, even where the national claims thereto overlap. Clearly, the development of private enterprise in space would not be served by imposition of an economic tribute by various states. Finally, it should be noted that the non-appropriation doctrine is double-edged: While it prevents an entity from establishing a monopoly, it prevents the competition from establishing one, too.

The abrogation and abandonment of the non-appropriation doctrine would not result in fostering the activities of private entities in space. Nevertheless, rules must be established regarding the manner in which rights in property may be acquired and maintained, and to apply those rules to all entities, whether they be individuals, corporations, states, or international organizations.[12] The Moon Treaty contains the

---

exploration and use of outer space. *See id.* at art. I.

10. *See* G.H. STINE, CONFRONTATION IN SPACE (1981).

11. Declaration of the First Meeting of Equatorial Countries, Bogota, Columbia, December 3, 1976, *text reproduced in* N. JASENTULIYANA & R.S.K. LEE, II MANUAL ON SPACE LAW 383 (1979).

12. *See generally* H.L. VAN TRAA-ENGELMAN, COMMERCIAL UTILIZATION OF OUTER SPACE (1993); Filho, *On Private, States and*

most detailed provisions in the extant *corpus juris spatialis* for the regulation of the use of natural resources. Specifically, the states party to the Moon Treaty have agreed to undertake to establish an international regime to govern the exploitation of lunar resources.

THE MOON TREATY AND THE INTERNATIONAL REGIME

The Moon Treaty restates the non-appropriation language of the Outer Space Treaty and declares that the Moon and its resources are the common heritage of mankind.[13] Article 11.3 provides "Neither the surface nor the subsurface of the Moon, nor any part thereof or natural resources in place, shall become property of any State, international intergovernmental or non-governmental organization, national organization or non-governmental entity or of any natural person." Pursuant to this provision, neither land on the Moon, *i.e.*, the surface, nor mineral or other resources in place, may be owned by any public or private entity. The use of such resources is not prohibited, although such use may be subject to regulation by an international regime, which could be established in the future.

The specific purposes of the international regime are set forth in article 11.7 as:

> (a) The orderly and safe development of the natural resources of the Moon;
>
> (b) The rational management of those resources;
>
> (c) The expansion of opportunities in the use of those resources; [and]
>
> (d) An equitable sharing by all States Parties in the benefits derived from those resources, whereby the interests and needs of the developing countries, as well as the efforts of those countries which have contributed either directly or indirectly to the exploration of the Moon, shall be given special consideration.

It must be noted that the Moon Treaty neither expressly requires the establishment of an international regime, nor does it impose a moratorium on the use of lunar resources pending the establishment of such regime.[14] However, it is clear that some form of jurisprudential framework will be necessary for the recognition and enforcement of rights in the use of extraterrestrial resources. Outer space is supranational in nature. When national security concerns are taken into consideration, it is apparent that all states, as sovereign entities, can be expected to demand some role in the regulation of space activities. In addition, the right to use and explore space should not be restricted to those who happen to have the technology today, to the exclusion of all others. States and other entities may have a legitimate right and expectation to be able to operate or participate in the operation of space activities in the future. Nevertheless, the jurisprudential framework which ultimately is developed does not necessarily need to constitute or include the international regime identified in the Moon Treaty.

International Public Interests in Space Law, in PROCEEDINGS OF THE 38TH COLLOQUIUM ON THE LAW OF OUTER SPACE 238 (1996); Doyle, *Legal and Policy Implications of Treating Natural Resources as the Common Heritage of Mankind*, in PROCEEDINGS OF THE 29TH COLLOQUIUM ON THE LAW OF OUTER SPACE 31 (1987); Haanappel, *Creating the Appropriate Regulatory Climate for Outer Space Activities Conducted by Private Enterprise*, in PROCEEDINGS OF THE 31ST COLLOQUIUM ON THE LAW OF OUTER SPACE 286 (1989).

13. Moon Treaty, *supra* note 5, at art. 11.1.

14. *See* Finch & Moore, *The 1979 Moon Treaty Encourages Space Development*, in PROCEEDINGS OF THE 23RD COLLOQUIUM ON THE LAW OF OUTER SPACE 13 (1981); *but see* Rosenfield, *A Moon Treaty? Yes, But Why Now?*, in PROCEEDINGS OF THE 23RD COLLOQUIUM ON THE LAW OF OUTER SPACE 69 (1981).

The range and depth of the issues to be considered in the acquisition and enforcement of rights in extraterrestrial resources show the need for adequate representation of all concerned entities in any body attempting to determine these matters. At a minimum, any regulatory body must assure the recognition, respect and enforcement of rights to utilize extraterrestrial resources which are granted to the constituent entities. Appropriate safeguards must be devised to protect the natural environments of celestial bodies, and to prevent interference by one entity with the activities of another. Furthermore, a mechanism must be developed for the resolution of disputes which will arise between parties involved or otherwise interested in the utilization of extraterrestrial resources.[15]

The level of regulatory detail that may be imposed by a future legal regime is impossible to predict. As summarized by Jenks,

> Distinctions may well be necessary between use which is by its nature exclusive and use which can be shared simultaneously, use which involves the resource used being consumed and use which leaves it available for further use, use which involves some transformation or deterioration and use which has no such effect. It is difficult to elaborate on the matter in any precise detail until it is known what can be used and how.[16]

LIABILITY

The Outer Space Treaty provides that states are internationally responsible for national activities in space, whether conducted by governmental agencies or non-governmental entities.[17] In addition, the Outer Space Treaty and the Liability Convention provide that the launching state internationally is liable for damages caused by space objects on the surface of the Earth, to aircraft in flight, or to other space objects. The Liability Convention does not impose liability on the launching state for damages caused to its nationals or other entities involved in the activity giving rise to the damages.[18] Nor does the Liability Convention apply to situations where the damage is caused other than by a "space object" or its component parts. Thus, the liability imposed by the Liability Convention is primary and unlimited, however, it does not apply in all circumstances.

The imposition of unlimited liability is a significant departure from maritime and aviation standards. International aviation traffic has operated since 1952 under the terms of the Rome Convention, which provides for limitations on the liability of the organization to whom the aircraft is registered for damage caused by the operation of the aircraft.[19] Similarly, liability under

---

15. *See* G.H. STINE, SPACE POWER (1981).

16. Jenks, *supra* note 7, at 275.

17. Outer Space Treaty, *supra* note 1, at art. VI.

18. DeSaussure, *Do We Need a Strict Limited Liability Regime in Outer Space*, in PROCEEDINGS OF THE 22ND COLLOQUIUM ON THE LAW OF OUTER SPACE 117, 119 (1980).

19. Convention on Damage Caused by Foreign Aircraft to Third Parties on the Surface, *opened for signature* October 7, 1952, art. 11, 310 U.N.T.S. 181 [hereinafter referred to as the "Rome Convention"]. The Rome Convention establishes a five tiered structure of liability limitations, based on the weight of the aircraft. The Montreal Protocol to Amend the Convention on Damage Caused by Foreign Aircraft to Third Parties on the Surface, *opened for signature* September 23, 1978, ICAO Doc. 9257, reduced the number of categories to four. The maximum liability provided by the Montreal Protocol is approximately $29,300,000. The Rome Convention did not receive widespread approval. Although it entered into force, the treaty has not been accepted by many industrialized nations, including the United States, Canada, the United Kingdom, or Germany. Among the reasons for the lack of support is the criticism that the liability limitations are too low. Of course, the

maritime law has been limited as a matter of both domestic and international law.[20] Liability for damage within the expressed limitations generally is absolute. Thus, commercial airline and ship operators, as well as private individuals, must arrange for their own insurance coverage to manage the risks inherent in their operations. This philosophy appears to have worked well by placing the risk of loss on aircraft and ship owners who must maintain and operate their craft in accordance with the national and international regulations and standards. The question therefore can be raised whether or not a limited liability regime should be applied to the realm of space activities.[21]

The activities of non-governmental entities in space are subject to the authorization and continuing supervision of the appropriate state of nationality.[22] The domestic law of the United States requires that private ventures obtain a license to conduct a launch of a payload into space.[23] A necessary component of a launch license application is that the applicant demonstrate financial responsibility, which can be established by obtaining insurance.[24] The amount of insurance is determined by the government based upon a risk analysis of the maximum probable loss which may be caused by a particular launch.[25]

By statute, the amount of insurance is limited to a maximum of the greater of $500,000,000 or the largest amount available at reasonable cost in the global marketplace for third party liability claims, and $100,000,000 for property damage claims in favor of the U.S. government.[26] In addition, the licensing statutes require that all parties to a licensed launch activity execute a reciprocal waiver of claims on behalf of themselves, their contractors, sub-contractors, customers, and the contractors and sub-contractors of the customer, pursuant to which each entity agrees to be responsible for property damage and personal injuries it sustains resulting from an activity carried out under the license.[27] The waiver by the U.S. government,

---

limitations of liability do not apply in cases of intentional damage. *See generally* I.H.PH. DIEDERIKS-VERSCHOOR, AN INTRODUCTION TO AIR LAW 125-36 (1993).

20. *See* DeSaussure, *supra* note 18, at 120-21.

21. *See generally id.*; *see also* G.H. STINE, HALFWAY TO ANYWHERE (1996); Hurwitz, *An International Compensation Fund for Damage Caused by Space Objects*, in PROCEEDINGS OF THE 34TH COLLOQUIUM ON THE LAW OF OUTER SPACE 201 (1992); Cocca, *Full Compensation to Total Responsibility*, in PROCEEDINGS OF THE 26TH COLLOQUIUM ON THE LAW OF OUTER SPACE 157 (1984); Dula, *Management of Inter and Third Party Liability for Routine Space Shuttle Operations*, in PROCEEDINGS OF THE 20TH COLLOQUIUM ON THE LAW OF OUTER SPACE 201 (1978).

22. Outer Space Treaty, *supra* note 1, at art. VI.

23. *See* Commercial Space Launch Act, 49 U.S.C. §§ 70101, *et seq; see also* 14 C.F.R. §§ 400 *et seq.* For a discussion of domestic legislation in other states, see von der Dunk, *Two New National Space Laws: Russia and South Africa* in PROCEEDINGS OF THE 38TH COLLOQUIUM ON THE LAW OF OUTER SPACE 251 (1996).

24. 49 U.S.C. § 70112(a).

25. 49 U.S.C. § 70112(c).

26. 49 U.S.C. § 70112(a)(3).

27. 49 U.S.C. § 70112(b)(1). For a discussion concerning the application of the reciprocal waivers, *see Martin Marietta Corporation v. Intelsat*, 978 F.2d 140 (4th Cir. 1992), *as amended* 991 F.2d 94 (1993); *see also* Bostwick, *Liability of Aerospace Manufacturers: McPherson v. Buick Sputters into the Space Age*, 22 J. SPACE L. 75 (1994); Meredith, *Spacecraft*

however, is limited to the amount of a claim in excess of the required insurance coverage.[28] A procedure has been established by which the U.S. government will provide for the payment of successful claims against a licensee in excess of the amount of required insurance, subject to a maximum of $1,500,000,000.[29]

A Proposed Notice of Rulemaking concerning Financial Responsibility for Licensed Launch Activities recently was issued.[30] Included among the proposed regulations is a form for the reciprocal waiver of claims. This form of waiver provides that where a licensed launch activity involves either the U.S. government, its contractors, or a federal launch facility, the government is not entitled to indemnification from the license holder.[31] Thus, although the regulations generally relate to tort claims between entities involved in a launch activity, the form of reciprocal waiver indicates that the license holder will be relieved of liability to indemnify the government for claims of third parties in excess of the required insurance.

The above described regulatory framework creates a *de facto* limited liability regime for launch license holders. This limitation would be effective as between the licensee and the U.S. government, especially if the cross waiver provision is judicially enforceable.[32] That is, the government has international responsibility, and in certain instances liability, for claims which are in excess of or otherwise not covered by the requisite insurance. Whether or not the self-imposed limitation of $1,500,000,000 over and above the insurance would be sufficient to cover these claims, it is doubtful that this limitation will carry any significance in either diplomatic negotiations or before a properly constituted Claims Commission under the Liability Convention.[33] Thus, it can be expected that claims in excess of this self-imposed limitation will be allowed where appropriate under international law. Nevertheless, the licensee will be able to rely upon the reciprocal waiver to avoid responsibility to indemnify the government for such excess claims.

The existing regulatory framework generally is concerned with activities relating to the launch of payloads, primarily satellites, and not to the operations of objects while in orbit. This focus on launch activities is exemplified in the Proposed Notice of Rulemaking. In the discussion concerning proposed regulation 440.11, regarding the duration of insurance coverage, it is noted that the licensee will be required to maintain the insurance until completion of the

---

Failure-Related Litigation in the United States: Many Failures, but Few Suits, in PROCEEDINGS OF THE 38TH COLLOQUIUM ON THE LAW OF OUTER SPACE 22 (1996).

28. 49 U.S.C. § 70112(b)(2).

29. 49 U.S.C. § 70113(a)(1) (expressed in 1989 dollars).

30. See 61 Federal Register 38991-39021 (July 25, 1996), proposing the establishment of a new Part 440 to 14 C.F.R. §§ 400, *et seq.*, which will implement the statutes discussed in the text.

31. *Id.* at 39021, Appendix II, § 6.

32. There is some question as to whether the reciprocal waiver will be applicable to damages arising from gross negligence. The proposed regulations state that claims for gross negligence are not excluded from the reciprocal waiver. However, waivers of claims for gross negligence may not necessarily be permitted as a matter of state law. *See Martin Marietta v. Intelsat*, 991 F.2d at 100 (finding that liability for gross negligence cannot be waived pursuant to Maryland law). This issue may be subject to conflicting decisions by the state courts. The lack of uniformity in interpretation of the applicable regulations could be a significant negative factor in space commercialization, and at a minimum will place increased emphasis on choice of law provisions in contract negotiations.

33. See Liability Convention, *supra* note 4, at arts. XIV *et seq.*

licensed activities or until the risk of liability is sufficiently small that financial responsibility is no longer necessary. It further is noted that such period generally will be thirty days or less from successful orbital insertion of the payload.[34] Thus, the regulatory framework is unclear and imprecise in relation to the operations of payloads or other commercial activities conducted in outer space.

AUTONOMY

Autonomy is the core of self-determination. The ability to achieve it is perhaps the strongest motivation for developing human settlements in space. In the past, the exploitation of natural resources has often been confused with self determination for the purpose of building a system of social relationships. While numerous examples can be devised which will involve both, they are separate and distinct. The right of self-determination is not necessarily intertwined with the right to use resources for profit.

To the extent that a commercial operation involves the permanent relocation of individuals from Earth (or other settlements) to a facility in space or on another celestial body, questions of the right of the settlers to exercise self-government necessarily will arise. The concept of autonomy and self-government as a preferred modality for permanent space settlements increasingly has been gaining support.[35] In space, the habitat and entire social structure can be devised together with the community design, in order to promote justice and harmony in the interrelationships between the settlement inhabitants and the entities interested in the establishment and operation of the facility. In this way, the lessons of history can prevent mistakes of the future, as mankind has an opportunity literally to design an entire way of life.

The application of terrestrial law to a permanent space community is derived from the perspective that an external legal structure will be superimposed upon the facility. However, extant jurisprudential philosophies will prove to be inadequate in the context of a settlement in space, as national and/or international instrumentalities cannot accommodate all the probable situations which likely will arise and require immediate resolution.[36] Furthermore, the passage of time involved in the process of terran resolution of conflicts would delay unnecessarily the administration of justice within the settlement.[37] It is unrealistic to assume that settlers will accept a situation wherein they do not share in the decision-making mechanisms for the internal functioning of the community. Manifestly, the determination of applicable law must consider the

---

34. 61 Federal Register at 39008.

35. *See generally* Esquivel de Cocca, *Human Society on Mars: New Legal Needs for a Different Mankind*, in PROCEEDINGS OF THE 35TH COLLOQUIUM ON THE LAW OF OUTER SPACE 335 (1993); DeSaussure & Ulrich, *Transition of Control and Jurisdiction Over Space Settlements*, in PROCEEDINGS OF THE 34TH COLLOQUIUM ON THE LAW OF OUTER SPACE 55 (1992); Fasan, *Human Settlements on Planets: New Stations or New Nations*, 22 J. SPACE L. 47 (1994); G.N. PATTERSON, PRIORITIES IN GEOLUNAR SPACE (1989); G.S. ROBINSON, LIVING IN OUTER SPACE (1975); G.S. ROBINSON & H. WHITE, JR., ENVOYS OF MANKIND (1986); Sterns & Tennen, *The "Art of Living in Space:" A Preliminary Study*, in PROCEEDINGS OF THE 21ST COLLOQUIUM ON THE LAW OF OUTER SPACE 245 (1979); Tamm, *Outer Space Colonization: A Planned Unit Development*, in PROCEEDINGS OF THE 22ND COLLOQUIUM ON THE LAW OF OUTER SPACE 217 (1980). *See also* Sterns & Tennen, *International Law and 'The Art of Living in Space:' The Recognition of Settlement Autonomy*, 9 SPACE POLICY 213 (1993).

36. *See* Shurley, Natani & Sengel, *Ecopsychiatric Aspects of a First Human Space Colony*, in SPACE MANUFACTURING FACILITIES (SPACE COLONIES) 259 (J. Grey ed. 1977).

37. *Cf.*, Chen, *Pending Issues Before the Legal Subcommittee of the United Nations Committee on the Peaceful Uses of Outer Space*, 5 J. SPACE L. 29 (1978).

alternative that a permanent space settlement will have the need for new law, unique unto itself.

The primary goal of continuity of settlement existence will be maintained by considering the settlement like unto another state, with the power to determine its own internal course. In this way, the space entity will be able to embark upon a rational and reasoned existence, and develop its own jurisprudential philosophy, derived from the collective experiences, needs, desires and goals of the inhabitants, rather than have determinations forced upon it in reaction to terrestrial events. Therefore, the space community should have separate and distinct control over those traditionally local areas of concern which will affect directly the proper functioning of the settlement on a daily basis, and the power to exercise limited home rule in an application of the concept of functional jurisdiction.[38]

The establishment of a settlement in space is an activity of unprecedented proportions, and necessarily will require a close, cooperative relationship between the founding terrestrial entity and the settlement. The emergence of settlement competence also will require consideration of the relationships between the settlement, the founding entity, and any nation or other ens desiring to conduct relations with the settlement. These goals may be accomplished by an international agreement of recognition and capacity, which will grant the settlement exclusive juridical competence for its internal and external functioning. Upon the receipt of recognition of its capacity as a legal regime, capable of conducting its own internal administration and external relations, the settlement will evolve from a mere habitable structure to an *exinde civitas politicae*, a political city-state in space. Such autonomy will enhance the ability of mankind to utilize extraterrestrial resources and promote the commercial development of space.

CONCLUSION

The present law of outer space is neither expressly "pro" nor "anti" free enterprise because it was not drafted to be a comprehensive regulation of private uses of space resources. As the commercial space age develops, some modifications and clarifications of existing space law clearly will be necessary. Elements of maritime and aviation law may provide meaningful analogies and examples of the manner in which the development of applicable laws, and the activities of governments, can either promote or stifle commercial ventures in space.

It is unlikely that the international community will abandon the non-appropriation doctrine that stands at the foundation of the *corpus juris spatialis*, and which continues to promote international peace and security. However, the future legal regime which will govern the use of extraterrestrial resources must include adequate provision for the representation and participation of all interested parties, whether public, private, national, international or transnational. The domestic laws of states also will have an important role to play in promoting and creating incentives for private investment in space. A robust space economy ultimately will lead to the establishment of permanent settlements on celestial bodies and other locations, and issues concerning the right of the settlers to autonomy and self-government necessarily will arise. The extant *corpus juris spatialis* provides a firm basis on which the issues presented in the emerging age of commercial space can be considered and resolved.

---

38. *See* I.A. CSABAFI, THE CONCEPT OF STATE JURISDICTION IN INTERNATIONAL SPACE LAW 64 (1971); *cf.* AZ. CONST., Art. XIII, § 2 (authorizing home rule).

Session 2:
CASES AND METHODS OF DISPUTE SETTLEMENT IN SPACE LAW

Chairman: K. H. Bockstiegel, Germany

IISL-96-IISL.2.02

DISPUTE SETTLEMENT AND SPACE ACTIVITIES: A NEW FRAMEWORK REQUIRED?

by

Professor Dr. Sylvia-Maureen Williams
Chair of International Law - University of Buenos Aires *

I. The present situation

The question of dispute settlement in the field of space activities has been a matter of permanent concern to the IISL and the Space Law Committee of the International Law Association. Both these bodies have made contributions to the progressive development of international law in this area which, together with the work of other specialised institutions at the national and international levels, provide a sound basis for the study of this problem on the eve of a new millennium.

The provisions embodied in the outer space treaties in force today appear insufficient. This is particularly so if we have in mind the growth of commercial activities in outer space, in which private enterprises participate directly. The 1967 Space Treaty, or Treaty on General Principles, lays down a number of guidelines which go no further than referring the question to the traditional methods of dispute settlement listed in article 33 of the U N Charter (1), to be read together with the underlying obligation to negotiate in good faith. There exists an additional duty to hold consultations, stemming from the 1967 Treaty , but only when States have reason to believe that damage may be caused to the Earth environment (2) as a result of their activities in outer space. The 1972 Liability Convention, for its part, implied a slight step forward at the time of its conclusion in spite of not going beyond a conciliation procedure (3). Finally, the 1979 Moon Agreement did not make any effective progress in this regard as no binding mechanism for dispute resolution was agreed upon in this text.

The principle of international co-operation -now seen by an important part of the doctrine as a legal obligation, and usually referred to as a "general obligation to co-operate"- is still far too weak. The magnitude of the consequences of never-ending stages of negotiations and consultations are sometimes difficult to predict.

The solution adopted by the Intelsat Agreements is indeed more realistic. Failing direct negotiations, arbitration is compulsory on a few assumptions including legal disputes between the parties to the Governmental Agreement, in other words, between subjects of public law, and between parties to the Special Agreement (which may, of course, be private companies).

----

* **The author is grateful to the University of Buenos Aires for the support given to carry out research in this area.**

It is true that Intelsat arrangements are predominantly technical. Thus, sensitive political issues are less frequent in this area. However, as observed earlier, the present pace of space activities indeed justifies, in a number of cases, the need for a more effective legal framework for dispute settlement in general. This means that new law should be created in connection with disputes between states and international organisations resulting from activities in outer space.

II. The goals in mind

In August 1996 the International Law Association celebrated its 67th Conference in Helsinki. In accordance with the mandate stemming from the 66th ILA Conference (Buenos Aires, 1994), the Space Law Committee was entrusted with the task of revising the ILA Convention on the Settlement of Space Law Disputes adopted in Paris in 1984, at its 61st Conference.

The aim of the Committee was to establish, in the most realistic manner, to what extent the Paris text had survived the times and whether any adjustments or changes to this instrument were necessary in the present stage of development of space activities.

Some of us here today have taken part in the Helsinki Conference. Others have sent in their comments and suggestions. The net result is an interesting spectrum of ideas from which useful common denominators may be drawn after a deep analysis of coincidences and divergences between members.

At the end of the day a Resolution was adopted by the Conference requesting the Space Law Committee to elaborate a Revised Draft Convention on the Settlement of Disputes related to Space Activities (this slight amendment to the original title, suggested by Dr. Jasentuliyana, was agreed at the Helsinki Conference).

III. A need for change or for minor adjustments?

As pointed out at the outset, commercial activities in outer space are the sign of the times. Private enterprises are becoming involved in this area with increased frequency. One of the most illustrative examples today is provided by the exploitation of the geostationary orbit, especially insofar as telecommunications are concerned. Equally commercial are the legal problems originated by these activities, e.g., advertising, copyright, intellectual property in general, and others.

Disputes arising from private activities in space which do not confront subjects of public law and therefore, are unlikely to raise issues involving sovereignty, do not appear unmanageable in light of the present legal system. Indeed, the rules and procedures applicable to international commercial arbitration seem, with certain adjustments, appropriate in this new field.

On this point, the views of the experts converge. Professor Böckstiegel considers that the greater flexibility shown by private enterprises due to the important economic interests involved in the practical uses of outer space is prompting lawyers to look for more realistic and agile solutions, such as those applied in international business law (4). This stand coincides with Professor Cocca's position, elaborated in his answers and comments to the Helsinki Space Law Report, where he stresses the need to give pride of place to the problem of dispute settlement between states.

Professor Malanczuk holds a similar view as to disputes between private enterprises. In his opinion, where disputes between a state and a private enterprise were concerned, good reasons justified the drawing up of a special system to cover investment disputes with the ICSID, even though about one third of this type of disputes had been dealt with under the auspices of the ICC (5).

On general lines, it is fair to say that the doctrine is almost unanimous in that the question of dispute settlement between private companies carrying out activities in outer space is nowadays adequately covered by the existing law. This consensus was reflected within the ILA Space Law Committee in its Report submitted to the Helsinki Conference (6). Consequently, only minor adjustments would be required in this area.

The question is infinitely more complex when we enter the domain of public international law. Here, the lack of effective mechanisms is clearly manifest. The problem is aggravated by the possibility of political issues being brought up in certain sensitive areas such as remote-sensing and direct broadcasting.

In this field a definite step forward ought to be taken to move away from the danger of falling back into a stage of autointerpretation of the law. In other words a change, and not just a minor adjustment, is needed. Therefore, new law should be developed in connection with disputes between subjects of public international law within a down-to-earth framework which takes due account of the modern, and indeed inexorable, trend proclaiming the relativism of state sovereignty in the contemporary world (7).

The 1984 Paris Convention laid down a system which includes non-binding dispute resolution by resort to conciliation (in article 4) and binding mechanisms which may be found in article 5 et seq. of this instrument. The latter, in addition to establishing the jurisdiction of the ICJ and arbitration procedures, envisages the possibility of setting up an International Tribunal for Space Law. States and international organisations (8) are free to choose one or more of those means by written declaration at the time of signing, ratifying or acceding to the Convention.

In order to move closer to the objectives in mind, a minor change is hereby suggested to article 3 of the Paris Convention. Both in paragraphs 1 and 2 of this article it is spoken of "expeditiously" when referring to the compulsory exchange of views to be held by the parties to a dispute before starting conciliation procedures. It is submitted that this requirement be made less subjective and more terminant. To this end it would be advisable to follow the Inmarsat example in establishing a precise time-limit (9) which, in the case of the 1984 Paris Convention, could be thirty days.

With a view to making the Paris text more effective which, in practice, means to have the maximum support from the international community and ease the way to ratification, the present writer considers that the exclusion clause included in article 1. 2 (a, b and c) of the Convention should, for the time being at least, be kept. The provision in question means that any State could leave out specific space activities or specific space areas and declare it will not be bound by certain sections of the Convention. This point was the object of a lively discussion within the ILA Space Law Committee at the Helsinki Conference as well as in the work carried out previous to this Meeting.

Opinions are conflicting on this matter (10).

Professor Umberto Leanza, for example, in his comments to the afore-mentioned Helsinki Report, squarely opposed the possibility of excluding any space activity from the scope of the Convention suggesting, instead, the inclusion of a list of disputes in respect of which the Space Law Tribunal would be competent. Professor Kopal, for his part, proposed to draw up a "list of exclusions".

Both these scholars openly favour the setting up of a special chamber within the future Tribunal for Space Law Disputes. Indeed, the idea is sensible and worthy of support. However, prior to the creation of this Tribunal, it is advisable to think in terms of a special chamber for space law disputes within the ICJ, as is presently the case where environmental law issues are concerned. This idea is advocated by Professor Böckstiegel in his presentation entitled "Equipping the Court to deal with Developing Areas of International Law" (11) submitted in April 1996 on the occasion of the 50th anniversary of the ICJ.

From a strictly legal point of view Professor Leanza's position on the deletion of the exclusion clause seems impeccable. So does Professor Kopal's, in his effort to compromise opposite views. Yet, in the world of today, it is not unreasonable to suppose that both these possibilities -namely, to have a list of disputes for which the Tribunal would be competent or, conversely, a list of exclusions- are likely to conspire against the main target which is to achieve the widest possible support for this Convention, particularly from those countries engaged in space activities.

Consequently, it is contended that article 1 of the 1984 text should remain unchanged for the moment (12). At a later stage - and hopefully in a not too distant future if we have in mind the increasing investments in this field and enormous interests in play - States will no doubt be more inclined to adopt harsher restrictions to their sovereignty in pursuance of a more effective dispute settlement system.

The task of convincing States to choose binding procedures by means of the declaration envisaged in the Paris Convention is not easy. Progress is expected to be slow and gradual in spite of the sometimes astronomic economic interests referred to before. In this challenge, it is perhaps helpful to have in mind the provisions of the Intelsat Agreement in connection with dispute settlement, to be read together with other useful examples such as the system laid down for dispute settlement in the 1991 Madrid Protocol for the Protection of the Environment in the Antarctic. These are important precedents in our quest for a more effective mechanism for dispute resolutiom between persons of public international law.

IV. Other matters debated in 1996 in Helsinki

The discussion which followed the presentation of the Space Law Report at the Working Session of the 1996 ILA Conference was enlightening in many aspects and provides food for thought on extremely topical questions.

Among the major issues involved, some of which have already been touched upon, attention was focused on the various aspects of "entities other than States" having access to dispute settlement procedures under the 1984 Paris Convention, in accordance with the wording of article 10.2 (13). The conclusion was that the door is left open for private entities to take part in such procedures. The scope of this provision will no doubt facilitate our task.

The foregoing question prompted the participants to discuss the need for a "genuine link" - such as nationality - concerning the private entities in question. The increasing role of NGOs was mentioned in this respect. In fact, NGOs could not, under the Paris Convention, become High Contracting Parties but could nevertheless be parties to a dispute settlement procedure pursuant to the Convention. In this way a practical solution is provided without entering the slippery groundsrelating to the sovereign rights of subjects of public international law.

V. Conclusions

Most of the provisions of the ILA Convention on the Settlement of Space Law Disputes (Paris 1984) , now renamed as the Convention on the Settlement of Disputes related to Space Activities (Helsinki 1996), are applicable in the present time.

Therefore, a new international instrument is not necessary. Rather, work should be directed to making a few adjustments in the existing system. Disputes between private companies engaged in the exploitation of outer space are today conveniently covered by the law applicable to international commercial arbitration.

Conversely, efforts should now concentrate on dispute settlement between subjects of public international law involved in space activities with a view to convincing them of the advantages of having compulsory dispute settlement mechanisms in this field.

However, having in mind the importance of getting the widest possible support from the international community and easing the way to ratification of the Paris text, it is advisable to start at a low level of compulsion and then, gradually, move up the scale.

Consequently, the exclusion clause included in article 1 of the 1984 Paris Convention should, for the moment, be maintained.

The establishment of a summary procedure to determine disputes, as envisaged in article 50 of the Paris Convention, appears a suitable way to avoid delays, particularly in certain areas where long-lasting controversies may lead to untold consequences (14).

The idea of a future Tribunal for Space Law Disputes, as provided in the ILA Paris Convention is worthy of consideration. In the meantime the role of the International Court of Justice should be strengthened, particularly through the creation of a special chamber dealing with space law disputes.

VI. Notes

1. Article III of the 1967 Space Treaty.

2. Article IX of the 1967 Space Treaty.

3. In fact, one of the greatest criticisms made by the doctrine to this Convention is the recommendatory nature of the Claims Commission's awards unless the parties, beforehand, have agreed to the contrary.

4. K.H. Böckstiegel mentions, inter alia, the International Chamber of Commerce, the London Court of Arbitration and UNCITRAL. See this author's presentation entitled "Equipping the Court to deal with Developing Areas of International Law - Space Law", during the Colloquium INCREASING THE EFFECTIVENESS OF THE COURT , organised in celebration of the 50th Anniversary of the International Court of Justice, The Hague, 16-18 April 1996.

5. P. Malanczuk, in his answers to the ILA Space Law Committee Questionnaire, ILA 67th Conference, Helsinki, August 1996.

6. See Cocca, Christol, Malanczuk, Böckstiegel and the Rapporteur in the Report of the Space Law Committee of the ILA to the Helsinki Conference, August 1996.

7. The members of the ILA Space Law Committee were firm on this point. Christol, in the second reading of the Helsinki Space Law Report, observed that in three cases the European Space Agency had declared itself bound by international agreements within the United Nations aegis, viz. Rescue, Liability and Registration, adding that Eutelsat had taken a similar step with respect to the Liability Convention. This would entitle them to bring up claims against the parties and viceversa. Christol strongly favours the idea of the parties to the Liability Convention giving their support to the 1984 ILA Convention on the Settlement of Space Law Disputes.

8. This is in accordance with article 36 of the Paris Convention.

9. The dispute settlement system laid down for Inmarsat establishes one year as the maximum span over which negotiations should extend. After this, any party to the dispute may start arbitration procedures. Conversely, in Intelsat, no time-limit exists for negotiations.

10. On this question the opinion was divided within the ILA Space Law Committee. See comments of the members in the 1996 Helsinki Report.

11. K.H. Böckstiegel, op.cit. in note 4.

12. Article 1, paragraph 1 of the 1984 Paris Convention reads as follows:

> 1. This Convention applies to all activities in outerspace and all activities with effects in outer space, if such activities are carried out by High Contracting Parties (HCPs), by nationals of HCPs or from the territory of HCPs.
>
> 2. Any HCP, on depositing its instrument of ratification, may declare
> (a) that it excludes from the applicability of this Convention space activities of a specific kind described in such declaration,
> (b) that it limits the applicability of this Convention in certain space activities or to specific areas of space law as may be dealt with in such declaration,

(c) that it will not be bound by certain sections or articles of this Convention described in such declaration.

13. Article 10, paragraph 2 of the Paris Convention provides

> The dispute settlement procedures specified in this Convention shall be open to entities other than HCPs unless the matter is submitted to the International Court of Justice in accordance with article 6.

14. Article 50, paragraph 3 of the Paris Convention establishes

> With a view to the speedy dispatch of business, the Tribunal shall form annually a chamber composed of five of its elected members which may hear and determine disputes by summary procedure. Two alternative members shall be selected for the purpose of replacing members who are unable to participate in a particular proceeding.

Buenos Aires, 1st October 1996

IISL-96-IISL.2.03

CASES AND METHODS OF DISPUTE SETTLEMENT IN SPACE LAW

By Dr. Hassan Safavi*
President, Air Space Research and Planning
International Arbitrator

ABSTRACT

The expansion of commercial and other beneficial uses of outer space inevitably will lead to disputes between various participants. States and other entities may have interests in particular disputes. In this regard, space law has substantial similarity to air law. Certain disputes arising from activities involving aircraft are resolved in domestic law, however, while others are resolved by international law.

The unification of domestic laws of various countries in the field of international activities facilitate their mutual cooperation and avoid any conflict arising from such activities. States tried to resolve their problems previously by negotiation, conclusion of bilateral or multilateral agreement, and finally by conclusion of international conventions or treaties. Alternatively, where the cooperation of various countries is based on the rules and procedures mentioned in international conventions or treaties, the contracting states prepare their domestic laws in accordance with such instruments. Consequently, the unification of domestic laws of the different countries is obtained. The liability rules mentioned in the Warsaw Convention concerning damage caused to passengers, cargo and mail which is textually mentioned in domestic flight is the best example to prove the necessity of unification of domestic laws of different countries.

In this paper, the various categories of cases and methods of dispute settlement in air and space law are compared and contrasted. Similarities as well as differences are identified, and the relative superiority of one legal regime over the other in specific circumstances is discussed. Finally, proposals are made for the formulation of necessary international rules to supplement the existing space law.

I. INTRODUCTION

In space law, disputes arising from space activities can be divided into different categories:

A. Disputes occurring from civil space activities;

B. Disputes occurring from criminal acts;

C. A combination of the two above mentioned cases; and

D. Disputes resulting from the application and interpretation of principles mentioned in international conventions and treaties.

The major sources of international rules regarding the cases and methods of dispute settlement are mentioned in the 1972 Liability Convention.[1] In the preamble of this Convention it is written that "the establishment of [these] rules and procedures will contribute to the strengthening of international cooperation in the field of the exploration and use of outer space for peaceful purposes. . ."

In this Convention, after giving a definition of the term "damage" in article 1(a) as a loss of life, personal injury or other impairment to health or loss or damage to the property of States or persons, natural or juridical, or property of international intergovernmental organizations, prescribes a rule which is mentioned in articles 8 and 9 for the presentation to a launching state a claim for compensation of damage. According to article 9, "A claim for compensation for damage shall be presented to a launching state through diplomatic channels." The determination of disputes is generally the same as in arbitration procedures.[2]

1. The rules regarding the compensation of claims is mentioned in article 12 of the Liability Convention. According to this article:

> The compensation which the launching State shall be liable to pay for the damage under this Convention shall be determined in accordance with international law and the principles of justice and equity, in order to provide such reparation in respect of the damage as will restore the person, natural or juridical, State or international organization on whose behalf the claim is presented to the condition which would have existed if the damage had not occurred.

This principle does not have a counterpart in air law. In this matter the space law has superiority to air law.

2. Article 23, subsection 2 of the Liability Convention prescribes that "No provision of this Convention shall prevent States from concluding international agreements reaffirming, supplementing or extending its provisions." Subsection 1 of this article provides that "The provisions of this Convention shall not affect other international agreements in force in so far as relations between the States Parties to such agreements are concerned."

Different structures for the purposes of activities, and the organization, management and methods of settlement of disputes can be found in various international space conventions. Examples include the INTELSAT Agreement of 1971[3], the INMARSAT Convention of 1976[4], the EUTELSAT Convention of 1982[5], and the EUMETSAT Agreement of 1983[6].

Finally, in the case of disputes occurring between states parties to the Outer Space Treaty of 1967[7] and 1972 Liability Convention, where

---

1. Convention on International Liability for Damage Caused by Space Objects, March 29, 1972.

2. *See generally* articles 15 - 20 of the Liability Convention.

3. Agreement Relating to the International Telecommunications Satellite Organization, *entered into force* February 12, 1973.

4. Convention on the International Maritime Satellite Organization, September 3, 1976.

5. Convention Establishing the European Telecommunications Satellite Organization, *entered into force* September 1, 1985.

6. Convention for the Establishment of a European Organization for the Exploitation of Meteorological Satellites, *entered into force* June 19, 1986.

7. Treaty on Principles Governing the Activities of States in the Exploration and Use of Outer Space, Including the Moon and Other Celestial Bodies, January 27, 1967.

they do not arrive at agreeable conclusions, but where the subject nevertheless corresponds to the cases mentioned in the Charter of the United Nations,[8] resort should be taken of article 33 which recommends negotiations, investigation, mediation, and other peaceful means of dispute resolution. Thus, the Complainant party can refer to the United Nations Secretary General, or to the Hague Tribunal, for appropriate measures to be taken for the settlement of the disputes.

II. Penal Acts

Crimes and offenses committed aboard spacecrafts are submitted to the domestic laws of countries, as there are no international rules in this subject. In air law, there are several international conventions relating to crimes and offenses committed against aircraft, crew, passengers, and cargo.

The Tokyo Convention of 1963 concerns any kind of crime committed aboard aircraft in flight which causes danger to aircraft, crew, passengers, cargo, etc.[9] In 1970, the Hague Convention was adopted which, according to article 1, declares that any person aboard an aircraft in service who, by means of violence or threat of violence, takes in his possession control of the aircraft, commits a crime.[10]

In 1971, the Montreal Convention was adopted which concerns the security of an aircraft or causing damage to an aircraft in flight or to air navigation facilities. According to article 1 of this Convention, any person who intentionally commits the following acts is recognized as a criminal:

A. By violence commits any act against passengers of an aircraft in flight which can put in danger the security of the flight;

B. To destroy an aircraft in service or to cause damage to said aircraft in some way that makes the flight impossible;

C. To put any material or substances in an aircraft in service which will destroy the aircraft or to cause danger to the aircraft in flight; and

D. To give any fictitious information which puts the security of the flight in danger.

These international rules do not exist in space law.

III. Procedures for Determination of Criminal Disputes: Competent Authorities

Among the primary objectives of all countries is to guarantee the security of their airspace and the safety of flight within that airspace. In order to achieve this, they try to restrain the accomplishment of crime, and take measures to prevent criminals from escaping from punishment. In international air law the following states are recognized as competent authorities for prosecuting and judgment of criminal acts:

A. State of registration of aircraft;

B. State in which the crime takes place and creates effects in its territory;

C. State in which the criminal resides permanently or is a subject of that state;

D. State in which the crime is committed against its subjects and matters;

E. State in which the crime puts the security of the state in danger; and

F. State in which the crime is committed against the rules of security of the flight.

---

8. Charter of the United Nations, June 26, 1945.

9. Convention on Offenses and Certain Other Acts Committed Aboard Aircraft, September 14, 1963.

10. Convention for the Suppression of Unlawful Seizure of Aircraft, December 16, 1970.

IV. OBSERVATIONS

The use of outer space, including the moon and other celestial bodies, has many advantages for the people of all countries in the world. Among the important benefits currently obtained are the use of outer space for communications and transportation. The commercialization of outer space is becoming a reality.[11] The Liability Convention concerns the compensation of damages caused by space objects. But many problems regarding civil and penal acts as I mentioned above is submitted to the domestic laws of each country. This situation can cause conflicts between different states. In this regard, see article 8 of the 1967 Space Treaty.

The formulation of necessary international rules will facilitate international relations between developed and developing countries in outer space activities.[12] Therefore, for safeguarding the security of spaceflight and in order to protect the interests of all the countries it is necessary to conclude an international convention relating to crimes and offenses committed aboard spacecraft. Article 4 of the 1967 Outer Space Treaty forbids the placement "in orbit around the Earth any objects carrying nuclear weapons or any other kinds of weapons of mass destruction" but it does not forbid the carriage of arms, munitions or explosive materials adequate to single destruction. This act is prohibited in air law and is considered as crime. It should be prohibited in space law.

V. CONCLUSION

The five space treaties such as the 1967 Outer Space Treaty, the Agreement on the Rescue of Astronauts,[13] the Liability Convention, the Registration Convention,[14] and the Moon Agreement[15] are the major principles of international space law. The 1967 Outer Space Treaty can be viewed as furnishing a general legal basis for the peaceful use of outer space and providing a framework for the developing law of outer space. The four other treaties could be said to deal specifically with certain concepts included in the 1967 Treaty. The 1984 Moon Agreement, for example, concerns the exploration, use and exploitation of its mineral resources and other benefits.[16] This Agreement has been ratified by only 9 states as of January 1, 1994.[17]

The review of the Moon Agreement is necessary in order to establish an international regime acceptable to the international community.[18] The methods of dispute

---

11. *See generally* H.L. VAN TRAA-ENGELMAN, COMMERCIAL UTILIZATION OF OUTER SPACE - LAW AND PRACTICE (1993).

12. Safavi, *Legal Aspects of International Cooperation in Space*, in PROCEEDINGS OF THE 26TH COLLOQUIUM ON THE LAW OF OUTER SPACE 255 (1984).

13. Agreement on the Rescue of Astronauts, the Return of Astronauts, and the Return of Objects Launched Into Outer Space, April 22, 1968.

14. Convention on Registration of Objects Launched into Outer Space, January 14, 1975.

15. Activities of States on the Moon and Other Celestial Bodies, *entered into force* July 11, 1984.

16. For a discussion of article 11, *see, e.g.*, Matte, *Legal Implications of the Exploration and Uses of the Moon and Other celestial Bodies*, in PROCEEDINGS OF THE 35TH COLLOQUIUM ON THE LAW OF OUTER SPACE 471 (1993).

17. These are Australia, Austria, Chile, Mexico, Morocco, the Netherlands, Pakistan, the Philippines, and Uruguay. In addition, France, Guatemala, India, Peru, and Romania have signed the Moon Agreement.

18. Safavi, *Review of the Moon Agreement - Some Legal Considerations*

settlement occurring from execution of the subject mentioned in article 11 of the Moon Agreement should protect the rights and benefits of all countries irrespective of their economic or scientific development on the basis of equality and in accordance with international law.

In October, 1985, this author presented a paper concerning "Legal Problems Of Registration of Objects."[19] In 1988 Dr. M. Bourely presented a paper relating to the same subject[20]. It is not possible to apply the rules and methods of dispute settlement in cases where the satellite launched into outer space is not registered in the United Nations' registration book. Other problems in international space law which will require dispute resolution include problems concerning space debris which cause danger to the active satellites in orbit around the earth.[21]

The cases and methods of dispute settlement in space law are the consequences of space activities. If such activities do not exist, there are no rights, no responsibilities, and no dispute to be resolved in the human society. It is obvious that there is interconnection between different problems that exist in space law, and it is appropriate to an environment whose nature is so extraordinary. The extension of international law to outer space has been gradual and evolutionary commencing with the study of questions relating to legal aspects, proceeding to the formulation of principles of a legal nature, and then incorporating such principles in general multilateral treaties.

Taking into consideration different aspects of space law in relation with the methods of settlement of disputes, I do believe that the conclusion of a new international convention pertaining the rules and procedures to safeguard the security of spaceflight and to prevent the commitment of criminal acts against spacecraft, astronauts, passengers, cargo, and the establishment of an independent international organization for management of outer space activities such as International civil Space Agency (I.C.S.A.) which I proposed several times in my previous papers, is the reasonable solution to resolve different problems in relations with space activities.

Concerning the Juridical Status of the Moon Agreement, presented to the 38th Colloquium on the Law of Outer Space, Oslo, Norway, October, 1995.

19. PROCEEDINGS OF THE 28TH COLLOQUIUM ON THE LAW OF OUTER SPACE 199 (1986).

20. *Is it Necessary to Re-Negotiate the Convention on Registration?*, in PROCEEDINGS OF THE 31ST COLLOQUIUM ON THE LAW OF OUTER SPACE 227 (1989).

21. Diederiks-Verschoor, *Legal Aspects of Environmental Protection Regarding Debris,* in PROCEEDINGS OF THE 30TH COLLOQUIUM ON THE LAW OF OUTER SPACE 131 (1987). *See also* Karl-Heinz Bockstiegel, The Draft of the International Law Association for a Convention on Space Debris.

IISL-96-IISL.2.06

LIABILITY FOR COPYRIGHT INFRINGEMENT IN THE CASE OF TV TRANSMISSION VIA SATELLITE (ESSEL VISION'S CLAIM ON INTERSPUTNIK)

by Dr. Gennady P. Zhukov*, Victor S. Veshchunov**

History of Dispute

In 1993, India's Essel Vision (a subsidiary of ZEE TV) stated that its right for public demonstration of films in India had been violated by Asia United Media Ltd. (AUM) registered in the UK. AUM leased communications channels from Intersputnik. It was stated that Intersputnik bore joint responsibility with AUM that was in breach of copyright. According to the plaintiff's lawyers who referred to a provisional authority by the Bombay High Court the case could be submitted to a Russian court if Intersputnik did not take appropriate measures.

The plaintiff's statement at the Bombay High Court could be reduced to the idea that video copyright holders had no right to transmit video cassettes through satellite and cable TV, as defined in Section 14c) of the Copyright Law of India. In the plaintiffs' opinion the copyright for the video cassettes was transferred to the owners only for direct-to-home service.

* Professor of international law, Hon. Director, IISL
** Legal Advisor, INTERSPUTNIK, member, IISL

The views expressed in this paper are the authors' own and in no way commit INTERSPUTNIK

In the decision of October 27, 1993, the Bombay High Court found the plaintiffs' arguments convincing but did not pass any final award. At the same time, the plaintiffs objected (even considering arbitration proceedings) against film satellite transmissions via channels originated in Russia whenever AUM had no appropriate copyrights.

At Intersputnik's request, the President of AUM advised that his company had all necessary rights to demonstrate TV programs in India and flatly repudiated the alleged copyright violation.

Comment

Disputes of this kind between broadcasting companies who accuse each other of being in breach of copyright will become more frequent as TV broadcasting service is expanded. In our particular case, we wanted to draw your attention to the fact whether the owner of telecommunication facilities (in particular, Intersputnik) is responsible for copyright matters in principle including the contents of the program and copyright observance by the program customer.

1. Mutual obligations of the Parties involved in satellite TV service and their liability are defined in a contract. According to the Contract with AUM, Intersputnik's obligations include only satellite operation in terms of technology; the satellite is used just as a technological facility to distribute AUM's programs in the territory of India.

The Contract reads: "Intersputnik shall not be liable for copyright matters" (Article 6). Intersputnik is entitled by its promoters to provide service while the contents of the transmitted signal is the responsibility of the clients.

2. The Brussels Convention on the Distribution of Programme-Carrying Signals Transmitted via Satellite of 1974 does not impose any responsibility on satellite operator (in our case Intersputnik) as a provider of technological service, for eventual violation of copyrights and associated rights of third parties while transmitting TV programs. The Convention does not include any specific provisions to protect authors' copyright and associated rights of third parties. The purpose of the Convention is to prevent unauthorized transmissions of programs. Strictly speaking, this Convention is the principal source of legal documentation applicable to this case. Moreover, Intersputnik as an intergovernmental organi-zation is a subject of international public law. In our opinion, the Convention does not imply any responsibility of entities which technically transmit programme-carrying signals via satellite for eventual violation of the rights of third persons in relation to broadcast-programmes.

3. Development of advanced technology leads to convergence between FSS and DTH satellites. This fact was confirmed by member states of the European Convention relating to Questions on Copyright Law and Neighboring Rights in the Framework of Transfrontier Broad-casting (1994, Strasbourg). This makes it necessary to consider further legal aspects of broad-casting via satellite from the viewpoint of copyright law and neighboring rights.

   The Strasbourg Convention recognizes that copyright and neighboring rights shall, as far as transfrontier broadcasting by satellites are concerned, be protected in conformity with provisions of the Bern Convention for the Protection of Literary and Artistic Works (Paris Act, 1971) and the Rome Convention for the Pro-tection of Performers, Producers of Phonograms and Broadcasting Organizations, 1961.

   In the context of the problem under review, these conventions as well as the World Copyright Convention (Geneva, 1952) use the term "to air" synonymous to "making public" or "issuing" (e.g. Article 11-bis of the Bern Convention, Article 7 of the Rome Convention, Article 6 of the World (Geneva) Convention).

   Both scholars and practical workers believe that programme-carrying signals inaccessible to public can not be regarded as "aired" in the sense of international copyright convention.

All the above international conventions deal with programs transmitted by satellite service providers/operators and no liabilities are imposed on them for the breach of third parties' rights.

Conclusion

The existing norms of international law do not impose any liability on Intersputnik, as a provider of technical satellite service, for the breach of copyright and associated right owners.

This is also confirmed by Article 6 of Contract for the Allotment of Intersputnik Space Segment Capacity to Asian United Media Ltd., UK, which precise that "Intersputnik shall not be liable for any copyright matters".

The contract goes still farther since it provides for a detailed arbitration procedure of any disputes and/or discords which may arise between INTERSPUTNIK and the AUM.

This special case illustrated by us may present interest to other satellite communications organizations, both international or private.

IISL-96-IISL.2.07

TENDENCIES OF DISPUTE SETTLEMENT IN PRESENT „EASTERN EUROPEAN" SPACE LAW

Dr. Mahulena Hošková*

Abstract

The substantial socio-economic changes, which occurred in the countries of the former Soviet block in recent years brought about *inter alia* certain changes in the understanding of dispute settlement procedures. One of the best examples of this evolution is Intersputnik - the telecommunication organisation of the former socialist block. In contrast to its former legal basis, detailed dispute settlement procedures are under preparation as a result of the far-reaching re-construction of its organisational structure. Certain mechanisms of dispute settlement were introduced also into the bilateral space co-operation agreements concluded by the Russian Federation in the years 1992-1993. As regards international treaties concerning space activities concluded between the successor States of the former Soviet Union, both in the Agreement On Joint Activities in the Exploration and Exploitation of the Outer Space, entered into by 9 such states in Minsk in 1991, and the Agreement Concerning Arrangements for Maintaining and Using Space Infrastructure Facilities in Pursuance of Space Programs of 1992, specific negotiations mechanisms have been introduced. Furthermore, the European Space Agency has concluded a great number of agreements on various levels, with partners from the former COMECON states; they reflect ist long experience in formulating provisions on dispute settlement as shown by the pertinent regulations of the General Clauses and Conditions for ESA Contracts. Taking into account the available multi- and bilateral co-operation agreements as well as information on the dispute settlement procedures involving private subjects, this paper seeks to analyse these tendencies and endeavours to draw some general conclusions concerning these developments in relation with the legal subjects from the former COMECON states.

1. Introduction

Notwithstanding the political and economical barriers existing before 1989, there had been considerable co-operation among the specialists from various geographic areas with their counterparts from the Middle and Eastern European countries on various levels since the beginning of the space era. The strategical relevance of space exploration and the differences in the legal traditions lead, however, to a general reluctance of the co-operating partners to bind themselves by detailed justiciable legal obligations; as a consequence, the joint activities were usually performed on a rather informal basis: The duties of the parties, if at all formulated, were usually inserted into protocols on the sessions of the respective working groups or agreed upon by an exchange of letters. The legal character of these documents oscillated

---

* JUDr. (Prague), CSc.; Member IISL.
Max Planck Institute for Comparative Public Law and International Law, Heidelberg, Germany.

between statements without legally binding force and special forms of agreement. Generally speaking, one of the consequences of this situation was that - as far one can judge on the basis of the information accessible - usually no mechanisms were provided for the settlement of disputes which might have occured during the implementation of the joint projects.

After 1989, the situation changed profoundly.: Privatisation dramatically diversified the scene of the Middle and Eastern European subjects involved in space activities and called for a more precise regulation of the legal framework of the international co-operation. This has been the case not only with regard to for the meritorial rules (obligations), but, as a consequence, also as regards for the dispute settlement procedures. More frequently, rules concerning the treatment of differences relating to the interpretation and implementation of such agreements were introduced into the texts of these legal instruments. The variety of these mechanisms reflects the diversity of the relations which occured in the course of the space co-operation - they represent almost all possible combinations of the relations between states, international organisations and legal persons[1].

2. Examples of Dispute Settlement Mechanisms in the Space Co-operation Agreements of the Former COMECON-States as Parties of these Agreements

a) The states of the former Soviet Union, among them especially Russia, inherited after 1991 one of the most monumental space programs. This „heritage" did not represent only the results of its indisputable successes and enormous experience, but also the desperate lack of financial resources. Thus, international co-operation, both on the level of agreements among the former USSR states and agreements, involving especially Russia, with the western partners became often the only possibility to save a part of this potential.

In conformity with these policies signed the Russian Federation in 1991/93 a group of bilateral agreements that established the framework for her co-operation with the space agencies of the - for future common activities most promising - countries[2]. Although all these documents create the legal basis for the implementation of the common projects, the models of the regulation of the dispute settlement mechanisms provided for vary to a considerable extent:

Article 8 of the Agreement between the Russian Space Agency[3] and the German Agency for Space Affairs (DARA) on Co-operation in the Exploration and Exploitation of Outer Space of 1 March 1993[4] stipulates that in case of disputes concerning the interpretation and implementation of this agreement „...the Parties shall enter without delay into consultations." If these fail, and unless otherwise provided by specially agreed procedures for particular projects, each unresolved problem will be brought to the attention of the Directors-General of both Agencies „...in order to reach a joint final solution."[5]

In contrast to the Russian - German Agreement, the Agreement between the Government of Japan and the Government of the Russian Federation on the Co-operation in the Field of the Exploration and Exploitation of Outer Space for Peaceful Purposes[6] of 13 October 1993 contains only a more general provision that calls for diplomatic negotiations in the event of differences concerning the implementation of the common projects.: According to its article 8, both governments shall, if necessary, address in diplomatic negotiations all problems which might arise in connection with this agreement[7].

Another way of dispute settlement was chosen in the intergovernmental Agreement between the United States of America and the Russian Federation Concerning Co-operation in the Exploration and Use of Outer Space for Peaceful Purposes of 17 June 1992[8], the annex of which deals primarily with the problems connected with intellectual property. As in the German - Russian Agreement, article I lit. d of the Annex put the emphasis on consultation between the Parties; if, however, these fail, the dispute shall, on the basis of an agreement between the Parties, be submitted to an arbitral tribunal for binding arbitration in accordance with the applicable rules of the international law. Unless the Parties otherwise agree, the UNCITRAL arbitration rules will be applied[9].

The French national space agency CNES is intensively co-operating with Russian subjects on the basis of agreements or contracts. Nothwithstanding the fact that so far no real dispute settlement procedures have been initiated, the pertinent clauses constitute common elements of these documents. For instance, under the agreement between CNES and the Russian Space Agency concerning the SCARAB project, in case of a dispute the first step would lead towards an attempt to settle the matter by the program committee of the project. If necessary, the problem should be brought before the steering committee of the project; in the third instance, the president of the CNES would decide. The general policy is, however, even if problems occurr, not to interrupt the co-operation and instead of resorting to the formal dispute settlement procedure, to seek for a mutually acceptable solution that does not constitute an unbearable financial burden for anyone of the Parties.

b) A basically different approach with regard to the dispute settlement was taken by the signatories of the agreements concluded under the auspices of the Commonwealth of Independent States (CIS): Neither the Agreement on Joint Activities in the Exploration and Exploitation of the Outer Space of 30 December 1991[10] concluded in Minsk (the Minsk agreement), practically simultaneously with the CIS´s creation among nine successor states of the USSR, nor the Agreement concerning Arrangements for Maintaining and Using Space Infrastructure Facilities in Pursuance of Space Programs of 15. 5. 1992[11] (the Tashkent Agreement) concluded among 10 former USSR states, nor the Agreement on the Exploitation of System of Military Communication Satellites of 12 March 1993[12] contain any of the „traditional" dispute settlement clauses.

Nevertheless, certain mechanisms for the joint problem-management have been provided for:: Article 6 of the „Minsk Agreement" contains e.g. a statement that the States Parties will co-ordinate their activities aimed at the settlement of international legal problems of space research and exploitation[13]; obviously, the actual legal relevance of this rather general obligation of the Parties, namely „to co-ordinate" their activities with the view to settle these „international legal problems", depends upon its future interpretation and application. Another interesting solution has been provided in the already mentioned „Tashkent Agreement" of 1992; its article 5 incorporates the rules of the Convention on International Liability for Damage Caused by Space Objects of 1972[14] (Liability Convention): Under this agreement, a special multilateral commission set up by the States Parties for the determination of the amounts of compensation shall be created; as far as space activities are concerned, this Commission will follow the provisions of the Liability Convention. It would be interesting to see, however, if also its composition would correspond to the creation of the Claims Commission under Articles XV. and XVI. of the Liability Convention or if a different *ad hoc* solution would be found.[15]

Among the important bilateral agreements regulating the space activities of the former Soviet-block states, it is necessary to mention the Agreement on the Order of Exploitation the Baikonur Cosmodrome signed by the Russian Federation and the Republic of Kazakhstan on 25 May 1992[16], followed by the Treaty between the Government of the Russian Federation and the Government of the Republic of Kazakhstan on the leasing of the Baikonur Complex of 10 December 1994[17]. Because of the framework character of the first of these two agreements, its principles are referring in all sensitive points to special rules. Consequently, Article 4 of this Agreement stipulates that for the settlement of property and economy problems specified in article 2 (e.g. implementation of the right of use of the cosmodrome, implementation of the property rights) a special organ will be created on the cosmodrome, the composition and procedural rules of which will be governed by the law of Kazakh Republic[18].

3. Examples of Dispute Settlement Mechanisms in the Space Co-operation Agreements between International Organisations and former COMECON-States as Parties of these Agreements

a) An active role in the space co-operation with the Eastern partners has been played traditionally by the European Space Agency (ESA). Article XIV(1) of the Convention of the European Space Agency which entered into force in 1980, provides that „the Agency may, upon decisions of the Council taken by unanimous votes of all Member States, co-operate with other international organisations and institutions and with Governments, organisations and institutions of non-member States, and conclude agreements with them to this effect".[19] Pursuing this policy, ESA concluded already in 1990 the Agreement between the European Space Agency and the Government of Soviet Socialist Republics concerning Co-operation in the Field of the Exploration and Use of Outer Space for Peaceful Purposes[20] which entered into force on 25 April 1990 for the period of 10 years and substituted an Agreement constituted by an exchange of letters between the USSR Academy of Sciences and the European Space Research Organisation in 1971. Article 12 of the Agreement of 1990 contains a rather general clause that the Parties, in case difficulties arise in the implementation of co-operation under this Agreement, shall enter into consultations at the request of either Party of this Agreement[21].

In a diplomatic note to ESA dated 28 April 1992, the Government of the Russian Federation stated that it was taking over the rights and obligations arising out of the above-mentioned Agreement of 1990 and explicitly designated the Russian Space Agency for the implementation of that Agreement. With regard to the invitation extended to the Government of the Russian Federation on December 1993 by the signatories of the Intergovernmental Agreement on the Space Station to become a partner in the International Space programme under the relevant international agreements, ESA concluded on 5 October 1994 with the Russian Space Agency an Agreement on Co-operation on Manned Space Infrastructure and Space Transportation Systems[22].

Taking into account the vital dependence of the success of this project on the realisation of all of its elements, the agreement contains a relatively detailed procedure of dispute settlement. Its Article 12 provides that the parties shall consult in advance any matter likely to have a bearing on the arrangements for the Agreement. In case that, inspite of these consultations, a dispute concerning the interpretation or application of this Agreement or its annexes arises, it should be referred first to the co-chairmen of the established specialists-working groups and then to the Co-ordinating Committee consisting of the directors in charge of the Programmes involved in the co-operation activities. If these negotiations fail, the next step should be the settlement by the Directors General of the agencies - parties of the Agreement.

In case that even these mechanisms do not lead to the envisaged result Article 12 provides for an arbitration clause: Any dispute that cannot be settled in accordance with the foregoing steps shall be referred,, at the request of either Party, to an arbitration tribunal which consists of two arbitrators appointed by the Parties and the third arbitrator who will be appointed by them and chair the tribunal. In case of failure to appoint the third arbitrator, he will be appointed by the President of the International Court of Justice. The seat and procedural rules will be chosen by the Tribunal itself; the only rule of procedure contained in the Agreement itself is that it shall take its decisions by a majority of its members, who shall not abstain from voting[23] . The decision of the tribunal shall be final and binding on both Parties.

This model of a two-steps settlement of disputes concerning the interpretation and implementation of an agreement allows enough space for consultations and negotiations before starting the arbitration procedure and does not limit e.g. the scope and time-limits of the „failure" of the negotiations, in connection of which the dispute could be submitted to arbitration. For these reasons, it has been introduced further agreements signed by the ESA on one side and the Russian Federation on the other side: e.g. in the Arrangement between the ESA and the Russian Space Agency for the Conduct of Joint Experiments on the BION-10 Mission of 13 March 1993[24] (Article 16) or in the Arrangement between the ESA and the Russian Space Agency Concerning Co-operation in the Development and Operations of the Service Module Data Management Systems (DMS) for the Russian Segment of the International Space Station (ISS), and of the Space Vehicle Docking System signed by the Parties on 1 March 1996 (Article 21).

b) A different category of relations and corresponding legal regulations represent the agreements of the ESA with the countries associated to the European Union such as Hungary and the Czech Republic. The Agreement between the ESA and the Government of the Republic of Hungary Concerning Co-operation in the Field of the Exploration and Use of Outer Space for Peaceful Purposes signed on 10 April 1991[25] remains in ist part concerning the dispute settlement mechanisms on a general level stipulating that disputes shall be settled in the course of consultations between the Parties[26] .

A similar agreement between the ESA and the Czech Republic is presently under preparation. With the view to the envisaged approximation to the European Union, it seems most probable that a more detailed provision on dispute settlement will be agreed upon by both Parties taking into account the general features of the relevant provisions in the above-mentioned instruments concerning the co-operation with the Russian Space Agency.

c) In 1971 the USSR and eight other COMECON member states founded the international intergovernmental organisation for space communications - Intersputnik. After 1989, the organisation became the subject of substantial changes: Its new composition was influenced not only by the German re-unification, but changed also due to the dissolution of the Soviet Union and of the former Czechoslovakia. Moreover, in 1989 the use of the Intersputnik system was opened also to non-members of COMECON such as Algeria, Iraq and India[27] . Not only these facts, but also the profound socio-economic changes within the member states themselves lead to the re-structuralisation of its legal system: The initial Agreement on the

Establishment of the „Intersputnik" International Organisation of Space Communications signed in Moscow on 15 November 1971[28] should be adapted to the new conditions and supplemented with an „operational agreement", the Parties of which should become various telecommunication entities of the member states. Presently, the final draft of these new documents has been prepared and will be submitted to the session of the Council of Intersputnik in the autumn of this year.

Corresponding to the structural changes in Intersputnik, a new system of dispute settlement is foreseen which will probably reflect, in its significant features, on the solutions adopted in Intelsat, Inmarsat or Eutelsat and will be inserted into the new operational agreement. Thus, the scope of the disputes which shall be settled under the mechanisms of this agreement will probably not differ from the solutions chosen in the agreements of these international telecommunications organisations, namely, it will be limited to the disputes arising in connection with the rights and obligations under the Agreement. In contrast to these texts, however, it is expected that the Intersputnik system will explicitly mention obligatory consultations between the Parties of the Operational Agreement as a first step of the procedure. Only if these fail within a certain time limit and if the parties will not come to a mutually acceptable solution by other means, each Party to the dispute might submit the matter to arbitration.

There is no serious doubt that with respect to the composition of the arbitration tribunal a solution will be accepted that does not differ substantially from the „classical" arbitration bodies. As usually, each Party will probably nominate one arbitrator within a certain time; these two persons (or more depending on the number of Parties to the dispute) will appoint the -"neutral" one(s); if they fail, such person(s) must be appointed by an impartial body - with regard to the composition of Intersputnik, probably by its Director General. It will be interesting to see whether the legal norms will be specified on the basis of which the arbitration body will render its decisions. It goes without saying that the provisions of the „basic" agreement of 1971 as well as of the operational agreement itself must be respected. Moreover, with a view to the general characteristics of such arbitration tribunal, it is to be expected that the decisions of the future Intersputnik arbitration body will be final and binding upon the Parties.

Obviously, the final form of Intersputnik's dispute settlement mechanisms depends on the position of the future Parties of the Operating Agreement; modifications are still possible. It would, however, be quite surprising if the final outcome would differ considerably from the solutions adopted within the framework of Intelsat, Eutelsat and Eumetsat.

4. Examples of Dispute Settlement Mechanisms in the Space Co-operation Agreements between an International Organisation and Russian Legal Persons as Parties of these Agreements

In order to simplify the process of concluding the contracts, the European Space Agency elaborated a document called „General Clauses and Conditions for ESA Contracts"[29] ; its Article 13 offers detailed rules for an arbitration negotiation between the contractors. Without mentioning any variant of the obligatory consultations, at the request of either party shall be any dispute arising out of the interpretation or execution of a contract submitted to the arbitration. The seat of the Arbitration Tribunal shall be specified in the contract itself; subsidiarily, it shall sit in a country of the legal seat of the Contractor or where the contract is to be executed. For the procedure of the arbitration the application of the rules of the Conciliation and Arbitration of the ICC are recommended, unless no other arbitration has been foreseen in the contract itself. The award resulting from the arbitration procedure shall be final and binding on the parties; its enforcement shall be governed by the rules of procedure in force in the state in which it is to be executed.[30]

In the relations with the legal persons from the Russian Federation, these General Clauses and Conditions for ESA Contracts have been applied with certain modifications which lead *inter alia,* in case of a dispute, to the exclusion of the application of the presently still evolving domestic Russian law. Thus, as regards the contractual relations, the General Clauses are, as a rule, applicable; however, with respect to the law pertaining to arbitration, some contracts provide for the application of the „neutral" legal system of a third country, preferably Sweden, as in the case of the Hermes Project of 1992 or of the Contract between the ESA and the RKK Energia concerning EUROMIR Missions of 7 July 1993. In the EUROMIR Contract, the provisions of the „General Clauses" of the ESA have been, moreover, substituted by the following model (Article 13): The first step of the dispute solution should be negotiations; only if these fail - it should be noted that there is no time limit set - the dispute shall be referred to the Arbitration Tribunal in Stockholm. Each of the disputing Parties appoint an arbitrator; if any of these Parties fails to appoint its arbitrator, he will be chosen by the President of the Chamber of Commerce in Stockholm who will also appoint an umpire, if the Parties fail to do so. The decision taken by a majority of votes of the Tribunal shall be final and binding upon both Parties.

According to Article 6 of the Agreement on Co-operation on Manned Space Infrastructure and Space Transport Systems of 1992[31], the General Clauses and Conditions for ESA Contract shall also apply - unless the Parties otherwise agree and with the exception of the provisions concerning intellectual property issues - to the contracts awarded by ESA to the Russian industry.

5. Examples of Dispute Settlement Mechanisms in the Space Co-operation Agreements between Legal Persons as Parties of these Agreements

In the relations between two legal persons if one of them is a contractor from the former USSR and the other a subject from an EU-state, the Rules on Conciliation and Arbitration of the Swedish Chamber of Commerce and Stockholm as a „neutral" seat of the Arbitration Tribunal are generally agreed upon: The common model of an arbitration clause in such a case includes usually negotiations as the first step of the dispute settlement procedure; if these fail, such dispute will be settled by one or more arbitrators appointed in accordance with these Rules. By settling a dispute, the arbitrators shall apply the Swedish law for the interpretation of the agreements.

A frequent alternative to the Swedish law as the legal system used for dispute settlement procedures is the law of Switzerland. In such a case any dispute arising in connection with or out of the performance or the interpretation of the contract which could not be settled amicably shall be finally settled under the rules of Arbitration of the International Chamber of Commerce by the arbitrators appointed in accordance with these Rules. The seat of the litigation will be Geneva, the applicable law the Swiss Code of Obligations.

It is interesting to note that the English legal system (as the London Court of Arbitration) have been hardly chosen for dispute settlement procedures involving legal persons from the Russian Federation. With the view to the only limited range of available data it seems, however, not possible to draw any general conclusions from this result of the present study.

In November 1992 the USA, Japan, the Russian Federation and the European Community signed the Agreement Establishing the International Science and Technology Center. With respect to the specific structure of this entity, the Draft Model Agreement for Projects of the International Science and Technology Center with Institutions in the Russian Federation and in other Interested States of the CIS from 1994 contents a specific regulation concerning the disputes settlement procedure: Article 12 of this draft agreement defines the scope of its dispute settlement procedures by the term „the disputes arising during the performance of the Agreement"; as examples of these disputes it mentions first a claim by the Institute for any payments deemed due, second an interpretation of a provision of the Agreement and finally a request for relief or approval related to the Agreement. These claims, demands or requests shall be submitted to the Chief Procurement officer of the Centre who will respond to them generally in four weeks. The decision of the Centre is not necessarily final,: it might be appealed to the Governing Board of the Centre within four weeks of the communication of the Centre's decision. Only the decision of the Governing Board shall be final and binding; pending the final settlement of disputes, the performance of the Agreement shall proceed diligently.

6. Conclusions

The last sentence of Article 12 of the Draft Model Agreement for Projects of the International Science and Technology Center with Institutions in the Russian Federation and in other Interested States of the CIS from 1994 might be symptomatic, to a certain extent, for the dispute settlement mechanisms involving a subject from the former COMECON countries. The general policy seems to be aimed at not to endanger the implementation of the common projects and not to interrupt the co-operation. In practice, the primary reason for this approach is, without any doubt, the interest to continue the good co-operative relations, the preparedness of the partners from the former COMECON-States to offer an alternative solution, together with the flexibility of their counterparts to adapt the mode of implementation of the projects to the changed conditions. Moreover, a certain role could play the differing financial possibilities of the respective partners and the fact that even a positive arbitration award would not always lead to the expected financial results.

Therefore, the impact in all these legal documents, irrespective of their nature and contents, has been laid primarily on consultations which serve in many of these agreements as the only means for dispute settlement. In other types of agreements, only if the consultations fail, they will be followed by another form of procedure. Since most agreements do not set a time limit within which such consultations have to yield success or otherwise must be declared as having failed, consultations might be - in reality - the only means of dispute settlement. Only with regards to the few agreements that provide for such time limits, arbitration is in fact a viable means for dispute settlement.

Specific forms of solving mutual problems were chosen among the states of the former USSR the legal form of which could be as a whole described as „negotiations".

Also as regards the relations with subjects from the former COMECON-states the general principle remained unchanged: The more concrete the obligations, the more important the financial engagement - the more detailed the procedure of dispute settlement. Finally, it should be stressed that it seems less important that - on the basis of this limited empirical research - the „classical" mechanisms have - until now - never been applied in the practice of space co-operation with subjects from or among the former COMECON countries and that the tradition of informal problem management continues to play its dominant role - a fact that could also serve as proof for the quality of the mutual co-operative relations. What should be pointed out, however, is the indisputable value of the above-discussed dispute settlement regimes that consists in their function as a guarantee that, if all efforts fail to bring about a mutually acceptable solution by means of consultation or negotiation, the way to obtain a justiciable result remains open.

---

[1] For the general overview of dispute settlement mechanisms in space law see Böckstiegel, Karl-Heinz, Arbitration of Disputes Regarding Space Activites, in: American Institute of Aeronautics and Astronautics (ed.), Proceedings of the 35th Colloquium on the Law of Outer Space, October 1993, Graz, (8 pp). (1994).

[2] Zickler, Achim, Schrogl, Kai-Uwe, Aspekte deutsch-russischer Raumfahrtkooperation (Das deutsch-russische Agenturabkommen vom 1. März 1993 im internationalen Kontext), ZLW 43 (1993), 268-292.

[3] See Decree of the Council of Ministers (the Government of the Russian Federation) of 25. 3. 1993, No 250.

[4] The German text of this agreement is reproduced in ZLW 43(1993), 288-291.

[5] Article 8 reads as follows (Translation by the author):
„Dispute Settlement:
In case of disputes about the interpretation and implementation of this agreement the Parties enter without delay into consultation and use all efforts in order to find a consensus for possible differences of their opinions. If for a particular case, no special procedure for the settlement of the differences of their opinions was established, all disputes concerning the implementation of this agreement and the realisation of the agreed projects, which could not be settled through consultations, will be brought to the Directors-General of the RKA and the DARA, or to persons whom they appoint, for a joint review in order to reach a joint final solution.“

[6] The German text of this agreement is reproduced in ZLW 43(1993), 291-292.

[7] Article 8 reads as follows:
„Both Goverments address, if necessary, through diplomatic negotiatins various problems which arise from this agreement.“

[8] See ZLW 43(1993), 285-288.

[9] “ I. Scope
d) Disputes concerning intellectual property arising under this Agreement should be resolved through discussions between the concerned participating institutions or, if necessary, the Parties or their designees. Upon mutual agreement of the Parties, a dispute shall be submitted to an arbitral tribunal for binding arbitration in accordance with thee applicable rules of international law. Unless the Parties or their designees agree otherwise in writing, the arbitration rules of UNCITRAL shall govern.“

[10] Russian text in Moskovskij zurnal mezdunarodnogo prava (1994) 4, 165-168.

[11] English text see ECSL (Bulletin of the European Centre of Space Law) 10(1992), Russian text in Moskovskij zurnal mezdunarodnogo prava (1994) 4, 169-171

[12] Bjulleten mezdunarodnych rozgovorov (1994) 5, 7-10.

[13] Article 6 reads as follows:
„The States Parties to the present Agreement undertake to develop their activities in space research and exploitation in accordance with existing international norms, and to coordinate their activities aimed at settling international legal problems of space research and exploitation.“

[14] The United Nations Treaties on Outer Space (1984), 13-22.

[15] Article 5 reads as follows:
„Compensation for damage resulting from breaches of the normal operating procedures for space infrastructure facilities and buildings and relating to the implementation of space programmes shall be made by the responsible Party to the victim. The compensation amounts shall be determined by the special multilateral commission set up by the States Parties to this agreement under the aegis of the Inter-State Space Council. The commission shall, with regard to space activity, be guided by the provisions of the Convention on International Liability for Damage caused by Space Objects.“

[16] For the text see Moskovskij zurnal mezdunarodnogo prava (1994) 4, 120-123.

[17] For the text see Moskovskij zurnal mezdunarodnogo prava (1994) 4, 125-126.

[18] Article 4 reads as follows:
„The Republic Kazakhstan shall create under her valid legislation a special organ on the cosmodrome for settling all property and economy questions connected with the Art. 2 of the Agreement.“

[19] Convention of the European Space Agency, ESA (1991).

[20] ESA/LEG/123, Paris 18 May 1990.

[21] Article 12 reads as follows:
„The Parties shall enter into consultations at the request of either Party in case difficulties arise in the implementation of the cooperation under this agreement.“

[22] ESA/C(94)52.

[23] Article 12 reads as follows:
„1. The Parties shall consult each other in advance on any matter likely to have a bearing on the arrangements for and conditions of cooperation under this agreement. Any dispute about the interpretation or application of provisions of this Agreement and the Annexes thereto shall be referred first to the co-chairmen of the working groups referred to in Article 5 and than to the Coordinating Commitee. Any dispute that cannot be resolved at that level shall be referred for settlement to the Directors General of these two agencies.
2. Any dispute that cannot be settled in accordance with the provisions of section 1 shall be referred, at the request of either Party, to an arbitration tribunal as provided for in sections 3 to 7.
3. The Party initiating arbitration proceedings shall notify the other Party of the name of its designated arbitrator. Within thirty days of such notification, the other Party shall communicate the name of its arbitrator. Within thirty days of the appointment of the second arbitrator, the first two arbitrators shall appoint the third arbitrator (who shall not be a national of a country of either Party and shall not be of the same nationality as either of the first two arbitrators). The third arbitrator shall chair the tribunal.
4. If the second arbitrator is not appointed within the stipulated time limit or the two arbitrators fail to agree within the stipulated time limit on the appointment of the third arbitrator, such appointment shall be made at the request of either Party by the President of the International Court of Justice at the Hague from among persons of international reputation who are not of the same nationality as either Party.
5. The arbitration tribunal shall decide where it is to sit and shall adopt ist own rules of procedure. It shall be the judge of ist own jurisdiction and shall apply the provisions of this Agreement or any other relevant agreement concluded between the Parties, as well as the regulations applicable under international law.
6. The tribunal shall take its decisons by a majority of its members, who shall not abstain from voting and shall be free to explain the reasons for their votes or not. The tribunal shall deliver its decisions in writing. Such decisions shall be final and binding on both Parties. The arbitration tribunal shall interpret its decisions at the request of either Party.
7. Save where the arbitration tribunal otherwise decides by reason of the special circumstances of a case, the costs of the tribunal and the remuneration of its members shall be borne equitably by the Parties.. Notwithstanding the foregoing, each Party shall bear ist own representation and procedural costs.
[24] ESA/LEG/153.
[25] On file with the autor.
[26] Article 7 reads as follows:
„Disputes:
Disputes concerning the interpretation or application of this agreement shall be settled by mutual consultations between the Parties.“
[27] See Hošková, Mahulena, Intersputnik - new legal developments; in: American Institute of Aeronautics and Astronautics (ed.), Proceedings of the 38th Colloquium on the Law of Outer Space, October 2-7, 1995, Oslo 1996, (11 pp). (1995).
[28] See TIAS 859/860 (1973), No. 123343.
[29] ESA/C/290 Rev.5.
[30] Article 13 reads as follows:
„Clause 13: Arbitration
13.1 Any dispute arising out of the interpretation or execution of the contract shall, at the request of either party, be submitted to arbitration.
13.2 The contract shall specify the country where the Arbitration Tribunal shall sit; normally the Arbitration Tribunal shall have its seat in the country where the Contractor has its legal seat or where the contract is to be executed.
13.3 If no other arbitration is foreseen in the contract, any dispute arising out of the contract shall be finally settled in accordance with the Rules of Conciliation and Arbitration of the International Chamber of Commerce by one of more arbitrators designated in conformity with those rules.
13.4 When arbitration other than in accordance with the Rules of Conciliation and Arbitration of the International Chamber of Commerce is provided for in the contract, the procedure of the Arbitration Tribunal shall be that of the country mentioned in subclause 13.2.
13.5 The award shall be final and binding on the parties; no appeal shall lie against it. The enforcement of the award shall be governed by the rules of procedure in force in the state/country in which it is to be executed.“
[31] ESA/C(94)52.

Session 3:
Legal Aspects of Sharing Benefits from the Conduct of Space Activities

Chairman: E. Gaggero, Uruguay
S. Doyle, USA

IISL-96-IISL.3.01

HIGH RESOLUTION REMOTE SENSING: NEW ASPECTS AND PROBLEMS.

Mikhail M. Fomtchenko, Aleksey S. Movlyav *
Sovinformsputnik, Moscow, Russia

Abstract

The discussion about high resolution remote sensing data must consider today's situation and prospective for the distribution of 2-meter and better ground spatial resolution data. 2-meter resolution space survey data first appeared internationally in 1992. This data quickly became a part of everyday use. Today significant need for this data and significant new prospects for its use in the future are obvious. High resolution remote sensing data is becoming more and more popular, and the field of its application is becoming wider and wider. Within the last years several possibilities for development of better than 2-meter resolution space survey systems appeared. Realization of these possibilities in conjunction with the modern information technologies will change radically the image of Remote Sensing. Data accessibility, its technological variety and diverse application potential will require new efficient mechanisms of cooperation. For further effective progress with respect to high resolution Remote Sensing this is extremely important. Taking into consideration substantial experience accumulated in a framework of international cooperation in the field of space communication, civil aviation and other aspects of international economic cooperation, it seems to be now time to utilize that experience in the field of remote sensing, especially high resolution remote sensing. Creation of specialized international organization is considered as one of possible ways. In establishing mechanisms of international cooperation the guiding principle should be cooperation for peaceful purposes and for the benefit and in the interests of all countries.

Introduction.

Today remote sensing of the Earth from Outer Space is an extensive branch of industry, who has in possession various technical means and applications. The whole complex of these technologies is developing rapidly and dynamically. It is also reality, that space remote sensing of the Earth constitutes integral part of the world economy, having passed from the phase of scientific research to an application tool used to resolve several social tasks. At the same time, the pace of development of remote sensing has not slowed down. The end of the cold war and "total warming" open the way for application of former military technologies for the benefit of the world community. Each new step of technical progress causes diverse opinions on its necessity, usefulness and degree of danger. Automobiles were also declared as "harmful"

*M. M. Fomtchenko, General Director of Sovinformsputnik
A. S. Movlyav, Director of Sovinformsputnik, Foreign Affairs,

sometimes, because they frightened horses. High resolution remote sensing does not escape from this fate.

The first question occurred was "is the high resolution necessary at all, is it justified to spend great resources of the world community for further increasing space data resolution?". Existing satellite systems resolve many tasks. There are various aerial survey technologies. Some may argue there is no absolute necessity for high resolution spacecraft for Earth observation since new international relations do not require such expensive kind of observation as space observation is. Nevertheless the events of the last years show that high resolution data is not only needed, but that it can impart new features for remote sensing as such. Not substituting and not forcing out aerial photography, space data has a number of advantages: large observation areas, accessibility for the surveying of any region of the Earth, variety of spectral bands, economic efficiency. Life shows that different technologies coexist updating and enriching each other.

The prospects for the appearance in the nearest future of 10 - 20 varied remote sensing satellites including commercial and governmental are quite real. Having different operational characteristics in terms of resolution (from 20 m to 1 m and better), spectral band, revisit time, information delivery time, swath, accuracy, etc., they will mutually complement or support each other for different applications. At the same time quality changes are taking place in on-ground data processing infrastructure. One can say that it becomes a sub-space of the international information space. Due to development of newest telecommunication technologies, already today technically it becomes possible to obtain and deliver the data to the user within 24 hours, or may be in real-time mode. On the other hand methods of data processing and deriving of value-added product offer a wide range of services. Already today modern technology allows the user to apply remote sensing data without special training, having only the most common technical equipment. From the point of view of the user, remote sensing would be rather not a type of space exploration and complexity, but a branch of industry like communication, which is used in different spheres of everyday life, from scientific research to education and entertainment. Thus, practice gives a positive answer to the question about improving of remote sensing data resolution.

At the same time, another fundamental question may be asked: where is the limit of the information spatial resolution improvement? We speak of physical, optical limits, as well as juridical limits protecting private information and the privacy of individuals and legal entities. What are the rules and regulations of obtaining and providing of high resolution remote sensing data? And in this field high resolution represents practically a new situation. Until now on the international level experts and lawyers were talking about the states interests and protection of nations and Sates. The main problem was the correlation of the state protection and freedom of information exchange. In the future, because of the high level of details of space information on the one hand, and its easy availability on the other hand, the problem will include an adequate level of personal "privacy". This article does not contain the answers to this questions, but proposes a way to develop and draw up these answers in new economic, technical and political conditions for remote sensing existence as a way of life.

What Is the High Resolution Remote Sensing.

The definition of the concept "high resolution remote sensing" includes "remote sensing", "resolution" and "high resolution". Let's start from the terms "resolution" and "high resolution".

Resolution

Resolution is one of the basic parameters being used in developing of the systems and data application. There are different types of Resolution: spatial, spectral, photometric, etc. Hereinafter as the Resolution we understand the size of the minimum distinguishable point object of the Earth surface visible on the picture taken from Space. This definition is quite conditional and it does not pretend to any degree of perfection. It is necessary to mention that there is not any definition generally accepted in the world, neither technical, nor juridical[1]. The term "resolution" was the main technical parameter during the discussion of the problem of the satellite information distribution in the 70's and early 80's , as well as within the last years. The new growth of interest to the resolution of remote sensing data was caused by the appearance of data with 2-meter resolution[2]. We call this data "high resolution data" like many other people do. Nevertheless, here the situation is also undefined in a sense of what "high resolution" means. The term "high resolution" is in often used between the specialists, but the meaning that is understood is different.

The term "high resolution" appeared a long time ago, probably together with the appearance of observation from Space in the 60's. It seems to be useful here to review briefly the history of remote sensing from the point of view of the resolution improvement and its "striving to zero".

Brief historical review.

The first Earth observation spacecraft "Corona" was launched by USA in august 1960[3]. Initially its images had 25 ft (approximately 8 meter) and were improved later to 6 ft (approximately 2 meter). On April 26, 1962 the Soviet Union launched its first Earth observation satellite "Zenith"[4] which had approximately the same characteristics. So, already in the 60's there was data with 2-meter resolution , which we call today "high resolution", and some people use an expression “ultra-high" or "super high" resolution.

At the same time the idea to use Earth observation satellites for a wide range of civil applications was born. Further improvement of resolution has been made in two ways: "hidden" improvement of observation systems for military purposes; and "open" development of remote sensing systems for natural resources research and environment monitoring. Satellites for the study of atmosphere, oceans surface and glaciers became a separate type of vehicle. In this field onboard sensors with resolution from 100 meters to dozens of kilometers are usual. Thus, for the specialists in meteorology 20 meter resolution is "high", and 2 meter resolution is "super high". The same situation in terms takes place among the specialists in a field of other planets exploration.

Wide civilian use of remote sensing data began in 1972 with the launch of the first spacecraft of Landsat series. Its best resolution is estimated at approximately 30 meters. Starting from 1975 in the USSR remote sensing satellites "Fram" for civil applications came to be in use. And later "Resurs F1" and "Resurs F2" came to be launched. Resolution of the data supplied by these satellites was about 5 meters.

The next step was the launch in 1986 of the French "SPOT-1" satellite with 10-meters resolution in panchromatic spectral band. Generally speaking, for remote sensing the middle of 80's was the second important milestone after the launch of first Earth observation satellites. Some events played a key role. In 1984 in the United States the Land remote sensing commercialization act was adopted[5]. In 1986 - the launch of SPOT-1 satellite and the adoption by the U.N. General Assembly of the Principles relating to remote sensing of the Earth from Outer Space. In 1987 - the appearance of free-accessible Soviet 5-meter resolution data. Today it is obvious that exactly at that time Earth remote sensing started its road to commercialization.

Finally, in the 90's three events took place. In August 1992 the Government of Russian Federation allowed open use of 2-meter resolution data for international cooperation. At the present time this data, both archival and newly acquired, is the best resolution data available for international usage. In February 1995 the President of the United States of America has issued a directive about declassification of archive 2-meter resolution data, acquired in the 60's-70's[6]. In 1994 the Department of Commerce of the United States of America has granted licenses for development of non-governmental Earth observation systems with 1-meter resolution[7].

<u>The concept of High resolution remote sensing.</u>

It is necessary to mention that all kinds of data with different resolution (1, 2, 5, 10, 20, 30-120 meters) listed above and a lot of other data already have and will have their own application value for resolving different types of civil tasks. The main purpose of the resolution criteria development was the national security considerations. The main role here belongs to national legislation regulating distribution of information, particularly space data. On the international level in the Principles relating to remote sensing of the Earth from Outer Space there is only the criteria that activities (remote sensing) shall not be conducted in a manner detrimental to the legitimate rights and interests of the sensed State[8].

There were a lot of other proposals: to distinguish data as "global", "regional", "local", or to distinguish resolution as "high", "medium", "low"[9]. There was a proposal to divide the resolution as: low resolution (approximately 1 km), high resolution (about dozens of meters), very high (better than 10 meters)[10], and some other systems.

The words "very", "ultra", "super" and others were mainly tended to be used because of the effect of sensationalism. Especially as with the word "spy" or "reconnaissance" they may cause some concern and even fear. Our conviction, confirmed by a five year experience, is that high resolution data brings benefit to the world community. The very fact that such information is now available gives evidence of positive changes in the world, mutual trust and, correspondingly, helps nations to come together.

Taking into particular account the needs for regulation of remote sensing activities we think that high resolution remote sensing data is data with ground spatial resolution less than two meters.

<u>The term of "remote sensing".</u>

As was already mentioned, remote sensing will radically change in the future. One of the aspects of this change is the appearance of two new categories of the participants to this activity. These two categories are non-governmental providers of data and numerous, practically unlimited group of individuals as data users. Consequently, the legislation should protect legal rights and interests of not only governments but private persons. In the same context the meaning "remote sensing" itself should be considered. Legal definition of the term "remote sensing" is given in the Principles relating to remote sensing of the Earth from Outer

Space. It has remote sensing function having a particular purpose: "...for the purpose of improving natural resources management, land use and the protection of the environment;"[11]. These fields continue to be of practical importance for high resolution data. But it is a particular feature of only high resolution data that the range of its applications is significantly wider. But this fact does not diminish public significance of the "Principles...". From our prospective, taking into consideration the changes now taking place in the field of remote sensing, application and interpretation of the Principles should be broader, at least until special regulations appear. But definitely with the generally accepted exclusions like meteorology and Earth observation for national security conducted by governmental organizations.

Today it seems that there is not any need for additional legislation or regulations for distribution of the data which became normal (2-, 5-, 10-meter resolution). May be in the future data with better than 2-meter resolution will become normal. But, now it seems that its distribution may contribute to possibilities of conflict occurring.

The principle of freedom in collection of remote sensing data is generally accepted and, obviously, should remain the same with respect to high resolution data. At the same time, the problem of high resolution data distribution, as well as remote sensing data distribution generally, remains open. All the more, in respect of high resolution data the problem is broadening due not only to resolution sharpening but also to the development of the modern information transmission channels and technologies. Consequently, other conflicts of interests may occur. For example, private person being a citizen of one state can receive from a foreign operator remote sensing information relating to government or private activities in his country. The current laws of different countries offer different ways of how to resolve these questions. And in the laws of many countries these issues are not regulated at all. Future norms should expand to high resolution remote sensing with respect to its distribution.

Another topic is commercialization, which is rapidly increasing. As are the matters of liability and intellectual property rights. Insurance requires international regulations. Also, space activity has to become a subject of not only International Public Law, but International Private Law. Nevertheless all these questions should be considered taking into account sharing benefits of space activities.

So, new remote sensing requires new definitions and new approaches differentiated on the industrial and inside of the industry branch levels. The development of these approaches will be done by different means. From our point of view time has come for the institutionalization of international cooperation in remote sensing. For high resolution remote sensing it is not only possible, but it is necessary to do.

Institutional mechanism of international cooperation in remote sensing of the Earth.

Preliminary considerations

The assumption that it is necessary to develop a constantly working mechanism of cooperation of high resolution remote sensing participants is based on the following considerations. Roughly they can be grouped under three headings - technical, economic, political. In the future an international fleet of remote sensing satellites and corresponding ground facilities will offer to users great opportunities. Cooperation of the operators in managing of the satellites will allow to make surveys more effective and reliable in case of malfunctioning, bad weather conditions, natural or ecological disasters. In addition to that, coordinated technical policy will allow joint advantages of different systems, which significantly differ from each other in technical parameters, to the good of the international community. Although here we are talking about pure civil use of the data, it was already mentioned in the media, that during crisis situations, even existing civilian systems working together to resolve one and the same task achieved much more efficiency, despite the apparent power of defense systems[12]. Probably, there is no need to mention the high level of expenses and, correspondingly, the necessity to fund the costs rationally and in the most optimal way by both developing and developed countries.

No less important is the development of coordination and cooperation in political and legislative spheres of remote sensing. Distribution of high resolution data has already caused a number of international law discussions[13]. Today, main reasons, probably, is that the technical specialists from different countries are not prepared yet to discuss all the technical details regarding the use of high resolution information both because of the political motives and for the reason of commercial competition. Nevertheless, it is necessary to look for a common approach. The best but most difficult way is to harmonize national rules. As like in other fields it can be done through the acceptance of international agreements, through the development of model laws, recommendations, specific standards, procedures, etc. Widening of industrial use of Space requires working out in detail of space law depending on type of space activity. The specifics of remote sensing, as has been mentioned earlier, are that this activity is carried out in close connection both on the Earth and in space. With respect to future high resolution remote sensing this particular feature becomes even more typical. Further widening of the use of this information requires the mechanism of consultations for finding a balance of different interests: the balance between sensing and sensed parties (states, entities, individuals), between developed and developing countries, between users and investors, etc.

Thus the development of a constantly working and evolving mechanism of international cooperation in the field of high resolution remote sensing would be extremely desirable, i.e. mechanism of joint activity in scientific, technical, economic, political and legal fields of high resolution remote sensing, aimed to provide peaceful activity in the field of high resolution remote sensing in the interests and for the benefit of all countries and nations.

Common approach

Earlier, the ways of establishing of such a mechanism were proposed. For example, there was a proposal of founding of an International Agency of Space Observation[14]. There were more global proposals to create World Space Organization, one of directions of which could be remote sensing[15]. There was also proposal to use the Secretariat of the United Nations as a World center of remote sensing[16].Two comments in this connection.

First. In our case more preferable, at least at this stage, would seem to be an organization that is engaged in high resolution remote sensing only but on a permanent basis and over the complete set of questions, including those which are in connection with current space and on-ground operations. An International Space Organization could become a basis for cooperation. But its establishing would seem to be a much more complicated task and the functions proposed here would make the solution more complicated. In the future, when the International Space Organization will be established all or at least part of the functions can be transmitted to it, such as informational, administrative, etc.

Second. Main purposes for creation of the International Agency for Space Observation are the political purposes. That means international agreements fulfillment control, armament restriction, decreasing of international tension[17]. But the main purpose of the institutional cooperation mechanism proposed here is the development of conditions for further development of international high resolution remote sensing in the interests of economic and social development of all countries and all people in the world. The main purpose is economic cooperation. It is also necessary to take into consideration changes in international relations and the world economy, which have taken place within the last years.

The most attractive model seems to be the critical use of the experience of Inmarsat, Intelsat, ICAO and MAGATE. The two first ones provide a convenient way of how to separate foundation documents to an intergovernmental treaty and an operational agreement, whose participants can be governments, as well as national organizations duly authorized by states. The first document provides legal status for the organization, and the second document provides conditions for everyday functioning issues. But, unlike the above said organizations, the international organization proposed is not to be aimed to create and operate its own space segment. Probably in the future, when this form of cooperation will be tested and will prove its effectiveness, the issue of its own satellites launch will be raised. Ground information infrastructure should exist including, probably, its owned or rented receiving stations and communication channels. At the first stage the main goal should be coordination of action in technical and political areas in order to operate remote sensing systems in the most effective way to the interest of the world community.

The experience of ICAO and MAGATE demonstrates proper work organization for distribution of information and consulting for a wide circle of questions, in training and for support of developing countries.

It is possible, that the establishing of a permanently acting entity could begin from the signing of an operational agreement or any other similar document establishing the order of interaction of the parties when operating remote sensing systems. In addition it should create a basis for deepening cooperation in all directions and involvement of the majority of providers and users.

Of course, detailed working out of questions of accession, participation, working organs, procedural, financial and many other components requires significant efforts from the specialists from different countries. At the same time, in making detailed proposals it is necessary to keep in mind tendencies of our reality. Particularly, the tendency of commercialization which is manifested in a most significant degree in the use of high resolution remote sensing. In this connection it seems to be possible that the parties of the operational agreement would be not only the states and their entities, but non-governmental organizations also. Definitely, they should be properly authorized by the government and work under state control in accordance with the provisions of space law.

Conclusion.

Obviously, the mechanism of cooperation proposed above is not the only possible way. What is more, it should not be the only one. The procedure of bilateral and multilateral relations, the work in COPUOS, UN organizations for the use of remote sensing data should be continued in the future. Establishing of an international specialized organization is not a simple task. Nevertheless, the experience of Russian organizations working with all the existing kinds of remote sensing data, including high resolution data, demonstrates significantly higher efficiency in joint and coordinated use of the data, technique and technology. As it was said, this approach allows us to open new horizons for space remote sensing of the Earth surface. Application of this approach on an international scale will lead to much greater effect.

As it is obvious, high resolution Earth remote sensing appeared practically at the same time with the beginning of the space era. Since that time international space law has made considerable progress in the creation of a basis for international cooperation, but provides no specific regulation for particular fields of space activity. Some directions, such as meteorology, space communications, even legal theory and practice of orbital settlements, which appeared much later, have now a much stronger real fundament for cooperation development than does Earth remote sensing.

Basic principles of international space law, despite the significant scientific and technical progress and dramatic changes in international life taking place within a last years, still remain constructive basis for development of progressive industrial models of space activity. All the many years of history for Earth remote sensing, its latest development in the field of high resolution deserves more attention. Having more than thirty year experience it is necessary to apply to high resolution remote sensing international cooperation in all the spheres, for cooperation for peaceful purposes to the benefit of all states, all nations and all people.

Endnotes

1. See, Doc. A/AC.105/250 and Add.1, A/AC.105/251,A/AC.105/260, A/AC.105/358

2. See, Space News, 1993, 26/4-2/5,v.4, n.17, p.7, Space News, 1996, 11-17/3, v.7,n.10, p.7, New Scientist, 1987, 5/11, v.116, n.1585, p.28,29, Aviation Week & Space Technology, 1987, 2/11, v.127, n.18, p.26,27.

3. Remarks by Admiral William O. Studeman, ADCI Speech, 2/24/95 and General information of EROS Data Center.

4. See, Maxim V. Tarasenko "The Military aspects of the Soviet Cosmonautics", Moscow, 1992 (in russian).

5. Land Remote Sensing Commercialization Act of 1984//Public Law. 98-365 (H.R.5155). 17 July 1984.

6. US President Executive Order on Imagery Declassification, White House, 02/23/95.

7. See, Space News, 1994, 3-9/10, v.5, n.40, p.8,17, Aviation Week & Space Technology, 1995, February 13, v.144, n.7, GIS World, February 1995, p.p.42-47.

8. G.A. Res. 41/65, adopted on December 3,1986, and, see, Doc. A/AC.105/572.

9. See, a proposals of Soviet Union at 1978-1981 sessions of the Scientific and Technical Subcommittee, also review of this issue, see, Doc. A/AC.105/176 and A/AC.105/358

10. Earth Space Review, 1993, v.2, n.4, p.p.20-25.

11. See, supra note 8, at Principle 1(a).

12. See, Aviation Week & Space Technology, 1991, July 13, v.137, n.2, p.p. 46,47,50,51,53-59,61-65, Earth Space Review, 1993, v.2, n.3, p.11-19.

13. See, Space News, 1996, v.7: 17-23/6, n.24, p.p.1,18, 1-7/7, n.26, p.p.1,18, 5-11/8, n.31, p.p.3,35, 12-18/8, n.32, p.2.

14. See, for example, Doc. UN A/S-10/AC.1/7, A/S-15/34, and Doc. of the Conference on Disarmament CD/OS/WP/.39 (Soviet proposal on creation of International Agency of Space Observation) CD/OS/WP.40 (French proposal on creation of International Satellite Monitoring Agency), CD/PV.410.

15. See, in particular as review E.Kamenetskaya "Outer Space and International Organizations. Problems of International Law.", Moscow, 1980 (in russian).

16. See, Doc. UN A/AC.105/C.2/L.73 of June 26,1970.

17. See, supra note 15 Doc. CD/OS/WP/.39, and CD/OS/WP.40.

IISL-96-IISL.3.02

SHARING OF REMOTE SENSING DATA CONCERNING ENVIRONMENTAL PROTECTION FOR PUBLIC BENEFIT

by
dr. Gabriella Catalano Sgrosso*
University of Rome, Italy

Abstract

A wider and inexpensive distribution of remote sensing data concerning the protection of the Earth's environment may be a concrete realisation of the international co-operation which extends to all countries the benefits deriving from a peaceful use out outer space.

After examining the inter-dependence between environmental protection, remote sensing and public benefit, the legal basis of the obligation to distribute the data will be studied.

The Principles on Remote Sensing of the United Nations do not mention the issues concerning the international commercialisation of the data, the notion of public benefit or intellectual property. There is a generic solicitation towards co-operation. The obligation for immediate diffusion of the data to the involved States is only foreseen for information which can help to prevent harmful events or natural catastrophes. In this case international co-operation is more active and various initiatives, which are considered in this paper, have begun their course.

A detailed study of the most emblematic data distribution policies (United States, France, ESA) shows an increasingly strong opening, albeit carried out in different manners, in favour of research in disciplines concerning the Earth.

The initiatives of rules of the European Union concerning satellite data and the protection of environment prove the developing interest in this sector for a growing international co-operation.

*Researcher of International Law Faculty of Economics, University of Rome, Italy; Director IISL

Link between public benefit, protection of the Earth's environment and Remote Sensing

The agenda item of "Outer Space Benefits" has already been faced various times during the past years by the Legal Subcommittee of the UNCOPUOS. During the Spring Meeting of 1996 a Draft Resolution was drawn up to be presented to the United Nations General Assembly[1]. The "Declaration on International Co-operation in the Exploration and Use of Outer Space for the Benefit and in the Interests of All States, Taking into Particular Account the Needs of the Developing Countries" moves from art. 1 of the Outer Space Treaty so that the States can commit themselves concretely and ensure that the exploration and application of outer space may benefit all countries. The main point of the Draft Resolution is that these benefits can be enjoyed by all countries, and especially by the developing ones, only thanks to a strengthened international co-operation. It is true that the countries are free to determine all the aspects of the co-operation (art. 2) but this, among the other aims, must facilitate the exchange of expertise and technology among States on a mutually acceptable basis (art. 5).

The approval of the Resolution could be a positive answer to the requests of the group of 77 developing countries meeting each year to establish a new international order for Outer Space; they claim that Outer Space is to become an instrument for social and economic development for those countries who are lacking.

In order to go beyond generic propositions a more constructive approach for co-operation would be that of finding out specific fields, where common interests are present, where the co-operation itself could take place[2].

One of the branches in which each

member of the international community has acknowledged mutual dependence and the necessity to co-operate in order to reach a common interest, the interest in survival, is environment. The protection of environment is one of the most urgent problems of the modern world, both for the developing and the industrialised countries. It has serious and complex aspects, on one hand because at times the pollution phenomenon reaches catastrophic proportions or often exceeds the sphere of sovereignty of each State involving the sovereignty of other countries or common areas, and on the other hand because a higher authority is missing from the international point of view for the prevention, control and removal of its causes.

In order to be protected the environment must be studied, its deterioration identified and its remedies discovered. The lack of balance existing on Earth is due either to natural causes or to the irrational use of its resources by mankind[3]. Remote sensing can intervene and give an important contribution to be completed with actions on Earth to establish the state of environment. By giving many and precise details it allows a faster and more effective, and at times less expensive, intervention[4]. Therefore the link between the two branches is stressed.

The use of remote sensing has become extremely important for many countries which have developed more and more sophisticated satellite programs.

The National Aeronautics and Space Administration (NASA), the National Oceanic and Atmospheric Administration (NOAA) and the Earth Observation Satellite Company (EOSAT), the commercial distributor of Landsat data, are the major actors in the provision of Earth remote sensing data in the United States. With the Landsat satellite data progress is made in the research on Earth part of the Mission to Planet Earth program.

France uses SPOT satellites for remote sensing and the private law company SPOT IMAGE is entrusted with the distribution and commercialisation of the data.

The RADARSAT is the first Canadian Earth observation satellite and the first civilian operated radar-equipped satellite.

The Japanese Space Agency (NASDA) has launched four meteorological geostationary satellites, two maritime observation satellites (MOS-1, MOS-2) and a remote sensing satellite for Earth resources (JERS-1); at present the NASDA is developing the Advanced Earth Observation Satellite and the American-Japanese Tropical Rainfall Measurement Mission.

The European Space Agency (ESA) entered remote sensing in 1991 with the launch of the ERS1 satellite the data of which contributed to the reconstruction of a particular vision of Earth and of the changes in its environment. With the help of the altimeter the satellite gave information on the sea bed of the Arctic Ocean under a thick cover of sediments, water and ice. The microwave beam of the high resolution SAR instrument of the ERS 1 penetrates the clouds whereas the optic sensors are unable to do so and therefore offers useful information for the tropical eco-system. Thanks to the ERS data scientists are able to calculate the deformations of the Earth's surface caused by Earthquakes and the speed of the movements of glaciers; they can draw three-dimensional charts (DEM) and observe the tectonic movements of whole continents with interpherometry. It is now possible to keep the petrol pollution and the complex climatic changes under control. The recently launched successor ERS 2 is a copy of the first satellite with some innovations concerning an instrument for the global measurement of the ozone levels, an infrared radiometer to enhance the systematic control of vegetation and a PRARE instrument which will render the instruments on board more precise. During the 1992 Space Conference in Granada another great European program for Earth observation was established: the first satellite of the ENVISAT program will be launched in 1998.

The acknowledgement of the necessity of preserving the state of our environment, be it oceanic, continental or atmospheric, has caused a growing need for global observation.

The legal problem we are interested in is to see how the satellite data, especially the data concerning the protection of the Earth's environment, may be largely distributed and used for the benefit of all the States in accordance with the Outer Space Treaty and with the above mentioned recent draft resolution of the United

Nations.

Starting from the United Nations Resolution of the Principles on Remote Sensing and from its rules which try to extend, with more or less clarity, the benefits of remote sensing to all countries, we shall examine the policy of distribution and commercialisation of data carried out by some countries, those which have launched their satellites for the longest time, and by the ESA.

The United Nations Principles on Remote Sensing concerning environmental protection

The main legal reference on an international level is the Resolution 41/65 of the General Assembly of the United Nations, adopted on December 4th 1986 on "The Principles on Remote Sensing of the Earth from Outer Space". Detailed studies on the principles having been carried out in other occasions, we shall therefore only examine those principles concerning the distribution of the data[5].

With remote sensing the States will pursue the purpose of improving natural resources management, land use and the protection of the environment (principle 1,a). The offset of the principle, which is remarkably controversial, is found in principle II where it is stated that remote sensing activities shall be carried out for the benefit and in the interest of all countries and in principle V where the States, carrying out remote sensing activities, are asked to promote international co-operation. If a wider distribution to all countries of the remote sensing data concerning environmental protection were to be carried out these aims would be substantially already reached. Unfortunately the dispositions of the resolution of the principles do not help very much in this sense.

Principle XII indicates, rather generically, that all States must have access to the data on a non-discriminatory basis and on reasonable cost terms. The principles do not impose any obligation to gratuity or mutual exchange of data. They do not mention questions concerning the international commercialisation of the data, the notion of public service, the tariff regulations and the intellectual property. The rules have been imposed by practise by the single States or by the ESA or they are included in some national regulation.

The consultation with a State whose territory is sensed in order to make available opportunities for participation and enhance mutual benefits to be derived therefrom (principle XIII) is not compulsory for the State carrying out the remote sensing.

The promotion of international co-operation, including technical assistance and co-ordination in the area of remote sensing (principle VIII) is entrusted to the United Nations and the relevant agencies within the UN system and to the initiative of each State[6].

An opening towards a help policy is offered by the second part of principle XII where it is stated that when giving access to the observed States to the primary data and the processed data concerning the territory under their jurisdiction, the State participating in remote sensing activities must take into particular account the needs and interests of the developing countries. In this case the reasonable cost terms must be particularly favourable[7].

Two positions face the problems of environment more directly. Principle X establishes that remote sensing shall promote the protection of the Earth's natural environment. For this purpose States participating in remote sensing activities that have identified information in their possession that is capable of averting any phenomenon harmful to the Earth's environment shall disclose such information to the States concerned. Principle XI indicates that remote sensing shall promote the protection of mankind from natural disasters. The States participating in remote sensing activities shall transmit data and information in their possession to the States affected by natural disasters or likely to be affected by impending natural disasters. No mention is made of the conditions for disclosing such information; however, because both cases involve information concerning environmental protection and therefore relevant to a public heritage it would be logical for the information to be disclosed free of cost[8].

On the subject of natural disasters the United Nations have established some initiatives for international co-operation. The Department for Humanitarian Affairs (DHA), a specialised office of the Secretary General of the United Nations responsible for all disaster-related matters has been created. One of the main purposes of this office is to mobilise, direct and co-ordinate external assistance provided by the United Nations system in response to disasters. The DHA helps to prevent potential catastrophes by studying and foreseeing them. In this activity and in the four phases of the management of catastrophes, preparedness, mitigation, response and recovery, a remarkable support is given to the DHA by the new technologies of remote sensing. The Department acts in co-ordination with other international organisations, most of which belong to the United Nations. Finally, the DHA participates in the International Emergency Readiness and Response Information System, a system uniting a growing number of international organisations for crisis management who adhere voluntarily to disclose and obtain the useful information[9].

In the last years the developing countries have requested the United Nations for a Third Conference on the Peaceful Use of Outer Space (UNISPACE III). The changed international political situation and the advance of new technologies must be taken into consideration in the Third Conference leading to the use of the new means offered by outer space for universal concern. One of the branches of application is the protection of environment and natural catastrophes[10].

The principle of international co-operation has led various International Intergovernmental Organisations to commit themselves to specific studies on Earth's environment. The World Climate Research program has been promoted by the World Meteorological Organisation (OMM); the United Nations have created a program for environment (PNUE), UNESCO has carried out various initiatives and the Forum of Space Agencies (SAF) has included the Mission to Planet Earth project in its program. This leads us to think that, at least in the branch of environmental studies, the policy of the States is leading towards international co-operation.

One last observation is to be made on the compulsory value of the United Nations Resolution of the principles on remote sensing. In actual fact it has a recommendation value even though, having been adopted by "consensus", it expresses the legal opinion of all the community. Should the following study on the policy adopted by the States and by the ESA for the diffusion of the remote sensing data show an increasing attitude favouring scientific research for the Earth's environment it could be claimed that a customary norm is being established. The States are realising that the protection of the Earth's environment is compulsory and that it involves all mankind, and therefore any behaviour in favour of research (distribution of data free of cost or on extremely advantageous cost terms) is to be seconded.

Data distribution policy of the United States, France and ESA

The market of space data concerning Earth observation is in full progress and it has not yet reached a sufficient maturity for the application of the laws of the market. At present the procedures change considerably from one country to another, and at times from one operator to another in the same country; they vary according to the nature of the data of the programs, of the categories of the users or of the use of the information. For the purpose of this study we shall consider the policy of the United States and of France, two countries which have launched remote sensing satellites in outer space for the longest time, in order to stress the apparent differences.

Since the beginning of the Eighties the **United States** carried out a policy similar to the one applied to research satellites. The 1984 Land remote Sensing Commercialisation Act laid down more precise dispositions for the Landsat program and transferred the distribution and commercialisation of the data to a private commercial society (EOSAT). This policy, called two tier policy, established at that time the sale of the data at a small cost to the American government and its affiliated institutions and at a commercial rate, on a global and non-discriminatory basis, for other users.

This law does not imply a protection of the remote sensing data by use of copyright, which would have created a legal protection *erga omnes* and a free exploitation by its owner, but through the use of the confidential trade secret procedure. The information is a confidential trade secret of EOSAT and its reproduction would cause a misappropriation of the trade secret itself. The American legislator, fearing that the holders of the data could make illicit profits, preferred to chose this form of protection[11].

In 1992 the commercial policy of Landsat was rediscussed due to the pressure of the scientific community and a new "Land Remote Sensing Act" was issued. The American law insists on the research concerning environmental changes and presses for a systematic supervision. The law transfers the responsibility of the program from the Department of Commerce to the Department of Defence and confirms a precise regime of licence for the administrative enjoying of totally private remote sensing systems, the latter having to act in accordance with the principle of equal access to the data. As for the distribution of the data the United States have adopted a free access policy, often free of charge, which is particularly generous for the users because the costs are completely sustained by the American government. The law of 1992 establishes that the access to data is to be carried out at the cost of fulfilling user requests. This excludes any other non direct cost such as the amortisation of the space system and the land stations or the commercial margin[12].

The NASA develops and operates experimental satellites and conducts scientific researches on Earth as part of the Mission to Planet Earth program in co-operation with many countries. The policy followed is that of a distribution of the data as vast as possible and at the lowest price for the use reserved to research. The data must be available for any user without restrictions and without pre-existing agreements. The new approach acknowledges the international character of research on global change and the necessity of exchanging information rapidly. For the future Earth Observing System (EOS) also the NASA has established a policy of free access, nearly free of cost, a policy which they defend on an international level.

The operational programs of the NOAA also encompass those satellites used for weather monitoring and prediction. According to the 1992 Land Remote Sensing Policy Act these programs may not be commercialised or privatised. The NOAA distributes the meteorological data in real time on a restricted basis and offers in non-real time distribution services to users at a cost calculated on the marginal cost of the service. This information is distributed without restrictions on it use and distribution. Thanks to the intervention of the government the American companies are therefore favoured by a free access free of cost to all information of meteorological character. This distribution has influenced the policy of the other States and therefore, no competition being possible, the distribution of meteorological products is free and without restrictions.

A Presidential Directive dated May 5th 1994 establishes the fusion of civilian and military programs of meteorological satellites in the Polar orbit including missions of environmental surveillance. This decision will have repercussions on the diffusion of data for meteorological satellites. The possibility of a selective diffusion in case of political crisis or conflicts has been foreseen. In the framework of the new European meteorological system METOP/EPS the United States have requested, for the instruments they grant, the possibility of refusing - in times of political crisis or conflicts - access to data which could be useful to their enemies and dangerous for the security of the United States, albeit guaranteeing its use to Americans and their Allies. Europe is considering the possibility of accepting this proposal which allows the use of the data at an interesting cost but which restricts the independence of the EUMETSAT in the matter of diffusion of the data.

The policy of the United States is however extremely open, but its offset is the problem of the financing of future satellites. This will have to be faced nearly exclusively in the public balance because private investors are less interested in the operation of remote sensing systems turning to more economically productive applications.

In **France**, on the contrary to what happened in the United States, no law regulates the legal regime of the activities of the SPOT remote sensing satellites. The law of July 3rd 1985 on the "logiciels" protected by copyright is applied analogically also to the collection of the remote sensing data. An important effort for harmonisation has been carried out in a circular by the Prime Minister dated February 14th 1994 concerning the diffusion of public data. The circular is an important reference point, but only when the data is of public nature.

The private commercial company SPOT IMAGE in which public organisms of different provenance are associated (remote sensing, industries, French banks and foreign partners) has a licence for the distribution, on a world basis, of the data coming from the SPOT satellites whose copyrights belong to the Centre National d'Etudes Spatiales (CNES). The SPOT IMAGE negotiated sub-licences with the foreign reception stations and with the distributors for the reproduction, distribution and sale of the satellite data in well defined areas. The distribution must be carried out without discrimination, according to the UN Principles, but on a commercial basis. The prices of the products are the market prices: SPOT IMAGE creates specific products upon request of the scientific community but only the products concerning the Eighties have a lower price[13].

The French policy is changing. There is an interesting study conducted by an inter-department group on the present and future policy for the diffusion of Earth observation data[14]. It stresses the importance of the State investments for the development of space systems for the observation of Earth, but the main principle of the diffusion is based on the necessity for a return on the investments. This implies that the producing organisation has the ownership of the primary and processed data and this must also be taken into consideration by the organisation producing the processed data. The protection of the data is carried out by coding and also legally through the protection of the right of intellectual property. Because this does not seem to be apt to protect the primary data the French government will have to support the European directive on the protection of the data base and its extension also to the remote sensing data. The principle of non-discriminatory access to the primary and processed data and to the analysed information must be ensured for all the users; the diffusion may only be restricted for national security reasons.

The three types of programs to be realised are especially important for our study. The strictly **experimental** studies are destined to **scientific research**, their return consist in the progress of research and techniques. The remote sensing data will be given to the scientific community free of cost or at reproduction cost. The officially selected researchers will publish the results they have reached. The **pre-operational or operational** programs answer missions of **general interest** established by international agreements and in accordance with the commitments taken in the international agreements concerning meteorology, the study of the climate, the preservation of bio-diversity and the fight against desertification. In these cases the return consists in the exchange or common disposition of data and knowledge. The remote sensing data is divided in three sub-groups: the data with free access, free of cost or at the cost of reproduction for each user; the data which is accessible at the same conditions only to a complex of identified users, for well defined purposes and in the framework of co-operation; the data distributed at a high cost or on the basis of bilateral exchanges. Special conditions are granted only to educational and non lucrative research which must not benefit commerce or industry. Favourable conditions are established for the services of those States who are partners in international agreements for co-operation and assistance in accordance with specific criteria. Finally the **pre-operational or operational** observation programs whose data is to be distributed on the basis of a **financial return.** These programs acquire high resolution images of the surface and specialised data concerning meteorology, the ocean and the Earth's resources.

Therefore it may be remarked that the French policy, even in its future projection, is less open that the American one. Despite establishing special conditions for the distribution of data for researchers who work on environmental protection, it does not specify any fixed criteria for the definition of the subjects which becomes extremely discretionary.

The **European Space Agency**

distributes the data of the ERS Satellites according to a policy approved in June 1994 by the Directive Council of the Earth Observation Programme[15]. It is interesting to examine the general principles laid down in the document, the classification of the users and the established prices.

In the name and in favour of the States participating in the ERS programs the ESA has the right of property of the two satellites of which the matriculation was ensured. The two satellites are under the jurisdiction and control of the ESA according to the dictate of the Space Conventions of the United Nations and the ESA can establish the rules for their use.

The distribution of data is carried out on a non-discriminatory basis and without overlooking the rules of international competition. In order to ensure the protection of the satellite's data against any unauthorised reproduction and distribution the Agency shall keep the full property of the satellite data including the rights of intellectual property. The formula chosen is that of copyright even though the criticisms to the system, especially for the primary data, have lead the ESA to contact the European Commission so that the protection systems foreseen by the directive proposal, now approved directive, for the data base, are extended also to the remote sensing data[16].

The Agency grants the receiving stations with whom an agreement has been stipulated a licence to receive, use and reproduce under certain conditions and upon payment of a canon, the data over which the ESA holds copyright. The official distributor of the data is the ERSC Consortium made up of EURIMAGE, for the distribution in Europe and in the Mediterranean Area, RADARSAT for North America and SPOT IMAGE for the rest of the world. However the price policy of the consortium is established by the ESA[17] which still takes care of the classification of the users and of the distribution of the data to the scientific world. As for the classification, the ESA has followed two basic principles: the States participating in the ERS program and having therefore already financed the latter do not pay the royalty on the price of a standard product of ERS; free or favourably based costs must be applied to the non commercial users belonging to the scientific world[18].

Other than the commercial users, who acquire the data at full price from the Consortium and the internal users who have the data free of cost for the evaluation of the functioning of the instruments, the ESA has classified and established the conditions for the following categories. The **Main researchers** are research groups using the ERS data for basic researches on oceanography geology, hydrology, glaciology, studies on climate, batimetry, meteorology and other topics concerning the Earth. All the European and non-European scientists who have introduced a research project passing the ESA approval receive the data free of cost; they must ensure that the data is only used for research purposes and not forwarded to others. The approved projects are over 300 but the new advertisement for the availability of the ERS1 data in 1994 led to the presentation of 400 new projects. Approximately 300 other organisations or institutions using the ERS data for practical applications in cartography, agriculture, land use, geology and environmental monitoring belong to the category of **pilot projects**. They have the right to receive data free of cost if they acquire the necessary experience in their applications. Both these categories must update the ESA on the progress of their work and the ESA publishes their results. In order to promote the use of the data and to encourage the development of innovative techniques a third category of users has been introduced for **research and demonstration exploitation of the data** outside the two fields used by the previously mentioned categories. The ESA and the commercial distributor examine the projects of the candidates and the chosen ones enjoy privileged access because they only pay the reproduction cost. In order to consider the national investments carried out in the ERS program and to promote the use of the ERS data, the organisations of the participating States which ensure the **operational services** have access at cost price but with a limitation on the use for specific services. Free of cost data is granted to the **meteorological services** of the countries belonging to the OMM, to EUMETSAT and the European Centre for meteorological forecasts. The data must be used for the forecasts and may not be transferred.

The number of users and the exploitation of the ERS data has gone fare beyond the initial forecasts. The request coming from research, especially for the topics concerning the Earth, has increased remarkably. This has led to a generalised policy of cost reduction and to a limitation of the role of the ERSC Consortium. Even the new ENVISAT program seems to be more oriented towards experimentation rather than to commercialisation and we can conclude that globally the ESA policy is addressed more an more towards a system of co-operation and communication with the research world.

Community Regulations on the matter

In order to strengthen its role in environmental research the European Union could internationally protect the interests of the users of the land remote sensing data useful for the research itself. The Commission could establish its own position on the price policy and develop the already open consultations with the ESA in order to find a formal agreement on the roles of the two organisations[19].

At present we are still far from this kind of co-operation and there is no Community regulation specifically considering remote sensing satellite data. The initiatives of the Community, which we shall herewith examine, that is to say the directive on the protection of a data-base and the two regulations for environment, have only indirectly involved the present topic.

The most frequent form of protection of the remote sensing data, protecting from improper appropriation, reproduction and distribution, is the right of intellectual property. The Bern Convention of 1886 and its subsequent modifications would allow protection through copyright. However, the assimilation of the technical organisation of a computer archive, consisting in a data base, to a literary work has been rather criticised. The Convention mentions "a collection of works" and not a "collection of data" and wishes to protect originality, the creation of the work, the fruit of the intervention of a human mind. With an extensive interpretation which considers the technical evolution that the "works" have suffered, one could think that this kind of protection could be applied also to a certain number of data bases with a high documentary added value (processed data and analysed information) where it is possible to find human intervention and originality, but this is hardly applicable to computer products which are the fruit of an automated process, such as the primary data[20]. The States are certainly free to extend the protection also to the data not answering the characteristics established by the Convention with the risk, however, that they do not make use of the obligation of protection and of the mechanisms of reciprocity in the countries of the Union.

An interesting solution to the problem could be offered by the already mentioned Directive of the European Parliament and Council of 11 March 1996 concerning the legal protection of a data base[21]. The directive distinguishes between a data base, considered as a work of collection and protectable by the member States under the profile of copyright, and the computer contents of the data base itself. If these contents are not already protected the directive establishes a *sui generis* right, that is to say the right of the creator of the data base to forbid the extraction and reuse for commercial purposes of the matters resulting from the data base for 15 years. This right does not have the aim of protecting the creation and originality of the work but more so the investment made for the collection of the raw data. It is placed between the right to incorporeal property and the action for unlawful competition. The States can foresee some exceptions to the "sui generis" right, among which the extraction for teaching and research purposes (art. 9).

Although the ESA has suggested the European Community to introduce a clear reference to the remote sensing raw and processed information in the definition of a data base (art. 1,2) [22], the directive is rather generic. This does not exclude the possibility that the collection of remote sensing primary data could enjoy such protection [23].

With the Decision of the Council of December 15th 1994 the European Union, evermore interested in environment topics, adopted a specific program for scientific research, technological development and demonstration on climate and environment

(1194-1998)[24]. For the purposes of the programme it is necessary to open activities of international co-operation with international organisations and third party countries. Of the four topics on which the programme is based one (c) concerns space technologies applied to environmental monitoring and research. Other than increasing the use of the remote sensing data to improve the methods of forecast, monitoring and management of catastrophes and natural risks, the program wishes to improve the European technological and scientific capacity for the elaboration and interpretation of the Earth Observation (EO) data and to define its purposes. The other aim is to develop the data concerning the EO with European interest by improving the quality and the costs/benefits ratio of the deriving information. In order to reach these aims, which must answer the interests of the European Environmental Protection Agency, the European Union wishes to support the Commission and the States for the creation of a more effective policy and to increase the use of the data gained form Earth observation for the development of a branch of services giving such information.

The freedom of access to information on environmental matters had already been ensured, in the Community, by the Directive 330 of the Council dated June 7th 1990 with the purpose of "guaranteeing freedom of access to information concerning environment in possession of public authorities and the diffusion of the same"[25]. The information on environment coming from remote sensing may be included in the information of the public authorities, also included in the data base, concerning the state of the environment and the activities or measures damaging it. This information must be given to any requesting natural or artificial person without the latter having to prove their interest. The information may be refused for certain reasons such as public security, the protection of commercial and industrial interests, the protection of individuals and their privacy. However, the directive underlines the exceptionalness of the secret in respect of the general character given to the information. The cost of the information must be "reasonable". Subsequently, with the decision 94/90 of February 8th 1994 the Commission extended the access of the public also to the documents of the Council and of the Commission and established that a reasonable cost is 10 ECU for 30 pages[26].

The dispositions of the directive on the access to information have been resumed in the Convention on Civil Liability for damage resulting from activities dangerous to the environment open to the signature of the States in Lugano on June 21st 1993. The access of the public to the information tends to favour any form of prevention and reductive intervention of the damage and to grate further means for proof to the eventual victim or operator[27]. The convention, which foresees the adhesion also of States who are not members of the European Council has the aim of reaching an adequate compensation for the damages connected to the alteration of environment but also for the damages caused to persons or goods and of the costs of the measures taken for the prevention of the damage. A regime of objective responsibility has been established therefore independently from the proof of liability and under a certain limited number of exceptions. The person exercising the control of the activity causing the damage is the liable one.

Conclusions

The practise followed in the distribution of the remote sensing data is at present extremely different from one country to the other. The United States have a policy of free access often free of cost which could be favourable for the users because the costs are supported by the American government, but this often has the purpose of ensuring a pre-eminence of the United States in the field. The French policy is more selective and it aims at making the users participate in the financing of the costs of the observation systems.

On the other hand the attention of the public opinion and of politicians has been awakened by revealing signals concerning a possible deterioration of the Earth's environment. Therefore on a national and international level more and more programs are developed for the safeguard of environment and the stabilisation of climate. The interest is no longer of each person but of all mankind and therefore initiatives for the co-ordination of national and international programs of Earth observation have increased. The researchers working in this field must be advantaged for the use of many and precise elements such as remote sensing can offer.

Many European governments and the ESA have shown attention to this problem and they have adopted a policy of distribution of the data which acknowledges the necessity of covering part of their financial investment in the Earth observation systems and also recognises the necessity to maximise the return of the investments in a non monetary sense. Because the main purpose of the public investment in Earth observation is to maximise the public benefit a wider use of the data is one of the ways to reach this aim. For this reason the purpose of the policy of those States and of the ESA tends to establish preferential categories for some users because of the social value of the research. Usually, a special treatment consisting in giving the data free of cost or at reproduction cost, is offered to the research community and to those operational organisations operating for public benefit and on a non commercial basis. This category at present basically includes meteorological services is now ready to encompass other organisations due to the growing interest in environmental monitoring.

On the contrary of what happens in other branches of space applications, such as meteorology and telecommunications, the community of users of satellite observation does not have an organised structure. The observation of Earth must be the privileged field for international co-operation in order to share the costs of the space systems and to avoid duplications and also to reach a larger exchange of the data concerning the Earth's environment and to strengthen the programs, for the benefit of developing countries, for a better management of the resources and their environment.

These aims are pursued by international organisations among which the most important is the Committee on Earth Observation Satellites (CEOS) with the purpose of optimising space observation among the States members and serving as a focal point for the community of the users[28]

The need to centralise in regional or international organisations the co-ordination of these space activities, which may be specifically for public benefit, is increasing[29]. The same above mentioned Draft resolution of the United Nations of Spring 1996 suggests in art. 8 that COPUOS should become "a forum for the exchange of information on national and international activities in the field of co-operation for the exploration and use of outer space".

NOTES

[1]Legal Subcommettee UNCOPUOS, 34th sess., Vienna, 18 March-4 April 1996, A/AC. 105/C.2/L.202, 27 March 1996.

[2]SAINT-LAGER, Les pays en développement et le droit des activités spatiales , in DUTHEIL DE LA ROCHERE, Droit de l'espace , Paris 1988, p. 316.

[3]For the technical and legal issues of the link between the remote sensing and the environment see: "Actes du Colloque International le droit face aux techniques de télédétéction par satellite au service de l'environnement, Strasbourg, 2-3-4-juin 1993" sous la direction de COURTEIX "Droit, télédétéction et Environnement, 1994 (later on: Actes du Colloque de Strasbourg) e *ibidem* KISS, Le droit international de l'environnement et la télédétection, p. 79

[4]MARTIN, Télédétéction et protection de l'environnement, in Les petites affiches, 22 juin 1994,n°74

[5]CATALANO SGROSSO, Aspetti giuridici del telerilevamento, in Diritto dello spazio. Recenti sviluppi e prospettive, Proceedings of the Colloquium of Rome 13-14 March 1992, edited by CATALANO SGROSSO, Padova 1994 , CATALANO SGROSSO, Mise en ouvre des principes des Nations Unis de 1986 sur la télédétéction, in Actes du Colloque de Strasbourg, note 3, p. 197

[6]GOROVE, Developments in Space Law, Issues and Policies, Dordrecht, Boston, London 1991, p. 306

[7]MARTIN, Droit des activités spatiales, Paris 1992, p.179

[8]WINTER, Access of the public to environmental data from satellite remote sensing, in Journal of Environmental Law, vol 6, n 1, p. 43

[9]SCOTT, Natural disasters, in Actes du Colloque de Strasbourg, note 3, p. 73

[10]JASENTULIYANA, Recent Developments in United Nations Activities relating to Outer

Space, presented to 38th International Colloquium on the Law of Outer space, Oslo 1995

[11]Agreement for Purchase and Protection of Satellite Data between the Department of Commerce and EOSAT, sept. 1985, 27

[12]"Land Remote Sensing Policy Act" 1992, Pubic Law 102-555, Section 2, Finding 13 states: " To maximize the value of the Landsat program to the American public, unenhanced Landsat 4-6 data should be available, at a minimum to United States government agencies, to **global environmental change researchers**, and to other researchers who are finencially supported by the United States Government, at the cost of fulfilling users requests, and unenhanced Landsat 7 data should be made available to all users at the cost of fulfilling user request". see ROBOK SHAFFER, The American Distribution system for satellite remote sensing data, in Actes du Colloque de Strasbourg, note 3, p. 123

[13]DUFRESNE, Le système de distribution des données et produits SPOT, in Actes du Colloque de Strasbourg, note 3, p. 149

[14]"Politique de diffusion des données d'observation de la Terre à partir de l'espace"Rapport du groupe interministériel, avril 1995

[15]ESA/PB EO (90)57, rév. 6, Paris, 9 may 1994

[16]ESA/AF (93) 13, p.3

[17]EURIMAGE, Assessment of the Correct Commercial Prices for ERS 1/2 Products, summary report, oct.1995

[18]FERRAZZANI, The European distribution system (ERS), in Actes du Colloque de Strasbourg, note 3, p. 115

[19]See the study of Logica Space and Communications Limited for Commission of European Communities:"Issues in Earth Observation data policy for Europe", executive summary, november 1992, study n° ETES-0018

[20]See Martin, Droit des activités spatiales,note 7, p. 188

[21]Directive 96/9/CE of European Parliament and Council on the Legal Protection of Data Base, 11 march 1996, in O.J., L77/20, 27 march 1996; Initial Proposal: COM(92), 24 final, 393, 13 may1992, in OJ , C156, 23 june 1992, p. 4, modified proposal: COM(93) 464 final, 4 oct. 1993, in OJ, C 308, 15 nov. 1993, p. 1

[22]MEJIA-KAISER,Proprietary Rights in Remote Sensing Images, in Proceedings of the 38th Colloquium on the Law of Outer Space, Oslo 1995

[23]Art. 1 and art. 2 of directive; see GAUDRAT, La protection des données de télédétection par recours aux Conventions internationales, in Actes du Colloque de Strasbourg, note 3, p. 277, who criticises the double protection system in favour of a global and specific solution of all the satellite production based on the protection of the investment.

[24]94/911 EC, Dec.of Council, 15/12/1994, in OJ, n. L 361/1, 31/12/94

[25]EEC 90/313, dir. of Council, 7/6/1990, in OJ, n.L 158, 23/6/90;see WINTER, Access of the Public to Environmental Data from Remote Sensing", in Actes du Colloque de Strasbourg, note3, p.249

[26]EC 94/90, dec. of Commission 8/2/1994, in O.J.n. L 46, p.58

[27]Convention on Civil Liability for damage resulting from activities dangerous to the environment, open for signature at Lugano, 21/06/93, conditions for entry in force: 3 ratifications. Chart of signature by Council of Europa (05/03/96): 8 signatures (Cyprus, Finland, Greece, Iceland, Italy, Liechtenstein, Luxembourg, Netherlands). For the satellite images as a new method of proof for the defence of the environment see: COURTEIX, Vers la reconnaissance juridique d'un nouveau moyen de preuve pour la défense de l'environnement: les images satellitaire, in Revue franç. de droit aér. et spatial, 1995, p. 5

[28]REVAH -CHEVREL, Mecanismes actuels de coopération dans le domaine de l'observation de la terre et perspectives, in Actes du Colloque de Strasbourg, note 3, p. 259

[29]COURTEIX, Towards an international satellite monitoring system of the environment, in Proc. of the 33th Colloquium on the law of Outer Space, Dresde 1990,p.148; KOPAL, Vers une Autorité mondial de surveillance de l'Environnement, in Actes du Colloque de Strasbourg, note 3, p. 265; HASHIMOTO, Verification System from Outer Space. Revival of International Satellite Monitoring Agency, in Proc. or th 37th Colloquium on the Law of Outer Space, Jerusalem 1994, p. 250.

IISL-96-IISL.3.03

U.S. REMOTE SENSING DATA FROM EARTH OBSERVATION -- LAW, POLICY AND PRACTICE

By Margaret A. Roberts
Attorney/Advisor
National Aeronautics and Space Administration
Washington, D.C.

Abstract

U.S. law and policy is presented on the collection and dissemination of Earth remote sensing data by the U.S. Government. The principles of "Open Skies" and "Non-Discriminatory Availability of Data" are detailed, as well as placed in context with other contemporaneous legal theories.

National Aeronautics and Space Administration (NASA) practice is also addressed. Data rights are examined for NASA-sponsored Earth observation satellite programs beginning with the 1960 launch of TIROS-1. What becomes apparent is that practice has varied depending on the program objectives, participants and funding availability.

The last part of the paper looks to the future to see what policies are being put in place which will determine data access in planned Earth observation programs, most notably the Earth Observing System (EOS). Factors which can conflict with public access to data, such as periods of exclusive scientific use and the desire for private sector investment in satellite programs are briefly discussed.

Introduction

The National Aeronautics and Space Administration (NASA), the federal agency responsible for U.S. civilian aeronautics and space (National Aeronautics and Space Act, 42 U.S.C. 2451 § 102(b) (1958)), has since its creation in 1958, utilized the space environment to better understand the Earth and its natural processes. One area of focus has been the collection and analysis of data taken of the Earth over long periods of time. One of the earliest examples occurred in 1960 with the launch of the Television and Infrared Observation Satellite (TIROS) designed to permit weather forecasting from space. Since that time, there have been a number of Earth observing programs, the most recent of which is the Mission to Planet Earth (MTPE) program. MTPE is a scientific program to provide multispectral, comprehensive, global observations of the Earth as part of an effort designed to understand the effects of both human-induced and natural environmental change. Involving participation from more than 20 international agencies, MTPE is designed to be far-reaching and achieve the broadest possible exchange of data. Determining the exact means by which the data will be widely distributed has been the subject of much discussion and negotiation among the MTPE parties. Participating countries, driven by local law and practice sought different outcomes. What is NASA's position? How has NASA's position evolved over time? This paper discusses NASA's practice with distributing Earth remote sensing data, from 1960 to the present, for programs involving partnerships. In this context, a partnership can be a program undertaken with significant contribution from a foreign government, an agency of the U.S. Government, or in one instance, a private company. "Data" refers to unenhanced data which is either unprocessed or preprocessed. NASA's practice is placed in context by presenting U.S. law and policy in this area. Because interest in Earth observing data is growing dramatically, there are sometimes conflicting interests, namely concerning public and/or private sector commercial access to government-generated data. These issues are also discussed.

This paper is not a statement of official U.S. policy. The opinions expressed herein are solely those of the author.

Mission to Planet Earth/Earth Observing System

NASA's cornerstone Earth observation program is the MTPE. "The basic scientific goal of MTPE is to understand the Earth as an integrated system, including the effects and couplings of the solid earth, land surface, oceans, atmosphere, and biota."[1] To accomplish this task, the data collection segment of MTPE must be diversified, which indeed it is. It includes . . ."EOS [Earth Observing System], Earth probes, geostationary satellites, and aircraft-and ground based programs . . ."[2] EOS alone provides a series of 17 satellites and supporting ground and data systems that will develop a 15-year environmental data base, focusing on climate change.[3] Because of the very large scope of the MTPE/EOS program, benefits derived from its data are expected to be great. It is intended that MTPE science can "provide an objective starting point for the development of sound global environmental policy" as well as "make important contributions to the reduction of hazards to human life and property from natural events such as earthquakes, volcanic eruptions, severe storms, and floods."[4] Program success will be based on the quality and quantity of the measurements taken, achieving broad dissemination and use, as well as success in analyzing and understanding the implications of the data.

In 1994, NASA concluded negotiations with its international partners on an overarching policy for International EOS (IEOS) data distribution. In the best of all worlds, for reasons of simplicity and clarity, there would be a uniform policy for all international participants. One permitting open, nondiscriminatory data distribution to all scientific users at the cost of reproduction and distribution would maximize use of the data. This was the approach advanced by NASA and the U.S. It would also provide an easily recognizable taxpayer return on NASA's investment. On the other hand, NASA's Earth observing programs undertaken to meet a demonstrable NASA mission or program requirement traditionally permitted principal investigators periods of exclusive use. Such periods are traditionally viewed as a mechanism to attract the best scientists in a given discipline. This provides them an opportunity to pursue specific peer-reviewed research objectives, as well as verify the accuracy of the recorded data prior to dissemination. Balancing these interests has proven challenging.

In addition, several countries such as those which are members of the European Space Agency, permit government-generated data to be copyrighted, which restricts subsequent distribution. Some countries also require the data-providing organization to recover its costs. Therefore, a scientist in the MTPE program who receives foreign IEOS data might have to agree to abide by any specific limitations imposed as a precondition of use and/or pay user fees. In contrast, the U.S. opposes the imposition of user fees, and by statute, works prepared by U.S. government employees as part of their official duties are not permitted copyright protection in the United States.[5] Moreover, NASA has stated that it does not intend to assert any protection internationally.[6] Thus distribution of data generated by the U.S. government is not subject to licensing restrictions either domestically or abroad.

U.S. Law and Policy

The basis of the U.S. position on nondiscriminatory data availability can be found in two early space policy pronouncements -- the United Nations (U.N.) established principle of "Open Skies" and public access to the results of NASA activities as provided in NASA's organic statute, the NASA Space Act of 1958, 42 U.S.C. § 2451 et. seq.

Open Skies refers to the right of a country with ownership of an Earth remote sensing satellite to collect and subsequently distribute data taken from space of the rest of the world. According to the U. S. Department of State, President Eisenhower first proposed Open Skies at the 1955 conference in Geneva. At that time, it was rejected by the Soviet Union.[7] Four years later, in a U.S. Policy on Outer Space, the Eisenhower Administration began to explore the appropriate position for the United States.

> An initial problem, in which all states have an interest, involves the permissibility of various activities in outer space. With respect to this problem, the report of the United Nations Ad Hoc Committee on the Peaceful Uses of Outer Space expresses the following view which the

U.S. has supported: 'During the International Geophysical Year 1957-1958 and subsequently, countries throughout the world proceeded on the premise of the permissibility of the launching and flight of the space vehicles which were launched, regardless of what territory they passed over during the course of their flight through outer space. The Committee, bearing in mind that its terms of reference refer exclusively to the peaceful uses of outer space, believes that, with this practice, there may have been initiated the recognition or establishment of a generally accepted rule to the effect that, in principle, outer space is, on conditions of equality, freely available for exploration and use by all in accordance with existing or future international law or agreements.'

. . . Although the U.S. has not to date recognized any upper limit to its sovereignty, a principle of freedom of outer space, such as that expressed by the United Nations Ad Hoc Committee, suggests that at least in so far as peaceful exploration and use of outer space are concerned, the right of states to exclude persons and objects may not obtain. However, the full implications of a principle of freedom of outer space, in contrast with a principle of national sovereignty over outer space, remain to be fully assessed. It is possible that certain military applications of space vehicles may be accepted as peaceful or acquiesced in as non-interfering. On the other hand, it may be anticipated that states will not willingly acquiesce in unrestricted use of outer space for activities which may jeopardize or interfere with their national interests.[8]

The above policy statement demonstrates the initial considerations the U.S. addressed in supporting U.N. establishment of an Open Skies approach. However, certain issues such as how broadly "peaceful" or "non-interfering" uses of outer space would be interpreted were unresolved. Other nations disputed the underlying basis for Open Skies. According to Carl Christol, the different assertions regarding an individual state's right to sense, or in the alternative "not be sensed" are based on varying interpretations of the same legal theory, that of national sovereignty.[9] The U.S. position -- one equating sovereign rights with the right to acquire data from space -- is documented in 1978, in Presidential Directive NSC-37. The objectives of the policy, as stated are "(1) to advance the interests of the United States through the exploration and use of space and (2) to cooperate with other nations in maintaining the freedom of space for all activities which enhance the security and welfare of mankind."[10] By 1978, the U.S. had asserted its right to pursue the exploration and use of outer space for both peaceful purposes and in support of its right of self-defense. Specifically, the basic principles, as outlined include "rejection of any claims to sovereignty over outer space or over celestial bodies, or any portion thereof, and rejection of any limitations on the fundamental right to acquire data from space. The space systems of any nation are national property and have the right of passage through and operations in space without interference. Purposeful interference with space systems shall be viewed as an infringement upon sovereign rights."[11]

Those opposing the Open Skies theory, according to Christol, claim a right of "national privacy" or "the sovereign right of a State to be let alone."[12] In 1978, nine countries -- Cuba, Czechoslovakia, the German Democratic Republic, Hungary, Mongolia, Poland, Romania, and the Soviet Union -- formalized their position through a United Nations Convention on the Transfer and Use of Data of the Remote Sensing of the Earth from Outer Space. The treaty proclaimed that prior consent by the sensed state was required for disclosure of data having a resolution of greater than 50 meters.[13] The U.S. and other spacefaring nations refused to accept their position.

The United States continues to assert the Open Skies principle. In addition to the referenced 1978 Presidential Directive, it can be found in the national space policies issued since that time, to include the most recent National Space Policy released on September 19, 1996.[14]

The U.S. position on Open Skies was reaffirmed in the 1967 Outer Space Treaty. Article 2 states that "Outer space, including the moon and other celestial bodies, is not subject to national appropriation by claim of sovereignty, by means of use or occupation, or by any other means."[15] This principle reiterates the right of a country to explore and use outer space to include passage through and operations in space over territory situated outside national boundaries. In fact, according to Christol, "During the negotiations attending the drafting of the agreement, and in subsequent State practice, it has become clear that the space environment is perceived in international law as a *res communis* . . . as an area available for inclusive uses, rather than for exclusive uses."[16] Thus the Outer Space Treaty limitations on space activities are few. Article 1 "authorizes the exploration, exploitation and use of the area and the resources of the area provided such 'activities' are carried out, as Article I specifies, 'for the benefit and in the interests of all countries, irrespective of their degree of economic or scientific development, and shall be the province of all mankind.'"[17] As one of approximately 95 countries to have ratified the Outer Space Treaty, the U.S. and most spacefaring nations espouse these principles.

In addition, in 1986, the U.N. General Assembly tied key provisions of the Outer Space Treaty to activities associated with Earth remote sensing. The U.N. adopted 15 Principles relating to remote sensing of the Earth from space. These principles include an explicit statement that remote sensing activities have to be conducted in accordance with Article 1 of the Outer Space Treaty. In addition, nations are directed to conduct their activities on "the basis of respect for the principles of full and permanent sovereignty of all States and peoples over their own wealth and natural resources, with due regard to the rights and interests, in accordance with international law, of other States and entities under their jurisdiction. Such activities shall not be conducted in a manner detrimental to the legitimate rights and interests of the sensed State."[18] U.S. policy provides that the sensed state be provided a copy of the data it has collected through overflights. That position is incorporated in the Open Skies Treaty, signed by 27 nations in Helsinki, Finland on March 24, 1992. Signatories include nations from the former Warsaw Pact and NATO. In addition, other parties to the treaty, upon request, have the right to the data collected by the observing state. The treaty was ratified by the United States in December 1993, but has not yet entered into force.

A second doctrine affecting NASA practice is incorporated in NASA's organic statute, the NASA Space Act of 1958, 42 USC § 2451 et. seq. It directs NASA to undertake broad dissemination across-the-board in its work in aeronautical and space programs. Specifically the Space Act requires NASA to work with the scientific community in planning and undertaking measurements and observations using aeronautical and space vehicles as well as "provide for the widest practicable and appropriate dissemination of information concerning its activities and the results thereof."[19] Thus from its inception, NASA was recognized as a public resource whose value to the public, in part, would be measured by how successfully it disseminates information, not only domestically but also abroad. Section 205 of the Space Act grants NASA authority to enter into international agreements. In the "policy and purpose" section of the Act, Congress directs NASA to accept as one of its objectives the conduct of aeronautical and space activities to include "Cooperation by the United States with other nations and groups of nations in work done pursuant to this Act and in the peaceful application of the results thereof."[20]

These principles are reflected in NASA's Strategic Plan which recognizes that MTPE serves the public at large. "The ultimate beneficiaries of Mission to Planet Earth are the present and future generations of people on Earth. The primary customers of Mission to Planet Earth are those who use environmental information to make decisions, especially national policy makers in the Administration and Congress and their international counterparts. The world science community also uses Mission to Planet Earth data and information to produce assessments, forecasts and analysis, and to develop new understanding."[21]

Given these two overarching principles, has NASA consistently conducted its business in consonance with them, as documented in its agreements with partners? If not, are there subsequent U.S. law and policy changes that dictated NASA practice?

NASA Practice

The very first satellite launched by NASA was the polar orbiting, Television and Infrared Observation Satellite (TIROS) launched in 1960. The first in a series, TIROS was designed to permit weather forecasting from outer space. The program was conducted as part of an agreement, dated April 1959, between NASA and the Advanced Research Projects Agency (ARPA) of the Department of Defense (DoD). Under the terms of the agreement, TIROS data was shared by both NASA and the DoD. Specifically, section 2 of the agreement required "close cooperation and full exchange of information between NASA and DOD." To effectuate full exchange of data, a committee with NASA and DoD participation was established. The agreement stated that:

> In order to insure the complete availability to DOD and NASA of all information developed under Project TIROS and to insure that the respective interests of both are fully recognized in carrying out the Project, the following arrangements are agreed to: a) A committee will be established under NASA chairmanship, with representation from both DoD and NASA, to advise NASA on technical matters related to Project TIROS, including DOD requirements, and to make any necessary arrangements for the close cooperation and full exchange of information between NASA and DOD.[22]

The TIROS program served NASA well in terms of establishing a standard for achieving "full exchange of data" among the participating entities.

During the next two decades, a series of TIROS satellites were launched which permitted continuity in weather forecasting. In 1961 however, after TIROS was recategorized as operational, responsibility for the program was transferred from NASA to the U.S. Weather Bureau. NASA was given responsibility, in 1964, for the next experimental meteorological satellite program, called Nimbus. The last in the series, Nimbus-7, was launched in 1978.

According to Richard Chapman, cited in "TIROS-NIMBUS: Administrative, Political, and Technological Problems of Developing U.S. Weather Satellites", TIROS was a great success and "literally created a worldwide appetite for weather satellite data and evoked worldwide praise."[23] President Dwight Eisenhower acknowledged NASA's 'startling strides' in weather forecasting, satellite communications and deep space probes in his January 12, 1961 address given just prior to the end of his term. He specifically called out the successful launching of TIROS-I and TIROS-II, which in his opinion, "promise[d] to revolutionize methods of weather forecasting."[24]

President John Kennedy likewise, took a keen interest in satellite technology. In his January 30, 1961 State of the Union Address, he invited all nations, including the Soviet Union, to join the U.S. in developing a weather prediction program, a new communications satellite program and planetary probes.[25] The President understood the potential value of space technology to people of all nations. He requested additional appropriations from Congress in May, 1961, not only to send a man to the moon and back within a decade, and for communications, but also to accelerate the weather prediction program to permit "world-wide weather observation" at the earliest possible time. . . "Such a system [of weather satellites], the President recognized, will be of inestimable commercial and scientific value; and the information it provides will be made freely available to all the nations of the world."[26]

It was not long before President Kennedy's vision was realized. By 1963, the United States was providing direct reception of weather data, free of charge, to users around the world. Currently there are more than 1,000 direct readout stations in over 130 countries. Users include public and private entities, as well as domestic and foreign governments.

Thus since the beginning of the meteorological satellite program, a tradition of making information "freely" available throughout the world was embraced at the highest levels of the U.S. Government. Weather information continues to be made available at no cost for public use and at the cost of reproduction for commercial use. The approach for U.S. Earth remote sensing programs, although not the same, has undergone changes which have brought it closer to achieving the maximum distribution possible.

A subsequent Earth remote sensing program, undertaken by NASA in conjunction with the Departments of Interior and Agriculture, was the Earth Resources Technology Satellite (ERTS) launched in July, 1972. The program was designed to "determine the desirability and configuration of an operational space-based earth resources survey system, and the problems associated with handling data from such a system."[27] According to Pitt Thome, quoted in a doctoral thesis, "NASA's Administrator, at the time of the ERTS program decided to make the data available to the public at the same time it was provided to selected Principal Investigators. His rationale was that if there was economic value in the data, as widely anticipated, he did not want NASA to be in a position of selecting potential beneficiaries of such economic value."[28] As a result, data was provided to the public, without restrictions, and at essentially the cost of fulfilling a user request, until 1984.

In May, 1972, NASA issued a policy directive addressing the availability to the public of all NASA-acquired Earth Resources Survey Imagery. It was to be made available at the cost of reproduction, both domestically and abroad, without restrictions except for national security concerns.

> Photographic products acquired by NASA for research and experimental use in the Earth Resources Survey Program from surface, airborne, or space-borne platforms, will, except as may be prohibited by law or regulations, be freely available for purchase by private and public parties, both foreign and domestic. Such photographic products will be placed in the public domain as soon as practicable after acquisition and before other use is made thereof. . .[29]

The policy also addressed the sale of imagery in the public domain. It could be provided free of charge by NASA and other Federal agencies engaged in the program: for purely educational or informational activities in the public interest; where there is a binding agreement between the government and another party in support of U.S. programs; where a foreign or domestic agreement exists calling for exchanges of data; when determined to be in the national interest; and when billing costs would exceed the return from charges. Government agencies providing imagery without reimbursement were given the responsibility to ensure the proprietary rights to the data were protected.[30]

The ERTS program generated a great deal of interest and excitement, according to a December 11, 1969 Memorandum for the President.

> . . . although the extent of the programs' future utility is not yet proved, progress in the field already has kindled a high degree of enthusiasm among proponents in the U.S. and has attracted considerable attention abroad. The enthusiasm centers on the belief that we are now on the threshold of a break-through in our capability to investigate, understand, and therefore to deal more effectively with, the earth's resources. Remote sensing by satellite (in conjunction with remote sensing by aircraft) offers not only promise of assisting in the acquisition of significant new information about resources. Perhaps, more important, it opens the door, for the first time, to a means by which regular inventory of resources might be taken, and therefore management of resources can be achieved to a degree far beyond anything previously thought attainable. The result, therefore, could be potentially and ultimately a major contribution to the solution of a number of the earth's food, water, and other resources problems as well as contributing to improvement of environmental quality.[31]

In September 1969, in a speech before the United Nations, then President Richard Nixon shared his vision for embarking on a truly global Earth resources satellite effort.

> The United States will (1) share the adventures and benefits of space and (2) as an example of our plans 'take actions with regard to earth resource satellites as this program proceeds and fulfills its promise' (3) dedicate the program to producing information not only for the U.S. but also for the world community; and (4) put 'several proposals in this respect before the United Nations.'[32]

Some of the "follow-up steps" to the U.N. speech were identified as well:

> To formulate and seek support for a resolution of the General Assembly which would, inter alia,

invite Member States with experience in the field to make such experience available to the other Member States and encourage the latter to become familiar with the field; encourage examination of programs and participation where feasible and practicable in their development including programs relating to airborne sensing techniques; invite Member States to join in exploring the problems of data analysis dissemination and application of data; and request the Outer Space Committee to continue its studies regarding the possibilities of further international cooperation.[33]

It is interesting to note that many of these same goals exist for current U.S. civil remote sensing programs including MTPE.

The ERTS program was later renamed LANDSAT, which stands for Land Remote Sensing Satellite System. The LANDSAT spacecraft carried multispectral scanners to provide high spatial and spectral resolution of both land and ocean mass. The LANDSAT program, like TIROS, was developed with the understanding that broad data dissemination would be an integral part of the program. Initially, during the time it was considered to be a research and development asset, LANDSAT was managed and operated by NASA. Data was transmitted to ground stations and sold by the Department of the Interior, through its Earth Resource Observation Systems (EROS) Data Center. "American users received data either directly from the satellite at no cost or at very low cost from NASA or the U.S. Geological Survey Earth Resources Observation System Data Center."[34] NASA entered into agreements with foreign ground stations which permitted them to collect data directly from the satellite as it passed overhead for an access fee of $200,000 per year. As a precondition to any ground station agreements, the station operator had to accept the U.S. nondiscrimination policy in its subsequent distribution and sales.[35] In addition, in limited circumstances, NASA provided grants to universities, non-profit organizations and State and local governments to receive LANDSAT data either free of charge or at reduced prices.[36]

President Jimmy Carter likewise supported development of remote sensing systems on a global basis. In an "Announcement of Administration Review" dated June 20, 1978, the President determined that:

> The United States will develop and operate on a global basis, active and passive remote sensing operations in support of national objectives . . . Data and results from the civil space programs will be provided the widest practical dissemination to improve the condition of human beings on Earth and to provide improved space services for the United States and other nations of the world.[37]

The Carter position was reiterated in the U.S. Civil Space Policy issued in October of that same year. It included as one of its first tenants a promise to "Emphasize space applications that will bring important benefits to our understanding of earth resources, climate, weather, pollution and agriculture, and provide for the private sector to take an increasing responsibility in remote sensing and other applications."[38] The policy committed the U.S. to continue to provide data from the developmental LANDSAT program for all classes of users. Simultaneously, NASA and Commerce were directed to prepare a plan to look at means for encouraging private sector investment and participation in civil remote sensing programs. The LANDSAT program had been the subject of much debate regarding whether or not it could be managed by the private sector. Although the Federal Government was the predominant user of the data, it was thought that a great many more commercial users could be identified and encouraged to buy the data.

In 1979, as a first step in a process to privatize LANDSAT, the Carter Administration announced plans to transfer the system to an agency with experience in satellite operations, the National Oceanic and Atmospheric Administration (NOAA), within the Department of Commerce. The Commerce Department was directed to "seek ways to further private sector opportunities in civil land remote-sensing activities, through joint ventures with industry, a quasi-government corporation, leasing, etc., with the goal of eventual operation of these activities by the private sector." The policy also committed the U.S., in the interim, to continue to provide LANDSAT data to foreign users as well as promote "development of complementary and cooperative nationally operated satellite systems so as to increase benefits for all nations."[39]

Transfer of LANDSAT to NOAA was achieved in 1982 as part of then-President Ronald Reagan's National Security Decision. In addition to the transfer, the policy included a commitment to provide public direct readout of Federal civil Earth remote sensing data to foreign users and ground stations.[40] In February, 1988 President Reagan released a subsequent space policy and commercial space initiative. The U.S. position remained the same with respect to its data policy. In addition, the administration declared an end to Federal subsidization of LANDSAT.

> The directive states that the United States Government will: (1) encourage the development of commercial systems which image the Earth from space competitive with or superior to foreign-operated civil or commercial systems; (2) discuss remote sensing issues and activities with foreign governments operating or regulating the private sector operation of remote sensing systems; and (3) continue a research and development effort for future advanced, remote sensing technologies. Commercial applications of such technologies will not involve direct Federal subsidy.[41]

In order to address the directive forbidding government subsidies, NOAA sought to bring the LANDSAT prices in line with the then-current operating costs of the program. In 1982, it began charging foreign receiving stations three times more than previously for the application fee. In addition, each station was charged a fee for the data it subsequently sold or distributed.[42] That same year, Earth Observation Satellite Company (EOSAT) was selected by the Department of Commerce to commercially operate LANDSAT. Contract negotiations were concluded in September, 1985 which gave EOSAT authority to operate and exclusively market LANDSAT 4 and 5 systems. EOSAT set prices for LANDSAT 1 through 6 data as well.

However, by this time, Congress had enacted the Land Remote-Sensing Commercialization Act of 1984 (P.L. 98-365), which among other things, mandated nondiscriminatory access to LANDSAT data, even for private sector operators. "Non-discriminatory basis" was defined as meaning "without preference, bias, or any other special arrangements (except on the basis of national security concerns pursuant to section 607) regarding delivery, format, financing, or technical considerations which would favor one buyer or class of buyers over another."[43] This required EOSAT to set one price for all customers.

In addition to codifying the nondiscriminatory data access policy, the purpose of the Land Remote-Sensing Commercialization Act of 1984 was to provide a phased transition of the LANDSAT program from one managed and funded by the government, to a fully commercial system. Private operators could obtain government approval to operate remote sensing spacecraft by getting a license from the Department of Commerce. Where it made sense to have private systems, the Act directed the government to avoid setting up competing systems. In an effort to guarantee that the government would not compete, limitations were placed on its use of Federal experimental remote-sensing space data. Such data could only be used for related Federally-funded research and development (including applications) and/or cooperative research programs. In addition, the data could be sold en bloc, to any U.S. entity willing to market the data on a nondiscriminatory basis and consistent with national security and international interests. Congress hoped that by clearly delineating and narrowing the parameters for scientific use, the data would have commercial value as well.[44] This legislation illustrates the approach taken by the Congress to reach a balance between private sector commercial interests and scientific research goals. Whether Congress accomplished something that was ultimately in the best interests of the public has been open to debate. Certainly scientific use of government-generated data was affected negatively by EOSAT's pricing scheme. EOSAT had to recoup its operating costs, whereas previously, data was provided to government-sponsored scientists and researchers at a price which reflected the existence of large Federal subsidies.

Congressional oversight of the LANDSAT program continued unabated. In October, 1987, Congress passed amendments to the Land Remote-Sensing Commercialization Act of 1984 (P.L. 100-147), to clarify its intent that the system operator (EOSAT) was supposed to provide data for government-sponsored research and development programs. In addition, the Act explicitly limited subsequent use and distribution to preclude the data from being incorporated into commercial products. Specifically, EOSAT was instructed to provide data for any research and development program if the following conditions were met:

> (1) a complete and timely disclosure of the results of such research and development is made in the open technical literature or is otherwise made publicly available; (2) the system operator or marketing entity provides to the Secretary an annual report of all research and development data transactions including the nature of any cooperative agreements and the prices charged for data; and (3) the data are not used for commercial purposes or in substantial competition with data available from a licensee under this Act.[45]

In October 1992, Congress reversed itself; it repealed the Land Remote-Sensing Commercial-ization Act of 1984. In its place, a new act, the Land Remote Sensing Policy Act of 1992 (P.L. 102-555) was passed which gave management of LANDSAT 7 to NASA and the DoD. The Congress acknowledged that the expense of the data sets was discouraging their widespread use -- a situation that would not change in the near future because full commercialization was not then achievable. LANDSAT 6, the first of the LANDSAT series to be fully built and operated by a commercial entity, had failed. The Administration committed to maintaining LANDSAT data by supporting LANDSAT 7 construction and operation. The Act seeks to maximize the value of the program to the American public by providing LANDSAT 7 data to all users at the cost of fulfilling a request. The legislation specifies the following:

> (a) LANDSAT 7 DATA POLICY. -- The LANDSAT Program Management, in consultation with other appropriate United States Government agencies, shall develop a data policy for LANDSAT 7 which should -- (1) ensure that unenhanced data are available to all users at the cost of fulfilling user requests; (2) ensure timely and dependable delivery of unenhanced data to the full spectrum of civilian, national security, commercial, and foreign users and the National Satellite Land Remote Sensing Data Archive; (3) ensure that the United States retains ownership of all unenhanced data generated by LANDSAT 7; (4) support the development of the commercial market for remote sensing data; (5) ensure that the provision of commercial value-added services based on remote sensing data remains exclusively the function of the private sector; and (6) to the extent possible, ensure that the data distribution system for LANDSAT 7 is compatible with the Earth Observing System Data and Information System.
> (b) In addition, the data policy for LANDSAT 7 may provide for -- (1) United States private sector entities to operate ground receiving stations in the United States for LANDSAT 7 data; (2) other means for direct access by private sector entities to unenhanced data from LANDSAT 7; and (3) the United States Government to charge a per image fee, license fee, or other such fee to entities operating ground receiving stations or distributing LANDSAT 7 data.[46]

As for LANDSAT 4 - 6 data, (although LANDSAT 6 subsequently failed) an exception to the EOSAT pricing scheme established under the "nondiscriminatory" distribution policy is permitted so that data can be provided more cheaply to U.S. Government agencies, global environmental change researchers, and other researchers sponsored by the U.S. Government. This class of users can obtain data at the cost of fulfilling a request. In addition, the LANDSAT Program Management was directed to begin negotiations with EOSAT to bring the LANDSAT 4 - 6 data policy in line, over the life of the EOSAT contract, with the LANDSAT 7 data policy.[47]

Experimental space remote-sensing data no longer has to be sold en bloc through a competitive process to any entity wishing to market the data on a nondiscriminatory basis. In its place, Congress has promoted fuller commercial participation from various business sectors able to use the unenhanced data. Such businesses are often interested in generating "value-added" products.

Likewise government-sponsored researchers again have access to LANDSAT data on terms that permit their science goals to be met. The LANDSAT 7 MOU, which will define the data dissemination terms and conditions, in consonance with the Land Remote Sensing Policy Act of 1992, has not yet been finalized. LANDSAT 7 is scheduled for launch in 1998.

During the signing ceremony for the Land Remote Sensing Policy Act of 1992, President George Bush articulated the highlights of the legislation. It will encourage future commercial opportunities in remote sensing by "supporting investments in new remote sensing technologies, removing unnecessary restrictions on the dissemination of privately gathered data; streamlining the licensing process for private remote sensing systems; and encouraging growth of the market for remote sensing data by pricing Federally provided data at the cost of fulfilling user requests, but no higher."[48]

The LANDSAT program highlights the difficulty of trying to bring scientific and commercial interests together. Subsequent efforts were made with other Earth observing programs, such as the Seastar (synthetic aperture radar)/SeaWiFS (Sea-viewing Wide Field-of-view Sensor) project. Signed in 1978, the 5-year contract will permit NASA, after the spacecraft is operational, to purchase ocean color data for government research purposes from a private source, Orbital Sciences Corporation (OSC). At the same time, OSC intends to market the data for commercial use as well.[49] Advanced funding by the government allowed OSC to secure the private financing required to design and begin building the satellite. The planned launch date was August 1993, but it has since slipped to February 1997.

The NASA/OSC contract permits NASA, in limited circumstances, to provide temporary real-time acquisition of data to specific authorized research users "where there exists adequate protections to ensure that the data will be used for research purposes exclusively, and when there is a compelling research requirement for real-time use by specified research users."[50] Otherwise 2 to 4 weeks processing time is built into the data availability schedule to permit OSC the opportunity to sell the same data to commercial users in real-time, and thereby provide them the greatest opportunity for making a profit.

NASA solicited proposals for no-cost research use of the SeaWiFS data through a "Dear Colleague" letter dated August 10, 1992. Data access terms were delineated as follows: researchers can obtain data, which for the most part will have a 4 km resolution, from the NASA archives (at preapproved ground stations) "at a cost which does not exceed the incremental cost of filling the individual user request." Such data will be provided after a delay of 2 to 4 weeks. NASA also agreed to obtain written agreements from each of its users guaranteeing that the data would only be used for research purposes.[51] Another category of data users are institutions and individuals. They can be granted authority to "directly receive encrypted data broadcast by the SeaWiFS satellite as it passes overhead. Non-U.S requests must be endorsed by an agency of the national government in the country. These data will be at 1 km resolution, but coverage will be limited to local data acquisition within the ground station mask. Costs for the ground station must be incurred by the requester. NASA may require a copy of the data received."[52]

Whether or not this is successful is to be seen since the satellite launch date has been so delayed. Success will have to be evaluated against NASA's scientific goals and OSC's commercial requirements. The unique SeaWiFS approach of time phasing data was initially applauded. However, OSC's repeated technical difficulties with the sensor and the possible availability of sea color data from the more recent launches of other remote sensing systems raise questions if this approach will ever receive a true market test.

Another unique example of a data distribution method began with the 1981 launch of a group of Earth observation experiments on the shuttle called the

Earth Spaceborne Imaging Radar series. These programs were begun as part of a research and development effort to evaluate the utility of radar remote sensing technology for Earth observations and mapping. The first spacecraft was designated SIR-A; the second, SIR-B, flew in 1984; and the third, SIR-C, flew in 1987. Only SIR-C was done in partnership with another entity. By way of comparison, the data access provisions for SIR-B and SIR-C are provided below.

The SIR-B, according to the 1984 agreement, was built to "measure the radar backscatter characteristics of preselected test site areas at variable angles of incidence."[53] Data distribution was bifurcated. Principal and Co-Investigators, whose proposals were pre-approved through a peer review process were given direct access to SIR-B data for the purpose of carrying out their pre-authorized research. They were not permitted to duplicate or give SIR-B data furnished by NASA to other individuals except those identified in their research proposal. A World Data Center was established to provide data, under restricted terms, to the general public and other interested parties in the scientific community.[54]

It was determined that SIR-B was subject to the applicable provisions of the Land Remote Sensing Commercialization Act of 1984 (P. L. 98-365). As a result, NASA limited its distribution of data to pre-selected Principle Investigators and prepared to conduct an "en bloc" sale of data for alternate uses. The "en bloc" sale was never conducted before the Act was repealed by the Land Remote Sensing Policy Act of 1992.[55]

In 1987, a SIR-C Memorandum of Understanding (MOU) was signed between NASA and the Federal Minister for Research and Technology (BMFT) of the Federal Republic of Germany. The Shuttle Imaging Radar was combined with the German provided X-band Synthetic Aperture Radar (X-SAR). It was intended that the SIR-C mission "provide multiple angles of incidence, multiple wavelength and multipolarization capability."[56]

As provided in the MOU, the science data rights permitted Principle Investigators an exclusive period of one year to validate and analyze the incoming data. Following that period, Germany controlled distribution of X-SAR data and the United States of SIR-C data to individuals outside the joint program. NASA intended to generally release SIR-C data immediately following the restricted period. The agreement read as follows:

> (1) Designated investigators will have a period of one year, beginning with the receipt of data in a form suitable for analysis, to perform verification and calibration and to engage in science activities in a manner coordinated between NASA and BMFT. General release of suitable X-SAR data sets is planned through DFVLR (Deutsche Forschungs- und Versuchsanstalt fuer Luft- und Raumfahrt). General release of suitable SIR-C data sets is planned in conformance with U.S. legislation governing release of experimental data by NASA. With regard to general distribution following the period of investigator activities, it is expected that NASA will arrange for X-SAR dissemination. NASA and BMFT may wish to engage in further data exchange of SIR-C and X-SAR data for experimental purposes. (2) Data provided to designated investigators under terms of this agreement can be used for experimental purposes only and will not be provided to any third party.[57]

The data provisions of the MOU were amended, by exchange of letters, in 1994 in keeping with NASA's movement toward broad data dissemination and use.

> Designated investigators will have a period of three months of exclusive data use beginning with the receipt of data in a form suitable for analysis, to perform verification and calibration and to engage in science activities coordinated between NASA and DARA. General release of suitable X-SAR data sets is planned through DARA/DLR and ASI. General release of suitable SIR-C data sets is planned through NASA. With regard to general distribution, following the period of investigator exclusivity, data sets will be placed in an appropriate archive and made available to users at no more than the marginal cost of filling the specific user request. During the period of investigator activity, designated investigators will

be given priority treatment over other users in receiving data products needed to conduct their investigations. NASA and DARA may wish to engage in further data exchange of SIR-C and X-SAR data for experimental purposes.[58]

For SIR-C, initial MOU provisions limiting data dissemination and use were amended to reflect the changing trend toward open data access policies espoused by the U.S. This situation will repeat itself in the next partnership as well.

An MOU was signed in March, 1987 between NASA and the French Centre National D'Etudes Spatiales (CNES) for a new Earth remote sensing program called TOPEX/POSEIDON. According to the MOU, the primary objective of the TOPEX/POSEIDON project was "to measure the surface topography of the global oceans for three years with sufficient accuracy and precision to enable the determination of the ocean's general circulation as well as its mesoscale variability." This was to be achieved through "radar altimetry, precision satellite tracking, and precision orbit determination."[59] Both NASA and CNES provided radar altimeters and tracking systems; the U.S. also provided a microwave radiometer. Data distribution rights mirrored those of the initial SIR-C/X-SAR program. Principal Investigators were given a period of exclusive use after which NASA would make the data generally available to the scientific community. Specifically the provisions read as follows:

> . . . (c) All TOPEX/POSEIDON Investigators will be expected to share data with one another, under procedures to be developed by the TOPEX/POSEIDON Science Working Team (SWT), in order to maximize the planned scientific return from the mission. The SWT will have exclusive use of the data for a period of time as mutually agreed but not to exceed twelve months after launch. NASA will make such data available to the general scientific community through NASA's Ocean Data System (NDOS) and/or such other U.S. facility, as appropriate. CNES will make such data available to the general scientific community through the French Ocean Data System (AVISO) under development. It is noted that NASA and CNES will take appropriate steps, as mutually agreed, to ensure compatibility between AVISO and NDOS.[60]

Although the Science Working Team was given exclusive data rights for a period of up to one year, they subsequently waived those rights and the data was made available to all users through the EOSDIS facility at the Jet Propulsion Laboratory immediately following the calibration period.[61] According to NASA program managers, "CNES and NASA had been very active in international discussions of data access for global change research and would have had difficulty justifying restrictive policies for TOPEX/POSEIDON with their public political positions encouraging widespread sharing of scientific data for research."[62]

Following the TOPEX/POSEIDON program, NASA negotiated an agreement with the USSR for the METEOR-3/TOMS -- Total Ozone Mapping Spectrometer Mission. An Implementing Agreement was signed on July 25, 1990 between NASA and the State Committee for Hydrometeorology of the Union of Soviet Socialist Republics (USSR). The program objective was to provide "continued mapping of global ozone from space and studying global and regional changes in the ozone as well the establishment of avenues of communication between the Parties at both scientific and technical levels to help resolve the question of global ozone modification."[63] NASA provided the TOMS/FM-2 instrument and interface adapter module. STATE HYDROMET USSR provided the spacecraft (Meteor-3), and the launch vehicle (Cyclone). Data sharing between countries was more limited than was provided in previous agreements with other countries. Probably this can be explained by the fact that the agreement was entered into during the height of the Cold War between the U.S. and U.S.S.R. Article XVII outlined each party's respective data rights.

> NASA and STATE HYDROMET USSR will each be entitled to receive all raw flight data from TOMS on the Meteor-3 and may reproduce, use and disclose the data for any purpose at their discretion. It is the intention of the Parties that the raw, processed, and analyzed data will be made available to the international scientific

community as noted in Article XIII and through publication or other appropriate means.[64]

Article XIII provided for the following concerning data analysis:

> NASA will reduce all the telemetry data to ozone values and will deliver archival ozone data tapes to National Space Science Data Center (NSSDC). NASA will provide to STATE HYDROMET USSR the TOMS radiance tables (look-up), a description of the physics and a description of the reduction algorithm which are in the public domain.[65]

Cooperation with respect to the sharing of analyzed data was kept to minimum. By comparison, "For EOS, NASA will acquire all data from its platforms and share the processing and archiving responsibilities with the foreign instrument providers."[66]

As the subject of her doctoral thesis, Dr. Lisa Shaffer, NASA's Director of MTPE Division, Office of External Relations, analyzed data access terms for NASA programs and determined that access varied depending on whether the program was undertaken to meet NASA mission requirements exclusively (autonomous programs) or if partnerships with foreign entities or agreements with other Federal agencies were involved. She concluded that:

> Autonomous programs have proprietary periods for Principal Investigators, while client and partner programs have open access policies. This may in part be a historical trend toward more open policies, since earlier programs tended to be autonomous, and more recent programs all involve partners. This reflects both the growing capability of NASA's potential international partners and the sophistication of the international scientific community. The difference in data access terms can also be explained by the desire of partners and clients to ensure their unrestricted ability to use output of their joint endeavor.[67]

In March 1991, NASA issued an internal NASA Management Instruction (NMI) stating its revised policy on dissemination of NASA-acquired experimental Earth remote sensing data to the public. NASA policy is determined according to the intended user. For all users participating in cooperative research programs or Federally-funded research, development, and application programs, spaceborne remote sensing data is to be made available as soon as practicable after acquisition and without any period of exclusive use. Furthermore, distribution costs are not to exceed the marginal cost of reproduction and distribution. In limited circumstances, the above-referenced users can get the data and products free of charge -- for educational or informational activities in the public interest; as part of a quid-pro-quo where a binding agreement exists; and when it is determined to be in the national interest of a government agency participating in the U.S. Global Change Research Program. Finally, as a precondition to access, the above users are required to specify that they would not engage in commercial applications of NASA-provided data without authorization.[68] Thus even for Earth remote sensing programs exclusively designed to meet NASA mission requirements, there can be no provision for exclusive access to data by the government-sponsored principle investigators. The other category of user addressed in NMI 8000.3 is one permitted by the Land Remote-Sensing Commercialization Act of 1984. The NASA policy specifies that spaceborne experimental remote sensing data could also be made available according to the terms of the Act (15 U.S.C. 4263)(although that Act has since been repealed).

NASA policy changed in that the NMI directs it to provide data free of charge in limited circumstances (previously, under NPD 8000.1, the data would have had to have been in the public domain), broadens the research user group to include those participating in applications or cooperative research programs, prohibits any period of exclusive use, and defines how the costs of disseminating the data will be assessed.

The Administration issued its own set of directives in its February 11, 1991 Presidential Directive on Commercial Space Policy Guidelines. The guidelines set forth the U.S. position with respect to commercial use and exploitation of space technologies. "The U.S. Government encourages private investment in, and broader responsibility for, space-related activities that can result in products and services that meet the needs of government and other customers in a competitive market." However, "As a matter of policy, the U.S. Government pursues its commercial space objectives without the use of direct federal subsidies."[69]

U.S. policy was documented in a set of principles outlined by the Assistant to President Bush for Science and Technology, Dr. Allan Bromley, and as part of a broader policy encompassed in the Paperwork Reduction Act (PRA) of 1995 (44 U.S.C. § 3501 *et seq.*), with implementing regulations provided by the Office of Management and Budget (OMB) in Circular A-130 (February 8, 1996). The Bromley principles are entitled "Data Management for Global Change Research Policy Statements." They were issued as U.S. policy on July 2, 1991. Their stated purpose is to "facilitate full and open access to quality data for global change research." Seven principles are articulated which address the full scope of data management considerations. The principles include a commitment to high-quality, long-term data sets; full and open sharing; preservation of all data needed for long-term global change research; easily accessible data archives; use of national and international standards for media processing and communication of global data sets; provision of the data at the lowest possible cost; and availability of data as soon as it becomes widely useful.[70]

The Clinton Administration likewise placed high priority on global change research. Its U.S. Global Change Research Program (USGCRP) includes participation and coordination among several agencies of the U.S. Government. In a May 28, 1992 National Space Policy Directive, the Administration outlined its reasoning behind the creation of the USGCRP.

> The U.S. Global Change Research Program (USGCRP), is a key component of the nation's overall approach to global stewardship and is one of the nation's highest priority science programs. The program's goal is to provide a sound scientific basis for developing national and international policy relating to natural and human-induced changes in the Earth system. The ultimate success of the USGCRP depends upon an integrated set of ground and space-based observation and research programs. The United States is planning on implementing a series of satellite missions that include NASA's Mission to Planet Earth, related environmental satellites, and activities of other agencies to provide these global observations for the next several decades. For purposes of this document, these systems are collectively referred to as the Space-based Global Change Observation System (S-GCOS).[71]

The implementing guidelines expect Federal agency participation in the USGCRP and interagency coordination. They also encourage Federal agencies to explore potential international cooperation in space-based global change observation.

Likewise, numerous international organizations are tackling the problems associated with coordinating and implementing a truly global initiative. Issues such as determining international standards for data processing, archiving and dissemination needed to be addressed. In September 1994, a multinational group, the Committee on Earth Observing Satellites (CEOS) agreed on principles for operational environmental use of data for the public benefit. Although not legally binding, the principles give an indication of the degree to which the U.S. data access policy is in sync with the international community. The CEOS agreed to do the following:

> Take into account the needs of users of data for operational environmental use for the public benefit . . . make data available on time scales compatible with user requirements and within agency capabilities . . . CEOS data supplier should provide easily accessible information and the data and related mission parameters . . . recognized standards should be used to the greatest extent practical . . . appropriate data provision mechanism should be used to optimize the use of data for operational environmental use for the public benefit . . . programs should have no exclusive period of data use except where there is a need to provide for data validation. An initial period of exclusive data use should be limited and explicitly defined. The goal should be release of data in some preliminary form within three months after the start of routine data acquisition.[72]

The international principles articulate on the one hand, objectives that mirror U.S. data access policy. On the other hand, the principles permit, within the overarching guidelines, interpretation and implementation to vary depending on national law and policy. This runs counter to U.S. goals for accomplishment of a broad-based global Earth remote sensing program -- one that fully utilizes all resources.

In October 1994, the U.S. entered into the first of several MOUs with foreign partners on the IEOS program. This first significant cooperation, with Japan, was called the Advanced Earth Observing Satellite (ADEOS). NASA provided a scatterometer and the Total Ozone Mapping Spectrometer (TOMS). Japan, through its National Space Development Agency (NASDA) provided the launch vehicle. ADEOS was developed by NASDA in order to establish platform technology for future spacecraft and inter-satellite data relay technology for transmitting Earth observation data, and to contribute to the observation of global environmental change. The U.S.-provided scatterometer was designed to take "190,000 measurements per day of the speed and direction of winds within about 1.5 inches of the ocean surface . . . " The TOMS sensor "will help extend the unique data set of global total column ozone measurements begun by a TOMS carried aboard NASA's Nimbus-7 satellite in 1978."[73]

The ADEOS MOU incorporated by reference, the 1994 data distribution provisions drafted by the Earth Observation International Coordination Working Group (EO-ICWG). These Data Exchange Principles (DEP) are intended to be included in each IEOS MOU. In addition, EOS investigators are required to agree to the DEP as a pre-condition to their selection for the program. The DEP provides for the following:

> [1] All IEOS Data will be available for peaceful purposes to all users *("users" does not include commercial users in this context)* on a non-discriminatory basis and in a timely manner.
> [2] There will be no period of exclusive data use. When the need to provide validated data is recognized, any initial period of exclusive data use should be limited and explicitly defined. The goal should be release of data in some preliminary form within three months after the start of routine reception of instrument data.
> [3] All IEOS Data will be available for the use of each of the Agencies and its designated users at the lowest possible cost for non-commercial use in the following categories: Research, Applications, and Operational Use for the Public Benefit . . .
> [8] All data required by the Agencies and their designated users will be made available on condition that the recipient agrees to applicable intellectual property rights, terms and conditions and/or proprietary rights consistent with these Data Exchange Principles, and ensures that the data shall not be distributed to non-designated parties, nor used in ways other than those for which the data were provided, without the written consent of the Data Providing Agency."

Key definitions include the following:

> "*Non-discriminatory Basis* means that all users in a clearly defined data use category can obtain data on the same terms and conditions, and the categories are defined in such a way that all potential users will be included in categories with access to data."
>
> "*Non-commercial Operational Use for the Public Benefit* is the utilisation of data to provide a regular service for the public benefit as distinguished from conferring an economic advantage on a particular user or group of users."
>
> "*Applications Use* of data is a limited proof of concept study toward: 1) the solution of an applied program to demonstrate the utility of the data; or 2) the demonstration of the operational use of the data." [74]

As for commercial access to IEOS data, terms and conditions are not included in the DEP. Therefore, instrument providers can establish access terms so long as the data dissemination is nondiscriminatory.

There are several IEOS platforms from different partner agencies which are subject to the DEP. IEOS platforms and corresponding instruments include: The NASA Earth Observing System (EOS), beginning with EOS-AM1; the ENVISAT-1 element of the ESA Polar Orbit Earth Observation Mission (POEM) programme, the NOAA Polar-orbiting Operational Environmental Satellites (POES), beginning with NOAA-N, the Japanese Earth Observing System (JEOS) [beginning with the Advanced Earth Observing Satellite (ADEOS)]; and the NASA/Japanese Tropical Rainfall Measuring Mission (TRMM). International agencies include the European Space Agency (ESA), the European Organization for Exploitation of Meteorological Satellites (EUMETSAT), NASA, the National Oceanic and Atmospheric Administration (NOAA), the Japanese Science and Technology Agency (STA), the National Space Development Agency of Japan (NASDA), the Ministry of International Trade and Industry of Japan (MITI), the Japan Environment Agency (JEA), the Japan Meteorological Agency (JMA), and the Canadian Space Agency (CSA).[75]

As for NASA's predominant portion of the program, the EOS elements consist of 17 instruments to assess global climate change. The program begins with the launch of EOS-AM in June 1998, which is a partnership program with Japan and the U.K. Other spacecraft in the series include EOS PM, EOS Color, EOS AERO, EOSALT, and EOS CHEM.[76] The computer and data collection system is called the EOS Data Information System, or EOSDIS.

In addition to designating specific programs subject to the IEOS DEP, the partners have agreed to attempt to include future Earth observation missions as well into the overall IEOS framework (to include acceptance of the IEOS DEP).[77] Thus, by 1994, a new revised framework was put into place for spaceborne Earth imaging to bring the U.S. and its international partners closer to the free exchange of data that prevailed in the earlier U.S. meteorological satellite programs. Scientists pursuing preapproved research (basic and applied), and researchers involved in the operational use of Earth observing data for the public good are provided for as part of the overall mission of the IEOS. However, as stated, the principles permit international partners to observe national laws and policy that to some degree, run counter to the program goals. Examples include requirements to pay user fees and observe copyright restrictions. For its part, the United States intends to provide all MTPE data from U.S. sources to researchers and scientists without restriction, at the cost of dissemination, and without regard to intended use.[78] "NASA plans to contract with a vendor to distribute data from the U.S. EOS platforms; the vendor will serve domestic and foreign commercial users under the same terms and conditions."[79]

In the international context, NASA continues to be active in advocating the free and unrestricted exchange of environmental data within the international community.[80] "The EOS program had a clear objective of obtaining and sharing the broadest possible suite of data for long-term monitoring of the Earth and its environment. The needs of the scientific research component of the EOS program exceeded the funding and capability of the space segment which NASA could develop. NASA is using its offer of full and open data sharing to push its international partners to follow the same approach. In this case, broad data availability is a fundamental NASA objective, extending to data beyond that provided by the NASA satellites."[81]

Across-the-board, the U.S. federal sector has a strong policy for public dissemination of data acquired at taxpayer expense. The Paperwork Reduction Act of 1995 (P.L. 104-13) addresses public access to government information generated in all sectors of the government. Two of its stated purposes are to:

> ensure the greatest possible public benefit from and maximize the utility of information created, collected, maintained, used, shared and disseminated by or for the Federal Government . . . and provide for the dissemination of public information on a timely basis, on equitable terms, and in a manner that promotes the utility of the information to the public and makes effective use of information technology."[82]

Implementing the Paperwork Reduction Act, Office of Management and Budget (OMB) Circular A-130 establishes a uniform, governmentwide policy for the reproduction and distribution of government information. It states that:

Government information is a valuable national resource. It provides the public with knowledge of the government, society, and economy -- past, present, and future. It is a means to ensure the accountability of government, to manage the government's operations, to maintain the healthy performance of the economy, and is itself a commodity in the marketplace."[83]

The open and efficient exchange of scientific and technical government information, subject to applicable national security controls and the proprietary rights of others, fosters excellence in scientific research and effective use of Federal research and development funds.[84]

In order to effectuate these principles, federal agencies, in essence, are instructed to be more user friendly and to promote the free flow of information between the government and the public. They are cautioned to avoid charging fees or royalties or setting up practices which interfere with the availability of information to the public on a timely and equitable basis. OMB advised all agencies that where user fees are required, the rates should not exceed the cost of dissemination, nor should they include the costs associated with the original collection and processing of the information.[85]

Thus, even though a program does not fall within the IEOS DEP, the same principle of full and open availability of data in a timely manner is found in U.S. domestic law and policy, and affects all U.S. agreements in the area of Earth remote sensing. NASA's practice has indeed evolved over time, to the point where there is a standard approach to data access.

The most comprehensive U.S. policy document addressing space data access issued in the Clinton Administration is the recent U.S. Space Policy Presidential Directive, issued on September 19, 1996. It again reiterates the value to the U.S. of space-based Earth observation and commits to providing government-generated civil Earth remote sensing data to users on a nondiscriminatory basis. In this instance, users include commercial firms as well.

The United States requires a continuing capability for space-based Earth observation to provide information useful for protecting public health, safety, and national security. Such a capability contributes to economic growth and stimulates educational, scientific and technological advancement. The U.S. Government will: . . . Support the development of U.S. commercial Earth observation capabilities by . . . providing U.S. Government civil data to commercial firms on a non-discriminatory basis to foster the growth of the "value-added" data enhancement industry; and making use, as appropriate, of relevant private sector capabilities, data, and information products in implementing this policy.[86]

NASA is also directed to "make use of relevant private sector remote sensing capabilities, data, and information products and establish a demonstration program to purchase data products from the U.S. private sector . . ."[87] Here, the government is trying to capture growing private sector capabilities to lower mission costs. Initial program emphasis by NASA on the attainment of scientific and foreign policy goals has shifted toward a recognition that private sector interests are not necessarily incongruent. The taxpayer can expect to share in the benefits of government-generated data, in terms of enabling a quality of life that is improved through scientific inquiry and discovery. Others can expect to be given the opportunity to participate and/or have access to the results of government activities as well.

Public/Private Partnership Considerations

The final part of this paper will focus on future policies that are being put in place which could affect data access in planned Earth observing programs. Much of what has been discussed, most notably the September 1996 National Space Policy, the IEOS DEP and OMB Circular A-130 are still very new. Yet, especially in the area of commercial remote sensing, changes to current policy are being sought by the private sector. As private industry becomes more capable in its ability to offer the government Earth remote sensing products and services, both it and

NASA have sought to redefine their relationship and find mutually beneficial public/private partnerships.

In part, the increased attention given to closing the gap between public and private sector participation in Earth imaging can be attributed to the increasing sophistication of private sector providers. NASA has responded by evaluating, across-the-board, the potential role of the private sector in MTPE. Working with industry, NASA has drafted a "Commercial Strategy for Office of Mission to Planet Earth." The strategy includes a description of the MTPE "Implementation Principles and Policies." It outlines nondiscriminatory data access in the first paragraph and, in addition, addresses the long-term activities NASA will undertake in promotion of the commercial space industry:

> MTPE will plan to acquire and provide scientific data products by the most cost-effective means available. The objective of the data policy is to maintain an appropriate balance between the scientific need for open low cost data with the commercial need for proprietary rights. As a matter of policy MTPE will:
>
> - provide science and commercial users with unrestricted access to science data acquired through MTPE capabilities;
> - provide MTPE-acquired Earth science data for the cost of dissemination;
> - establish rights to distribute proprietary science data acquired from commercial sources on a unique case-by-case basis. The respective contribution by each partner will be a key determinant in the balance between open and proprietary data.
>
> Within its obligation to meet critical science objectives, MTPE will not compete with, but will in fact support development of a competitive commercial remote sensing industry. MTPE will:
>
> - make best efforts to purchase data and value-added services from the commercial sector when that data meets MTPE science requirements;
> - seek out purchase arrangements where NASA is not the dominant customer over the long term;
> - not arbitrarily withdraw support from MTPE efforts or activities which are critical to commercial success, subject to national policy direction and the availability of appropriated funds; and
> - avoid establishing commercial monopolies or forcing partnerships among commercial providers by its actions.[88]

Finally, the shift in emphasis toward incorporation of commercial interests can be seen in the NASA Strategic Plan. Recall that the 1995 plan identified the MTPE beneficiaries as follows:

> The ultimate beneficiaries of Mission to Planet Earth are the present and future generations of people on Earth. The primary customers of Mission to Planet Earth are those who use the environmental information to make decisions, especially national policy makers in the Administration and Congress and their international counterparts. The world science community also uses Mission to Planet Earth data and information to produce assessments, forecasts and analysis, and to develop new understanding.[89]

The 1996 plan includes a similar section outlining MTPE beneficiaries. In this instance however, primary customers are defined much more broadly to include commercial firms and other non-scientific users. The plan states that:

> The ultimate beneficiaries of MTPE are the present and future generations of people on Earth. The primary customers are researchers seeking answers to key Earth science questions, commercial firms using MTPE data and technology to expand their businesses, public sector managers exercising stewardship of our national resources, and educators teaching the next generation of scientists, engineers and citizens. The outcome is the major contribution

to the scientific foundation for sustainable development.[90]

What are some of the potential commercial products and services that NASA is considering? Generally they include private sector (1) data processing, archiving and distribution of government remote sensing satellite imagery; (2) secondary use of NASA-generated data for commercial purposes to include the value-added industries; and (3) sales of industry-generated Earth remote sensing imagery to NASA.

As an example of the first category, it was originally intended that the data collected as part of the EOS program would be sent to government-run data processing and distribution centers, called Distributed Active Archive Centers (DAACs) for further distribution to intended users. Private sector companies have more recently expressed an interest in competing for the business rather than having the government operate the DAACs. The National Research Council evaluated the situation and subsequently recommended that responsibility for the DAACs (characterized as product generation, publication and user services) be determined through an open competitive process.[91] In response, NASA has outlined a plan to implement these recommendations and to select privately-run data centers for the MTPE program.

With respect to secondary uses of scientific data, NASA is planning to issue a Cooperative Agreement Notice in 1997, seeking proposals for development of commercial applications from EOS science data.[92] These data can be processed further, analyzed for a specific customer, and presented in the form of tailored charts, maps, or graphs, thus adding value to the original data. Estimates vary as to how large a market might exist for a value-added industry. Potential customers include map makers, land developers, resource managers, fisheries, mining companies, and others.

NASA and industry efforts to define a policy for data access by commercial users could be affected by newly enacted law, signed by the President on October 2, 1996. Entitled the Electronic Freedom of Information Act (FOIA) Amendments of 1996 (P.L. 104-231), it broadens the scope of FOIA (5 U.S.C. § 552) which provides private citizens a guaranteed right of access to government agency records, except where specific exemptions are provided by statute. The 1996 amendments change the definition of agency record to include records maintained in electronic format. A goal of the new legislation is to provide on-line access to government information. Yet, depending on how the implementing regulations are drafted, the government could be required to provide space Earth remote sensing data to any requester under the provisions of the Act. Under FOIA, fees charged to a requester are kept to a minimum to encourage public inspection and oversight. At most, for commercial use of any data, the fees include "reasonable standard charges for document search, duplication, and review . . ."[93] As a result, efforts to establish a separate data access policy for such programs as MTPE could be hampered.

Finally, NASA is exploring ways to purchase science data directly from the private sector. In two instances, NASA has already done this -- through the Seastar/SeaWiFS contract and the Student Explorer Demonstration Initiative. In its fiscal year 1997 budget, NASA requested a separate appropriation of $50 million to permit additional private sector purchases. As a means of getting industry input about possible opportunities, NASA issued a Request for Information. Seven private Earth imaging companies have received licenses from the Department of Commerce per the licensing scheme established under the Land Remote Sensing Policy Act of 1992. Any of these seven could potentially sell their imagery services to the government. At least one of these operators plans to deploy a satellite with the capability of providing one-meter resolution images, which far exceeds the 30-meter resolution capability of both LANDSAT 5 and 7.

A potential obstacle to data purchases by NASA is commercial intellectual property rights which restrict subsequent use and dissemination. Depending on the rights sought by the commercial provider, NASA may find that requirements to include company logos, pay licensing fees, or limit data usage might prove prohibitive. As commercial providers work to secure the greatest return on their investment, NASA's commitment to nondiscriminatory availability of scientific data cannot be compromised. NASA has taken steps to address this issue in one new program called Earth System Science Pathfinder (ESSP) Program. The ESSP was initiated so that spaceborne imaging missions could be accomplished with greater frequency -- every 2 years -- and at low cost, using innovative methods. Proposers were encouraged to cofund and/or provide like-kind resources as part of the program plan. The understanding was that by providing commercial opportunities (while still accomplishing the science objectives) proposers would be motivated to share the costs of development and mission operations. Through this shared funding mechanism, NASA is able to sponsor a greater number of missions and generate more scientific data than if the programs were to be undertaken as traditional NASA procurements. In its ESSP Announcement of Opportunity, dated July 19, 1996, NASA outlined data access requirements. Data from ESSP missions which are fully funded by the government will be distributed according to the IEOS DEP. For those missions which include significant private investment, NASA will consider innovative data management approaches so long as the data is immediately available to users at the cost of reproduction.

> U.S. Government information must be disseminated without restriction at no more than the cost of dissemination. Therefore, data from ESSP missions fully funded by the U.S. Government will be distributed in the same way as other NASA MTPE data. However, for data from missions in which there is significant U.S. private sector investment, NASA will consider innovative data management approaches that afford protection of commercial opportunities while still maximizing non-proprietary scientific return. The mission science team approved by NASA must have immediate and complete access to the basic data and products defined and produced by the mission. NASA encourages unique proposals for other distribution arrangements, such as purchase of data on delivery, as long as the full data set is ultimately available for long-term archival and open distribution. As with any NASA program, higher level products developed from Government-provided data by users outside of NASA-funde investigations are not subject to Government dat policies or controls.[94]

The above discussion provides an indication of wher NASA is headed in its efforts to promote and utiliz the commercial space industry. Privatization o LANDSAT provéd difficult and was never full accomplished. Hopefully the lessons learned wi make future government/private sector partnerships i this area more successful. At the same time, NAS will endeavor to make sure that MTPE and othe Earth remote sensing mission objectives are met an the current data access principles incorporated i future agreements with international partners an industry. Finally, NASA will be an advocate abroa for immediate availability of government informatio at no more than the cost of dissemination.

References

[1]NASA, Mission to Planet Earth: Strategic Enterpris Plan 1996-2002 9 (1996).

[2]NASA, MTPE EOS Reference Handbook 6 (Ghassem Asrar & Reynold Greenstone eds., 1995).

[3]NASA Facts (NF-209) (January 1994).

[4]NASA, Mission to Planet Earth: Strategic Enterpris Plan 1996-2002 9 (1996).

[5]Copyrights Act of 1976, title I, § 101, 17 U.S.C. § 105 (1994).

[6]Letter from Nina Lawrence (NASA) to Scott Pace (RAND Corporation) of October 3, 1995.

[7]U.S. Department of State, Fact Sheet (March 15, 1993).

[8]National Security Council, U.S. Policy on Oute Space (NSC 5918) 8, 9 (December 17, 1959).

[9]Carl Q. Christol, The Modern International Law of Outer Space 720 (1982).

[10]Presidential Directive (NSC-37), National Space Policy (May 11, 1978).

[11]Id.

[12]Christol at 720.

[13]Convention on the Transfer and Use of Data of the Remote Sensing of the Earth from Outer Space, June 28, 1978, U.N. Doc. A/33/162.

[14]National Science and Technology Council Fact Sheet (NSTC-8), National Space Policy 1, 2 (September 19, 1996).

[15]Treaty on Principles Governing the Activities of States in the Exploration and Use of Outer Space, Including the Moon and Other Celestial Bodies, October 10, 1967, U.N., T.I.A.S. 6347.

[16]Carl Q. Christol, 9 Annals of Air & Space Law 217, Article 2 of the 1967 Principles Treaty Revisited (1984).

[17]Glenn H. Reynolds & Robert P. Merges, Outer Space: Problems of Law and Policy 80 (1989).

[18]Space Activities of the United Nations and International Organizations 269 (United Nations ed., 1992), U.N. Doc. A/AC.105/521.

[19]National Aeronautics and Space Act of 1958, § 203(a)(2) and (3), 42 U.S.C. § 2473 (1994).

[20]Id. at § 102(d)(7).

[21]NASA, Strategic Plan 9 (1995).

[22]TIROS Meteorological Satellite Project Agreement between the Department of Defense and NASA (April 13, 1959).

[23]Lisa R. Shaffer, Earth Observations Satellite Data Policy: Process and Outcome 60 n. 6 (1994) (unpublished Ph.D. dissertation, The George Washington University).

[24]Text of President Eisenhower's Jan. 12 State of the Union Message in CQ Almanac at 936 (1961).

[25]Text of President Kennedy's Jan. 30 State of the Union Message in CQ Almanac at 860 (1961).

[26]Address of the President of the U.S. Before a Joint Session of the Senate and House of Representatives Relative to Urgent National Needs, H.R. Doc. No. 174, 87th Cong., 1st Sess., 11-12 (1961).

[27]Memorandum for the President (NSC-U/SM-53), International Space Cooperation (Feb. 10, 1972).

[28]Shaffer dissertation at 28.

[29]NASA, Policy Directive: NASA Earth Resources Survey Program Imagery, Notice 72-6, 37 Federal Register 9695-6 (May 16, 1972).

[30]Id.

[31]Memorandum for the President (S/S 19133), Earth Resources Surveying (December 11, 1969).

[32]A Report of the NSSM 72 Committee on International Cooperation (December 5, 1969).

[33] Id.

[34]Office of Technology Assessment, U.S. Congress, Remotely Sensed Data from Space: Distribution, Pricing, and Applications: An OTA Background Paper 11 (1992).

[35]Robert J. Aamoth et al., Vol. 2 American Enterprise, The Law, and the Commercial Use of Space 52 (Phillip D. Mink ed., 1986).

[36]Office of Technology Assessment, U.S. Congress, International Cooperation and Competition in Civilian Space Activities (OTA-ISC-239) 280 (1985).

[37]14 Weekly Compilation Pres. Docs. 1135 (June 20, 1978).

[38]The White House Fact Sheet, U.S. Civil Space Policy 1 (October 11, 1978).

[39]Weekly Compilation Pres. Docs. 2149 (November 20, 1979).

[40]The White House Fact Sheet, National Space Policy 4 (July 4, 1982).

[41]The White House Fact Sheet, Presidential Directive on National Space Policy 3 (February 11, 1988).

[42]OTA, International Cooperation and Competition in Civilian Space Activities at 282.

[43]Land Remote-Sensing Commercialization Act of 1984, § 104(3)(A), 15 U.S.C. § 4204 (1988) (repealed 1992).

[44]Id. at § 502 and 503.

[45]National Aeronautics and Space Administration Act of 1988, § 504, 15 U.S.C. 4264 (1988) (repealed 1992).

[46]Land Remote Sensing Policy Act of 1992, § 105, 15 U.S.C. § 5615 (1994).

[47]Id. at § 103.

[48]Weekly Compilation Pres. Docs. 2181 (October 28, 1992).

[49]Gene Carl Feldman, Background of the SeaWiFS Project (visited on September 14, 1996) <http://seawifs.gsfc.nasa.../SEAWIFS_ BACKGROUND.html>.

[50]Dixon M. Butler, SeaWiFS Dear Colleague Letter (August 10, 1992) <http://seawifs. gsfc.nasa .... ENTS/DEAR_COLLEAGUE.html>.

[51]Shaffer dissertation at 39.

[52]Butler, SeaWiFS Dear Colleague Letter.

[53]NASA, Provisions for Participation in the Shuttle Imaging Radar-B Experiment 2 (March 1984).

[54]Id. at 6.

[55]Shaffer dissertation at 33, 34.

[56]Memorandum of Understanding Between NASA and The Federal Minister for Research and Technology of the Federal Republic of Germany for Cooperative Flights of the Spaceborne Imaging Radar (SIR) with the X-Band Synthetic Aperture Radar (X-SAR) 2 (October 6, 1987).

[57]Id. at 7.

[58]Letter from Dr. Kennel (NASA) to Professor Stoewer (DARA) of January 26, 1995.

[59]Memorandum of Understanding Between the U.S. NASA and the French Centre National D'Etudes Spatiales for Joint Development of the TOPEX/POSEIDON Project 2 (March 23, 1987).

[60]Id. at 13.

[61]Shaffer dissertation at 36.

[62]Shaffer dissertation at 122 (based on personal interviews with Charles Yamarone and William Patzert, TOPEX managers at NASA).

[63]Agreement Between NASA and USSR State Committee for Hydrometeorology, Meteor-3/TOMS Implementing Agreement 1 (July 25, 1990).

[64]Id. at 11.

[65]Id. at 10.

[66]Shaffer dissertation at 142.

[67]Shaffer dissertation at 169.

[68]NASA Management Instruction on NASA Earth Science Data Program - Delegation of Authority (NMI 8000.3) Effective March 22, 1991-1995 (March 21, 1991). (Expiration date extended to December 31, 1996; superseded NPD 8000.1 dated May 10, 1972).

[69]Presidential Directive (NSPD-3), U.S. Commercial Space Policy Guidelines 2 (February 11, 1991).

[70]Office of Science and Technology Policy, Executive Office of the President, Data Management for Global Change Research (July 2, 1991).

[71]Presidential Directive (NSPD-7), Space-Based Global Change Observation 1 (May 28, 1992).

[72]CEOS Plenary Meeting Data Exchange Principles, Resolution on Principles of Satellite Data Provision in Support of Operational Use for the Public Benefit (September 28, 1994).

[73]NASA News Release 96-105, Oceans Winds and Ozone to be Measured by U.S. Instruments Aboard Japanese Earth Observation Satellite 2 (August 13, 1996).

[1]Memorandum of Understanding Between National Space Development Agency of Japan and NASA for Cooperation in the Advanced Earth Observing Satellite (ADEOS) Program App. (October 25, 1994).

[5]Id.

[6]NASA, MTPE EOS Reference Handbook at 16.

[7]ADEOS MOU at App.

[8]Lawrence letter.

[9]OTA, Remotely Sensed Data from Space at 12.

[0]Letter from Humphries (NASA) to Monk (European Parliament) of June 29, 1995.

[1]Shaffer dissertation at 116-117.

[2]Paperwork Reduction Act of 1995, § 2, Pub. L. No. 104-13, 109 Stat. 163.

[3]Circular A-130 at § 7b (February 8, 1996).

[4]Id. at § 7k.

[5]Id. at § 8(a)(7)(a), (c).

[5]NSTC-8 Fact Sheet at 11.

[7]Id. at 3.

[8]NASA, Draft Commercial Strategy for Office of Mission to Planet Earth (OMTPE) 3, 4 (1996).

[9]NASA, Strategic Plan 9 (1995).

[0]NASA, Strategic Plan 11 (1996).

[1]National Research Council, A Review of the U.S. Global Change Research Program and NASA's Mission to Planet Earth/Earth Observing System 24 (July 19-28, 1995).

[2]NASA, Draft Commercial Strategy for OMTPE at App.

[3]5 U.S.C. § 552 (1994).

[94]NASA, Announcement of Opportunity Earth System Science Pathfinder Missions (ESSP) 10, 11 (1996).

Additional Resources

For a good discussion of LANDSAT, see Kathleen M. Eisenbeis, Privatizing Government Information: The Effects of Policy on Access to LANDSAT Satellite Data (1995).

Also see Paul F. Uhlir, The Public International Law of Civilian Remote Sensing: An Overview, Vol. 2, American Enterprise, The Law, and the Commercial Use of Space 25 (Phillip D. Mink ed., 1986).

IISL-96-IISL.3.04

SHARING BENEFITS OF THE GLOBAL NAVIGATION SATELLITE SYSTEM WITHIN THE FRAMEWORK OF ICAO

Jiefang Huang*

Abstract

The development of the Global Navigation Satellite System (GNSS) may bring a profound change to air navigation and greatly promote the safety and efficiency of civil aviation. The international law-making process must keep up with the development of space technology. A legal framework, preferably within the auspices of the International Civil Aviation Organization (ICAO), is necessary in order to assure universal accessibility, reliability and continuity of the GNSS services. At present, as a transitional arrangement, the regulatory framework of GNSS is largely based on the non-binding policy and guidelines of ICAO, as well as the exchange of letters between ICAO and the State or States which provide GNSS services. In the long run, the international community will have to decide how to implement a civil global navigation satellite system. On the basis of its constitutive instrument and its previous practice, ICAO is fully competent in planning, co-ordinating, facilitating and regulating GNSS services for civil aviation purposes.

1. Introduction

In the early 1980's, the international civil aviation community realized the increasing limitations of the current systems of air navigation and started to explore, through ICAO, the possibility of improvement. In 1987, the ICAO Future Air Navigation Systems Committee identified the use of satellite technology to provide communication, navigation, and surveillance (CNS) services as "the only viable solution" that will enable one to overcome the shortcomings of the present air navigation systems and fulfil the needs and requirements of the foreseeable future[1]. The satellite based system was subsequently designated as ICAO Communications, Navigation, Surveillance and Air Traffic Management (CNS/ATM) Systems.

CNS/ATM Systems consist mainly of a marriage of space technology and computers[2]. The Global Navigation Satellite System (GNSS) is the key element of the system. GNSS is an electronic aid which may be used to determine in the course of aircraft flight the real-time position of the aircraft, the course and distance to the desired destination, and the deviation from the desired track. GNSS will render obsolete much of today's ground base navigation radio services and promote efficiency and safety in the sky. At present, there are two satellite navigation systems: the Global Positioning System (GPS), developed by the United States, and the Global Orbiting Satellite Navigation System (GLONASS), developed by the Russian Federation[3].

GNSS is one form of the use of outer space. The United States and the Russian Federation have respectively offered their systems for the use by the international community free of direct charge for a period of 10 years in the case of GPS and 15 years in the case of GLONASS. This initiative has enabled all countries, particularly those without space capabilities, to enjoy the benefit of space technology. In this sense, it has given effect to the principle enshrined in Article 1, paragraph 1 of the Outer Space Treaty that the exploration and use of outer space shall be carried out for the benefit and in the interest of all countries.

2. Legal Issues

At operational level, however, many issues remain to be resolved in order to provide a legal guarantee that GNSS may be used as primary means of air navigation. Under international law, the sovereign rights of a State include the right to regulate and control the provision, operation and

* The view expressed here is that of the author and should not be attributed to ICAO.

management of air navigation services within its territory. In the case of GNSS, the navigation facilities for most States, at least as far as the space segments are concerned, would be controlled and operated by one or more foreign countries, representing a dramatic step away from past practice in the application of the principle of sovereignty. Naturally, this situation gives rise to certain concerns, particularly in view of the fact that the GNSS services currently available for the international aviation community have originated from systems designed and operated for military purposes. A related concern is that when GNSS becomes the sole air navigation system and the traditional ground facilities are dismantled, the discontinuation of GNSS services, if decided unilaterally by a provider State, could mean the shutting down of the entire air transport system using such GNSS services. To address these issues, it is necessary to set up a legal framework.

3. Transitional Arrangements

To keep up with the development of GNSS, one of the important steps taken by the ICAO Council is the adoption on 9 March 1994 of the Statement of ICAO Policy on CNS/ATM Systems Implementation and Operation[4]. The Statement declares that the principle of universal accessibility without discrimination shall govern the provision of all air navigation services provided by way of CNS/ATM Systems. The Statement also reiterates that implementation and operation of CNS/ATM Systems which States have undertaken to provide in accordance with Article 28 of the *Convention on International Civil Aviation* (the Chicago Convention) shall neither infringe nor impose restrictions upon States' sovereignty, authority or responsibility in the control of air navigation and the promulgation and enforcement of safety regulations[5]. Furthermore, the Statement affirms that continuous availability of service from the CNS/ATM Systems shall be assured. Thus ICAO has provided certain policy safeguards for State sovereignty, as well as universal accessibility to, and continuity of, GNSS services.

However, the Statement of ICAO Policy is not a binding instrument, although it may carry strong political weight and high persuasive value. To provide a more definitive assurance, ICAO has made transitional arrangements by exchanging letters respectively with the United States and the Russian Federation. The exchange of letters with the United States on 14 October and 27 October 1994 states that the United States intends, subject to the availability of funds as required by United States law, to make the Standard Positioning Service of GPS available for the foreseeable future, on a continuous, worldwide basis and free of direct user fees[6]. Similarly, the exchange of letters with the Russian Federation on 4 June and 29 July 1996 also confirms that the Government of the Russian Federation offered the world aviation community the provision of the standard-accuracy GLONASS channel "on a non-discriminatory basis for a period of at least 15 years with no direct charges collected from users, subject to the allocation of resources, as required under the legislation of the Russian Federation"[7]. The United States and the Russian Federation have also respectively declared that the availability of their systems is not intended in anyway to limit the right of any State to control aircraft operations and enforce flight safety regulations in its sovereign airspace[8]. Further, they have respectively committed to take all necessary measures to maintain the integrity and reliability of the services and each of them expects that it will be able to provide at least six years notice prior to termination of its services[9].

It should be noted that the exchange of letters with the Russian Federation "will constitute a mutual agreement" whereas the exchange of letters with the United States will comprise mutual understanding "in lieu of an agreement"[10]. In this respect, a writer from the United States has made the following comments:

> "By using letters in lieu of a formal agreement, the FAA and the Administration may be walking a fine line between demonstrating a firm commitment by the United States and executing a formal executive agreement that might have domestic political consequences".[11]

Furthermore, the offers by the United States and the Russian Federation for the provision of GNSS services respectively contain the proviso of "subject to the availability of funds as required by United States law" or "subject to the allocation of resources, as required under the legislation of the Russian Federation". The applicability of this proviso may be subject to a future interpretation.

Nevertheless, the exchange of letters represent a significant step in the establishment of a legal framework with regard to GNSS. They contain legal commitments concerning universal accessibility to, and continuity of GNSS services. They strike a balance between the realization of early benefit from GNSS and necessary protection of the users' interest. They do not, and in my view, cannot replace the consideration of the long-term legal framework for GNSS, which is currently the mandate of the Panel of experts established by the ICAO Council on 6 December 1995.

4. The Long-term Legal Framework for GNSS

It is the ICAO's established policy that GNSS should be implemented as an evolutionary progression from existing global navigation satellite systems, including the United States' GPS and the Russian Federation's GLONASS, toward an integrated GNSS over which Contracting States exercise a sufficient level of control on aspects related to its use by civil aviation[12]. Accordingly, the consideration of the long-term legal framework should address the issue of control. The establishment of a new international organization for GNSS, which may be similar to INMARSAT, may resolve the issue of control. However, this will depend upon whether the international community has sufficient political will and financial means to do so. The past experience has also indicated that it is both difficult and time-consuming to conclude a new multilateral convention that will form the constitutional instrument of an organization. In view of this, it is the policy of ICAO that the CNS/ATM Systems shall, as far as practicable, make optimum use of existing organizational structure, modified if necessary[13]. It is submitted that within the framework of the Chicago Convention, a number of options, which are not mutually exclusive, exist for achieving different degrees of international control.

Article 15 of the Chicago Convention provides that upon representation by an interested Contracting State, the charges imposed for the use of airports and other facilities shall be reviewed by the Council, which shall report and make recommendations thereon for the consideration of the State or States concerned. The term "other facilities" may of course include the elements of GNSS[14]. Therefore, with respect to the user charges related to GNSS, there is a reviewing mechanism in place, which may be used by Contracting States.

If the Contracting States so wish, ICAO's responsibility may be extended beyond the power of review and recommendation. Under Article 84 of the Chicago Convention, any disagreement relating to the interpretation or application of provisions of the Annexes that are applicable to GNSS may be decided by the Council if any State concerned so requests. Further, ICAO Assembly Resolution A1-23, which is still in force, authorizes the Council to act as an arbitral body on any differences arising among Contracting States relating to international civil aviation matters submitted to it, when expressly requested to do so by all parties to such differences. Therefore, it is possible for Contracting States to give jurisdiction to the ICAO Council for settlement of disputes related to GNSS. In this way, certain judicial or quasi-judicial control of GNSS activities related to aviation may be achieved.

Chapter XV of the Chicago Convention makes it possible for ICAO to be more dynamically involved in administrative aspects of GNSS services. Article 71 states that if a Contracting State so requests, the Council may agree to provide, man, maintain, and administer any or all of the airports and other air navigation facilities including radio and meteorological services, required in its territory for the safe, regular, efficient and economical operation of the international air services of the other Contracting States, and may specify just and reasonable charges for the use of the facilities provided. In this connection, reference should be made to the joint financing arrangements used for Iceland and Greenland. While the air navigation facilities are jointly financed by the Contracting Parties to the Joint Financing Agreements, and operated by Denmark and Iceland, the Secretary General of ICAO is responsible for generally supervising the operation of the services; a section in the Secretariat carries out the day-to-day administrative functions involved. It estimates actual costs, evaluates requests for new capital expenditures or resources, prepares the assessment levels for Contracting Parties, determines the level of user charges and arranges for the handling of funds and payments to the provider States[15]. It has been suggested that the same or similar arrangements could be applicable to GNSS, wherein the ICAO Council may assume the function of administrative control over the facilities related to GNSS.

In summary, international control of GNSS within the ICAO system may range from non-binding review to active administration. It depends upon the Contracting States to decide which option is acceptable.

5. Concluding Remarks

GNSS presents both opportunities and challenges. It provides benefits to all mankind, but such benefits can only be continuously ensured within an appropriate long-term legal framework that provides for certain degree of international control. In this respect, ICAO may, within its constitutional mandates, develop and implement a legal framework for GNSS services and give effect to the principle of shared benefits among Contracting States.

References

1. ICAO Doc. FANS(II)/4-WP/9, para. 1.2.1
2. Address by the President of the Council of ICAO, Dr. Assad Kotaite, to the "Sociedade Brasileira de Direito Aeroespacial" on ICAO's Role with respect to the Institutional Arrangements and Legal Framework of Global Navigation Satellite System (GNSS) Planning and Implementation (21 May 1996, unpublished).
3. ICAO Doc. LC/29-WP/3-3, paras. 4-1 - 4-3
4. ICAO Doc. LC/29-WP/3-2
5. *Ibid.*, paragraphs 1 and 2
6. ICAO Doc. C-WP/10396, Attachment 1 to State Letter LE 4/49.1 - 94/89
7. ICAO Doc. PRES AK/522, Attachment
8. See *supra* notes 6 and 7.
9. *Ibid.*
10. *Ibid.*
11. Epstein, J.M., "Global Positioning System (GPS): Defining the Legal Issues of its Expanding Civil Use", 61 *JALC* 243, at 274-275
12. See *supra* note 4, paragraph 6.
13. *Ibid.*, paragraph 5
14. See *supra* note 2, at 7.
15. ICAO Doc. A31-WP/15, para. 2.4

– – – – –

IISL-96-IISL.3.05

REVIEW OF ARTICLE I OF THE OUTER SPACE TREATY

MEGUMU NAKAMURA

Nihon University, College of Law, Tokyo, Japan

Abstract

Article I of "The Outer Space Treaty" includes two significant provisions as to sharing benefits from space activities: "for the benefit and in the interests of all countries" and "the province of all mankind". This paper analyzes and re-interprets these two phrases.

Special attention is paid to the ITU Regime named the "Allotment Plan" for geostationary orbits and for radio frequency bands, which was established at WARC-ORB-85, 88. According to this Regime, at least one geostationary orbit and one radio frequency have been distributed to each country.

This Regime may be criticized for creating much "deadwood" in geostationary orbits and radio frequencies; nevertheless, it can be considered a major contribution to international cooperation in sharing benefits from space activities, especially from the viewpoint of equity between present and future generations.

1. Introduction

The Legal Subcommittee of the UN-COPUOS adopted in 1988 the new agenda named "Consideration of the legal aspects related to the application of the principle that the exploration and utilization of outer space shall be carried out for the benefit and in the interests of all States, taking into particular account the needs of developing countries"(1). In the negotiations conducted under this new agenda, how to share benefits derived from space activities has become one of the most important topics(2).

This paper therefore analyzes and re-interprets "The Principle of Freedom of Exploration and Use of Outer Space" (hereafter called "the Freedom Principle"), which is included in Article I of "The Outer Space Treaty"(3) (hereafter called the Space Treaty), from the viewpoint of sharing benefits from space activities; how to concretely share the benefits among all countries. This Principle is one of the most important rules in the Space Treaty; nevertheless, it is impossible for many developing countries to explore and use outer space freely and to obtain benefits from such space activities without cooperation with developed countries. In this analysis, attention is paid to two phrases in this Principle: "for the benefit and in the interests of all countries" and "the province of all mankind". For they might be related to the sharing of benefits from space activities by all countries.

2. The Principle of Freedom of Exploration and Use

"The Freedom Principle" in Article I of the Space Treaty is generally interpreted to include three rights of states: "freedom of access", "freedom of exploration", and "freedom of use"(4). However, these freedoms have one restriction: "space activities shall be carried out for the benefit and in the interests of all countries, and shall be the province of all mankind". That is to say, this restriction can be considered to lay stress on space activities by all states.

Nevertheless, it is very difficult for many developing countries to employ these freedoms, for they do not have enough scientific skills and economic power. This restriction should therefore lead to international cooperation in space activities among all states. As Prof. Diederiks observes, the legal content of "the province of all mankind" is international cooperation in exploration and use of outer space without discrimination against any state and the duty to take the interests of all other states into account(5).

Concerning international cooperation, the Space Treaty makes the following provisions. Firstly, Article X provides that states parties shall afford an opportunity to observe the flight of space objects launched by other states parties. But such an opportunity for observation shall be determined by agreement between the states concerned. Secondly, Article XI provides that states parties shall offer information about their space activities to the international community. But this offer is conditioned by a clause, namely "to the greatest extent feasible and practicable". Thirdly, Article XII provides that all stations on the moon and other celestial bodies shall be open to representatives of other states parties. However, it is impossible for representatives of developing countries to visit the said space stations without riding together in space vehicles of other states. Therefore, almost all the rules for international cooperation in the Space Treaty, which includes many conditions, would provide for not active but passive cooperation in space activities between states.

As mentioned above, "the Freedom Principle" offers all states the rights of freedom of access, exploration and use. However, it is only some developed countries which can actually exercise these rights. For many developing countries, international cooperation is needed in order to exercise these rights. Nevertheless, international cooperation under the Space Treaty is not clearly defined, especially to what extent states have to cooperate each other(6).

3. Related rules in the Moon Agreement

Another provision concerning sharing benefits from space activities can be found in Article XI of the Moon Agreement(7): "the common heritage of mankind", the meaning of which is briefly examined(8).

Article XI, Paragraph 1 of the Moon Agreement states that "the moon and its natural resources are the common heritage of mankind", and

Paragraph 5 requires that an international regime to govern the exploitation of these resources shall be established by States Parties. On the occasion of its establishment, an equitable sharing of benefits by all States Parties, whereby the interests and needs of the developing countries, as well as the efforts of the contributing countries, shall be given special consideration according to Paragraph 7(d).

These rules provide for an equitable sharing of benefits by all states, but concrete rules for this sharing are not stipulated in the Moon Agreement; States Parties to the Agreement undertake only to establish the regime till the exploitation of those resources is about to become feasible under Paragraph 5 of the same Article. Therefore, in order to realize an equitable sharing of benefits from the exploitation of these resources, it will be necessary at least to set up a regime similar to the U.N. Seabed Authority under the Law of the Sea Convention(9).

In contrast, Article IV, Paragraph 1 of the Moon Agreement follows two phrases in Article I of the Space Treaty: "the province of all mankind" and "for the benefit and in the interests of all countries". Furthermore, it states that "due regard shall be paid to <u>the interests of present and future generations</u> as well as to the need to promote higher standards of living and conditions of economic and social progress and development" (underlined by author). And Paragraph 2 of the same Article also states that "states parties shall be guided by the principle of cooperation and mutual assistance in all their activities concerning the exploration and use of the moon".

The legal contents of the Moon Agreement are much stricter than those of the Space Treaty. Because equity between present and future generations is taken into account in the rules of the Moon Agreement, and the principle of cooperation and mutual assistance in space activities is also emphasized by them. The concept of "Intergenerational Equity" can be considered to be unique and significant not only in environmental law(10) but also in space law(11), to which special attention is paid in the following part.

4. The ITU Regime for geostationary orbits and radio frequency bands

In this part, the Regime of the International Telecommunication Union (hereafter ITU) for geostationary orbits (hereafter G-Orbits) and radio frequency bands is examined from the viewpoint of equity between present and future generations, which is mentioned above.

Over the years, one of the main purpose of the ITU has been to avoid interference with radio frequencies. To meet this need, the International Frequency Registration Board (IFRB) has been formed. The duty of the IFRB has been to accept the registrations of radio frequencies by any stations, and to publish them to the international community(12). Through this Registration System, the registered station has obtained a vested right to the specific frequency. In other words, "firstcome, firstserved" has become the principle in this matter. Therefore, many developing countries are worried about the possible exhaustion of radio frequencies by developed countries if this Registration System is also applied to space communications in addition to short- and middle-wave communications.

In 1973, the ITU adopted a new

convention, "The Malaga-Torremolinos Convention"(13), during the preparation of which controversies between developed and developing countries as to G-Orbits and radio frequencies occurred. That is to say, the former insisted that they were "re-usable resources", but the latter insisted that they were "limited natural resources" and that the equitable sharing of them should be open to all countries. In the end, the claim of the developing countries prevailed, and Article 33, Paragraph 2 of the Convention was adopted as follows:

"In using frequency bands for space radio services Members shall bear in mind that radio frequencies and the geostationary satellite orbit are limited natural resources, that they must be used efficiently and economically so that countries or groups of countries may have equitable access to both in conformity with the provisions of the Radio Regulations according to their needs and the technical facilities at their disposal (underlined by author)."

Furthermore, the ITU adopted an amended convention, "The Nairobi Convention"(14), in 1982. In this Convention, the last phrase of Article 33 Paragraph 2, "according to their needs and the technical facilities at their disposal", was deleted and replaced by the phrase "taking into account the special needs of the developing countries and the geographical situation of particular countries". This amendment could be looked at as resulting in a significant change in the meaning of the principle of equitable access. By emphasizing the special needs of the developing countries, this amendment requires that equity be measured not simply in terms of efficiency and economy(15).

Reflecting these amendments, the World Administrative Radio Conference for the Broadcasting-Satellite Service (WARC-BS), which was held in 1977, has introduced a "Planning" system for frequency bands of 11.7-12.5 GHz. Under this system, at least one frequency band has been distributed to all states, irrespective of their technical abilities(16).

At that time, some developed countries, especially the United States, criticized this system for creating much "deadwood" in the frequency bands for the broadcasting-satellite service, and United States did not agree with such "Planning" in Region 2 (the North and South Americas). But United States finally agreed to it in 1983 in order to avoid interference with the frequencies, because the "Planning" in Region 1 (Africa, Europe, the Middle East, and Russia) and Region 3 (Asia and the Pacific) had already been established.

Moreover, as for G-Orbits, the World Administrative Radio Conferences on the Use of the Geostationary-Satellite Orbit (WARC-ORB-85, 88), which were held in 1985 and 1988 respectively, have established a Regime called the "Allotment Plan". According to this Regime, at least one G-Orbit has been distributed to each country, too.

Therefore, the principle of equitable access to G-Orbits and radio frequency bands by all states has been established instead of the principle of "firstcome, firstserved"(17).

Through this ITU Regime, "the Freedom Principle" in Article I of the Space Treaty has obtained a more positive interpretation: every state has the right to begin space activities at any time when it acquires the technical and economic abilities. In other words, a state which has already started space activities cannot insist upon a vested rights to them, and has to modify its space activities in order to guarantee opportunities to new states.

Consequently, this interpretation of "the Freedom Principle" is worthy of attention from the viewpoint of equity between generations. For the opportunities of states to participate in the space activities will be guaranteed in the future.

5. Conclusion

In the 1996 session of the Legal Subcommittee of the UNCOPUOS, the Chairman of the Working Group submitted a Working Paper for a Draft Resolution called "Declaration on International Cooperation in the Exploration and Use of Outer Space for the Benefit and in the Interests of All States, Taking into Particular Account the Needs of Developing Countries"(18).

In this Draft Resolution, international cooperation in space activities is also emphasized. However, as Paragraph 2 states that "States are free to determine all aspects of their participation in cooperation … ", it is not necessarily clear to what extent states have to cooperate each other and how the benefits derived from space activities should be shared.

Therefore, the above-mentioned ITU Regime can be considered a major contribution to international cooperation in sharing benefits from space activities, especially from the viewpoint of equity between present and future generations. Because G-Orbits and radio frequency bands are "limited natural resources" and "re-usable resources" at the same time, International Administration is necessary in order to manage their use not only by all states but also by all generations.

References

(1) U.N. Doc. A/AC. 105/411, paras. 41, 46.

(2) Jasentuliyana, N., "Article I of the Outer Space Treaty Revisited", Journal of Space Law, Vol. 17, 1989, p. 144.

(3) 610 UNTS 205.

(4) Cheng, B., "The 1967 Space Treaty", Journal du Droit International, 1968, p. 576.

(5) Diederiks-Verschoor, I.H.Ph., "Implications of Commercial Activities in Outer Space, Especially for the Developing Countries", Journal of Space Law, Vol. 17, 1989, p. 125.

(6) Christol, C.Q., Space Law: Past, Present, and Future, Deventer, 1991, pp. 69-70.

(7) 18 ILM 1434.

(8) See, Danilenko, G.M., "The Concept of the 《Common Heritage of Mankind》 in International Law", Annals of Air and Space Law, Vol. XIII, 1988.

(9) U.N.O.R. A/CONF. 62/122 (7 Oct. 1982).

(10) See, Weiss, E.B., In Fairness to Future Generations: International Law, Common Patrimony, and Intergenerational Equity, UNU-Tokyo, 1989.

(11) See, Informal consultations by Chile on new items for the agenda (U.N. Doc. A/Ac. 105/639, p. 39).

(12) White, R.L., et al., The Law and Regulation of International Space Communication, Boston, 1988, p. 85, ff.

(13) 1209 UNTS 32.

(14) UNTS, not yet published. (Registered Number to U.N. Secretariat: 26559)

(15) White, op cit., p. 189.

(16) Jakhu, R.S., "The Evolution of

the ITU's Regulatory Regime Governing Space Radiocommunication Services and the Geostationary Satellites Orbit", *Annals of Air and Space Law*, Vol. VIII, 1983, p. 402-406.

(17) Smith, M.L., "Equitable Access to the Orbit/Spectrum Resource", *Proceedings of the 30th Colloquium on the Law of Outer Space*, 1987, p. 263.

(18) U.N. Doc. A/AC. 105/C. 2/L. 202.

IISL-96-IISL.3.06

THE INTERNATIONAL REGULATION OF AN EQUITABLE UTILIZATION OF NATURAL OUTER SPACE RESOURCES

Henri A. Wassenbergh
International Institute of Air and Space Law, University of Leiden, The Netherlands

Introduction

The question is "how?", when one reads about an equitable regulation of the exploitation of scarce or limited natural resources and the sharing of the benefits thereof.
An answer could be: let the free market decide.
As to outer space resources, this can only work after States will have enabled private enterprise to freely compete on a "level playing field".

Article VI of the Outer Space Treaty of 1967 opens the possibility for States to deploy 'national' space activities, also by non-governmental entities by enacting national space legislation. As States widely differ as to the ability to be active in outer space, 'nationality' is not a good basis or criterion for regulation aimed at creating a 'level playing field' for private enterprise.
Therefore States shall have to promote cross-border alliances between 'national' entities, to give them more equal chances.

The Legal SubCtee of the UNCOPUOS had on its agenda since 1989 the discussion of principles regarding international cooperation in the exploration and utilization of outer space. It is the intention to give with such principles substance to article 1 of the OST of 1967, where it stipulates that 'the exploration and use of outer space shall be carried out for *the benefit and in the interests of all countries'*.

Dr. N. Jasentuliyana speaks of ensuring *equal access to the benefits* of space technologies for all countries. (10 Space Policy 7, 1994).
He obviously limits access to the benefits of space technologies, as it is more difficult to give 'equal' access to the technologies themselves as the transfer of technology may be a security problem.

A working group of the Legal SubCtee has been busy trying to find a wording which may lead to concrete and workable results which are acceptable to all States, i.e. the different groups of States, Brazil leading the developing countries and France and Germany as the voice of the industrialized countries.
The Moon Agreement of 1979/84, in its article 11, 'solves' the problem by imposing a moratorium on the exploitation of the celestial bodies in the solar system, while the States Parties undertake to establish an international regime to govern the exploitation of the natural resources of the celestial bodies as soon as such exploitation becomes feasible.
No action is taken so far to arrive at such an international regime.

The undertaking to come to an international regime is based on the declaration in the article that the celestial bodies, including their orbits around or other trajectories to or around them, and their natural resources are the *common heritage of mankind.*

'Natural resources' do not include man-made facilities in outer space: Artificial satellites and space stations do not belong to the common heritage of mankind, not even when they use outer space resources.
The Moon Agreement, and therefore neither this principle, have universal validity, however. The principle as worded, moreover, lacks substance to give it legal effect.

The UNCOPUOS principles of 1996

The 'benefit problem' results from the 'freedom' of outer space for States. As a result of this freedom, States with the ability to reach outer space pursue their own interests, with the result that there now are space powers and non-space powers.

As a consequence of the equal and non-discriminatory freedom of outer space for exploration and use, the more powerful, more advanced and more active space powers stand to obtain more benefits than less powerful and less active space powers, creating next to the 'haves' and the 'have-nots', among the space powers a few dominant ones. The less powerful like a number of the European States try to look after their interests in outer space through international co-operation in the ESA.

The Legal SubCtee of the UNCOPUOS drafted a Declaration of principles with respect to the exploration and utilization of outer space for the benefit and in the interests of all States, taking into particular account *the needs* of developing countries.
The UN Declaration focuses on inter-State cooperation, but fails to oblige States to enter into such cooperation.
Moreover, it gives priority to the needs of the developing countries.
What are these needs?
One example is Tongasat, filling the gap left by Intelsat in Asia.

The Declaration is a "should" document, it gives no 'right' to access/participation/share of benefits with respect to the exploitation of outer space resources.
The UNCOPUOS/General Assembly of the UN can do no more than express the desire in a Declaration that the space powers "should contribute to promoting and fostering international cooperation on an equitable and mutually acceptable basis"; and "aim, inter alia," at :
(a) Promoting the development of space science and technology and its applications." ; and
(b) Fostering the development of relevant and appropriate space capabilities in interested States; and
(c) Facilitating the exchange of expertise and technology among States on a mutually acceptable basis." 1)

The international cooperation, according to the Declaration, "should be conducted in the modes that are considered most effective and appropriate by the countries concerned, including, inter alia, governmental or non-governmental; commercial and non-commercial; global, multilateral, regional or bilateral; and international cooperation among countries in all levels of development."
Anyhow "States are free to determine all aspects of their cooperation on an equitable and mutually acceptable basis". States are free to find 'the most effective cooperation'. 2)
Contractual terms "should be in full compliance with the legitimate rights and interests of the parties concerned, e.g. with intellectual property rights."

These texts of the principles are vague and general and reflect desiderata (the use of "should", instead of "shall"), which moreover, are essentially repetitive of what already exists in legal outer space instruments.
The principles, as desiderata, ought to be self-evident among civilized nations, the basic social need being that the space powers educate the non-space powers about what they are doing and about the results thereof, that they share their scientific and technological knowledge and that they assist the non-space powers in developing *indigenous capability,* enabling them to participate in space activities and receive adequate benefits from space activities.

These principles, adopted by the general Assembly of the UN, can hardly be considered to add new obligations for, more especially, the space powers, nor new rights for the developing countries.
They do not constitute a new binding legal regime adding new and binding rules to the provisions of existing space conventions.

Agreement on a Declaration of principles regarding cooperation, in our opinion, can easily be reached as the principles are just that, i.e. 'principles', which, as such, need not immediately be translated into action as long as there are no practical proposals or a concrete planning of how the principles can best be implemented.

The principles are formulated in such a way that they remain completely non-committal, open-ended and merely reflecting the good intentions of the States. They give general guidance *if* action is taken.
They do not bind States to take such co-operative action, however.

What is needed in our opinion, and would be more practicable, is to internationally 'de-nationalize' space activities by placing private enterprise under the international responsibility of the State of incorporation of the entity and from where the activities are being deployed, while enabling non-governmental entities to enter into cross-border cooperative arrangements for the utilization, that is the commercial exploitation of the outer space resources. 3)

Private enterprise of different States will only enter into such co-operations if it is in their mutual benefit to become a multi-national entity.
States, therefore, should promote the opportunities for private enterprise to obtain benefits from space activities, deployed under cross-border co-operative arrangements.
Such approach is far better than pursuing a space-power struggle between States.
The UN Principles can merely act as an exhortation to in principle not exclude (the private enterprise of) any State, while giving indications as to the objective of such cooperation.

Again in our opinion, instead of adopting vaguely-worded principles, it would be better to create opportunities of direct access by private enterprise of all States to outer space resources, i.e. to the exploitation and the benefits thereof.

The approach to international space law taken in 1967 must be modernized to accommodate private enterprise in outer space, to compete in a level playing field.

There is no longer the confrontation between East and West leading to forced compromises. (e.g. Article VI of the OST).

Private enterprise is to be given direct access to outer space activities in order to exploit the natural space resources.

To this end a distinction must be made between what States should do and what should be left to private enterprise.

International legal instruments should make a distinction between:

(i) international outer space law for States to cover the technical/operational and infra-structural as well as environmental aspects of commercial outer space activities, which activities have to be regulated internationally and should be placed under international governmental supervision, while agreeing on easily amendable SARPS;

In other words, governments have the task to ensure the licensing and authorizing of private entities to be active in outer space and the registration of *civil* space objects/spacecraft, give the (traffic) "rules of outer space", ensure the security of space activities, provide the needed infra-structure, promote an international level playing field, guarantee fair competition internationally, arrange for standardization of licensing and registration requirements and oblige private enterprise to conform to regulations for the protection of the environment;

and

(ii) supplementary international legal instruments to bring private enterprise into outer space under standardized regulations concerning:
the economic aspects of commercial outer space activities, which should be left to private enterprise and be regulated in international legal instruments to guide national legislations, which should be based on standard provisions agreed upon internationally, taking into account article 1 of the OST and other obligations of the States involved, under existing international space law, as well as the principles mentioned-above.

Present space law

Present space law must be read as making a distinction between outer space (the solar system) as an area, outer space as a medium and outer space as a natural resource.

In the OST outer space is treated as an area, which States have freedom to explore, without the right to appropriate parts of outer space. moreover the OST treats outer space as a medium which may be used by States in which to sojourn or to transit.
Only the Moon Agreement deals with outer space as a natural resource.
When drafting the OST, natural resources were amply discussed, but finally left out as the time was not ripe to include provisions on their exploitation.
Even the later Moon Agreement in its article 11.5. refers to an international regime for the exploitation of natural resources, "as such exploitation is about to become feasible", but the UNCOPUOS in 1995 still found no need to take this matter up in accordance with article 18 of the Moon Agreement.

This means in the light of the Moon Agreement article 11.3. that 'a contrario' the OST leaves free the appropriation of natural resources, at least of the celestial bodies.
If earth orbits are a natural resource, the OST does not apply to these resources as such, but only as part of outer space as an area and a medium. To the extent that these resources are scarce or limited, Article I of the OST applies.

The *freedom* of article I, *second* paragraph, of the OST means that every State has an equal right to do what it likes in outer space, as long as its national or international activities do not adversely affect other States.

In our opinion the only workable interpretation of article I, *first* paragraph (in view of private space activities and in connection with its second paragraph,) of the OST is that it does not require a 'sharing of benefits', but only requires that all space activities and their results are public so that everybody can share the news of discoveries and experiences.
The obligations with respect to the benefits of the exploration and use of outer space and the interests of all countries and this exploration and use being the province of mankind, for private enterprise, should be interpreted by keeping in mind the following distinction:
(a) one may benefit as a client against payment for the product;
(b) one may benefit by receiving full information;
(c) one may benefit by receiving technology;
(d) on may benefit by actually participating in an activity;
(e) one may benefit by receiving a share of the money earned from commercial space activities.

States may wish to claim the benefits mentioned under (b), (c) and (d) above, while private enterprise may claim them all.

Article II of the OST forbids *national appropriation* of outer space, including the celestial bodies. This article does not deal with natural resources, nor with private enterprise, however: that is why Article 11, para 3, of the Moon Agreement specifically adds the non-appropriation of natural resources, and non-governmental entities and natural persons, while limiting that non-appropriation to natural resources 'in place', in order to protect outer space as a free area and medium and keep room for the exploitation of the natural resources under an international regime.
The most natural approach to the problem of the 'haves' and the 'have-nots' with respect to outer space resources would be for the space powers to apply a system of technical assistance and foreign aid also in the field of space exploration and use, *in casu* to the non-space powers, including the developing countries.

Legitimate shares?

It seems futile to try and define a State's *right to participate in space activities or even a State's right to a share of the benefits,* for it is impossible to translate each State's 'territorial, c.q. economic imperative', which drive States' policies, especially if given a free field of action, into an equitable participation in the activities or equitable share of the benefits of the space activities.
Under a regime of freedom the basis of a State's share of the activity, or of the benefits of the activity, is its 'power', its capability to act, c.q. to take its share, or alternatively its qualification for international co-operation as a dependent partner, or simply 'charity'.
Such 'charity', which ultimately may be in the self-interest of the space powers, should be directed to the needs of the non-space powers for specific assistance and to the need to reduce on our planet the gap between the rich and powerful on the one hand and the poor and weak on the other.

To claim parts of outer space, as did the equatorial States with respect to segments of the Geo-orbit, is not the way to go.
Positive discrimination, e.g. in the allocation of parts of scarce resources and participation in limited resources, could be a way to help small States (cf. the slots in the Geo-orbit, allocated to Tonga).

A far better approach than to try and divide (the benefits of) outer space among all States, will be, however, to allow private enterprise direct access to outer space, be it under supervision of the 'home-State' of the enterprise. 3)

The 'infra-structure' (launching sites, spaceports, navigation aids, ground stations, launchers) necessary for private enterprise to reach outer space and be active in outer space, should then be 'internationalized', i.e. be made available by the States to all licensed private undertakings, regardless of their nationality and on a non-discriminatory and national treatment basis.

The privatization of space activities

To the growing extent that 'space activities', that is 'activities in outer space as well as activities elsewhere, but directly related to the activities in outer space', can be deployed profitably, there is a growing interest among private enterprise to become active in such commercial space activities.

For private enterprise, that is non-governmental entities, to become active in outer space, it is necessary, under present international space law, that a State authorizes, under its national laws, the activity in outer space and supervises the activity.

Private enterprise, being totally dependent on the authorization by a State, while individual States are in totally different positions with respect to space activities, will not find a *level playing field* when entering the private commercial space activities market.
An *international* legal framework for private commercial space activities, so far, does not exist under public international space law, let alone that a level playing field is established beyond Articles I and II of the Outer Space Treaty.

Like in international air transport, trans-border co-operation between private companies of States with different positions in respect of competitiveness, will be necessary for many to be successful in the exploitation of outer space resources under international competitive conditions.
Such international co-operation can create a more level playing field for private enterprise of whichever country.
For no longer on a basis of nationality, but on the basis of international co-operation will the exploitation of outer space resources be developed.

National rivalry between States, the efforts to increase the State's space power is to be replaced by international competitiveness between private, non-governmental entities. Like in aviation this could develop into *regional* competitiveness. 4)

It may be important for States to be the 'home-State' of certain space activities, without, however, becoming the absolutely liable State for damage caused by the private activities to third parties.
This will have to be arranged by agreement between the Parties, i.e. the States having licensed, under their national space legislation, the private companies taking part in the cross-border co-operative venture.
For instance, the liability of the launching State should no longer extend to the total duration of the space activity, originating from the launch. The launch and the liability of the launching State also should legally be considered as to have terminated after the separation of the space object/spacecraft from the launch vehicle. 5)

Conclusion

Present international space law requires an international supplement to cover private space activities, if States wish to promote space activities by ('their') private enterprise.

This supplement must facilitate the international co-operation between private entities licensed under national space legislations, by prescribing standard clauses for such national space legislation, giving private enterprise free access to outer space under similar conditions, and freeing international private enterprise from governmental economic guardianship in outer space.

Private enterprise requires freedom in its own right.

Also present space activities deployed by (inter)governmental organizations should be 'privatized' as much as possible, without affecting the international public interest of the society of States. 6)

We shall have to give a new 'definition' to the role of States and of the international inter-governmental organizations in the world, involved in space activities, and in our case more especially of the European States, Members of the EU, and of such inter-governmental organizations in Europe.

The EU, after the example of the USA, wants privatized air carriers to enjoy the free internal market and benefit from free competition.
The EU, moreover, abolished regionally the nationality of air carriers, i.e. within the Union.

These measures, like in the USA, led to airline concentrations and under open skies regimes to cross-border alliances of air carriers of the US and the EU. Why not go the same way with private companies active in outer space ?

---

1) See UN Doc. A/AC. 105/639, 1996, Annex, page 37, resp. articles 3, 5, 4 and 2.

2) See on international space cooperation also Megumu Nakamura: "Review of Article I of the OST." Abstract, IAF/IISL Beijing Conference, 6-11 October 1996.

3) Cf. the Barcelona Traction Case 1970, p. 42: "The traditional rule (of international law. Wh) attributes the right of diplomatic protection of a corporate entity to the State

under the laws of which it is incorporated and in whose territory it has its registered office. These two criteria have been confirmed by long practice and by numerous international instruments."

In our opinion, the nationality criterion for air carriers and for space companies should be replaced in the international regulation of the economic aspects of international air transportation, resp. the international regulation of private space activities, by these criteria.

4) The Chinese Minister of the Commission of Science, Technology & Industry for national Defense, Mr. Ding Henggao, said that China's space industry is still behind the advanced countries (US, Europe, Japan and Russia) in the technical level, scale of economy, investment scale & industrialization. (See "Aerospace China", Summer 1996.) He sees the space technological industry as a strategic industry, which affects the balance of power. International co-operation is welcome if it serves the development of China's satellite technology and its application.

5) Present outer space law should no longer speak of a State's space object ('its' space object) other than if reference is made to a State space object or any space object during the launch by a State enterprise.

6) E.g. Among telecommunications providers, Intelsat, as an inter-governmental 139 nation organization, deciding by time-consuming consensus as members decide in favour of direct national benefit, may lose out to the competition of fiber optic cable for high-traffic, trunk, point-to-point routes and private enterprise active in satellite communications. This competition is faced not only in the commercial market place, but especially also in the regulatory market place.

(See Maury Mechanick of Comsat, in Via Satellite, pp. 12/14, of February 1996 and 'Intelsat debates restructuring', in Via Satellite of July 1996, p. 12).

Intelsat is to split into two entities, one governmental and one private.

IISL-96-IISL.3.07

PRIVATIZING AN INTERNATIONAL COOPERATIVE? THE CASE OF INTELSAT

by

Jonathan F. Galloway*

Abstract

Privatization, commercialization and de-regulation are the buzz words in the communications satellite business these days. What do these policies and market forces portend for the future of INTELSAT, an international cooperative of 139 states? It seems that some services can be privatized and made subject to market forces while other services which are more collective in nature will have to be organized differently. Sharing benefits will take place both by government plans and market forces. INTELSAT has been a great success but in the new more competitive environment it must restructure and it cannot rest on its laurels.

---

*Professor of Politics, Lake Forest College, Lake Forest, IL, USA and AIAA, IAA, IISL.

History

How commercial and entrepreneurial has the market for communications satellite services been? When communications satellite service was established in the United States, Comsat was given a monopoly for sending traffic in and out of the country. It was the carriers' carrier. AT&T, ITT, Western Union and other carriers had to go through Comsat. So, although Comsat was a private corporation listed on the New York stock exchange, it had a preferred position because of the Communications Satellite Act of 1962.[1] Although Congress intended that the corporation be commercial, it also intended that it should serve certain public purposes such as providing services to less developed countries. Such services might not be justified from a purely market-oriented perspective. In the wording of the Act itself, Congress "declares that it is the policy of the United States to establish, in conjunction and cooperation with other countries, as expeditiously as practicable a commercial communications satellite system, as part of an improved global communications network, which will be responsive to public needs and national objectives, which will serve the communications needs of the United States and other countries, and which will contribute to world peace and understanding."[2] One would not privatize some of these goals. Further one would not want to commercialize a collective good because, by definition, due to the lack of scarcity, there can be no free market price to allocate consumption and send signals to the market.

In keeping with the goal of expeditiously establishing a global system, INTELSAT was set up as an international cooperative in 1964.[3] INTELSAT, itself, was a monopoly which pursued not only market-oriented ventures but also certain collective goals such as providing service to remote and isolated areas.

The 1990s

It is now more than 30 years since Comsat and INTELSAT were established. In the intervening years, market and political forces in the United States and in other countries have worked to increase the number of actors in the satellite communications arena. Comsat is no longer the only carrier authorized to engage in point-to-point services. It is no longer authorized to be the sole link within the U.S. to INTELSAT. Further, INTELSAT is no longer the center piece of the global communications satellite system. We have INMARSAT[4] and various regional organizations such as EUTELSAT[5] and ARABSAT.[6] We also have INTERSPUTNIK, the international system which was based on the communist states.[7] With the end of the Cold War and the breakup of the USSR and the mellowing of Russia, this organization became a more marginal actor in the global communications satellite sector. In July, 1991 the USSR joined INTELSAT. Russia, viewed as the successor state to the Soviet Union, took over its seat in 1992.

Are these international entities public or private enterprises? This questions is important for, in theory, privatized actors can provide services more efficiently to the public. Government-owned systems may be inefficient due to subsidies, the need to fund public services, corruption, patronage, etc. The existing picture is very complex. Organizations like INTELSAT, INMARSAT and ARABSAT have been set up by international agreements between states. Other enterprises such as Alpha Lyracom, PanAmSat, Societe Europeene des Satellites and Orion are private. Then, there are some public entities such as Tongasat which have been established by entrepreneurs from other countries in order to gain access to a nation's orbital slots guaranteed to it by the International Telecommunications Union (ITU). For communications to work on an integrated, global basis, all these entities have to network and to coordinate with each other, whether they are public or private or some sort of strange mix. In reality, as the market has become more competitive, public organizations such as INTELSAT have had to act like private entities if users are to continue to avail themselves of their services. For instance, INTELSAT leases space to over 35 countries for domestic services. While it is mainly a global organization, the market does not readily recognize borders, and so what is domestic, what is regional and what is global tends to blur and be lost in the heavens.

Let us look at another case in point. Motorola believes that the market exists for hand-held satellite terminals tied into a global network. The company plans to launch a system named IRIDIUM. This will have 66 satellites in low earth orbit. At the ITU's 1992 World Administrative Radio Conference (WARC) in Spain, frequency space in the L band was authorized for this type of personal communications service. INMARSAT, an international organization established by states, saw this system as a competitor to its various mobile offerings. Therefore, INMARSAT decided to establish its own such system, ICO Global Communications. To counter this, IRIDIUM is going to offer the service for less than INMARSAT. Other spinoff market entries are Globalstar and Mobile Communications.[8] Perhaps when the invisible hand in the commercialization of outer space works its way through this market, at the global level we shall see what Arthur C. Clarke has prophesized, "With the historic abolition of long distance charges on 31 December 2000, every telephone call became a local one, and the human race greeted the new millennium by transforming itself into one large, gossiping family."

New Services

Commercialization in the 1960s was largely a matter of providing point-to-point communications. Channels delivered telephone, telegraph and television traffic. With additional frequency bands being allocated and with new public and private enterprises entering the market, many new services are now provided. In the 1970s, we saw the introduction of maritime services through INMARSAT. This organization is now offering land mobile and aeronautical mobile traffic as well. Other services include fax, radio broadcasting and direct broadcast satellite. Combined with the personal communications services promised by IRIDIUM and INMARSAT, the ability to send TV programs directly to dishes on individual homes and apartments introduces the next stage of the commercialization of communications satellites on a global basis. We may even see HDTV services provided worldwide. Direct broadcast satellites (DBS) already provide service in certain countries such as Britain, Japan, and the United States.

Clearly, communications satellites present the number one success story of the commercialization of outer space. This process started in 1962 in the United States and it has spread to many other countries and to many regional and international organizations. While not all these enterprises are in the private sector, they do exist in increasingly competitive markets so that even government-owned systems have to be price conscious if they wish to survive.

There are some government systems that serve collective needs and that will never be totally privatized. These are defense systems. They account for a great share of the traffic on a day-by-day basis, and they use a significant amount of the frequency space. Today we can estimate that most traffic within and between nations is business traffic, followed by government-to-government messages, and then come personal services of an individual sort. With the end of the Cold War, the military is giving up access to some frequency space. Individualized and personal traffic will take up more of the market, but we are still quite a long way from the realization of Arthur C. Clarke's dream of a global village. Even then, some skeptics will see television as dominating the market. The communications infrastructure will be global and planetary but the messages being carried may point to one television wasteland writ large. Of course, if this becomes the case, it would be the choice of the market. The wasteland would be a market failure from the point of view of community values if not economic profits.

A Newer Technology

There is another technology in place that the market may prefer to communications satellites. Fiber optic cables are handling more and more traffic. Capacity has been doubling every two years. Each strand of glass fiber can carry 525 Mbs of digital video which equals at least twelve TV channels, and one fiber optic cable can have up to 96 strands. However, fiber optic cables have their disadvantages. Economically, the cost of laying fiber is $70,000 to $100,000 a mile.[9] The cables can be cut inadvertently. The main drawback is that the cables are not good for many types of service, e.g., mobile traffic to ships, planes, or cars and trucks. Fiber optic is the preferred technology for high density, long-haul routes, e.g., New York to London or Los Angeles to Tokyo, but it will not connect every country to each other, which is one of the goals of the Communication Satellite Act of 1962. One will not see fiber optic cables replace satellites or satellites replace fiber optics. What we shall see is an integrated communications network where each technology will have its own niche.

Finances

From a financial perspective, the communications satellite sector in the United States is quite lucrative. In 1992, for instance, it was estimated that $1 billion went to commercial satellite manufacturers and $1.7 billion was spent on ground equipment. Of course, the governmental sector still predominates across the board when one looks at total space expenditures. In 1990, the U.S. space budget was $30 billion, $18 billion of which went to the Department of Defense and $12 billion to NASA. By 1996 with the Cold War over, the total was only slightly less although one has to adjust for inflation. These figures are the totals for all programs and include various satellite communications systems. For instance, within the defense establishment, there are the Defense Satellite Communications System (DSCS) and the Military Strategic and Tactical Relay System (MILSTAR), and within NASA, there are the Advanced Communications Technology Satellite (ACTS) and the Tracking and Data Relay Satellite (TDRS). Strangely enough, NASA, which is a research agency, is in some sense a commercial actor because it has leased transponders on its TDRS satellites to TRW and Columbia Communications.

In terms of finances, the commercialization of communications satellites still meets a limit where government is involved either in providing its own satellites or in terms of being a dominant public customer for private communications satellite services.

More Privatization? More Sharing?

The workings of the market and domestic, international and transnational lobbying and proceedings before courts and regulatory commissions had, by the mid-1990s, further broken down the exclusiveness of the Comsat/INTELSAT relationship. The past president of Comsat proposed privatization.[10] In the U.S., the Commission on Reinventing Government proposed in 1995 "(1) privatizing INTELSAT and INMARSAT and eliminating the privileges and immunities and special access to spectrum and orbital slots currently enjoyed by those organizations and (2) eliminating Comsat's exclusive status as the sole U.S. investor and provider of INTELSAT and INMARSAT services...."[11] Further, the Federal Communications Commission is pushing increasing commercialization and privatization of satellite services not only within the United States and between the United States and other countries but in a "global, seamless network of services."[12] The FCC wants to encourage competition in a global market and this competition will replace regulation because it will more efficiently serve the public interest by lowering rates.

Last year at the Oslo colloquium of the IISL, Francis Lyall proposed that the public interest required that INTELSAT be treated as an international public utility.[13] Now "utilities are hybrid enterprises because they combine two universal features. First, they are regulated by their constituencies through public utility commissions or other forms of public sector input. In return for accepting regulation, they are given monopolies and are guaranteed a certain level of profit..."[14] Professor Lyall's suggestion would seem to relate to the public purpose of providing noncommercial services to remote areas. Insofar as this relates to current proposals for INTELSAT's restructuring, perhaps this feature, i.e., of an international public utility, would be preserved in INTELSAT, the IGO, while the profitable part of INTELSAT, INTELSAT, Inc. would be progressively privatized.[15] In essence the successful commercial parts of INTELSAT services will be turned over to the market place while the public purpose parts such as aiding less developed countries will be kept in a cutback operation called colloquially "Mother Intelsat." This seems to be the path toward which we are heading although the details will not be known till1997.

At the end of 1996, there is still much controversy over whether INTELSAT's privatization will lead to a competitive market or to a monopolistic or oligopolistic structure. PanAmSat, recently acquired by Hughes Electronics Corp., a unit of General Motors, has contended that if INTELSAT's privatization leads to only one firm being spun off this will mean that the market will be too concentrated.[16] INTELSAT favors one privatized affiliate but it is too early to tell how all of INTELSAT's 139 members will deal with this issue and related ones such as phasing out INTELSAT's diplomatic privileges and immunities and the 14(d) consultation process concerning technical and economic compatibility with INTELSAT as created by the 1971 treaty.

In a pure market, with no collective goods the government would set the rules and the private actors in the market would then decide on the best technology. However, governments and international organizations not only regulate carriers, as in the case of the FCC and the ITU vis-a-vis the frequency spectrum and orbital slots, they also subsidize particular actors and particular technologies. For instance, NASA is obligated under the 1958 National Aeronautics and Space Act to engage in the research and development of manufacturing processes which will aid U. S. industry. And, in most countries, government-owned Postal Telegraph and Telephone administrations (PTTs) have been the designated entities handling international communications. Some of these PTTs are being privatized, as is the case with Nippon Telephone & Telegraph (NTT) in Japan and

British Telecom (BT) in England, and, as this process continues in the coming years, we shall see more market-based commercialization. However, one can expect governments to be very interested in which companies win market contracts. Will they be private companies from the home country, or foreign-based firms? Only if and when transnational firms become truly global firms will the planet be set to ignore or transcend political boundaries.

Conclusions

Satellite communications has partially fulfilled its promise - the promise of pioneering thinkers and dreamers such as Arthur C. Clarke, the promise of the Communications Satellite Act of 1962, and, it might be said, the promise of most of the world's states as set out in the Outer Space Treaty of 1967, in which it is stated that the "use of outer space...shall be carried out for the benefit and in the interest of all countries..." There are still promises to keep, e.g., Clarke's concerning the global village, but the technology is laying the infrastructure for bringing the world closer together. Sovereignty is still significant, but less so. There are still national economies competing with each other in protectionist and neo-mercantilist ways, but boundaries and corporate identifications are becoming more confused. The services provided by communications satellites such as mobile maritime, mobile aeronautical and hand-held global telephones point to a new world information order not created by governments alone, but by governments, markets and peoples. The commercialization of satellite communications satellites in a mixed political and economic environment has been a great success story. INTELSAT has been part of that story. But it cannot rest on its laurels. After restructuring, INTELSAT will become just another actor in the market and not the single actor forseen in the 1960s. Sharing benefits will be the outcome of market forces and government and international plans - not one or the other.

ENDNOTES

1. "Communications Satellite Act of 1962," 76 STAT. 419.

2. Sec. 102 (a).

3. "Agreement Establishing Interim Arrangements for a Global Commercial Satellite System," 15 U.S.T. 1705, T.I.A.S. 5646. These interim arrangements were superseded by the Definitive Arrangements in 1971. See "Agreement Relating to the International Telecommunications Satellite Organization "INTELSAT," 28 U.S.T. 2248, T.I.A.S. No. 8542.

4. "Convention on the International Maritime Satellite Organization (INMARSAT)," 31 U.S.T. 1, T.I.A.S. 9605, 1976.

5. Convention and Operating Agreement of the European Telecommunications Satellite Organization (EUTELSAT), 1982.

6. Agreement of the Arab Corporation for Space Communications (ARABSAT), 1976.

7. Agreement on the Establishment of the "INTERSPUTNIK" International

System and Organization of Space Communications, 1971.

8. Renee Saunders, "Comsat Prepares for Debut of Planet 1 Service, "Space News, vol. 7, no. 34, September 2-8, 1996, p. 14. Also see Jeff Cole, "Mobile Communications, Armed with Funding, Seeks FCC License, The Wall Street Journal, September 16, 1996, p. B6.

9. Jonathan F. Galloway, "Commercializing Outer Space," National Forum, vol. LXXII, no. 3 (Summer, 1992), 34-36.

10. Bruce L. Crocket, statement in Hearing before the Subcommittee on Telecommunications and Finance of the Committee on Energy and Commerce, U. S. House of Representatives, "Future of Satellite-Based Services (Part 2)," 103rd Congress, 2nd Session, July 28, 1994, p. 112.

11. Commission on Reinventing Government. "Creating a Federal Communications Commission for the Information Age," February 1, 1995. Appendix A, p. 2, Item 10.

12. FCC, "In the Matter of Market Entry and Regulation of Foreign-Affiliated Entities," Report and order released November 30, 1995. II FCC Rcd. no. 7, 3873 (1996) at p. 3875.

13. Francis Lyall, "Privatization and International Telecommunications Organization," Proceedings of the Thirty-Eighth Colloquium on the Law of Outer Space (Washington, D.C.: American Institute of Aeronautics and Astronautics, 1996), pp. 168-174. Lyall writes, "My own feeling, however, is that the best safeguard for the concept of a global system, serving the world without discrimination, would be for INTELSAT to continue, more or less as an international public utility, deemed to be owned by mankind, for the benefit of mankind, and irrespective of the technical legalities."

14. Paul Hawken, The Ecology of Commerce: A Declaration of Sustainability, (New York: Harper Business, 1993), p. 191.

15. See INTELSAT 2000 Working Party, "INTELSAT Future Structure, Executive Summary," February 16, 1996.

16. Jeff Cole, "Intelsat's Privatization Beams in Rivals' Cries of Foul," The Wall Street Journal, October 17, 1996, p. B4.

BENEFIT SHARING: THE MUNICIPAL MODEL

IISL-96-IISL.3.09

D.J. O'Donnell
United Societies in Space, Inc.[1]

Abstract

The principle of benefit sharing from usage of space resources is well settled space policy. The "benefit of mankind" is part of Article I of the Outer Space Treaty of 1967. The "Common Heritage of Mankind" was introduced in the Moon Agreement of 1979 and may be defined in the UN Convention on the Law of the Sea, 1982. The concept is not only established, it is also praiseworthy. It is asserted that administration of this policy must be accomplished by an agency like a trustee of the resources for the benefit of all. Administration by individual nations and/or by the UN may not be appropriate, nor legally adequate. A municipal authority like the Lunar Economic Development Authority, Inc. (LEDA), which can provide site specific allocations to the space venue developers on a professional and completely independent basis, is recommended. An analogy is made to the town of Castle Rock, Colorado. The policy basis for this municipal undertaking is stronger than that of national and international UN administration; there is less chance of discrimination; sharing is based on recourse to space resources; there is no recourse to national treasuries; and a relevant space governance paradigm is enabled with the proposal.

Administration by the Courts

The legal basis for benefit sharing as a principle of international space law is well established. It is a part of the Outer Space Treaty of 1967, our constitution for space regulation.[1] It was part of a UN General Assembly Resolution before that.[2] It appears in later treaties, resolutions, and international agreements, notably the Moon Treaty of 1979 under the concept of Common Heritage of Mankind.[3] This last treaty may or may not have failed, but the UN continues to advance the concept as a universal treaty burden and integral part of *Corpus Juris Spatialis* as a lien on the appropriate percentage of manufactured goods using space resources.[4]

It has been asserted that the treaty burden is not self-executing because the wording is too general and no legally enforceable standards can be applied to it.[5] The Moon Treaty has been cited as the problem that ended an era by bringing to a halt the viability of the UN process of generating treaties for the

---

Author Declan J. O'Donnell, JD, is a member of the International Institute of Space Lawyers; President of the World-Space Bar Association; President of United Societies in Space, Inc.; and principal attorney in Declan Joseph O'Donnell, P.C., 6841 South Yosemite Suite 3-C, Englewood, Colorado 80112, USA.

peaceful use of outer space.[6] No space treaties have been passed by consensus or otherwise since then.

The satellite industry has incorporated a form of benefit sharing into its mosaic of doing business in LEO (low earth orbit). The treaty burdens of international cooperation, resource non-appropriation, and benefit sharing of profits were accommodated by allowing nations to participate as shareholders and directors.[7] This brand of satisfaction is now a standard for performance in the communication satellite industry. No court cases have been decided and none are expected because the entire concept of benefit sharing is probably not self-executing, although this is untested in any court.[8]

The underlying problem is a cloud on every nation's general fund. If the International Court of Justice in a future case decides that the Article I treaty provisions of the 1967 treaty are self-executing, or that the "Common Heritage of Mankind" phrase in the 1979 treaty is binding, and that the satellite industry has not demonstrated any substantial compliance, an adverse judgment could result. This would be a money judgment against the satellite organizations and, per force of the 1967 treaty, against each sponsoring nation jointly and severally. It would be in favor of all nations, not just the plaintiffs and not just those who signed the 1967 or 1979 treaties.[9] Such a result has no time limit because there is no statute of limitations on such treaty breaches and because usage of the orbits is ongoing and will involve long term future damages as well as past damages.

Continuation of this cloud on title to space business profits is not tolerable. It increases the uncertainty of legal opinions and dampers business generally. Perhaps the worst result is the possibility of litigation forever in the future in almost any court, especially in national courts of Third World countries. A default judgment or consent decree among selected nations would threaten national treasuries worldwide. Any judgment amount would be immense and could be collected worldwide. Perhaps the difficulty in enforcing treaty judgments will reduce the value of this cloud. Non-payment of treaty judgments is one of the more difficult, recurring, and structural difficulties with the treaty system as a whole.[10] The value of the benefit sharing treaty burden might be deemed to constitute a general obligation on the general credit of the sponsoring nations in favor of all nations. This could then be supported by a judgment of the International Court of Justice pursuant to an international class action by the UN: the Security Council has no veto over litigation. Such a judgment would result from the treaty burden and be collectible against assets of the defendant nations wherever found. Under this scenario, the fact that the defendant state reserved rights or asserted a different interpretation or enacted contrary domestic legislation is irrelevant. The judgment will rest on international law only and be interpreted by judges. This litigation is inevitable at some future date.

Focus on Space Resources

The legal impediments notwithstanding, space resources will be utilized. The orbits around earth are already so crowded that frequency allocations are hotly contested and in need of more and better regulation. The International Telecommunications Union Regime is now supplemented by a parallel paradigm within the USA, the Federal

Communication Commission. This is a convenient supplement to UN auspices but it was born out of real need.[11]

Benefit sharing as a treaty burden is not a decreed accomplishment in the communication satellite industry. In fact, the compliance as defined may be more nominal than substantial: there is no "actual sharing" as contemplated by the 1982 UN Agreement on the Law of the Sea and its definition of "Common Heritage." Instead, a version of financial international cooperation by allowing nations to invest capital in satellite organizations and receive future dividends and societal benefits is the stated mode of compliance.[12] Is this going to satisfy the Third World when all orbits and all frequencies are gone to others? There is a litigation risk that it will not.

Physical space resources will be used up as well. When the parade to space starts, when access becomes more economical, and when the challenge to participate and the fear of losing out is heightened, a rush of space developers may emerge: the Moon will be settled and developed quickly. The space science and technology community has already advocated the liberal usage of space resources in such a migration.[13] Therefore, the administration of benefit sharing must focus on the resources and how they are allocated well before the developers arrive. Otherwise, physical resources may soon be compromised, perhaps lost forever, before the non-spacefaring nations and humankind can enjoy the benefits promised to them since 1967.

The experience gained in the satellite industry is important. Frequency bands and relevant orbits have become scarce. Benefit sharing was not based on resource allocations. Management of space debris was neglected. Administration of benefit sharing was far too informal and voluntary. This aspect needs to be corrected for physical space resources particularly at the Moon, our next obvious target.[14]

Individual State Administration of the Benefit Sharing Treaty Burden

Benefit sharing as a treaty burden may not be self-executing. The general principle sounds more like a sermon than a law.[15] Therefore, in order for individual states to administer a formula for space resource allocations and benefit sharing burdens, each will need to adopt domestic legislation declaring what its policy will be and then enter into another international agreement as to which states it will extend that policy to in space, under what conditions, and in respect to which space resources at what venue. The combinations of incongruous and contradictory results may be very large. The weight of translating the nation to nation treaty system into an effective *Corpus Juris Spatialis* may be so heavy that it jeopardizes the entire concept.[16] As the more venue specific body of law called astro law develops, these treaty burdens may also become less important, if not irrelevant.

Sovereign states may impose self-interest on top of the benefit sharing principle. For example, one may require satisfaction in kind in some part, thus requiring that part of the space resource be allocated to it here on Earth. Non-spacefaring nations may also require a cash up front payment as a fee to negotiate the treaty burden because it will have expenses. A nation may claim a royalty on gross revenues, much like in the tradition of the worldwide mining industry. Another nation may call for a lump sum settlement of its claims. Yet another nation may desire a capitalized life of the project royalty amount to be paid up front. The point is that the legal principle does not contain any measurable restraint on the beneficiary nations' desire for benefits.

If one nation tried to administer benefit sharing for all nations, it would run the risk of improperly administering its duties. This is a legally substantial risk since every nation is a beneficiary of benefit sharing so any single nation would have a conflict, or an appearance of conflict, if it assumed the role of trustee or manager. The resulting damages could be substantial. If this nation was also the spacefaring nation that exploited the space resource, that problem would be exacerbated. The ethical and legal analysis of conflict could be a real problem. The benefit sharing administration is like a trustee's function and the law would impose a fiduciary duty. That high level of liability brings with it equitable remedies such as asset tracing, project-wide accounting, injunction, mandamus, and execution. The risks are substantial.

United Nations Administration of the Benefit Sharing Treaty Burden

The UN may not want to undertake space resource allocation and benefit sharing treaty burden administration. It sponsored the treaty. It adopted the General Assembly Resolution that set up the concept. UNCOPUOS is thought of as our upper legislative house, a senate for outer space. The only executive office likely to serve in this capacity is the Division of Outer Space Affairs. It may be deemed an agent of the UN which, in turn, is an agent of member states. As a space policy, it may be wise for the UN to remain aloof and act more as a senate.

Furthermore, UN membership does not include all nations.[17] Even those larger spacefaring nations, such as the USA, may not have adequate influence in the UN to effect any kind of plan for space resource management.

A proposal has been made for the creation of new executive offices at the UN for space resource management and space governance generally.[18] The IOSSA could be tailored• to include a master planning function at least. It has been 17 years since UNCOPUOS has launched a space treaty and none are pending. The committee's working group of the legal subcommittee has proposed a draft resolution for the General Assembly. It deals with international cooperation and benefits in the interests of all states. However, it does not nominate any UN office to administer these benefit sharing treaty burdens. It is unlikely the UN will seek executive authority in this particular because individual states have not spoken on the subject, there are no consensus standards, and its own authority is unclear in the face of substantial liability for misadministration.

The Municipal Model for Administering Benefit Sharing Treaty Burdens

The municipal model refers to a direct governance entity administration of space resources at their *in situ* venue. This may be a unique application but the model itself is widely trusted and may be considered traditional.

Castle Rock, Colorado

My home town, much like yours, benefit shares each time a developer applies for approval of project plans. Castle Rock, Colorado, has a municipal ordinance that requires 10% of the land be dedicated for schools, police, and such; 20% for parks; and 10% for buffer zones which require approved landscaping. Another 20% is allocated for open space although this percentage may overlap into some of the other areas. The town council approves the developments after recommendation by a professional staff having completed a process of several layers of reviews. A planning commission hearing is always a challenge and the water certification is a basic first step in the process. However, when the council does approve the development, permits issue, licenses and inspections follow, and legal certainty attaches. The town council is comprised of citizens, the staff is made up of professional persons, and the town is enabled under Colorado State Law. It has a court system and also a mayor. Many towns predate the state and county and their national governments and they still fit into this model functionally.

Our town is financed 5% from property taxes, 35% from a sales tax, 35% from state and federal sources, and 25% from utility use fees. The residents *qua* residents only account for 50% of this budget: 5% from property tax, 20% from sales tax (because the other 15% comes from tourists), and 25% from utility fees. In contrast, all of the budget is expended on Castle Rock business for the benefit of current and future residents, to be shared in common by all people who utilize the town.

Another interesting feature of this municipal model is that the town is subject to State of Colorado development laws and to a Douglas County Master Plan for real estate in its region; but, otherwise it is exclusively in charge. The USA and the UN are not. It is almost universally a practice that municipal governments control zoning and building and real estate development.

Benefit Sharing in Space

Many adjustments to this model will be necessary in space. For example, a larger consensus on a master plan for space and for each space venue should be developed either in advance or as we go project by project. The town council, so to speak, should be reflective of the world citizenry and our space industries. The staff might need to have a specialized space background. However, these adjustments can be made as we design an appropriate entity to perform the function.

Sources for funding of the governance structure in space may include user fees, rents, and royalties associated with the development of space resources. Moreover, like the Castle Rock model, off-site revenue sources may also be used such as grants and Earth nation contributions. This would sustain the effort until a balance can be achieved with space resource based funding. The budget may be modest until the venue is developed and regulated, no doubt.

A benefit sharing formula, however, can be asserted and implemented in advance. Conceivably, half of the space resources may be set aside. This is consistent with the Castle Rock ordinances and it approximates the maximum burden permitted by municipalities generally in our societies. Developers of space resources should be able to count on having half of the properties for their private property uses, however complicated that may be in outer space.[19]

The application of the reserved half may be complicated, but not something to prevent development proposals from coming forward. In other words, we can work on how to apply the public half of these resources while the rest of the world and our space industrialists propose what they want, and how they want to develop space. The tandem evolution may lead to a synergy.

The suggestion of a liberal 50:50 ratio of public and private (perhaps "non-public benefit shared property" is better terminology) is based on the idea that the treaty burden could not be interpreted to be any more than that. Fifty percent is far higher than the typical public mineral rights royalty, which usually run 2-25%, and it approximates the usual municipal burdens on developed land in a city. The 101 nations that ratified the Outer Space Treaty of 1967 are almost all free enterprise democracies which rely on a free economy and a foundation of private property. They are all accustomed to striking a sort of economic equilibrium with their private sectors. Therefore, a burden over 50% would be too high. A formula of less than 50% allocated to public uses may be subject to criticism, on the other hand, as too low because the developer has no direct cost basis in the resource. Humankind, in effect, donated that asset to the project so long as the municipal jurisdiction is effective.

The LEDA Proposal

The LEDA, Lunar Economic Development Authority, proposal reflects a municipal style entity with special quasi-public authority. It is proposed by USIS, United Societies in Space, Inc., and tendered to congresses and parliaments worldwide for sponsorship. It is less than a town but more than a space agency for coordinated civilian development of the Moon. It involves a large corporate board of directors with representatives of each participating nation, as well as persons to represent humankind generally. It has executive and judicial branches, as well as authority to raise money. A professional staff will be sought. Its mission is to assume authority of the cislunar venue, plan its logical development, and help finance projects that qualify for that objective.

The host nations for this authority and four others will be participating nations and a Metanation to be formed as a space commonwealth or federation of nations to deal with jurisdiction in outer space. This long range future entity is proposed by USIS and work has already begun on its design and function.[20] It may be operational by 2010 AD according to its sponsor. Viewgraph No. 1 depicts the essential elements of that space governance proposal.

LEDA will move forward with or without Metanation. The host nations of Earth are adequate sponsorship for such an authority, even if fewer than all of them participate. The English Channel Tunnel (called the Chunnel Project) operated in international territory with very few national sponsors. Moreover, note that less than half the nations on Earth have ratified the Outer Space Treaty of 1967; nevertheless, it is commonly referred to as our constitution of space law. Hopefully, LEDA will gain a broad base of consensual and shared legal authority for its important mission for the benefit of all.[21] There is no doubt that it will effect benefit sharing at the point of development as its mission. Viewgraph No. 2 depicts its structure.

Risk Management

The municipal model of space resource allocation and benefit sharing administration, whether by LEDA or some similar entity, will tend to limit legal risks. The liberal formula for dedicating half of the resource back to authority for the benefit of all uses up the burden, so to speak. No further burden should be required so the general credit of spacefaring nations will not be threatened. For example, if Lockheed Martin, as a USA licensed space developer, undertook a project on the Moon, perhaps placing oxygen producing plants at the Apollo 17 landing site on the Moon, and it cleared the 50:50 dedication processes at LEDA in order to obtain approval of its project, no greater burden should be asserted against the US Treasury. The project is already encumbered to its reasonable limit in a legal sense. If LEDA gains wide support in the space community, this result would be certain.

Licensed developers such as Lockheed Martin should not object. They recognize that municipal services will be needed at the Moon. The price to be paid may seem high but it now includes a premium benefit not previously available: legal certainty in space development activity. Their contribution will make the Apollo 17 site accessible to all nations as LEDA (or some similar municipal style entity) applies the public benefit sharing funds to ready the premises for others, particularly non-spacefaring nations and all of humankind.

There is significant risk management benefit to the developers favor. It is assured that some relevant governance infrastructure will grow up at its project's venue. A rising tide of traditional municipal services will have a good effect on its project, give comfort to its investors, and solidify the future for expansion purposes, if desired.

Obviously, the greatest risk reduction accrues to all nations and to future generations of humankind. It is less likely that they will be cheated out of their benefit sharing of lunar based space resources: Improvements will be in place for their usage when they arrive. These may include free oxygen at the Apollo 17 landing site.

Conclusion

Benefit sharing is a part of space policy and space law. Whether or not it is judicially enforceable is not as important as whether it is a good idea. If it is to be preserved as a policy, its administration must be in good hands and under a reasonable formula. State administration has questionable merit and UN administration may not be appropriate. An independent quasi-public Lunar Economic Development Authority has been proposed. It would effect a municipal style space resource allocation subject to treaty benefit sharing burdens. This functional satisfaction of the burden would reduce the salient risk of litigation and national treasury recourse for space licensee activities off-world. The municipal model also adds to planning, zoning, permitting, regulating, inspecting, and policing the space venue development. A relevant future space governance paradigm would be accommodated accordingly and the Common Heritage of Mankind may be salvaged from almost certain extinction as a good idea but not self-executing as a law.

Viewgraph No. 1

New words to be added to the lexicon on space policy dialogue worldwide:

1. **SPACE METANATION:** An entity to be created for the purpose of managing our space resources and governing the venue known as outer space as trustee for all.

2. **SPACE DEVELOPMENT PLAN:** A comprehensive plan to develop settlements at the moon and Mars and in GEO and LEO from 2010 AD for 100 years using then state of the art technology under Metanation auspices.

3. **SPACE AUTHORITIES:** Five quasi-public corporations to be assigned venue specific municipal planning, zoning, and permitting tasks with ability to raise money and provide funding for qualifying projects at the venues, all under host nation and Metanation auspices. The five authorities indicated are:
    - **LEDA**, Lunar Economic Development Authority
    - **MEDA**, Mars Economic Development Authority
    - **GOODA**, Gerard O'Neill Orbit Development Authority
    - **LPA**, Lunar Port Authority (for SSTOs)
    - **MHA**, Metanation Headquarters Authority (and theme park)

4. **SPACE MONETARY SYSTEM:** The Metanation banking system through a MetaBank of space money to be authorized for use in outer space.

5. **SPACE COMMON LAW:** A general background common law to be adopted by the Metanation for the venue of space. The likely basis will be USA common law at August 4, 2000 AD.

6. **UNITED SOCIETIES IN SPACE, INC.:** A Colorado non-profit corporation with a mission of creating the Metanation and the five authorities and assembling the Space Development Plan. In order to accomplish this it features the following programs:
    - Ten Countdown Conferences
    - Constitutional Convention at August 4, 2000 AD
    - College of Delegates
    - Council of Regents
    - Corps of Observers
    - SPACE GOVERNANCE Journal (with the WSBA)

7. **WORLD-SPACE BAR ASSOCIATION:** A Colorado non-profit corporation with an agenda to promote good governance, law, and order worldwide and to assist in the making of astro law. It was formerly known as the World Bar Association. Its programs include:
    - Founding and sponsoring United Societies in Space, Inc.
    - Annual and Global Space Essay Contests.
    - Space Humanitarian Award
    - Various space law research projects
    - Lobbying for space causes

VIEWGRAPH NO. 2

LEDA Management Structure

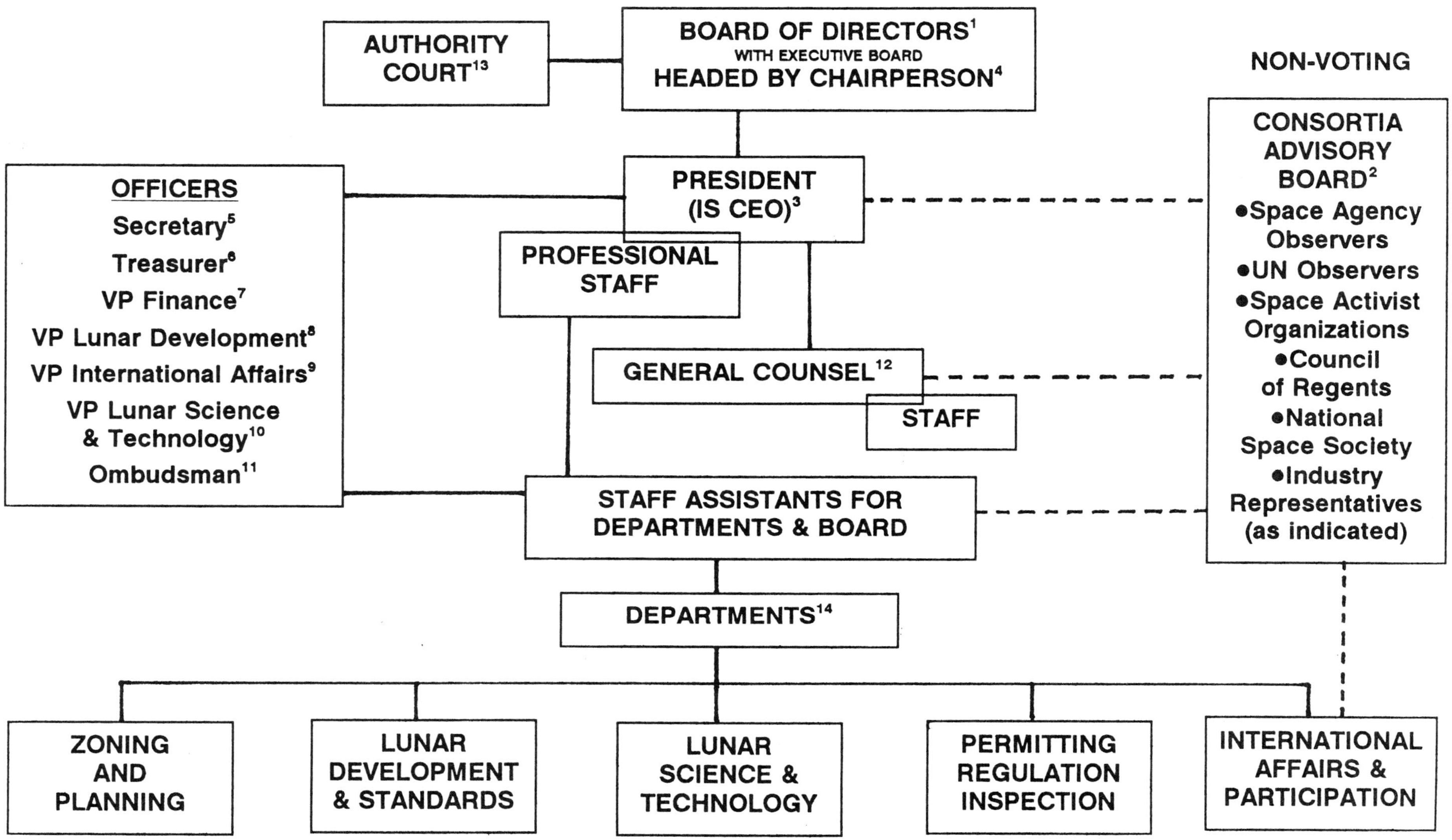

1. The Board of Directors will have the responsibility for overall management of the LEDA. Appointees by the participating Nations will control this Board: Each will appoint six. We foresee about 100 nations participating because that is how many have already signed the Outer Space Treaty, 1967. The original board is already in place running the Colorado Not-for Profit Company. The third world appointees represent a bonus consistent with the benefit sharing tenor of space treaties. The advisory consortia committee will have three of its members on the voting board. These will be taken from the National Space Society appointees, probably.

An executive committee of the Board will be comprised of three members of the Board. A staff is to be provided. This committee will work directly with the president and general counsel. Several other special committees of the Board are provided. These will work with the VP's for Finance, Lunar Development, International Affairs and Lunar Science and Technology.

2. The Advisory Consortium is a non-voting group of advisors to the board and to the managers. Each appointee will represent a space and governance entity. Fifteen from the National Space Society will be appointed to the voting board, also. The NSS Board of Directors is invited to serve on the advisory consortia board. Likewise, the sponsor World Bar Association has nominated the USIS Council of Regents to same. These groups may change or expand in the future, but their constituencies are relevant and they have an ongoing interest in space governance. Finally, space industry representatives will serve as advisors also.

3. The President is the Chief Executive Officer of the enterprise. He is elected by the Board of Directors. He will appoint the Vice Presidents, the General Counsel and employ the staff.

4. The Chairman of the Board is elected by the Board.

5. The Secretary is elected by the Board and reports to it regarding all record keeping functions of the enterprise.

6. The Treasurer is elected by the Board and reports to it regarding the overall management and banking of monies.

7. The VP for Finance is appointed by the President and reports to the office of the President. This VP coordinates revenues and budgets as proposed by the President. He works with a three number committee of the Board of Directors. This office will coordinate all bond market and securities underwriting activities and will coordinate with the general counsel's office.

8. The VP for Lunar Development is appointed by the President and works with a committee of the Board. The mission of this office is to create a consensus development plan for the moon, one that may be similar to the NASA baseline scenario, (S.P.509). Then bids would be let for development of the consensus plan. Common standards are to be promulgated. A zoning, building, and architectural control process is supervised by this

department. This will be reviewed by the Council of Regents, NSS, and space activists on the advisory committee.

9. VP for International Affairs is appointed by the President and works with a three board member committee. This office will coordinate national participation in the financial, development, and settlement aspects of LEDA, as well as consult with space agency representatives on the advisory committee.

10. VP for Lunar Science and Technology is appointed by the President and works with a three board member committee, as well as with the industry representatives on the advisory committee. All plans and contracts for lunar development must be approved here before any LEDA funds can be committed to them.

11. The Ombudsman is elected by the Board. This office will deal with special problems, complaints, and lobbying requests from those who can not otherwise access the LEDA administration.

12. The General Counsel is appointed by the President. Two associate general counsel are contemplated, as well as a legal staff, in order to deal with the special problems involved in lunar development. Astro law, international law, securities law, tax law, and quasi-governance authority law are some of the topics to be handled as they apply to LEDA. General counsel will also serve the legal needs as requested from the Chairman of the Board and President of the consortia advisory committee.

13. The Authority Court is an administrative law department with judicial authority to interpret and apply LEDA ordinances, rules and regulations, as well as handle violations and civil disputes generally. An appeals procedure to the World Court will be sought.

14. The departments include line authority over municipal functions such as zoning, planning, standards, development, science and technology and regulation of safety. There is also another department to coordinate international cooperation and participation on a professional basis.

References

1. The Outer Space Treaty, 1967, Article I, formally entitled "Treaty on Principles Governing the Activities of States in the Exploration and Uses of Outer Space, including the Moon and other Celestial Bodies, January 27, 1967."

2. UNGA #1962 (XVII), A Declaration of Legal Principles Governing the Activities of States in the Exploration and Use of Outer Space, 1963.

3. The Moon Treaty, 1979, Article XI, formally entitled "Treaty Governing the Activities of States on the Moon and Other Celestial Bodies, 1979."

4. Dembling, P.G., Report to the Scientific and Technical Subcommittee of UNCOPUOS, 1994, reported in the *Journal of Space Law*, Vol. 22-2, 1994, p. 129. To the contrary see, Dekanozov, R.V., "Juridical Nature and Status of the Resources of the Moon and Other Celestial Bodies." IISL 23 (1980), p. 5.

5. Goldman, N.C., *American Space Law: International and Domestic,* 2nd edition, Univelt, San Diego, 1966, p. 70.

6. ibid, p. 94.

7. There are no identifiable benefits actually paid to all nations and/or mankind by satellite organizations, albeit in kind benefits result to society. See, Doyle, S.E., "Benefits to Society from Space Exploration and Use," *Acta Astronautica,* 1989, Vol. 19-9, p. 749; Doyle, S.E., "Space Law and the Geostationary Orbit: The ITU's WARC-ORB 85-88 concluded," *Journal of Space Law,* Vol. 17-1, 1989, p. 13; and Doyle, S.E., "Equitable Aspects of Access to and Use of the Geostationary Satellite Orbit," IAF, IAA-87-642, Brighton, UK, 1987.

8. Jasentuliyana, N., "Review of Recent Discussions Relating to Aspects of Article I of the Outer Space Treaty," IISL 26, (1983), p. 7 at p. 9.

9. The treaty beneficiaries are all countries as a class with no exclusion for those producing the space resources as the burdened parties.

10. Robinson, G.S., and White, H.M., *Envoys of Mankind,* Smithsonian Institution Press, Washington, D.C., 1989.

11. Rothblatt, M., "Lex Americana: The New Legal Regime for LEO Satellite Communications Systems," *Journal of Space Law,* Vol. 23-2, 1995, p. 123.

12. See, Reference No. 7.

13. Space resources appropriation has been the principal component of the following Space Settlement Scenarios: Mission to the Moon Programme, SP1150, ESA, 1992; Space Resources, Materials, McKay, M.F., McKay, D.S., and Duke, M.B., including the following contributions: "Exploring, Evaluating and Mining Non-Terrestrial Resources" by Richard E. Gertsch, "Lunar Exploration for Resource Utilization" by Michael B. Duke, "Asteroid Resources" by John S. Lewis, "Benefaction and Extraction of Non Terrestrial Materials" by William N. Agosto, "The On-site Manufacture of Propellant Oxygen From Lunar Resources" by Sanders D. Rosenberg, Robert L. Beegle, Jr., Gerald A. Guter, Frederick E. Miller, and Michael Rothenberg, "Lunar Cement" by William N. Agosto, "Iron and Alloys of Iron" by Sankar Sastri, and "Bioprocessing of Ores-Application to Space Resources" by Karl R. Johansson, NASA

S.P.-509, Vol. 3, 1992, pp. 242-258; Robert Zubrin of Lockheed, Martin Marrieta re: terra-forming Mars by mass industrialization and restructuring on the surface, and S. Nadis, "Mars, the Final Frontier," *New Scientist*, 2/5/94, p. 28; Michael Simon, "Utilization of Space Resources in the Space Transportation System, NASA S.P. 509 Vol. p. 97; Garvey, J.M., "Adaptation of Space Technology for Lunar Operations," NASA Second Conference on Lunar Bases and Space Activities, 1992, p. 25; Sirko, R.J., "Lunar Base Reference Design," IAF No. 92-0515, 1992; Repic E.M., Richter P., Roy C., "The Lunar Resource Base, Stepping Stone to Mars," IAF No. 92-0542; Criswell, D.R., "Lunar Solar Power Satellites," *Journal of Practical Applications in Space*, Vol. 3:4, 1992, p. 63; Kulcinski, G.L., "Helium 3 Fusion Reactors - A Clean and Safe Source of Energy in the 21st Century," 9th National Space Symposium, U.S. Space Foundation, Colorado Springs, Colorado, 4/13/93; O'Neill, G.K. "High Frontier - Human Colonies in Space," Space Studies Institute, Princeton, N.J., 1976/1989; Stephensen, D.G. "Lunar Manufacture of Helium 3," *Journal of Practical Applications in Space,* Vol. 2:2 1991, p. 41; Bova, B., "The Vision of Spaceflight" in *Blueprint for Space*, Smithsonian Press, 1992, p. 19; President George Bush, "America at the Threshold," U.S. Government Printing Office, 1989; The National Commission on Space, "Pioneering the Space Frontier," Banta Books, N.Y. 1986; Hartmann, W., "Out of the Cradle," Publ., N.Y. 1984; Wernher von Braun, Space Frontier (rev. ed.), Holt, Rinehart, & Winston, N.Y., 1963; Arthur C. Clarke, "Profiles of the Future: An Inquiry into the Limits of the Possible," Harper and Rowe, N.Y., 1963; (to name a representative sample only).

14. The National Space Society has adopted the following theme in 1995: "Back to the Moon, this Time to Stay."

15. See, Reference No. 5 and 8.

16. O'Donnell, D.J., "Overcoming Barriers to Space Travel," *Space Policy Journal*, Vol. 10-4, Nov. 1994, p. 252.

17. The UN started with 52 signatures in 1947. It grew to 130 nations in 1967 when the Outer Space Treaty was adopted. There are 267 nations worldwide. Many UN Nations are subject to expulsion for non-payment of dues, including the USA. Clearly the UN does represent the class of nations as a matter of international law whether or not all nations are signed or in good standing. The point is that UN membership in fact is dangerously non-representative on a head count basis, or may appear so.

18. The IOSSA, International Organization for Sentient Space Activities, and, IARC, International Agreement for Recognition and Capacity, were proposed 16 years ago and remain dormant at the UN. See, Sterns, P.M., and Tennen, L.I., "International Recognition of the Art of Living in Space: The Emergence of Settlement Competence," 22 IISL (1980), p. 221.

19. O'Donnell, D.J., "Property Law in Outer Space: A-E-I-O-U and Sometimes Y as a Rule," *Space Governance Journal,* Vol. 3-1, July 1996, p. 14.

20. O'Donnell, D.J., and Harris, P.R., ""Metanation" and Other Words," IAA-96-IAA.5.1.05, Beijing, 1996.

21. Goldman, N.C., "A Lawyer's Perspective on USIS Strategies for Metanation and the Lunar Economic Development Authority," *Space Governance Journal,* Vol. 3-1, July 1996, p. 16: "The Metanation and the Lunar Economic Development Authority can answer many practical questions which are simply untouched by extant space law," p. 17.

IISL-96-IISL.3.10

BRAZILIAN-CHINESE SPACE COOPERATION: AN ANALYSIS OF ITS LEGAL PERFORMANCE *

José Monserrat Filho **
Brazilian Society of Aerospace Law (SBDA)
Brazilian Society for the Progress of Science (SBPC)

"The whole moral universe, the whole political universe, the whole human universe, are based today on paper rags."
Rui Barbosa, Brazilian statesman (1849-1923)

Abstract

This paper aims to examine some of the most important juridical issues raised during the short but yet rich Brazilian-Chinese space cooperation history. It tries to assess the effectiveness of the agreements signed by these countries on space matters.

At the same time, it seeks to present the political and legal concepts which were in the foundations of the main phases of this history.

Introduction

The current Brazilian government, according to the Republic's President, Fernando Henrique Cardoso, has a clear commitment to support a program for the indigenous development of space science and technology. Brazil already started its space activities in the sixties. However, the successful launching of its first satellite, the SCD-1 (1), did not occur before February 9, 1993, and the launching of its first space vehicle (VLS) is hoped to take place next year. Today Brazilian space activities, as a whole, rank between the 9th and 10th position among similar national space programs in the world. Its annual budget, which lies between US$ 150 to 200 millions, has regained the level it had at the end of the eighties, as the Brazilian Space Agency recently informed.

The consciousness of the absolute necessity of international space cooperation for the future of the country's space program have increased in Brazil. At the same time, more and more Brazilian space specialists and officials understand that international space cooperation should be oriented not just by occasional offers, but answering national needs. Futhermore, they think that cooperation should not mean technical assistance, but joint development. (2)

For these reasons, it seems that Brazilian space authorities presently give the highest priority to the space cooperation with the People's Republic of China.

Having launched its first space vehicle in 1964 and its first satellite in 1970, China became the 5th space power. Nowadays, space technology became a priority in its current plans to improve national economic and social development. Particular attention is paid towards applied as well as applications satellites and is keen on pursuing cooperatives endeavors, although it intends to retain its autonomy. (3)

Therefore, it is not by chance that China and Brazil have already gone a long way in their joint construction of two remote sensing satellites. The project, named Chinese-Brazilian Earth Resources Satellite (CBERS), has been approved by both countries' governments in 1988. Many contrivances came forth along the eight years since.

At the beginning, it was presumed that the first satellite could be launched in December 1992. A schedule revaluation performed at the beginning of 1993, after a long paralysis in the project, set the first launching to October 1996. There were new delays.

To a certain point, this was no surprise, considering the originality of a space cooperation between two developing countries. Brazilian diplomat Celso Luiz Nunes Amorim, whose participation on the initial negotiations with China was very assertive, as a especial secretary to International Issues at the Ministry of Science and Technology, has made a faultless prevision, in an article published in August 1988: "The actual realization of the (CBERS) project will certainly involve practical difficulties which we

---

 This paper was presented at the 39th International Colloquium on the Law of Outer Space, Beijing, China, October 7-11, 1996.

** Member of IISL, Master of International Law, Professor of Space Law at the Brazilian Society of Aerospace Law, director of the magazine Ciência Hoje (Science Today) and the newsletter Jornal da Ciência Hoje (Journal of Science Today), published by the Brazilian Society for the Advancement of Science (SBPC). Address: Av. Oswaldo Cruz, 73/701, CEP 22250-060, Flamengo, Rio de Janeiro, RJ, Brazil. Phones: 55-21-552-9036, 55-21-295-4442. Fax: 55-21-541-5342.
E-mail: <monserrat@ax.apc.org>

cannot even anticipate, even though the high level support received by it allow us to trust that the necessary means to its completion will not lack, from either side."(4)

Both aspects of these predictions came to fact. The encumbrances, in fact, have been not few nor small, but, after all, the project has already advanced several steps and has accomplished phases which importance one cannot minimize. Today it seems absolutely irreversible.

Till last September, Brazil has concluded its part in the construction of all equipments destined to the qualification model of the first satellite, and delivered it to China. The qualification phase will be finished at the beginning of 1997, at the Chinese facilities. Then, the phase of construction of the flight model will be started. The first satellite could be launched, then, by at the end of 1997 or at the beginning of 1998. The second satellite should go up two years later, that is to say, at the year of 2000. The chances that these predictions will come to fact are considered large, mainly because there have been no lack of the necessary means.

The good results achieved so far, mainly during the last years, led both sides to think about two subsequent satellites, CBERS 3 and 4. At the same time, the creation of a binacional enterprise to explore the products from the new remote sensing system is under study.

Today the space cooperation is the most prominent part of a wider bilateral collaboration policy which both countries officially consider as "strategic partnership".

How did Brazil and China come so far? How did they overcome the problems and hindrances that delayed the CBERS implementation? How did a project, adopted under such enthusiasm and so many hopes, felt under a dangerous climate of waiting and indecisions — that almost made it sink — but was, in time, resumed, and gives now a clear indication that it is solidly irreversible?

This history may be told and studied under many aspects. Here, it will be examined under the juridical point of view. We will follow the sequence of agreements signed by both countries governments and institutions, in order that the CBERS project should be made real, and see how did they work.

The Brazilian-Chinese space agreements are the first high technology ones between developing countries. The experience and the products of this cooperation program surely will have a considerable influence over the future space activities of both countries and may turn out an example and a reference to other developing countries.

Two quotations would be proper here:

1) Another prophecy soon coming to fact, from Ambassador Celso Luiz Nunes de Amorim: "By the time (the two sino-brazilian satellites) are in orbit, they will provide the most significant example of a South-South cooperation in the whole planet." (5)

2) Some recommendations made by the program of priority actions regarding the cooperation South-South, from the 1990 report "The challenge to the South" (6), approved by the South Commission - created in 1987 by a group of well known scientists and statesmen from several countries:

a) "All developing countries should provide legal, technical and taxing initiatives that would foster joint-ventures and the completion of technology transfer agreements between southern enterprises."

b) "The South should develop a scientific cooperation strategy centered in areas of greater mutual interests, where research and innovation could provide tangible benefits, through the addition and the conjugation of resources".

A consistent evaluation of the effectiveness of the Brazilian-Chinese space agreements is, by these reasons, even more necessary and relevant. This is what I intend to outline here, centered mainly on the Brazilian side, but far from assuming to exhaust the matter. It goes beyond doubts that the Brazilian-Chinese space cooperation deserves many further and deeper researches, under many different aspects, including juridical and political, so that its enormous experience potential and learnings should be profited the most.

Pacta sunt servanda

Agreements must be honoured. That is the essence of the *rule pacta sunt servanda*, one of international law's oldest principles, as defined in the Article 26 of the 1969 Vienna Convention on the Law of Treaties: "Every treaty in force is binding upon the parties to it and must be performed by them in good faith".

The treaty, as said by the super realistic Hans J. Morgenthau, is "the main instrumentality by which the international law is created."(7) Today, the written agreements are seen as the principal sources of international law, as well as the most democratic ones, since the States participate directly in its elaboration.

Nevertheless, even so, they are not always duly respected. This failure is critical to multilateral as well as to bilateral agreements. It can signify frustration, breaking off an entire chain of understandings from which concrete results could be expected, as well as the benefits, not only for the concerning countries, but also for international relationships as a whole. It is especially crucial with reference to agreements on high technology fields.

Of course, bilateral agreements, as well as laws of reciprocity, are relatively strong, being laws of limited partnership, whose members' common end is a set of mutual interests. (8) It is usually easier to comply with bilateral agreements. Yet, it does not necessarily happen this way, even when the agreement deals with extremely important affairs.

In fact, agreements, including bilateral ones, may have different levels of respect. Sometimes they are implemented, not exactly as they have been established, and only some degrees of its compromises have been respected. Quite frequently, the Parties have complied with some of the obligations, but not with others, due to some new difficulty or reasoning, leaving it clear, however, by their actual deeds, that they are not giving up the entire agreement.

For this reason, we not only can, but we must analyze those implementations. The process could be named "performance of an international agreement".

Appraising the performance of international agreements is quite necessary, after all, because these agreements are, nowadays, the most important basis for achieving cooperation on practically all matters, including, of course, space ones. Not only by chance, the same Vienna Convention on the Law of Treaties recognizes, in its preamble, the importance of treaties as a "means to develop peaceful cooperation among nations, independent of their constitutional regimes".

Oscar Schachter remarks that "the governments which enter into cooperative arrangements through treaties or otherwise, do so, not because of their moral idealism, but because of the predicaments in which they find themselves."(9) If so, we gave still another argument to require the assessment of these arrangements.

Moreover, such an assessment is essential in relation to agreements signed to achieve the goals set for space projects, which comprise a range of high costs, difficulties and risks. That is the case of the Brazilian-Chinese space agreements.

The sources

The legal history of Brazilian-Chinese space cooperation is formed by the following eleven main documents:

1) **Agreement** on Scientific and Technological Cooperation Between The Government of The Federative Republic of Brazil and The Government of The People's Republic of China, done in **Beijing**, on **March 25, 1982**;

2) **Complementary Agreement** on Scientific and Technological Cooperation, done in **Beijing**, on **May 29, 1984**;

3) **Work Report** on Sino-Brazilian Joint Project for Development of CBERS Satellite, done in **Beijing**, on **March 4, 1988**;

4) Protocol on Approval of Research and Production of the Earth Resources Satellite Between The Government of The Federative Republic of Brazil and The Government of The People's Republic of China, done in Beijing, on July 6, 1988;

5) Cooperation Agreement for the China-Brazil Earth Resources Satellite Between the Chinese Academy of Space Technology of China (CAST) and The Institute for Space Research of Brazil (INPE), done in Beijing, on August 22, 1988;

6) Supplementary Protocol on Approval of Research and Production of the Earth Resources Satellite Between The Government of The Federative Republic of Brazil and The Government of The People's Republic of China, done in Brasilia, on March 5, 1993;

7) Protocol on the Main Points For the Further Joint Development of the China-Brazil Earth Resources Satellites Between Chine Space Administration of The People's Republic of China and The Ministry of Science and Technology of The Federative Republic of Brazil, done in Brasilia, on September 15, 1993;

8) Protocol on Further Developments of The China-Brazil Earth Resources Satellites and Related Matters Between Chine National Space Administration of The People's Republic of China and The Ministry of Science and Technology of The Federative Republic of Brazil, done in Beijing, on November 9, 1993;

9) Protocol Between The Ministry of Science and Technology of The Federative Republic of Brazil and The China National Space Administration of The People's Republic of China (CNSA) on Cooperation in the Peaceful Applications of Outer Space Sciences and Technology, done in Brasilia, on November 23, 1993; and

10) Framework Agreement Between The Government of The Federative Republic of Brazil and The Government of The People's Republic of China on Cooperation in the Peaceful Applications of Outer Space Science and Technology, done in Beijing, on November 8, 1994. (10)

11) **Agreement** Between The Government of The Federative Republic of Brazil and The Government of The People's Republic of China on Technical Security in Connection with The Joint Development of Earth Resources Satellites, done in **Beijing**, on **December 13, 1995**.

12) **Minutes of Understanding** on the Strengthening and Expansion of the Brazil-China Space Technology Cooperation, done in **Beijing**, on **December 13, 1995**.

How did these agreements function? In which level have they been observed? What was its effectiveness? By answering these questions we can evaluate the legal performance of Brazilian-Chinese space cooperation until now. This analysis will be done as we show the phases of the legal history of Brazilian-Chinese space cooperation.

At this moment, it is interesting to note that most of these agreements have been signed, in Brazil's behalf, by four Ministers of foreign Affairs — Ramiro Saraiva Guerreiro (1979-84), Roberto de Abreu Sodré (1986-90), Fernando Henrique Cardoso (1992-93) and Luiz Felipe Lampreia (1995-) - and by one Minister of Science and Technology — José Israel Vargas (1993-). I call the attention to the fact that, from 1988 until today, in addition to the already mentioned, Brazil had three other Ministers of Foreign Affairs — José Francisco Resek (1990-92), Celso Lafer (1992) and Celso Luis Nunes

Amorim (1993-94) — aside four other Secretaries of Science and Technology - Decio Leal Zagottis (0989-90), José Goldemberg (1990-91), Hélio Jaguaribe (1991-92) and Edson Machado (1992-93).

By contrast, in China's behalf, the agreements have been signed by two Ministers of Foreign Affairs - Huang Hua and Qian Qichen (from 1988) - and one Administrator of the China National Space Administration - Liu Jiyuan.

This information shows the high level of administrative continuity in China, beneficial to the fulfillment of the signed agreements. About Brazil, we can say that the administrative interruptions after 1988 had ill effects upon the cooperation process, started that year, but the administrative continuity after 1993 has, undoubtedly contributed a lot for the progress of the CBERS project.

A history in four chapters

From the proclamation of The People's Republic of China until August 15, 1974, Brazil has kept severed its diplomatic relations with that country. In August 1961, there was an important attempt to an approach. Brazil's vice-president, João Goulart, has visited China, and, in addition to a bank agreement, authorized the establishment of a commercial office at an important Brazilian city. But in March 1964, the winning military movement, that promoted the automatic alignment with the United States, arrested nine Chinese civil servants that have come to set the commercial office. Ten years later, the world had already gone through the first petroleum shock, and the north-American president himself, Richard Nixon, had visited China. The then Brazilian government, under the late general Ernesto Geisel, had an attitude quite different from its predecessors. It defended a project of national autonomy on strategic sectors. It was he who elaborated and approved the first large spatial program in the country, the Complete Brazilian Space Mission, known as MECB. And it was also he who decided - not without strong internal reactions, mainly within the Army - to resume relationships with China. (11)

However, the first Brazilian-Chinese agreement on scientific and technological cooperation wasn't signed until seven years later, on March 25, 1982. Yet, this agreement is very cautious and doesn't mention space cooperation.

According to its Article I, the scientific and technological cooperation between both countries will be carried out "in fields to be decided through diplomatic channels." Its Article II, listing the ways the scientific and technological cooperation will be developed, foresees in its seventh and last item "other forms of scientific and technological cooperation to be agreed by the Parties", leaving that way an open door to any fields of cooperation, including space.

Finally, its Article III allows the Parties to conclude the Complementary Protocols, "in which basis the cooperation shall develop". It also establishes that these Protocols will be negotiated and approved through diplomatic channels or by the Brazilian-Chinese Commission on Scientific and Technological Cooperation, which was created at that time. The Brazilian Ministry of Foreign Affairs and the Chinese Ministry of External Economical Relations and Trade were designated as "executive bodies" of the Agreement.

Two years later, in May 29, 1984, Brazilian and Chinese Governments have signed the first Supplementary Protocol to the 1982 Agreement. They agreed to intensify its cooperation and to this end had elected seven areas, including space. (12)

At the same time, the Brazilian Government had designated, as executive organism for the future space cooperation projects with China, the Brazilian Commission of Space Activities (Cobae), acting through the Technical Aerospace Center (CTA) and the National Institute for Space Research (INPE). Meanwhile, the Chinese Government had designated its Ministry of Space Industry to the same task. (Later, in 1993, that ministry has been transformed in China National Space Administration, the Chinese space agency.)

It was agreed that this cooperation would be carried out in the following areas: Communications satellites, remote sensing satellites and image processing, launching vehicles and its systems, sounding rocks and other techniques. This Complementary Protocol didn't, however, define any projects.

This Supplementary Protocol, even though it represented a step forward, didn't immediately produce any tangible assets, however.

So far, this was the pre-history of the Brazilian-Chinese space cooperation. The actual history didn't start until 1985, and may be divided into four periods: 1985-88, 1988-89, 1989-92, 1992-96. (13)

The first period (1985-88)

In March 15, 1985, after 21 years under a military regime, a civil government was inaugurated in Brazil and the first Ministry for Science and Technology was created in the country's history. One of the first acts of the new minister, ruling over de National Institute of Space Research (INPE), was to consider the Chinese proposals, so that the possibilities and general intentions registered in the Complementary Protocol of 1984 could come to fact under a cooperation program.

The first Brazilian minister for Science and Technology, Renato Archer, valued highly the international cooperation. On his inauguration speech he stated: "... (we cannot) hope that the higher developed nations turn themselves into donors of such valuable goods, as are knowledge and know-how. What we want from them are mainly an understanding position towards our problems and our solutions to it, giving way to a mature cooperation, based on mutual advantages, were the richer nations wouldn't give anything for free, but wouldn't either try to establish rules on how we should conduct our development. This is the posture we hope for, both at the bilateral level and the multilateral courts were the questions concerning Science and Technology are discussed. This same principle of respect to the national options of each country shall preside the collaboration agreements we intend to keep with countries at the same progress level as ours." (14) This point of view, clearly presided over the relationships between Brazil and China, which soon became activated.

In July 1986, the minister Renato Archer visits China and starts a cycle of technical negotiations aiming to the elaboration of a real space program cooperation.

Such an effort results in the Work Report on Sino-Brazilian Joint Project for Development of CBERS Satellite, signed in Beijing, in March 4, 1988, by three representatives for Chinese Academy of Space Technology (CAST) and three for the Brazilian Space Research Institute (INPE).

The following are the principal issues agreed in the Work Report:

1) The Chinese-Brazilian earth resources satellite (CBERS) is to be jointly developed "on the basis of equality and mutual benefits";

2) The CAST will share responsibility for 70% and the INPE for 30% of the total project cost, which includes expenses for development of satellite (two flight models) and purchasing two launching vehicles and the launch services;

3) The CBERS will be utilized by both parties. When it flies over the two parties' territories, each party may use its own earth station to receive the remote sensing and DCS system data. The use of the satellite by a third country and delivery of remote sensing products to a third can only be allowed under the approval of both parties;

4) A "Project Committee" has to be established as highest level authority of the project, consisting of representatives from both countries, with the responsibility to organize and implement the project while exercising its leadership and supervision.

5) The mark of fulfilling the project is that CBERS has had a qualification test in orbit and has been delivered for utilization;

6) None of the parties is allowed to cease implementing the program of the project, otherwise will bear all the responsibility resulted from its independent ceasing of the project and will compensate to the other party for all the losses;

7) Any amendment or addition to the project must be unanimously approved by the Project Committee;

8) The Work Report will be annexed to the Agreements and has the same legal effect as the Agreement after they are signed by both Governments.

This Work Report includes two annexes:

1) CBERS Technological Requirements, which presents its mission objectives, its overall system, satellite description;

2) Engineering Management, with the Development Program and Plan, as well as the phases of construction.

Based on this Work Report, the first consolidated space cooperation project between Brazil and China came forth. In July 6, 1988, the Brazilian and the Chinese Foreign Ministries signed, in Beijing, at the presence of the Brazilian President Jose Sarney, the "Protocol on Approval of Research and Production of the Earth Resources Satellite Between the Government of the People's Republic of China". This Protocol was negotiated by the Brazilian Ministry of Science and Technology through the INPE and with the support of the Ministry of Foreign Affairs. The Brazilian Commission for Space Activities (COBAE), which was headed by the Chairman of the Joint Chiefs of Staff (EMFA), approved the plan to develop space cooperation with China, in spite of the opposite vote from the Ministry of Aeronautic representative.

The Protocol encompasses only two points, being a small document:

1) It approves de CAST-INPE Work Report of March 4, 1988; and

2) It designates the INPE and the CAST as the executing agencies for the joint program. They were entrusted with celebrating the necessary acts for its implementation.

In the brief Protocol introduction, Brazil and China reaffirm "their determination to strengthen bilateral ties in the field of high technology". That is the reason why this space relationship was seen at the time as an example of cooperation between two developing countries in a high technology field.

A step further was to be taken just a month later, in August 22, when the Cooperation Agreement, a document exclusively executive was signed between CAST and INPE, for the CBERS. This agreement, not only reaffirms and enhances the CAST-INPE Work Report of March 4, but establishes a practical legal basis for the implementation of the Project as well.

Its Article 3 lists the following eight appendices, "which have the same legal effectiveness as this Agreement": CBERS Technical Requirements; CBERS Development Plan; Organization; Tracking, Telemetry and Command (TT&C) and Operational Management; Division of Work; Financial Share; Regulation on Personnel Exchange; and Product Assurance.

The Appendix 1 defines two CBERS mission objectives:

* The use of advanced space remote sensing techniques to inventory, develop, manage and monitor the Chinese and Brazilian earth resources in agriculture, forestry, geology, hydrology, geography, cartography, meteorology and environment, etc.

* The promotion of the development and application of space remote sensing and space tech-

nology in China and Brazil.

The CBERS Development Plan (Appendix 2) had planned the launching of the first satellite to be done in December1992. This proved to be a mistake, due to the fact that the Taiyuan Satellite Launch Center, from where the CBERS should be launched, doesn't usually function at that period of the year.

In Article 4, it was, for the first time, established the amount for the total project investment, US$ 150 millions — US$ 100 millions for the development and the assembling of two satellites, and US$ 50 millions for the purchase of two Chinese launchers and launching services. It was also registered that China would be responsible for 70% of the total costs, 30% being Brazil's due. It was stated, however, that "if the contribution provided by each party in the implementation of the Project, due to mutual subcontracting, doesn't correspond to its accorded share, the difference shall be covered with money, materials, goods or services".

It is known, today, that the Project's costs went beyond those calculated before. Brazil has already invested about US$ 64 millions, from 1988 till 1995, and shall invest US$ 33,5 millions more, from 1996 till 1999. To this, it must be added other costs amounting to approximately US$ 35 millions, from important items as the construction of the Brazilian wide field camera (WFI), integration and test of CBERS 2 in Brazilian facilities, ground stations, new contracts on the structure of satellite and applications and commercialization of the CBERS products. However, both parties haven't, so far, redefined this matter through another agreement.

The purchase of the two launching vehicles and launching services was left to a later, distinct agreement, within the same financial partition as the original Project.

This launching contract ended up by being signed almost five years later, in November 9, 1993.

The Articles 10 and 13, on delicate questions as "Defaults" and "Disputes" were written in poor legal terms, certainly because it was intended to be the most cordial it could be, aiming to prevent by all means any type of confrontation, as well as the ending of the agreement itself. I think it worth to quote them here, so that the spirit in which they were written can be perceived.

Article 10 says:

'If either party fails to fulfill any commitment required in this Agreement, and if such Party fails to remedy such failure within a reasonable period after being notified by the other party in written form, the other party shall have the right to terminate the present Agreement.

It is a very serious step to terminate the Agreement. Both parties shall do whatever they can to avoid that. If either party wishes to consider the termination of the Agreement, an urgent Project Committee shall be held to discuss if the termination can be prevented. Otherwise, a detailed procedure for the termination shall be worked out."

Article 13 says:

All disputes arising in connection with the present Agreement and during the implementation of the Project shall be solved through friendly consultation. In case an agreement is not reached, all disputes shall be analyzed and solved by the Project Committee. If the disputes are still persisting, both parties shall report to their government".

Until now all the defaults and disagreements, even the most serious, have been dealt with and solved through friendly consultations and negotiations.

The main important case of difference on interpretations on the CAST-INPE Agreement was on the definition of responsibilities for the tracking, telemetry and command of the satellites in the second phase of the mission (from the separation of the satellites, including the complete in-orbit tests, to the delivery of the satellites to the users).

This question wasn't solved until several years later.

Why this kind of project?

Let's open an especial chapter to examine why is that Brazil and China decided to adopt this kind of project.

Brazil had some good reasons for that decision:

1) The need to develop indigenous capabilities on the construction of remote sensing satellites, greatly enlarging its accumulated experience on working with satellite applications, started in the beginning of the seventies. By 1972, Brazil was the third country, behind USA and Canada, to have an operational system for receiving data from remote sensing satellites (Landsat);

2) The first Brazilian space program, named Brazilian Complete Mission (MECB), approved in 1979, had, as its main object, the construction of four satellites - two Data Collecting and two Remote Sensing Satellites. Brazil has, furthermore, as part of the MECB, prepared qualified human resources, as well as some modern facilities, which could also help to accomplish an international cooperative space project;

3) The CBERS could contribute to maintain the MECB, in the case the hypothesis of its unfeasibility, as some have supposed at the time, should come to fact (14);

4) The two CBERS satellites would cost considerably less than the four MECB satellites. This was very important, considering the Brazilian budgetary difficulties (15)

5) The political willingness to participate in a great international space project, capable to impart new stimulus to Brazilian space activities and to rise them to a qualitative higher level.

6) The strategic conviction that the cooperation with China in remote sensing , based on

strong mutual interests, could open new opportunities to reach space technologies, otherwise impossible to establish or to buy in developing countries. The Brazilian space program has been thwarted by the seven most development countries (G-7), the USA being the first of them, by the Missile Technology Control Regime (MTCR), as to the assembly of the VLS (Satellite Launching Vehicle), to begin with. (16) By the time the Protocol was signed, in July 6, 1988, the then Brazilian President, Jose Sarney, stated to the Press that the cooperation with China, thanks to an effort authentically shared, could brake those restrictions the developed Nations had built against the advanced technologies transfer. He added that the so much praised south-south cooperation - until then limited, except for a few modest technical assistance and student and in-the-job trainees exchanges - was going thorough high technologies boundaries to get inside the more advanced spheres of research and space technologies. (17)

China also had strong reasons for going for such a cooperation with Brazil:

1) External cooperation was, at that time, and still is welcome, as a means to speed up the development of Chinese capability in satellite application, as China considers its "services and operations in the field of meteorology, navigation and remote sensing, essentially dependent on foreign satellites."(18)

2) Brazil could be a competent and efficient partner in the assembly of application satellites, since it already have some technical and industrial experience in this field, and could even contribute with financial resources;

3) Brazil could bridge China's possibilities on getting further technological resources from other countries, with whom it didn't have the conditions for transacting this kind of goods before.

The second period (1988-1989)

The effective implementation of CBERS didn't begin until this period. It started with the CAST-INPE Cooperative Agreement of August 22, 1988, which establishes all the objectives, plans, structures, work ways, schedules and regulations of the project. This was the time when the different teams have been created and started working.

The CAST-INPE Cooperative Agreement has incorporated the organization structure proposed by the Work Report on March 4.

The Project Committee is the highest authority level for the joint development of the CBERS. It turned out to be known as "Joint Project Committee" and by the acronym "JPC". It is formed by eight members - four from each party. Each party appoints one chairman. Under the JPC there are two Project Managers. Under the Project Manager are placed the Engineering Technical Group (ETG) and the Engineering Management Group (EMG).

The JPC defines the general policies and issues orders and instructions, as well as approves the execution of cooperative plan and all the reports from the ETG and EMG.

There are two Project Managers - a manager from China and an associate manager from Brazil. They hold great responsibilities. While working together, they set the project implementation, verify all the system level reports from the two engineering groups, approve all the subsystem level documents, as well as coordinate and solve the problems raised within the joint development.

The Engineering Technical Group may have up to 16 members from each party and is composed by one chief head from China and one associate head from Brazil. The ETG is composed by two subgroups. The System subgroup deals with mission analysis, orbit design, configuration design, integration, assembly and verification, interface with launcher, interface with launch site and others. The Satellite subgroup looks after the structure, thermal control, power supply, tracking, telemetry and command (TT&C), on-board data holder (OBDH), circuits & cables, altitude and orbit control subsystem (AOCS), payloads and ground electric support equipments (GESE).

The Engineering Management Group is composed of up to five representatives from each party, with one chief head from China and one associate head from Brazil. This group works out the development plan; arranges detailed programs for each phase and each year; inspects the implementation of the plan; organize review meetings, maps out the product technical documents; coordinates and handles all management affairs.

The JPC conducts its work in the form of meetings, held alternatively in both countries and chaired by the chairman of the host country. The resolutions discussed and decided at each meeting are written in the form of minute, which orientates the subsequent development of the project. Until now seven meetings have been held, as shown in the following box:

Joint Project Committee (JPC) Meetings

1) August 24-25, 1988, in Beijing, China;
2) August 2-8, 1989, in São José dos Campos, Brazil;
3) June, 11-16, 1990, in Beijing;
4) February 25-March 2, 1993, in São José dos Campos;
5) July 26-August 6, 1993, in Beijing;
6) October 18-21, 1994, in São José dos Campos;
7) September 26-28, 1995, in Beijing.

Therefore, two JPC meetings have taken place during this period (1988-89): the first one in August 24-25, 1988, in Beijing, immediately after the signature of the CAST-INPE Cooperation Agreement of August 22, and the other, one year later, in august 2-8, in São José dos Campos.

It happened that, in January 1989, the then Brazilian President, José Sarney, introduced considerable changes in his government structures. The Ministry of Science and Technology merged into the Ministry of Industry and Commerce to form the Ministry of Economic Development, Science and Technology. It didn't last beyond a few months, for the National Congress ended up by refusing it, forcing the government to go back on its decision of fusing both ministries and to create a Secretary of Science and Technology to replace the Ministry of Science and Technology, aside from creating back the Ministry of Industry and Commerce. This ministerial reform, however, had a negative effect, as a whole, over the scientific and technology sector, which went aimless during quite a long period, a victim of disorientation, uncertainties and indefinitions. Priorities and agreements previously assumed had, to a great extend, lost its sense, including the space cooperation with China. As a result, the Brazilian party didn't give the project the importance it has given it at the year of 1988 anymore. This way, during 1989, as asserted by the technicians involved in the project at that time, it went on by inertial momentum, spending up the fuel accumulated at the previous year. This can be viewed by the degree of implementation of the CBERS Development Plan at the period. (See the table below)

Until the end of 1989, phases A and B were concluded, but phase C tasks, foreseen for this period, couldn't be done. From one side, the qualification and contracts with the Brazilian firms selected to assemble the necessary pieces, parts and subsystems didn't start. From another, the assembly and launching of the first satellite at the beginning of the nineties became impossible, as it was predicted. The main cause: Brazilian government didn't release the financial resources it was committed to do. (20)

Third period (1990-1992)

In March 15, 1990, the new President of Brazil, Fernando Collor de Mello was inaugurated. The Ministry of Science and Technology, reborn in December 1989 at the José Sarney government, was once more turned into a Secretary of Science and Technology. To head it, professor José Goldembeg was invited, who didn't put CBERS among his priorities. So, the new government kept unchanged the low level of attention the project had in 1989 and refused it all the means. Brazil, this way, didn't meet its responsibilities and didn't perform the tasks foreseen at the CAST-INPE Agreement. The project was then practically paralyzed because of the obvious failure from the Brazilian side.

The Chinese side got to the point of thinking to demand the payment of a fine, from Brazil, as a reparation in regard to the delay on the implementation of CBERS. There was a legal basis to that. According to Article 7 of CAST-INPE Agreement, "it is the duty of each party, among others, ... to bear the responsibility for any consequences and losses caused by itself during implementation its committed duty." By failing to honor its contractual duties, the Brazilian party had, at least, gone through a deliberate neglect, liable to some kind of penalty. But the demand for a fine or reparation, as far as it is known, was never formalized.

Chinese government, it appears, was very pa-

CBERS Development Plan

Phases	Objectives	First schedule
Phase A	Mission specification and others	
Phase B (Definition phase)	* Determine satellite system scheme and technical specifications * Determine subsystem's preliminary scheme and subsystem's technical specifications	**February 89**
Phase C (Detailed design phase)	* Determine subsystem scheme and their technical specifications * Determine preliminary design scheme of equipment and their technical specifications * Develop subsystem equipments * Complete integration and test of the structure model (SM), thermal test model (TM) and electric test model (EM)	**April/May 90** **February 91**
Phase D (Manufacturing phase)	* Freeze the equipment schemes and their technical specifications * Manufacture the equipment for Flight Model (FM) subsystems * Integrate and test FM * Launch FM	**December 91** **September 92** **December 92**
Phase E (Flight phase)	* Mission management during the normal operation in orbit after orbit injection * In orbit test	

tient and wise on its way to treat the crisis that had fallen over both countries about the CBERS. It was probably thought that it would be better to bet on a change on positions from Brazilian government, timely, than to get from it some financial compensation that could take the controversies to a point of no return, and lose everything, this way.

In this period, the Chinese President, Yang Shan Kun, visited Brazil and the Brazilian Foreign Minister, José Francisco Rezek, visited China, being received in the highest governmental level. Yet the abnormal situation didn't change.

Brazil has never stood at the uncomfortable situation of having to pay any fine or reparation, but it certainly suffered moral and material discomforts, aside the serious diplomatic embarrassment, for not having met such an important international commitment. (21)

During this period, the JPC had met only once, in June 11-16, 1990, in Beijing. There was already a lot that the JPC, being exclusively technical and executive, could perform. However, there was nothing they could do without any money. All that both countries had agreed to, so far, was under the threat of not coming to fact. The survival of CBERS became dependent on a political decision at the highest level of Brazilian government.

The Brazilian management of the project used constructively this opportunity to discuss with the Chinese side three relevant proposals:

1) To explicitly establish the technological transfer as one of the CBERS objectives, improving, this way, the 1988 agreement;

2) To integrate and test the second satellite (CBERS-2) at the Integration and Test Laboratory (LIT) of INPE, having the technical teams of both countries working together; and

3) To broaden the Brazilian participation in the satellite tracking and command activities.

These claims were so reasonable that they ended up by being accepted. Nevertheless, they cannot be used at all as a justification to disrespecting the agreements.

As says Fabíola de Oliveira, "the CBERS program gained impetus in 1991, when Brazilian firms started to be contracted for the fabrication of equipment for that part of the satellite under the responsibility of INPE". (22) It seems to be a polemical assertion. In fact, during the second semester of 91, contracts amounting to US$ 15 millions were signed, for the assembly, by Brazilian companies, of the CCD (Charged Coupled Device) chamber, of computers and of the test systems. That was doubtless a positive deed, for it helped to avoid the total dismantling of the project from the Brazilian side. But it was still a quite weak sign, because it didn't reflect a clear position from the government part towards the resuming of the project.

The critical general picture remained unchanged. It could be shown by two facts: 1) In 1992, the Brazilian government didn't plan any resources to CBERS; and 2) JPC, the most important executive part of the project, after the meeting on June 11-16, 1990 didn't come together again until two years and eight months later, in February 25-March 2, 1993, while it has been a consensus that it should meet at least once a year.

Fourth period (1992-1996)

This is the period of the resuming or the CBERS project and the steps ahead, towards its consolidation. Which would be the turning point for the moving of the previous period to this one? It is not easy to answer this question.

It must be said that the Brazilian Ambassador Roberto Abdenur, during his long mission in Beijing, from January 1989 to August 1993, was a untiring advocate of the space cooperation with China. At that time, during more than two years, he was a lonely fighter. He wasn't supported in his efforts by the highest levels of Brazilian Government. He just had the backing of INPE management personal. This way, the persistent work of Roberto Abdenur can be seen as a very important factor to the CBERS survival. He was so convinced of the far-reaching relevance of the Brazilian-Chinese cooperation in high technology fields that he coined the expression "strategic partnership" to qualify the kind of relations that should be adopted between two countries. This expression was right way accepted by the Chinese Vice-First Minister of Economic Affairs, Zhu Ron Gji, who used it in a meeting with the then Brazilian President, Itamar Franco, in Brasilia, early 1993.

In September 1992, at the beginning of the yearly session of United Nations General Assembly, the Chinese delegation met the Brazilian one and apparently exerted strong pressure on them to normalize the space cooperation between both countries.

Surely enough, right at the beginning or October a committee, lead by the then Secretary of Science and Technology, Edson Machado, was sent to China to promote the necessary understandings toward the CBERS project with Chinese officials.

In December 1992, President Collor was impeached by the National Congress, being forced to leave the government to be charged with corruption. His successor, vice-president Itamar Franco, even before being inaugurated, had shown an enthusiastic intention on supporting the CBERS.

In December 1992 and in January 1993, two Brazilian technical delegations (from INPE) have been in Beijing, reestablishing operational contacts and reorganizing the tasks and the project conditions. Soon after, the JPC itself resumed its activities at a historical meeting in February 25-March2, 1993, in São José dos Campos.

Closing this resuming cycle, the Supplementary Protocol of March 5, 1993, was signed in Brasilia by both Brazilian and the Chinese Foreign Ministers. It was the most important act of the visit to Brazil of the Chinese Foreign Minister, Qian Quichen. The Brazilian Foreign Minister at that time was the present day President of the Republic, Fernando Henrique Cardoso.

This Protocol meant the official renewing of the Brazilian-Chinese space cooperation. By the Protocol, the Parties decided to make all necessary efforts in order that the first flight model of the CBERS be placed in orbit by October 1996. This intention certainly expresses both side's wishes to accelerate the implementation of the project after such a long delay. As we know today, this plan, however, was not accomplished.

This Protocol ratifies the Brazilian proposition in order that the activities of assembly, integration and testing of the second flight model of the CBERS take place at the Laboratory of Integration and Testing (LIT) or INPE, with the additional costs under Brazilian responsibility. It was also noted that the Parties have made progress on the question of control orbit revision of the CBERS, as was Brazil's wishes.

As a first step towards reaffirming the CBERS, this Protocol announces that the Ministry of Science and Technology of Brazil and the Ministry of Aerospace Industry of China will sign a Protocol on Main Points for the Further Development of the CBERS.

Six months later, in September 15, 1993, actually, the new Protocol was signed - again in Brasilia - by the Brazilian Ministry of Science and Technology and the China National Space Administration (which, at that time, had replaced the Ministry of Aerospace Industry). This new Protocol ratifies the agreed decision of the 5th JPC Meeting held in July 26-August 6, 1993, in Beijing. Its expressed objective was "to speed up" the development of the CBERS.

To this end and to assure the launching of the first satellite in October 1996, the Protocol records that "both sides shall endeavour to allocate sufficient financial resources to garantee the work schedule for the development of the satellites and the subcontracted items". By the end of 1993, other contracts were signed, amounting to US$ 16 millions for the assembling of the structure, power supplier, transponders for data collection, all the aerials, solid state power amplifier (SSPA).

In general, from 1993 on, the flow of resources from the Brazilian side went much better, apart from a few delays, which, notwithstanding, didn't jeopardize the high priority given to the project. However, the plan to launch the first satellite in October 1996 was not accomplished for technical and other reasons rather than financial ones. In 1995, the chief Brazilian company contracted for the fabrication of equipment for the CBERS project, ESCA, went bankrupt. This resulted on a delay of at least six months. ESCA was a branch of the American Raytheon Corporation in Brazil.

This Protocol of September 1993 reaffirms the agreed decision to assembly, integrate and test (AIT) the second flight model of satellite (FM2) at LIT of INPE. It also establishes that (a) the task or AIT of FM2 should be performed during a maximum period of 14 months from the date of the arrival of FM2 equipment in Brazil and that (b) after the completion of AIT work, FM2 shall be shipped to China by charter flight for launching.

Both sides hoped that, within one year of the signature of this Protocol, a separate agreement concerning satellite safety and protection of proprietary rights should be signed and be effective after the approval by their respective governments. This hope didn't come true at the scheduled time. The intergovernmental agreement on technical security in connection to the joint development of CBERS was signed over two years later, in December 12, 1995.

As a last point in the Protocol of September 1993, both sides had confirmed that in the first half of November 1993, they would sign, in Beijing, the contract of CBERS Launching Services. This point has been strictly fulfilled. The contract was signed in November 9 of that year.

1993 was the year of reconstruction. It ended up with the signature of two other Protocols, in November 9 and 23, respectively in Beijing and Brasilia. Both of them display a nature of understanding and perspectives from both countries. The November 9 Protocol, "on further developments" of the CBERS records that "the Chinese side agrees, during the launching of CBERS-1, to carry, as passenger load, a Brazilian scientific experiment micro-satellite with approximately 60 kg of mass".

According to this Protocol, "both sides agree to set up a joint group in the first half of 1994 and to make joint efforts to advertise the products of CBERS in the international market so as to enlarge its potential users". However, this joint group has not yet been created. Besides, it was agreed that "the Brazilian agencies concerned and CAST would establish a team in order to prepare an all-encompassing feasibility report for the joint development of a communication satellite, and would provide the feasibility report in the first half of 1994. That issue hasn't yet been fulfilled either. In 1994, the then president of the Brazilian Telecommunication National Company, (EMBRATEL), Renato Archer, has visited China, envisaging a possible joint project in that field. However, as President Fernando Henrique Cardoso was inaugurated on January 1st, 1995, the differences between Brazilian and Chinese telecommunications policies became more evident than ever before, which, if doesn't make it impossible, it certainly makes it difficult to reach an agreement.

The November 23rd Protocol, rather broader than the previous one, is similar to a framework agreement. Its Article 1st says that "the Parties shall encourage, with due account for the widely accepted international laws and rules, exchange and cooperation in the exploration and use of outer space for peaceful purposes on the basis of equality and mutual benefits, in accordance with the laws and regulations in force in each country and through their respective competent organizations in the areas of space science, technology and applications..." In the same sense, its Article 3 affirms that "the parties will endeavor to coordinate their positions on the matter regarding the peaceful uses of outer space in the relevant bodies of the United Nations system". This Protocol, therefore, seems deeply concerned to present very clearly the peaceful and legally adequate purposes of the Brazilian-Chinese space cooperation. We can suppose that it would be necessary to dissipate the suspicions of developed countries, mainly the United States, on the eventuality of a future military space cooperation between Brazil and China. It should be remembered that Brazil, soon after this, in February 10, 1994, assumed unilaterally the compromise of following the rules of the missile Technology Control Regime (MTCR), aiming at being accepted as an informal organization.

After the Protocol of November 1993, just one year later, the framework Agreement on cooperation in the peaceful applications of outer space science and technology came forth under the same spirit, signed in November 8, 1994. For the first time, the Agreement mentions the Brazilian Space Agency (BSA) as the organism designated by the Brazilian Government to implement the agreement. The RSA was founded in February 10, 1994. In practice, however, it has been seen that the chief role at conducting the CBERS project has been played by the Ministry of Science and Technology. Just as did the Protocol, the Agreement establishes the creation of a joint working group to develop the binational space cooperation, but until now this haven't been done.

In January 1995, it was defined, through a contract, that Brazil would also have autonomy in the tracking and command processes of CBERS satellites.

The two more recent documents from the list of Brazilian-Chinese space agreements point to the considerable level of confidence achieved by both countries. The Agreement on Technical Security in Connection with the Joint Development of Earth Resources Satellites and the Minutes of Understanding on the Strengthening and Expansion of the Brazil-China Space Technology Cooperation were both signed at the same day, December 13, 1995, during the visit of the Brazilian President, Fernando Henrique Cardoso to China.

The Brazilian Ministry of Science and Technology and the Commission of Science, Technology and Industry for National Defense of People's Republic of China were appointed as the executive organism for the Agreement on Technical Security. According to its Article I, this Agreement is applicable to all stages, including the development assembly, integration and test (AIT), transportation and launching of the CBERS satellites, as well as the CBERS satellites' engineering models and flight models, the satellites' support equipment, auxiliary equipment and all components, parts, software, technical data, technical parameters, plants, information, as well as every other matter bearing on the security and economic interests of both Parties. Article II settles that neither Party shall gain access to and acquire any item developed or assembled by the other Party without its consent. Article III lists the items that both Parties shall classify by appropriate degree of confidentiality. This Article also foresees that three months before starting the assembly, integration and test of the finalized prototype of the satellites, both Parties shall reach an specific agreement for technical security in order to carry out all this operations, covering the safety and monitoring requirements of the satellite's models in the course of transportation between Brazil and China as well as during ground operations in both countries. The Agreement establishes that the launching of the satellites CBERS 1 and 2 will take place at the *Tai Yuan* Satellite Center in China. In accordance with the Article VI, 'any disputes arising from the interpretation and implementation of this Agreement shall be settled through negotiation by both Parties'.

On the other hand, the Minutes of Understanding considers the tasks set at the 7th JPC Meeting, held in September 1995 in Beijing, as the foundation for the expansion of bilateral space cooperation. It records the intention of both Parties to establish a joint group to perform a study to ascertain the feasibility of two additional satellites (CBERS 3 and 4). The costs of the two additional satellites' development and launching would be shared by both sides on equal basis (at the current system, China is in charge of 70% and Brazil of 30% of the project's costs). It also points out that 'both sides decided to establish a bilateral enterprise with a view to marketing the CBERS joint-developed products internationally '. It is still reiterated, in addition, that both sides will continue the expansion of cooperation in the five areas stipulated in the Protocol of November 1994. As for the telecommunication satellites, both sides agreed that they will further explore the cooperation in the third generation of Brazilian telecommunication satellites and in the low-earth-orbit satellite mobile telecommunication system (Echo System), approved by the Brazilian Government.

Conclusions

Both Brazil and China - each one having its way and making worth its best political and technical talents, accomplished a terrific job at saving, resuming and enlarging its historical joint project on space cooperation.

As for Brazil, since 1993 it has made a remarkable effort to meet, as well and as quickly as possible, its part at the enterprise. However, to make the reached conquests worthy, it seems necessary and convenient to promote a strict evaluation of the faults, inadequacies and inefficiencies recognized in both sides that still compromises the best accomplishment of the cooperation. This would certainly help to perfect and vitalize all the institutions, steps and staffs involved in the project. This way, both countries will be able to reach a proper level of legal performance for the demands on agility, efficiency and competitiveness of the space activities of our time, and thus, turn its joint work even more into an example.

Notes

1) Oliveira, Fabiola, *Brazil Reaches the Space - SCD-1 Data Collection Satellite*, National Institute for Space Research (INPE) and Proposta Editorial, São Paulo:1996.

2) Briefing from the Strategic Studies Center at the Presidency of Republic Secretary of Strategic Affairs about the Symposium on International Space Cooperation Perspectives, held in Brasilia, in July 23, 1996.

3) Yilin Zhu, *Fast-track development of space technology in Chine*, *Space Policy*, Vol. 12, N° 2, May 1996, pp. 139-142.

4) Amorim, Celso Luiz Nunes, *Por que a China?*, Revista Brasileira de Tecnologia (review published by National Council for Scientific and Technological Development - CNPq, of the Ministry of Science and Technology), Vol. 19, N° 8, August 1988, pp. 48-49.

5) Id Ibid.

6) *O Desafio do Sul* (*The Challenge to the South*), The South Commission 1990, Portugal: Edições Afrontamento, 1990, p. 207.

7) Morgenthau, Hans J., *Politics Among Nations - The Struggle for Power and Peace*, New York: Alfred A. Knopf Inc., Sixth Edition, 1985, p. 297.

8) Hoffmann, Stanley, *International Systems and International Law, in The Strategy of World Order - 2 International Law*, edited by Richard A. Falk and Saul H. Mendlovitz, New York: World Law Fund, 1972, p. 162.

9) Schachter, Oscar, *International Law in Theory and Practice*, The Netherlands: Martinus Nijhoff Publishers, p. 61.

10) *Journal of Space Law*, Volume 23, Number 1, 1995, pp. 117-120.

11) Conde, Carlos, *Diálogo com Pequim: resistências e avanços* (Dialog with Beijing: resistance and advancements), Revista Política Externa (Review of External Politics), Vol. 3, N° 3, December, 1994. pp. 125-130.

12) The other areas were: agriculture, cattle-raising and fishery; forestry; health; electric energy; microelectronics and computing; standardization.

13) Biton Tabio has divided the process of CBERS Program implementation in three periods: 1988-90, 1990-92 e 1992-95 (Biton Tabia, Jorge Rubem, *O Desenvolvimento de Sistemas de Produtos Complexos: o Caso do Satélite Brasileiro* (The Development of Systems of Complex Products), in Coutinho, Luciano; Cassiolato, José Eduardo; and Silva, Ana Lucia G. da, (coordenadores), *Telecomunicações, Globalização e Competitividade* (Telecommunications, Globalization and Competitiveness), Campinas, São Paulo: Papirus, 1995, p. 249).

14) Archer, *Renato, Ciência e Tecnologia - Soberania e Bem-Estar* (Science and Technology - Sovereignty and well-being), Ministry of Science and Technology, INPE, Vol. I, 1996.

15) Biton Tabia, Jorge Rubem, Id Ibid, p. 249.

16) Biton Tabia, Jorge Rubem, Id Ibid, p. 250.

17) Monserrat Filho, José, *The Place of the Missile Technology Control Regime (MTCR) in the International Space Law*, Proceedings of The 36th Colloquium on The Law of Outer Space, October 16-22, 1993, Graz, Austria, AIAA, pp. 89-92. Published in *Space Policy*, Volume 10, Number 3, August 1994, pp. 223-228.

18) Amorim, Celso Luiz Nunes, Id Ibid.

19) Fast-track development of space technology in China - Report of Secretary-General of Science and Technology Commission of Chinese Academy of Space Technology, in Space Policy, May 1996, pp. 139-142. The report says: "At present, services and operation in the field of meteorology, navigation and remote sensing are essentially dependent on foreign satellites. China's own applied satellites have been built slowly. Not only we not satisfy domestic demands, but also whole domestic markets ay be lost and a favorable development opportunity missed – which is not appropriate to China's international position as a spacefaring nation – unless the development of applied satellites can be speeded up."

20) Biton Tabia, Jorge Rubem, Id Ibid, p. 252.

21) Monserrat Filho, José, *O Acordo Espacial Brasil-China* (Brazilian-Chinese Space Agreement), *Jornal do Brasil*, 11/2/93.

22) Oliveira, Fabiola, *Brazil Reaches the Space - SCD-1 Data Collection Satellite*, National Institute for Space Research (INPE) and Proposta Editorial, São Paulo:1996, p. 42.

TOWARDS A CODE OF CONDUCT FOR THE EXERCISE OF INTELLECTUAL PROPERTY RIGHTS (IPR) IN SPACE ACTIVITIES -- MODERATION OF THE MONOPOLY ?

by Bradford Lee SMITH

Alcatel Alsthom Recherche, Intellectual Property Department

Paris- France

[1]Abstract

Intellectual Property Rights (IPR) are regarded as an insurance for high-risk industrial investments in technology. However existing patent law affords no firm basis for territorial extension to extra-terrestrial activities on orbit and beyond.

In order to attract substantial private investments for commercial space activities, legal certainty is a prerequisite, in particular in order to accurately assess potential infringement liability. The existing legal framework is a patchwork of unilateral territorial extensions (cf. US Space Bill), doctrine based on maritime law, a smattering of US case law, and the one shot InterGovernmental Agreement (IGA) for the international space station Alpha. This explosive mixture is likely to raise more legal problems than it solves.

It must not be forgotten that IPR is a competitive weapon, whose principal goal is to secure and enforce a temporary monopoly for the owner. As such, in its known forms, IPR is fundamentally antithetical to the "common benefit" tenants of the Outer Space Treaty (OST). This contradiction will be illustrated with a few real-life examples (HAC, TRW). These examples reinforce the conclusion that national patent laws and the provisions of the OST may readily lead to conflict. But how may such conflicts be resolved ?

Legal certainty may be best obtained by establishing a universal legal framework by treaty among nations having an interest in space activities. Further, the drafting of such a treaty should include provisions for the sharing of progress in space technologies for the benefit of all mankind, in conformity with the spirit of the OST.

The author proposes that the traditional IPR monopoly be diluted by a "code of conduct" consisting of treaty provisions for the use of IPR in space applications. Inspiration may be found in other fields with a similar broad interest for mankind, for example human genomes, medicinal plants, telecommunications standardisation, etc. Compulsory cross licensing could be proposed among signatory nations under fair and reasonable terms and conditions, perhaps with a predefined royalty scheme based on a percentage of profits (rather than a percentage of revenues).

Such a clearly defined sharing policy is necessary to allow would-be spacefaring nations now in the starting blocks to catch up to those whose space supremacy has

Bradford Smith is a Senior Patent Counsel in the Intellectual Property Department Alcatel Alsthom Recherche, Paris, France.

been acquired by decades of defense-related, taxpayer funding during the cold-war space race. Continuing to apply traditional IPR monopoly thinking to space activities will only perpetuate competition and conflict in place of cooperation and sharing of benefits of space activities for the common benefit of mankind.

Basic Principles

In order to examine conflicts which may arise between application of existing Intellectual Property (IP) law and the basic tenants of the Outer Space Treaty (OST), we shall first recall the principles as expressed in the various legal instruments, as well as some specific US IP-related legislation and the IP clauses of the InterGovernmental Agreement (IGA) for the international space station Alpha.

OST Article 1, Paragraph 1 states, in what has been called the "Space Benefits" clause :

> "The exploration and use of outer space ... shall be carried out for the benefit and in the interest of all countries, irrespective of their degree of economic or scientific development, and shall be the province of all mankind."
>
> Outer space... shall be free for exploration and use by all states without discrimination of any kind, on a basis of equality and in accordance with international law, ..."
>
> There shall be freedom of scientific investigation in outer space ... and States shall facilitate and encourage international co-operation in such investigation."

Article II continues :

> "Outer space ... is not subject to national appropriation by claim of sovereignty, by means of use or occupation, or by any other means."

On the other hand, the basic principles underlying national IP law may be illustrated by one of the most venerable texts on the matter, the United States Constitution (1787). Article 1, section 8, paragraph 8 states :

> "Congress shall have power ...to promote the progress of science and useful arts by securing for limited times to authors and inventors the exclusive right to their respective writings and discoveries"
> (emphasis added)

President Bush, when commenting on his signature of the US Space Bill, [2] explained how this bill would promote progress of science and useful arts by securing a temporary monopoly for US commercial entities which would apply also to space in the same manner that they would receive if their activities were conducted on earth (i.e. in the US).

The motivation for the US Space Bill as expressed by President Bush, was to obtain legal certainty that US patent law protection would be extended to Outer Space for US entities under certain broad conditions. The US Space Bill adds an article [3] to US patent law, which reads in part :

> " Any invention made, used or sold in outer space on a space object or component thereof under the jurisdiction or control of the United States shall be considered to be made, used or sold within the United States for the purposes of this title, [3] except with respect to any space object or component thereof that is specifically identified and otherwise provided for by an international agreement to which the United States is a party, or ... carried on the registry of a foreign state in accordance with the Convention of Registration of

---

[2] S459, Nov. 16, 1990, publ. in BNA vol. 41, pp. 90-93 (11/22/90).

[3] 35 U.S.C. 105

Objects Launched into Outer Space."...

The US Space Bill thus follows the "flagship principle" [4] as applied to vessels on the high seas, or aircraft flying over international waters. This "flagship principle" is pursued to its logical limits in the provisions governing applicable law (including, but not limited to IPR law) in the IGA for the international space station Alpha, which states [5] :

> "... for purposes of intellectual property law, an activity occurring in or on a Space Station flight element shall be deemed to have occurred only in the territory of the Partner State of that element's registry, except that for ESA-registered elements any European Partner State may deem that the activity to have occurred within its territory.
>
> For avoidance of doubt, participation by a Partner State, its Cooperating Agency, or its related entities in an activity occurring in or on any other Partner's Space Station flight element shall not in and of itself alter or affect the jurisdiction over such activity provided for in the previous sentence."

Industry Expectations from IPR

In practice, industry has certain needs and expectations which motivate the investments required to obtain and use Intellectual Property Rights (IPR). Thinking habits of space industry players come from the historical roots of the terrestrial practices of earth-bound industry. In the present environment, space players are still surrounded on all sides by terrestrial practice. And most space IPR practitioners have started their own trade with terrestrial practice.

In addition to identified past and present contributions to industry expectations, I think it is safe to say that there are many expectations which come from simply unfounded hopes, or plain old "wishful thinking".

So what about the content of industry expectations ? A partial list must include at least the following main expectations; whether justified or not.

Industry and practitioners alike cite the alleged "protection" of R&D investment. This may mean simply the recovery of the R&D investment, or, on the other hand, may be extended to include the future fruits of such an investment. Visionaries and optimists may go so far as to speak of ensuring not only the autonomy, but also the very survival of the enterprise as something which can and should be protected by acquisition of IPR.

A more justified expectation is that IPR should confer a competitive advantage, either to win contracts or to otherwise exclude competitors from using a cost-saving innovation or an improved technical solution.

Further commercial and marketing advantages are also often cited by industrial firms and the inventors themselves. For example, the overall image of the firm is enhanced by IPR generated within the firm. Or that granted patents and even pending patents constitute a proof of competence in the "field" which upon closer examination, may be revealed to be only casually related to the filed patent or to the invention itself.

Perhaps the most realistic expectation one could have is the usefulness of IPR in a defensive mode---against third party attacks on the basis of third party rights. Having a well-garnished patent portfolio can be useful in coming to a friendly agreement when approached by a hostile third party, if it can be argued that the third party is also a potential infringer, or that he could benefit from accepting a cross-license instead of continuing with litigation.

Finally, as reflected in President Bush's statement concerning the US Space Bill, it is hoped that IPR may also be used to

---

[4] cf. Senate Report on S 459, publ. in BNA vol. 41, p. 91 (11/22/90) : "Extraterritorial application of the patent laws".

[5] IGA art, 21, para. 2 (1988).

attract private investment for commercial space endeavors by minimising risks and maximising opportunities for obtaining economic returns.

Possible Conflicts

Is there conflict between 1) IPR use ; 2) OST ; 3) principles of IPR ? Between industry expectations and the existing legal framework for exercise of IPR in space endeavors ?

There would seem to be a fundamental conflict between a temporary monopoly granted to the owner of IPR, and the broad general terms of the OST Space Benefits clause. In some cases, IPR may also conflict with the non-appropriation clause of OST (Art. 2). We will illustrate such possible conflict by reference to a couple of real cases in the following paragraphs, which may also lead us to ask if there may be a contradiction between the use of IPR in space, and the basic underlying principle of IPR itself, i.e. to promote the progress of science and the useful arts.

Our first example concerns a US patent granted to TRW in July 1995 [6]. The main claim of this patent may be interpreted as reserving an orbital "shell" surrounding the earth between the altitudes of 5600 and 10,000 nautical miles, for virtually all conceivable practical applications in the field of satellite-based communications to mobile handsets.

As soon as the patent was granted, a foreign (non-US) competitor, ICO Global Communications Ltd., was warned that its planned satellite system was considered to be a potential infringement of that patent. The warning was followed by a lawsuit to enforce the monopoly, and to exclude that foreign competitor from implementing a global mobile satellite communications system having satellites in the forbidden (appropriated) altitude range mentioned in the main claim.

This action based on legitimately obtained US IPR seems to be in direct conflict with both the non-appropriation (Art.II) and the Space Benefits (Art. I) provisions of the OST.

The TRW-ICO conflict was recently settled, according to press reports, by the conclusion of a "non-agression" pact between the currently identified major players proposing global mobile communications satellite systems : Odyssey (TRW), Irridium (Motorola), ICO (Inmarsat), Globalstar (Space Systems Loral et al.), Teledesic (Bill Gates et al.), ... But will such a non-agression pact also be graciously extended to any and all newcomer competing systems ? For the moment, the answer depends primarily on the goodwill of the patent owners, and not on the terms of the OST which apparently do not prevent them from exercising thier enforcement rights before a US Federal Court.

Our second example concerns the famous Hughes Aircraft Company (HAC) Williams patent [7], concerning a method for obtaining and maintaining satellite attitude on orbit. Proper attitude is necessary in order to allow the satellite to properly aim its directional antennas in order to fulfill communications missions, and in some platform architectures, to orient the solar energy collectors to supply electrical energy to the payload.

Once again, shortly after this patent was granted in 1973, HAC attacked the US Government for infringement in the same year, followed by multiple attacks on foreign entities. In this case, litigation dragged on for years, practically during the whole term of the patent, and by the time the first judgement was handed down in 1983, there were 108 alledgedly infringing craft, although when the litigation started there were only 14 satellites incriminated.[8] HAC had not sought an injunction or a temporary restraining order to prevent the launches of the additional satellites, and was rewarded

[6] US-A-5,433,726 to Horstein et al.

[7] US-A-3,758,051, 1973.

[8] For discussions of the Hughes case, cf. BNA vol. 52, pp. 250-252, idem vol. 46, pp. 428-430, idem vol. 36, pp. 555-556, idem vol. 26, pp. 491-492.

financially by the substantial (multibillion dollar) damages awarded.

However, it would have theoretically been possible, especially concerning foreign entities, to request the court to halt the alleged infringing activities pending final judgement of the case. If this had happened, in view of the necessity of a method for maintaining the satellite attitude in order to fulfill communications missions, this patent could be seen to hinder, rather than to promote, the progress of science and the useful arts, at least during its term of enforcement.

These two examples serve to illustrate that in practical situations in the use of IPR, conflicts may arise with the basic tenants of the OST, and even with the fundamental underlying principles of IPR itself.

Existing attempts to obtain legal certainty for IPR in space activities through extension of territorial sovreignty via the flagship principle (e.g. US Space Bill, IGA) present only ad-hoc, piecemenal solutions concerning the forum for IPR enforcement. However these efforts do not attempt to address the fundamental underlying conflicts illustrated above.

Analagous Conflicts in Other Fields

Space endeavors are not the only field in which conflicts arise in the application of IPR to activities having an interest for all mankind. Perhaps we can learn from these analagous situations and the methods attempted to resolve the ethical problems arising.

In a first example, US patents have recently been granted concerning therapeutic uses of certain medicinal plants imported from India, and their pharmaceutical derivatives. The Indian medical profession, according to press reports, is stunned with disbelief, as these plants and their medicinal properties have been known and used indigineously for centuries. Indian doctors are now working to find prior published accounts in order to invalidate the patents, but they are encountering some difficulty as the use of such plants is in fact a folk tradition handed down through generations. As such, these traditional uses are more likely to be referred to in allegories and in novels that in medical treatises.

The reader will probably be aware of the highly mediatised attempts by the US National Institutes of Health (NIH) to patent thousands of human gene fragments as they were identified, without even a hint as to their function or usefulness. In fact, the corresponding patent applications were computer-generated directly from experimental results, practically without human intervention.

The filing of these patents caused great emotions in the international community for ethical reasons, and led to diplomatic intervention from foreign governments (France in particular). The applications were withdrawn, so that the issue of their patentability was never finally decided by the USPTO (although rejected in the first Office Action).

In a technical field a bit closer to space endeavors, namely that of telecommunications standardisation, conflicts have arisen from the standardisation of patented methods and technology. The owners of such patents then find themselves in a position of absolute domination, as such standards render the use of the patented method or technology mandatory.

This problem has been addressed by a number of standards bodies, of which the most recent example is that of ETSI (the European Telecoms Standardisation Institution). In long, hard-fought negociations between the various industry players and telecoms operators which make up ETSI, a compromise was eventually found. Dominant industry players, in particular some of the US firms, did not want to see any dilution of their IPR strength and resulting market domination. At one point, they were nearly ejected from ETSI for this predatory attitude and their unwavering stance.

Finally, a compromise was reached, including declaration of relevant IPR during the standardiation process, and a committment from holders of standard-relevant IPR to make licenses available under fair and reasonable terms and conditions. If such committments are not given, then the patented technology or method is barred from standardiation.

Possible Resolutions of IPR in Space

In order to resolve apparent or potential conflicts with fundamental principles which may arise from the use of IPR in space activities, we propose that a code of conduct be elaborated for such use.

This code of conduct should reflect the basic principles and rely on them for its terms. We are committed to promoting the progress of science and the useful arts, while rewarding inventors for their efforts, and procuring Space Benefits for all mankind. Any appropriation of any region of space for any use should be formally precluded. Patentability incompatible with the basic principles should be excluded. Such exclusion would be most effective if operated in the patent examination phase.

A first step is reflected in the UN Declaration on International Cooperation in the Exploration and Use of Outer Space for the Benefit and in the Interests of All States, Taking into Particular Account the Needs of Developing Countries, [9] which states in particular :

> in Para. 2 : " States are free to determine all aspects of their participation in international cooperation ... on an equitable and mutually acceptable basis. Contractual terms in such cooperative ventures shold be fair and reasonable and they should be in full compliance with the legitimate rights and interests of the parties concerned, as, for example, with intellectual property rights. "
>
> And in Para. 5, last alinea : "International coooperation, while taking into particular account the needs of developing countries, should aim, *inter alia*, at the following goals ...
>
> ... Facilitating the exchange of expertise and technology among States on a mutually acceptable basis. "

[9] A/AC.105/L.211, 11 June 1996.

We urge the necessity of a harmonisation, a uniformisation of applicable law, which could be obtained through the efforts of an international treaty organisation such as UNCOPUOS.

Modest Recommendations

Whereas the space industry is a truly global endeavor at present, the playing field is not level for all of the global players. This is related to several problems above, plus favouritism of governments and contracting organisations towards their own national champions.

The best we could hope for in a free market economy of space-related endeavors would be to reap the (until now) illusory expectations of industry and private investors as exposed above. This would surely be limited in practice, but industry would like to be able to use IPR to protect its R&D investments, to gain competitive advantages such as marketing and commercial advantages, and to be able to continue industrial pursuits without fear of third party aggressions on IPR issues. These expectations must remain compatible with the basic principles of promoting the progress of science and the useful arts, while ensuring appropriate rewards for inventors, and allowing all states to reap Space Benefits regardless of their respective levels of scientific or economic development.

As exposed above, a major and necessary step towards achieving such a situation is to **establish legal certainty** for IPR issues in space-related activities. Obtention and enforcement of IPR must be clarified in view of disparate territorial principles.

The obvious question to be resolved is that of the universality vs territoriality or nationality question. However in view of the general interest of space-related activities to mankind as a whole, as reflected in the terms of the Outer Space Treaty, we should perhaps consider at length the possibility of developing a fair scheme which strikes a balance between the private interests which generate innovation at the expense of financial and human resources, and which hope to capitalize on those investments ; and the wider interests of the planet, perhaps through some sort of compulsory licensing scheme under fair and resonable terms and conditions.

The best solution may well be to **establish space and its accesses (launch sites, vehicles) as a single territory with a single, uniform law**. This could be an international treaty elaborated for example by COPUOS, and administered and interpreted by **a single, universal enforcement body** such as an international court of law or an international arbitration authority. Perhaps such an arbitration authority could be created under the auspices of the World Trade Organisation (WTO), aided by the World Intellectual Property Organisation (WIPO) for the IPR aspects.

To further facilitate the application of IPR law in Outer Space, it may be considered expedient to create a "Space Patent" , which could be for example a designation on an international patent application under the Patent Cooperation Treaty. Such designation would indicate that the resulting patent would be interpreted and enforced by the above arbitration authority according to the above single uniform law, concerning space objects and space activities, instead of being judged according to national law in a national court.

The UNCOPUOS Declaration is a first step to show the way to proceed. The field of IPR and space activities is only beginning to take on its economic and ethical importance. The time is ripe for efforts from the Legal Subcommittee to balance the needs and rewards of the various actors in space activities and to work out a legal framework which can take them into the 21st century with minimum conflict and maximum progress and cooperation.

THE 1996 UN-DECLARATION ON "SPACE BENEFITS" ENDING THE NORTH-SOUTH DEBATE ON SPACE COOPERATION

Dr. Marietta Benkö, Attorney-at-Law, Cologne
Dr. Kai-Uwe Schrogl, German Space Agency DARA, Bonn

Abstract

At its 1996 session, UNCOPUOS adopted by consensus a "Declaration on International Cooperation in the Exploration and Use of Outer Space for the Benefit and in the Interests of All States, Taking into Particular Account the Needs of Developing Countries". It was recommended for adoption at the 1996/97 session of the UN General Assembly.

This Declaration finalizes the agenda item in the UNCOPUOS Legal Subcommittee which has become known as "Space Benefits". It provides an authoritative interpretation of the cooperation principle in Article I of the Outer Space Treaty. It furthermore puts an end to the North-South confrontation in shaping the international order for space activities.

The authors, members of the German delegation to the UNCOPUOS Legal Subcommittee, describe in this paper the background of the agenda item "Space Benefits", analyse the first draft resolutions by a group of developing countries, explain the philosophy of the German-French counter-proposal of 1995, report about the merger of the two approaches during the 1996 session of UNCOPUOS and introduce the Declaration in its final form.

1. Putting "Space Benefits" on the Agenda (1988)

The agenda setting process in the UNCOPUOS Legal Subcommittee (LSC) has - as it is quite common in the UN - so far been a political tightrope-act. Not the straight solution of legal problems but the maintenance of an equilibrium between regional interests has clearly been in the forefront. So, after UNCOPUOS had adopted the Principles on Remote Sensing in 1986, this group provided the next agenda item replacing „Remote Sensing“ especially since the group of Western countries could not agree on any new approach or even a common proposal. Nevertheless, it was obviously difficult for the developing countries to find an appropriate subject.

Having failed to see their interests adequately reflected in the existing body of space law the developing countries approached the basic question, which was rather posed than answered in the first article of the Outer Space Treaty: On the one hand outer space is free for exploration (para. 2), on the other hand space exploration shall be carried out for the benefit and in the interests of all countries (para. 1). Raising the statement of para.1 over the statement para. 2 therefore was the not yet clearly defined aim of the developing countries, when in 1988 the agenda item "Consideration of the Legal Aspects Related to the Application of the Principle that the Exploration and Utilization of Outer Space Should be Carried out for the Benefit and in the Interest of all States Taking into Particular Account the Needs of Developing Countries" appeared on the agenda of the LSC.

The longer the text of an agenda item is, the more controversy it surely contains. In this case the industrialized countries softened the subject in so far that they only allowed for the "Consideration of the legal aspects ...". For years, the industrialized countries used this wording to support their position that the LSC should consider and discuss but not dare to draft any sort of legal text. Without any ideas of their own at that stage, the developing countries were assisted by the UN Office for Outer Space Affairs in finding a position[*] .

2. The Questionnaires on International Cooperation (1988-1991)

The lack of orientation - due to the political deadlock - in the first phase of discussions produced what so often is done to avoid embarrassment: questionnaires were sent out[†] . A first questionnaire on national frameworks for space activities[‡] and a second one on the States' assessment of existing treaties in the field of space activities[§] . When the chairman of the Working Group on "Space Benefits" presented his analysis of the answers to these two questionnaires in 1992 [¶] , the results were already obsolete because the developing countries had already figured out a bold new approach.

3. The Draft Set of Principles by the Developing Countries and Its First Revision (1991-1994)

The developing countries became serious about integrating the issues of outer space into their concept of New International Orders (like for the world economy, the High See or the information and communication sys-

[*] See *Nandasiri Jasentuliyana*, Article I of the Outer Space Treaty Revisited, in: Journal of Space Law (17,2) 1989, pp.129-144.

[†] For an assessment of this phase see *Kai-Uwe Schrogl*, "Space Benefits" - A New Aspect of Global Politics, in: German Foreign Affairs Review (42,4) 1991, pp.373-382.

[‡] Distributed in September 1988. The replies are documented in UN Doc. A/AC.105/C.2/15 and Add. 1-13 of 9 February 1989 ff.

[§] Distributed in December 1989. The replies are documented in UN Doc. A/AC.105/C.2/16 and Add. 1-10 of 27 February 1990 ff.

[¶] UN Doc. A/AC.105/C.2/L.187 of 22 January 1992.

tem)[**]. Nine developing countries presented a working paper containing a draft for "Principles Regarding International Cooperation in the Exploration and Utilization of Outer Space for Peaceful Purposes"[‡‡]. This draft set of principles was rich in New International Order language aiming at forced cooperation and an automated transfer of financial and technological resources from North to South. This came as a shock for the industrialized countries since such a strong attack on the freedom of space exploration and utilization had not been expected. Doubting that the LSC had any mandate to discuss such texts, the industrialized countries refused to even talk about the working paper. When the developing countries realized that they had gone too far and produced a less aggressive revision of their working paper in 1993[§§], they had to concede that their attempt for a redistributive revolution in international space cooperation had failed[¶¶].

4. The German-French Counter-Proposal and the Developing Countries' Response (1995)

Although the developing countries could not in any way persuade the industrialized countries to accept their approach, the four sessions from 1991 to 1994, when the draft set of principles was discussed in the LSC made clear that passivity was detrimental to the international climate as well. Industrialized countries realized that they could act up as well by exhibiting their broad programmes with developing countries. Making clear that numerous developing countries already participated in bilateral space projects and that industrialized countries do provide considerable amounts of money for building satellite utilization capacities in developing countries (i.a. through multilateral programmes like the UN Space Applications Programme), the industrialized countries set a new tone for the debate: the North is already making considerable efforts voluntarily and cooperation has to be beneficial for both sides.

In this situation Germany and France decided to present - at the 1995 session of the LSC - a working paper containing a draft "Declaration on International Cooperation in the Exploration and Use of Outer Space for the Benefit and in the Interests of all States, Taking into Particular Account the Needs of Developing Countries"[***]. The German-French working paper rested on two basic considerations: first, that States are free to determine all aspects of their international cooperation, whether it is bilateral or multilateral or whether it is commercial or non-commercial, including of course development cooperation; second, that States shall choose the most effective and appropriate mode of cooperation in order to allocate resources efficiently[†††]. Glad that at last a dialogue had begun, the co-sponsors of the developing countries' working paper - now led by Brazil, which (a space-power itself) was less redistribution-minded and diplomatically more constructive - presented a far more conciliatory second revision[§§§]. Time for a merger was however not yet right at that session. First of all there were still some fields of disagreement and secondly States are not very quick in acting, when matters like the reconciliation of different ideological positions are concerned. Therefore, the attempt by the chairman of the working group to more or less simply add the two texts in a voluminous but rather incoherent version had of course to be doomed. Anyhow, it was above all meant to put pressure on the two parties to find their own solution quickly[¶¶¶].

5. The Merger of the Two Texts (1996)

A merger happened surprisingly quick in 1996. It was prepared in the LSC among the German, the French and the Brazilian delegations in March[‡‡‡] and finalized in the plenary of the Main Committee of UNCOPUOS in June on the basis of the merged text, which - with a few square brackets - had been introduced in the LSC as a chairman's paper[****]. The final text of the Declaration, adopted in the UNCOPUOS Main Committee in June 1996 is annexed to this paper. It will, after having passed the Political Committee, be presented to the UN General Assembly for adoption during its 1996/97 session. The possibilities that the Political Committee or the General Assembly itself might change the text is rather small.

With regard to the text adopted in UNCOPUOS, we should not look at details, as to which text is taken from which paper. For example: the title of the legal text originates from the German-French working paper and

[**] See the analysis by *Stephan Hobe and Kai-Uwe Schrogl*, "Space Benefits" - Towards a new international order for space, in: Space Communications (11,1) 1993, pp.3-11.

[‡‡] UN Doc A/AC.105/C.2/L.182 of 9 April 1991.

[§§] UN Doc.A/AC.105/C.2/L.182/Rev.1 of 31 March 1993.

[¶¶] For an analysis of the working paper and its first revision see *Kai-Uwe Schrogl*, "Space Benefits", in: *Marietta Benkö and Kai-Uwe Schrogl (eds.)*, International Space Law in the Making, Editions Frontières, Gif-sur-Yvette 1993, pp.195-231. The two texts are annexed to that article. For a different view see *Nandasiri Jasentuliyana*, Ensuring equal access to the benefits of space technologies for all countries in: Space Policy (10,1) 1994, pp. 7-18.

[***] UN Doc. A/AC.105/C.2/L.197 of 27 March 1995.

[†††] For an in-depth account on the backgroud of the German-French working paper see *Marietta Benkö and Kai-Uwe Schrogl*, "Space benefits" - towards a useful framework for international cooperation, in: Space Policy (11,1) 1995, pp.5-8.

[§§§] UN Doc. A/AC.105/C.2/L.182/Rev.2 of 23 March 1995.

[¶¶¶] For a more detailed report on the results of the 1995 session of the LSC see *Marietta Benkö and Kai-Uwe Schrogl*, The UN Committee on the Peaceful Uses of Outer Space: Progress on "Space Benefits" and Other Recent Developments, in: German Journal for Air and Space Law ZLW (44,3) 1995, pp.291-305. The texts of the German-French working paper and the second revision of the developing countries' working paper are annexed to that article.

[‡‡‡] The two parties had each presented slightly modified versions of their texts from 1995: UN Doc. A/AC.105/C.2/L.197/Rev.1 of 19 March 1996 by Germany and France and UN Doc. A/AC.105/C.2/L.182/Rev.3 of 22 March 1996 by Brazil and at that time already 11 other developing countries (but with the exception of Argentina, which - a co-sponsor of the original working paper - left the group in 1995 in order to press for a more conciliatory approach).

[****] UN Doc. A/AC.105/C.2/L.202 of 27 March 1996.

the structure resembles more the developing countries' proposal. It is far more important that all member States of UNCOPUOS finally agreed on the basics of a liberal regime, such as it was pointed out in the German-French proposal, and had to a great extent already been reflected in the later drafts of the developing countries.

The Declaration is introduced by a preamble pointing out the relevant provisions of international law and stressing equally the demand for more international (mutually beneficial!) cooperation (para. 8) and the fact that international cooperation is already well-established (para. 7). The Preamble also mentions (para. 6) international organizations as participants in international space cooperation. The Declaration itself, however, only speaks of States since they are the ones to adopt it as a Resolution in the UNGA. However, it is evident, that international organizations, like the European Space Agency, are - through their member States - as free to determine their cooperation as are their single member States.

The text of the Declaration itself

- presents in para.1 the basis for international cooperation;

- stresses in para.2 the freedom of cooperation and - as a novelty in space law - refers to intellectual property rights as legitimate right and interest of States in this field, which is of importance for all fields of space technology but of particular importance for the field of earth observation data;

- makes clear in para. 3 that the space powers must not forget to integrate the developing countries into space exploration. However, this para. does not intend to force cooperation but instead focusses on an already broadly developed net of space cooperation, bilaterally or - as already mentioned - through international activities like the UN Space Applications Programme;

- introduces in para. 4 effectiveness as a basic principle for international cooperation, thus providing an instrument for countering fancy demands like e.g. for the creation of a World Space Organizations. So this para. could be regarded as containing the "subsidiarity principle" for international space activities. This para. - also for the first time in UN space law making - sets commercial space activities on one level with State activities (however without changing anything in the way, the Outer Space Treaty has regulated State responsibility). This has a more political than legal impact but it is a tribute to the changed environment;

- enumerates in para. 5 the fields of international cooperation and makes again clear what efficiency means;

- calls upon als players in para. 6 to use space services for development cooperation. This will for example also help space agencies in industrialized countries to stimulate the use of satellite data by their development aid ministries and agencies most of which still have rather conservative tendencies in selecting their tools;

- supports in para. 7 the efforts of UNCOPUOS;

- asks all States in para. 8 to support the UN Space Applications Programme, which for example Germany - one of the parents of this Declaration - fulfilled in 1996 through hosting the 6th UN/ESA Workshop on Basic Space Science in Bonn.

6. The Expected Impact of the 1996 Declaration

The Declaration should - at least in the point of view of their drafters - have basically three broader impacts:

1. It marks the end of a North-South debate which had focussed on the introduction of forced cooperation and transfer of ressources. By now providing an authoritative interpretation of the cooperation principle of Art. I of the Outer Space Treaty the Declaration prevents further confrontation on a general political level.

2. It cements the freedom of the exploration and utilization of outer space but at the same time reminds the space powers - in a productive and mutually fruitful manner - to fulfill their obligation to conduct their activities for the benefit of all countries, which means that the space powers should foster international cooperation - on an equitable and mutually acceptable basis. This means that developing countries interested in space activities have now higher incentives to put their energies in a, by own efforts well-prepared, "demand-pull" instead of waiting for a politically induced "technology push". This will make many of them more equal partners in cooperation, the space powers are ready to accept. Maybe this will even lead to the only reasonable way for them to become active in space, which is to pool resources on a regional basis (as even the industrialized countries of Europe had to do).

3. In parallel to the adoption of the Declaration, UNCOPUOS took the basic decision to organise a third UNISPACE Conference alternatively in 1999 or in 2000. While the UNISPACE Conferences of 1968 and even more so of 1982 had been used as platforms for conflicts over distribution, UNISPACE III will - thanks to the Declaration - be able to avoid an ideological debate on the international order for outer space and concentrate instead on the benefit, space applications can provide for all mankind.

Annex

UN Doc. A/AC.105/L.211 of 11 June 1996 "Text of Declaration on International Cooperation in the Exploration and Use of Outer Space for the Benefit and in the Interests of All States, Taking into Particular Account the Needs of Developing Countries"

The General Assembly,

Having considered the report of the Committee on the Peaceful Uses of Outer Space on the work of its thirty-ninth session and the text of the Declaration on International Cooperation in the Exploration and Use of Outer Space for the Benefit and in the Interests of All States, Taking into Particular Account the Needs of Developing Countries, as approved by the Committee and annexed to its report,

Bearing in mind the relevant provisions of the Charter of the United Nations.

Recalling notably the provisions of the Treaty on Principles Governing the Activities of States in the Exploration and Use of Outer Space, including the Moon and Other Celestial Bodies,

Recalling also its relevant resolutions relating to activities in outer space,

Bearing in mind the recommendation of the Second United Nations Conference on the Exploration and Peaceful Uses of Outer Space, and of other international conferences relevant in this field,

Recognizing the growing scope and significance of international cooperation among States and between States and international organizations in the exploration and use of outer space for peaceful purposes,

Considering experiences gained in international cooperative ventures,

Convinced of the necessity and the significance of further strengthening international cooperation in order to reach a broad and efficient collaboration in this field for the mutual benefit and in the interests of all parties involved,

Desirous of facilitating the application of the principle that the exploration and use of outer space, including the Moon and other celestial bodies, shall be carried out for the benefit and in the interests of all countries, irrespective of their degree of economic or scientific development, and shall be the province of all mankind,

Adopts the Declaration on International Cooperation in the Exploration and Use of Outer Space for the benefit and in the Interests of All States. Taking into Particular Account the Needs of Developing Countries, set forth in the annex to the present resolution.

Annex

Declaration on International Cooperation in the Exploration and Use of Outer Space for the Benefit and in the Interests of all States, Taking into Particular Account the Needs of Developing Countries

1. International cooperation in the exploration and use of outer space for peaceful purposes (hereafter „international cooperation") shall be conducted in accordance with the provisions of international law, including the Charter of the United Nations and the Treaty on Principles Governing the Activities of States in the Exploration and Use of Outer Space, including the Moon and Other Celestial Bodies. It shall be carried out for the benefit and in the interests of all States, irrespective of their degree of economic, social or scientific and technological development, and shall be the province of all mankind. Particular account should be taken of the needs of developing countries.

2. States are free to determine all aspects of their participation in international cooperation in the exploration and use of outer space on an equitable and mutually acceptable basis. Contractual terms in such cooperative ventures should be fair and reasonable and they should be in full compliance with the legitimate rights and interests of the parties concerned as, for example, with intellectual property rights.

3. All States, particularly those with relevant space capabilities and with programmes for the exploration and use of outer space, should contribute to promoting and fostering international cooperation on an equitable and mutually acceptable basis. In this context, particular attention should be given to the benefit for and the interests of developing countries and countries with incipient space programmes stemming from such international cooperation conducted with countries with more advanced space capabilities.

4. International cooperation should be conducted in the modes that are considered most effective and appropriate by the countries concerned including *inter alia*, governmental and non-governmental; commercial and non-commercial; global, multilateral, regional or bilateral; and international cooperation among countries in all levels of development.

5. International cooperation, while taking into particular account the needs of developing countries, should aim, *inter alia*, at the following goals, considering their need for technical assistance and rational and efficient allocation of financial and technical resources:

Promoting the development of space science and technology and of its applications;

Fostering the development of relevant and appropriate space capabilities in interested States;

Facilitating the exchange of expertise and technology among States on a mutually acceptable basis.

6. National and international agencies, research institutions, organizations for development aid, and developed and developing countries alike should consider the appropriate use of space applications and the potential of international cooperation for reaching their development goals.

7. The Committee on the Peaceful Uses of Outer Space should be strengthened in its role, among others, as a forum for the exchange of information on national and international activities in the field of international cooperation in the exploration and use of outer space.

8. All States should be encouraged to contribute to the United Nations Programme on Space Applications and to other initiatives in the field of international cooperation in accordance with their space capabilities and their participation in the exploration and use of outer space.

Session 4:
OTHER LEGAL MATTERS

Chairman: T. Kosuge, Japan
E. Fasan, Austria

IISL-96-IISL.4.02

PARALYSIS BY PHANTOM:
PROBLEMS OF THE ITU FILING PROCEDURES

by

Francis Lyall*
Professor of Public Law
University of Aberdeen
Aberdeen AB24 3UB
Scotland, U.K.

Abstract

The international procedures through which intended satellite systems are notified to the ITU, and later systems have to be co-ordinated with earlier, is in danger of paralysis through notification of systems which are unlikely to be implemented. This abuse of procedures is presently under consideration in the ITU. Proposed solutions, 'due diligence' by states in investigating proposals submitted to them, or a suitable 'filing fee' are considered. The paper suggests that in addition recourse might be had to the doctrine of 'implied powers' of international organisations, to justify the ITU itself refusing to accept such notifications. As it notes, this paper now contains material not available at the time of its initial delivery.

Director, IISL.
Corresponding Member, IAA.

Introduction

The International Telecommunication Union plays a major role in the functioning of telecommunications generally. Its roles in the allocation of radio frequencies, in ensuring the propriety of frequency assignments, in the use of those assignments, in the matter of orbits, and in the coordination of systems are fundamental to the modern use of outer space, and particularly for the various space telecommunication networks. To fulfil these roles the ITU has developed various mechanisms and procedures. Unfortunately some of these procedures have, within recent years, been abused. It is time to seek to abate this nuisance, which in an international sense is a 'public nuisance' although it has been to an extent been acquiesced in by those who should know better.

The problem (properly the problems) outlined below has been identified by the ITU. The Plenipotentiary Conference of the Union which was held in Kyoto in 1994, adopted Resolution 18, calling for a review of various important issues concerning international satellite coordination. Three objectives were identified for this review: equitable access and the efficient establishment and development of satellite networks; that coordination procedures should meet the needs of administrations while preserving the interests of other services; the examination of technical advances in relation to allotment plans to see whether they provide a flexible and efficient use of the spectrum and the geo-stationary orbit. These objectives comply with the requirements of the ITU's basic documents.

Simultaneously, the Kyoto Conference also adopted Resolutions 15 and 39. The first of these involves a review of the rights and obligations of all the members of sectors of the ITU so as to enhance the responsiveness of the ITU to the changing telecommunications environment. Financial questions are not irrelevant in that review. However, under Resolution 19 separate but linked consideration is being given to the strengthening of the financial base of the Union.

Work has proceeded under each of these three Resolutions, but none of the reviews has reached the point of final recommendations. The 1995 Radiocommunication Assembly established a Special Committee on Regulatory/Procedural Matters, and inter alia charged that Committee with work under the three Resolutions. The Special Committee has sought the views of the ITU members and named two Rapporteurs to prepare draft reports for the Special Committee meeting in January 1997. On the basis of discussion then, and probably with other input, the Director of the Radiocommunication Sector will make a final report to the World Radiocommunication Assembly later that year.

When the initial form of this paper was drafted interim reports and submissions by interested parties were not available to me. Some now are, particularly through Internet access.[1] I have, however, thought it best to retain the broad-brush approach of the Beijing paper, while inserting some (but not all) reference to the newly available documentation. The sketch of the matter presented in China has provided not to be wholly inaccurate, and in sketch form may be more useful for this forum rather than an attempt to track detail. Those wishing to pursue the matter in further detail are directed to the ITU web-site.[2]

The Problem

By Article III of the Outer Space Treaty, International Law applies in Outer Space, and that principle would now appear to have become customary international law as well as being treaty-based. Under Article VI of the Treaty states bear international responsibility for national activities in Outer Space, and are under a duty to authorise and continuingly to supervise their nationals' use of Outer Space. Telecommunications is a major area in which states discharge these obligations. Naturally, however, the bald words of Articles III and VI are too imprecise. For detail of the obligations one has to look at International Law as made within the framework of the International Telecommunication Union, obligations which in their principle go back to the origins of the ITU.

Under the ITU Radio Regulations, as amended, a state Member of the ITU notifies to the Bureau of the ITU Radiocommunication Sector its intention to assign the use of a particular frequency or more usually a set of frequencies, and, where appropriate, an orbital slot on the geostationary orbit, to an operator for use by a space system. This procedure is engaged in whether the intended operator is the state itself, whether the operator will be an international organisation for which that particular state acts,[3] or whether the operator will be some other entity such as a company amenable to the licensing jurisdiction of the state.

When the Radiocommunication Sector of the ITU receives such notification, the notification is checked for conformity with the Table of Allocations of the Radio Regulations, and the Master International Frequency Register is also checked to see whether any other system has previously been registered to use those frequencies and orbit. Any problem with each other systems is followed up. Receipt of the notification is brought to the attention of member Administrations. If there is no apparent difficulty with the notice the ITU enters the assignment as received in the appropriate register, the Master International Frequency Register, and the information is published by the ITU in its weekly bulletin.

Of course, just as one terrestrial radio station may intrude on another, any space system may impinge on another space system, and the coordination of systems is important. Under the ITU system, the use of the radio spectrum requires systems using compatible or similar frequencies properly to integrate what they do so as to secure the efficient use of the radio spectrum.[4] Causing interference to other systems is also specifically prohibited.[5] And, of course, apart from the legal obligations, the fixed and unalterable laws of physics form a constraint. It is not too much to say that in space telecommunications, the prescripts of physics are the ultimate ius cogens!

These matters antedate the opening of space. Terrestrial radio systems interfere with other as it is, but matters would be much worse had not states at an early stage in radio history established the Table of Allocations, and the procedures for the notification of assignments to the ITU.[6] Further, it was early and easily accepted that priority of notification of an assignment which confirmed to the Table of Allocations, meant that assignment should be protected from harmful interference. Priority of notification came therefore to assume great importance. Indeed, it has come to be referred to in the somewhat pejorative expression - 'first come, first served'. This formulation is overstated, but it is true that states coming later into the ITU forum have on occasion felt that their needs were not equitably protected, the older states having already 'notified' frequencies and orbital positions which the newcomers might have wanted to use. Further, through substitution of satellites a state may continue to use slots and frequencies that were originally notified for a previous satellite.

Nonetheless, until recently the principle of priority through notification worked well, preventing much dispute and squabbling, since it meant that potential disputants were not working from a position of equality. One state did have a priority in the matter. This did not mean that a state having priority was under no duty to seek to accommodate the requirements of the newcomer. It did, however, mean that the newcomer was under greater pressure to make concessions in discussions between them. The onus in the matter was clear. The later had to contact the earlier. The earlier can to some extent stand on its rights. And of course, other existing systems have a greater authority than planned, or even more hypothetical, systems. The existing and even the well-nigh existing deserves greater consideration than the possible or the may-be.

In the past, when these procedures and requirements were being worked out, not too many states were involved in licensing and in notifying systems. In addition there were not too many systems to be dealt with. Now, the demand for space systems is considerable and this has been aggravated by geography. God did not see fit to distribute habitable land equally round the globe, so centres of population are not regularly distributed round the world. It follows that orbital positions which 'see' population centres, or which can encompass both sides of an ocean, are more useful than others. These positions are therefore sought by many satellite systems.

The problem has therefore emerged that some states have proved willing to notify the ITU of intended assignments of orbits and frequencies for a projected system, when the system exists only in a tentative form (if that) in the mind of their proposers. The intention has been, it seems, to obtain whatever advantage can be got through making notification to Geneva and getting the system entered on the Master International Frequency Register. As we have seen, under the 'rules' the registered notification has 'priority' and later systems have to seek coordination with these 'prior' systems.

Of course, this is an abuse of the system. The system of notification/registration worked on the basis of proven and 'real' requirements. However, just as some countries have notified systems beyond their own requirements for national telecommunications so as to gain financially through leasing or otherwise engaging in business, so others have sought to gain a priority by notifying systems which have barely entered the planning stage, let alone progressed through it.

Five major variants of the fundamental problem arise.

First, states which have more fully planned and in a sense therefore 'real' systems to notify, have found themselves under an obligation to coordinate their systems with systems which exist only on paper - hence the phrase 'paper satellites'.

Second, the fact of the quasi-spurious nature of a filing is not always obvious. This can deter others from proceeding with a system proposal.

Third, the result could be a 'compromise' solution in which the earlier 'system' is 'modified' in the abstract in exchange for a real concession by the other side.

Fourth, the filing and coordinating procedures within the ITU has become clogged by the administrative procedures which any filing triggers. The detail of a notified system have to be checked against the Table of Allocations and any other regulations, as well as against the detail of any relevant prior notified systems. The ITU has also had to cope with its duty to seek to arrange an accommodation between competing systems. ITU effort is wasted when one of these is a phantom, but has been through the notification and registration procedure, and the other is a later, but nonetheless a 'real' system lacking only the magic protection of priority of notification to the ITU.

Fifth, a related problem is that systems once established do not always fully conform to the parameters indicated in the notification filed with the ITU. This is not quite the same problem as the others, but could be tackled to an extent by the same solutions as the others.

The problem of filings which do not result in working systems has been known about for some years, and is now being attacked through the work of the Radiocommunication Advisory Group (RAG) with a view to action by the ITU. I outline the main proposals so far as I understand them, and add another of my own.[7]

Due Diligence

As indicated above, it is the responsibility of a state to supervise and license the activities in Outer Space of those subject to its jurisdiction. It is the right and duty of states alone to engage in the ITU filing process. It has therefore been thought that, were states properly carrying out their functions - exercising due diligence in the exercise of their responsibilities - the problem would be diminished if not elided.

This is an attractive suggestion. But of course it does imply that some states have been less than diligent in the past. While some may bridle in anger at such a suggestion, it is a fact of life that that is indeed the cause of the present problem. What assurance is there that states which have not exercised 'due diligence' in the past will suddenly change their behaviour?

Cynicism aside, it can be argued that what must be sought is a means through which 'due diligence' can be encouraged.

A US Discussion paper in 1996 outlines certain possibilities,[8] which others have later agreed with. In particular it is suggested that the information required to be notified to the ITU by an 'assigning' state could be extended. This would go some way to show that a proposal is real, and that it has already gone some way towards implementation. Thus, were launch dates and completion dates for stages of spacecraft and other construction supplied as well as the current bare information as to location, and frequencies, there would be a greater assurance that the notification is of a system that will be proceeded with.

While this is attractive, it has some problems. Present regulations require notification up to nine years in advance of commissioning the system, and it may be unrealistic to demand detail that far in advance. (The Radio Regulations Board has suggested four years).[9]

On the other hand some provision could be included under which particular information was to be supplied closer to completion of the project. That would permit a running check to be kept on progress. A notification which failed timeously to supply information on progress could then simply be deleted, and its 'assignments' made available for others without the need to coordinate with the prior and now expired system.

However, there is a fundamental problem with such an idea. The initial filing would still require ITU action, and the clogging of the system by filing would not be eased.

An alternative variant of this possibility is to keep such checks on the genuineness of a proposal within the competence, and therefore perhaps the confidentiality of the state administrations. States could be encouraged to require more information to be supplied and substantiated within the national licensing or authorising procedure before proceeding to notify the ITU, and without passing on that data to the ITU. Such information could be kept confidential in detail on commercial grounds. Of course, the cloak of 'commercial confidentiality' could in turn be itself abused, but there may be more to gain by requiring that a state at least certify that it has been satisfied as to such matters as the commercial viability of the applicant, of the project, and the detail of the planning and scheduling of the system. Should the project not be proceeded with the state would have been shown to have failed in its duty, and that alone might be a sufficient sanction.

The trouble is, of course, that it would seem that some states have already failed to be embarrassed by it being known that they engage in such unscrupulous, and I would say, immoral failure to exercise 'due diligence'. Would more publicity for such failures be a solution?

Whatever one thinks of these points, a renewed stress on 'due diligence' coupled with some more obvious indicators as to full compliance with the duty, has some advantages. In form the 'due diligence' approach is simple. It emphasises state responsibilities which already exist both under the Outer Space Treaty and the ITU system. Some might also stress that in that 'due diligence' puts the onus on states rather than on an international organisation, it thus recognises state sovereignty and guards against its diminution.

On the other hand, we got where we are at present by trusting states. Some more transparency is needed so that they can be seen to do their duty. And, even if other mechanisms are brought into play, increased transparency in all forms of governance is rarely a bad thing. In the case where a an actual working system is found not to correspond with the information in the notification to the ITU, publicity may also be useful.

But there remains one huge flaw in such an emphasis on 'due diligence'. Not only does it assume (or encourage) states to do their suty, It assumes that all states are equally competent in supervising, checking and scrutinising the material involved. That patently is not so, and the problem is likely to get even worse as enterpreneurs persuade small states to make use of their rights under the ITU system to license speculative endeavours. In the discussion of this paper in Beijing, it was suggested that the solution would be for states of marginal competence to hire consultants to do the work for them. However, a) that assumes that a state is willing in effect to admit its inability adequately to discharge its international obligations, b) it still leaves the state with the duty of evaluating the advice it is given, and c) it assumes that the "consultant" interest is undividedly devoted to the international interest in the matter. None of these need be so.

Filing fee

Another set of proposals would attach a filing fee to any notification to the ITU.[10] Were those setting up the space system to have to meet a significant financial cost as part of the filing process, that might well deter some at least of the more outrageous or frivolous proposals.

Various forms of the filing fee can be conceived. The fee might be a 'good faith' deposit, returnable to the system operator once the system was operational. Interest on the deposit would help offset the costs of processing the notification. Again, if a working system is found not to conform to its notified data, the filing fee should be forfeit.

On the other hand, the fee could simply be a 'processing fee' which could accurately reflect the cost of putting the notification through the ITU procedures, and thereby help ITU finances through making those who produce the work pay for its execution. Cost recovery for facilities provided has its attractions.[11]

Finally some mixture of the two extreme 'filing fee' approaches could be taken - a proportion of the fee returnable in due course while some proprtion would be retained to offset the ITU costs. This could also be adapted to the case where the system as activated does not quite fit the original notification. Thus were the system not brought into service within a specified period, or were its characteristic found not to conform to the filing, the deposit would be forfeit in whole or in part to the ITU.

What might be a suitable figure for the fee is, of course, a question. A UK/Luxemburg paper [12] speaks in terms of returnable deposit of 2% of the cost of each satellite in the system multiplied by a charge for the amount of spectrum space sought computed in units of 1000 MHz. If the fee were not to be returnable, it could be set somewhat differently, relating it clearly to processing cost. In any case it would be wise perhaps, as the US/Luxemburg paper suggests, to exempt from the calculation the first 1000 MHz of spectrum sought for either national services only, or in the case of systems to be set up for the use of less-developed countries.

Implied Powers?

Although it is likely that the problems of the phantom satellite will be tackled by legislative changes within the framework of the ITU, I find myself wondering whether in a suitably obvious, not to say clamant, case the ITU itself might not take action, for example, by refusing to process a filing which it suspects does not represent a fully and genuine intention to establish a space system. Alternatively it might include in its procedures the requirement of additional information that would allow it to form a view as to the reality of a notification which has been sent to it, and proceed accordingly. If either or both possibilities outlined under the separate headings above are not adopted, or prove inadequate, could not the ITU itself act?

The principle is, of course, that an international organisation not only has the powers expressed in its constituent documents. In addition, by international law, it has the powers which it requires in order to fulfil its function.[13] The ITU has therefore more powers than are expressed in its Constitution and Convention. Already it has exercised discretion in a matter of filing. When the Kingdom of Tonga filed for a large number of assignments, the matter was referred back to the Kingdom, and an agreed solution arrived at.[14] The same could be done in the case of a notification which is suspected to lack reality.

Were the ITU to exercise such a power, other questions might then be tackled. Could the ITU not refer back a notified assignment which goes beyond the telecommunications requirements of a Member State, or where the state may reasonably be doubted to have the competence properly to supervise the activities of its licensee? This would prevent the use of a state as a 'post-box', and the exploitation of a state's 'rights' under international law in an environment where states do not have rights - outer space.[15] I would prefer to see such a development, but suspect that I will wait a long time to see it.

Conclusion

The problem of processing filings which are unlikely ever to eventuate in actual working satellite systems is real. Steps are being taken to deal with it. If formal steps are not taken the ITU itself could lawfully take some steps that might help deal with the matter.

NOTES

1 See below, n.7.

2 See http://www.itu.ch.

3 Thus the US acts for INTELSAT, the UK for INMARSAT, and France for EUTELSAT.

4 ITU Constitution, arts. 1.2.a) and b) and 44.

5 ITU Constitution, art.45.

6 This was first done through the International Radio Union which fused with the International Telegraph and Telephone Union to form the ITU at simultaneous conferences of the two Unions held in Madrid in 1932. The current system was basically established during the re-formation of the ITU following the Second World War.

7 What follows may be more fully followed in such ITU documents as the "Final Report of Region 3 Forum for Resolution 18" (Kyoto, 1994) Region 3-APSCC-Doc.13; Rapporteur, SC-5 "Rapporteur's Initial Draft Report", Doc. SC-RG5/33; and "Special Committee on Regulatory Procedural Matters devoted to Resolution 18 (Kyoto, 1994), Rapporteur Group SC-4, Preliminary Report of the Rapporteur" (David M. Leive) 13 September 1996, Doc. SC-RG4/39. See also the draft paper "Views of the Radio Regulations Board on Resolution 18 (Kyoto, 1994)" Doc. RRB96/22-E.

8 "The Use of "Due Diligence" in Frequency Coordination of GSO FSS Satellite Networks", USA, Doc. RAG96-1/19.

9 See the draft "Views of the Radio Regulations Board on Resolution 18 (Kyoto, 1994)" Doc. RRB96/22-E.

10 Cf. Luxembourg material cited in n.12.

11 Cf. the Canadian paper, "Review of the Financial Foundations on the Union", ITU-2000, Doc. 3-E, 21 October 1996.

12 "Due Diligence Considerations", U.K./ Luxembourg June 1996, submitted as part of the work of RAG96. Cf. "Some Further Aspects of the Financial Approach to Due Diligence" Luxembourg, RES18-R1/7-E and "Some Financial Considerations Arising from Consideration of Resolution 18 that Relate to the Review under Resolution 39," ITU-2000, Luxembourg Doc 2-E.

13 Reparation for Injuries Suffered in the Service of the United Nations, 1949 ICJ Rep. 174; (1949) 43 AJIL 589.

14 M.L. Smith, 'Legal and Policy Developments in International Satellite Communication' 1991 34 Proc. Int. Inst. Sp. Law 342-7 at 345-6; D. Riddick, 'Why does Tonga own Outer Space?', 19 Air and Space Law 15-29.

15 As outer space cannot be subject to claims of sovereignty, a state can not have any 'right' in outer space (art. II, Outer Space Treaty).

Development of Broadcasting Laws related to Satellite Television in the ASEAN Countries

Dr.Mieke Komar Kantaatmadja
Prof. of Law, Dean of the Faculty of Law
Universityof Padjadjaran,Bandung,
Indonesia

Abstract

Satellite broadcasting services in the Asean (South East Asia Nations)region are developing rapidly .The member countries,such as Thailand,Malaysia ,Singapore,the Philippines,and Indonesia ,each having their own satellite are at present updating their respective laws ,in order to keep up with the fast development. Private participation to enhance competition domestically and regionally is essential. This paper will deal with the basic elements of the existing laws..

Introduction

This paper is inspired by the papers and discussions presented at the seventh General Assembly and Conference of the ASEAN Law Association in Kuala Lumpur, Malaysia, in December 1995 . Telecommunication services have increased tremendously in the last two decades in the South East Asian Region,(known as ASEAN.) so have satellite broadcasting and cable broad[1]casting services.

It is known that telecommunication and broadcasting laws related to satellite broadcasting in the more industrialized countries, such as the European countries ,the US and Canada are more developed than similar laws in the ASEAN countries. The latter laws were often in the early stage drafted after the laws of those industrialized countries .However due to their different national goals and needs the ASEAN member countries now have each their own specific telecommunication and broad casting laws .One thing they have in common is that their national laws are all in the process of updating and amending to keep in breast with the fast technological developments and the heavy competion faced in the region. It is interesting to note that the development of telecommunication in general and in particular satellite broadcasting and cable television are developing so rapidly , whilst the specific laws

[1] Copyright 1996 Mieke Komar

regulating to these activities often lack behind.
Moreover, other related laws such as the copyright laws of these countries should also be updated, and at the same time facing the requirements of the TRIPs (GATT) **1)** the process of revising these laws become even more complicated.

It is widely known that the Indonesian PALAPA communication system, often referred to as the first regional telecommunication system in this area **2)** has promoted the use of broadcasting via satellite in the ASEAN countries. Intended as a domestic satellite system, this system was first introduced in 1976 and since then was also used by its neighbouring countries , based on bilateral lease agreements of space segment capacity on the Indonesian Satellite System . The PALAPA system A series, followed by the B and the C series transponders are leased a.o. to Malaysia, the Philippines, Cambodja, Papua Nugini , Vietnam as well as Australia, U.S.A. and New Zealand. **3)** Before the launching of its own satellites,Thailand was one of its customers too.Indonesia will launched its direct broadcasting system in 1997.

Thailand has launched its own communication satellite system for domestic and broadcasting services: the THAICOM I in 1991 followed by THAICOM 2 in 1994.
With a lifetime of 15 years these satellite systems have footprints coverage over Thailand,Laos,Cambodia, Mynmar., Vietnam, Malaysia, the Philippines, Hongkong Korea, Japan and the East coast of China. Domestic telecommunications services are obliged to be transmitted through the Thaicom transponders **4)**
Malaysia owns its Malaysian satellite ,MEASAT 1 which provides the Malaysian public with more than 20 channels **5)** Whereas Singapore is in the process of launching its ASIA PACIFIC MOBILE TELECOM (APMT) in 1998 and SINGAPORE TELECOM 1 (K.U - BAND) in 1998 too. And the Philippines owns its AGILA space communication system and will launch the MABUHAI system in 1998 . **6)**
With footprint coverages overlapping each other, one can envisaged the com - pition in this area at present and in the near future

Broadcasting Laws

Thailand 7)

Thai laws directly regulating space telecommunication services comprise the Radio Communications Act of B.E.249B (1955)as amended by the Radio Communication Act of B.E. 2535 of 1992.Television and cable broadcasting services are regulated by two principal laws, the Broadcasting Act B.E. 249B (1955),as amended in 1987 and the Royal Decree Establishing Mass Communication Organization of Thailand (MCOT)(1977) and several ministerial regulations,such as the Ministerial Regulation number 12 B.E. 253G (1993)
These laws are at present in the process of amendment to keep up with the development of television and cable broadcasting technology. The aim is also to give the opportunity for the participation of the private sector in the opera tion of state-owned basic television stations.

Responsible authority : the licensing of applications under the Broadcasting Act and the MCOT lies with the Public Relations Department and the MCOT respectively . A license is required for the broadcasting of radio television . (Section 5 of the Broadcasting Act). Pay-tv licenses are licensed by the Public Relations Department, however currently operating cable TV operators have entered into concession contracts with the MCOT ,and their service related activities were therefore not regulated under the Broadcasting Act.. The Radio Communication Act of B.E. 2535(1992) which regulates that a license is required for the manufacturing, possession, use, import, export or commerce of radio communication devices, is followed by Ministerial Regulation no 24 B.E. 2535 (1993) which explicitly exempt from obtaining a license for possession, use, import and export: a) a via satellite television receiver only (TVRO)-for household use only and b)a cable TV receiver-

Definition of Broadcasting : under the above Broadcasting Act and the Ministerial Regulation number 12 B.E. 2539 (1993), no person shall provide radio television broadcasting to service the public or community without the license from the licensing official. The broadcasting of radio television by transmitting hertzian waves into the atmosphere of which the programme is broadcast regularly or permanently and can be received by any person by using a televison set provided or to be on sale in general shall be deemed the said broad - casting to service the public or commu-nity... Furthermore, this Act defined... "broadcasting of radio television to service the public or commun - ity"...(Section 5)..: 1) being the broadcasting of programme to any community with the broadcast signal through wire or conductor at the level over 75 dBu and with more than one signal amplifier;... 2) being the broadcasting of programme by means of relaying, rebroadcasting or adapting the sound or radio television programme to be broadcast through the atmosphere or to be procured or produced by the broadcaster; ...3) being the broad - casting of programme to members by means of subscription with or without subscribing fees, maintenance fees or any other consideration,or for free... Radio television service refers to broadcasting of radio television to the public.

..

Mr. Julponocgsathom **8)** views that the above regulations do not cover pay- TV, as their main purpose was to regulate the basic free television services and not pay-TV. In reality Thai cable are broadcasting their programmes by micro waves since the commencement of operation and not over the cable as the name suggests. It is for this matter that the cable operators are licensed by the MCOT, which has the authority to carry out mass communication projects and to which the Broadcasting Act and the re-lated regulations do not apply. This is one of the reasons that present broad-casting laws should be updated.

Malaysia 9)

Responsible Authority: Malaysia 's broadcasting activities are regulated in the Broadcasting Act 338 of 1988. This Act specifically states that a license is required for the broadcast of any matter in Malaysia. This Act also provides for the penalty in the case a person broadcasts without the required license.It includes a penalty fine or imprisonment .The Minister of Information is the responsible official for Broadcasting in Malaysia. The Ministry also controls private broadcasts.

Definition of broadcasting :This Act defines "broadcast matter" as any sign or signal transmitted by a broadcasting station whether for aural or visual reception or both, and includes any music, theatrical or other entertainment concert, lecture, speech, address, news and information of any kind so transmitted for reception by the general public.
Part IV regulates "television broadcast receiver" as any apparatus used for the visual and aural reception of broadcast matter transmitted by radio waves through either, wire and cable or by means of any other electro-magnetic waves in the electro- magnetic spectrum designated for broadcasting services.A license is required for activities of installing, working or dealing in radio broad - cast receivers or television receivers . This Act also prohibits any person who is in possession of any radio broadcast receiver or television broadcast receiver or the occupier of any dwelling house or premises in which radio broadcast receiver or television broadcast receiver, without a license. It also refers to licenses in respect to the same matter issued under the Telecommunications Act of 1950.

Interesting to note is the Malaysian media ideology **10)** as stated in the operating policy of RTM channel 1 and 2 ,which operate under the following main objectives : a) to explain in depth, and with the widest possible coverage , the policies and programmes of the government in order to ensure maximum understanding by the public; b) to stimulate public interest and opinion in order to achieve changes in line with the requirement of the government; c) to assist in promoting civic consciousness and fostering the development of Malaysian arts and culture; d) to provide suitable elements of popular education, general information and entertainment;and e) to aid national integration efforts in a multiethnic society through the use of the national language.
It seems that the use of parabol disks for household -use is not allowed ,but this will be amended in the new law which is now under study in Malaysia. New guidelines will be set up governing transmission of television programs by private stations,.as well as covering cable -tv broadcasting.

Singapore. 11)

On October 1,1994 the Singapore Broadcasting Authority Act was passed establisihing the Singapore Broadcasting Authority (SBA) to regulate the broadcasting and cable industry in Singapore.,which was revised in 1995 Cap .294. Whereas in l992 by Act no 12 of 1992 the Telecommunication Authority of Singapore chapter 323 was promulgated, which was later amended in 1994.

Responsible Authority : under this Act it is established that the SBA has the powers to license almost every type of broadcasting and cable transmission activity known under the present state of technology. The license is not transferable without consent of the SBA. The penalty fee for breach is high or imprisonment. The SBA Act also regulates the protection of cable operator's rights,and provides that no person shall in the course of any trade or business, import, manufacture, sell, offer for sale or let for hire any unauthorised decoder.

Definition of Broadcasting is widely defined in this Act to include any programme signal transmitted by any means received by persons having appropriate equipment

Broadcasting service is defined as " a service whereby signs or signals transmitted, whether or not encrypted, comprise a) any programme capable of being received, or received and displayed, as visual images, whether moving or still; b) any sound programme for recep tion; or c) any programme, being a combination of both visual image (whether moving or still) and sound for reception or reception and display, by persons having equipment appriopriate for receiving, or receiving and displaying, as the case may be, that service , irrespective of the means of delivery of that service"

In conjunction with the functions , duties and powers of the Authority and in particular with Part V11 of the1994 Act on Frequency Planning, art.35 which states that ..(1) the Telecom - munication Authority of Singapore , in consultation with the Authority (SBA), assign to the Authority specific fre - quencies in the electromagnetic spectrum and satellite orbits for the purpose of broadcasting having regard to the international allocation plans set by the International Telecommunication Union as well as national requirements. (2) The authority may re-assign to any person the frequencies in the electromagnetic spectrum and satellite orbits assigned under subsection(1) in accor - dance with this Act. This makes it unequivocally clear that the Authority regulates and controls the use of satellite orbits and frequencies for cable and satellite broadcasting, and the Authority has the legal right to re-assign satellite orbits.**12)**

Any broadcasting service licensee licensed by the SBA may broadcast or transmit satellite signals from Singapore for distribution regionally or interna - tionally. However it is an offense to operate a satellite antennae in Singapore without a license. Also any broadcasting service licensee may receive satellite signals from the region or internationally. Unlicensed use of TVRO antennae is an offence under the Act . Furthermore TVRO Antennae licensees may receive satellite signals, depending on the size of the satellite they install, and the programmes or satellites they are permitted to access.

The law also provides rules regarding to ownership and control of broadcasting companies in detail.

The privatization process started when Singapore' national broadcaster Singapore Broadcasting Corporation was privatised in 1994, this was to enable competion and encourage better production. Cable tv has been introduced in Singapore and these programmes are widely used in the neighbouring countries. Cable transmission is planned to wire homes in Singapore via fabric optic in 2005. In line with the Government's decision to promote Singapore as a broadcasting hub in this region, changes in its Laws and related regulations are expected to come.

The Philippines 13)

The writer was not able to acquire the Philippines broadcasting law in time for this paper.A relevant law available was the Republic Act no 7925,:An Act to Promote and Govern the Development of Philippine Telecommunications and the Delivery of Public Telecommunications Services of 1995.

Definition of Broadcasting:
"Broadcasting" is referred to in this Act as an undertaking the object of which is to transmit over- the-air commercial radio or television messages for reception of a broad audience in a geographic area. The Act further states that a "Franchise" is a privilege conferred upon a telecommunications entity by Congress, authorizing that entity to engage in a certain type of telecommunication service. Taking into account that satellite broadcast is a part of telecommunictions, and except regulated differently in other laws and regulations, in the writer's view any person engaging in said satellite broadcasting activities should acquire a license for his operations. However this Act does not specify to whom a broadcaster should apply for a specific license to operate. Furthermore,this Act regulates that no single franchise shall authorize an entity to engage in both telecommunications and broadcasting, either through the airwaves or by cable.

The Philippines Telecommunication national policy states that telecommunication is essential to the economic development, integrity and security of the Philippines, and as such shall be developed and administered as to safeguard, enrich and strenghten the economic cultural, social and political fabric of the Philippines. Having said that, the writer believes that the relevant broadcasting laws of this country must have covered all the other aspects vital to broadcasting and in particular satellite broadcasting and cable tv. With the Agila and the Mabuhai systems (in 1998) in orbit their broadcasting laws will surely be updated to meet the new activities to come.

INDONESIA 14)

At present Indonesia has tabled a new draft Law on Broadcasting to Parliament., which is expected to come into effect soon. Several ministerial decrees of the Ministery of Information on the operation of television broadcasting are still in force, a.o. the Decree no lll/Kep/menpen/l990 . This decree has modified earlier decrees, such as the Decree of the Director Jendral of Information no 18 of 1986 on the use and operation of the Parabol Antennae for receiving television broadcasting. A short review on the 1990 decree added with the proposed draft law on broadcasting will give us an inside on the broadcasting rules in Indonesia. Taking into account the practice of legal drafting in Indonesia, a basic Law often refers to implementing regulations issued by Government Decrees ,which are drafted later and will contain more specific requirements . Awaiting these implementing regula- tions to come into force the basic law often states that earlier decrees are still in effect, insofar they are not contrary to the contents of said basic law.

Responsible Authority : the Government of Indonesia cq. The Department of Information has the function and responsibility for the development and control of broadcasting in Indonesia.. A license to operate radio, television and pay-tv broadcasting activities is required by the Minister of Information This license may not be assigned to others.
The license to use radio frequencies and or broadcasting equipment and other transmission devices is regulated by Law no 3 1989 on Telecommunication Services ,and should be obtained from the Ministery for Tourism, Post and Telecommunication. A severe fine or imprisonment is provided for unlicensed users.

..

Definition of Broadcasting : means the operation of sending broadcast through broadcasting facilities or transmission facilities on land or in space by means of the use of electromagnetic waves , cable transmission, fibre optic and or other media for the reception of the public with the use of radio broadcasting receivers and or television broadcasting receivers ,either with or without the assistance of an apparatus.

These services may be operated by government owned bodies and private owned Indonesian companies.
Prohibited is to set up private owned broadcasting companies for the interest of a single political party,ideology, religion, or personal interest or group interest. Ownership or control over private owned broadcasting companies leading to or establishing a monopoly is prohibited. Cooperation among Indonesian broadcasting ,technical and service providers companies are allowed with the approval of the government. Foreign programmes imported from abroad have to comply to the same rules applicable to domestic television broadcasters and need a permit from the National Censorship Board. Program content should not be detrimental to the relationship between Indonesia and other countries. Cable tv may be operated by both government owned and private companies with the approval of the government.
Furthermore, foreign companies may undertake broadcasting activities in Indonesia with the approval of the Ministery of Information , they may set up representatives offices or place their correspondences and the Indonesian satellite facilities for international broadcast services , both for "up link" as well as using "portable up link "transmissions. Foreign broadcasters who intend to market their services in Indonesia should operate with Indonesian companies

Each broadcasting company shall acquire a right of broadcast for every program in accordance to the Laws on Copy Rights of Indonesia The use of parabol antennaes by the public is allowed as they are privately owned . For commercial use a approval is need- ed from the government.`The public may also use parabol antennaes for distribution purposes.Private companies and provincial government offices may have their own privately financed parabol system distribution at places not covered by TV-RI (the government owned broadcasting company). A license is needed for such a construction,also for Close Circuit Systems.

Spill over of foreign broadcasting programs into Indonesian territory as well as Indonesian programs into foreign territory should be avoided.

Unintentional or intentional spillovers should be regulated based on bilateral agreements between the receiving and broadcast sending states

Conclusions

This short and not in-depth study shows that the above countries'laws may not have the answers to all the existing legal issues present . However as stated earlier these laws are in the process of amending . Private sector participation will be encouraged to meet the competition faced both domestically and in the region. National policies will be redrafted to devise new guidelines encouraging private participation to meet the challenge of information and telecommunication technology. Copy rights law will be updated in line with international conventions and other related laws. Finally, it is sufficient to conclude that the ASEAN region is "broadcast friendly".

Footnotes

1) See, GATT/ TRIPs rules, a.o. art.9, 11, and art. 14; etc.

2) John L. Mclucas, **Space Commerce ,** Harvard University Press,Cambridge, 1991,pp.84-85

3) Mieke Komar Kantaatmadja,**An Overview of the Existing Laws and Regulations relating to Satellite and Cable Television in Indonesia**,,The seventh General Assembly and Conference,Asean Law Association, Kuala Lumpur , Malaysia, Dec 6-10, 1995(abbr.A.L.A. Gen.Ass. 1995)

4) Piyatida Julponocgsathom, **Development of Law in the Asean Countries in the Context of Satellite/CableTelevision - Thailand,** A.L.A. Gen.Ass., 1995.

5) Abu Bakar Munir, **Satellite/Cable Television:The Development of Laws-Malaysia,** A.L.A. Gen. Ass.1995

6) Data from P.T.Telkom Indonesia,

7) Piyatida Julponocgsathom, supra no 4.

8) idem

9) Abu Bakar Munir, supra no 5.

10) idem

11) Linda Nai,**Development of Satellite Broadcasting and Cable Television in Singapore,** ALA.Gen Ass.1995.; Gerald Chew, **The Development of Laws in Asean Countries in the Context of The Singapore Position**, ALA.Gen.Ass 1995.
The Singapore Broadcasting Authority Act no 15 of 1994,re.ed. 1995 cap.294 ; Telecommunication Authority of Singapore Act, Chapter 323, Act no 12, 1992, am. By 15 of 1994.

12) Gerald Chew, idem

13) Republic Act no 7925,An Act to Promote and Govern the Development of Philippine Telecommunications and the Delivery of Public Telecommunications Services ,25 1994.

14) Mieke Komar Kantaatmadja, supra 3 ;

GLOBAL NAVIGATION SATELLITE SYSTEM (GNSS) INTERFERENCE TESTING: LEGAL ISSUES

by

PAUL B. LARSEN*

GEORGETOWN UNIVERSITY LAW CENTER

I. Introduction

II. Background

III. Effects of GNSS Testing

IV. Legal Issues

- A. Regulatory
  1. International Regulation
  2. National Regulation
- B. Liability Issues
  1. International Liability
  2. National Liability

V. Recommendations

VI. Review

I. Introduction

On March 29, 1996 the White House issued a Presidential Decision Document which established "comprehensive national policy on the future management and use of the U.S. Global Positioning System (GPS) and related U.S. Government augmentations." The Decision Document described GPS as a dual-use system, the primary purpose of which is the military use. However, the civilian use of GPS is growing rapidly and becoming an essential element of the Global Information Infrastructure; civilian use includes such diverse activities as air traffic control, mapping and surveying, and global change research. GPS augmentation is an important expansion of GPS capability. 1/

While this paper refers to GPS, it is assumed that the reader will know that the kind of issues that apply to GPS also apply to other Global Navigation Satellite Systems (GNSS). The analysis will consider the entire basic GPS system including the GPS satellites, their navigation payloads, the ground stations, and their control stations, as well as augmentations systems.

II. Background

Disruption of the GPS navigational signals is cause for great concern because there are no plans for a back-up navigational system. Back-up systems are considered redundant. Users will have to be prepared for the GPS to be interrupted during testing for interference and for maintenance. These activities are necessary to maintain and promote the over-all safety and efficiency of the GPS system.

The Presidential Decision Document states that the U.S. Government (the Department of Defense) will take "measures to prevent the hostile use of GPS and its augmentations." 2/ This

appears to refer to Governmental measures to prevent terrorists and unfriendly forces either to interfere with the GPS signals or to use the GPS for their own purposes. Such measures will require testing the system for possible illegal uses. Such testing could interfere both with military and civilian uses of GPS. Consequently interference testing will be conducted by the operator of the GPS system, the Department of Defense. Clearly such testing will have to be coordinated with all civilian as well as military users. Failure to communicate with all reasonably foreseeable users could have legal consequences. The same notification issues exist for shutdown that is part of technical maintenance. Technical maintenance is to occur to preserve GPS accuracy, integrity, and availability. 3/ The 1995 NAPA/NRC report defines these three terms as follows:
(1) Accuracy is the degree of conformity between the estimated or measured position or velocity of a platform at a given time and its true position and velocity.
(2) Integrity is the ability of a system to provide timely warnings to users when the system should not be used for navigation.
(3) Availability of a navigation system is the percentage of time that the services are usable, for example, an indication of the ability of the system to provide usable service within the specified coverage area. 4/
.

The Presidential Decision Document makes the following assignment of responsibilities for GPS: The Department of Defense will maintain the GPS system and will operate the navigation service, including the testing of the GPS signals. The Department of Transportation (DOT) is responsible for non-military uses of GPS including development of the GPS augmentations. 5/

The President assigned responsibility for civilian coordination and communication of GPS testing to DOT. This assignment is consistent with the NAPA /NRC Report which holds DOT responsible for monitoring the civil GPS signal and for cooperating with DOD to insure its integrity, accuracy and availability and concludes "that the most important Government action required is to improve the performance of the basic GPS satellite system to provide the highest levels of position accuracy, signal integrity and signal availability that can be technologically achieved at reasonable cost without negatively impacting national security." 6/

Therefore it is within the mandate of the Presidential Decision Document to place a high priority on resolving testing interference issues in order to provide GPS standard service " for peaceful civil, commercial and scientific service on a continuous, worldwide basis." 7/ It probably does not need to pointed out that a continuously operating GPS system is one in which service is not interrupted .

It is critical for the rapid growth and development of the GPS system that the capability of "continuos operation in all foreseeable contingencies" be maintained. For that purpose the NAPA/NRC Report recommends that more GPS monitoring stations be added to the existing operational control segments of the GPS system. 8/

The International Civil Aviation Organization (ICAO) defines continuity of service (also referred to as reliability) as the ability of a navigation system to provide required service over a stated uninterrupted period of time. The continuity level is stated in terms of the probability of maintaining the radiated signals. 9/ The average navigational reliability of GPS is stated as being 99,97% . 10/

Finally, it is possible that GPS navigational accuracy may experience unintentional, unwanted interference from terrestrial and other sources so that the GPS receiver cannot accept navigational or positioning information. Unintentional unwanted interference may come from UHF transmitters. 11/

III. Effects of GNSS Testing

Interruptions to military navigation may be small since GPS is virtually controlled by the Department of Defense. For civilian users it is possible to reduce the magnitude of intentional GPS interference by testing at remote areas where the navigational needs are small. Testing, like maintenance of streets and roads, may also be done at times and during seasons when the traffic requirements are the lowest.

The Department of Transportation is responsible for notifying civilian users. The Federal Aviation Administration and other air traffic control authorities can be expected to know about GPS interference testing and to pass information on to aircraft users. Likewise the Coast Guard and other maritime navigation authorities can be expected to inform mariners. DOT regularly issues NOTAMS to pilots and notices to mariners. However, non-transportation users may suffer because they are not naturally in the chain of information from the DOT. Surveyors, and even more so farmers and recreational users, will be difficult to notify of interruptions..

Legal Issues

A. Regulatory

A number of international treaties have some authority over navigation afforded by GPS. Consequently these treaties and their institutions also have some authority over interruptions of the supply of navigation. A number of national laws and institutions also have authority and therefore responsibility for interruptions. Both kinds of regulatory authorities will be discussed here. 12/

1. International Regulation.

The international treaties with relevant authority over GPS, and in turn authority over interruptions of GPS, are:

1. The U.N. Charter which applies in outer space. Article 2 of the Charter obligates States to resolve their differences by peaceful means. Thus GPS interruptions which amount to acts of aggression are prohibited. Furthermore, under the 1967 Outer Space Treaty, Article VI, 13/ States have assumed responsibility for national activities in outer

space. The United Nations through the United Nations Committee for Peaceful Uses of Outer Space exercises an active role in all space issues. 14/

2. International conventions on liability, registration and aid to astronauts are relevant to GPS navigation and will be further discussed below. 15/ These treaties do not establish regulatory institutions. 16/

3. The International Telecommunications Convention 17/ governs the use of radiofrequencies through the institution of the International Telecommunications Union (ITU). Thus ITU is concerned with disruptions of and interference with the GPS radio signals

4, The 1944 Convention on the International Civil Aviation (Chicago Convention) 18/ governs navigation of aircraft. The Convention has established the International Civil Aviation Organization (ICAO) as the competent body to establish international minimum air navigation standards (article 44) As described above 19/ ICAO Annex 10 defines the concept of continuity of air navigation services.

5. The Convention on the Intergovernmental Maritime Organization (IMO) 20/ establishes international maritime navigation standards. IMO is concerned with interruption of maritime GPS navigation signals that constitute dangers to maritime navigation .

6. Under the aegis of the Treaty of Rome 21/ the European Union also is exercising authority over Global Navigation Satellite Systems. In the 1995 Madrid Agreement between the United States and the European Union the two parties decided to establish a working group to coordinate and cooperate on all GPS issues. Any interruption of or interference with the GPS navigation system may be an issue for coordination.

2. U.S. Domestic Regulation

Use of radio frequencies are regulated by the Communications Act of 1934 22/ . The Act establishes the Federal Communications Commission (FCC) to regulate the use of radio frequencies, including interference with the use of radio frequencies. While the FCC would not regulate military uses of GPS it would have concerns with civilian interruptions.

The Federal Aviation Act 23/ establishes the Federal Aviation Administration (FAA) which regulates GPS navigation by aircraft . The FAA regulates the use of GPS, including its augmentation, in the United States . The FAA is directly involved in regulation of interruptions and interferences with GPS, because of potential adverse effects on aviation safety.

U.S. maritime laws 24/ establish controls over maritime navigation by the U.S. Coast Guard. Like the FAA the Coast Guard is involved in the regulation of interruptions and interferences with GPS signals because of potential adverse effect on maritime safety.

Operation of the Intelligent Vehicle System (IVS) will also be affected by interruptions and interferences with the GPS signal. The IVS system is under the oversight of the Department of Transportation's Federal Highway Administration. Likewise, the use of GPS by trains is of concern to the Department of Transportation (Federal Railroad Administration)

Non-Transportation GPS users may look to the Department of Transportation for resolution of their concerns with GPS interruptions and interferences because the Presidential Decision Document assigned DOT to "serve as the lead agency within the U.S. Government for Federal civil GPS matters," and in cooperation with other U.S. agencies to "coordinate U.S. Government-provided GPS civil augmentation systems." 25/

B. Liability Issues

1. International Liability

Virtually all states are parties to the 1967 Outer Space Treaty 26/ . Under its Article VII contracting States are internationally liable for damage done by space objects whether such damage happens in outer space, air space on the surface of the earth. Furthermore, under the 1972 Liability Convention, Article II, States have agreed that: "A launching state shall be absolutely liable to pay compensation for damage caused by its space objects on the surface of the earth or to aircraft in flight." 27/

Claims for damages are more likely to be brought under national law. Many countries have now removed legal barriers to direct law suits against governments for their torts. In the United States claims may be brought against the U.S. Government under the Federal Tort Claims Act 28/ A claim against the U.S. Government is barred if the Governmental activity is discretionary. However, U.S. case law has held the U.S. Government liable for negligently provided air traffic control service. It appears that the Presidential Decision Document's assignment of responsibility to the Department of Defense to "Develop measures to prevent the hostile use of GPS and its augmentation" would be a discretionary decision made at a high decision-making level. 29/ Whether failure of the DOT to inform known GPS users of known disruptions and interferences resulting in injuries would also be discretionary, is a different matter. In the Supreme Court case of Indian Towing v. United States, 350 U.S. 61 (1955) the Court decided that the discretionary exception to governmental liability would not apply in cases in which "one who undertakes to warn the public of danger and thereby induces reliance must perform his 'good Samaritan task' in a careful manner."

In Indian Towing the Supreme Court concluded that once the Government had undertaken to operate the navigation aid (the lighthouse) "it was obligated to use due care to make certain that the light was kept in good working order; and, if the light became extinguished, then the Coast Guard was further obligated to use due care to discover this fact and to repair the light or give warning that it was not functioning. If the Coast Guard failed in its duty and damage was thereby caused to petitioners, the United States is liable under the Tort Claims Act." 30/ The application of the Supreme Court's line of reasoning is directly relevant to the duty to inform known GPS users of known disruptions.

The next issue then becomes the Government's liability to the GPS users who are not identified and known. Here the liability issue becomes one of foreseeability. The question is: could the Government reasonably foresee that claimants would suffer if not informed? If claimants' damages were not foreseeable then they would not come within the Government's duty of care.

V. Recommendations

Clearly a continuously performing system is required if a reliable satellite navigation system is to exist and function without a back-up system. The system would have to meet the ICAO Annex 10 minimum test for continuity, specified by the GPS operator, DOD, as a reliability of 99,97%. 31/ That means that the system would have to be up and functioning virtually 100% of the time. To achieve this high level of performance:

1. Interruptions should be limited as much as possible and should be scheduled for remote locations, at low traffic times and seasons.

2. An effective communication tree should be established to distribute information about known disruptions to the extent possible

a. For that purpose the military and civilian authorities should work closely together

b. The civilian authorities should create both international and national coordination systems that include all civilian users

3. Liability for failure to perform would act as a hammer to compel a virtually 100% GPS system.

VI. Summary

On March 29, 1996 President Clinton announced U.S. policy on management of the Global Positioning System. While GPS will continue as a dual use system, the integration of GPS into peaceful civil, commercial and scientific applications is assured. The decision document clarified the roles and responsibilities of the Departments of Defense and Transportation.

This Presidential Decision Document announced that the Department of Defense will take measures to prevent the hostile uses of GPS and its augmentations. Thus the focus of this paper is on the legal consequences of intentional interference with GPS and also with technical testing to assure accuracy, integrity and availability of the GPS system.

ICAO Annex 10 sets as a goal that the navigational system should be continuously operational and DOD has specified the global average reliability of GPS to be 99,97%, in other words the systems should be continuously operational virtually all the time. Thus there is almost no space for interruption of the GPS system whether for intentional interference testing nor for unintentional interference testing.

When there must be interruptions the main GPS users may be fairly easily reached for information. The greater adverse effects of interference testing may well be on the more remote civilian users such as surveyors, farmers and recreational users.

A number of international and national institutions have some responsibility for the consequences of interruptions to the GPS system These institutions range from international institutions such as ICAO and IMO and the E.U. to national institutions such as the DOT, the FAA, and the U.S. Coast Guard.

Potential liability for negligent GPS operation and negligence in informing GPS users acts as a pressure for the GPS system to perform virtually 100% of the time.

For that purpose, the paper makes three recommendations:

1. Schedule intentional interruptions so that they cause as little interference as possible

2. Establish an effective communication tree to inform virtually all users of interruptions that may affect them

3. Let potential liability act as a hammer to keep the GPS system operational virtually 100% of the time.

FOOTNOTES

*) Currently at the Max Planck Institute for Private International Law, Hamburg. None of this paper should in any way be attributed to any organization or agency with which the author is associated.

1. White House Press Release, March 29, 1996

2. Id.

3. National Academy of Public Administration/ National Research Council, The Global Positioning System, Charting the Future, Summary Report, at 7.

4. Id. at 23. The NAPA/NRC Report describes these three as the most important needs for commercial and civil GPS users.

5. Supra n. 1.

6. NAPA/NRC Report supra n. 3 at 17, and 27.

7. Supra n. 1

8. NAPA/NRC Report supra n. 3 at 24 - 27.

9. ICAO Annex 10, Vol. 1, 22 (1987).

10. Assistant Secretary of Defense for Command, Control, Communications and Intelligence, Global Positioning Service Signal Specification, Section 4.0 at B-11 to B-14; also see NRC Report, The Global Positioning System at 163, National Academy Press (1995).

11. NRC Report supra n. 10 at 163.

12. For extensive discussion of regulatory institutions, see Larsen, Positioning Satellites:

Current Institutional Issues, 1994 Coll. on the Law of Outer Space.

13. Treaty on Principles Governing the Activities of States in the Exploration and Use of Outer Space, Including the Moon and other Celestial Bodies, 18 UST 2310, TIAS 6347, (1967); Jasentuliyana and Lee, Manual on Space law, at 851.

14. Larsen, supra n. 12

15. Convention on International Liability for Damage caused by Space Objects, 24 UST 2389, TIAS 6347 (1972); Agreement on the Rescue of Astronauts, the Return of Astronauts and the Return of Objects Launched into Outer Space, 19 UST 7570, TIAS 6599, 672 UNTS 121 (1969); Convention on Registration of Objects Launched into Outer Space, 28 UST 695, TIAS 8480, Manual on Space Law, at 23.

16. Larsen, supra n. 12

17. 1932 Telecommunication Convention, 151 LNTS 4, as amended; latest amendment was in 1992. For discussion see Lyall, The International Telecommunication Union Reconstructed, Proceedings of the Thirty-Sixth Coll. on the Law of Outer Space, at 78.

18. 51 UNTS 295, 51 Stat. 1180, TIAS 295.

19. At n. 9.

20 Convention on the Intergovernmental Maritime Organization, 9 UST 621, TIAS 4044

21. Rudden/Wyatt, Basic Community Laws at 20.

22. 47 U.S.C. 151.

23. 49 U.S.C. 40101

24. 14 U.S.C. 2, 81 - 90.

25. Supra n. 1.

26. Supra n. 15.

28. 28 U.S.C. 2671 et seq..

29. Dalehite v. U.S., 346 U.S. 15 (1952).

30. Indian Towing v. United States, 350 U.S. 61 (1955), at 69.

31. Supra notes 9 and 10.

IISL-96-IISL.4.07

DAMAGES AND INTELLECTUAL PROPERTY: AN UP-DATE ON HUGHES AIRCRAFT COMPANY vs USA

by

Carl Q. Christol
Distinguished Professor Emeritus of International Law and Political Science
University of Southern California
Los Angeles, California 90089-0044
Attorney at Law, Member, IISL, IAA, AIAA

Abstract

In August of 1993 the U.S. Court of Claims made findings based on the unlicensed use by the government of the United States of a patent entitled "Velocity Control and Orientation of a Spin-Stabilized Body." The Court held that Hughes Aircraft Company, as owner of the patent, could collect damages for the unlicensed use of the patented device on orbiting satellites.

In the damages phase of the case the Court of Claims created a formula for arriving at "just compensation" to be paid to the Company. The Court issued a ruling on June 17, 1994, which made a substantial award to the Company, but which left unresolved other elements of the claim for damages. The litigants were advised to attempt to resolve their differences.

The parties were not successful in bridging their differences. The Company filed an appeal in the United States Court of Appeals on October 31, 1994. These pleadings were supplemented on February 13, 1995. In each instance the government filed opposing briefs. These pleadings identified how the complex concept of "just compensation" might be construed. The Court of Appeals by mid-summer, 1996, had not issued a judgment in the matter.

Introduction

The Hughes Aircraft Company has been engaged in a marathon-like course of litigation since 1976 against the government of the United States dealing with patent rights relating to an object mounted on a satellite used to control the velocity and the orientation of a spin-stabilized space object.[1] In 1993 the Court of Claims rendered a judgment in favor of the Hughes Aircraft Co.[2]

The 1993 decision relied on existing patent law. Although that law was inadequate in many respects, and was later amended, it was held that national space activity, including the use of a patented spin-control system on a satellite while in earth-orbit, was subject to U.S. legislation. This was true despite the use of the patented item beyond the territory of the launching State, which, in this case, was the United States.[3]

<u>Hughes Quest for Adequate Compensation</u>

With the 1993 decision establishing the liability of the U.S. government for the unlicensed use of the Williams patent, the litigants turned to the question of damages. The initial response of the Court of Claims occurred on June 17, 1994.[4] In this segment of the litigation Hughes sought monetary damages of $1.2 billion. Hughes also tried to demonstrate that it might be entitled to as much as $6 billion. During the unlicensed use of the patent the using satellites had a value in the neighborhood of $3.5 billion.

In the 1994 decision reliance was placed on 28 United States Code #1498(a) which dealt with the use or manufacture of patented objects.

In arriving at sums ultimately to be paid to Hughes the Court of Claims indicated that the final computation of an appropriate award was to be determined by the parties, or, if there were no agreement, they were to identify their respective positions on the proper award. For the guidance of the parties the Court identified general criteria.

First, if there were an established royalty rate applicable to a "patent in suit," that rate would usually be adopted as the best measure of reasonable compensation. In the instant case this formula was inapplicable because there had not been an established royalty rate nor had there been any other royalty compensation arrangement. Second, this being the case, the rate was to be determined through a process of hypothetical negotiations between an assumed "willing buyer" and an assumed "willing seller," as of the date of the initial infringement, but taking into account the events occurring after the original infringement.

Third, the royalty rate was to take into account the entire cost of each infringing space object rather than the relatively minor costs associated with the manufacture of the components constituting the altitude control system.

Fourth, the Court fixed a percentage limit on payments to Hughes. It was 1.2% of the total cost of the space object, based on correspondence with spacecraft contractors, at the time of the issuance of the patent in September, 1973, at which time Hughes had offered to license its patent. Included in this package was one case in which Hughes had identified the patentee's royalty rate under the patent. The Court emphasized the relevance of the early offers made by Hughes to potential licensees.

Finally, the Court, in placing the burden on the litigants to arrive at a settlement, took note of the absence of guidance in section 1498 concerning the computation of damages. According to the tribunal congressional intention required only that a claimant receive "reasonable and entire compensation."[5]

With these considerations in mind the Court determined first that the applicable royalty rate should be 1% of the value of the spacecraft utilizing system; second, that a uniform rate of compensation would apply for delay damages[6] during an identified time period; and, third, should depend on federal legislation governing the amount of interest taxpayers are entitled to receive following an overpayment of taxes.

On this last point the court was explicit. It stated that the plaintiff was to receive delay damages computed at an annual rate of 7.5% over the period from September 11, 1973 through December 31, 1975; at an annual rate of 8.5% from January 1, 1976 through January 31, 1980, compounded on January 31 of each year, and commencing on February 1, 1980 in accordance with the tax overpayment rate prescribed from time to time as set forth in 26 U.S.C. ##6621 and 6622(a). The Court fine-tuned its formula by adding that it contemplated that a judgment would be entered for the total amount of damages calculated as of March 31, 1994, plus interest on that sum, taking into account the tax overpayment rate compounded daily from March 31, 1994, until paid.[7]

The Appeal of Hughes Aircraft Company

On October 31, 1994 Hughes filed an appeal in the United States Court of Appeals for the Federal Circuit. The Company urged that the formula employed by the Court of Claims did not contemplate or constitute just compensation. In support of this contention it was argued that the factors deemed controlling by the trial court did not take suitable account of the real worth of patented property, and, hence did not measure the extent of the loss to the company from the unlicensed use of its property.[8]

The Company contended the trial court erred in its determination that a 1% royalty was appropriate in light of the royalty rates contained in three licensing offers made by it during a period of pending litigation and a period of "widespread infringement" by the government. These factors were seen as depressing the true worth of the patent. The Company urged that it had sought a 3% royalty, that this offer had been rejected by aerospace companies, and that, since it was a rough measure of the value because of the above-identified circumstances, that a 3% royalty rate should have been the "floor" adopted by the trial court.[9] In support of this view that company urged that the 3% figure was the minimum that it had ever indicated as being acceptable. Thus, it contended that a justly compensating royalty would presumably exceed that floor.[10] Underlying the Company's contention was the proposition that the Williams patent was an important invention and that it had significantly facilitated instantaneous global communications and navigation.

Response of the U.S. Government

In response to the arguments made by Hughes the government urged that the trial court property weighed the evidence in fashioning a "just compensation" royalty.[11] Underlying this conclusion was the contention that the value of the Williams patent was not as large as Hughes had endeavored to prove. In order to sustain this outlook the government presented historical information respecting both successful and unsuccessful space launches.

The government also argued that the trial court's awarding of delay compensation to Hughes constituted a "windfall," and that on appeal this issued should be addressee *de novo*.

Response of Hughes Aircraft Company

In its reply brief, dated February 13, 1995 (Nos. 94-5149, 95-5001), in its capacity as Plaintiff-Appellant, the Company urged that the Government had engaged in "assiduous selectivity" respecting the operational characteristics of satellites employing gravity gradient equipment.[12]

The Company also considered that the Government was engaged in a "deconstructionist enterprise" when it traced the history of successful communications satellites.[13] These arguments were addressed to the value to space endeavors and to a larger body of uses of a patent allowing for the changing of a satellite's orientation so that it could be inserted into a final orbiting position.

In addressing the figure to the be placed on delay compensation the Company suggested that the government's *de novo* approach constituted "an invitation to judicially legislate, for all section 1498 cases, niggardly uniform rates bearing no relationship to the harm done to patent owners by virtue of government takings."[14] While objecting to a *de novo* approach by the United States Court of Appeals on the grounds that this would be "inappropriate," because of the absence of legislation, the Company urged that the establishment by the Court of Claims of delay compensation was to be upheld. Behind this contention was the view that the trial court had made a determination of just compensation "at uniform rates established in precedent. . ."[15]

One of the more interesting aspects of this extremely lengthy litigation, which in 1996 had been going on for thirteen years, relates to the trial court's determination that compound interest should be paid as previously indicated.[16] This aspect of the trial court's decision was not disputed by the Government.

In its effort to minimize the sums due to the Company the government argued that if royalties had been paid in the past the Company would have been obliged to pay income taxes on such royalties and that earnings derived from royalties would also have been subject to taxation. Thus the government suggested that the amount compounded should be discounted accordingly, that is, that the sums constituting the assumed taxes should not be made a part of the ultimate compensation payable to the Company. The litigants also presented other taxation issues to the court. Their intricacy, respecting identification and application, is so vast as to preclude further comment here. However, it may be for this reason that the Court has not resolved the litigation as of the Summer of 1996. Over 17 months have elapsed since the litigants presented their last briefs to the Court.

Conclusion

This case, which originally produced an interest for those identified with the development of national and international space law, and which confirmed that a nation's patent laws can have extra-territorial application, namely, where the patented device is employed in outer space, has currently been focused on formulas for the allocation of damages.

The federal courts dealing with the remaining issues have not been able to have recourse to detailed legislation on the subject, although there are numerous court decisions which bear tangentially on the subject of patent violations. Also, the enormity of the monetary damages sought by the Company has induced the Federal Court of Appeals to proceed very gingerly.

At this numbingly late hour the saga of the Williams patent and its use for the benefit of outer space activity has not been brought to a close. Like other cases characterized by novelty and complexity this case has taken on a life of its own.

Notes

1. *Hughes Aircraft Co., v. United States*, 534 F. 2d 889, 192 USPQ 296 (Ct. C. 1976). Even before 1976 Hughes Aircraft Company, acting with the inventor of the spin-control system, Mr. Donald T. Williams, a Hughes Aircraft Co. scientist, was engaged in litigation with the National Aeronautics and Space Administration. See 423 F. 2d 1253, 165 USPQ 326 (CCPA 1970); 463 F. 2d 889, 175 USPQ 5 (CCPA 1972). Between 1973 and 1994 the Hughes litigation was considered by the U.S. Court of Claims ten times.

2. 29 Fed. Cl. 197 (1993).

3. C.Q. Christol, "Judicial Protection of Intellectual Property: Hughes Aircraft vs. USA," *Proceedings of the 37th Colloquium on the Law of Outer Space* 145 (1995).

4. Hughes Aircraft Company vs. U.S.A. 31 Fed. Cl. 481 (1994). The Court's order was made on August 5, 1994.

5. *Id.* at 484.

6. By "delay damages" was meant compensation for harms occurring at an earlier date, e.g., starting with the use of the unlicensed patent down to the time when the sums owing from the conduct are actually paid to the successful litigant.

7. *Id.* at 495.

8. Brief for Appellant/Cross-Appellee, Nos. 94-5149, 95-5001, October 31, 1994, pp. 1-2.

9. *Id.* at 1.

10. *Id.* at 48.

11. *Government Brief* at 16.

12. *Id.* at 6.

13. *Id.* at 7.

14. *Id.* at 24.

15. *Id* at 24, citing cases.

16. *Supra*, p. 4.

IISL-96-IISL.4.08

SPACE DEBRIS: DISCUSSIONS IN THE UNITED NATIONS IN 1996

Luboš Perek[1]
Astronomical Institute
Academy of Sciences, Prague, Czech Republic

Abstract

This year the Scientific and Technical Subcommittee discussed the measurements of space debris with a view to provide the understanding of data and of the effects of this environment on space systems. In the Legal Subcommittee, while conducting consultations on new items for the agenda, some delegations proposed to review existing norms of international law applicable to space debris with the aim to clarify the issues involved and help to improve the interpretation and application of existing norms. The Legal Subcommittee, however, has not reached consensus in this matter. The Committee on the Peaceful Uses of Outer Space expressed its agreement with the reports of both Subcommittees and its satisfaction with the report prepared by the Secretariat on steps taken by space agencies for reducing the growth of the damage potential of space debris. The paper concludes with a brief review of possible perspectives and of an issue which might elude a satisfactory solution.

A. Scientific and Technical Subcommittee

Election of the Chairman

The thirty-third session of the Scientific and Technical Subcommittee was held in Vienna from 11 to 23 February 1996. After the resignation of Professor Carver last year, the Subcommittee elected as its new Chairman, Professor Dietrich Rex of the Federal Republic of Germany. In his professional life, Professor Rex is heading the Institute for Spaceflight Technology and Nuclear Reactor Technology at the Technical University of Braunschweig, Germany. He serves as Chairman of the European Space Agency Space Debris Advisory Group and is a member of the US National Research Council's Committee on Space Debris. He and his colleagues are authors of many highly important scientific papers on space debris. At a time when Space Debris is a priority item, the Subcommittee has a chairman who is an eminent expert in the field. A fast progress of the Subcommittee in that field can be anticipated.

Views of Delegations

About twenty delegations participated in the discussion on Space Debris. Only a few contributions can be mentioned here:

The Russian Federation proposed to establish an international centre for providing information and advance warning on explosions in space, on fragmentation of space objects and on possible collisions of space objects with space debris. Also an exchange of data on space debris was advocated with a view to make the catalogues of space debris more reliable, consistent, and complete.

Indonesia considered important to adopt an explanation of the term "space debris". The view was expressed that designating an object as "space debris" should not depend on the identification of the owner. The following wording was proposed:

"Space debris are all man-made objects, including their fragments and parts, whether their owners can be identified or not, in Earth orbit or re-entering the dense layers of the atmosphere, that are non-functional with no reasonable expectation of their being able to assume or resume their intended functions or any other functions for which they are or can be authorized".

Some delegations stressed the importance of reorbiting geostationary satellites into disposal orbits after the termination of their useful lifetimes. India proposed to reorbit to more than 300 km while Japan recommended a higher altitude of at least 500 km beyond the geostationary orbit. The latter is a somewhat higher and safer altitude than that proposed in the IAA Position Paper on Orbital Debris (300 km) but requires more fuel. It should be noted in this context that space debris in the geostationary orbit were discussed under the item on Space Debris and not under the item on the Geostationary Orbit.

The US reported in detail about results obtained with the Haystack Debris Radar which is so powerful that it can detect a pea (0.65 cm) at 650 km distance. Because of the increased accuracy, some of the debris can be assigned to individual breakup events, and previously unrecognized debris sources can be discovered. NASA completed the development of the Liquid Metal Mirror Telescope for observing orbital debris. It will be possible to observe objects of 2.5 cm at 900 km altitude and of 10 cm in the geostationary orbit. In February 1995, the second mission of the Orbital Debris Radar Calibration Spheres was launched. Three spheres and three dipoles of different sizes were deployed from the Shuttle. They were observed by ground based radars and optical telescopes . The observations were used for calibrating their scales and consequently improving their interpreting capabilities.

The Czech delegation stressed the importance of preventive measures but pointed out that a large number of inactive objects is already in orbit. Their highest density occurs at about 800 to 1500 km where the average lifetime is very long, of several hundred years at least. During that time secondary collisions will multiply the number of debris. Methods for removing those objects from orbit have been already studied but further research is needed. The scientific community should be encouraged to study these methods with an emphasis on efficiency and cost effectiveness.

Some delegation supported the view that the Legal Subcommittee should be informed of the discussions in the Scientific and Technical Subcommittee and that a set of international rules should be adopted in order to reduce the risk posed by orbital debris and to support a rational use of outer space. That view was, however, not shared by all delegations. Some considered it premature at present and insisted on a thorough discussion of all important technical aspects of the problem by the Scientific and Technical Subcommittee before deciding on any possible further steps.

Technical Presentations

Several technical presentations[2] supplemented the information provided by delegations.

Prof. Dr. Walter Flury, speaking for the European Space Agency, gave an overview of measurements of space debris and effects of the environment on space systems. He treated in detail ground-based measurements, in particular those made by radar and by optical telescopes, space-based measurements by radar, by optical means by infrared sensors and particle detectors, and those derived from spacecraft returned from space. He concluded with an analysis of possible damage to space systems. He found that impacts by debris of 1 cm size can seriously damage a spacecraft, while larger debris can destroy it.

Dr. Dieter Mehrholz of the Research Institute for High Frequency Physics in Germany, reported on research activities of the Research Establishment for Applied Science, in particular on the Tracking and Imaging Radar system. It uses a 34 m antenna for tracking objects down to 5 cm at 2500 km distance and to 1 m objects in the geosynchronous orbit. The imaging data can be used for checking the functionality of the spacecraft and for identification purposes.

Dr. S. Banerjee and A.S. Ganeshan of the ISRO Satellite Center in Bangalore, India, reported on a Hybrid Model to find Spatial Distribution of Debris from a Breakup. The paper lays down the background for the development of a new analytical method for studying small debris which are not listed in catalogues and have to be studied statistically.

Dr. Andrew Potter of the Johnson Space Center, NASA, presented a Summary of the United States Space Debris Measurements Programme. The programme uses radars for low earth orbits, optical telescopes for deep space, and surfaces returned from space for identifying man-made particles in impact pits. Many results have been already arrived at: There are over 100.000 debris in LEO down to 1 cm size. An unsuspected source of debris was discovered near 900 km altitude, possibly from Rorsat nuclear reactors. A study of surfaces returned from space yields evidence for swarms of microdebris and some microdebris in highly elliptical orbits. Damage on Shuttle windows shows that the microdebris population is underestimated and that it is growing. An additional capability for studies of debris at geosynchronous altitudes is needed. Very little is known about debris population in Molniya and geotransfer orbits, although one geotransfer breakup has been accidentally detected.

Dr. Fernand Alby of the Centre Spatial de Toulouse, CNES, France, spoke on Modelization of Space Debris and Comparison of Observations. Impact craters on exposed surfaces are being searched for and impacting particles identified. The observed flux of particles in space is compared with theoretical models. At the same time, detectors of debris are studied with a view to mount them on satellites to obtain informa-

[2]A/AC.105/638, of 7 May 1996.

tion on the debris population, in particular in the geostationary orbit.

Dr. Richard Crowther of the Defence Research Agency, United Kingdom, reported on The Unique Hazards Associated With Satellite Constellations. A constellation is a collection of satellites performing a common function, such as global positioning, earth observation, personal communications by means of hand-held phones, etc. Several constellations are planned for launch in the near future, requiring tens or hundreds of satellites with lifetimes of 5-8 years. Each system would require frequent launchings of new satellites and frequent deorbiting of satellites approaching the end of their useful lifetimes. Unless the system has a built-in mechanism for restricting the number of debris, the collision risk would increase substantially. The paper gives estimates of collision probabilities. New constellations will add a new dimension of com-plexity in managing the space debris en-vironment but operational practices can reduce the hazard.

Mr. George Levin, NASA Headquarters gave a summary of the United States National Research Council Report on Space Debris 1995[3]. The Report presents the most recent and detailed information. It puts its authority behind previously recommended measures, in general confirming the conclusions of the IAA Position Paper on Orbital Debris. It makes several recommendations for improving knowledge of the debris environment, for improving spacecraft protection against the impact of debris, and for reducing the future debris hazard. In the last area, it advocates:

- Reduction of debris on a multilateral basis in order not to penalize those engaging in mitigation measures,
- Prevention of explosions,
- Minimizing of mission-related debris,
- Minimizing unintentional release of surface materials, such as paint,
- Avoiding intentional breakups, in particular those producing debris with long lifetimes,
- Reorbiting of spacecraft and rocket bodies in Low Earth Orbit after their functional lifetime and achieving an international consensus on the magnitude of such maneuvers, and,
- Until a verifiably superior strategy is produced, reorbiting spacecraft and rocket bodies in the geostationary orbits at least km beyond that orbit.

Other Documents

Several documents on space debris, some of them in connection with nuclear power sources, were before the Subcommittee:

National Research on Space Debris, Safety of Nuclear-Powered Satellites, Problems on Collisions of Nuclear-Powered Sources with Space Debris[4]. Contains replies from Canada, Chile, Germany, Japan and the United Kingdom.

Interpretation and Development of the Safety Principles for Nuclear Power Sources in Space, working paper by the United Kingdom[5].

Collisions between nuclear power sources and space debris[6], working paper by the Russian

---

[3]Orbital Debris: A Technical Assessment, National Research Council, National Academy Press, Washington, D.C., 1995, ISBN 0-309-05125-8, 224 p.

[4]A/AC.105/619 of 21 Nov 1995 and Add.1 of 1 Feb 1996.

[5].A/AC.105/C.1/L.203 of 9 Feb 1996.

[6]A/AC.105/C.1/L.204 of 13 Feb 1996.

Federation.

Brief Review of the Work Done by Russian Scientists on the Problem of the Technogenic Pollution of Near Space[7], working paper by the Russian Federation.

Space Agencies

The implementation of concrete steps for reducing the amount of space debris in future missions is in the hands of those space agencies which provide the launching of spacecraft. They can influence the design , launching and operation of satellites. These may be the reasons why many delegations expressed their appreciation of the document[8] on Steps Taken by Space Agencies for Reducing the Growth or Damage Potential of Space Debris. It reports on preventive measures adopted by space agencies on a voluntary basis, without awaiting the out-come of the discussions in the United Nations.

A few specific examples follow:

- Venting of hypergolic upper stages and discharging of batteries in order to prevent explosions in orbit,
- Measures for avoiding the generation of new debris, such as ballistic re-entry trajectories, trapping of explosive bolts, using of recoverable satellites,
- Measures for decreasing orbital lifetime of inactive spacecraft,
- Re-orbiting of geostationary satellites into disposal orbits, and
- Shielding of vital parts of satellites.

[7]A/AC.105/C.1/L.205 of 13 Feb 1996

[8]A/AC.105/620 , of 21 November 1995.

This is regarded as an important event because space agencies have shown that they are approaching the problem of space debris with a high degree of responsibility and that they have not only the power but also the will to preserve outer space in a state fit for future space activities. Several delegations therefore supported the proposal that space agencies should be brought into a closer contact with the Subcommittee. The Subcommittee decided to invite a representative of the Inter-Agency Space Debris Coordination Committee to give a presentation at the next session of the Subcommittee.

Technical Report

The most important part of the work of the Subcommittee consisted in preparing a structured Technical Report[9] in agreement with last year's decision to follow a multi-year Work Plan. Accordingly, the Technical Report deals briefly with previous history and explains why it has to be structured. It contains also an explanation of the term "space debris". As recently as last year, a proposal to explain what is the common understanding of the term failed to find the agreement of the Subcommittee. This year, the Report (see footnote 5, para 95) states:

"It is understood that space debris are inactive man-made objects, such as spent upper stages, spent satellites, fragments or parts generated during launch or mission operations, or fragments from explosions and other breakups".

No size limits of space debris have been expressly stated. Evidently, the upper limit is the largest man-made spacecraft, if and when it

[9]A/AC.105/637, of 4 March 1996, para 94-138.

becomes inactive. The lower limit in size can be inferred from the text of the Report. It deals with impacts of submillimeter-size particles and with craters and holes extending from several millimeters down to micrometers. Thus the smallest debris are the size of dust particles.

This year , only the part dealing with Measurements of space debris was detailed, while Modelling and Mitigation will be filled in the next two years.

B. The Legal Subcommittee

The Legal Subcommittee has held its thirty-fifth session from 18-28 March. It did not have space debris on its agenda but it discussed topics for new items to be put on the agenda in the future. Two of these topics deal with space debris:

Review of Existing Norms of International Law Applicable to Space Debris. The item was proposed by the delegation of the Czech Republic in an unofficial background note[10]. The purpose of the item is to examine the problem of space debris from the perspective of existing international law which could be applicable to space debris. The following questions could be discussed:

- Does the definition of "space object" as contained in instruments of space law cover space debris?
- Do provisions of the 1967 Outer Space Treaty concerning the avoidance of harmful contamination of outer space and adverse changes in the environment of the Earth apply to the problem of space debris?
- Should the protection of ownership of space objects, and of their component parts, also be extended to space debris?
- Should liability for damage caused to a space object and/or its crew by space debris depend on the proof of fault as in the case of a collision of two space objects?

The consideration of these and other questions would serve to clarify the issues involved and improve the interpretation and application of existing norms. It would not amount to the drafting of new provisions. The item could be limited to 2-3 meetings at two sessions of the Subcommittee. It would help the main Committee to decide possible further steps after it examines the Technical Report prepared by the Scientific and Technical Subcommittee which could be finished in 1998.

Legal Aspects of Space Debris. The item was proposed every year since 1993 but there never was a consensus on the matter because some delegations were of the opinion that the Technical Report by the Scientific and Technical Subcommittee has to be completed before any legal considerations can be initiated.

C. The Main Committee

The Committee on the Peaceful Uses of Outer Space has held its thirty-ninth sessions from 3 to 14 June. It discussed space debris in the agenda item "Report of the Scientific and Technical Subcommittee" and in the item "Report of the Legal Subcommittee" when new items for the inclusion in the agenda of the Legal Subcommittee were under consideration.

In brief, the Committee agreed with the Scientific and Technical Subcommittee that international cooperation was needed to de-

---

[10]A/AC.105/639, of 11 April 1996, Annex E.

velop appropriate and affordable strategies to minimize the impact of space debris; that there was need for further research; that national research should continue and its results made available to all interested parties; and that the Inter-Agency Orbital Debris Coordination Committee (IADC) should be invited to give a presentation to the Subcommittee at its next session. The Committee expressed its satisfaction with all documents on space debris which were before the Subcommittee and with the first part of the Technical Report.

As regards possible new items for the agenda of the Legal Subcommittee, the Committee noted the opinion of some delegations that a new item entitled "Review of existing norms of international law applicable to space debris" should be put on the agenda of the Subcommittee in 1997. Other delegations considered that proposal premature.

The Committee agreed that proposals for new agenda items should have a multi-year work plan which should address, i.a., the objectives of the work to be undertaken, any reports to be provided by the Secretariat or Member States, and the possible end product.

For the sake of completeness, let us mention that the Committee entrusted the Chairman to undertake intersessional informal consultations among the members of the Committee with the aim of reaching consensus, i.a., on agenda structures. These consultations could lead to important decision of the Committee at its session in 1997, including new agenda items for the Legal Subcommittee.

D. Perspectives

It can be anticipated that the Technical Report will be completed in 1998 and that it will be examined by the COPUOS and a decision will be made about further steps to be taken on space debris. At the same time, Space Agencies, in particular members of the IADC, can be expected to coordinate and extend their measures for restricting the generation of debris and for mitigating their harmful impact. They already realize that such practices have to be adopted by all because there is no significant effect if they are adopted only by one operator. An optimistic point of view is justified as regards a significant restriction of generation of space debris in the future.

The situation is different with regard to space debris which are already in orbit and which have no maneuvering capability. It is true that a few objects have been retrieved by the Space Shuttle but these were exceptions. In general, the cost of retrieving a worthless piece of debris by a manned spacecraft is prohibitive. Deorbiting by means of a tether is theoretically possible but no successful experiments have been conducted and the cost involved will probably be very high. Drag augmentation by large balloons[11] or sweeping small debris by large spread films have the inherent difficulty of a potential encounter with an operating spacecraft.

Ground-based methods for removing debris have been proposed, such as directing a powerful laser beam on a piece of debris and evaporating it or at least changing its trajectory and reducing its lifetime. Since such a laser could be looked upon as an antisatellite weapon and an unauthorized removal of debris could be considered to constitute a breach of the Outer Space Treaty, an application of this or a similar method would require international discussions and agreements.

---

[11] J. Loftus Jr., Space Debris Mitigation, Int. Astronaut.Congress, Oslo 1995, paper IAA.95-IAA.6.5.01.

Briefly, no adequate and affordable methods for removing passive debris from orbit exist at present. On the other hand, orbiting debris may become very dangerous. According to several recent investigators[12,13,14] debris will start colliding among themselves, producing large numbers of fragments. As a consequence, the collision probability for active satellites will increase considerably. At present, there are about 2000 tons of debris below the altitude of 2000 km presenting a combined cross-section of 10.000 square meters. With this amount of mass, which is a critical factor, the safety of future operations in space seems to be in jeopardy and research on a wide basis seems to be indispensable.

An appeal should be directed to the scientific community, specifically to international scientific organizations, such as the IAF, IAA, COSPAR, or, in fact, to the IADC, to try to find new , or substantially improve the existing, ways for removing large as well as small passive objects from outer space. The new inventions, if and when they are made, will, of course, have to be assessed from the point of view of cost and effectiveness as well as from the legal point of view.

---

[12]D.J. Kessler: Collisional cascading: The limits of population growth in Low Earth Orbit. COSPAR, The Hague, Netherlands, paper MB 2.2.2(1990).

[13]D. Rex and P. Eichler: The possible long term overcrowding of LEO and the necessity and effectiveness of debris mitigation measures. Proc. of the First European Conference on Space Debris, Darmstadt, Germany, 5-7 April 1993, 607-615.

[14]P. Eichler and R. Reynolds: Mid- and long-term debris environment projections using the EVOLVE and CHAIN models. Int. Astronaut. Congress, Oslo, Norway 1995, paper IAA-95-IAA.6.4.07.

IISL-96-IISL.4.09

The Draft of the International Law Association for a Convention on Space Debris(Buenos Aires) Can it Meet the Needs o f 21st Century?

Ali Akbar Golrounia*, Managing Director
Atlas Aviation Group
Dr. Mohsen Bahrami†, Associate Professor
Mechanical Engineering, Amir Kabir University of Technology
Tehran, Islamic Republic of IRAN

ABSTRACT

The next century will be dominated by an ever increasing of space activities and will witness a considerable boost in commercialization in space affairs.
As the result, government control will be severely effected by the commercial interest of private entities, specially when we realize that the future private sectors in space activities are mainly dominated by multinational organization which make the necessary governmental and international control even more complicated.

The needs for an international binding instrument to monitor and control the space activities in such a way that while controlling the environment from space debris and contamination/pollution, does not hinder of the process of using the outer space for benefits of mankind.

As this draft is being prepared for such a purpose, there are doubts that it will be able to meet the challenge of space activities in the Twenty First century.

This study will provide analysis and comments on different part of the draft instrument such as:

* Definition of environment.
* Space activities originated out of jurisdiction or control of any state.
* Obligations and responsibilities of states in regard to commercial and non-governmental entities.

Suggestions are made for changes to be applied to the draft instrument to accommodate the needs of the space activities in Twenty First Century.

---

* Member, IISL; Founding Member, IRIASS; International Arbitrator, ICAO.

† Senior Member, AIAA; Member, ASME; Founding Member, IRIASS; Head, Air Space Educational Planning Committee, High Council of Educational Planning, IR. IRAN

INTRODUCTION

The beginning of space activities is marked by the lunching of Sputnik-1. It is also fair to say that Sputnik was the first source of space debris. After close to fifty years of constantly growing space industry and increasing space activities, the subject of space debris as a hazard to environment has become of great concern to all nations, regardless of the degree they are involved in developing and/or using space technology.

The subject has been getting more alarming in recent years, since number of private parties involved in different areas of space industry is growing rapidly. We are witnessing private sector to take over many parts of the industry that traditionally were in government control. Of course this is normal considering the level of the development of the technology. Private and multinational corporation, and even self reliant government organizations have enjoyed the rapid growth in space based communication, remote sensing, weather forecasting, space based tele-medicine and etc. Many more areas are being introduce such microgravity, Navigation and Air Traffic Control, etc. What is usually left out of this success story, is that for each of this services their is a certain amount of debris and pollution/contamination involved. This means that the earth environment is facing a threat of new dimensions and magnitude that is compatible to technology developed, unmatched in the history of mankind.

From 7184 objects observed, only 350 are operative satellite, and 1427 are non-operative satellite and more that 5407 are debris[1]. Major part of the debris has been produced by explosion of satellite. The debris population is the greatest between 500Km and 1200Km orbit. Debris in LEO and GEO are the most dangerous ones. New measures of environment protection is obviously needed.

It should be noted that albeit all its hazardous potential for the environment, space technology creates many new possibilities and venues for protection of the environment. As a matter of fact following the United Nations Conference on Environment and Development at Rio de Janeiro, from 3 to 14 June 1992, a report on application of space technology in implementation of Agenda 21 is being prepared at the request of the Committee on Peaceful Uses of Outer Space[2].

The question of environment protection in face of growing space activities has also been addressed in international treaties. Article IX of Treaty on Principles Governing the Activities of States in the Exploration and Use of Outer Space, including the Moon and other Celestial Bodies(adapted in 1967) requires: "... States parties to the Treaty shall pursue studies of the outer space, including the moon and other celestial bodies, and conduct exploration of them so as to avoid their harmful contamination and also adverse changes in the environment of the earth resulting from the introduction of extraterrestrial matter and, where necessary shall adopt the appropriate measures for this purpose. ..."

Article 7 of the Agreement Governing the Activities of States on the Moon and other Celestial Bodies (adapted in 1979) requires "...States Parties shall also take measures to avoid harmfully affecting the environment of the earth through the introduction of extraterrestrial matter or otherwise..."

More recently use of nuclear power in space has become of some concern such that UN General Assembly Resolution 47/68 of 14 December 1992, Principles Relevant to Use of Nuclear Power Sources in Outer Space, was adopted. Principles 3 and 4 of this resolution make indirect attempt to take some measures to reduce the risk to environment.

Many studies has shown the importance and situation of the space debris[3,4], as well. These reports are mainly prepared due to the fact that the operative environment for new activities is becoming ever more dangerous.

Obviously, In spite of all the progress in different sectors of the industry, and wide spectrum of the technology and applications, proper attention has not been paid to the environmental issues. The first serious international step taken concerning the protection of the earth and outer space environment, is the ILA Draft Instrument, i.e. "Buenos Aires International Instrument on Protection of the Environment from Damage Caused by Space Debris"

This draft even though commendable in its own right, and a long step from a situation of ignorance and negligence to the environment, which is the characteristics of the development stage of any technology, is not properly worded and does not seem to change the status quo for the future of more commercialization and privatization of space industries. The sprite of the draft is to consult and to inform, which is not necessary a new idea in space treaties and agreements. Article IX of Outer Space Treaty requires the parties to consult others when they consider their planned space activities may be harmful to them. Not too many reports are documented in this regard.

In the present work, after a critical view of some parts of the draft , some suggestion are made , which are considered necessary to make the instrument more efficient.

THE INSTRUMENT RECONSIDERED

In finalizing the draft one should note with the rapid growth of technology and industry, before this instrument can become effective the situation will be considerably different. Thus we need to prepare the instrument in such a way that it will be more applicable in the real world of tomorrow.

In Article 1.d, environment is defined as " both the outer space and earth environments within or beyond national jurisdiction." It is not clear if this definition includes the moon or other celestial bodies, which will be of increasing importance in the near future. There will be a lot of activities on the moon and other celestial bodies, which require the implementation of considerable amount of equipment and material along with human resources. These items can be the potential sources of pollution/contamination and debris. At the same time they may suffer from pollution/contamination and debris from other sources, as well. Therefore, we suggest that the instrument should explicitly specify the moon and other celestial bodies are included in the definition of the environment.

We propose that Article 1(d) be restated as follows:

"Environment for the purposes of this instrument is, the outer space including moon and other celestial bodies, and earth environment within or beyond national jurisdiction."

Article 3 part 2 falls short of considering space activities which may originate or take place in areas under jurisdiction of no particular state. High seas and outer space are of such significance. A lunch from high seas or outer space, which may result in damage to environment and/or property can not be handled by this instrument. This situation may arise, when a private party attempts a lunch from a point out of jurisdiction of no state, which results in a failure and damaging debris and pollution/contamination. The instrument is not explicit in defining the responsibilities, in particular if the lunching party is not willing to abide with the instrument.

NATIONAL REGULATORY BODY

The next century will certainly be dominated by an even increasing level of space activities and will witness a considerable boost in privatization and commercialization of space affairs. This easily can be observed by the current trends in space faring nations. A contract goes to private sector to manufacture the next generation space shuttle in United States. Many space industrial centers in Russia are turning to more self reliance from government budgeting. European Space Agency has long history in commercial space activities. Needless to say china as a rather new comer to the commercial arena has made a considerable success in offering wide range of space services. India is making strong headway to offer her own services, probably we will witness her success in shorter time than is expected.

Article 3 imposes on states and international organizations parties to this instrument to protect the environment from damages caused by debris as result of their space activities. This means all states and international organizations parties to the instrument have the obligation to make sure that their space activities and that of organizations under their control and/or jurisdiction are properly guided and monitored.

In this time of increasing rate of commercialization and privatization of space activities the wording of this article is not clear enough of how to achieve its goals. What standards and guiding regulations are to be used? How different private organization know what level of debris is acceptable in the future? For that matter how a government knows what level of debris to expect and to accept from different organizations to fulfill the goals of the instrument?

Therefore rules, regulations, standards and guidelines are needed to make it possible for both commercial organizations and governments to know how to perform and control. A NATIONAL REGULATORY BODY is essential to establish appropriate rules, regulation and standards, as well as to control and monitor the activities of the commercial sector in their national jurisdiction, to control and reduce the damage and risk caused by debris resulted from their space activities.

It is note worthy[5] that so far five states, i.e. Russian Federation, Republic of South Africa, Sweden, United Kingdom ad

United States are in possession of national space legislation.

INTERNATIONAL REGULATORY BODY

As stated above, rules, regulations and standards are the essential tools for any government and private sector to control and to perform their space activities with regard to control of space debris, in a meaningful way; and the fact that space activities is not limited to national boundaries and national jurisdiction. Therefore uniformity in rules, regulations and standards are essential among states and international organizations parties to this instrument. This uniformity is more important considering the obligations which article 4 of this instrument imposes on all states and international organizations to prevent, inform, consult and negotiate in good faith.

As the current trends already show, next century is going to witness unprecedented increase in volume and privatization of space activities. However, one should bear in mind that "... to inform and to consult in good faith..." as Article 4 of the instrument is requiring, are not necessarily the strong points of competitive private sector; particularly in area such as outer space and high seas that no government has any judicial control. Therefore, time is crucial for the international community to take proper measures for protection of the environment, in form of an INTERNATIONAL REGULATORY BODY(IRB).

This international body should be established as part of the instrument to coordinate the national governments to control and guide their space activities, thus to fulfill the goals of the instrument.

Furthermore, the IRB can and must establish proper guidelines and regulations for high seas and outer space activities, which are under no governmental jurisdiction and control.

IRB as part of its activities can offer advise and consultation, which in particular is useful for the newcomer to space arena, to direct their space activities properly; and set the stage for more meaningful cooperation among space faring nations for the purpose of environmental protection.

It should be noted that the creation of an international space agency has been suggested many time[6]. However, it seems that the time is not ready for such an all-out effort. But a meaningful cooperation in form of the suggested regulatory body can enjoy a wider support of all parties due to its goal of protection of environment.

SPACE EXPLORATION AND ENVIRONMENT PROTECTION

The history of human civilization and in particular technology development has taught us that any development has its own environment degradation and damages. Space exploration in its own right has been of no difference. The fact that the instrument is the subject of discussion is the proof of this claim. However we have learned while to accept this fact, we should try to reduce the environment damage and even to look for remedies.

At this special point in time, that we have new frontiers to explore we need to establish flexible mechanism with regard to future technology development to protect our environment and that of the future generations, while not hindering the space activities. This requires that all states and organization to cooperate in good faith to create such mechanism in form of the aforementioned International Regulatory Body.

The role of the IRB is to have an updated assessment of the current environment hazards and technological abilities and potentials. With this information proper standards can be introduced which are to be met in targeted times. Obviously, these standards are to be followed by the states and international organization. This will guaranty us a course which notonly improves the current situation, but also generate less and less debris and pollution/contamination as time goes by.

REFERENCES

1. Gabriella Catalano Sgrosso, Liability for Damage Caused by Space Debris, International Institute of Space Law Colloquium, Paper No. IISL-95-IISL.2.04, Oslo, Norway, 1995.

2. Boutros Boutros-Ghali, International Cooperation Space Activities for Enhancing Security in the Post Cold War, Report of the Secretary-General, United Nations, A/47/27, pp11.

3. Space Debris, The Report of the ESA Space Debris Working Group. ESA Publication ESA-SP-1109, Nov. 1988.

4. Orbital Debris, A Technical Assessment, Committee on Space Debris, Aeronautical and Space Engineering Board, Commission on Engineering and Technical Systems, National Research Council, National Academy Press, Washington, DC, 1995.

5. Frans G. Von der Dunk, Two New National Space Laws: Russia and South Africa, International Institute of Space Law colloquium, Paper No. IISL-95-IISL.4.09, Oslo, Norway, 1995.

6. Cyril E. S. Horsford,Is I.C.A.O. the Model for an International Space Agency? International Institute of Space Law Colloquium, Paper No. IISL-95-IISL.3.09, Oslo, Norway, 1995.

IISL-96-IISL.4.10

JAPANESE SPACE POLICY -WHERE IS SHE GOING?

HASHIMOTO, Yasuaki*
Associate Professor
The National Institute for Defense Studies
Tokyo, Japan

Abstract

Passing 25 years from 1970 when the first satellite was launched into the orbit, Japan developed and successfully launched H-II from Tanegashima Space Center in 1994. During those period, Japanese space policy has experienced a big shake from independent development to technology import from US, and back again to independent development. In general, the H-II rocket which was manufactured by 100 % domestic technology, brings Japan from the old era (experimental stage) to the new era (practical use stage).

Fundamental Policy of Japan's Space Activities, which decides such policy as mentioned, was revised in January, 1996 this year after an interval of 7 years. This revised outline confirms the result of Japanese space technology until present and identifies the future direction and framework of her space activities for a period of coming ten years on the basis of a long-term perspective towards the 21st century. However, when comparing with the last Fundamental Policy in 1989, there seems no big change in it, and a long-term perspective is also not seen there. The description varies on some important points in international space law, like international cooperation, protection of environment, commercial use, etc. In addition, the immaturity as well as the necessity of broader discussion are felt because, for example, neither this Fundamental Policy nor The National Defense Program Outline treated any national and international security matters concerning outer space.

Considering the present time when Japan enters into the practical use of outer space, such as application, commercial use and launching service, it is doubtful whether new Fundamental Policy was properly planned or not. It seems necessary to use several measures by which the public opinion, opinions from industry field and deeper debate on the security are reflected in the law and policy making.

New Fundamental Policy of Japan's Space Activities

The policy concerning the Japanese space development is decided by Fundamental Policy of Japan's Space Activities. This outline is written by Space Activities Commission[1].

The views expressed in this paper are those of the author and do not represent the ones of any organization with which the author is affiliated.

* Member, International Institute of Space Law, Member, Society for the Study of Law & Policy on Space Utilization (Japan)

It is 1978 that Fundamental Policy of Japan's Space Activities was planned for the first time. Afterwards, the Commission revised this Fundamental Policy twice on 1984 and 1989. Those revisions were to respond to the changes in the space development and use in Japan and the world. Upon the same reasons, new Fundamental Policy in January this year[2] was drafted and approved in order to identify the future direction and framework of Japan's space activities for a period of coming ten years on the basis of a long-term perspective towards the 21st century[3] .

Setting-up Chapters -The Structure

New Fundamental Policy consists of 6 chapters in it. They are,

Preface

1 Basic Policy and Implementation of Space Development

2 Development of Space Development Activities

3 Institutional Structure of Space Development

4 Promotion of International Cooperation

5 Encouragement of Space Activities in Private Sector, and

6 Preparation for Promotion of Space Activities.

When comparing title of each chapter with previous one, there is not a big difference. The almost same name is applied since Chapter 2. The setting up of previous Policy was

2 Space Development Activities

3 Organizational Framework

4 International Cooperation

5 Private Sector, and

6 Social Environment.

Especially, those changes are smaller in Japanese compared with English.

Moreover, the Chapter 1. does not have a big change either (in previous Policy: that was Fundamental Principles). It is thought that the present Policy succeeded to overall in structure.

New Direction of Fundamental Policy

Though there is not so big change in its structure, some policy changes are seen in the present Policy.

The first to be enumerated is recognition of the change in international environment. New fundamental Policy thinks that The US and Russia are now turning their emphasis in space development from military projects and matters of national prestige to cost/benefit context and high technology development by converting space technology from military use to commercial application. Those two countries as well as Europe and China are thought to put their resources to civilian use in future space activities.

Further, considering the international projects like the space station, international cooperation is respected in it. Upon the above mentioned recognition, the Policy says that Japan has to play an active role in international space endeavours from a global standpoint[4].

Policy Change in Each Field

High priority areas are listed up in Section 1 of Chapter 2, and afterwards concrete contents of the activities are described in Section 2. Following are the main points in each field.

First of all, Subsection 1. Earth Observation and Earth Science, while developing a series of satellites, insists on establishing an information network for data use. This is a point that was not referred in the previous Policy which devoted attention only to satellite technology. In addition, the Policy offers a global earth observation system in harmony with other countries, which is one area of international cooperation. Regarding the reason why the description of meteorological satellites decrease, this technology reaches completely the practical use level.

Subsection 3 is devoted to the Moon Exploration. In this part, unmanned exploration and an international lunar observatory are planned.

About Communication, Broadcasting and Navigation (Subsection 4), much attention has been paid to the active development and use of personal satellite-based mobile communication, GPS, etc.

Subsection 6. Manned Space Activities newly enumerates acquiring experience and know-how through JEM (Japanese module of the space station) and the US space shuttle, and describes space medical science.

Subsection 7. Basic Technology for Satellite and Subsection 8. Space Infrastructure are planning development of satellites, transportation systems in the future. The new tendency in both subsections is a declaration of cost reduction. When a new satellite is built, cost reduction is essential, and cost cutting is also indicated in the transportation system. It is new that Subsection 8 describes H-IIA launch vehicle[5], J-1 launch vehicle, HOPE-X[6] (an experimental part of the reusable type transportation system), HTV[7] for supplying logistics to the space station and a space plane. In addition, new landing field for HOPE-X and a monitoring system of space debris are listed up as new items.

In Chapter 3. Institutional Structure of Space Development and Chapter 4. Promotion of International Cooperation, the enhancement of national and international cooperation is requested. Especially, the reinforcement of cooperation with Asia-Pacific regions in some fields is pointed out in Chapter 4[8].

Chapter 5. (Encouragement of Space Activities in Private Sector) newly refers providing the private sector the opportunities for verification and experiments, actively personnel exchange between NASDA and the private sector and commercial launch service.

For the Preparation for Promotion of Space Activities (Chapter 6), it enumerates, as promotion measures, Internet, science museums, aero-space related centers, use of "Space Day"[9], etc. In the field of manpower training, additional effort to foster personnel of humanities and social science such as space law and space psychology. Additionally, it is the first time that the space insurance is expressed in the Policy. This might be a result of recognition of entering the practical use stage.

Evaluation of New Fundamental Policy

As mentioned above, while keeping the same structure as a previous one, New Fundamental Policy has some changes and additions in part. Those changes and additions are made basing upon the history of space development inside Japan and related international environment for recent 7 years.

Whether Fundamental Policy is an appropriate compass for Japanese space policy should be carefully examined. Only this Policy can clarifies the Japanese attitude responding the obligation of international space law, because there has been no fundamental law concerning the space development in Japan[10].

Commercialization

Though the revised outline recognizes that the US and Russia are converting space technology from military use to commercial application. And further, there is growing emphasis among major space powers (US, Russia, Europe and China) on civilian use in future space activities, the direction of Japanese effort for commercialization remains ambiguous. The Policy declares that in its Preface "We should renew the significance of space development and recognize a world wide trend to emphasize both civilian use and international cooperation in space activities. We have to play an active role in international space endeavours by enhancing the current level of our space technology and know-how, and by pursuing real utilization of space from a global standpoint."[11] However, the actual content of commercialization is not described. The definition of civilian use and commercial application is assumed to be vagueness. It only points out the necessity of cost reduction, active participation of private sector and introduction of space insurance. The border line between two categories, one is left for the national responsibility and the other is commercialized for private sector, is not drawn though Chapter 5 which newly introduced commercial launch service. Under such situation, the enterprise which positively executes the space activity is not to appear easily while some are included in national space projects as contractors or subcontractors.

Protection of Environment

Recently, the environmental issue has been important as a problem of pollution prevention of outer space itself by debris as well as a problem of the environmental protection of the earth by using remote sensing data from outer space.

New Fundamental Policy spares one paragraph for conducting research on space debris monitoring systems[12]. Moreover, the environment problem is referred in each part and it offers the global observation system with other nations. Those are descriptions to consider the international contribution in this field.

International Cooperation

Regarding cooperation, Chapter 4 as a whole provides its promotion. To compare with the previous Policy, joint establishment of observation system is newly proposed in this field. And the new Policy intends to expand cooperation especially with Asia-Pacific Regions[13]

Peaceful Character

International space law has made an effort to prevent outer space from the military expansion. That spirit appears to the Preface and Article 4 of Outer Space Treaty in 1967. Fundamental Policy, in only one sentence, says that Japan promotes its space development within a scope of peaceful purposes[14]. The description concerning peace and security is not seen in other parts at all. Japan interpreted 'peaceful' in outer space treaty as 'non-military' and does not change that interpretation at present. After the private sector came to use some space technologies generally, such space use is allowed to the military sector for the first time[15]. However, it should be discussed whether we continue this interpretation or not, even after Japan herself develops enough technology for launching satellites by which security data can be acquired from outer space. If 'peaceful' is interpreted as 'non-aggressive', information gathering from outer space can be done by Japanese military sector. New Fundamental Policy in 1996 does not refer at all on this issue, at the time when it is understood that the regional stability and security are kept with satellite data and analyzed information from that data. The National Defense Program Outline[16], which decides the Japanese defense policy, also does not describe the space utilization yet, though that use is insisted on in the advisory report "The Modality of the Security and Defense Capability of Japan" submitted to the Prime Minister by his Advisory Group of Defense Issues[17]. The appropriate policy on this matter should be discussed inside and outside the Diet sufficiently and should be reflected not only in the Fundamental Policy but also in the National Defense Program Outline in the near future.

This policy regarding the security use of outer space by Japanese military sector has related to the wide spread concern about the Self Defense Forces themselves. While the Advisory Group of Defense Issues submitted its report to the Prime Minister for considering the outer space utilization for national security[18], there remains a strong concern for the military activities among the public opinion in Japan.

The good example was the failure in search and picking up the HYFLEX this year. On 12 February, 1996, the experimental equipment called HYFLEX (HYpersonic FLight EXperiment) was launched by J-1 rocket successfully. This launch was an experiment for acquiring the necessary data for future development of HOPE (H-II Orbiting Plane). After this HYFLEX was landed on the Pacific Ocean safely, NASDA lost it because it sunk into the deep sea. Though NASDA announced that they could get most of the data transmitted by electric wave, there was still unrecoverable damage for this failure. During this mission, Self Defense Force was never requested for support. It is natural that they might find and pick up the HYFLEX if they were asked cooperation in advance. Seeing the same case in US where Navy cooperates the national space activities positively, this example shows the Japanese unique attitude against the Forces.

As well known, it is needless to say that the national space activities which accompany the high risk need all related resources even in the country. However, in Japan, the appropriate situation where the Defense Forces support space activities and the public accepts the security use of outer space, seems far from the present.

Conclusion

The fundamental Policy of Japan's Space Activities in 1996 is thought to be the first Policy decided after Japan started practical use of outer space. This Policy successfully outlined continuous, mid-term targets for a period of coming 10 years, of which the term is intended by the planner, Space Activities Commission, from the beginning. On the other hand, Japan's long-term vision and philosophy in her space activities are not clear though this Policy is a steady forecast based upon the present technical achievements. It is rather difficult to see the policy and guidelines for the future legal structure which can appeal to the public domestically and internationally.

In order to solve the problem, the system by which the public opinion is considered and entered into the Policy is needed. In this case, the Diet where the public opinion as well as the opinion from the industries are reflected should be involved more in the policy and law making process.

Note

1. The Space Activities Commission (SAC) was founded in 1968 under the Law for the Establishment of SAC. This commission is composed of five members including a chairperson. The chairperson is the Director General of Science and Technology Agency.
2. The present Policy was revised on January 24, 1996.
3. Paragraph 15 of Preface.
4. *ibid.*
5. H-IIA is an advanced H-II launch vehicle to launch a 20 ton payload into low Earth orbit or a 4 ton payload into geostationary orbit with a drastic cost reduction.
6. HOPE is a H-II Orbiting Plane to develop the unmanned reusable winged space plane.

7. HTV is a H-II Transfer Vehicle with rendezvous and docking functions.
8. (5) of Chapter 4.
9. 12 September.
10. Though the Diet resolution recommended to make the Fundamental Law for Outer Space Exploration, there still is no such law in Japan.
11. Paragraph 12 of Preface.
12. Chapter 2, Section 8 Space Infrastructure, (3) Support System, (iii) Monitoring Space Debris.
13. note 8, *supra.*
14. Chapter 1, 1-1. Basic Policy
15. In 1985, Japanese government announced in the Diet that interpretation.
16. This Outline was approved by the Cabinet on 28 November, 1995.
17. The Modality of the Security and Defense Capability of Japan -The Outlook for the 21st Century (August 12, 1994)-
18. Chapter 3 The Modality of Defense Capability in the New Age, Section 3 Maintenance and Qualitative Improvement of Self-Defense Capability, (4) Specific Measures of Reform.

IISL-96-IISL.4.11

NATIONAL INSTITUTIONS RESPONSIBLE FOR SPACE ACTIVITIES : A COMPARATIVE LAW APPROACH

by

Michel BOURELY* and Simone COURTEIX**

* Docteur en Droit,
Former Legal Adviser to the European Space Agency,
Member IISL.

** Director of Research at the National Center for Scientific Research (CNRS),
Director of the Center for Study and Research of Space Law (Institute of Comparative Law), Paris, France,
Professor of Space Law, Member IISL.

ABSTRACT

States have always been the initiators of space activities and, despite the emergence of private sector operators in some countries, continue to be engaged in space activities on their own behalf. The institutional framework for space activities in different countries can be compared by examining the following characteristics :

(1) general conditions concerning (a) the extent of state involvement (closely tied to each country's history), (b) the nature of the involvement (direct or indirect), which may have developed differently according to whether or not the state has a national space agency, and (c) the type of space regulations in effect;

(2) the institutional framework of the State, generally, with regard to the involvement at various levels of political and administrative authorities, and the institutional framework of public or semi-public bodies created specifically for space activity purposes (budgetary concerns play a major role with respect to both frameworks);

(3) the nature of the relations between the State and the private sector, which differs greatly according to the importance given to military or commercial purposes, and the development of non-governmental space activities and the consequent institution of regulations providing for the "supervision" and "authorization" of such space activities, in order to

comply with international space law treaties; and

(4) the development of international cooperation both on a multilateral and bilateral level, which has had a significant influence on space institutions and which has led to the sharing of authorities with regional and international bodies.

I INTRODUCTION

States have been the initiators of space activities since they have existed, either exclusively in some countries or partly in others. However, in that case, they keep the control of the activities in some determined sectors (military notably) while they share, at the same time, the other sectors with the private operators.

The role of the States has been predominant during the "Cold War Period", which has been characterized by a rivalry between USSR and the USA, as much on the level of prestige as on the level of military abilities. Nowadays, the competition between the two great powers does not have the same reasons to be anymore, and one can see a worldwide cooperation among States being developed in definite sectors, whereas there is a fierce competition among the actors of the private sector in other sectors of activities.

However, as it is asserted in the "Outer Space Treaty" of 1967, it belongs to the States and only to them to: bear, on one hand, international, political and juridical responsabilities for all national space activities -whether they are carried out by governmental agencies or non-governmental entities- and to ensure that the provisions of the treaty are enforced; on the other hand, it belongs to them to authorize and supervise the space activities of the non-governmental entities placed under their jurisdiction, and finally to supervise that the international organizations they are participating are complying with the provisions of the treaty. It is obvious that this triple duty applies to all the international agreements -which goal is to govern the exercise of space activities- signed by the States whatever their form is.

In consequence, whatever their direct involvement in outer space is, as actors, the States Parties of the 1967 Treaty have to participate to the drawing up and the enforcement of the international rules applicable to space activities. However, these States are, of course, free to organize, as they wish, within their national framework, the implementation of the obligations contracted under the international agreements. The actual world practice lets us notice that a great variety of situations exists, resulting from the range of answers given to this state obligation.

We can observe that, in some countries, national specialized structures exist, generally named "Agency", and that they are responsible for space activities. However, they can get very varied legal forms and different powers according to the kind of space activities undertaken by the State itself. In other countries, there are no agencies of this kind, the responsability of the State being shared between the already different existing national entities, which more often are ministerial departments.

The choice between these two forms obviously depends upon, first of all, the political regime of each country, and therefore upon the power of intervention given to the public authority; it also depends upon the existence and vitality of the private sector, as well as the degree of freedom granted by the State.

Within this Colloquium, it seemed to us interesting to inform the IISL Members of the results of a study which has just been done by the Center of Study and Research on Space Law (CERDE) of Paris (France) in cooperation with the European Center for Space Law (ECSL), and which results will be published later on.

The present Report will, first, briefly set out the different ways which can be used by the States in order to comply with their obligations relating to the national organization of space activities in their respective countries (I). It will then describe the conditions of the intervention of the States in the exercise of these activities (II). These questions will, of course, be studied in details in the work above mentioned.

PART I THE ORGANIZATION, BY THE STATES, OF THEIR SPACE ACTIVITIES

The intervention of the States in space activities, which will take place on their territory or which will be undertaken by their nationals, is expressly foreseen by articles VI, VII, and VIII of the 1967 Outer Space Treaty to which, it shall be recalled, nearly all the States of the world - including the space powers- are parties.

As it is known, this intervention has to take place either if the State plays the role of actor and undertakes itself the space activities, or if it only supervises, on its territory, their execution by entities which are outside the State properly said: ie. autonomous governmental agencies, private sector, international organizations.

However, the intervention of the State can take many diverse forms. It has however to be underlined that the organization of space activities is not related to the existence or the lack, in a country, of a specific national legislation. Such a legislation does not exist in all the space powers and in that case the intervention of the State relies upon the existing general texts.

1- THE GENERAL STRUCTURES

The institutional framework within which the space activities of the States are carried out, includes, first of all, general structures that are, for most of them, related to the principal political and constitutional authorities of the States. In consequence, it is not surprising to notice that even the heads of States themselves possess very asserted prerogatives in space affairs. One of the recent example of this tendency consists in the great powers given by the 1991 constitution of the Russian Federation to its President, completed by the authority given to the government in this matter. Of course, these powers are not exclusive of those traditionally given to Parliaments in democratic regimes; the prerogatives of the Parliament generally consist in the vote of a Funding Act which estimates the budgetary envelop fixing the appropriations given to space activities. Parliaments also play a general role of control, quite often by means of specialized committees.

Concerning the governmental structures in charge of the administration and control of programs and space activities, we have no intention here to enter into the detail of these functions. However, a preliminary remark has to be made: concerning public entities, departments, boards or offices which are in charge of space matters, we have to make a strict distinction between the democratic regimes, whether they are presidential or parliamentary regimes. In the first case, we can notice an important gathering together of the prerogatives within the hands of the President, who is assisted by different offices or boards which turn around him: this is the case of the USA where we know the decisive role played by bodies such as the Presidential Executive Committee, the National Board for Security, the Office of Management and Budget, the Office of Science and Technology. This tendency, during the recent period of the Clinton administration, has only grown stronger. Such kind of observation could be made toward the new Russian organization, even if it is still too early to conclude on the lessons given by the development of the Russian institutions.

In parliamentary regimes, a more important role is given to the government by means of classical departments. Within the development of space activities, from their origin, the departments being in charge of the scientific research in general have been given, at first, the supervision of a space sector mostly composed of research activities. This situation has notably prevailed in most of the Member States of the European Space Agency (ESA) such as France, Great Britain, Italy or Federal Germany; and also in other countries which have undertaken a significant space program, such as Japan.

This situation has evolved with the time being when industrial and commercial aspects have taken an increasing place in the space programs. This development can also be noticed in France when, from 1962 to 1969, the supervision of space activities was assumed by a State Secretary in charge of scientific research, atomic and space questions, while since 1969, that function was entrusted to the Department of Industrial and Scientific

Development. It can also be noticed that, in Canada, and during the present period, it is the Department of Industry which is assuming the supervision of these activities.

Within the framework of complex governmental structures, other departments are in charge, at different levels, of the administration of space affairs: Department of State, Post Office Department, Department of National and University Education, Department of the Treasury for budgetary aspects,... However, a particular place has to be reserved to the department in charge of National Defense. Indeed, in consideration of the primordial interest granted by the principal powers to the strategic and political aspects of outer space, a particularly active role, sustained by important budgetary appropriations, is played by authorities in charge of the military sector. To illustrate this situation, one has only to remember the huge resources at the disposal of the Soviet military and industrial complex, and also the prerogatives and means which are today still at the disposal of the Pentagone. In the same range of ideas, it has to be underlined that, in France since 1993, the National Center for Space Studies (CNES) has been placed, for most of its activities that interest the Department of Defense, under its supervision. Otherwise, it is true that a contrary tendency consisting in the transfer of military activities to civil activities can also be noticed here and there: Russia is offering, for example, during these last few years, the spectacle of a partial dismantling of its enormous military potential - if one thinks for example to the SS-18 and SS-20 missiles- and a reconversion to civil aims. A country such as Argentina has recently given up the construction of its program of CONDOR missiles in order to dedicate itself to scientific, remote sensing and telecommunications satellite projects. This second tendency is, however, less important than the first one and does not necessarily imply that Departments of Defense of those countries are given up the military aspects of their space programs.

Finally, we will add that, in consideration of the increasing international dimension taken by space affairs, due to both the strategic interests that they are developing and a constantly growing cooperation among States, the Departments of States are more and more implied in the management of space policy of their respective country.

It can also be observed that the deep involvement in space policy, of the Department of Defense as well as the Department of States, is one of the specific characteristics of space affairs marked both by their dual and international nature.

Of course, the increasing complexity of space affairs and the more and more numerous departments which are in charge of, make essential the establishment of coordination footbridges in order to insure a coherent and efficient implementation of the space policy. On this connection, the creation in France, in 1989, of a Space Committee, a structure of coordination among the departments in charge of the preparation of the governmental rulings related to the French space policy, has to be noticed.

The diversity of the aspects which have to be taken into account, when defining a national space policy, has finally given rise to the multiplication of advisory bodies, intended to prepare the rulings taken by the executive power or consulted by the parliamentary houses within the framework of their jurisdiction in space matters. The USA, from this point of view, are a particularly stricking example of a proliferation of such bodies aiming to cover all the implied sectors in the definition, the development and the supervision of the American space policy.

2- THE SPECIALIZED BODIES

The willingness of the States to carry out space activities has often been realized by setting up a specialized body for space affairs. The States which have endowed themselves with such a body are extremely numerous. Without giving an exhaustive list of them, we will just remind the most known and, first of all, the eldest one which is the American NASA, then come the French space agency (the CNES), the British National Space Council (BNSC), the Japanese NASDA, and more recently the Italian ASI, the German DARA, the Russian RKA, the Brazilian, Canadian and Indian space agencies. At the opposite, some countries which have undertaken a space effort, have not judged it necessary to create a specialized space agency: among them we will quote Belgium, Spain, Denmark, Switzerland, ..., China being an intermediate case having wished to endow itself both with an industrial company for the marketing of the launchers, the "Great Wall of China", and more recently a National Civil Administration for Space Activities. The disintegration of USSR has finally allowed a certain number of States of Eastern Europe to take some initiatives in order to endow themselves with autonomous structures. Different kinds of space agencies, research bodies and companies have been therefore created in Poland, in Rumania, in Hungary, in the Czech Republic, and in Ukrain.

The setting up of space agencies has been done using extremely diverse methods. This diversity is the result of the different dates of founding of these agencies, at time implying for each one its own particular historical context. At a juridical level their methods of formation have also been characterized by a certain heterogeneity: it is sometimes the result of an enactment, and sometimes of a mere administrative ruling. Finally their legal status strongly varies from an agency to another: departments as well as autonomous bodies, public institutions (France), even commercial companies (Germany) can be found.

Despite this diversity, these agencies have in common a certain number of purposes.

Their main missions and functions, pursue the establishment of space programs, the assessment of budgets, the promotion and implementation of projects realized by space industries. Finally they keep close relationships with international space organizations, either for the realization of programs, or within the framework of their partnership to international programs: this is in particular the case of the European space agencies of the Member States of the European Space Agency.

The functions of the agencies, corresponding to these different missions, can be analyzed as it follows:

-In a first category, functions of reflexion and coordination can be found: they concern the preparation of governmental rulings within the framework of the working out of a national space policy, taking into account the opinions of the various departments, boards, and offices in charge of this working out; secondly they are related to the preparation of the governmental position and its representation within the international institutions or within the programs of international cooperation of which they also have to follow the implementation, as well as the development of their own programs; thirdly, the agencies have for mission to promote, inside as well as outside the country, the space industry of their own country. Within this action, they have to give incentives to the efforts of industries by granting contracts of study and technology. Of course, they also have, for the same reason, to participate to the definition of a national industrial policy in the space sector.

-In a second category, space agencies have more operational functions: in that respect, they manage the national space effort either directly, implementing projects with their own resources, or making them executed under contracts with industrial firms which they control. They can found subordinated bodies or subsidiary companies in charge of the promotion of these commercial uses (so the companies Spot Image or Arianespace have been created in France). Finally they give effect to international obligations resulting from the international agreements, particularly by granting licences for space operations, by supervising the beneficiaries of these licences and finally by keeping a registration list of the space objects.

This double mission of the national space agencies is not without leading to some critical problems for the European States members of the ESA.

As a matter of fact, the problem to resolve is indeed to share out, rationally and with efficiency between the European programs of the Agency and the national programs of the Member States, the fundings and others resources -which, of course, are limited- at the disposal of these States for their civil and military space activities. Then, it is obvious that the answer relies upon factors that are specific to each Member State, which is leading to a great disparity among them. The ESA only being ruled by its own convention and being outside the legal order of the European Union (which scope in space matters is besides limited), the disputes in this field can only be solved within the framework of the Agency itself, no exterior body being entitled to arbitrate them.

Concerning the legal status and the organization, properly said, of the national space agencies, the diversity is the outstanding feature. Indeed, we are meeting with a certain number of common procedures, and particularly the relations which necessarily have to exist between the Funding Act and the appropriations foreseen for the functioning of these agencies. In a certain number of cases, we are also in presence of cooperative contributions of public and private funds for the realization of space programs under the aegis of the agencies. Finally, common procedures of control on the utilization of these funds can also be found. On the other hand, it can easily be understood, if we consider for example the sizes of agencies such as the NASA, the Dutch space agency or the Argentinian and Indonesian space agencies, that no common measure exists in fact among these agencies as regard to their manpower, the budgetary funding which they assume the management, and the complexity of the implementation of the programs. In order to have an idea of this complexity for States such as the USA, Japan or Russia, one only has to list the different bodies which must be consulted while defining or executing the space programs. Finally, the development of the commercialisation of space activities has led to specific problems in countries, such as the USA, where a growing tension is taking place between a private sector which wants to act in a more and more independent way, as its role is growing, and a NASA, which wants to preserve its prerogatives but sees its status call in question again. There is no doubt that the relations between the private and public sector, and the increasing tendency of the private sector to cast off the states' restraints to its development, will constitute one of the major problems of the years to come. Will we see in a certain number of States (USA, France, Great Britain, Japan,...) a public sector that will, more and more, dilute itself with a private sector which thinks that it is the only one able to take the initiatives corresponding to the development of the space sector in the decades to come?

PART II : THE INTERVENTION OF THE STATES IN THE EXERCISE OF SPACE ACTIVITIES

It is obvious that the States will still try, for a long time, to keep under their direct control a certain number of activities related to their sovereignty or which nature cannot concern the private sector, either by mean of Departments or by mean of specialized Agencies. However, even when the State is implied, it can take no further interest in the control of some space activities which have consequences on the common interest. Finally, there is the case when space activities are carried out by several States within the framework of an international cooperation.

1- THE ACTIVITIES RESERVED TO THE STATES

All activities related to National Defense, to the exploration of outer space in general and to strictly scientific space research are undeniably under the only responsability of the States, the private sector having no competence for them.

This fact is obvious for military activities, which we have moreover seen that they have been playing a decisive role in the development of civil activities. The same remark also applies to activities related to the sole exploration of outer space -and not to its use-. Finally, this is also the case of scientific activities which, as fundamental research, cannot be undertaken by the private sector; these activities being, by definition, opposite to the concept of return on investment.

2- THE ACTIVITIES OF THE PRIVATE SECTOR

If we consider activities which are under the responsability of the private sector because of their nature, we have to remember that, except States which until a recent period, ie. up to the disintegration of USSR, were unwilling to create a private sector in the field of space matters, nearly all the other States have estimated that it was not only unavoidable but also necessary that a sector properly of private nature, with commercial purposes, be set up close to a public sector. This has been the case both in States where the principle of free entreprise is highly proclaimed, and in those States which want to maintain a strong state presence going further than the traditional sectors devolved to the States (activities belonging to the defense).

Of course, according to States, the private sector has known diverse expansion conditions, but it also has been tied down to a certain number of common obligations. Concerning activities which are under the market logic, it can be noticed that a certain number of programs are more adaptable to this logic because of their nature, without, however, a strict distinction between the programs of private nature and those of public nature. As an example, it can be noticed that, on the one hand, the telecommunication industry is undoubtedly under the market logic but that, on the other hand, its satisfactory development is still, quite often, depending upon a state support: with this respect, we are particularly aware of the way the order of operational systems of satellite launchers and of satellites for purposes which are under the state authority (and in particular for the defense) amply benefit to the American industry. Similar examples could be found in other countries such as Japan, where the capital role played by the Ministry of International Trade and Industry (MITI) in the promotion of the Japanese space industry and for its penetration on international markets, is well known. In France, the CNES, which in its beginning has incited the industry to increase its competences, is now entertaining with the private sector, but not in an exclusive way, promotor to executioner relationships, notably by contractual means and by using more and more various forms of partnership. In the same way, we can observe in Canada, similar modes of cooperation on a contractual basis, aimed particularly to carry out activities of research or development of facilities by the private sector on behalf of the Canadian Space Agency.

States could not only limit themselves to promote actions of private activities, or of research activities of a partnership according to various procedures. For reasons related to the nature, the economic and financial importance of space investments and related to the consequences on an international level of space activities, a certain number of States, including those where a preferential role is given to the private entreprise, have judged necessary to establish a political and legal framework for private commercial space activities. Indeed, the 1967 Outer Space Treaty binds the States to authorize and supervise the space activities of the non-governmental entities under their jurisdiction. As a result of this, specific provisions have been taken in the USA with the Nasa Act, the Comsat Act, the Launch Service Act and the Remote Sensing Act. These texts concern general enactments, completed by other texts adopted by Administrations (FCC, NOAA, ...) and by the States of the Federation. The same kind of provisions have been taken by States such as Great Britain, Sweden, and more recently Russia, particularly for the grant of licences.

Some States have not, however, established such a legislative framework, either because the States in these countries are the only ones to undertake space activities, or because the entities undertaking these activities are, in fact, closely controlled by the State. This is precisely the case which prevails in France, as regard to the activities of Arianespace or Spot Image. This lack of specific legislation does not, however, means that the States have given up to exercise their supervision on the activities of private entities. Indeed, in some States, such as France, a specific legislation is unnecessary in order to make compulsory, on their territory, the international provisions of the 1967

Treaty; the international agreements that they have signed being likely to be immediately enforced in their own country.

However, it has to be noticed that this does not mean that a national specific space legislation, in order to complete or modify the national law, and in order to adjust it to the exercise of space activities, would not be useful in some countries.

3- THE INTERNATIONAL COOPERATION

Finally, space activities are obviously strongly marked by their international nature. Therefore they have been promoted for an international cooperation already specially foreseen in the 1967 Outer Space Treaty and which have taken different forms. They are carried out within the framework of bilateral intergovernmental relations, mainly on a par with space agencies. They have been also strongly developped within a multilateral framework, either by means of agreements, or by the way of creation of new and specialized structures, such as international organizations. The development of this international cooperation has had a significant influence on space institutions of States, which has also led to the sharing of authorities with regional and international space bodies.

CONCLUSION

From the above mentioned study, and from this paper which purpose is to summarize its results, three conclusions can be drawn:

(1) The first conclusion is that the institutional framework for the exercise of space activities is mostly characterized by a great diversity. Indeed, it goes from mere recourse to the existing institutions to the creation of agencies excusively devoted to space matters, the status of these agencies -when they exist- being itself extremely varied.

(2) The second conclusion is that few countries have enacted a specific space legislation, and this for very different reasons. Moreover, it has to be recognized that such legislations do not have only for purpose to create an institutional framework, but also to complete the national existing legislations in order to take into account the juridical specificities of space activities.

(3) The third conclusion is that the States are and remain the actors of the exploration and use of outer space, but their role, in reason of the emergence of private activities, is now becoming secondary. On the other hand, the States, even outside them, are and remain bound by the 1967 Treaty to authorize and supervise space activities which are carried out in outer space.

SUMMARY OF THE U.S. AD-HOC WORKING GROUP MEETING ON REVISING THE U.N. PRINCIPLES ON THE USE OF NUCLEAR POWER SOURCES IN OUTER SPACE

Gary L. Bennett
Metaspace Enterprises
5000 Butte Road • Emmett, Idaho 83617-9500 • U.S.A.

Abstract

In 1990 the U.N. Committee on the Peaceful Uses of Outer Space adopted a draft set of principles relevant to the use of nuclear power sources (NPS) in outer space. Unfortunately, this draft set of principles contained some technical flaws which would have made them unworkable as written. As a result, U.S. technical experts convened an ad-hoc working group meeting on 8 January 1991 to develop a more technically accurate and consistent set of principles. This working group followed the 1990 draft U.N. principles paragraph by paragraph in developing its technical changes. The working group adopted the guiding principle of only making the minimum number of changes even though the majority of U.S. technical experts recognized that the entire U.N. set of principles needed to be rewritten to be technically accurate, realistic, and consistent. The output of this meeting served as one of the major inputs for U.S. policy makers in working within the U.N. to modify or clarify the 1990 draft principles so that they would be technically realistic and accurate. This paper summarizes the work of the ad-hoc working group of U.S. experts in an effort to provide some of the historical supporting documentation for the reasons that the U.S. changed its approach on the NPS principles at the United Nations from 1990 to 1991.

Introduction

Following the adoption by the United Nations (U.N.) Committee on the Peaceful Uses of Outer Space (COPUOS) of a draft set of principles relevant to the use of nuclear power sources (NPS) in outer space in 1990, U.S. technical experts, most of whom had not been consulted by the U.S. delegation during the adoption process, convened a meeting on 8 January 1991 in Albuquerque, New Mexico to discuss the draft principles. The meeting, which became known as the (U.S.) Ad-Hoc Working Group Meeting, was held because the technical experts had learned in late 1990 that the draft principles were to be incorporated into a U.N. General Assembly (UNGA) resolution, contrary to earlier promises from representatives of the U.S. Department of State (DOS) that they would ensure that the principles were buried in a report.[1]

The Ad-Hoc Working Group Meeting, which was held in conjunction with the Eighth Symposium on Space Nuclear Power Systems in Albuquerque, New Mexico, was designed to familiarize U.S. technical experts with the principles and, where necessary, to develop corrective language to make the politically motivated principles technically valid. Both because of time constraints and its critical nature, the U.S. Ad-Hoc Working Group elected to focus exclusively on Principle 3: "Guidelines and criteria for safe use". The plan was to take the revised technical language developed on Principle 3 in this meeting to the policy organizations in the U.S. Department of Energy (DOE), the U.S. Department of Defense (DoD), and the National Aeronautics and Space Administration (NASA) for further action.

Representatives from DOE, DoD, and NASA attended along with people from various government laboratories and contractors. The U.S. Department of State (DOS) had been invited to participate but declined. Earlier, DOS representatives had said they would abide by whatever technical agreements were reached jointly by DOE, DoD, and NASA. The list of attendees is given in Appendix 1.

The author was asked to chair the meeting and to provide background information on the earlier U.N. work on developing NPS principles. The source for much of this background material can be found in Ref. 2. The attendees then reviewed the 1990 draft set of U.N. principles, specifically focusing on Principle 3 ("Guidelines and criteria for safe use"). For reference purposes the 11 principles as finally adopted by UNGA are (1) Applicability of international law; (2) Use of terms; (3) Guidelines and criteria for safe use; (4) Safety assessment; (5) Notification of re-entry; (6)Consultations; (7) Assistance to States;

(8) Responsibility; (9) Liability and compensation; (10) Settlement of disputes; and (11) Review and revision (see also Appendix 4).[3]

Mindful of the admonition from various policy organizations that it might not be possible to make any changes in the draft principles, the Ad-Hoc Working Group adopted as a fundamental ground rule that only a very minimal set of substantive changes in Principle 3 would be allowed so that the policy people could focus on the "hard points", i.e., the most technically inaccurate of the language in the U.N. draft Principle 3. Each proposed change had to be defended by the proposer and if it could not be defended as an essential change then it was dropped by the Ad-Hoc Working Group. Thus, while many of the attendees expressed dissatisfaction with the entire draft set of U.N. principles and said all of the principles should be completely rewritten to be technically accurate and consistent, they did agree in a spirit of compromise to the minimal set of revisions to Principle 3 provided in Appendix 2 of this paper.[4]

These revisions to Principle 3 were taken back to DOE, DoD, and NASA Headquarters for further action. Since these revisions to Principle 3 provided a minimum common agreement among the technical experts from the three agencies the revised Principle 3 became the de facto common technical underpinning for some of the subsequent U.S. statements and U.S.-initiated changes to the draft U.N. principles. While the U.S. decided for political reasons not to change the most controversial principle (Principle 3: "Guidelines and criteria for safe use"), the thinking behind the Ad-Hoc Working Group's revisions to Principle 3 can be found in U.S.-initiated revisions to other paragraphs and the overall preamble of the U.N. principles as adopted by the U.N. General Assembly (UNGA) in 1992 in which most of the meaning of Principle 3 was changed or clarified.

The following section explains the changes which the U.S. Ad-Hoc Working Group proposed to the draft 1990 U.N. Principle 3. The complete text of the revised version of Principle 3 developed by the Ad-Hoc Working Group is given in Appendix 2.[4]

Explanation of Proposed Changes in Principle 3: Guidelines and Criteria for Safe Use

The following subsections provide background information (in the author's words based on notes taken during the Ad-Hoc Working Group meeting) on some of the reasons for the changes which the U.S. Ad-Hoc Working Group made in Principle 3 ("Guidelines and criteria for safe use") of the 1990 U.N. "Draft Principles Relevant to the Use of Nuclear power Sources in Outer Space". The explanations are keyed to the numbering system used in the 1990 U.N. draft version of Principle 3 that was available to the U.S. Ad-Hoc Working Group. Principle 3 is divided into three main sections or "paragraphs" which follow the preamble (Principle 3 is the only principle with its own preamble). The full text of Principle 3 as adopted by the U.N. in 1992 is given in Appendix 3.

Preamble

The 1990 preamble, which focused on restricting the use of NPS, was judged to be extremely negative toward the use of nuclear power in space. Unlike the original 1981 U.N. technical consensus on principles governing the use of NPS in outer space which the U.S. delegation and all other COPUOS delegations had supported, the preamble to the 1990 Principle 3 would force users to find any other "reasonable way" to power spacecraft.[3] In contrast, the 1981 U.N. Working Group report said that the decision to use NPS in outer space should be a technical one (all other factors equal).[5,6] The proposed new preamble listed in Appendix 2 puts the safety goal in a positive vein, that is, enhancing safety and environmental protection.[4] (Author's note: Given the naturally occurring and very high nuclear radiation of the Van Allen Belts, solar flares, Jovian radiation belts, etc., many of the attendees found it incongruous that the U.N. was attempting "to minimize the quantity of radioactive material in space" as stated in the Preamble.[3])

1. General goals for radiation protection and nuclear safety

Section 1.1 uses the word "hazards" which is not quantitatively defined.[3] The term "risks" was substituted in the second sentence by the U.S. Ad-Hoc Working Group because it has a quantitative definition (basically probability multiplied by consequences). (In keeping with the objective of minimizing changes the word "hazards" was left in the first sentence.)

Section 1.1 also requires that any "hazards" be kept below "acceptable levels" in "foreseeable operational or accidental circumstances".[3] The Ad-Hoc Working Group judged that the term "foreseeable" connotes everything one can envision beforehand. In U.S. safety analysis reports a wide range of postulated accidents are considered, some of which border on the incredible but they are still "foreseeable" in the sense of prescience or foreknowledge. If all "foreseeable" operational or accidental circumstances have to be considered then it is doubtful if a reasonable nuclear power source can ever be built just as one could not build a reasonable automobile if all foreseeable accidents had to be mitigated by design.

Since the U.S. Government does not have official dose limits for accidents (just as it does not have accident limits on airplane or automobile crashes) the reference to dose limits was deleted by the Ad-Hoc Working Group and replaced with a concept used in radiation health physics, namely, "as low as reasonably achievable". (It is interesting to note that less than two months after the Ad-Hoc Working Group meeting the representative from the International Atomic Energy Agency to COPUOS independently supported the U.S. Ad-Hoc Working Group's position by stating that "The sole use of the individual-related dose limits, rather than the complete ICRP [International Commission on Radiological Protection] system of radiation protection (including source-related constraint), is, in the Agency's view, inappropriate and does not conform with the aims of the ICRP recommendations . . . Secondly, as the ICRP has recently issued new recommendations on dose limitation . . . It might, therefore, be problematic to issue guidelines and criteria of safe use of NPS in outer space that would be outdated from their inception".[7])

Regarding the last sentence of Section 1.1, several of the attendees at the Ah-Hoc Working Group Meeting observed, as noted earlier regarding the Preamble, that the prohibition of the U.N. principles against "a significant contamination of outer space" was inconsistent with the fact that many parts of outer space are already highly filled with radiation (e.g., Van Allen radiation belts, solar storms, etc.)

Section 1.2 applies the "appropriate radiation protection objective for the public recommended by the International Commission on Radiological Protection (ICRP)" to the normal operation of an NPS including reentry.[3] Consistent with the policy-dictated objective of preparing only a minimal number of changes the Ad-Hoc Working Group added a clarifying phrase "to the public" at the end of the paragraph to make it clear that the ICRP standards apply only to the general public and then only in normal operation situations. Astronauts and radiation workers, for example, have different (and higher) radiation standards. The Ad-Hoc Working Group was well aware that the ICRP had no rigid standards for accidents because accidents are almost by definition events that are out of control.

Section 1.3 established for the first time radiation exposure limits for accidents.[3] The Ad-Hoc Working Group deleted the paragraph on dose limits because the U.S. Government (and all other rational agencies) have no official dose limits for accidents. In any of the radiation protection standards the Ad-Hoc Working Group was aware of, no limits were set for accidents because (as noted above) by definition an accident is an unintentional event, one that is out of control or off-normal. Just as there are no regulations restricting injuries or fatalities in automobile crashes or airplane crashes there are no dose limits for radiation accidents.

Section 1.4 requires that "Systems important for safety shall be designed, constructed and operated in accordance with the general concept of defence-in-depth" and that "foreseeable safety-related failures or malfunctions must be capable of being corrected or counteracted by an action or a procedure, possibly automatic".[3]

The U.S. Ad-Hoc Working Group replaced the word "foreseeable" with the word "credible" for the same reasons discussed in Section 1.1.

Based on the text of Section 1.4, the Ad-Hoc Working Group judged that the draft 1990 U.N. Principle 3 intended to apply the terrestrial concept (and not some new space concept) of "defense-in-depth" to space nuclear power. In one of the U.S. definitions of defense-in-depth for terrestrial nuclear power facilities three independent levels of safety are required.[8] As an example of the potential impact of Section 1.4, such a definition would require that a new cladding physically separated from and redundant to the existing fuel cladding be developed for the current U.S. radioisotope thermoelectric (RTG) heat source design which has already shown itself to be the safest RTG yet flown. Similarly, at a minimum, the then-planned U.S. design for the SP-100 space nuclear reactor power system, which already had multiple safety features, would have had to be drastically modified to include a heavy containment vessel in addition to the fuel cladding and the pressure vessel in order to meet the requirements of Section 1.4. All other identified U.S. and Russian space nuclear reactor designs would have suffered similar drastic design changes. (The reader interested in the RTG and SP-100 safety features is referred to Ref. 9.)

Adding to the confusion of Section 1.4 is that unlike most reactors, RTGs are passive devices with no moving parts so there should not be a requirement for them to have active safety systems when passive safety systems have been shown to do the job; hence, the Ad-Hoc Working Group changed the U.N. words to "corrected by design". (In fact, a case could be made that adding active safety systems to an RTG could degrade the safety margin because, for example, active safety systems have some probability of failure.)

The other changes made by the Ad-Hoc Working Group (e.g., changing "must" to "should", "*inter alia*" to "consideration of" and "shall" to "may") basically make the paragraph more realistic; some things (e.g., reality) just cannot be legislated.

2. Nuclear reactors

Section 2.1 limits the use of nuclear reactors to interplanetary missions, sufficiently high orbits (SHO) and low-Earth orbits (LEO).[3] The Ad-Hoc Working Group replaced the phrase "in low Earth orbits" with the phrase "in any orbit or flight trajectory" to allow the use of other than low-Earth orbit and also to allow for nuclear propulsion missions which may need to use a "flight trajectory" rather than an "orbit".

Section 2.2 requires that "The sufficiently high orbit must be such that the risks to existing and future outer space missions and of collision with other space objects are kept to a minimum".[3] The Ad-Hoc Working Group changed this sentence to give the mission planner sufficient flexibility while still requiring consideration of orbital debris. Since there will probably be orbital debris everywhere (particularly when future missions have to be considered) the original U.N. paragraph was not practical. If taken literally, Section 2.2 means that many existing NPS in orbit about the Earth violate Principle 3.

Section 2.3 states that "Nuclear reactors shall use only highly enriched uranium 235 as fuel. The design shall take into account the radioactive decay of the fission and activation products".[3] While the Ad-Hoc Working Group was aware that in 1990 the choice of "shall" or "should" had yet to be decided by the U.N., the Ad-Hoc Working Group believed rather strongly that in this instance the word should be "should" in order to give some flexibility in the choice of fuel (e.g., Section 2.3 excludes low-enriched uranium 235 which is not a problem). For certain futuristic mission scenarios other fissionable materials might be desirable.

Section 2.4 states that "Nuclear reactors shall not be made critical before they have reached their operating orbit or interplanetary trajectory".[3] As written, this section would prohibit zero-power testing before launch. Zero power testing is a means of checking to ensure that the reactor systems work while operating at such a low ("zero") power that there is very little fission product buildup. The original U.N. paragraph would have had the effect of forcing a country to launch multi-million dollar reactors on multi-billion-dollar spacecraft with no assurance that the flight reactors would work. In some mission scenarios, the reactor would be needed to boost the satellite (via some form of nuclear propulsion) to a SHO so if the reactor did not operate because of the failure to perform preflight zero-power checkout tests then SHO could not be reached. The Ad-Hoc Working Group changed this sentence to allow for zero-power testing to ensure the operability and safety of the flight reactor(s).

Section 2.5 states that "The design and construction of the nuclear reactor shall ensure that it can not become critical before reaching the operating orbit during all possible events, including rocket explosion, re-entry, impact on ground or water, submersion in water or water intruding into the core".[3] The changes proposed by the Ad-Hoc Working Group acknowledge the use of nuclear reactors in nuclear thermal propulsion or nuclear electric propulsion; hence, such systems may need to be operated in the "flight trajectory" and not just in orbit. The phrase "all possible events" would lead to an unending list of anything anyone can think of no matter how far-fetched; therefore, the word "credible" was used to bring this sentence into the real world.

Section 2.6 requires "a highly reliable operational system to ensure an effective and controlled disposal of the reactor".[3] In keeping with the objective of minimizing changes, the Ad-Hoc Working Group made no changes to this section (paragraph), although some of the attendees noted that the word "disposal" was not defined and so could mean anything.

3. Radioisotope generators

Section 3.1 states where radioisotope generators may be used and calls for "ultimate disposal".[3] In keeping with the objective of minimizing changes, the Ad-Hoc Working Group made no changes to this section (paragraph). Some of the attendees at the Ad-Hoc Working Group Meeting noted that the term "ultimate disposal" was not defined and so could mean anything, including leaving the NPS in orbit.

Section 3.2 states that "Radioisotope generators shall be protected by a containment system that is designed and constructed to withstand the heat and aerodynamic forces of re-entry in the upper atmosphere under foreseeable orbital conditions, including highly elliptical or hyperbolic orbits where relevant. Upon impact, the containment system and the physical form of the isotope shall ensure that no radioactive material is scattered into the environment so that the impact area can be completely cleared of radioactivity by a recovery operation".[3]

The Ad-Hoc Working Group replaced the word "foreseeable" with the word "credible" for the reasons discussed in Section 1.1 (see also the discussion on Section 2.5). The Ad-Hoc Working Group recognized that absolute containment cannot be guaranteed in all "foreseeable" accidents so it used words to give the designers some flexibility to minimize the consequences of postulated accidents while preserving the overall safety goals. For similar reasons the IAEA and the ICRP recognize the impossibility of absolute containment and complete cleanup in terrestrial nuclear facilities in all "foreseeable" accidents. Such a requirement is akin to requiring absolute protection of all passengers in an airplane crash.

It is interesting to note that in the case of the Soviet reactor-powered satellite Cosmos 954, which reentered over Canada in 1978, the Canadian government eventually quit trying to clean up the debris and concluded that what was estimated to be left was not worth the expense of cleaning up.[10] Similar flexibility must be given to future decision makers.

Consequences of the Ad-Hoc Working Group Meeting

As a result of the meeting of the Ad-Hoc Working Group the knowledgeable technical experts in the U.S. Government became united around a specific document (Appendix 2) which allowed them to press their respective policy organizations to argue for the necessary changes to make Principle 3 technically realistic and meaningful. Following the meeting on 8 January 1991, the U.S. delegation insisted on a number of changes to the overall principles. Since other delegations would not countenance changes to Principle 3 no matter how necessary, the U.S.-led changes were made in other paragraphs and the overall preamble to the principles.

The overall preamble to the 11 U.N. principles (not the specific preamble to Principle 3) was changed to a more positive and specific preamble with these words:[3]

"The General Assembly,

"Recognizing that for some missions in outer space nuclear power sources are particularly suited or even essential due to their compactness, long life and other attributes,

"Recognizing that the use of nuclear power sources in outer space should focus on those applications which take advantage of the particular properties of nuclear power sources,

"Recognizing that the use of nuclear power sources in outer space should be based on a thorough safety assessment, including probabilistic risk analysis, with particular emphasis on reducing the risk of accidental exposure of the public to harmful radiation or radioactive material,

"Recognizing the need, in this respect, for a set of principles containing goals and guidelines to ensure safe use of nuclear power sources in outer space,

"Affirming that this set of Principles applies to nuclear power sources in outer space devoted to generation of electric power on board space objects for non-propulsive purposes, which have characteristics generally comparable to those of systems used and missions performed at the time of the adoption of the Principles,

"Recognizing that this set of Principles will require future revision in view of emerging nuclear power applications and of evolving international recommendations on radiological protection,

"Adopts the Principles Relevant to the Use of Nuclear Power Sources in Outer Space as set forth below."

The third paragraph of U.N. Principle 2 ("Use of terms") was changed to state that "For the purposes of principle 3, the terms 'foreseeable' and 'all possible' describe a class of events or circumstances whose overall probability of occurrence is such that it is considered to encompass only credible possibilities for purposes of safety analysis. The term 'general concept of defence-in-depth' when applied to nuclear power sources in outer space considers the use of design features and mission operations in place of or in addition to active systems, to prevent or mitigate the consequences of system malfunctions. Redundant safety systems are not necessarily required for each individual component to achieve this purpose. Given the special requirements of space use and of varied missions, no particular set of systems or features can be specified as essential to achieve this objective. For the purposes of paragraph 2.4 of principle 3, the term 'made critical' does not include actions such as zero-power testing which are fundamental to ensuring system safety".[3]

These and other U.S.-developed changes had the effects of

- Making the use of NPS a technical decision as the 1981 U.N. technical report[5] stated.
- Eliminating nuclear propulsion and future

NPS (those not currently in existence) from the Principles

- Requiring future revisions to recognize that trying to legislate rigid standards of radiological protection was inconsistent with the evolving national and international standards of radiological protection.
- Defining the terms "foreseeable" and "all possible" to mean, in effect, "credible".
- Defining the term "defense-in-depth" to give the necessary flexibility for space applications.
- Defining the term "made critical" to allow zero-power testing of reactors before launch.

The preamble also brings in the basic concept that the principles are to provide safety goals and guidelines rather than (by inference) arbitrary numerical dose limits that have no relationship to accidents. The preamble also mentions the term "risk" rather than the undefined word "hazards" and the preamble describes the need for probabilistic risk assessments (which is the U.S. approach).

In a number of formal statements, the U.S. has stated its view that the principles are non-binding and recommendatory only and that the words "shall" and "must" should be replaced by the word "should".[11,12] The U.S. delegation has also taken exception to rigid dose limits applied to any accident.[11,12,13]

While the U.S. reluctantly went along with the principles for political reasons it formally expressed its reservations and interpretation in this statement during the final adoption process: "The United States did not block the consensus recommendation of the Committee to forward the principles to the General Assembly, nor will the United States oppose their adoption here. On some points, however, it remains our view that the principles related to safe use of nuclear power sources in outer space do not yet contain the clarity and technical validity appropriate to guide safe use of nuclear power sources in outer space. The United States has an approach on these points which it considers to be technically clearer and more valid and has a history of demonstrated safe and successful application of nuclear power sources. We will continue to apply that approach".[14]

In effect, the U.S. is going to continue to follow its own proven safety practices which it believes are consistent with the overall *goals* of the U.N. principles. The U.S. will not necessarily be guided by the specifics of the U.N. principles since as this paper has shown many of the specifics are technically inaccurate or misleading. Unfortunately, because certain delegations would not accept the U.S.-proposed changes that would have made the principles technically accurate, realistic, and consistent, the U.N. now has a set of principles which are inaccurate, inconsistent and unworkable, a fact that has been noted rather forcefully elsewhere.[15,16]

Concluding Remarks

Overall, the meeting of the (U.S.) Ad-Hoc Working Group achieved its objective of providing a common set of changes to U.N. draft Principle 3 ("Guidelines and criteria for safe use"). Most of this minimal set of changes requested by the Ad-Hoc Working Group was incorporated into the overall principles (generally in the overall preamble or in Principle 2 ["Use of terms"]). In other areas where the U.S. was not able to make the requested specific changes (e.g., "shall" versus "should", Section 1.3, Section 3.2, etc.), U.S. delegates presented formal statements describing how the U.S. intended to interpret the principles. This process also showed that it is possible for knowledgeable, rational technical experts to work together to correct a political document that contained many technical flaws. As the author has stated elsewhere, "Whether the issue is NPS, remote sensing, orbital debris, the definition and delimitation of outer space, or direct broadcast satellites, it is essential that qualified technical experts be involved in the development of any international principles affecting that area".[16]

Acknowledgments

The author acknowledges his gratitude to the attendees of the Ad-Hoc Working Group Meeting (see Appendix 1) for taking the time to discuss, debate, and agree on a minimal set of changes and then to take these changes to their respective agency policy groups for implementation. Specifically, the author would like to thank George C. Allen of Sandia National Laboratories for providing excellent and rapid administrative support to the meeting.

References

1. G. L. Bennett, "A Technical Review of the U.N. Principles on the Use of Nuclear Power Sources in Outer Space", IISL-95-IISL.4.15 and IAF-95-R.1.04, paper presented at the 38th International Colloquium on the Law of Outer Space and the 46th International Astronautical Congress, Oslo, Norway, 2-6 October 1995.

2. G. L. Bennett, J. A. Sholtis, Jr., and B. C. Rashkow, "United Nations Deliberations on the Use of Nuclear Power Sources in Space: 1978 - 1987" in *Space*

Nuclear Power Systems 1988, edited by M. S. El-Genk and M. D. Hoover, Chapter 13, pp. 45-57, Orbit Book Company, Malabar, Florida, 1989.

3. "Report of the Legal Subcommittee on the Work of its Thirty-First Session, Chairman's text, Principles Relevant to the Use of Nuclear Power Sources in Outer Space", U.N. Document A/AC.105/L.198, 23 June 1992. A partial listing of the principles (U.N. Document A/47/20) is presented in the *Journal of Space Law*, Vol. 20, No. 2, pp. 211-215, 1992. The final form of the U.N. principles, as passed by the Special Political Committee of UNGA on 30 October 1992, is in U.N. document A/47/610.

4. "Revision to the Draft Principles Relevant to the Use of Nuclear Power Sources in Outer Space" prepared at the Ad-Hoc Working Group Meeting held during the Eighth Symposium on Space Nuclear Power Systems in Albuquerque, New Mexico, 8 January 1991.

5. "Report of the Working Group on the Use of Nuclear Power Sources in Outer Space on the Work of its Third Session", Annex II of Report of the Scientific and Technical Subcommittee on the Work of its Eighteenth Session, U.N. Document A/AC.105/287, United Nations, 13 February 1981.

6. G. L. Bennett, "The 1981 United Nations Report: An Historical Consensus on the Safe Use of Nuclear Power Sources in Space" in *Proceedings of the Ninth Symposium on Space Nuclear Power Systems*, edited by M. S. El-Genk and M. D. Hoover, American Institute of Physics Conference Proceedings 246, Part Two, pp. 662-667, proceedings of a conference held in Albuquerque, New Mexico, 12-16 January 1992.

7. International Atomic Energy Agency, "IAEA Statement to the Scientific and Technical Sub-Committee of the Committee on the Peaceful Uses of Outer Space", United Nations, New York, 19 February - March 1991. (Note: The U.S. copy is marked 25 February 1991.)

8. U.S. Atomic Energy Commission, *The Safety of Nuclear Power Reactors (Light-Water Cooled) and Related Facilities*, WASH-1250, U.S. Atomic Energy Commission, Washington, D.C., July 1973.

9. G. L. Bennett, "Safety Status of Space Radioisotope and Reactor Power Sources", paper number 900464 in *Proceedings of the 25th Intersociety Energy Conversion Engineering Conference*, Volume 1, pp. 162-167, proceedings of a conference held in Reno, Nevada, 12-17 August 1990.

10. W. K. Gummer, F. R. Campbell, G. G. Knight, and J. L. Ricard, *COSMOS 954, The Occurrence and Nature of Recovered Debris*, INFO-0006, Atomic Energy Control Board, Canada, 1980.

11. R. Lange, "Statement by Robert Lange, United States Adviser at the Twenty-Eighth Session of the Scientific and Technical Subcommittee of the United Nations Committee on the Peaceful Uses of Outer Space, on Agenda Item 7, Nuclear Power Sources in Outer Space, February 26, 1991", USUN Press Release 08-(90), United States Mission to the United Nations, New York, New York, 26 February 1991.

12. R. Lange, "Statement by Robert Lange, United States Adviser at the Thirtieth Session of the Legal Subcommittee of the United Nations Committee on the Peaceful Uses of Outer Space, to the Working Group on Nuclear Power Sources in Outer Space, April 10, 1991", USUN Press Release 18 (91), United States Mission to the United Nations, New York, New York, 10 April 1991 (includes U.S. working paper, U.N. document A/AC.105/C.2/L.185, 10 April 1991).

13. P. G. Smith, "General Statement by Mr. Peter G. Smith, United States Representative to the Twenty-Ninth Session of the Scientific and Technical Sub-Committee of the United Nations Committee on Peaceful Uses of Outer Space, February 25, 1992".

14. K. Hodgkins, "Statement by Kenneth Hodgkins, United States Adviser to the 47th Session of the United Nations General Assembly, in the Special Political Committee, on Item #72, International Cooperation on the Peaceful Uses of Outer Space, October 28, 1992", USUN Press Release #116-(92), United States Mission to the United Nations, New York, New York, 28 October 1992.

15. S. Aftergood, "Space nuclear power and the UN, A growing fiasco", *Space Policy*, pp. 9-12, February 1992.

16. G. L. Bennett, "Reaching the outer planets -- with or without the U.N.", *Aerospace America*, pp. 26-30, 43, July 1996.

Appendix 1
List of Attendees at Ad-Hoc Working Group Meeting

(**Note**: The organizational listings are for identification purposes only and do not imply any organizational endorsement. These listings are those of the attendees at the time of the meeting on 8 January 1991.)

Douglas M. Allen, SDIO/TNK
George C. Allen, Sandia National Laboratories (SNLA)
Hal Bengelsdorf, ERCE
Gary L. Bennett, NASA Headquarters
Colette Brown, DOE Headquarters
Hatice Cullingford, NASA/LMEPO
Leven Gray, NASA Headquarters
Lt. Col. Ernest D. Herrera, USAF/PL/TAP
Frank Jankowski, USAF/PL/TAPN
Inara Kuck, USAF/PL/TAP
Stephen J. Lanes, DOE Headquarters
Robert G. Lange, DOE Headquarters
Jim Lee, SDIO/TNK
Lt. Col. Roger X. Lenard, SDIO/TNG
Al Marshall, SNLA
Bill McCulloch, SNLA
Greg Reck, NASA Headquarters
J. C. Sawyer, NASA Headquarters
Lt. Col. Joseph Sholtis, AFISC/SNRA
Greg Sullivan, Xerad, Inc.
Earl J. Wahlquist, DOE Headquarters
Abe Weitzberg, NUS Corporation
Col. Robert Winchester, AFISC/SNR

Appendix 2
Revision to Principle 3 of the 1990 Draft Principles Relevant to the Use of Nuclear Power Sources in Outer Space

The following is the revision to the 1990 U.N. draft Principle 3 ("Guidelines and criteria for safe use") prepared at the (U.S.) Ad-Hoc Working Group Meeting held on 8 January 1991 in Albuquerque, New Mexico during the Eighth Symposium on Space Nuclear Power Systems.[4] It must be emphasized that the Ad-Hoc Working Group operated under the rigid guideline of making only a very few substantiative changes. Many of the attendees believed that all of the principles (not just Principle 3) needed to be completely rewritten to be technically accurate, realistic, and consistent. At the Ad-Hoc Working Group meeting, it was recommended that additional text from the 1981 U.N. working group guidelines[5] be added to the preamble. The text was not available when this revision was typed and so that text is not included here.

Author's note: The Ad-Hoc Working Group assumed that the U.S. delegation would be successful in changing "shall" and "must" to "should" or "may". Since those changes were not accomplished, this text contains those modifications. Some minor editorial changes of a grammatical nature have also been made. An additional change from Ref. 4 is the author's highlighting through italics or brackets where the changes were made (including where, for convenience, the Ad-Hoc Working Group used acronyms as was done in the 1990 draft U.N. text instead of spelling out the phrases as in the 1992 U.N. final text).

Principle 3: Guidelines and criteria for safe use

In order to *enhance the safety of nuclear power sources (NPS), which include nuclear reactors and radioisotope power sources used for space power or propulsion, the decision to use NPS should be based on the technical merits with due consideration for safety and environmental aspects.*

1. General goals for radiation protection and nuclear safety

1.1 States launching space objects with *NPS* on board *should* endeavour to protect individuals, populations and the biosphere against radiological hazards. The design and use of space objects with *NPS* on board *should* ensure, with a high degree of confidence, that the *risks* in [*Deletion*] operational or accidental circumstances, are kept *as low as reasonably achievable (ALARA).*

Such design and use *should* also ensure with high reliability that radioactive material does not cause a significant contamination of outer space.

1.2 During the normal operation of space objects with *NPS* on board, including re-entry from the sufficiently high orbit *(SHO)* as defined in paragraph 2.2, the appropriate radiation protection objective for the public recommended by the International Commission [on] Radiological Protection (ICRP) *should* be observed. During such normal operation there *should* be no significant radiation exposure *to the public.*

1.3 To limit exposure in accidents, the design and construction of the *NPS* systems *should* take into account relevant and generally accepted international radiological protection guidelines.

[*Deletion of dose limits.*]

The probability of accidents with potentially serious radiological consequences [*Deletion*] *should* be kept extremely small by virtue of the design of the system.

Future modifications of the guidelines referred to in this paragraph *should* be applied as soon as practicable.

1.4 Systems important for safety *should* be designed, constructed and operated in accordance with the general concept of defence-in-depth *for aerospace systems.* Pursuant to this concept, *credible* safety-related failures or malfunctions *should* be [*Deletion*] corrected *by design* or counteracted by an action or a procedure, possibly automatic.

The reliability of systems important for safety *should* be ensured *by consideration of* redundancy, physical separation, functional isolation and adequate independence of their components.

Other measures *may* also be taken to raise the level of safety.

2. Nuclear reactors

2.1 Nuclear reactors may be operated:

(i) On interplanetary missions;
(ii) In sufficiently high orbits (SHO) as defined in paragraph 2.2;
(iii) *In any orbit or flight trajectory* if they are stored in *SHO* after the operational part of their mission.

2.2 The *SHO* is one in which the orbital lifetime is long enough to allow for a sufficient decay of the fission products to approximately the activity of the actinides. *The selection of the SHO should take into consideration* the risks to existing and future outer space missions and [*Deletion*] collision with other space objects [*Deletion*]. The necessity for the parts of a destroyed reactor also to attain the required decay time before re-entering the Earth's atmosphere *should* be considered in determining the *SHO* altitude.

2.3 Nuclear reactors *should* use only highly enriched uranium 235 as fuel. The design *should* take into account the radioactive decay of the fission and activation products.

2.4 Nuclear reactors *should* not be *operated at power, except for zero-power testing* before they have reached their operating orbit or [*Deletion*] trajectory.

2.5 The design and construction of the nuclear reactor *should* ensure that it cannot become critical before reaching the operating orbit *or flight trajectory considering credible launch accidents,* including rocket explosion, *inadvertent* re-entry, impact on ground or water, submersion in water or water intruding into the core.

2.6 In order to reduce significantly the possibility of failures in satellites with nuclear reactors on board during operations in an orbit with a lifetime less than in the *SHO* (including operations for transfer into the *SHO*), there *should* be a highly reliable operational system to ensure an effective and controlled disposal of the reactor.

3.1 Radioisotope generators

3.1 Radioisotope generators may be used for interplanetary missions and other missions leaving the gravity field of the Earth. They may also be used in Earth orbit if, after conclusion of the operational part of their mission, they are stored in a high orbit. In any case, ultimate disposal is necessary.

3.2 Radioisotope generators *should* be protected by a containment system that is designed and constructed to withstand the heat and aerodynamic forces of re-entry in the upper atmosphere under *credible* orbital conditions, including highly elliptical or hyperbolic orbits where relevant. Upon impact, the containment system and the physical form of the isotope *should minimize radioactive material release into the environment so that the debris can be retrieved.*

Appendix 3
UN Principle 3: Guidelines and criteria for safe use

[The following is the text of Principle 3 as taken from Reference 3. Note that the numbering system of the subparagraphs is different from that of Appendix 2 because the U.N. text that Ad-Hoc Working Group was given had used Arabic numbers rather than lower case letters for the subparagraphs.]

In order to minimize the quantity of radioactive material in space and the risks involved, the use of nuclear power sources in outer space shall be restricted to those space missions which cannot be operated by non-nuclear energy sources in a reasonable way.

1. General goals for radiation protection and nuclear safety

(a) States launching space objects with nuclear power sources on board shall endeavour to protect individuals, populations and the biosphere against radiological hazards. The design and use of space objects with nuclear power sources on board shall ensure, with a high degree of confidence, that the hazards, in foreseeable operational or accidental circumstances, are kept below acceptable levels as defined in paragraphs 1 (a) and (c).

Such design and use shall also ensure with high reliability that radioactive material does not cause a significant contamination of outer space.

(b) During the normal operation of space objects with nuclear power sources on board, including re-entry from the sufficiently high orbit as defined in paragraph

2 (b), the appropriate radiation protection objective for the public recommended by the International Commission on Radiological Protection shall be observed. During such normal operation there shall be no significant radiation exposure.

(c) To limit exposure in accidents, the design and construction of the nuclear power source systems shall take into account relevant and generally accepted international radiological protection guidelines.

Except in cases of low-probability accidents with potentially serious radiological consequences, the design for the nuclear power source systems shall, with a high degree of confidence, restrict radiation exposure to a limited geographical region and to individuals to the principal limit of 1 mSv in a year. It is permissible to use a subsidiary dose limit of 5 mSv in a year for some years, provided that the average annual effective dose equivalent over a lifetime does not exceed the principal limit of 1 mSv in a year.

The probability of accidents with potentially serious radiological consequences referred to above shall be kept extremely small by virtue of the design of the system.

Future modifications of the guidelines referred to in this paragraph shall be applied as soon as practicable.

(d) Systems important for safety shall be designed, constructed and operated in accordance with the general concept of defence-in-depth. Pursuant to this concept, foreseeable safety-related failures or malfunctions must be capable of being corrected or counteracted by an action or a procedure, possibly automatic.

The reliability of systems important for safety shall be ensured, inter alia, by redundancy, physical separation, functional isolation and adequate independence of their components.

Other measures shall be also be taken to raise the level of safety.

2. Nuclear reactors

(a) Nuclear reactors may be operated:

(i) On interplanetary missions;

(ii) In sufficiently high orbits as defined in paragraph 2 (b);

(iii) In low-Earth orbits if they are stored in sufficiently high orbits after the operational part of their mission.

(b) The sufficiently high orbit is one in which the orbital lifetime is long enough to allow for a sufficient decay of the fission products to approximately the activity of the actinides. The sufficiently high orbit must be such that the risks to existing and future outer space missions and of collision with other space objects are kept to a minimum. The necessity for the parts of a destroyed reactor also to attain the required decay time before re-entering the Earth's atmosphere shall be considered in determining the sufficiently high orbit altitude.

(c) Nuclear reactors shall use only highly enriched uranium 235 as fuel. The design shall take into account the radioactive decay of the fission and activation products.

(d) Nuclear reactors shall not be made critical before they have reached their operating orbit or interplanetary trajectory.

(e) The design and construction of the nuclear reactor shall ensure that it can not become critical before reaching the operating orbit during all possible events, including rocket explosion, re-entry, impact on ground or water, submersion in water or water intruding into the core.

(f) In order to reduce significantly the possibility of failures in satellites with nuclear reactors on board during operations in an orbit with a lifetime less than in the sufficiently high orbit (including operations for transfer into the sufficiently high orbit), there shall be a highly reliable operational system to ensure an effective and controlled disposal of the reactor.

3. Radioisotope generators

(a) Radioisotope generators may be used for interplanetary missions and other missions leaving the gravity field of the Earth. They may also be used in Earth orbit if, after conclusion of the operational part of their mission, they are stored in a high orbit. In any case ultimate disposal is necessary.

(b) Radioisotope generators shall be protected by a containment system that is designed and constructed to withstand the heat and aerodynamic forces of re-entry in the upper atmosphere under foreseeable orbital conditions, including highly elliptical or hyperbolic orbits where relevant. Upon impact, the containment system and the physical form of the isotope shall ensure that no radioactive material is scattered into the environment so that the impact area can be completely cleared of radioactivity by a recovery operation.

Appendix 4
List of U.N. Principles Relevant to the Use of Nuclear Power Sources in Outer Space

The 11 principles consist of:[3]

Principle 1 - *Applicability of international law* - basically states that the use of NPS will be carried out in accordance with international law

Principle 2 - *Use of terms* - defines a number of terms, in particular ". . . the terms 'foreseeable' and 'all possible' describe a class of events or circumstances whose overall probability of occurrence is such that it is considered to encompass only credible possibilities for purposes of safety analysis". In addition the definition of the term "general concept of defence-in-depth" allows flexibility in achieving this goal by allowing consideration of ". . . the use of design features and mission operations in place of or in addition to active systems, to prevent or mitigate the consequences of system malfunctions. Redundant safety systems are not necessarily required for each individual component to achieve this purpose. Given the special requirements of space use and of varied missions, no particular set of systems or features can be specified as essential to achieve this objective". Finally, the term "made critical" mentioned in paragraph 2 (a) of Principle 3 ". . . does not include actions such as zero-power testing [prior to the launch of the reactor] which are fundamental to ensuring system safety".

These definitions, which are discussed in the context of the technical assessments presented in this paper, were included at the request of the U.S. as a way to correct some of the technical flaws in Principle 3 without actually changing Principle 3 (which the other delegations did not want changed no matter how many technical flaws it contained).

Principle 3 - *Guidelines and criteria for safe use* - this principle begins with a somewhat negative preamble (it is the only principle with its own preamble) and then sets forth general goals for radiation protection and nuclear safety followed by specific safety criteria for nuclear reactors and for radioisotope generators. This is the principle that was and still is of the most concern to U.S. technical experts and, as such, it is the principle which is both discussed further and technically assessed in this paper.

Principle 4 - *Safety assessment* - requires a "thorough and comprehensive" safety assessment which is to be made publicly available prior to each launch. Principle 4 states that "This assessment shall respect the guidelines and criteria for safe use contained in principle 3".

Principle 5 - *Notification of reentry* - requires a timely notification of the reentry of radioactive materials to the Earth and provides a format for such notification.

Principle 6 - *Consultations* - requires States providing information under Principle 5 to respond promptly to requests for further information or consultations sought by other States.

Principle 7 - *Assistance to States* - requires States with tracking capabilities to provide information to the Secretary-General of the U.N. and to the State concerned and requires the launching State to promptly offer assistance. After reentry, other States and international organizations with relevant technical capabilities should also provide assistance to the extent possible when requested by the affected State.

Principle 8 - *Responsibility* - states that States shall bear international responsibility for their use of NPS.

Principle 9 - *Liability and compensation* - holds the launching State and the State procuring such a launch internationally liable for any damage, including restoration ". . . to the condition which would have existed if the damage had not occurred". Compensation includes ". . . reimbursement of the duly substantiated expenses for search, recovery and clean-up operations, including expenses for assistance received from third parties". (Note: In view of the reentry of the Soviet Cosmos 954 satellite over Canada, this was an interesting Principle for Canada to support because Canada neither achieved this level of cleanup nor did it request or get full reimbursement from the Soviet government.)

Principle 10 - *Settlement of disputes* - states that disputes ". . . shall be resolved through negotiations or other established procedures for the peaceful settlement of disputes, in accordance with the Charter of the United Nations".

Principle 11 - *Review and revision* - states that "These Principles shall be reopened for revision by the Committee on the Peaceful Uses of Outer Space no later than two years after their adoption". This principle was sold to the U.S. technical experts as the mechanism for U.S. technical concerns to be addressed eventually.

IISL-96-IISL.4.15

SOME LEGAL ASPECTS OF CONFIDENCE-BUILDING MEASURES CONCERNING OUTER SPACE

Jan Ondřej[+]

Abstract

Confidence-building measures /CBMs/ played an important role in the past in the era of cold war. These measures are also important today.

Very important are CBMs in connection with outer space. Appropriate CBMs with respect to outer space activities are potentially important steps towards the prevention of an arms race in outer space and for ensuring the peaceful use of outer space.

CBMs in connection with outer space play also a role in relation to arms-control agreements, obligations arising from the UN Security Council decisions, etc. Satellites in outer space may confirm the fulfilment of arms-control obligations or observe various crisis areas. The fulfilment of obligations enhance confidence among states. On the other hand, CBMs such as cooperative monitoring may support verification measures. There is a close connection between CBMs and verification of arms-control agreements.

Nowadays, there is a certain basis for CBMs in various agreements concerning outer space and disarmament. But a further development is necessary.

General consideration of confidence-building measures

CBMs are increasingly accepted as an important element in reducing suspicion and tension between nations and enhancing international peace and stability. Over the past three decades, states have initiated and adopted a number of bilateral and multilateral confidence-building measures.

CBMs have also played an increasing role in the security planning of states. While initially limited to bilateral arrangements pertaining to strategic nuclear weapons, they have more recently found application

---

+ Doctor of Law, Faculty of Law, Charles University, Prague, Czech Republic in multilateral context relating to conventional military forces.

The United Nations system has given increasing attention to the potential contribution of CBMs to stregthening international peace and stability.The positive experience that has emerged in a bilateral context and in certain regions has formed a basis for potential extension of this process to other areas and subjects.

The General Assembly noted in paragraph 93 of the Final Document of the First Special Session devoted to disarmament in June 1978 that "in order to facilitate the process of disarmament it is necessary to take measures and pursue policies to strengthen international peace and security and to build confidence among states.Commitment to confidence-building measures could significantly contribute to preparing for further progress in disarmament "./1/

The General Assembly also considered CBMs in other resolutions in later years.

CBMs have primarily political and psychological effects and although closely related,cannot always be considered as arms limitation measures by themselves in the sense of limiting or reducing armed forces.Improved confidence, however can have a positive impact on the subjective estimation of the intentions and expectations of other states.

CBMs can contribute to progress in concrete disarmament and arms limitation agreements.They can supplement disarmament and arms limitation agreements and thus may become an important way for progress in reducing international tensions. In the context of disarmament and arms limitation negotiations,such measures form part of an agreement itself,faciliting implementation and verification provisions.But CBMs cannot substitute for concrete progress in limiting and reducing armaments.In the face of unconstrained increases in the number of weapons or of continued improvements in the capabilities of weapons the distrust and apprenhension that is created will outweigh the contribution of CBMs.

CBMs seek to reduce misperceptions and misunderstanding,as a first step towards replacing suspicion with confidence by enabling the parties to be more transparent about their intentions in specific circumstances."In crisis situations or in post-conflict contexts,the ability of all parties to have accurate,timely information so that threatening actions can be avoided, or early warning of impending danger,may be central to the successful resolution of the dispute in question"./2/

The general goal of CBMs is to reduce or even eliminate the causes of mistrust,fear and tension between nations,and to enhance international peace and stability.

Another goal is to reinforce the existing confidence between states.It includes a wide spectrum of activities implemented among states in the political,legal, military,economic,social and cultural fields./3/

Relation between CBMs and verification

We can define verification as a process which establishes whether states parties are complying with their obligations under an agreement The traditional concept of verification is in the context of arms limitation and disarmament agreements which is carried out by the states parties or international bodies.

The process of verification consists of multiple steps which include collection of information relevant to obligations under arms limitation and disarmament agreements,analysis of the information and reaching a judgement as to whether the specific terms of an agreement are being met./4/

Verification is the process based on international treaty or other legally binding documents /Security Council decisions /. Compliance with the obligations of states strengthens confidence among them.In this connection "the primary aim of verification is to increase the level of transparency in relation to relevant activities"./5/

On the other hand,verification needs some degree of confidence among states.The states were not willing to accept more intrusive verification measures such as inspection in the era of cold war. The verification of arms control agreements were based especially on national technical means in outer space.The best example is the ABM treaty of 1972 or SALT I treaty of 1972.

The CBMs have primarily political and psychological effects. They are based especially on political documents e.g. the Stockholm Document of 1986.Sometimes the basis for CBMs is also an international treaty e.g.Treaty on open skies of 1992.This Treaty shows a close connection between CBMs and arms control.The purpose of this Treaty is inter alia,"to improve openess and transparency,to facilitate the monitoring of compliance with existing or future arms control agreements and to strenghten the capacity for conflict prevention and crisis management"./6/

There is also a close connection between verification and CBMs from the point of view of methods and technics.Some methods,technics and measures of CBMs are similar to the measures and technics of verification.For example inspections,information,consultations,observation etc.But there are other measures of the CBMs such as advance notice of military manoeuvres, exchange programs including those of scholars etc./7/ These measures are special for CBMs.

Confidence-building measures concerning outer space

The CBMs concerning outer space may play an important role in outer space itself but also in connection with the Earth.Very often activity in this connection is the observation of the Earth from outer space.

There is a freedom of outer space.All states have the right to explore and use outer space.Therefore observation from outer space by satellites for military or non-military purpose is not prohibited. Satellites are very suitable as one of the CBMs."The historical development shows us that at least U.S.A. and U.S.S.R. have recognized the observation from outer space as a confidence-building measure from 1972"./8/ Satellites for commercial purposes and also national technical means may serve as CBMs.For example,monitoring efforts in Iraq pursuant to Security Council resolution 687/1991/,and relevant IAEA activities in relation to the Democratic People´s Republic of Korea./9/

CBMs in outer space serve to

monitor the compliance of disarmament and arms limitation treaties.

As for outer space itself the potential importance of CBMs in outer space derives both from concerns over emerging trends in space activities,as well as from the need to prevent an arms race in outer space./10/

The legal basis for CBMs is included in various relevant outer space treaties.

The Outer Space Treaty of 1967 gives the states parties opportunity to observe the flight of space objects /art.X/.This Treaty provides on-site inspection on the Moon and other Celestial Bodies /art.XII/, consultations if an activity is potentially harmful to those of others /art.IX/.The state parties have an obligation to inform the United Nations Secretary-General of the nature,conduct,locations and results of their activities in outer space.The Secretary-General should be prepared to disseminate such information immediatelly and effectively /art.XI/.

The Registration Convention of 1975 established a framework for reporting to the United Nations Secretary-General information regarding the name of launching state,appropriate designator,date and location of the launching of objects in space,basic orbital parameters, general function,changes in orbital parameters after launch,recovery data of spacecraft /art.IV/.

The Hot Line Agreement of 1971 between U.S.A. and U.S.S.R. provides for the establishment of a satellite communication system to increase reliability of the Direct Communication Link.

Many U.S.A. - U.S.S.R./Russia/ treaties provide for verification by national technical means /NTMs/.

For instance the ABM Agreement of 1972 provides for verification measures by national technical means /art.12 para 1/ and establish the principle of non-interference with NTMs /art.12 para.2/. The concept of non-interference with NTMs is important since NTMs include ground and space-based systems.This concept also implicitly includes the protection of such space-based systems as reconnaissance satellites /art.12 para.3/ against any form of interference. Legitimacy was given by the parties to the Treaty to their satellite activities for monitoring arms limitation and disarmament agreements.Moreover,in order to promote the objectives and implementation of the provisions of the Treaty a Standing Consultative Commission is established /art.13/.Within the framework of this Commission the state parties consider questions concerning compliance with the obligations,provide on voluntary basis such information as either party considers necessary to assure confidence in compliance with the obligations assumed,etc./11/

Other bilateraly U.S.A. and U.S.S.R. treaties include similar provisions,e.g.SALT I of 1972, SALT II of 1979,INF Treaty of 1987, START I of 1991,START II of 1993.

Besides NTMs also remote-sensing satellites may be used for monitoring purposes and for enhancing confidence among states.The remote sensing of the Earth from space is based on the United Nations General Assembly resolution 41/65 of 1986 containing Principles Relating to Remote Sensing of the Earth from Space.These Principles provide inter alia, that"remote sensing activities shall not be conducted in a manner detrimental to the legitimate rights and interests of sensed State "/Principle IV/.State carrying out a a programme of remote sensing shall inform the Secretary-general of the United Nations and shall "make available any other relevant information to the greatest extent feasible and practicable to any other State,particularly any developing country that is affected by the programme,at its request"./Priciple IX/.

NTMs and satellites generally are very important CBMs and verification technics.The problem with NTMs and observation satellites is that only limited number of states possess such means.For this reason and in the absence of an international satellite monitoring agency, the group of experts suggested in 1990 that Member States of the United Nations operating observation satellites could undertake to provide their services,including possible access to their imagery./12/

As for institutional framework, there are various proposals concerning CBMs in connection with outer space.For instance in 1989,France proposed the creation of a Satellite Image-Processing Agency which would constitute the initial phase of an international institution for satellite monitoring.The French initiative clearly stated that the proposed agency "would be a confidence-building device and would not be intended to be the embryo of a verification system with universal competence attached to the United Nations".This Agency is to be understood as an agency to be created within the framework of confidence-building measures.It would be designed as a low-cost agency with three objectives. The first of these would be to collect and process data obtained from existing civilian satellites,and then to disseminate that material to the Agency´s members.Its second objective would be to serve as a research unit or centre charged with /a/ identifying groups of satellites which could contribute to the implementation of multilateral programmes,and /b/ designing various linkage agreements.The third objective would be to train national personnel to interpret space images and ascertain the extent to which the monitoring and verification of arms limitation and disarmament could be performed by means of satellites./13/

Conclusion

The United Nations should play an important role in further consideration and possible elaboration of specific confidence-building measures in the context of the prevention of an arms race in outer space and also in connection with security and disarmament generally.

The earlier proposal concerning the International Satellite Monitoring Agency should be re-examined.The possibility of establishing an international registry of orbital and functional data on vehicles and missions,which would receive submissions from tracking centres of Member States could be considered.This question deserves further consideration in view of its potential relevance to confidence-building.

The institutional mechanisms to encourage international cooperation among states in respect of space technology,including international transfer,should be also evaluated,taking into account the legitimate concerns about dual-purpose /civil and military/ technology.All states would have access to space for peaceful purposes on a cost-recoverable or reasonable commercial basis.States that need assistance in this respect could use appropriate forms of technical cooperation,which would take into account the needs of the developing countries and countries in transition.

References

1/Official Records of the General Assembly Tenth Special Session, Supplement No.4 /A/S-10/4/

2/Verification in all its aspects, including the role of the United Nations in the field of verification,Report of the Secretary-General,United Nations,General Assembly,A/50/377,22 September 1995,p.19

3/Comprehensive Study on Confidence-building measures,United Nations publication,Sales No.E.82.IX.3., United Nations 1982,p.6

4/Study on the role of the United Nations in the field of verification,United Nations,General Assembly,A/45/372,28 August 1990, p.20

5/Supra note 2,p.19

6/Treaty on open skies,in:Status of multilateral arms regulation and disarmament agreements,fourth edition 1992,vol.2,United nations publication,Sales No.93.IX.1 /vol. 2/,p.5

7/Y.Hashimoto,Verification systems from outer space-revival of International Satellite Monitoring Agency,IISL 1994,Washington 1995,p.250

8/Supra note 7,p.251

9/Supra note 2,p.89

10/Study on the Application of Confidence-building Measures in Outer Space,Disarmament,Study series 27,United Nations 1994, p.40

11/Supra note 10,p.23

12/Supra note 4,p.86

13/Supra note 10,p.51

IISL-96-IISL.4.20

U.S. National Space Policy and Bilateral Launch Service Agreements

Dennis J. Burnett and David Lihani*

Abstract

In the past 18 months, the United States has entered into new bilateral trade agreements with China, Russia and the Ukraine. These agreements set market quotas for launches of commercial communications satellites to geostationary orbits, establish requirements for "par-pricing" with Western launch providers and create structured consultations in the event of disputes. On September 19, 1996, President Clinton released his National Space Policy. That policy envisions the expiration of the bilateral trade agreements on launch services at the expiration of the present agreements in 2001. While launch service providers will need to plan to operate within the confines of these agreements for the next five years, satellite manufacturers and users with product or project cycles beginning up to three years prior to the first launch, undoubtedly will start to plan for a free trade regime.

* Dennis J. Burnett is a Partner and David Lihani is an Associate in the Washington, D.C. law offices of Pierson & Burnett, L.L.P. The firm specializes in matters affecting the space and telecommunications industries and can be reached through its presence on the world wide web at http://www.comspacelaw.com. The views expressed herein are solely those of the authors.

Introduction

On September 19, 1996, President Clinton released his National Space Policy[1] which assesses and attempts to balance United States military, commercial and civil space activities and goals. By this first post cold-war space policy assessment, President Clinton's administration has set forth its expectations for international cooperation, inter-agency governmental cooperation, and privatization in United States space programs. The new policy represents the culmination of a year-long review undertaken by the National Security Council and the National Science and Technology Council. The policy is spelled out in a classified Presidential Decision Directive and is expected to serve as the administration's platform for an upcoming bipartisan national space summit (scheduled for mid-December, 1996) and a conference on space exploration (scheduled for late-November, 1996).

National Space Policy

The new space policy contains several provisions relating to the United States national (civil) space programs and commercial space activities.

National Programs

With respect to the national (civil) space programs, the policy reaffirms a U.S. commitment to develop the next generation of launch vehicles and stresses the importance of building alliances between the United States and foreign countries on projects such as the International Space Station. The Administration supports cooperative projects for furthering human knowledge of space and supports programs of discovery which will result in obtaining in-situ measurements and sample returns from celestial bodies. The policy also reasserts the existing U.S. commitment to a long-term program of environmental monitoring from space.

Commercial Space

The new space policy encourages alliances between the government and the private sector. In order to foster private-sector investment in space activities, the government pledges to help expand commercial space activities, and to refrain from conducting any activities that deter commercial space activities except for reasons of national security or public safety.

The new policy states that United States Government agencies will be required to purchase commercially available space goods and services to the fullest extent feasible. Commercially available goods and services are defined as those currently offered commercially, or those that could be supplied commercially in response to a government request. It is the policy of the United States Governments not to directly subsidize commercial space activities.

Export Licensing

Exports of space systems and components continue to be regulated, and the United States Government will retain a strong presumption against the export of complete space launch vehicles or other components classified as Category I components under the Missile Technology Control Regime ("MTCR").[2] The U.S. Government will consider the export of other MTCR controlled components to MTCR countries only on a case-by-case basis.

Reusable Launch Vehicle

The development of a reusable space launch vehicle will continue to be a primary objective of the national U.S. space program, but the United States will not support the development or acquisition of space launch vehicle systems from nations that are not signatories to the Missile Technology Control Regime ("MTCR").

Trade Agreements in Launch Services

The President also expressed the intent to allow free and fair trade in commercial launch services to prevail when the bilateral agreements with China, Russia and the Ukraine expire at the beginning of the next decade. The United States entered into these agreements under the rationale that these countries had "economies in transition" that should be accorded access to the U.S. launch market but on limited terms. The goal was to promote free and fair trade in the international commercial space launch market but not to allow ruinous competitive pricing from economies that did not yet operate according to market principles.

The new Clinton National Space Policy foresees the end of the transition period and implementation of the goal of free and fair trade:

> "In support of this goal, the United States will implement, at the expiration of current space launch agreements, a strategy for transitioning from

negotiated trade in launch services towards a trade environment characterized by the free and open interaction of market economies. The U.S. Trade Representative, in coordination with the Office of Science and Technology Policy and the National Economic Council, will develop a strategy to guide this implementation"[3]

This is a definite policy shift in an attempt to reconcile the President's policies on trade and the existing regime of bilateral agreements. The new policy also strikes a better balance between competing U.S. satellite manufacturing and launch provider interests. The new policy creates a real challenge for the U.S. launch service providers who must prepare for eventual unfettered market entry of Chinese, Russian, and Ukrainian launch service providers.

While satellite manufacturers and satellite operators will not enjoy the full benefit of open competition for the next five years because of the constraints imposed by the bi-lateral agreements, those agreements do provide limited benefits to launch consumers during the transition period as these three market agreements, taken together, allow up to a total of 60 U.S.-built satellites to be launched by China, Russia and the Ukraine through the end of this century. The agreements are not intended to close the U.S. market but to stabilize the market in a period of transition. They are intended to provide satellite manufacturers with access to foreign launch vehicle and launch services providers from economies in transition, to provide safeguards against unfair or disruptive practices by those providers, and to ensure the flexibility of the agreements so as to take account of changing market conditions.[4]

The Bilateral Agreements

In the 18 months prior to the issuance of President Clinton's space policy, the United States has renewed bilateral commercial space launch services agreements with China and Russia and has entered into a new agreement with the Ukraine. The avowed purpose of these agreements was to balance the interests of the U.S. space launch, satellite, and telecommunications industries.[5]

The bilateral agreements were intended by the United States to be transitional measures with annual consultations built-in to review and consider market conditions. The transitional measure of a stabilized price comparison appeared to the United Sates to be necessary as the one-time non-market economies often receive funding or products from their governments. The theory was that the agreements would provide a period of adjustment by the market as China, Russia, and Ukraine evolved their internal markets adopted market pricing mechanisms.

In order to avoid a disruption of the market, the agreements were intended to provide some stability by placing quantitative limits and pricing controls on future launch services contracts. The U.S. Trade Representative's Office is directed to investigate the prices offered by China, Russia, and Ukraine.

The bilateral agreements are not favorable to U.S. satellite manufacturers who want increased access to foreign launchers. The Agreements are intended to strike a balance between competing interests by allowing the supply of launch services available to the U.S. satellite industry to grow in a controlled fashion. It was believed that such limited growth would protect the U.S. launch industry and at the same time not harm the leading world market position of U.S. satellite manufacturers.[6]

Bilateral Agreement with China

On March 13, 1995, the U.S. and China signed a Memorandum of Agreement regarding international trade in commercial launch services for the period from January 1, 1995 to December 31, 2001.[7] The Agreement replaced the first U.S.-China Memorandum of Agreement which was signed on January 26, 1989 and expired on December 31, 1994.

The U.S. Trade Representative's Office established guidelines, which became effective on April 27, 1995, to assist in the implementation of this bilateral agreement. The Trade Policy Staff Committee's Subcommittee on Commercial Launch Services (Subcommittee) is responsible for overall implementation of the agreement. The Subcommittee is chaired by the USTR. The Subcommittee has performed two key functions with respect to the agreement: (1) conducting an ongoing assessment of the operation of the agreement relative to U.S. goals and objectives; and (2) monitoring China's compliance with its specific obligations under the agreement.

The agreement provides that China shall offer launch services at prices "on a par" with those prices, terms and conditions prevailing in the international market for comparable commercial launch services. The agreement further describes the mechanism that is utilized in applying the "par-pricing" requirement for launches to geosynchronous earth orbit (GEO): an adjusted Chinese price falling within 15 percent of the lowest Western price is assumed to be in compliance with the bilateral agreement. That assumption is reviewed by the United States if clear evidence to the contrary is presented to the Subcommittee. In those instances in which the price differential is greater than 15 percent, compliance with the "par pricing" obligation will be evaluated in light of the comparability factors and values contained in the agreement.

The United States makes a preliminary evaluation prior to any decision to request special consultations. Information for an evaluation by the U.S. is collected by the Subcommittee through information exchanges, consultations (annual, semi-annual, special), and comprehensive reviews.

In July of this year, U.S. Trade Representative's Office met with its counterpart in Beijing to discuss implementation of the bilateral agreement. At these first consultations, the United States had three objectives: 1) to reconcile the Parties' projections of the size of the global markets for GEO and LEO (low-earth orbit) payloads; 2) to review China's participation in competitive bidding for launch contracts; and 3) to examine specific pricing issues for the burgeoning LEO market. The results of these consultations have not yet been made public .

The United States interprets the agreement to require that the 15 percent price differential is applicable only to the difference between Western and Chinese offer prices. If China's offer price is more than 15 percent less than the lowest Western price, the relevant comparability adjustments are to be made to the unadjusted Chinese or Western offer prices, as appropriate. Comparison will then be made of the prices adjusted only for the relevant comparability factors, and not for the 15 percent differential as well.

In the event of a perceived problem with compliance, the Subcommittee is responsible for notifying the TPSC and recommending consultations with China if appropriate. If consultations proceed and satisfactory resolution is not achieved or, if consultations are deemed to be inappropriate in the circumstances based on recommendations of the TPSC, the Committee may consider whether the USTR should initiate an investigation in accordance with United States law.[8]

The bilateral agreement places no direct limit on the number of commercial LEO launches, but stipulates that the Parties will reconvene in three-and-one-half years to discuss the issue. The agreement also allows China to increase its number of GEO launches if a shortage of launch vehicles occurs in the global market.

Bilateral Agreement with Ukraine

On December 14, 1995, the United States and Ukraine signed a bilateral commercial space launch agreement which established the entry for Ukraine into the global commercial launch market.[9] The agreement allows international customers to launch spacecraft on Ukrainian launch vehicles available from a Ukrainian space launch services provider, or provided by an integrated space launch services provider of a U.S.-operated launch platform at sea. By this agreement, Ukraine is positioned to potentially become a major commercial launch provider.

The United States agreed to negotiate the agreement with Ukraine only after Ukrainian officials agreed to abide by the terms and conditions of various arms control agreements.

The U.S.-Ukraine agreement was modeled on then-existing agreements between the United States and Russia, and the United States and China. Under the terms of the bilateral agreement, the Ukrainians are permitted to conduct up to five launches of spacecraft to GEO until the agreement terminates at the end of 2001.

The agreement also allows Ukraine to conduct an additional 11 GEO launches through an "integrated space launch services provider." The integrated space launch services provider must be a U.S.-led joint venture with Ukraine that meets certain criteria affecting ownership, control and services. These qualifying criteria are: (1) the U.S. partner must maintain control in fact; (2) the U.S. must be the source of a significant share of the goods and services employed in any launch; (3) a majority of the goods and services, including financing and insurance, must originate in market-economy countries; and (4) the joint venture must receive a launch license from the U.S. Department of Transportation. In the Protocol to the Agreement, the U.S. and Ukraine agreed that the International Sea Launch (ISL) venture meets the criteria.

The Sea Launch venture is led by Boeing, with Energia and Yuzhnoye of Ukraine providing the engines and rocket for an initial launch in 1998.[10] The Sea Launch concept involves a launch of the Ukrainian-built Zenit from a sea-based platform in the middle of the Pacific Ocean. Spacecraft will be prepared and integrated with the launch vehicle at a homeport in southern California. The platform and assembled vehicle will travel with a command and control ship to a selected launch point near the equator. To comply with the U.S.-Ukraine Agreement, Boeing maintains control of the Sea Launch venture and a significant percentage of the goods and services associated with each launch also are provided by U.S. companies.

If the commercial satellite launch market continues to expand significantly over the next several years, the agreement provides for up to four additional launches, three of which are required to be for U.S.-Ukraine joint ventures. Of the 20 total launches which can then be conducted using Ukrainian vehicles, 14 must be conducted for U.S.-led joint ventures.

The bilateral agreement does not limit the number of launches by Ukrainian launch vehicles for spacecraft to LEO. However, the agreement states that the total participation in the initial deployment of any single LEO telecommunications constellation by Ukraine, Russia, and China combined must be less than that of market-economy launch providers. Additionally, the agreement imposes limits on Ukraine's commercial launch activity to the use of the Zenit and Tsyklon launch vehicles and their upgrades. This limitation purposefully excludes the use of converted excess ballistic missiles or new types of launch vehicles.

Like the bilateral agreement with China, the U.S.-Ukraine bilateral agreement sets pricing guidelines, as well as launch quotas, to ensure that Ukraine's entry does not disrupt the international commercial space launch market As stipulated in the agreement, the bids, offers, or contracts for launch services must be comparable to those of market-economy launch service providers. For GEO launches, the price for the launch services must be within 15 percent of that of market-economy providers or be subject to special consultations. The special consultations may be convened at either the United States or Ukrainian request within 30 days on matters of particular concern, including prevailing international market conditions. The agreement also prohibits grants, subsidies or credits that distort the production or cost for commercial space launch systems.

Bilateral Agreement with Russia

After the United States renewed its agreement with China and entered into a new agreement with Ukraine, Russia sought to amend its existing bilateral agreement with the United States. Russia perceived that it was significantly disadvantaged in pursuing the international space launch markets because the quotas for China were significantly higher than those originally agreed to by Russia. With expansion of the launch agreements to now include Ukraine, and an increase in the number of launches permitted with China, Russia sought from the United States a larger number of commercial launches for Russian launch vehicles. Under the 1993-negotiated agreement already in place, Russia was allowed only nine launches to GEO until the end of 2000.

Russia and the U.S. agreed on January 31, 1996 to amend Russia's launch quota along similar terms afforded China. Under the renegotiated agreement, Russia received permission to conduct up to 16 launches to GEO through the year 2000.[11]

Russia also stands to gain from the Ukrainian agreement because Russia is a direct supplier of components and raw manufacturing materials for the Zenit, as well as the RD-171 first-stage engine of the Zenit and the Block-DM upper stage.

The United States and Russia also agreed, if the commercial space launch services market improves significantly beyond current expectations, Russia may conduct up to four additional launches to GEO for international commercial customers by the end of the year 2000.

The amended launch agreement enhanced the prospects of commercial launches on Russia's Proton launch vehicle. The 4-stage Proton is Russia's only vehicle capable of launching spacecraft into GEO. To gain funding and marketing services, the Russian companies Khrunichev State Scientific and Production Space Center (the Proton's manufacturer), and RKK Energia (the manufacturer of the Block-DM upper stage) formed a joint venture with Lockheed-Martin to market Proton launches under the name International Launch Services (ILS).

The first commercial launch of the Proton arranged by ILS occurred on April 9, 1996 when the Hughes-built Astra-1F communications satellite was successfully boosted into GEO from the Baikonur Cosmodrome in Kazakhstan for the Sociéte Europeéne des Satellites.

The bilateral agreement allows Russian space launch service providers to contract to provide launch services for up to three launches of satellites to LEO for the Iridium system. In addition, with regard to the initial deployment of LEO telecommunications constellations, the United States will assess whether participation by Russia in the deployment of any single LEO constellation is greater than the participation of market-economy launch providers.

Conclusion

As seen from the brief discussion above, the bilateral agreements negotiated by the United States with China, Ukraine and Russia have put in place launch quotas and pricing policies for at least the next five years. At the insistence of United States launch providers, the quotas and pricing policies were instituted to ensure the controlled entry of Chinese, Russian and Ukrainian services into the global, commercial space launch market.

The new National Space Policy appears to presage the end of the biliateral launch quotas and pricing restrictions by expressing the intention that the bilateral agreements will not be renewed beyond their present terms. Satellite manufacturers and satellite users who must contend with product design and constuction cycles of up to three years or more should begin to plan for the end of the bilaterals, taking into account, of course, that Presidents and their policies change from time-to-time.

---

1. National Space Policy, The White House, unclassified Fact Sheet prepared by National Science and Technology Council, released on September 19, 1996.

2. Guidelines for Sensitive Missile Relevant Transfers (April 16, 1987).

3. Id., *see* "Commercial Space Guidelines," paragraph (5).

4. Statements made by Donald Eiss, deputy assistant U.S. Trade Representative for industry and Catherine Novelli, deputy assistant U.S. Trade Representative for Central and Eastern Europe and Eurasia before the House Sub-committee on Space and Aeronautics, Washington, D.C., June 12, 1996.

5. Comment by U.S. Trade Representative Michael Kantor following the conclusion of the U.S.-PRC Commercial Space Launch

Agreement, January 30, 1995, U.S. Department of State "Press Release, Q's and A's," February 1, 1995.

6. Public Statement, Office of the United States Trade Representative, Executive Office of the President, "United States Reaches Agreement with Ukraine on a Commercial Space Launch Agreement," December 14, 1995. In a separate statement following the two-day session of the U.S.-Russian Joint Commission on Economic and Technological Cooperation, U.S. Vice-President Al Gore said that the amended U.S.-Russian commercial space launch agreement "will benefit the U.S. economy through new investments by joint ventures and by diversifying the supply of launch services available to America's satellite industry, allowing that industry to maintain its world leadership position." (White House Office of the Press Secretary, Press Conference by Vice President Gore and Prime Minister Chernomyrdin of Russia, January 30, 1996, Washington, D.C.).

A noticeable reaction to the reliability and diversity offered by the launch systems covered by the bilateral agreements is the satellite manufacturers willingness to sign multiple launch contracts. For example: Hughes Communications Inc. signed multiple launch contracts with Boeing Sea Launch for 10 launches; and Space Systems/Loral signed contracts for 10 launches with International Launch Services (ILS) and five with Sea Launch.

7. Memorandum of Agreement Between the Government of the United States of America and the Government of the People's Republic of China Regarding the International Trade in Commercial Launch Services, (March 13, 1995).

8. The investigation would be conducted under section 301 of the Trade Act of 1974, as amended.

9. Agreement between the Government of the United States and the Government of the Ukraine Regarding International Trade in Commercial Space Launch Services. (February 21, 1996).

10. The first launch by the Sea Launch venture will lift the Galaxy 11 satellite to orbit for Hughes Electronics Corporation in June 1998.

11. Agreement Between the Government of the United States of America and the Government of the Russian Federation to Amend the 'Agreement Between the Government of the United States of America and the Government of the Russian Federation Regarding International Trade in Commercial Space Launch Services, (January 30, 1996).

IISL-96-IISL.4.21

TANGIBLE AND INTANGIBLE PROPERTY IN OUTER SPACE

René Oosterlinck*
ESA Directorate of Administration, Paris, France

1. Introduction

Property in space is certainly one of the most important issues for the future not only in the context of the more classical form of tangible property such as minerals but also intangible property such as orbital slots on the geostationary orbit, frequencies, etc.

As far as the exploitation of mineral resources is concerned the similitude is striking between space law and the law of the High Seas and Antarctica. In studies on the law of the high seas and Antarctica very often reference is made to concepts of property used in Roman Law such as "*res nullius*" , "*res communis omnium*" etc.

A typical example of this is found in one of the most important historical sources of the law of the sea namely Hugo Grotius' "The freedom of the seas"[1] e.g. "....Vergil also says that the air, the sea, and the shore are what Romans call "common" to all men by natural law, or as we have said, "public" according to the law of nations; and indeed they call their use sometimes common, sometimes public. Nevertheless, although those things are with reason said to be *res nullius*, so far as private ownership is concerned, still they differ very much from those things which, though also *res nullius*, have not been marked out for common use, such for example as wild animals, fish, and birds. For if any one seizes those things and assumes possession of them, they can become objects of private ownership, but things in the former category by the consensus of opinion of all mankind are forever exempt from such private ownership on account of their susceptibility to universal use; and as they belong to all they cannot be taken away from all by any one person any more than what is mine can be taken away from me by you. And Cicero says that one of the first gifts of justice is the use of common property for common benefit.....".

Another quotation is, by analogy, to space activities even more relevant: "And in Plautus' Rudens when the slave says : - the sea is certainly common to all persons - the fisherman agrees; but when the slave adds: - then what is found in the common sea is common property -, he rightly objects, saying: - But what my net and hooks have taken, is absolutely my own -."[2]

The similitude between the fisherman and an astronaut removing samples on the moon is remarkable but what about the outcome??

The answer is not straightforward and a closer look to some concepts of Roman Law which are used in this context is desirable for a good understanding.[3]

2. Tangible Property

2.1. "Property" under Roman law

Under Roman Law "*res*" or things are classified into *res corporales* and *res incorporales.*
Within *res corporales* a certain number of things are excluded from trade "*res quarum commercium non est*", normally referred to as *res extra commercium.*[4]
Objects qualified as *res extra commercium* are sub divided into three distinct categories - (i) *res publicae,* (ii) *res divini iuris* and (iii) *res communis omnium.*
(i) Objects qualified as *res publicae* are common property of the roman people subject to governments regulations. This includes public roads, flowing rivers, lakes, water distribution conducts etc.
(ii) Objects qualified as *res divini iuris* are put under the protection of the Gods and include *res sacrae* mainly temples and objects used for worship, *res religiosae* - burial places which were sacred and could not be subject of trade *res sanctae* e.g. the city walls.
(iii) Finally objects qualified as *res communis omnium* are available to all and cannot be owned by anyone not even by a state e.g. the air, rain and flowing river water, the sea and shore. With the exception that over the shore the state exercised certain rights (*litora maris*).
Ownership is normally acquired through effective possession but this is not sufficient in itself, also required is that this possession results from a legal act - *iusta causa possessionis.* e.g. purchase - *pro emptore*, donation -*pro donato* etc. A special way of obtaining property is through occupation - *occupatio* of things which belong to no one. The latter are qualified as *res nullius* and may be subject to appropriation through effective occupation and the will expressed by the [new] owner to exercise ownership (*corpore et animo*).[5] There is thus either an absence of original title which could be transferred as is normally the case from the former owner to the new one, this because no one has ever claimed ownership, or the former owner has abandoned ownership (*res derelicta*). For this kind of acquiring property more stringent rules were applied.

As shown in the example quoted by Hugo Grotius the sea is considered as *res communis omnium* which means that it is not amenable to appropriation but what is in it is, including the water of the sea itself.
For a good understanding of the underlying reasoning a closer look at the meaning and use of the two notions *res nullius* and *res communis omnium* and on how they interact is necessary. At first sight one could conclude that

since the sea is *res communis omnium* which is part of the wider *res extra commercium* it could never become *res nullius*. Since if this would be the case the sea could become at least in theory subject of private ownership through occupation and consequently subject of trade which by definition is excluded.
In practice the Romans looked differently to the issue when considering the sea as a whole or when considering its constituents. In the former case they qualified it *res communis omnium* and in the latter *res nullius*. Or in more general terms "*res communis* differs from *res nullius* in that the source of the resources cannot be appropriated but the resources themselves are amenable to appropriation".[6]
This apparent contradiction finds, inter alia, its origin in the impossibility of satisfying one of the basic conditions for acquiring ownership of goods which belong to no one, namely, effective occupation. It goes without saying that this is for the sea as a whole impossible.[7] On the other hand this condition could be satisfied easily for fish and some quantity of sea water, e.g. "if you bring the sea (water) into your estate for private fish reserves then the interdict *uti possidetis* applies"[8]. These resources were looked at as inexhaustible and their appropriation was physically possible and would moreover only be partial leaving thus the possibility to others for future exploitation and use of the sea.
Hugo Grotius evokes however, though briefly, the possibility that fish could be an exhaustible resource of the sea but in his view this would not alter the legal status of the sea as a whole.

"And if it were possible to prohibit any of those things, say for example, fishing, for in a way it can be maintained that fish are exhaustible, still it would not be possible to prohibit navigation, for the sea would not exhausted by that use."[9]

The contradiction is thus only fictitious since the use of the sea keeps its status of *res communis omnium* untouched.
The freedom of navigation (use) was in the eyes of Hugo Grotius the most important result of the non appropriation thesis which he defended and which is at the origin of his work. It is amazing that this freedom which is essential for all space activities is not mentioned in any of the Outer Space Treaties. Maybe as Hamilton DeSaussure argues "it is so basic to the exploration and use of Outer space that it must be considered as inherent in the launching and orbiting of all space objects".[10]

2.2. Property of Celestial Bodies

What now about Outer Space ? One could consider Outer Space as the combination of interstellar space and celestial bodies. The interstellar space would be similar to the sea and the celestial bodies to *res nullius*. Or one could also assimilate Outer Space as a whole to the sea whereby the celestial bodies are its resources similar as the fish in the sea. In the first case only the interstellar space would be *res communis omnium* and in the second the entire Outer space would qualify for it. It being understood that in the latter case the celestial bodies would be amenable for appropriation similar as the fish of the sea. In conclusion, de facto, in both cases the celestial bodies would be *res nullius*. Notwithstanding this identical qualification there are however some fundamental difference between the resources of the sea as seen by the romans and celestial bodies.
First of all a celestial body, as for example the moon, is closer to the notion of *terra nullius* than *res nullius*.
Terra nullius is usually used for large pieces of land or islands for which no owner was known or recognised. The concept has been alive for centuries and is still used nowadays in disputes or settlements on sovereignty rights over land between states.
Secondly, the number of celestial bodies which could be of interest to men are very limited and thus certainly not inexhaustible.
In other words once ownership is acquired for part or in whole of a celestial body this part will automatically be excluded for others which clearly contradicts the principle of *res communis omnium* and the similarity with the inexhaustible fish in the sea. Remains thus only the first possibility amongst the two i.e. the interstellar space is in legal terms similar to the sea whereas the celestial bodies are *terra nullius*.[11]
Coming back to the *terra nullius* concept. As said this concept is normally used when referring to land although sometimes *res nullius* is also used. The way of acquiring ownership for large pieces of land is ,however, in practice different from movables or immoveables like buildings.
Historically title of sovereignty of *terra nullius* was acquired by a State when it discovered new land followed by effective possession.[12] Or as S. Pufendorf puts it: "The base seeing a thing of the knowing where it is, is not sufficient Title of Possession".[13]
Discovery alone never has conferred a complete title of sovereignty, it resulted only in a inchoate title. Effective occupation was for centuries the overriding principle. It is true that the effective occupation principle has somewhat be dilute over the centuries and that in some cases the mere fact that a State landed for the first time on an island without any further activity was considered sufficient to satisfy the condition of effective occupation.[14]
The Clipperton Island case is a typical illustration of this change. In that case the arbitrator concluded that "if a territory, by virtue of the fact that it was completely uninhabited, is, from the first moment when the occupying state makes its appearance there, at the absolute and undisputed disposition of that state, from that moment the taking of possession must be considered as accomplished and the occupation is thereby completed."[15]
For Outer space by analogy and under the assumption that celestial bodies are terra nullius the fact that a new celestial body is discovered does not give any rights other than the paternity of the discovery itself to the discoverer. An additional act would be necessary for acquiring property rights namely, an act of effective occupation.
A more recent case Denmark v. Norway concerning sovereignty rights over Eastern Greenland diluted even

more the condition of effective occupation. In this case Norway "occupied " in 1931, with a view of establishing sovereignty rights, Eastern Greenland which it considered as *Terra nullius*. Denmark brought the case immediately before the Permanent Court of International Justice. The Court redefined the notion of effective occupation by arguing that effective occupation required both intention and will to exercise sovereignty and manifestation of state activity and thus a contrario effective occupation was not really required.[16] The decision was criticised since it was difficult to accept that it would be possible to acquire sovereignty rights over on a piece of land bigger than Europe as a whole without any act of effective occupation. Or to put it differently "It would be altogether unreasonable if a State, by annexing a portion of such a vast land should obtain sovereignty over the whole country."[17]

In this case the fact that for western Greenland Denmark sovereignty rights were internationally recognised played certainly an important role in the decision making process of the Court. Another important consideration was the physical characteristics of the area which was very hostile and difficult to access.[18]

This case is understandably extremely important for space activities (same hostile place and of difficult access) for if a celestial body would qualify for *terra nullius* it would be sufficient for a state to only have the intention and the will to exercise sovereignty combined with at least some local effective occupation for acquiring sovereignty rights over the celestial body as a whole.

A step further in diluting the effective occupation would be to accept that by dropping an object made by a state on a *terra nullius* followed by a clear expression of that state of its will to establish title of sovereignty it would actually acquire such rights.

For Outer Space the question arose for the first time when a soviet spacecraft carrying a soviet flag stroke the moon as early as September 1959. This event led to considerable discussions notwithstanding the fact that the Soviet Union indicated from the beginning that it had not the intention to seek any claim of sovereignty through this act.

In order to avoid similar problems for the Apollo program when an American flag would be put on the moon a special bill was enacted in the United States. Sec. 8 of the US Law on the Implantation of the United States Flag reads as follows:

"the flag of the United States, and no other flag, shall be implanted or otherwise placed on the surface of the moon, or on the surface of any planet, by the members of the crew of any spacecraft making a lunar or planetary landing as apart of a mission under the Apollo program or as a part of a mission under any subsequent program, the funds for which are provided entirely by the Government of the United States. This act is intended as symbolic gesture of national pride in achievement and is not to be construed as a declaration of national appropriation by claim of sovereignty."

In conclusion there was a time where the qualification of celestial bodies as *terra nullius* was conceivable from a legal point of view and in line with customary international law, claims of sovereignty based on effective occupation could certainly have been recognised.

But already in the mid fifties even before the launch of the first satellite a theory was developed according to which territorial sovereignty should be excluded in Outer Space. "The first step... had been taken at the private level in 1954, on the occasion of the fifth Congress of the International Astronautical Federation (Innsbruck), where a theory was developed according to which Outer Space and celestial bodies should be considered an object of conquest by mankind for mankind. This thesis was embodied in the expression *res communis humanitatis...*".[19]

The extreme competition between the USA and the USSR in the conquest of space and the fact that neither was sure to win the race worked in favour of the exclusion of territorial sovereignty in Outer Space. Also in favour of the concept of *res communis humanitatis* was the profound change of the political scene which took place during the late fifties and early sixties. During that period many countries became independent and the third world started playing an important political role which was equally influenced by the East - West confrontation. It was also for these reasons inconceivable to defend a legal regime whereby one nation would be allowed to establish sovereignty rights in Outer Space. In order thus to avoid any uncertainty as to the outcome of the question of what effective occupation of Outer Space in whole or in part could lead made it necessary to define in a treaty the status of Outer Space. This was done in the Outer Space Treaty with the introduction of the principle of non appropriation of Outer Space, including the Moon and other celestial bodies, laid down in article 2 of the Outer Space Treaty "Outer Space, including the Moon and other celestial bodies, is not subject to national appropriation by claim of sovereignty, by means of use of **occupation** or by any other means" (emphasis added). National appropriation in this article clearly refers to the concept of territory and sovereignty[20] which is different from the concept of property in civil law.

The specific phrasing of article 2 clearly rejects, insofar as appropriation by a State is concerned, the qualification of celestial bodies as *terra (res) nullius*. In other words it is not possible for a State to acquire sovereign rights over celestial bodies through occupation.

The Outer Space Treaty changed thus the status of Outer Space celestial bodies from a historical and logical justified *res* or *terra nullius* to *res communis omnium stricto sensu.* [21, 22]

Legal issues are however seldom straightforward and unambiguous this is unfortunately also the case here. The wording of article 2 refers only to national appropriation but is silent as to appropriation by legal or natural persons. This ambiguity kept according to some specialists in space law for some time options open.[23] Nowadays it is generally accepted that appropriation by anyone of parts of outer space is prohibited.

The Moon Treaty is more explicit with respect to the surface and sub-surface of the moon which may not become the property of any State, international intergovernmental or non-governmental organisation, national organisation or non-governmental entity or of any natural person. The

Treaty reaffirms, however, that the Moon is not subject to national appropriation by any claim of sovereignty, by means of use or occupation, or by any other means. The specific phrasing used in article 11 reinforces the idea that by national, appropriation creation of sovereign rights should be understood.

2.3. Property of extra-terrestrial materials

2.3.1. Resources of Moon and other celestial bodies

A next question concerns the resources of Outer space i.e. celestial bodies are not amenable for appropriation but what about their resources? Stephen Gorove and Aldo Cocca considered that the prohibition of article 2 applied equally to resources from Outer Space, the Moon and celestial bodies. The opposite school of thought includes Daniel Goedhuis and Bin Cheng for whom, by analogy with the rules underlying the freedom of the high seas, the appropriation of natural resources merely formed part of the freedom of exploration and use of Outer Space[24].

The history of article 2 as recorded during the meetings show that it was the intention of at least some of the participants to give a wider scope to this article than its actual reading. At least at two occasion the matter was raised; in the first case explicitly by the Belgian Delegate to the Legal sub-committee and in the second case more implicitly by the French delegate to the committee. The Belgian Delegate stated that "His delegation has taken note of the interpretation of the term "non appropriation" advanced by several delegations -apparently without contradiction- as covering both the establishment of sovereignty and the creation of titles to property in private law.[25] The French Delegate mentioned in a long intervention on several issues that ".... there was reason to be satisfied that three basic principles were affirmed, namely : the prohibition of any claim of sovereignty or **property** rights in space .... ".[26]

Notwithstanding the history of article 2 which supported the views expressed by Gorove and Cocca no consensus was reached on the matter.

The legal status of the resources became a concern for many, once the Apollo program had started and that, for example, mining activities seemed to be feasible in the near future. This concern resulted in the Moon Treaty which contains certain provisions dealing with outer space resources.

The matter is, however, treated differently depending whether the purpose of the mining activities is intended for the immediate support of a space mission or whether it is for activities on earth.

The wording of the Outer Space Treaty is too vague and therefore difficult to be applied to mining directly. From the treaty mining would, according to certain scholars fall within "use" prohibited in article 2; others are, however, of a contrary opinion. Or as E. Galloway puts it "There was an assumption by some commentators that the 1967 Treaty did not cover the exploitation of natural resources because they under estimated the meaning of "use" ...whereas others are certain that the 1967 Treaty made an outstanding contribution to space law by including "use" as well as "exploration" as general terms applicable to all activities in outer space, including the Moon and other celestial Bodies." [27] What is not contested by anyone is the that term "use", when referring to the extraction of ore and other extra terrestrial material for scientific purposes is authorised. The quantity of the extracted material should however be in line with this purpose i.e. very limited. But when would this limit be exceeded? It is mainly this ambiguity which is at the origin of the Moon Agreement. The initiative came in 1970 from Argentina with the submission of a draft to the Legal Sub committee of COPUOS. After lengthy discussions the text was finally agreed on by the General Assembly on December 5, 1979, and opened for signature and eventually ratification by States on December 18, 1979. The Agreement has been signed and ratified by nine countries (Australia, Austria, Chile, Mexico, Morocco, the Netherlands, Pakistan, Philippines, and Uruguay) the minimum requirements for entering in force are thus satisfied.[28]

The small number of States party to the Agreement and the absence of the main space faring nations make, however, that the Agreement does not really became effective international law.

The unwillingness of the main space faring nations to adhere to the Agreement stems from the fact that it contains a number of provisions which are the least to say subject to contradictory interpretations.

Or as Menter puts it "A reading of the Moon Treaty without consideration of its negotiated history, reflects some key words or phrases that are without definition, infer a meaning other than intended, ambiguous or not clear in intend."[29]

Or in other words one should read the Moon Treaty only in combination with all the preparatory documents!

The Soviet Union indicated from the beginning that it preferred an Agreement limited to the moon excluding other celestial bodies. The USA was of the opinion that if an agreement would be concluded the Agreement should then cover all celestial bodies since it would soon be feasible to travel beyond the moon. The compromise reached was that the agreement would cover all celestial bodies until such a time when specific treaties or agreements would be set up to deal with other celestial bodies.[30]

Furthermore, a more theoretical debate took place on the question whether the Agreement should be limited to the solar system or on the contrary apply to the whole universe. Without to much difficulty the former was accepted. Interesting to note is that the application of the moon agreement extends to orbits around the moon or other trajectories to or around it.

The Moon Treaty deals, regretfully in a controversial manner, for the first time with the exploitation of natural resources.[31]

The qualification of the natural resources as "the common heritage of mankind" is one of the many examples in this respect.

The concept of common heritage of mankind was for the first time used by Pardo during the discussion held during the Law of the Sea Conference. He wrote in particular that it was the objective to replace the principle of freedom of the seas by the principle of common heritage of mankind in order to preserve a greater part of ocean space as a commons accessible to the international community. The commons of the high seas, however, would not be open to the whims of the users and exploiters; it would be internationally administered. International administration of the commons and the management of its resources for the commons good distinguished the principle of common heritage from the traditional principle of the high seas as *res communis*.[32]

For historical reasons the following extract from Hugo Grotius' Freedom of the seas and the following is certainly worthwhile reading.

"....Two conclusions may be drawn from what has thus far been said. The first is, that which cannot be occupied, or which never has been occupied, cannot be the property of any one, because all property has arisen from occupation. The second is, that all that which has been so constituted by nature that although serving some one person it still suffices for the common use of all other persons, is today and ought in perpetuity to remain in the same condition as when it was first created by nature. This is what Cicero meant when he wrote: "This then is the comprehensive bond that unites together men and men and all to all; and under it the common right to all things that nature has produced for the common use of man is to be maintained."

....Ovid : "Why do you deny me water? Its use is free to all. Nature has made neither sun nor air nor waves private property; they are public gifts" The poet uses public in its usual meaning, not of those things which belong to any one people, but to human society as a whole; that is to say, things which are called public are, according to the Laws of the law of nations, the common property of all, and the private property of none."[33]

The concept of common heritage of mankind as used in Outer Space is however considered as unique and its interpretation totally independent of the concept defined by the same wording in the Treaty of the High Seas.[34] E.g. the statement on the moon treaty adopted by the Section of Internal Law of the American Bar Association.

"c)The meaning of the term 'common heritage of mankind' is to be based on the provisions of this Agreement, and not on the use or interpretation of that term in any other context. Recognition by the United States that the moon and its natural resources are the common heritage of mankind constitutes recognition (A) that all States have equal rights to explore and use the moon and its natural resources, and (B) that no State or entity has an exclusive right of ownership, property or appropriation over the moon and its natural resources in place...."[35]

The insertion of the common heritage of mankind in the Moon Treaty was suggested in the original Argentine proposal [36] but was in fact only at a later stage formally proposed by the United States. The support of the United States was not followed by all, the USSR was in particular opposed to making explicit reference to this concept. In the end a compromise was reached whereby the concept would be limited by only making reference to it in article 11 and moreover limit it further by its sub paragraph 5. Article 11 reads:

"1. The moon and its natural resources are the common heritage of mankind which finds its expression in the provisions of this Agreement, in particular in paragraph 5 of this article"

.....

"5. States Parties to this Agreement hereby undertake to establish an international regime, including appropriate procedures, to govern the exploitation of the natural resources of the moon as such exploitation is about to become feasible. This provision shall be implemented in accordance with article 18 of this Agreement. "

The USSR agreed thus finally to the inclusion in the Moon Treaty of the concept of common heritage of mankind. The way it was done was however not acceptable to the USA who feared that the wording of article 11 would put a moratorium on the exploitation of the natural resources until a time when a special regime would be agreed on. Most, if not all, authors agree that there is no such moratorium but it would of course have been better if this would have been clearly spelled out in the Text.

The declaration by N. Hosenball, US delegate in the COPUOS, illustrates the USA's point of view in this matter:

"The draft treaty, as part of the compromise by many delegates, places no moratorium upon exploitation of the natural resources on celestial bodies pending establishment of an international regime. This permits orderly attempts to establish whether such exploitation is in fact feasible and practical by permitting experimental beginnings and then pilot operations, a process by which we will learn if it will ever be feasible to commercially exploit the mineral resources of celestial bodies. My Government will, when and if negotiations for such a regime are called for under Article XI and XVIII, make every effort to see that such a regime is successfully negotiated."[37]

One of the main shortfalls of the Moon Treaty is that it seems that exploitation of natural resources is acceptable as from now on an experimental basis but that the rules governing real exploitation would be established later. It is clear that such an approach only leads to the non-exploitation of the resources since no government or private enterprise would invest large amounts of money in a venture were the rules of the games will be established later, and by others.

The provisions of paragraph 7 of article 11 of the Moon Treaty makes it even more doubtful that investments will be made under those circumstances.

" 7. The main purposes of the international regime to be established shall include:

a. The orderly and safe development of the natural resources of the moon;

b. The rational management of those resources;

c. The expansion of opportunities in the use of these resources;

d. An equitable sharing by all States Parties in the benefits derived from those resources, whereby the interests and needs of the developing countries, as well as the efforts of those countries which have contributed either directly or indirectly to the exploration of the moon, shall be given special consideration."

If the same provision would have existed for the geostationary orbit prior to the first feasibility studies on geostationary satellites it is doubtful that they would exist today! Notwithstanding all the shortfalls of the Moon Treaty some provisions are a step forward in the ruling of natural resources of Outer Space.

First of all Article 6 which deals with the freedom of scientific investigation authorises explicitly the removal from the moon of samples of its minerals and other substances. It puts only a "moral" obligation on those who are carrying out such activities a of making samples available to other interested States. It also provides that States may in the course of their scientific investigations use mineral and other substances of the moon in quantities appropriate for the support of their missions.

Secondly the US proposed and obtained an amendment of paragraph 3 of article 11 of the treaty by specifying that only the resources in place are not subject of appropriation by any State, international organisation ....

This amendment is by far the most important one. It means that the prohibition of property rights would not apply to natural resources once they have been removed by States or private enterprises or others. Or in other words no property rights may be acquired in immoveables but once part of an immovable is transformed into movables, e.g. through mining, the latter is amenable for property.

But how much extra terrestrial resources will be needed in the future? In order to set the order of magnitude lets consider the construction of solar power systems. According to O'Neil in order to fill all the US needs for new electric generating capacity in the year 1990 about five power satellites would have to be put in to orbit that year alone, each weighing as much as an ocean liner.[38]

For its implementation O'Neil proposes to use materials, some 600.000 Tons a year, from the moon and bring them in high orbit around the earth. The energy required to do this is of course much less than if one would put this material into orbit from the earth.

It seems that the USA amendment of the Moon Treaty would mean that even for mining activities of this scope i.e. some 600.000 Tons per year this would not be considered as an appropriation of part of the moon.

In the context of the exploitation of resources the case of Spitsbergen (Svalbard) is also worthwhile considering in the sense that the rich natural resources have influenced considerably the legal status of the island. For many centuries the only interest in the island was whaling and fur hunting. For these purposes it was visited by nationals from many countries and was at that time considered as *terra nullius*. Some claims of territorial sovereignty existed but no State really tried to enforce them. By the end of the nineteenth century things changed with the discovery of large coal deposits which rapidly resulted in a conflicting situation. After lengthy negotiations a Treaty conceded the full and absolute sovereignty of Norway over the Archipel of Spitsbergen. The many exceptions foreseen in the Treaty undermined *de jure* the Norwegian exclusive territorial sovereignty. In particular ships and nationals of all contracting parties enjoy equal rights to fishing and must be permitted under the same conditions of equality to establish and pursue maritime, industrial, mining or commercial enterprises both on land and in the territorial waters. No monopoly may be established on any account or for any enterprise. The Treaty provides also that any taxes, dues and duties levied musty be devoted exclusively to the territories of Spitsbergen and not to exceed what is required for the object in view. The special status of Spitsbergen has sometimes be considered by some scholars as a possible model which could be transposed to Outer Space.

2.3.2. Property of asteroids

As an alternative asteroids could be considered as possible mining resource. The existence of relatively rich materials in water and carbon on the surfaces of a large number of asteroids represent, together with the expected deposits in the permanently shadowed areas of the lunar pole the nearest extra terrestrial source of the essential materials to be used in the colonisation of outer space.

Low cost transportation systems including solar sailing may make even relatively distant asteroidal sources competitive with lunar surface.

The production of the materials could either take place on the moon or asteroid or in outer space itself. In the latter case the raw materials would be transported to large manufacturing facilities in space.

The preconised use of asteroids poses the question of their legal status i.e. are asteroids celestial bodies or not.

The issue is rather important since if they are celestial bodies the provisions of the moon treaty would in the absence of specific rules be applicable automatically.

About 100.000 earth approaching asteroids larger than 100 meters in diameter exist. These numbers are probably correct to within a factor of 3 or 4.[39]

Asteroids are especially common between the orbits of Mars and Jupiter.

Brooks in 1966 argued that a medium sized asteroid could be considered as a floating mineral resource? In his opinion no legal impediment would seem to stand in the way of appropriating the entirety of an asteroid".[40] Since then the Outer Space Treaty and the Moon Treaty came about. J.H. Glazer feels, however, that the Outer Space Treaty does not alter Brooks' point of view with respect to movable asteroids since these natural objects are not ordinarily perceived of as celestial bodies.

N. Jasentuliyana [41] is of a contrary opinion; he advocates that the provisions of the Outer Space Treaty and in particular the wording of article 2 excludes that a state or company could claim the property of an asteroid. Notwithstanding this he implicitly agrees that his conclusion based on the interpretation of the Outer Space Treaty could be challenged. "In recognition of the ambiguity of the Outer Space Treaty, on the subject of mining on the Moon and other celestial bodies"

Fasan is inclined to make a difference between asteroids having long known astronomical specifications and/or those who received already a name and other asteroids. These asteroids should be considered celestial bodies whereas smaller ones should not.[42] It is evident that with the quantities of materials quoted above a small sized asteroid would be used entirely for the production of useful materials. In other words the mining of the asteroid would result in its disappearance.
As mentioned earlier the moon treaty excludes property rights in the surface and sub-surface of the moon which by definition are immoveables, but does not exclude property rights in parts of the surface or sub-surface of the moon once removed i.e. movables.
As far as asteroids are concerned large asteroids could be assimilated to the moon for which property rights can only exist in parts once removed whereas small asteroids could be assimilated to a movable and as such subject of property as a whole.

In conclusion, if our astronaut would have removed some samples on the Moon in 1969 he would not have acquired property but if the same astronaut would go back in 1996 he would become the legal owner of these samples. Or the natural resources of the Moon and other celestial bodies went from *res nullius* to *res communis omnium stricto sensu* back to *res nullius*.

3. Intangible property in outer space

Intangible property usually refers to something which is lacking physical existence, which cannot be apprehended by the senses. A typical example of intangible property is intellectual property such as patens, copyright etc.
In the context of space law intangible property comprises property rights in specific areas in outer space other then celestial bodies e.g. langrangian points, orbits including specific slots of certain orbits, trajectories and to a certain extend frequency spectrum. Intellectual property vested in patents or copyright in for example remote sensing data is not covered in this study.

Property rights in orbits and trajectories are not granted by any of the outer space treaties, in fact the Outer Space Treaty of 1967 is silent on the matter. This in itself is not sufficient to conclude that such rights may exist, on the contrary the concept of property in outer space is clearly against the spirit of the Treaty. The moon treaty on the other hand excludes explicitly exclusive rights in orbits around the moon and trajectories to or around it.
Notwithstanding this some form of property has been introduced recently in orbits. These rights find their origin in the application of ITU regulations and national patents the former with respect to the geostationary orbit and the latter for low and medium earth orbits.

Each space mission has its own specific trajectories and orbit requirements be it a transfer orbit or a final orbit.
The importance of trajectories and orbits should not be underestimated in the context of Outer Space exploitation since some of them are crucial for certain applications.
The best known and described orbit is the geostationary orbit, but other orbits are becoming from an economic point of view equally important. Trajectories comprises inter alia minimum energy trajectories for traveling to other celestial bodies and trajectories whereby energy is pulled out from celestial bodies through gravitational swings.

3. 1. Geostationary Orbit

The importance of this orbit was recognised at a very early stage and became with the frequency spectrum one of the main legal issues in Outer space Law.
At the 1971 conference the status of the geostationary orbit was also put on the agenda but ended without any concrete result except that the participants to the conference agreed on the non binding principle of non-discriminatory , equitable access to the geostationary orbit by recognizing that the radio frequency spectrum and the geostationary satellite orbit were limited natural resources that should be efficiently and equitably utilized.[43]
It was on the other hand considered premature to establish repartition criteria for the geostationary orbit.
The question on the legal status of the geostationary orbit was raised again in 1973 but this time at the Plenipotentiary Conference of the ITU which is the highest forum (Malaga - Spain) and progress was made with the formal incorporation of the guidelines as to the use of the geostationary satellites in the ITU Regulations itself.
"In using frequency bands for space radio services Members shall bear in mind that **radio frequencies and the geostationary orbit for satellites are limited natural resources, that they must be used efficiently and economically** so that countries or group of countries may have equitable access to both in conformity with the provisions of the Radio Regulations according to their need and the technical facilities at their disposal."[44]
The formal insertion in the ITU Convention of the principle of limited natural resources applied to the frequency spectrum and the geostationary orbit stems from the fear expressed by the developing countries that the application of the first come first served principle would have exhausted all possibilities at a time when they would have reach a level of technology sufficient to have access to it.
The use of the terms "limited" and "natural resources" is in retrospect not the most suitable.
The qualification of natural resources leads automatically -cf. the Bogota Declaration - to a tendency to apply to the geostationary orbit and the frequency spectrum rules which are applied to what is general understood by natural resources such as oil and mineral resources i.e. tangible exhaustible resources.
Some equatorial countries felt that their interest were not sufficient protected and decide to meet in order to study the matter in more detail and to agree on a common approach. This resulted on 4 December 1976 in the claim of the Equatorial Countries known as the Bogota claim which was formulated at their first meeting with the participation of Brazil, Colombia, Congo, Ecuador, Indonesia, Kenya, Uganda and Zaire.

"Bearing in mind the existence of sovereign rights over segments of the geostationary orbit, the equatorial countries consider that the applicable legal considerations in this area must take into account the following

The rationale behind this position is that the equatorial states are of the opinion that the geostationary ring as they call the geostationary orbit is an integral part of the earth and as such is not part of Outer space.

"The Geostationary ring is the product of the gravitational attraction of the earth, it is a natural resource, it's origin, nature and existence are inherent to the earth planet, like ground, the air and the water...". The sovereignty arises in the same manner as for other natural resource of earth such as atmosphere, ocean, coal, iron, petroleum, etc since the geostationary orbit is a natural resource and it stays permanently over determinate country.[45]

The US maintained on the contrary that "the geosynchronous satellite orbit is essentially a regime of satellite path not a physical natural resource".

The latter is certainly closer to reality than the thesis defended by the Equatorial Countries. The geostationary orbit in itself is not different from any other location in outer space. If a spacecraft moves on a orbit around the for instance the earth its movement is a result from the equilibrium at any given moment between the forces acting on it. These forces have two main opposite components, the gravitational and the centrifugal force which is the case for any orbit around a celestial body. In addition to these forces additional forces will act on the spacecraft leading disturbances in the orbit. The specificity of the geostationary orbit is that ...

The developing countries requested furthermore an a priori allocation of frequencies and geostationary slots. In other words frequencies and slots would be reserved for future use by developing countries based on their plans.

At a first glance the principle of a priori allocations seems an equitable solution. Unfortunately experience shows that plans seldom materialise as was originally foreseen. It is exactly here where the second part of article 33.2 of the ITU Conventions enters into play i.e. "... that they must be used efficiently and economically." The ITU Convention imposes three conditions on the use of the frequency spectrum and geostationary orbit i.e. equitable access, efficient use, economic use. These conditions are however not independent from each other and in many cases they will even be conflicting conditions. It became therefor clear that special effort had to be made to come to more objective criteria or conditions to allocate frequencies and orbital slots.

At the 1977 WARC on Broadcasting Satellites Services (BSS)[46] an allotment plan for the regions 1 and 3[47] was adopted whereby a certain number of well defined channels and geostationary slots were reserved for domestic satellite broadcasting services. The Member States of Region 2 decided for various reasons not to develop a allotment plan. In particular the fact that the 11.7 - 12.2 GHz frequency band was shared by the BSS and the Fixed Satellite Services (FSS) played an important role.[48] According the Member States a decision at that moment could jeopardize the development of one or the other and it was at this stage not possible to predict which one would justify the largest number of frequencies. The decision to allocate orbit slots and frequencies without any time limit is in contradiction with the provisions of the Outer Space Treaty which specifies that Outer Space is not subject to national appropriation ... by means of use or occupation or by any other means.

It was against this background that the WARC 1979 started its work. After lengthy discussions several non binding resolutions were adopted of which two are at the base of the 1985 and 1988 WARC. Resolution 2 dealt with equal rights of all states to use the orbit and spectrum resources.

Resolution 3 invited participants to convene a WARC to deal with the question of guaranteeing in practice equitable access to the geostationary orbit to all states i.e. first come first served versus a priori allotments.

The initiative came from the developing countries who considered an "a posteriori" approach a justification for the first come first served practice which they contested since many years. The developed countries and in particular the United States of America were opposed to an "a priori" allocation which in their opinion would be detrimental to the evolution of space telecommunications. In the meantime, at the 1982 Plenipotentiary Conference of the ITU the Member States took a next step towards the claims of the developing countries with the amendment of art. 33 by which the last paragraph was replaced by "taking into account the special needs of the developing countries and the geographical situation of particular countries."

The WARC on the use of the Geostationary-Satellite Orbit and the Planning of Space Services following Resolutions 2 and 3 adopted in 1979 took place as agreed beforehand in two sessions the first in 1985 followed by the second in 1988. Both sessions were dedicated to issues related to the use of the geostationary orbit. At the 1985 session it would be decided 1. which space services and frequency bands would be planned; 2. establish principles, technical parameters and criteria for planning; and 3. establish guidelines for regulatory procedures with respect to services and frequency bands not brought under planning. The 1988 session would implement the decisions taken at the first session.

The decisions finally taken at the World Administrative Radio Conference of 1985 and 1988 concerned only the use and exploitation of Fixed Satellite Services. These services are only part of the total satellite services package which exist.

The results of both session can be summarised as follows;

- guaranteed equitable access to specific orbit and frequency resources for a period of 20 years
- existing systems may continue their operations for a period of maximum of 20 years.

The a priori allocation has evolved in granting property rights in certain slots for a limited period in time. Some countries have exploited this possibility immediately by requesting a higher number of orbital slots than really justified for their own purposes.

The Kingdom of Tonga situated in the South Pacific is a typical example already in 1998 it attempted to claim some 30 geostationary satellite slots. INTELSAT reacted very severely against these claims. In a letter addressed to the ITU and the Chairman and Members of the International Frequency Registration Board (IFRB) INTELSAT pointed out that the slots were in their view not intended for satisfying TONGA'S own needs but rather as a means of financial speculation. " The Administration of the Kingdom of Tonga has initiated the ITU registration process on behalf of Tongasat for these orbital slots. I strongly believe that Tongasat's attempts to convert the ITU registration process into an opportunity for financial speculation in the geostationary orbit constitute an abuse of the ITU Radio Regulations and undermine the intended purpose of such regulations."[49]

INTELSAT's point of view is based on public statements made by TONGASAT and the fact that the latter offered the orbital slots or lease to interested parties. INTELSAT's letter quotes a TONGASAT document ; "In that particular portion of the orbital arc of most value to a communications satellite system, designed to serve most of the Asian countries, in addition to the Pacific and Asian countries and still reach the United States, Tonga has registered and therefore controls the last such remaining positions.

Thus Tonga possess the asset most critical to the establishment of an Asia Pacific regional communications satellite system - namely the orbital arc positions vital to economic success."

In a second letter to the Chairman and Members of the Frequency Registration board the Director General of INTELSAT expressed the view that " the attempt by Tongasat to gain control over an excessive number of orbital slots is contrary to the spirit of Article 29 of the ITU Convention (Nice 1989) ....Moreover, Tongasat's misuse of the publication and registration procedures of the Radio Regulations leads to the subversion of the spirit and intent of article 33 of the ITU Convention (Nairobi 1982)... and the underlying principles of Resolutions 2 and 4 of WARC - 79."

On the 5 July the Director general of INTELSAT informed Tonga's prime minister of the actions undertaken by INTELSAT against TONGASAT'S attempt to obtain the slots. Particular relevant is the argument used by INTELSAT for justifying its action; ".. My actions in this regard have not been intended to embarrass the Kingdom of Tonga, but the actions of TONGASAT, if allowed to be unchallenged, could establish a precedent that would seriously jeopardize the ability of all administrations to gain access to the geostationary orbit on an equal and equitable basis, and make technical coordination and efficient use of the frequency spectrum extraordinarily difficult"

The prime ministers cabinet reacted promptly in stating that it is TONGA's intend to set up an Asia Pacific regional satellite communications system similar as EUTELSAT, INMARSAT, PANAMSAT etc.

The main part of the letter confirms in strong words the feeling expressed at many occasions by other developing countries that the existing monopoly positions of developed countries and INTELSAT should be stopped.

"We do not agree ..that Tonga attempts to convert the ITU Regulation process into an opportunity for financial speculation. On the contrary, Tonga recognizes the past apparent abuse by several countries to lay claim to more orbital positions than they need, to the detriment of the developing countries....

It is no wonder that the INTELSAT signatories would subscribe to the views expressed in your letter. After all, they are anxious to protect their monopolistic positions in their countries, possibly to be challenged by Tonga and TONGASAT....

You speak of preventing such abuse from occurring. Tonga is operating in strict conformance with the radio regulations. The abuses seem instead to be on the side of those who feel threatened by competition.....

You are free to make whatever attempts you wish, to preserve INTELSAT's monopoly position. It is not up to you to judge whether it is likely that your monopolised positions will be perpetuated under the umbrella of the ITU and IFRB regulations."

Tonga nevertheless agreed under the international pressure to limit its claims to six slots only.

In the meantime TONGASAT has leased several of "its" slots to commercial entities such as APT Satellite Co. of Hong Kong.

The present situation is thus far from the noble principles underlying the ITU regulations i.e. equitable access, efficient use and economic use. The rights which are granted are similar to emphytensis which is a real right by which someone is entitled to use something as if it were his own. Interesting to note is that under roman law the shore had somewhat analogue legal status.

As explained above a State exercising sovereign rights over a territory enjoys all rights in the resources existing within the territorial limits of that territory and allowed under certain conditions the existence of private property. The sea and the shore however were excluded and could not become the private property of any one.

Hugo Grotius quotes and defends however an exception "If any part of these things is by nature susceptible of occupation, it may become the property of the one who occupies it but only in so far as such occupation does not affect its common use. Hugo Grotius concluded that it is permissible to build upon the shore if such buildings are without hindrance to public or common use of the shore. The owner of such a building may even become the owner of the ground on which it is build but this ownership will last only as long as the building last and remains occupied by its owner. Once it will be abandoned or destroyed by a will full act or by accident or natural disaster the property ends.[50]

In addition to the "misuse" of the a priori allocation by some states the a priori allocation principle has moreover led to a number of very often bona fide requests largely in excess of the total capacity of the geostationary orbit.

A way out would be to request a fixed deposit and proof that the slot will be used in a reasonable time form the acquisition date of the slot.[51]

Closely linked to the division of the geostationary orbit in slots is the frequency spectrum.

3.2. Frequency Spectrum

As mentioned earlier the frequency spectrum is also considered a limited natural resource and qualifies for *res communis omnium*.

Recent developments whereby part of the frequency spectrum have been auctioned tend to pave the way for a commercial exploitation of the frequency spectrum thereby endangering certain activities unless appropriate actions are undertaken.

A USA representative said he had made some calculations based on recent auctions and he came to the conclusion that the 2 GHz science service allocations would become a non affordable commodity if the same financial rules would apply to it.

The Australian policy in this matter may serve as an example how the spectrum has become an economic asset. The Australian government through its Spectrum Management Agency has initiated a number of actions with the objectives of:

- promoting spectrum efficiency;
- encouraging technical change;
- expanding freedom of choice;
- accelerating economic development;
- optimising the benefit to the general community.

The licenses have a maximum duration of 10 years with a possibility of renewal. The licenses are tradable and may be sold as one block, sub-divided or amalgamated with other contiguous spectrum blocks. In other words the licensee has rights similar to property rights.

The space sciences are for the moment not adversely affected by the new policy as is also the case for internationally operated services.

In the USA the FCC has auctioned only two direct broadcast licenses for some 735 million dollars. In an interview with Space News Donald Gips, the chief of the US Federal Communication Commission International Bureau stated that "Spectrum auctions might work for licensing domestic satellites services, but host of problems makes them unlikely for international satellite services."[52]

The huge amounts of money may encourage some states to try to apply the same approach for international satellite services.

At a meeting of ITU representatives, inter alia, on auctioning the Indian representative recalled that licenses in the international context is ruled by article 24 of the ITU/RR. Moreover the frequency spectrum had to be considered a natural resource available to all mankind. However, if done right, auctioning might be instrumental for arriving at a more efficient use of the spectrum. A delicate balance had to be kept between revenue-providing and non-revenue-providing users.

In order to avoid similar problems as the one encountered with the geostationary orbit it would be advisable to developed a set of rules in this field.

A solution could be to extend to the frequency spectrum the proposal advocated by S. Wiessner for the Geostationary orbit. He considers that the regime of the geostationary orbit goes beyond the *res communis* idea and favours the idea of res publica and given the international character *res publica internationalis*.[53] He proposes that part of the slots would auctioned and the revenue used for space research. Any solution should of course respect one of the basic principles of the Outer Space Treaty, i.e. guaranteeing equal access opportunities for all nations to Outer Space.

Apart from the geostationary orbit other orbits have high potential economic value for example for mobile communication systems; the low and medium earth orbits.

3.3. Low and Medium Earth Orbits (LEO, MEO)

Although it is not sure yet whether low and medium earth orbit systems may be financially viable[54] several companies have started investing money and protecting their intellectual property.

Recently some US patents have been granted TRW which gave a major concern to their competitors. Two of these patents were first published on 16 May 1995 but withdrawn by the Patent Office the same day. According to the Patent Office the withdrawal was a result of a routine quality control procedure; Both patents were finally re-published a few months later.

The TRW patents deal with medium earth orbit systems for wireless telephones. They are a continuation-in-part of a patent application dated May, 28, 1992 which is a continuation-in-part of an earlier patent application filed on April 22, 1991 abandoned.

According to TRW officials these patents would prevent others from using the medium earth orbits as the basis for providing worldwide mobile satellite communications to pocket-sized phones.[55]

If this would be the case the statement quoted by Alan Cane in the Financial Times would be true; "It is bizarre that a company could hope to patent thousands of square miles in space".[56]

The TRW patent concerns a satellite-based cellular telecommunications system comprising a number of satellites placed in a plurality of inclined orbits about the earth at an altitude of between approximately 5,600 and 10,000 nautical miles. The characteristics of the orbits, the number of satellites in earth orbit and the altitude of the satellites are part of the invention.

US Patent 5433726 of July 18, 1995 is of particular relevance, the background of the invention or the state of the art as quoted in the patent relates to low earth orbit systems.

"These proposed cellular telephone systems typically include a large constellation of telecommunications satellites in low earth orbit at an altitude between approximately 400 and 1000 nautical miles..."

This implicitly means that the inventor considers that the use of medium earth orbits for mobile telecommunication systems is not part of the state of the art and therefore new.

The invention itself may be best summarised by the first and main claim of the patent: "A method of providing medium-earth-orbit satellite-based communications be-

tween low-power mobile handsets having an omni-directional antenna and a gateway station through a satellite forming part of a satellite constellation, comprising the steps of:
- launching a plurality of satellites to an orbiting altitude between 5,600 and 10,00 nautical miles, wherein at least one satellite has a reduced antenna field of view (FOV) less than full earth coverage;
- orienting said satellites in a plurality of orbital planes which are inclined at a predetermined inclination angle with respect to the equatorial plane of the earth;
- receiving, by at least one of said satellites, radio frequency (RF) signals from a plurality of mobile handsets which transmit said RF signals using their omni-directional antennas; and
- overlapping a portion of a coverage region of a departing satellite with a portion of a coverage region of an arriving satellite, including assignment means having a predetermined criterion of assignment that calls placed to or from a user located within the coverage overlap region are assigned to said arriving satellite."

The patent contains in total 35 claims of which many include the use of medium earth orbits be it elliptical or circular orbits.

US Patent 5439190 of August 8, 1995 (one of the two patents which were re-published) describes a similar system but its claims do not refer to the medium earth orbit but are more system oriented.

Without going in to too much detail of the technicalities of patent law one can conclude that neither of the TRW patents claim the use "as such" of the medium earth orbit as "the" invention. It is in fact the combination of this kind of orbit and a plurality of satellites functioning in a particular manner which is claimed. It is, however, true that the scope of the claims is rather broad making it therefore difficult to escape infringement when using similar systems in the medium earth orbits or as Bruce Gerding -TRW managing director of the Odyssey programs, says "The scope of the patent protection in the US is broad enough to exclude other service providers deploying a commercial viable MEO system".[57]

The question "is it possible to patent the use of certain orbits or trajectories" should probably be answered affirmatively if the use is specified i.e. the orbits or trajectories in abstracto will in most countries be unpatentable.. This assumes of course that the use of this specific orbit or trajectory is not new and not obvious to the layman. Depending on the country in which the patent application is filed other conditions should be fulfilled for the invention to be patentable. Arthur Clarke could have patented, when for the first time he conceived in the early forties the use of the geostationary orbit for telecommunication by using one or more geostationary satellites. The same would be true for the Hohmann transfer orbit which is an elliptical transfer orbit to go from one planet to the other. The limited duration of patent protection would probably prevented him from making any money out of it. This is unfortunately the case for many pioneer inventions related to space applications, the concept of solar power satellites patented by Peter Glazer is a typical example of this.

Important to note is that patent rights are granted by states and their effect is limited to the territory of the state which granted the patent. In the USA the outer space patent act has extended the US patent law to spacecraft and/or activities on board of spacecraft registered by the USA. For this reason it is difficult to talk about property rights obtained by TRW in medium earth orbits (assuming that the wording of the claims would cover the use of medium earth orbits for mobile telephone communication as such) not only are these rights limited to certain applications, in other words, these orbits could be used for other purposes without infringing the TRW patents. Furthermore any spacecraft not registered in the USA could use the orbits even for mobile telecommunication purposes without infringing the US patent.[58]

The importance of patents in space applications calls for a special regime for intellectual property in outer space, recent developments makes this a matter of urgency. In my opinion the best solution would be to consider, insofar as intellectual property is concerned, outer space as a whole as one territory for which the World Intellectual Property Organisation (WIPO) would be responsible. WIPO would be empowered to deliver patents for outer space, special rules should be established for dealing with infringement issues. This solution would give legal stability which is absolutely needed for enhancing the scope of space applications.[59]

Conclusion

If we wish to enhance Space applications, a clear and precise legal situation including property rights should be established. Property rights were banned from the Outer Space Treaty for social and political reasons. The underlying reasons changed over the years and made it possible to include implicitly in the Moon Treaty the acquisition of property. Since then nothing happened on the international scene but, in the meantime some forms of property were introduced by using legal means not really foreseen for this purpose e.g. the ITU and patent law. Time has therefore maybe come to review the matter and to settle property rights in an appropriate legal form.

---

* The views expressed herein are those of the author and do not necessarily reflect those of ESA.

1 cf. The bilingual edition: Hugo Grotius "The Freedom of the Seas", Oxford University Press 1916.

2 This excerpt is quoted by several authors e.g. by L.F.E. Goldie in "Is there a general international law of original ownership? The possible relevance of general doctrines governing the possession of deep ocean-bed resources" proceedings of the..... coll. of the IISL, pages 287 - 289 and by Emilio J. Sahurie in " The International law of Antarctica" New Haven Press, page 369.

3 Not all are in favor of studying Roman Law concepts in relation to Space Law cf. Ryszard Hara in "Space Law and the Roman Law concepts" 27 coll. 1984 of IISL, pp. 51 - 57

concluded that reaching for roman law concepts when analyzing problems of space law is neither necessary nor useful. The absolute necessity may be contested but the usefulness in my opinion certainly not.

[4] Kaser & Wubbe Tjeenk Willink 1971, Romeins Privaatrecht.

[5] "Res nullius naturaliter fit primi occupantis".

[6] supra 2 Emilio J. Sahurie page 369.

[7] Supra 1 Hugo Grotius; page 39 "But where in this case is that corporal possession of physical appropriation, without no ownerships arise ? There appears to be nothing truer than what our learned jurists have enunciated, namely, that since the sea is just as unsusceptible of physical appropriation as the air, it cannot be attached to the possession of any nation".

[8] "as you possess it-you may keep it" Gaius, IV, 148.

[9] Supra 1 page 43.

[10] Manual on Space Law , N. Jasentuliyana and R. Lee page 6.

[11] This is based on our two possibilities approach one could however imagine other solutions.

[12] A prerequisite is of course that the things over which one wishes to acquire title of sovereignty were res nullius or terra nullius prior to the alleged discovery. This assumption is certain valid in most circumstances with respect to Outer Space.

[13] S. Pufendorf, De Jure Naturae et Gentium Libri Octo, quoted by Emilio Sahurie.

[14]In the Netherlands v. United States over the MIANGAS Islands, Max Huber insists on the inter-temporal basis i.e. the conditions which existed at a given moment are not sufficient to keep the property but they should follow the conditions required by the evolution of law. (A.A. II 829, 4 April 1928).

[15]In the Clipperton Island Arbitration the Mexican claim was based on the assertion that Spain had gained the title by the discovery and that title had been transferred to Mexico through state succession. Mexico could however not establish any proof of Spanish sovereignty over the islands whereas France could prove the rediscovery by a French officer who was sent to the island to claim it for France.

[16] supra 2 page 259.

[17] Smedal by Sahurie supra 2 , page 395.

[18] As the acts of sovereignty required to be effectively performed, the geographical circumstances of the are in dispute can be relevant, for it would not be logical to require the same intensity of exercise of sovereignty as elsewhere when an area is uninhabited, inhospitable and/or of difficult access.
Santiago Torres Bernardez "Territory, acquisition", in Encyclopedia of Public International Law, Vol 10 , North Holland, p 499 .

[19] S. M. Williams, "Celestial bodies" , Vol 11, p.52.

[20] "The supreme, absolute and uncontrollable power by which any independent state is governed", Black's law dictionary.

[21] Sylvia Maureen Williams came to the same conclusion in "The exploitation and use of natural resources in the new law of the sea and the law of Outer Space" 29 Colloq. IISL (1986), pp. 198-204.

[22] See also Space Lax Committee of the International Law Association (1970), 54 International Law Association Proceedings (The Hague), 430.

[23] In fact two opposite views existed for some time and had both its defenders, e.g. according to Gorove: "an individual ... could lawfully appropriate any part of Outer Space", Gorove, "Interpreting Article II of the Outer Space Treaty", (1696), 37 Fordham Law Rev.

[24] International and Comparative Law Quarterly, Vol. 36, Jan. 1987, pp. 142-151. The Law of Outer Space and Natural Resources, Sylvia Maureen Williams.

[25] Statement made by the Belgian delegate when the matter was raised in the Legal Sub-committee of the UN and quoted in Manual of Space Law , Volume III, page 65.

[26] Emphasis added - Statement made by the French Delegate on December 17, 1966 and quoted Manual of Space Law in volume III page 95.

[27] see Eilene Galloway; "Issues in implementing the agreement governing the activities of states on the moon and other celestial bodies " , proceedings of the 23 rd colloquium on the law of outer space , 1980, pp 19-24.

[28]Article 19 of the Agreement provides that it shall enter in force on the thirtieth day following the date of deposit of the fifth instrument of ratification.

[29] Martin Menter " Commercial Space Activities under the Moon Treaty " 23 rd colloquium of the IISL, 1980 , p 35 - 47.

[30] Article 1 reads " The provisions of this Agreement shall also apply to other celestial bodies within the solar system, other than the earth , except in so far legal norms enter into force with respect to any these celestial bodies ".

[31] e.g. preamble of the Moon Agreement; "Bearing in mind the benefits which may be derived from the exploitation of the natural resources of the moon and other celestial bodies."

[32] quoted in Emilio J. Sahurie "The international Law of Antarctica", Martinus Nijhoff Publishers, 1992.

[33] supra 67 page 27. The introduction also contains on page 2 an interesting passage "Now, as there are some things which every man enjoys in common with all other men, and as there are other things which are distinctly his and belong to no one else, just so has nature willed that some of the things which she has created for the use of mankind remain common to all, and that others through the industry and labor of each man become his own."

[34]see for further information J.F. Galloway "Political Philosophy and the Common Heritage of Mankind concept in International Law ", 23 rd colloquium of IISL, 1980, pp 25 - 28; and S.M. Williams" The Exploitation and Use of Natural Resources in the New Law of the Sea and the Law of Outer Space ", 29 th colloquium of IISL, 1986, pp. 198 - 204.

[35] Section of International law report to the House of Delegates, American Bar Association, April 1980. The understanding (A) is similar to one attached by the US Senate when ratifying the 1967 Outer Space Treaty.

[36] UN Doc. A/AC.105/C2/L71; "The natural resources of the Moon and other celestial bodies shall be the common heritage of all mankind".

[37] UN Doc. A/AC.105 PV.203 dated 16 July, 1979.

[38] Gerard O'Neil "Directions for Research" space manufacturing facilities space colonies 2 proceedings of the third Princeton/AIAA conference may 1977 pp 27-32.

[39] O'Leary "Mass driver retrievals of earth approaching asteroids " in Space Manufacturing facilities II, proceedings of the third Princeton/AIAA Conference 1977, pp 157-168.

[40] see Brooks, National Control of Planetary Bodies, 32 Journal of Air Law and Commerce.

[41] N. Jasentuliyana "International space law and cooperation and the mining of asteroids". Speech delivered to the

International Space University, 30 July 1990, Toronto, Canada.

[42] Ernst Fasan "Some legal Problems regarding the Moon", 23 rd colloquium of the IISL, 1980, pp 9 - 11.

[43] cf. Resolution Spa 2.1.

[44] Article 33 of the ITU Convention (emphasis added).

[45] (UN General Assembly Resolution 1721 (XVI), December 20, 1961) (R. Lauria White et al. "Evolving principles of space communication regulation in the ITU: 1959-1985" 31st coll 1988 pp 304 -311 .

[46] According the ITU Radio Regulations the Broadcasting Satellite Services provides signals intended for reception by the general public. through either individual or community reception; Fixed Satellite Services are intended for reception by a limited number of receivers such as telephone, telex, facsimile, video etc...

[47] Region 1 covers essentially Europe, Africa and the (former) Soviet Union , Region 2 North, Central and South America and Region 3 South and East Asia and the Western Pacific basin.

[48] The allocation of the frequency band for certain activities differs from one region to another and is subject to revision.

[49] Letter dated 8 June 1990 from Dean Burch, Director General of INTELSAT , addressed to the ITU and letter dated 12 June 1990 to the Chairman and Members of the IFRB.

[50]page 30 "It becomes therefore the property of the occupier, but his ownership lasts no loner than his occupation lasts, inasmuch as the sea seems by nature to resist ownership."

[51] This is already in the USA where the FCC to weed out spurious applications requires an 80.000$ deposit from all satellite proposals and also demand proof that the system developers have the money needed to build, launch and operate their system for at least one year. - Space News September 16-22,1996, p.4.

[52] Space News, Vol. 7 N°29, July 22-28,1996, page 1.

[53] S. Wiessner "access to a *res publica internationalis*: the case of the geostationary orbit" 29 th coll. 1986 pp. 147-153.

[54]Space & Satellite Business, December 1994/ January 1995, p. 28; "Can LEO systems be a roaring success?".

[55] Space News, May 1-7,1995, Vol. 6, N° 17, page & and page 20, "TRW's Patent Claim Stuns Inmarsat Unit".

[56]Financial Times, 8 May 1995, Alan Cane; "Clash over patent on space looms for telecoms groups".

[57] Infra 55.

[58] For a more in depth study on these issues, see "Patentability of orbits and trajectories" R. Oosterlinck, Lectures at the International Space University, to be published end 1996.

[59] R. Oosterlinck "Intellectual Property and Space activities", Proc. Of the 26th Coll. of IISL, 1983 pp. 161-164.

ADDENDA

REPORT OF THE DISCUSSIONS HELD AFTER THE SESSIONS OF THE 39TH COLLOQUIUM ON THE LAW OF OUTER SPACE

On the last morning of the IISL Colloquium, the Chairmen and Rapporteurs of each session gave a short summary of the papers presented and highlighted the issues that in their view merited further discussion. The IISL President, Mr. Jasentuliyana chaired the discussions. Below, an attempt is made to reflect the points that were raised, but it is of course impossible to give a complete overview of everything that was said. It is also possible that some comments are omitted, or do not entirely reflect the speaker's intention. Nevertheless this short overview may give an indication of current concerns within the International Institute of Space Law.

Property rights on the moon and other celestial bodies

The discussions focused on the need of clear regulation before private enterprise would start acting and on the finding that we have to know what to regulate before clear regulations are possible.

Dr. E. Galloway was of the opinion that too much emphasis was placed on the regulation of the natural resources of the moon without defining what those natural resources really are. She noted that it is not clear how to make profit on the moon. Although such inventions as solar power satellites may be used to make profit, this is an expensive and risky business. Before we start regulating we have to know the scientific and technical facts. *Prof. J. Galloway* replied that profit can be made from resources brought back from the moon, such as Helium 3. He suggested that first clarification of present science and technology for space development should be sought, before starting the discussion on rights and obligations regarding the moon and other celestial bodies. On the contrary, *Mr. R. Oosterlinck* held that regulation should come first, before exploitation is possible.

Prof. M. Andem emphasized the importance of international law and treaties for regulating states as well as the private sector. He stated that clear rules are needed, and that the elaboration of existing treaties would be the best solution. He held the view that space law should not be seen as a separate area of law, but together with all other areas of law, bearing in mind the common heritage of mankind principle. He added that cooperation with scientists is necessary in order to know what to regulate.

Dr. W. Wirin noted that although there has been irresponsible exploitation of natural resources on Earth, under space law states remain responsible, and hence must control the activity of private enterprises. On the other hand, some formulation or maximum charge for entrepreneurs is needed so that they can assess the risks of the endeavour; otherwise they will not engage in it. On the other hand, taking risk is inherent to commercial enterprise! He also agreed with Mr. Oosterlinck that waiting to know what we can find in outer space before regulating the exploitation simply denies the fact that we can find something in space. *Mr. N. Jasentuliyana* agreed on the need to take into account the interests of the private sector.

Dr. E. Galloway concluded these discussions by reminding that only 9 states have ratified the Moon Agreement because of the "common heritage of mankind" principle, and that this principle is NOT included in the Outer Space Treaty, as so many authors wrongly assert. She recommended that action be taken on the issue of the Moon Agreement.

Dispute settlement

Dr. Veschunov recalled that international satellite operators are subjects of public international law. The Brussels Convention of 1974 is important for this issue; it provides that a satellite operator as a provider does not bear responsibility for the possible violation of copyrights. There are mainly three entities involved in the process of providing a programme: (1) the manufacturer of the programme software, (2) the technical satellite operator, dealing only with the technical transfer of the signal from point to point, and (3) the distributor of the programme. Dr. Veschunov held that only the entities mentioned under (1) and (3) could be held liable. He also recalled that it is not impossible for an international organisation to be sued.

Sharing of benefits from space activities

Prof. F. Lyall recalled that the ITU system of "first come, first served" has been abused because people found out that they can make money out of it. *Mr. M. Nilsen* of Tongasat answered that in 1987, the motivation was that INTELSAT had not properly planned the repartition, and had not considered future needs. The positive impacts after the request of Tonga were transformed in negative ones from 1990 on. He stated that Tongasat was an adequate business solution in that area. *Prof. Lyall* held that among the more than 150 members of the ITU, not all have real needs for orbital positions, and *Mr. R. Oosterlinck* added that a good commercial success is not necessarily a good example of respect for the principle of sharing of benefits! Regarding the idea of a filing fee, *Mr. N. Jasentuliyana* believed that it might be useful, and added that if the fee is returnable, its amount is irrelevant.

Regarding Intelsat, *Prof. J. Galloway* stressed once more that public actors such as Intelsat must be price conscious. If Intelsat is privatized, it would result in an oligopoly. Thus, the Intelsat spin-off should be broken up. Mr. N. Jasentuliyana added that small nations will sell their shares in the Intelsat affiliate; this will result in privatization of the satellite market.

Space debris

Mr. A. Golrounia stated that in his view, the only way to realize protection of the environment in outer space is the introduction of fees. Those who launch a satellite could be required to pay a fee for the contamination they generate. The only way to realize this is to have an international forum which could adequately deal with the questions of private enterprises.

Dr. L. Perek added that concerning the prevention of pollution, two points must be stressed. The first concerns the participation of launching entities taking measures to limit the pollution. The scientific community is now in a position to check the pollution in outer space, and can thus verify whether regulations have been complied with or not. The adoption of a Code of Conduct between the UN and launching authorities may be an idea. The second point concerns the removal of actual debris from outer space (cleaning). At present, we do not know how to do that. The economic implications of the problem must be taken into account. In conclusion, Dr. Perek said that he was confident that cooperation will lead to limitation of debris. *Mr. N. Jasentuliyana* mentioned that technical standards rather than legal standards or SARPs are required to limit debris. *Mr. D. Burnett* proposed that insurance companies could give certificates in order to make sure there is money to clear up. The model already in force for the sea could be applied to outer pace. *Dr. Perek* replied that we would first have to determine how much the cleaning of outer space would cost!

Remote sensing

Dr. M. Vivod (Slovenia) proposed that some form of institutionalization of remote sensing is required.

Mr. D. Burnett (USA) expressed his concern that private space enterprises would not particularly welcome competition from a new public international organization. *Mr. N. Jasentuliyana* (UN/Sri Lanka) added that SPOT-Image and other private providers are already developing a world-wide market for space data.

Mr Vivod said that he did not specifically urge for a new organization, but only for the need for legislation in this field.

Legal framework for commercial space activities

Prof. H.A. Wassenbergh (The Netherlands) pointed out that a new approach to international space law is necessary. He illustrated his idea by referring to the Moot Court Competition on space law held the day before; it was striking that three judges of the International Court of Justice could find no solution to the problem (although that was of course not the purpose of the competition). In the case, we saw how the distinction between tort and contract law can be blurred. If absolute liability under the Liability Convention follows a satellite, current space law is inadequate to deal with reality. Therefore, we need new international space law. *Ms. T. Masson-Zwaan* (The Netherlands) reacted by agreeing that space activities are nowadays more commercially oriented, and it would be a good idea to complement existing law, but disagreed that current public international space law should be put aside. Bilateral contracts can supplement and clarify space law. *Prof. Wassenbergh* said that a distinction between governmental tasks and the commercial aspects is required. We can find the same distinction in the aviation field: ICAO adopts SARPs, and the economic problems are regulated through bilateral or open sky agreements. *Dr W. Wirin* (USA) was of the opinion that some restrictions on commercial activity are necessary, but agreed that governmental responsibility and regulation can stifle the emerging space industry.

Tanja Masson-Zwaan
IISL Secretary/Colloquium Coordinator

INTERNATIONAL INSTITUTE OF SPACE LAW
of the
INTERNATIONAL ASTRONAUTICAL FEDERATION

Standing Committee on the Status of International Agreements Relating to Activities in Outer Space

Annual Report - 1996

Andrei D. Terekov, Senior Legal Officer
United Nations Office of Legal Affairs

Background

At the meeting of the IISL Board of Directors held at Brighton, United Kingdom, in October 1987, the Board decided to create a standing committee of the Institute to prepare and submit at each annual Colloquium a report on the status of agreements relating to activities in outer space.

Institute members who can contribute substantively to the work of the committee are invited to serve on it. Membership is open to any interested IISL member. The committee members help collect, review and verify data concerning selected space agreements. Agreements of general global applicability or regional applicability are selected for reporting. Bilateral agreements are not included in the report. In general, the agreements included in the present report, and their status, are believed to be valid as of 1 January 1996.

Coded entries are used in the table as follows:

R = ratification, accession or succession
S = signature only
D = declaration of acceptance of rights and obligations

When no entry is made in a column opposite a state's name, that state has not signed that agreement, or is not a party to it, or that state has withdrawn from the agreement.

COMMITTEE MEMBERSHIP

Prof. Dr. K.-H. Böckstiegel
Institut für Luft- und Weltraumrecht
University of Cologne
Albertus-Magnus-Platz 5000
Cologne, 41 GERMANY

Prof. Carl Q. Christol
1041 Anoka Place
Pacific Palisades, CA 90272
USA

Prof. Dr. Aldo Armando Cocca
Lavalle 1527, piso 10
1048 Buenos Aires
ARGENTINA

Prof. Dr. Isabella Diederiks-Verschoor
President Emeritus, IISL
Leestraat 43, 3743 EH Baarn
NETHERLANDS

Dr. Stephen E. Doyle
3431 Bridget Brae
Shingle Springs, CA 95682
USA

Dr. Eilene Galloway
4612 29th Place, NW
Washington, D.C. 20008 USA

Prof. Dr. Andrzej Gorbiel
ul. Marysinska 90 m.69
91-850 Lodz POLAND

Prof. Dr. Vladimir Kopal
IAF General Counsel
Vidlicová 2200
16000 Prague 6 - Dejvice
CZECH REPUBLIC

Prof. Francis Lyall
Department of Public Law
University of Aberdeen
Aberdeen, AB92UB
SCOTLAND

Mr. G. Lafferranderie
Legal Adviser, ESA
8-10, rue Mario Nikis
Paris 75738
FRANCE

Dr. HE Qizhi
Legal Advisor
Department of Treaty & Law
Ministry of Foreign Affairs
Beijing
CHINA

Dr. W. von Noorden
Legal Adviser, INMARSAT
40 Melton St., Euston Square
London NW1 2EQ
ENGLAND

Prof. Dr. Neri Sybesma-Knol
Vrije Universiteit Brussel
Pleinlaan 2, 1050 Brussels
BELGIUM

Dr. A. D. Terekhov (Chairman)
Office of Legal Affairs
Room 3430G, UN Secretariat
New York, NY 10017
USA

Judge V. S. Vereshchetin
International Court of Justice
Peace Palace 2517 KJ
The Hague
NETHERLANDS

AGREEMENTS INCLUDED

1. 1963 NTBT - Treaty Banning Nuclear Weapon Tests in the Atmosphere, in Outer Space and Under Water; done at Moscow on 5 August 1963; entered into force on 10 October 1963. (14 UST 1313; TIAS 5433; 480 UNTS 43)

2. 1967 OST - Treaty on Principles Governing the Activities of States in the Exploration and Use of Outer Space, including the Moon and Other Celestial Bodies; done at Washington, London and Moscow on 27 January 1967; entered into force on 10 October 1967. (18 UST 2410; TIAS 6347; 610 UNTS 205)

3. 1968 ARRA - Agreement on the Rescue of Astronauts, the Return of Astronauts and the Return of Objects Launched into Outer Space; done at Washington, London and Moscow on 22 April 1968; entered into force on 3 December 1968. (19 UST 7570; TIAS 6599; 672 UNTS 119)

4. 1972 LIAB - Convention on International Liability for Damage Caused by Space Objects; done at Washington, London and Moscow on 29 March 1972; entered into force on 1 September 1972. (24 UST 2389; TIAS 7762; 961 UNTS 187)

5. 1975 REG - Convention on Registration of Objects Launched into Outer Space; done at New York on 14 January 1975; entered into force on 15 September 1976. (28 UST 695; TIAS 8480; 1023 UNTS 15)

6. 1979 MOON - Agreement Governing the Activities of States on the Moon and Other Celestial Bodies, done at New York on 18 December 1979; entered into force on 11 July 1984. (18 ILM 1434; UN doc. A/RES/34/68 of 14 December 1979, Annex)

7. 1971 INTL - Agreement Relating to the International Telecommunications Satellite Organization (INTELSAT) with annexes, and Operating Agreement Relating to the International Telecommunications Satellite Organization with annex; done at Washington on 20 August 1971; entered into force on 12 February 1973. (23 UST 3813, 4091; TIAS 7532)

8. 1976 INMR - Convention on the International Maritime Satellite Organization (INMARSAT) with annex, and the Operating Agreement on the International Maritime Satellite Organization with annex; done at London on 3 September 1976; entered into force on 16 July 1976. (31 UST 1, 135; TIAS 9605)

9. 1971 INTR - Agreement on the Establishment of the "Intersputnik" International System and Organization of Space Communications; done at Moscow on 15 November 1971; entered into force on 12 July 1972. (862 UNTS 3)

10. 1976 INTC - Agreement on Cooperation in the Exploration and Use of Outer Space for Peaceful Purposes (INTERCOSMOS); done at Moscow on 13 July 1976; entered into force on 25 March 1977. (16 ILM 1)

11. 1976 ARBS - The Agreement of the Arab Corporation for Space Communications (ARABSAT); done at Cairo on Wednesday, 14 Rabi Al Akhar 1396 H., corresponding to April 14, 1976; entered into force on July 16, 1976. (Space Law and Related Documents, U.S. Senate, 101st Congress, 2nd Session, 395 (1990))

12. 1975 ESA - Convention for the establishment of a European Space Agency (ESA) with annexes; done at Paris on 30 May 1975; entered into force on 30 October 1980. (14 ILM 864)

13. 1982 EUTL - Convention establishing the European telecommunications satellite organization (EUTELSAT); done at Paris on 15 July 1982; entered into force on 1 September 1985. (XI Annals of Air and Space Law 416 (1986); UK Misc. No.4, Cmnd. 9154 (1984))

14. 1983 EUMT - Convention for the establishment of a European organization for the exploitation of meteorological satellites (EUMETSAT); done at Geneva on 24 May 1983; entered into force on 19 June 1986. (Federal Republic of Germany <u>Bundesgesetzblatt</u>, Jahrang 1987, Teil 11, p. 256 (1987). This Convention has been published in the national bulletins of the ratifying States)

15. 1974 BRUS - Convention relating to the distribution of programme-carrying signals transmitted by satellite; done at Brussels on 21 May 1974; entered into force on 25 August 1979. (1144 UNTS 3)

The texts of all the above agreements, except 1974 BRUS, 1982 EUTL and 1983 EUMT, were published in Space Law and Related Documents, U.S. Senate, 101st Congress, 2nd Session, June 1990.

Status of International Agreements Relating to Activities in Outer Space

TREATY

STATE	(1) 1963 NTBT	(2) 1967 OST	(3) 1968 ARRA	(4) 1972 LIAB	(5) 1975 REG	(6) 1979 MOON	(7) 1971 INTL	(8) 1976 INMR	(9) 1971 INTR	(10) 1976 INTC	(11) 1976 ARBS	(12) 1975 ESA	(13) 1982 EUTL	(14) 1983 EUMT	(15) 1974 BRUS
Afghanistan	R	R					R		R						
Albania													R		
Algeria	S	R		S			R	R			R				
Andorra													R		
Angola							R								
Antigua and Barbuda	R	R	R	R	R										
Argentina	R	R	R	R	R		R	R							S
Armenia	R						R						R		R
Australia	R	R	R	R	R	R	R	R							R
Austria	R	R	R	R	R	R	R					R	R	R	R
Azerbaijan							R						R		
Bahamas	R	R	R				R	R							
Bahrain							R	R			R				
Bangladesh	R	R					R	R							
Barbados		R	R				R								
Belarus	R	R	R	R	R			R	R				R		
Belgium	R	R	R	R	R		R	R				R	R	R	S
Benin	R	R		R			R								
Bhutan	R						R								
Bolivia	R	S	S				R								
Bosnia and Herzegovina													R		R
Botswana	R	S	R	R			R								
Brazil	R	R	R	R			R	R							S
Brunei Darussalam							R	R							
Bulgaria	R	R	R	R	R			R	R	R					
Burkina Faso	S	R					R								
Burundi	S	S		S	S		S								
Cambodia				S											
Cameroon	S	S	R				R	R							
Canada	R	R	R	R	R		R	R				(1)			
Cape Verde	R						R								
Central African Republic	R	S		S			R								
Chad	R						R								

STATE	TREATY (1) 1963 NTBT	(2) 1967 OST	(3) 1968 ARRA	(4) 1972 LIAB	(5) 1975 REG	(6) 1979 MOON	(7) 1971 INTL	(8) 1976 INMR	(9) 1971 INTR	(10) 1976 INTC	(11) 1976 ARBS	(12) 1975 ESA	(13) 1982 EUTL	(14) 1983 EUMT	(15) 1974 BRUS
Chile	R	R	R	R	R	R	R	R							
China		R	R	R	R		R	R							
Colombia	R	S	S	S			R	R							
Congo			S				R								
Costa Rica	R		S	S			R	R							
Cote d'Ivoire	R						R								S
Croatia	R						R	R					R		R
Cuba		R	R	R	R			R	R	R					
Cyprus	R	R	R	R	R		R						R		S
Czech Republic	R	R	R	R	R		R	R	R	R			R		
Dem. People's Rep. of Korea									R						
Denmark	R	R	R	R	R		R	R				R	R	R	
Djibouti											R				
Dominican Republic	R	R	S	R			R								
Ecuador	R	R	R	R			R								
Egypt	R	R	R	S			R	R			R				
El Salvador	R	R	R	S			R								
Equatorial Guinea	R	R													
Ethiopia	S	S					R								
Fiji	R	R	R	R			R								
Finland	R	R	R	R			R	R				R	R	R	
France		R	R	R	R	S	R	R				R	R	R	S
Gabon	R		R	R			R	R							
Gambia	R	S	R	S											
Georgia								R	R				R		
Germany	R	R	R	R	R		R	R	R			R	R	R	R
Ghana	R	S	S	S			R	R							
Greece	R	R	R	R			R	R					R	R	R
Guatemala	R			S		S	R								
Guinea							R								
Guinea-Bissau	R	R	R												
Guyana		S	R												
Haiti	S	S	S	S			R								
Holy See		S					R						R		

STATE	TREATY (1) 1963 NTBT	(2) 1967 OST	(3) 1968 ARRA	(4) 1972 LIAB	(5) 1975 REG	(6) 1979 MOON	(7) 1971 INTL	(8) 1976 INMR	(9) 1971 INTR	(10) 1976 INTC	(11) 1976 ARBS	(12) 1975 ESA	(13) 1982 EUTL	(14) 1983 EUMT	(15) 1974 BRUS
Honduras	R	S		S			R								
Hungary	R	R	R	R	R		R		R	R			R		
Iceland	R	R	R	S			R	R					R		
India	R	R	R	R	R	S	R	R							
Indonesia	R	S					R	R							
Iran (Islamic Republic of)	R	S	R	R	S		R	R							
Iraq	R	R	R	R			R	R			R				
Ireland	R	R	R	R			R					R	R	R	
Israel	R	R	R	R			R	R							S
Italy	R	R	R	R			R	R				R	R	R	R
Jamaica	R	R	S				R								
Japan	R	R	R	R	R		R	R							
Jordan	R	S	S	S			R				R				
Kazakstan							R		R						
Kenya	R	R		R			R								R
Kuwait	R	R	R	R			R	R			R				
Kyrgyzstan							R		R						
Lao People's Dem. Republic	R	R	R	R					R						
Latvia								R					R		
Lebanon	R	R	R	S			R	R			R				S
Lesotho		S	S												
Liberia	R							R							
Libyan Arab Jamahiriya	R	R					R				R				
Liechtenstein				R			R						R		
Lithuania													R		
Luxembourg	R	S	S	R			R						R		
Madagascar	R	R	R				R								
Malawi	R						R								
Malaysia	R	S	S				R	R							
Maldives			R												
Mali	S	R		R			R								
Malta	R		S	R			R	R					R		
Mauritania	R						R				R				

STATE	TREATY (1) 1963 NTBT	(2) 1967 OST	(3) 1968 ARRA	(4) 1972 LIAB	(5) 1975 REG	(6) 1979 MOON	(7) 1971 INTL	(8) 1976 INMR	(9) 1971 INTR	(10) 1976 INTC	(11) 1976 ARBS	(12) 1975 ESA	(13) 1982 EUTL	(14) 1983 EUMT	(15) 1974 BRUS
Mauritius	R	R	R				R	R							
Mexico	R	R	R	R	R	R	R	R							R
Micronesia (Fed. States of)							R								
Monaco			S				R	R					R		
Mongolia	R	R	R	R	R				R	R					
Morocco	R	R	R	R		R	R				R				R
Mozambique							R	R							
Myanmar	R	R	S												
Nepal	R	R	R	S			R								
Netherlands	R	R	R	R	R	R	R	R				R	R	R	
New Zealand	R	R	R	R			R	R							
Nicaragua	R	S	S	S	S		R		R						R
Niger	R	R	R	R	R		R								
Nigeria	R	R	R				R	R							
Norway	R	R	R	R	R		R	R				R	R	R	
Oman				S			R	R			R				
Pakistan	R	R	R	R	R	R	R	R							
Panama	R	S		R			R	R							R
Papua New Guinea	R	R	R	R			R								
Paraguay	S						R								
Peru	R	R	R	S	R	S	R	R							R
Philippines	R	S	S	S		R	R	R							
Poland	R	R	R	R	R		R	R	R	R			R		
Portugal	S		R				R	R					R	R	R
Qatar				R			R	R			R				
Republic of Korea	R	R	R	R	R		R	R							
Republic of Moldova													R		
Romania	R	R	R	R		S	R	R	R	R			R		
Russian Federation	R	R	R	R	R		R	R	R	R			R		R
Rwanda	R	S	S	S			R								
Samoa	R														
San Marino	R	R	R										R		
Saudi Arabia		R		R			R	R			R				
Senegal	R		S	R			R	R							S

STATE	TREATY (1) 1963 NTBT	(2) 1967 OST	(3) 1968 ARRA	(4) 1972 LIAB	(5) 1975 REG	(6) 1979 MOON	(7) 1971 INTL	(8) 1976 INMR	(9) 1971 INTR	(10) 1976 INTC	(11) 1976 ARBS	(12) 1975 ESA	(13) 1982 EUTL	(14) 1983 EUMT	(15) 1974 BRUS
Seychelles	R	R	R	R	R										
Sierra Leone	R	R	S	S											
Singapore	R	R	R	R	S		R	R							
Slovakia	R	R	R	R	R			R	R	R			R		
Slovenia	R		R	R											R
Somalia	S	S	S				R				R				
South Africa	R	R	R	S			R	R							
Spain	R	R		R	R		R	R				R	R	R	S
Sri Lanka	R	R		R			R	R							
Sudan	R						R				R				
Suriname	R														
Swaziland	R		R				R								
Sweden	R	R	R	R	R		R	R				R	R	R	
Switzerland	R	R	R	R	R		R	R				R	R	R	R
Syrian Arab Republic	R	R	R	R			R		R		R				
Tajikistan									R						
Thailand	R	R	R				R								
Togo	R	R		R			R								
Tonga	R	R	R												
Trinidad and Tobago	R	S		R			R								
Tunisia	R	R	R	R			R	R			R				
Turkey	R	R	S				R	R					R	R	
Turkmenistan									R						
Uganda	R	R					R								
Ukraine	R	R	R	R	R			R					R		
United Arab Emirates							R	R			R				
United Kingdom	R	R	R	R	R		R	R				R	R	R	
United Rep. of Tanzania	R			S			R								
United States of America	R	R	R	R	R		R	R							R
Uruguay	R	R	R	R	R	R	R								
Venezuela	R	R	S	R			R								
Viet Nam		R					R		R	R					
Yemen	R	R	R				R		R		R				

STATE	TREATY (1) 1963 NTBT	(2) 1967 OST	(3) 1968 ARRA	(4) 1972 LIAB	(5) 1975 REG	(6) 1979 MOON	(7) 1971 INTL	(8) 1976 INMR	(9) 1971 INTR	(10) 1976 INTC	(11) 1976 ARBS	(12) 1975 ESA	(13) 1982 EUTL	(14) 1983 EUMT	(15) 1974 BRUS
Yugoslavia	R	S	R	R	R		R	R					R		R
Zaire	R	S	S	S			R								
Zambia	R	R	R	R			R								
Zimbabwe							R								
ORGANIZATION															
European Space Agency (ESA)			D	D	D										
European Telecommunications Satellite Org. (EUTELSAT)				D											

Notes: (1) Canada has a Cooperation Agreement with ESA, but is not a Member.

Addendum

IISL Program at UN COPUOS
Legal Subcommittee
1996 Session

On March 18., 1996 a Symposium „PROTECTION OF THE SPACE ENVIRONMENT was held shortly after the opening of the 35th Session of the Legal Subcommittee of the UN. Committee on the Peaceful Uses of Outer Space. The Symposium was organised by the International Institute of Space Law (IISL) and the European Center for Space Law (ECSL).

On request of the President of the IISL, *Dr. Nandasiri Jasentuliyana* the session was coordinated by *Dr. Ernst Fasan,* Honorary Director of IISL, and Mr. *Jitandra Thaker,* Legal Affairs Officer to the UN Office for Outer Space Affairs served as rapporteur.

Fasan was able to welcome the President of the Legal Subcommittee, *Dr. Vaclav Mikulka,* and many of its distinguished delegates and guests. He introduced the four speakers in the order of the agenda, namely: *Professor Dr. Lubos Perek,* of the Astronomical Institute of the Czech Academy of Sciences; *Dr. Gabriel Lafferanderie,* Chairman of the ECSL, and Legal Adviser of ESA; *Bryan Cheuvront III, Esq.,* Senior Counsel of Motorola, Inc.; and *Professor Dr. Vladimir Kopal,* General Counsel of the International Astronautical Federation.

Fasan pointed out that the topic of the Symposium PROTECTION OF THE SPACE ENVIRONMENT was not on the Legal Subcommittees Agenda for this year but he expressed his hope that the papers to be presented would informally give some background information for the distinguished audience.

After presentation of the papers by the four speakers, there followed a „questions and answers“ period, in which took part the distinguished delegates of China, *Prof Huang Huikang,* of Australia, *Dr. Mc. Intosh,* and the speakers.

In conclusion, the Chairman of the Legal Subcommittee, *Dr. Vaclav Mikulka,* expressed his appreciation for the information given. He added that the problems of space debris were of major concern, and he thanked the IISL for the choice of this topic.

A little reception closed the event.

IISL-ECSL Symposium on Space Debris: Issues of Policy & Law
Held on occasion of the thirty-fifth session of the Legal Subcommittee of COPUOS
Vienna International Centre, 18 March 1996

Space Debris: Discussion in the Scientific and Technical Subcommittee in February 1996

L. Perek[1]
Astronomical Institute
Academy of Sciences, Prague, Czech Republic

Election of the Chairman

The thirty-third session of the Scientific and Technical Subcommittee was held in Vienna from 11 to 23 February 1996. After the retirement of Professor Carver last year, the Subcommittee elected as its new Chairman, Professor Dietrich Rex of the Federal Republic of Germany. In his professional life, Professor Rex is heading the Institute for Spaceflight Technology and Nuclear Reactor Technology at the Technical University of Braunschweig, Germany. He serves as Chairman of the European Space Agency Space Debris Advisory Group and is a member of the US National Research Council's Committee on Space Debris. He and his colleagues are authors of many highly important scientific papers on space debris. At a time when Space Debris is a priority item, the Subcommittee has a chairman who is an eminent expert in the field.

Views of Delegations

About twenty delegations participated in the discussion on Space Debris. Only a few contributions can be mentioned here:

The Russian Federation proposed to establish an international centre for providing information and advance warning on explosions in space, on fragmentation of space objects and on possible collisions of space objects with space debris. Also an exchange of data on space debris was advocated with a view to make the catalogues of space debris more reliable, consistent, and complete.

Indonesia supported the opinion expressed at the thirty-second session of the Subcommittee (A/AC.105/605, para 95) and considered important to adopt an

[1] Member IAU, IAA, IISL.

explanation of the term "space debris". The view was expressed that designating an object as "space debris" should not depend on the identification of the owner. The following wording was proposed:

> "Space debris are all man-made objects, including their fragments and parts, whether their owners can be identified or not, in Earth orbit or re-entering the dense layers of the atmosphere, that are non-functional with no reasonable expectation of their being able to assume or resume their intended functions or any other functions for which they are or can be authorized".

Some delegations stressed the importance of reorbiting geostationary satellites into disposal orbits after the termination of their useful lifetimes. India proposed to reorbit to more than 300 km while Japan recommended a higher altitude of at least 500 km beyond the geostationary orbit. The latter is a somewhat higher and safer altitude than that proposed in the IAA Position Paper on Orbital Debris (300 km) but requires more fuel. It should be noted in this context that space debris in the geostationary orbit were discussed under the item on Space Debris and not under the item on the Geostationary Orbit. The proposal to do so was put before the COPUOS in 1995 (see Report of the COPUOS A/50/20, para 80).

The US reported in detail about results obtained with the Haystack Debris Radar which is so powerful that it can detect a pea (0.65 cm) at 650 km distance. Because of the increased accuracy, some of the debris can be assigned to individual breakup events, or previously unrecognized debris sources can be discovered. NASA completed the development of the Liquid Metal Mirror Telescope for observing orbital debris. It will be possible to observe objects of 2.5 cm at 900 km altitude and of 10 cm in the geostationary orbit. In February 1995, the second mission of the Orbital Debris Radar Calibration Spheres was launched. Three spheres and three dipoles of different sizes were deployed from the Shuttle. They were observed by ground based radars and optical telescopes and the observations were used for calibrating the scales and consequently for improving the interpreting capabilities of the radars and telescopes.

The Czech delegation stressed the importance of preventive measures but pointed out that a large number of inactive objects is already in orbit. Their highest density occurs at about 800 to 1500 km where the average lifetime is very long, of several hundred years at least. During that time secondary collisions can increase the amount of debris. Methods for removing those objects from orbit have been already studied but further research is needed. The scientific community should be encouraged to study these methods with an emphasis on efficiency and cost effectiveness.

Some delegation supported the view that the Legal Subcommittee should be informed of the discussions in the Scientific and Technical Subcommittee and that a set of international rules should be adopted in order to reduce the risk posed by orbital debris and to support a rational use of outer space. That view was, however, not shared by all delegations. Some considered it premature at present and insisted on a thorough discussion of all important technical aspects of the problem by the Scientific and Technical

Subcommittee before deciding on any possible further steps.

Technical Presentations

Several technical presentations supplemented the information provided by delegations:

Prof. Dr. Walter Flury, speaking for the European space Agency, gave an overview of the chapter of the work plan on measurements of space debris and effects of the environment on space systems. He treated in detail ground-based measurements, in particular those made by radar and by optical telescopes, space-based measurements by radar, by optical means, by infrared sensors and by particle detectors, and those derived from spacecraft returned from space. He concluded with an analysis of possible damage to space systems. While large debris can destroy a spacecraft, the impacts by debris of 1 cm size can seriously damage it.

Dr. Dieter Mehrholz of the Research Institute for High Frequency Physics in Germany, reported on research activities of the Research Establishment for Applied Science, in particular on the Tracking and Imaging Radar system. It uses a 34 m antenna for tracking objects down to 5 cm at 2500 km distance and to 1 m objects in the geosynchronous orbit. The imaging data can be used for checking the functionality of the spacecraft and for identification purposes.

Dr. S. Banerjee and A.S. Ganeshan of the ISRO Satellite Center in Bangalore, India, reported on a Hybrid Model to find Spatial Distribution of Debris from a Breakup. Small debris are not listed in catalogues and have to be studied statistically. The paper lays down the background for the development of a new analytical method for studying small debris.

Dr. Andrew Potter of the Johnson Space Center, NASA, presented a Summary of the United States Space Debris Measurements Programme. The programme uses radars for low earth orbits, optical telescopes for deep space, and surfaces returned from space for identifying man-made particles in impact pits. Many results have been already arrived at: There are over 100.000 debris in LEO down to 1 cm size. An unsuspected source of debris was discovered near 900 km altitude, possibly from Rorsat nuclear reactors. A study of surfaces returned from space yields evidence for swarms of microdebris and some microdebris in highly elliptical orbits. Damage on Shuttle windows shows that the microdebris population is underestimated and that it is growing. An additional capability for studies of debris at geosynchronous altitudes is needed. Very little is known about debris population in Molniya and geotransfer orbits, although one geotransfer breakup has been accidentally detected.

Dr. Fernand Alby of the Centre Spatial de Toulouse, CNES, France, spoke on Modelization of Space Debris and Comparison with Observations. The analysis consists in searching for impact craters on exposed surfaces and in identifying impact particles. The observed flux of particles in space is compared with theoretical models. At the same time, detectors of debris are studied with a view to mount them on all satellites to obtain information on the debris population, in particular in the geostationary orbit.

Dr. Richard Crowther of the Defence Research Agency, United Kingdom, reported on The Unique Hazards Associated With Satellite Constellations. A constellation is a collection of satellites performing a common function, such as global positioning, earth observation, hand held personal communications etc. Several constellations are planned for launch in the near future, requiring tens or hundreds of satellites with lifetimes of 5-8 years. Each system would require frequent launchings of new satellites and frequent deorbiting of satellites approaching the end of their useful lifetimes. Unless the system has a built-in mechanism for restricting the number of debris, the collision risk would increase in a substantial way. The paper gives estimates of collision probabilities. New constellations will add a new dimension of complexity in managing the space debris environment but operational practices can reduce the hazard.

Mr. George Levin, NASA Headquarters, gave a Summary of the United States National Research Council Report on Space Debris 1995[2]. The Report presents the most recent and detailed information. It puts its authority behind previously recommended measures, in general confirming the conclusions of the IAA Position Paper on Orbital Debris. It makes several recommendations for improving knowledge of the debris environment, for improving spacecraft protection against the impact of debris, and for reducing the future debris hazard. In the last area, it advocates:

* Reduction of debris on a multilateral basis in order not to penalize those engaging in mitigation measures,
* Prevention of explosions,
* Minimizing of mission-related debris,
* Minimizing the unintentional release of surface materials, such as paint,
* Avoiding intentional breakups, in particular those producing debris with long lifetimes,
* Reorbiting of spacecraft and rocket bodies in Low Earth Orbit after their functional lifetime and achieving an international consensus on the magnitude of such manoeuvres, and,
* Until a verifiably superior strategy is produced, reorbiting spacecraft and rocket bodies in the geostationary orbits at least 300 km beyond that orbit.

Other Documents

Several documents on space debris, some of them in connection with nuclear power sources, were before the Subcommittee:

---

[2]Orbital Debris: A Technical Assessment. National Research Council, National Academy Press, Washington, D.C., 1995, ISBN 0-309-05125-8, 224 p.

A/AC.105/619 of 21 November 1995 and Add. 1 of 1 February 1996, National Research on Space Debris, Safety of Nuclear-Powered Satellites, Problems on Collisions of Nuclear-Powered Sources with Space Debris. Contains replies from Canada, Chile, Germany, Japan and the United Kingdom.

A/AC.105/C.1/L.203 of 9 February 1996, Interpretation and Development of the Safety Principles for Nuclear Power Sources in Space, working paper by the UK.

A/AC.105/C.1/L.204 of 13 February 1996, on collisions between nuclear power sources and space debris, working paper by the Russian Federation.

A/AC.105/C.1/L.205 of 13 February 1996, Brief Review of the Work Done by Russian Scientists on the Problem of the Technogenic Pollution of Near Space, working paper by the Russian Federation.

Space Agencies

The implementation of concrete steps for reducing the amount on space debris in future missions is in the hands of those space agencies which do the launching. They can influence the design , launching and operation of spacecraft. These may be the reasons why many delegations expressed their appreciation of the document A/AC.105/620 on Steps Taken by Space Agencies for Reducing the Growth or Damage Potential of Space Debris. It reports on preventive measures adopted by space agencies on a voluntary basis, without awaiting the outcome of the discussions in the United Nations. This is regarded as an important event because space agencies have shown that they are approaching the problem of space debris with a high degree of responsibility and that they have not only the power but also the will to preserve outer space in a state fit for future space activities. Accordingly, several delegations supported the view, already expressed at the thirty-eight session of COPUOS (A/50/20, para 78), that space agencies should be brought into a closer contact with the Subcommittee. The Subcommittee decided to invite a representative of the Inter-Agency Space Debris Coordination Committee to give a presentation at the next session of the Subcommittee.

Technical Report

The most important part of the work of the Subcommittee consisted in preparing a structured Technical Report in agreement with last year's decision to follow the Work Plan. Accordingly, the Technical Report deals briefly with previous history and explains why it has to be structured. It contains also an explanation of the term "space debris". As recently as last year, a proposal to explain what is the common understanding of the term failed to find a wide support in the Subcommittee. This year, the Report states:

"It is understood that space debris are inactive man-made objects, such as spent upper stages, spent satellites, fragments or parts generated during launch or mission operations, or fragments from explosions and other break-ups".

No size limits of space debris have been expressly stated. Evidently, the upper limit is the largest man-made spacecraft, if and when it becomes inactive. The lower limit in size can be inferred from the text of the Report. It deals with impacts of submillimeter-size particles and with craters and holes extending from several millimeters down to micrometers.

This year , only the part dealing with measurements of space debris was detailed, while Modelling and Mitigation will be dealt with in the next two years. The text appears in the Report of the Scientific and Technical Subcommittee of its thirty-third session, section on Space Debris.

Conclusion

If and when the Legal Subcommittee takes up the matter of space debris, it will face a difficult task. The technical complexity of the phenomenon of space debris is evident. Most methods for reducing the risk of a collision or a close encounter of an active spacecraft with a piece of orbital debris are strongly dependent on the actual state of technology and science. In particular, they depend on the technical design of spacecraft and its parts. It seems that the amount of technical data and numerical parameters is higher in the field of space debris than in any other area on the present or past agendas of the COPUOS. The question of space debris will require a "sui generis" approach.

IISL - ECSL SYMPOSIUM - 18 March 1996

ESA Activities

Status and Organisation of the Inter-Agency Space Debris Co-ordination Committee (IADC)

Presented by G. Lafferranderie (ESA Legal Advisor)

ESA and its Member States have been actively addressing the space debris issue for several years, a matter by definition subject of an international cooperation (facilities, expertise within the spirit of the Outer Space Treaty). I would like to summarise the main actions undertaken by ESA in close cooperation with Member States and their national agencies in order to reach a better understanding of the issue. These actions will at a later stage lead hopefully to a common policy which will be the starting point for regulations at international level.

1) The genesis and development within ESA (involvement of national space agencies)

In 1986 the Director general of ESA decided to create a **Space Debris Working Group**, composed by ESA staff and experts from ESA member States, the objective of which was to assess the various aspects of space debris.

Based on the report of this working group, the ESA Council adopted in **1989 a Resolution on space debris** (entitled "Resolution of the Agency vis a vis the space debris issue", see Annex I) and approved a **document entitled "ESA Activities for space debris"** where the Agency objectives in the field of space debris were formulated.

These objectives are the following:

- to minimise the creation of space debris to ensure free access to space and reduce the risk for manned and unmanned space flight;
- to reduce the risk on ground due to re-entry of space objects;
- to reduce the risk for the geostationary satellites;
- to acquire through its own facilities and in cooperation with the other space agencies the data on space debris which are necessary to assess the extent of the problem and its consequences;
- to study the legal aspects of space debris;

  (on this last point I have to say that it has not been yet addressed)

A **two phase implementation plan** was foreseen, initially where **Phase 1** - Analysis and preparation - (=13,5 MAU) covered the period **1989-92**, and **Phase 2** (=15-20 MAU) - Implementation and operations - the **period 1993-95 mainly oriented towards international cooperation**. **A Phase 3**, has now been added covering the period 1996-1998 which will address the Low-Earth Orbit (LEO) region and the consequences of multi-satellite constellations (such as the Global Positioning System [GPS] or Iridium project). The international cooperation both on a European and world wide level will remain an essential element.

A crucial element of the Space Debris Plan is the **Space Debris Research Programme** whose general objectives include:

- to gain a better understanding of the space debris problem,
- to assess the level of risk for its own programmes
- to identify ways and methods to mitigate the space debris problem,
- to support the establishment of an overall ESA policy on space debris.

Two groups were created for the guidance and coordination of the Agency's activities in compliance with the formulated objectives: **the ESA Space Debris Advisory Group (SDAG)** with experts from member States representing the major entities in Europe with experience in space debris matters and the internal **Space Debris Coordination and Technical Analysis Group.**

I should here underline that the SDAG has a special coordination role with respect to space debris matters not only with national space Agencies of member states but also at international level with other space agencies (European and non-European like NASA).

It is interesting to note in this context that the progress in international cooperation was demonstrated at the occasion of the **salyut-7/Kosmos 1686 reentry**, where our European Space Operation Centre acted as the central hub for the data exchange between several space organisations and also subsequently organised an **international workshop on that matter in April 1991**. The same applied at the occasion of the uncontrolled reentry of the equipment module of the Chinese spacecraft in October

1993, as well as at the occasion of the very recent (on 12 March 1996) uncontrolled reentry of a Chinese satellite, where ESOC provided forecasts to ESA's Member States on time and location of the reentry based on the data from European facilities, US Space Command and Russia.

I should maybe also mention that ESA and NASA entered into an exchange of letters in 1992 (see Annex III) concerning the space debris issue and ESA has regularly been organising ad hoc **Space Debris Coordination Meetings** with the Japanese and American space agencies which were the predecessors of the IADC.

Particular emphasis on the **First European Space Debris Conference** which was held in Darmstadt at the **initiative of ESA from 5-7 April 1993**. This conference which was a considerable success gathered 251 experts from 17 countries. Its aim was to provide:

- a forum for the presentation of results from research on space debris;
- to assist in defining future directions of research;
- to identify methods of debris control, reduction and protection;
- and to discuss international implications and policy issues.

At this occasion a major step in the international cooperation was reached when the **first multilateral meeting** with representatives of NASA, the Russian Space Agency (RKA), Japan and ESA agreed to establish an **Inter-Agency Space Debris Coordination Committee (IADC)** (terms of reference in Annex II). It is envisaged to hold the second European Space Debris Conference in 1997.

I would briefly like to indicate which were the major achievements of ESA regarding the space debris issue:

- The Agency has established the DISCOS data base for space objects for its own use and entities in the Member States; it supplies information on the currently catalogued objects and is a basis for risk assessments.

- Debris preventive measures, such as venting of Ariane upper stage in synchronous orbit since flight 59 (in September 1993) and re-orbiting of geostationary spacecraft into a graveyard orbit above the GEO (the recent examples are GEOS-2 [+ 260 km, 1984], OTS-2 [+318 km, 1991], METEOSAT 2 [+334 km, 1991], ECS-2 [+ 335 km, 1993], OLYMPUS (-213 km, 1993), METEOSAT 3+4 (1995), have been implemented;

- Finally generic work on protective measures for manned vehicles has been carried out (shield testing and hypervelocity impact tests) at several facilities within the Member States. In the shielding area research activities have focused on the selection of optimum materials and the design of shields with minimum mass for given safety and damage tolerance;

ESA contributed to a comprehensive report[1] on space debris of the U.S. National Academy of Sciences. It offers clear recommendations for research on the space debris population, for methods to improve the protection of spacecraft, and on

---

[1] Orbital Debris. A Technical Assessment. *National Academy Press* 1995

methods to reduce the creation of debris.

2) The IADC

a) Form

The IADC constitute a very unique forum devoted to consultations at international level on orbital debris without creating any specific legal commitment for its Members and has therefore no legal personality.

b) Membership

This Committee has today increased the number of its Members and is now composed by eight members which are ESA, Japan, NASA, the Russian Space Agency (RKA), the Chinese Space Administration (CNSA), the French Centre National d'Etudes Spatiales (CNES), the UK Defense Research Agency (DRA) and the Indian Space Research Organisation (ISRO).

c) Purpose

IADC offers a forum for discussion and coordination of technical space debris issues and will soon hold its 14th meeting in Darmstadt, Germany. Such meetings are being held at intervals of about 8-10 months preferably coinciding with other international meetings. Location of meetings are rotating among Members as appropriate and the host of each meeting acts as the Chair of the meeting, and is responsible for coordinating the dates, location, and agenda of the meeting, drafting and distributing the minutes of the meeting. The primary purpose of the IADC is to exchange information on space debris research activities, to facilitate opportunities for cooperation in space debris research, to review the progress of ongoing cooperative activities and to identify debris mitigation options. It is also stated in the IADC terms of reference that any specific cooperative activities endorsed by the IADC will be implemented through arrangements negotiated between Member organisations. Members exchange data resulting from national orbital debris programs as appropriate. Data and information exchanged through the IADC are normally to be exchanged without restrictions as to use or disclosure. In the event that technical data is exchanged which is considered to be proprietary, and for which protection is desired, the data is marked with a notice indicating the use and disclosure restrictions, and the recipient agrees to abide by the terms of such notices.

d) Structure

IADC comprises a Steering Group composed by representatives of the Members and four technical working groups composed of 2-3 experts from each Member and dedicated to specific areas:

i) measurements of the environment,

ii) database and environment,

iii) protection,

iv) mitigation.

Within the framework of this cooperation the participants exchange relevant technical information and experience related to space debris and prepare common strategies to counter the space debris problem. Current activities focus on:

- a joint debris database,

- the discovery of significant new debris source in the heavily used near Earth orbital region of 700 km to 1100 km altitude which could be attributable to RORSATs[2],
- improve meteoroid and debris models,
- debris mitigation in GEO transfer orbits,
- optical observations and global inventory of the geostationary ring,
- debris management practices in the geostationary ring.

e) Legal commitment

It is important to note that the IADC terms of reference document the mutual interest on the part of its Members to exchange information on orbital debris, but that they do not establish any obligation or legal requirement to do so, nor do they establish any obligation to conduct any particular cooperative activity.

3) ESA and UNO work on space debris

As you know the topic *space debris* appeared in 1994 and 1995 on the agenda of the Scientific and Technical Subcommittee of the United Nations Committee on the Peaceful Uses of Outer Space (UNCOPUOS). At both sessions technical presentations to the space debris issue were given by ESA. The S&T Subcommittee adopted in

[2] Radar Ocean Reconnaissance Satellites

1995 a multi-year work plan:

- 1996: Measurements of space debris and effects of the environment on space systems
- 1997: Modelling of the space debris environment and risk assessment
- 1998: Space debris mitigation measures (protection, prevention, removal).

Conclusion

I shall conclude by stating that for the moment the necessary flexible international cooperation tool exists which allows us to understand the technical aspects and to coordinate national activities related to space debris. It remains to discuss at an appropriate time, in addition to the existing space law treaties if new instrument would be needed and if so what would its legal form be.

Any future legal regulation on that subject should be examined by the UNCOPUOUS which will still take some time. ESA will naturally in due course, subject to a mandate given by its member States, contribute to the elaboration of such new standards from a European perspective once the technical assessments of the space debris have been completed.

- Annex 1 -

ESA/C/LXXXVII/Res. 3 (final)

european space agency

COUNCIL

Resolution on the Agency's policy vis-à-vis the Space Debris issue

(approved on 29 June 1989)

The Council,

CONSIDERING that the problem of space debris has become world-wide one of the major issues regarding the environmental protection of outer space and has reached a level which requires serious considerations especially for manned missions,

WELCOMING the attention already devoted to this problem by the Agency and NOTING the on-going activities and preventive measures (i.e. ESA/PB-ARIANE-(89)26),

HAVING REGARD to the report by the Chairman of the Council Working Group on Space Debris set up following the invitation it made at its December 1986 meeting (ESA/C(89)44),

CONSIDERING that any action, such as elaboration of norms, will require careful assessment and coordination, in particular among all space-faring nations,

ESA/C/LXXXVII/Res. 3 (final)

I. ENDORSES the recommendations expressed by the Space Debris Working Group;

II. AGREES to the Agency's objectives and implementation strategy as contained in document ESA/C(89)24, rev. 1, i.e. in particular to obtain a better knowledge and understanding of critical issues, to reduce to the maximum possible extent the production of space debris and to promote exchange of information and cooperation with other space operators;

III. SUPPORTS the setting up, under the Director General's authority, of the necessary management structure to cope with all space debris aspects and of a space debris Advisory Group with outside experts;

IV. INVITES the Member States to continue seeking a common position, using IRAC, with regard to space debris matters at international level, in particular vis-à-vis the United Nations;

V. INVITES the Director General to make proposals within the annual budgets for implementing the approved objectives.

- Annex 2 -

IADC Terms of Reference
(draft update)

Revised March 10 1995

Terms of Reference for the Inter-Agency Space Debris Coordination Committee

This document constitutes the Terms of Reference (ToR) for the Inter-Agency Space Debris Coordination Committee (IADC)and establishes the basic principles related to its function.

The Terms of Reference of the Inter-Agency Space Debris Coordination Committee have been agreed at the 10-th IADC meeting at TSNIIMASH, Kaliningrad, October 25-26, 1993, and have been updated at the 12-th IADC meeting at NASA Johnson Space Center, Houston, March 8-10, 1995.

1.Purpose

The primary purpose of the IADC is to exchange information on space debris research activities between member space agencies, to facilitate opportunities for cooperation in space debris research, to review the progress of ongoing cooperative activities and to identify debris mitigation options.

2.Rationale

The members share a number of common interests in space debris research which may be developed into a variety of cooperative research activities. Such ventures are likely to increase in frequency and scope in the future. It is highly desirable to exchange information on current research activities so as to identify future cooperative activities. Therefore, the IADC is established to identify, plan, and assist in the implementation of joint cooperative activities that are of mutual interest and benefit.

3.Scope

The IADC will

a. review all ongoing cooperative space debris research activities between member organizations;

b. recommend new opportunities for cooperation;

c. serve as the primary means for exchanging information and plans concerning orbital debris research activities;

d. identify and evaluate options for debris mitigation.

Any specific cooperative activities endorsed by the IADC will be implemented through arrangements negotiated between member organizations.

Members should exchange data resulting from national orbital debris programs as appropriate. Data and information exchanged through the IADC will normally be exchanged without restrictions as to use or disclosure. In the event that technical data is exchanged which is considered to be proprietary, and for which protection is desired, the data shall be marked with a notice indicating the use and disclosure restrictions, and the recipient agrees to abide by the terms of such notices.

4.Membership

Members of the IADC are the European Space Agency (ESA), Japan, the National Aeronautics and Space Administration (NASA), and the Russian Space Agency (RKA), China, CNES (France), DRA (United Kingdom), ISRO (India since 27.02.1996).
New members may be included upon unanimous decision of the members of IADC.

Member delegations may include representation from other organizations or government agencies in their delegation.

More detailed criteria for membership are defined in Annex I.

5.Organizational structure

The IADC will comprise

- a Steering Committee composed of representatives of the members. The Steering Committee will include the points of contacts of the members listed in Annex II.

- four specialised Working Groups:

  Working Group 1: Measurements

  Working Group 2: Environment and Data Base

  Working Group 3: Protection

  Working Group 4: Mitigation.

Each Working Group shall be composed of 2-3 experts from each member. The terms of reference of each working group are given herein and as supplemented in Annex III. Present working group chairperson, deputy chairperson, and membership are listed in Annexes IV and V.

6. Meetings

Location of meetings of the IADC will rotate among the members of the IADC, as appropriate. The frequency and schedule of IADC meetings will be established by the Steering Committee. Meetings at intervals of about 8-10 months should be aimed for, preferably coinciding with other international meetings.

The host of each meeting will act as the chair of the meeting, and will be responsible for coordinating the dates, location, and agenda of the meeting and drafting and distributing the minutes of the meeting.

General meeting arrangements and associated meeting expenses will be borne by the host agency. Each member will be responsible for the travel and subsistence of its representatives attending the IADC.

7. Terms and Conditions

These Terms of Reference may be modified or terminated by mutual agreement of the parties. These Terms of Reference and all activities under these Terms of Reference may be terminated unilaterally by any member with three-months prior written notice. All debris cooperative activities for which separate agreements have been concluded, may continue after termination of these Terms of Reference, pursuant to the terms and conditions of those agreements.

These Terms of Reference document the mutual interest on the part of the members of IADC to exchange information on orbital debris. The Terms of Reference do not establish any obligation or legal requirement to do so, nor do they establish any obligation to conduct any particular cooperative activity.

Working Group 1

Measurements

Terms of reference

- The IADC Steering Committee has established Working Group 1 on Measurements
- The members of WG 1 are appointed by each member of the IADC.
- The Working Group nominates a chairperson and a deputy. The chairperson organizes and guides the activities of the Working Group.
- The Working Group establishes its own agenda. However, it may also receive tasks from the IADC.
- The Working Group reports through its chairperson to the IADC Steering Committee.
- Meetings of the Working Group can be attended by others when invited by a member of the IADC.

Scope and objectives

The scope of WG 1 are all measurement techniques, both functioning and currently under development, to gain information on man-made and natural objects in near-Earth space. This includes

- ground-based and space-based measurements and related techniques, e.g. radar, optical and infrared
- detectors and collectors for small-size particulates onboard space vehicles
- analysis of spacecraft surfaces exposed to the space environment.

Within the above scope the objectives of the WG are to

- review space debris research efforts in the area of measurement techniques
- identify, evaluate and recommend new opportunities for cooperation
- serve as means for exchanging information and plans concerning research activities in the area of measurements of orbital debris.

Required inputs

- Reports on research activities in member organizations with regard to measurements.

Expected outputs

- Identification, definition and review of cooperative research activities.

Working Group 2

Environment and Data Base

Terms of reference

- The IADC Steering Committee has established Working Group 2 on Environment and Data Base.
- The members of WG 2 are appointed by each member of the IADC.
- The Working Group nominates a chairperson and a deputy.The chairperson organizes and guides the activities of the Working Group.
- The Working Group establishes its own agenda. However, it may also receive tasks from the IADC.
- The Working Group reports through its chairperson to the IADC Steering Committee.
- Meetings of the Working Group can be attended by others when invited by a member of the IADC.

Scope and objectives

The scope of Working Group 2 is the characterization and modelling of meteoroid and debris around the Earth and storage and access of the data by electronic means. This includes

- meteoroid and debris models describing the spatial distribution and other characteristics, e.g. flux, size, albedo.
- short- and long-term evolution
- related mathematical methods
- collision prediction and risk assessment
- uncontrolled reentry
- establishment of joint data base for debris and meteoroids
- development of models which characterize explosions or collisions in space.

Within the above scope the objectives of the WG are to

- review research efforts in environment modeling and related data base
- identify, evaluate and recommend new opportunities for cooperation
- serve as means for exchanging information and plans concerning research activities in the area of environment modelling and related data base.

Required inputs

- Reports on research activities in member organizations with regard to environment modelling and related data bases.

Expected outputs

- Identification, definition and review of cooperative research activities.
- Concepts for extended and comprehensive data bases.

Working Group 3

Protection

Terms of reference

- The IADC Steering Committee has established Working Group 3 on Protection.
- The members of WG 3 are appointed by each member of the IADC.
- The Working Group nominates a chairperson and a deputy. The chairperson organizes and guides the activities of the Working Group.
- The Working Group establishes its own agenda. However, it may also receive tasks from the IADC.
- The Working Group reports through its chairperson to the IADC Steering Committee.
- Meetings of the Working Group can be attended by others when invited by a member of the IADC.

Scope and objectives

The scope of the activities of WG 3 comprises design and technology of shielding against meteoroids and space debris and the associated test methods.

Within the above scope the objectives of the WG are to:

- establish a common data base of world-wide test facilities
- optimize the shield design, its performance and test methods, including the use of computer codes
- coordinate test procedures for computer code validation
- establish a data base on impact test results
- develop and update shield design and test planning for improvement of crew safety and satellite/station system integrity
- study space vehicle fragmentation events including dynamics of structure at their impact with space debris and secondary debris
- coordinate test procedures for impact testing on pressurized structures
- study the feasibility of common shield designs, testing planning and test procedures
- review research efforts on hypervelocity testing and shielding
- identify, evaluate and recommend new opportunities for cooperation
- serve as means for exchanging information concerning actual on-orbit impacts and shielding design performance
- serve as means for exchanging information and plans concerning research activities in the area of protection.

Required inputs

The working group requires the following inputs:

- Design and performance data on current shield concepts.
- Description and capabilities of test methods.
- Description and capabilities of computer codes.
- Information on planned activities in the area of shield design, shield testing and establishing and upgrading of test facilities.

Expected outputs

The expected outputs are as follows:

- Data base on testing and shielding.
- Detailed acquaintance with existing shield design, performance and test facilities.
- Proposed shield design and test activities for improvement of crew safety and satellite/station system integrity.
- Proposal for implementing the proposed concepts.

Working Group 4

Mitigation

Terms of Reference

- The IADC Steering Committee has established Working Group 4 on Mitigation.
- The members of WG 4 are appointed by each member of the IADC.
- The Working Group nominates a chairperson and a deputy. The chairperson organizes and guides the activities of the Working Group.
- The Working Group establishes its own agenda. However, it may also receive tasks from the IADC.
- The Working Group reports through its chairperson to the IADC Steering Committee.
- Meetings of the Working Group can be attended by others when invited by a member of the IADC.

Scope and objectives

The scope of Working Group 4 is the study of all measures to reduce or avoid the creation of space debris or reduce the hazards created by space debris. This includes

- identification of space debris sources
- design and operations of space system to avoid or reduce the creation of space debris
- removal of man-made objects
- measures to prevent the creation of space debris
- measures to reduce the collision hazard
- guidelines for debris mitigation.

Within the above scope the objectives of the WG are to

- review space debris research efforts in the area of mitigation
- identify, evaluate and recommend new opportunities for cooperation
- serve as means for exchanging information and plans concerning research activities in the area of mitigation.

Required inputs

- Debris mitigation measures of member organizations.

Expected outputs

- Evaluation of debris mitigation measures.
- Handbook/guidelines for debris mitigation.

Annex I

Criteria for Membership in IADC

1. Scope

The purpose of the "Criteria for Membership in IADC" is to expand on Article 4 of the ToR of IADC, and to provide a more detailed and precise description of the criteria for membership in IADC.

Membership in IADC is addressed in Article 4 of the ToR.

2. Preamble

In the interest of efficiency the number of members of the IADC should be of a manageable size and, therefore, limited to appropriate nations and organizations consistent with the aims and objectives agreed in the ToR of the IADC. Where appropriate greater concentration in regional grouping should be aimed for.

IADC members complete necessary coordination (Intra-agency, Inter-agency, etc.) prior to IADC meetings.

3. Criteria for membership

a. Members are countries or national or international space organisations which are carrying out space activities, through either manufacturing, launching and operating spacecraft or manufacturing and launching rockets.

A member should be actively undertaking space debris research activities and contribute to an increased understanding of space debris issues.

A member may represent one or several countries.

b. A country is represented in IADC by itself or by one space organization. The delegation of any IADC member may, however, be comprised of delegates from other space organizations or other selected agencies of that country or of other countries.

c. International consortia sponsoring major satellite programmes (e.g. INTELSAT, INMARSAT, etc.) or relevant specialized agencies of the UN (e.g. International Telecommunication Union) may be invited to participate in IADC meetings when specific issues of interest are discussed.

ANNEX II

Contact Points of IADC Members

ESA: Dr. W. Flury, ESOC, Robert-Bosch-Str. 5, 64293 Darmstadt Germany

Fax +49 6151 902 625
Tel +49 6151 902 270
wflury@esoc.bitnet

Japan: Dr. S. Toda, NAL, 7-44-1 Jindaiji-Higashi-machi, Chofu, Tokyo, 182 Japan

Fax +81 422 44 4843
Tel +81 422 47 5911
toda@asuka.nal.go.jp

NASA: Mr. G. Levin, NASA HQ, Washington D.C. 20546, USA

Fax +1 202 358 2885
Tel +1 202 358 4478
glevin@osfms1.hq.nasa.gov

RKA: Mr. Y. Levitsky, RKA, Schepkina Str. 42, Moscow 129 857, Russia

Fax +7 095 251 8702
Tel +7 095 971 9315

Annex III

Format of the IADC Meetings and Procedures for the Working Groups

A Format of IADC Meetings

1. The host agency or country will act as secretary and prepare the minutes of the meeting for the approval of the Chair.

2. The agenda will be prepared by the Chair and provided to all the participants not less than three weeks prior to the meeting. The agenda will identify topics and speakers and time allocations for presentation. Not less than one third of the time should be allocated to discussion and plans.

3. The Chair will be responsible for reporting the groups activity to the plenary session; he may ask members of the group to make parts of the report.

4. The general plan for future meetings should be for four full days. The pattern of such a meeting would be:

Day 1 AM Plenary
PM Working Groups

Day 2 AM Working Groups
PM Working Groups

Day 3 AM Working Groups
PM Working Groups

Day 4 AM Plenary - Working Groups Report
Executive session of Plenary:
- o Draft minutes with summary
- o Recommendations
- o List of action items

PM - Review of proposals of cooperative projects between Steering Committee and Working Groups
- Tours of suitable facilities
- Closing session.

The objective is to provide enough time for meaningful discussion and the accomplishment of real work.

5. Establish a "rule" that all presentations have word charts and figures, as appropriate to summarize the remarks. In addition the speaker should provide three copies to the secretary.

B Procedures for the Working Groups

1. Elect a Chairperson to serve a term of two consecutive meetings and a Deputy who will succeed as Chairperson for the following term. A new Deputy will be elected for the following term, etc.

2. Normally a presentation should not last more than 15 minutes.

3. Discussion should define the most immediately important topics for the Working Group and who will prepare material for the next meeting to address those topics. Assign the appropriate actions to make the presentations for the next meeting.

4. The Working Groups are expected to pursue agreed upon activities by fax, e-mail and other correspondence and communication between meetings to perform agreed upon tasks.

5. Working Groups are not expected to have meetings outside of the context of the general meeting. The objective of the plan is to reduce the total number of meetings.

6. The basic function of each Working Group is to define mutually agreed upon work so that each participant can better understand the issues and the state of understanding so as to advise his authorities as to appropriate policy and action.

Annex IV

Chairpersons and Deputies of Working Groups
Status: March 11 1995

	Chairperson	Deputy
WG1 Measurement	Tadashi Takano The Institute of Space and Astronautical Science 3-1-1 Yoshinodai, Sagamihara Kanawage 229, Japan Tel +81 427 51 2911 Fax +81 427 59 4251	Prof. A.I. Nazarenko Russian Academy of Sciences, Center for Program Studies 84/32 Profsoyuznaya ul. Moscow 117810, Russia Tel +7 095 429 5400 Fax +7 095 420 2275
WG2 Environment & Data base	Heiner Klinkrad ESOC PO Box 406 64276 Darmstadt Germany Tel +49 6151 90 2295 Fax +49 6151 90 2625 HKLINKRA@ESOC	Robert C. Reynolds Lockheed 2400 NASA Road 1 C102, Houston TX 77085-3799 USA Tel +1 713 333 7071 Fax +1 713 333 7791 BOBR@SN.DNET.NASA.GOV
WG3 Protection	Viktor N. Dolgikh TSNIIMASH 4, Pionerskaya st. 141070 Kaliningrad Moscow region, Russia Tel +7 095 516 3043 Fax +7 095 274 0025	Jeanne Lee Crews NASA Johnson Space Center Mail Code SN3 Houston,TX 77058 USA Tel +1 713 483 5308 Fax +1 713 483 5276 CREWS@SN.DNET.NASA.GOV
WG4 Mitigation	Akira Takano Office of Research and Development System Engineering Department Tsukuba Space Center NASDA 2-1-1 Sengen Tsukubashi Ibaraki 305, Japan Tel +81 298 52 2239 Fax +81 298 52 2247	Walter G. Naumann ESA HQ 8-10, rue Mario-Nikis 75738 Paris Cedex 15 France Tel +33 1 5369 7350 Fax +33 1 5369 7678 WNAUMANN@ESA

Table 2. Chairperson and Deputy of Working Groups

Annex V

Membership in Working Groups of the IADC

Status: March 10 1995

	ESA	**JAPAN**	**NASA**	**RKA**
WG 1 Measurements	Jehn Schwehm	Arimoto (CRL) Takano (ISAS) Sato (Kyoto University)	Stansbery Vilas	Kuriksha Yurasov Shargorodsky
WG 2 Environment & Database	Drolshagen Klinkrad	Kibe (NAL) Kato (NASDA)	Potter Kessler	Veniaminov Khutorovsky Potchukaev
WG 3 Protection	Lambert Heusmann	Shirai (NASDA/MHI) Sato (NASDA)	Crews Christiansen	Dolgikh Ulanov
WG 4 Mitigation	Soons Naumann Flury	Yasaka (Kyushu University) Takano (NASDA)	Loftus Levin	Chekalin Moiseev Yakovlev

Table 1. Composition of Working Groups

- Annex 3 -

Correspondence with NASA

european space agency
agence spatiale européenne

CAB/INT/KB/MTL/5144

Mr. Peter G. Smith
Director International Relations
NASA H.Q.
Washington, D.C. 20546

U.S.A.

Paris, 15 JUIL 1992

Dear ~~Mr.~~ Peter Smith,

1. ESA and NASA agree to regularly hold coordination meetings on all debris aspects of mutual interest, in particular the knowledge of the terrestrial particulate environment, risk analysis of space projects, and prevention and protection. This cooperation includes exchange of research results.

2. ESA and NASA agree to continue cooperation in the studies of debris impacts on LDEF. ESA has provided LDEF thermal blanket material to NASA and results of their analyses. NASA will provide to ESA the results of their thermal blanket material analysis.

8-10 rue Mario-Nikis 75738 Paris Cedex 15 - ✆ (33.1) 42 73 76 54
Télécopieur (33.1) 42 73 75 60 - Télex ESA 202746 - Télégr. Spaceurop Paris

3. Cooperation will also continue on the analysis of IRAS data. For its part, ESA will continue to conduct analyses of the IRAS data, establish a database of debris sightings, and make the results of the analysis available to NASA.

4. ESA and NASA agree to exchange information involving orbital elements of satellites and space objects. For its part, NASA will provide electronic transmission of the Two-Line-Element (TLE) updates to ESA/ESOC. For its part, ESA will provide NASA access to ESA's DISCOS database, which contains among other elements, the TLE's and the Royal Aerospace Establishment's (RAE) Table of Earth Satellites. ESA may grant full access to DISCOS for users within the ESA establishments. For external users within the ESA Member States, full access to the DISCOS TLE requires the prior agreement of NASA. Annex 1 lists the current users with full access to the TLE data in DISCOS. In addition, any user of the DISCOS database may gain access to a limited number of TLE of space objects (on the order of 20). ESA is free to publish, in hard copy format, any data or information derived from the TLE catalog.

5. ESA and NASA also agree to continue the exchange of information and results concerning hypervelocity impact results. Efforts will be made to continue the standardization process for testing and reporting results, and developing a shared database of information.

6. ESA and NASA also agree to continue exchange of information on debris minimization through space vehicle design and operation.

7. Other areas of interest which will be studied by ESA and NASA are:

- optical and radar observation of space debris
- modelling of the space debris environment of the Earth including long-term evolution
- break up modelling
- risk analysis
- meteoroid and debris protection of manned and unmanned vehicles
- re-entry of space objects (trajectory calculation, break up modelling)
- geostationary orbit (re-orbiting, collocation)
- debris mitigation.

8. It is the intent of ESA and NASA that the data exchanged by them be exchanged without restrictions as to use or disclosure. In the event either side finds it necessary to exchange technical data that are either export-controlled or considered by the furnishing side to be proprietary, and

for which protection is desired, the furnishing side shall mark the technical data with a notice indicating the use and disclosure restrictions and the receiving side agrees to abide by the terms of the notice.

Release of public information regarding this cooperation may be made by each side for its own portion of the envisaged activities as desired and, insofar as participation of the other is involved, after suitable consultation.

Nothing in this exchange of letters shall be construed as granting or implying any rights to, or interests in, patents or inventions of the Parties or their contractors or subcontractors.

Nothing in this exchange of letters shall compel or authorize the disclosure of privileged or proprietary information, national security information, or information the disclosure of which is prohibited by applicable law.

Nothing in this exchange of letters authorizes the export of any item in violation of applicable laws and regulations; and both sides, upon timely coordination, shall use their best efforts to arrange for free customs clearance of items necessary to carry out this cooperation.

9. No exchange of funds is provided under this cooperation and it is understood that participation by either NASA or ESA is contingent upon availability of funding appropriations required to support their respective responsibilities. Neither side nor its contractors, subcontractors, experimenters, or any other participant(s) in these cooperative efforts shall hold the other liable for any injury, death, loss or damage which arises out of this cooperation. Further, these arrangements shall not be considered as creating any right or benefit, enforceable at law or in equity, by any person or entity against either side, its contractors, subcontractors, experimenters, or other participants in the cooperative effort.

References:

1. Proceedings of the first European conference on space debris - Darmstadt, Germany, 1993 - ESA

2. L'ESA et les débris spatiaux - ECSL NEWS Letter n° 3 - January 1990

3. Europe's contribution to the long Duration Exposure Facility (LDEF) Meteoroid and Debris Impact Analysis - W. Flury - ESA/ESOC

4. Formulation of an International Position Paper on Orbital Debris by the IAA Ad Hoc Space Debris Group - 42nd Congress of the International Astronautical Federation - October 5-11, 1991 - Montreal, Canada

1996 IISL-ECSL Symposium
Protection of the Space Environment

United Nations Office for Outer Space Affairs

Space Debris: Industry Viewpoint

Presented by
F. Bryan Cheuvront III, Esq.
Senior Counsel, Motorola, Inc
Chandler, Arizona

March 18, 1996
Vienna

Thank you for inviting me to speak to you about the challenging issues associated with space debris. Your willingness and interest in soliciting a perspective on this topic from industry is commendable. I hope that my remarks will provide you with some beneficial insight into the activities of industry which is attempting to use the space environment for the benefit of our global community of nations.

There have been numerous symposia and conferences around the world at which the topic of space debris has been discussed in detail and from differing perspectives. Motorola, an active member of the global space industry since 1958, understands both the business and technical aspects of the space environment. It has presented papers and participated as chairmen of and technical experts on various committees at these symposia and conferences. I would like to first review one of the historical and some of the more recent publications that address space debris. Then I will describe some extraordinary debris mitigation approaches actually employed by Motorola on the IRIDIUM® Program.

Space Debris Issues - Industry and Governmental Developments

I believe that the only published collective recommendation from industry sources on space debris is the 1992 AIAA Special Project on "Orbital Debris Mitigation Techniques: Technical, Legal, and Economic Aspects". In that paper, several actual space debris mitigation techniques were identified as being in use or under consideration by both the United States Government and various private industry organizations. This report mentioned several current and potential debris mitigation techniques associated with the spent upper stages of launch vehicles including:

1) intentional or guaranteed reentry into the atmosphere,
2) modifications to remove all excess propellants to minimize the risk of on-orbit explosions where reentry cannot be guaranteed,
3) use of separation devices and other launch vehicle design improvements to minimize the release of parts after reaching orbit, and,
4) using various programs to minimize on-orbit collisions including the Collisions On Launch (COLA) program and the Computation of Miss Between Orbits (COMBO) program.

In addition, it identified several operational debris mitigation techniques associated with satellites including, with respect to LEOs, the deorbit and controlled reentry of satellites, and the retrieval or reuse of such spacecraft. With respect to Geostationary (GEO) satellites, the report acknowledges that current techniques seem to focus primarily on maneuvering the spacecraft at its end of life to an orbit higher than the Geostationary orbit.

The National Research Council in the United States began an effort in 1993 to research the topic of space debris from a technical perspective. That effort resulted in the publication last year of an extremely thorough report titled "Orbital Debris - A Technical Assessment". That report set forth several recommendations - many of which can, will and are being implemented by industry on its own. The implementation of other recommendations, however, such as the further cataloging of the debris population at both the LEO and GEO orbits, will need government assistance or access to resources that the government currently controls.

The National Aeronautics and Space Administration (NASA) is in the process of preparing an Orbital Debris Handbook. That handbook, which has not yet been released publicly, is described in a progress report on its status as of last year, as including guidelines around five specific areas. Those areas are:

1) Debris released during normal operations,
2) Debris generated by explosions and intentional breakups,
3) Debris generated by on-orbit collisions during missions operations,
4) Post-mission disposal of space structures, and
5) Risk from reentering debris at post mission disposal.

The progress report on the handbook also indicates that a NASA technical memorandum titled "The Orbital Debris Assessment Reference Manual" will be prepared to provide assistance in developing debris mitigation and assessment efforts. It will allegedly consist of three volumes: Volume I titled "Assessment of Debris Mitigation Procedures": Volume II " Technical Background for Assessing Orbital Debris": Volume III "The Debris Assessment Software User's Guide."

In late February of this year the National Science and Technology Council's committee on Transportation Research and Development finally released it's "Interagency Report on Orbital Debris 1995". That report, which is an update of the

1989 report, suggests several approaches to minimize the continued growth of the space debris problem. It suggests that launch vehicles and spacecraft be designed so that they are "litter-free" (i.e., they not release separation devices or other potential debris once they become orbital.) It also suggests that LEO spacecraft and launch vehicle upper stages be deorbited, or, that all propellants and pressurants be expelled in the event they are not capable of being deorbited. Alternatively, it suggests that LEO satellites be reorbited into a safer orbital location that it describes as a "trash" orbit. This is similar to the approach taken with virtually all Geostationary satellites which are reboosted into higher orbits beyond the Geostationary orbital plane.

Of some intrigue is the suggestion in the report that several space "vacuum cleaners" could be developed to remove certain small and large objects from the low earth orbit areas. The report also suggests the possibility of significant increases in the space debris in LEO orbits due to the proliferation of proposed large LEO constellations. This concern is simply founded upon the large numbers of satellites that are scheduled to be launched to deploy the constellations supporting these programs in the next few years and during the period following their deployment with respect to the maintenance and operation of such constellations by replacing satellites as they approach the end of their useful life. As I will describe later, at least with respect to the IRIDIUM System, we have recognized this risk and undertaken aggressive efforts to significantly reduce the risk of adding to the space debris problem.

The report contains many other recommendations including the establishment of government and industry design guidelines on orbital debris and further international cooperation and discussion on this topic. Rather than commenting on any of the specific recommendations contained in this newly released report, I would simply suggest that, to the extent discussions on this topic are continued further in this forum or others, that you seek the input from all available industry sources in order to both understand the technical issues associated with this matter and to facilitate a practical solution that will be beneficial for us all. In the event the establishment of national or international standards on space debris mitigation is pursued, it is essential that some consideration be given to the ability of industry to conform to such standards on a prospective basis. A phased approach which gradually implements any such standards over a period of time would be much more readily embraced by industry and could be implemented much more effectively. To assist in your analysis of this topic further, let me describe for you a specific program now being developed by industry.

Space Debris Mitigation Efforts on the IRIDIUM Program

For the past six years I have been deeply involved in the development of the business and programmatic arrangements of one of the world's most ambitious space programs - the IRIDIUM Communication System being developed by Motorola. IRIDIUM is one of a number of low earth orbit (LEO) satellite-based telecommunications systems announced by industry and is expected to begin commercial service in 1998.

As you are probably all well aware, the issue of orbital debris is particularly significant for LEO satellites due to the thousands of individual pieces of debris located at that altitude. This is particularly significant for the IRIDIUM Communication System which will utilize 66 satellites in a constellation of six orbital planes at an altitude of approximately 780 km. In addition to the 66 satellites, roughly six spare satellites will be in orbit slightly below the orbit of the constellation. I'd like to share with you some of the specific orbital debris mitigation strategies that we are employing in the IRIDIUM program.

Early in the development phases of the IRIDIUM program, Motorola decided that it would implement a state-of-the-art orbital debris mitigation philosophy. Initially this concept required the selection of orbits which minimized the collision hazard for all the spacecraft in the constellation. For example, small adjustments were made to inclination and argument of latitude to create spacing distances between spacecraft of greater than 100 km at the North and South Pole.

Motorola also inserted a specific requirement in its design level space segment specifications which requires the implementation of debris mitigation approaches by all of our suppliers, including our launch service suppliers. The following is a sample of the wording contained in the specifications:

> "Subsequent to deployment of all of the IRIDIUM Space Vehicles, the launch vehicle upper stage must perform a deorbit maneuver placing the upper stage in a decay orbit."
>
> "Design analysis shall also be performed to demonstrate that the launch vehicle or related hardware does not generate any debris on orbit in excess of the limitations specified in the IRIDIUM Space Segment Specification."

We sought out experts knowledgeable about specific hazardous components such as the nickel-hydrogen batteries. As a result of the advice of the noted Russian scientist, Boris Tsenter, we modified the nickel-hydrogen battery design and incorporated key procedural recommendations into our operations plan.

Perhaps the most visible and widely acclaimed aspect of the debris mitigation practices implemented for the IRIDIUM system is the end-of-life deboosting of the spacecraft. This space debris mitigation mandate required us to include additional mass and fuel to accommodate the deboosting maneuvers associated with placing the spacecraft in a decay orbit that would ultimately result in its reentry into the atmosphere.

Recently we began discussions with Orbital Sciences Corporation regarding its ORBCOMM constellation of satellites that it is beginning to deploy which will occupy orbits close to the orbits of the IRIDIUM satellites. These discussions are on-going and we expect to engage in discussions with all members of industry and governments who would find benefit from sharing orbital data to insure to the maximum extent possible that on-orbit collisions are avoided.

These debris mitigation approaches, taken as a system requirement for a 66 satellite constellation, are unique. Nonetheless, they can be implemented on many satellite programs. Our experiences on the IRIDIUM program have demonstrated that there are several factors, however, that must be considered before any specific approach to debris mitigation is implemented effectively.

As you know, the development time and effort associated with current space-based activities extends over many years before the first satellite is ever launched. During that time significant design and production tradeoffs are evaluated by the engineering and operations staffs in their efforts to develop a spacecraft that performs the essential mission functions as efficiently as practical. During that time several interfaces with the launch vehicles that may launch the spacecraft are also designed.

A formal space debris mitigation philosophy and approach should, therefore, be adopted at the earliest point in the spacecraft development cycle to attain the maximum ability to implement practical debris mitigation approaches. Where such debris mitigation philosophies are not considered until later in the development cycle, the ability to implement such approaches is significantly reduced due to the costs and time associated with redesigning the spacecraft and launch vehicles.

In summary, I hope it is rather clear that, where active debris mitigation philosophies are incorporated in the early development efforts of new spacecraft and launch vehicle systems, significant and effective debris mitigation techniques can be employed in those systems at an acceptable cost. Further research into other debris mitigating techniques is being pursued by industry and should be implemented at appropriate times in the future. Finally, continued assistance from government and discussions between industry, government and academia will serve to increase the chances of implementing better and practical approaches to minimizing the space debris problem that we face today. However, it is not a problem that any one business enterprise or country can hope to solve on its own - it will require international communication and commitment to adopt those policies that can minimize the space debris dilemma for us all.

Thank you for your time and your attention.

Bryan Cheuvront is a Senior Counsel in Motorola's Law Department. He currently manages the law office located in Chandler, Arizona in support of the Satellite Communication Division of Motorola's Government and Space Technology Group.

SPACE DEBRIS: A REVIEW OF THE CURRENT REGULATORY STRUCTURE

By Dr. Vladimír Kopal [x]

Introduction

From the reports and studies, which have been published during the last decade, it has become evident that a thorough exploration of the problems relating to the protection of space environment against pollution by space debris has been a recognized subject of a deep concern of the world community.[1]

A visible, though rather slow progress in the discussions on this issue in the United Nations Committee on the Peaceful Uses of Outer Space /COPUOS/ was also reached and by a consensus decision taken in 1993, the Scientific and Technical Subcommittee of the COPUOS was entrusted to begin the consideration of this issue as a separate point of its agenda. In 1995 and 1996 the Subcommittee continued its consideration of "Space Debris" on a priority basis and adopted a work plan for the time span 1996-98 in order to advance this consideration. The up-to-date results of the deliberations of the Subcommittee on this point have been reflected in its reports.[2]

Present Legal Basis for Keeping Outer Space Clean and Safe and the Need for Its Further Development

Whatever conclusions may come out from the discussions in the scientific and technical area, when pondering the ways to keep outer space clean and safe, it is also necessary to consider the availability and possible development of adequate legal means for this purpose. A realistic approach to the study of legal aspects of the space debris issue should start by the following question: Is the present international law of outer space as developed in the United Nations sufficient for this endeavour, does it offer a solid basis for this kind of cooperation ? Or do such efforts require strengthening and supplementing of the existing rules, or even the elaboration of a new, special instrument ?

It should be recognized that the principles and provisions of the international law in force offer a certain guidance in this regard. The 1967 Treaty on Principles Governing the Activities of States in the Exploration and Use of Outer Space, including the Moon and Other Celestial Bodies, encouraged international cooperation in the peaceful exploration and use of outer space and according to its Article I, space activities should be carried out for the benefit and in the interest of all countries. The exploration and use of outer space shall be the province of all mankind. At the same time, the Outer Space Treaty enshrined in Article VI the principle of international responsibility for national activities in outer space as well as for space activities of international organizations. It should be emphasized that by national activities in outer space are meant not only activities carried

----

[x] Professor of Law, Doctor of Sciences, Prague, Czech Republic.

out by governmental agencies but also the activities performed by non-governmental entities, i.e. by private persons, physical or juridical, and the groups thereof. States Parties to the Outer Space Treaty are responsible for assuring that national activities are carried out in conformity with the provisions set forth in the Treaty, and the activities of non-governmental entities require authorization and continuing supervision by the appropriate State Party to the Treaty./Article VI./

Of a particular interest, in relation to the issue of space debris, may be the provision of para. 3, Article V of the Outer Space Treaty according to which States Parties to the Treaty shall immediately inform the other States Parties and the UN Secretary-General of any phenomena they discover in outer space, including the moon and other celestial bodies, which could constitute a danger to the life or health of astronauts.

Moreover, Article IX of the Outer Space Treaty, which enshrined the principle of cooperation and mutual assistance of the States Parties to the Treaty, and also stipulated due regard to corresponding interests of all other States Parties in all activities in outer space, spelled out a general principle for protection of the space environment. According to it "States Parties to the Treaty shall pursue studies of outer space, including the moon and other celestial bodies, and conduct exploration of them so as to avoid their harmful contamination and also adverse changes in the environment of the earth resulting from the introduction of extraterrestrial matter and, where necessary, shall adopt appropriate measures for this purpose." When analyzing this particuler text, can we conclude that by "harmful contamination" and "adverse changes in the environment of the earth resulting from the introduction of extraterrestrial matter" the drafters of this provision intended to also cover the effects caused by space debris ? Can we also assume that by adopting "appropriate measures" adequate steps for prevention and mitigation of space debris could be understood including some legal tools to be elaborated and applied in order to attain this goal ?

In this context, it should be recalled that Article IX of the Outer Space Treaty also provided for "appropriate international consultations" which might be offered or requested by States Parties to the Treaty for avoiding a potentially harmful interference with their space activities. Needless to say that such interferences might generate, or be caused by, space debris. Such consultations, however, are not obligatory.

The principles of international liability for damage caused by space objects or their component parts on the earth, in air or in outer space was also included in the 1967 Outer Space Treaty. This principle was further elaborated in the 1972 Convention on International Liability for Damage Caused by Space Objects which includes a number of provisions that may be considered as relevant to space debris. As explicitly stated in Article I of the Convention, the term "space object" includes component parts of a space object as well as its launch vehicle and parts thereof. Apparently, by an extensive interpretation of this provision, space debris which originate from space objects, their launch vehicles or the parts thereof, should be covered by this definition. However, is it possible to go in this interpretation so far as to qualify as component parts of a space object or parts of its launch vehicle the smallest fragments or even flakes of paint peeled off from such objects ? Moreover, will such small pieces of material be always identifiable as to their origin ? It is obvious that without an exact identification of a piece of space debris, it would be impossible to impute any liability for damage caused by such particals to anybody.

As is known, the 1972 Liability Convention, in its Articles II - IV, deals with two categories of damage, one caused by space objects on the surface of the earth or to aircraft in flight, the other caused elsewhere than on the surface of the earth to a space object of the launching State or to persons or property on board such a space object by a space object of another launching State. According to some authors, these provisions should also apply to damage caused by space debris. [3] However, according to the 1972 Convention, the liability provided for damage effected elsewhere than on the surface of the earth or to aircraft in flight shall only be applied in case of fault on the part of the launching State or the fault of persons for whom this State is responsible. But in most cases of damage caused by smaller space debris it will be very difficult or even impossible to identify the origin of the debris concerned and thus to ascertain who is at fault. Furthermore, the term "fault" has not been specified in the Convention. May it be assumed that both "intention" and "negligence" are supposed to be considered as a basis of fault? Or is it possible to go even further and apply in this regard the "objective" approach which has prevailed in the codification work of the UN International Law Commission on State responsibility ? [4]

On the other hand it should be observed that the term "damage", as defined in Article I of the 1972 Liability Convention, means only "loss of life, personal injury or other impairment of health; or loss of or damage to property of States or of persons, natural or juridical, or property of international intergovernmental organizations". It must be concluded from this definition that the term "damage" in the Liability Convention does not include damage caused by space activities to the space environment and to the environments of other areas, which lie beyond the limits of national sovereignty, such as Antarctica and the oceans. [5]

Some guidance for dealing with space debris can also be found in other UN space law instruments. The 1975 Convention on Registration of Objects launched into Outer Space, which established the duty of the launching State to register space objects both nationally and internationally /with the United Nations/, allows the State of registry to provide the Secretary-General of the United Nations with additional information concerning space objects carried on its registry. This State is even obliged to notify the Secretary-General "to the greatest extent feasible and as soon as practicable, of space objects concerning which it has previously transmitted information, and which have been but no longer are in earth orbit." In this connection it is to be recalled that the term "space object" is specified in the Registration Convention in the same way as in the Liability Convention, i. e. that it includes component parts of a space object as well as its launch vehicle and parts thereof. This provision of the Registration Convention might offer a certain basis for developing a practice of providing more detailed information about space debris remaining in outer space in connection with the decay of space objects. In this regard, however, the same question arises which was already mentioned with regard to the Liability Convention, namely what should be still qualified as space object or its part, and what lies beyond the reasonable limits of this notion.

Finally, attention should be also drawn to the last of the United Nations space treaties, the 1979 Agreement Governing the Activities of States on the Moon and Other Celestial Bodies, in spite of the fact that thus far, this instrument has collected but a limited number of adhesions. In relation to the moon, Article 7 of the Agreement goes further than the 1967 Outer Space Treaty went generally, for the States Parties to the 1979 Agreement, in exploring and using the moon, are obliged to take measures to prevent the disruption of the existing balance of its environment, whether by introducing adverse changes in that environment, by its harmful contamination through the introduction of extraenvironmental matter or otherwise. The word "otherwise" may include the pollution of the moon environment or some of its areas by generation of space debris. But will such pollution be that big to be qualified as "disruption of the existing balance" of the moon environment ?

In the same Article, the 1979 Moon Agreement also involves some other elements which are necessary for establishing an effective protection of the moon environment. It is, e.g., the duty to inform the Secretary General of the United Nations of the measures being adopted in connection with the above obligation, as well as the special duty to notify him in advance of all placements of radioactive materials on the moon and of the purpose of such placements. Moreover, as provided in para. 3 of the same Article 7, the idea of reporting to other States Parties and to the Secretary-General concerning areas of the moon having special scientific interest in order that consideration may be given to the designation of such areas as international scientific preserves for which special protective arrangements are to be agreed upon, also deserves our attention.[6]

As a whole, it is obvious that for the solution of all legal problems relating to the protection of outer space against space debris the provisions of the present international law of outer space are too general, raise a number of questions and are far from being satisfactory.

On the other hand, a certain step forward has been marked in the specific field of the use of nuclear power sources in outer space. Though the 1992 Principles dealing with this subject[7] are applicable only to a particular kind of instrumentalities /namely to"nuclear power sources in outer space devoted to the generation of electric power on board space objects for nonpropulsive purposes, which have characteristics generally comparable to those of systems used and missions performed at the time of the adoption of the Principles", some important innovations have been introduced by these Principles in comparison with the earlier space law instruments. They include, inter alia, the establishment of general goals for radiation protection and nuclear safety, the idea of storing of nuclear reactors and radioisotope generators in a disposal orbit after the conclusion of the operational part of their missions, and also a certain specification of the general principle of liability for damage as far as the determination of compensation for damage is concerned.

The problems relating to the use of nuclear power sources in outer space have several common points with problems of protection of the space environment against space debris, as was clearly demonstrated during the discussions of the Working Group on Nuclear Power Sources in the Scientific and Technical Subcommittee of the COPUOS. [8] A successful conclusion of these efforts in the form of a set of internationally agreed Principles Relevant to the Use of Nuclear Power Sources in Outer Space in 1992 offers an example for a similar approach to the problems of protection of the space environment against space debris.

Question of a Legal Definition of Space Debris

As already said, the up-to-date space legislation has known only the term "space object" which, according to Article I /d/ of the 1972 Liability Convention and the identical provision of Article I /b/ of the 1975 Registration Convention, includes "component parts of a space object as well as its launch vehicle and parts thereof". This term has been used as a fundamental element for establishing the principles and rules governing space activities and has also become one of the basic notions in the space law doctrine. The underlying philosophy of all present international law instruments relating to outer space has been based on a conviction that launching of space objects has been opening great prospects before mankind. For this reason, space activities should be promoted and guided by broad international cooperation in the scientific as well as the legal aspects of the exploration and use of outer space for peaceful purposes. /Preamble of the 1967 Outer Space Treaty./

In recent years, however, attention has been drawn to a growing population of remains of these objects which, having ended their missions, become useless "space debris" unless they perish during their descent, are boosted to a disposal orbit or are brought back to the earth. The present space treaties and other instruments of space law do not explicitly address this particular problem. Neither the space treaties concluded under the auspices of the United Nations, nor any other international agreements, nor the domestic law of individual spacefaring nations provide a definition of this notion and establish specific legal rules that should be applied to the ever increasing number of these objects which are not only of any use but may even cause harmful effects.

Fortunately, the scientific and technical community, both at national and international levels, has already investigated this problem in greater detail and produced a number of reports and studies that can be used as a basis for consideration of its legal aspects. [9] In some of these papers, the term "space debris" /which is sometimes also called "orbital debris"/ has been defined. Thus e.g. in the IAA Position Paper on Orbital Debris, this kind of objects includes "any man-made Earth-orbiting object which is non-functional with no reasonable expectation of assuming or resuming its intended function or any other function for which it is or can be expected to be authorized, including fragments and parts thereof. Orbital debris includes non-operational spacecraft, spent rocket bodies, material released during planned space operations, and fragments generated by satellites and upper stage break-up due to explosions and collisions." A similar definition has been used in the considerations of the Scientific and Technical Subcommittee of the COPUOS which understood that "space debris are inactive man-made objects, such as spent upper stages, spent satellites, fragments or parts generated during launch or mission operations, or fragments from explosions and other break-ups." [11]

Such an approach was also adopted by the Space Law Committee of the International Law Association /ILA/ when this important non-governmental organization was preparing a Draft International Instrument on the Protection of the Environment from Damage Caused by Space Debris. According to the final version of this document, which was adopted by the 66th Conference of the ILA at Buenos Aires in August 1994, the meaning of "space debris" includes "man-made objects in outer space, other than active or otherwise usefull satellites, when no change can reasonably be expected in these conditions in the foreseeable future". The scope of application of the ILA's Draft has been also adjusted to this definition, for the Instrument "shall be applicable to space debris which causes or is likely to cause direct or indirect, instant or delayed damage to the environment or to persons and objects. [12]

In light of this definition of space debris, Article VIII of the 1967 Outer Space Treaty, which guarantees the retaining of jurisdiction and control of States over space objects carried on their registry as well as the continuing ownership of space objects and of their component parts, must be carefully analysed and should be probably limited in its application with regard to the need for protecting outer space against space debris. Other United Nations Space Treaties /the 1968 Rescue Agreement, the 1972 Liability Convention, the 1975 Registration Convention/ as well should be reviewed in the same direction.

Conclusion

For these and other reasons, a special legal document on space debris is desirable, be it a comprehensive instrument that would deal with all aspects of space debris, or only an interpretative protocol to the existing space treaties with regard to their application to space debris. *Inter alia*, such a legal document should clearly establish from which moment a space object or its parts become non-functional and useless, and may be treated by anybody as space debris.

The elaboration and adoption of an exact legal definition of "space debris", which would be in harmony with the best scientific and technical knowledge, should then be accompanied by the formulation and adoption of new rules that would govern liability for damage caused by an inactive object or its parts and exclude space debris from the general protection guaranteed by the present international law of outer space to space objects and their parts.

The ILA Buenos Aires International Instrument on the Protection of the Environment from Damage Caused by Space Debris offers a good example how a legal document on the issue of space debris could be drafted.

References

1. See, e.g., Nicholas L. Johnson and Darren S. McKnight, Artificial Space Debris, Malabar, Florida, 1987; Space Debris. A Report From the ESA Space Debris Working Group, ESA SP-1109 /November 1988/; Report on Orbital Debris by Interagency Group /Space/ for National Security Council, Washington, D.C., February 1989; U.S. Congress, Office of Technology Assessment, Orbiting Debris: A Space Environmental Problem - Background Paper, OTA-BP-ISC-72, Washington, DC, September 1990; Proceedings of the First European Conference on Space Debris, Darmstadt, Germany, 5 - 7 April 1993, ESA SD-01, July 1993; International Academy of Astronautics, Position Paper on Orbital Debris, Prepared by an Ad Hoc Expert Group of the IAA Committee on Safety, Rescue and Quality, November 1993; David S.F. Portree, Joseph P. Loftus, Jr., Orbital Debris and Near-Earth Environmental Management: A Chronology, NASA Reference Publication 1320, December 1993; Orbital Debris. A Technical Assessment, Committee on Space Debris, Aeronautics and Space Engineering Board, Commission on Engineering and Technical Systems, National Research Council, Washington, D.C. 1995; Interagency Report on Orbital Debris by Office of Science and Technology Policy, November 1995.

2. Cf., in particular, Reports of the Scientific and Technical Subcommittee on the Work of Its Thirty-second and Thirty-third Sessions, UN doc. A/AC. 105/605, 24 February 1995, pp. 15-18, and UN doc. A/AC. 105/637, 4 March 1996, pp. 15-25.

3. See, e.g., S. Gorove, Definitional Issues Pertaining to "Space Object", Proceedings of the Thirty-seventh Colloquium on the Law of Outer Space, International Institute of Space Law of the IAF, October 9 - 14, 1994, Jerusalem, Israel, AIAA, p. 90.

4. In this context it is interesting to note the suggestion of Professor Bing Cheng to establish absolute liability, or at least a régime of presumed fault, for damage caused by space debris. /See "Space Objects","Astronauts" and Related Expressions, Proceedings of the Thirty-Fourth Colloquium on the Law of Outer Space, International Institute of Space Law of the IAF, October 5 - 11, 1991, Montreal, Canada, AIAA, p. 25. - As to the problem of fault see also Interagency Report on Orbital Debris by Office of Science and Technology Policy, November 1995, p. 46.

5. See Nandasiri Jasentuliyana, Environmental Impact of Space Activities: An International Law Perspective, Proceedings of the Twenty-seventh Colloquium on the Law of Outer Space, International Institute of Space Law of the IAF, October 7 - 13, 1984, Lausanne, Switzerland, AIAA, p. 395.

6. For the texts of all space treaties referred to in this paper as well the status of Parties to these instruments cf. United Nations Treaties and Principles on Outer Space, UN doc. A/AC. 105/572, United Nations, 1994.

7. See Principles Relevant to the Use of Nuclear Power Sources in Outer Space, in UN doc. A/AC. 105/592 quoted <u>supra</u>, note 6, pp. 47 s.

8. Cf., e.g., Report of the Scientific and Technical Subcommittee on the Work of Its Twenty-fifth Session, UN doc. A/AC. 105/409, 29 February 1988, Annex III, paras. 8-10 at p. 30; Report of the Scientific and Technical Subcommittee on the Work of Its Twenty-sixth Session, UN doc. A/AC. 105/429, 6 March 1989, Annex III, paras. 10-12, p. 33.

9. A substantive contribution to these efforts was made by convening, under the auspices of ESA, by its ESOC the First European Conference on Space Debris held in Darmstadt, Germany, 5 - 7 April 1993. See the voluminous Proceedings of this Conference /741 pp./, doc. ESA SD-01, July 1993. The second conference of this kind, organized by ESA/ESOC, is to be held again in Darmstadt, Germany, 17 - 19 March 1997. - First International Workshop on Space Debris was also held from October 8 to 11, 1995 in the building of the Space Research Institute of the Russian Academy of Sciences.

10. See International Academy of Astronautics, Position Paper on Orbital Debris. Prepared by an Ad Hoc Expert Group of the IAA Committee on Safety, Rescue and Quality, November 1993, p. 3.

11. Cf. Report of the Scientific and Technical Subcommittee on the Work of Its Thirty-third Session, UN doc. A/AC. 195/637, 4 March 1996, para. 15 at p. 17.

12. Cf. the text of Resolution No. 5 of the Conference of the International Law Association adopted in August 1994 and the final text of the International Instrument on the Protection of the Environment from Damage Caused by Space Debris. See also Statement by Prof. Dr. K. H. Böckstiegel as representative of the International Law Association /ILA/ at the 39th Session of the COPUOS, Vienna, June 1996.

MANFRED LACHS SPACE LAW MOOT COURT COMPETITION 1996

PARLIVIA V. CALIFORNIUM, *ET AL*

Case Concerning Liability for Commercial Space Endeavors

1. INTRODUCTION

The finals of the 5th Manfred Lachs Space Law Moot Court Competition were held in Beijing during the IISL Colloquium. Preliminary competitions had been organized in Europe by the European Centre of Space Law (ECSL) of ESA, and in the US by the Association of US Members of the IISL. The winners of these preliminaries were the University of Helsinki, Finland (Anna Markkanen and Satu Heikkilä) for Europe, and the University of Wyoming (Bastiaan Coebergh and Joseph Richer) for the USA. They met in Beijing before a bench composed of Judge Chr. Weeramantry, Judge G. Herczegh and Judge V. Vereshchetin of the International Court of Justice. The University of Helsinki won the competition. Financial and organizational support for the competition were granted by the Chinese Foreign Ministry, the University of Beijing, Air China and KLM Royal Dutch Airlines. ECSL and AUSMIISL sponsored the teams' travel to Beijing. Hereunder follow the case, written by Pamela Meredith, and the briefs of the winning teams.

2. THE PROBLEM

Issues presented:

1) Whether a claim can be presented under the Liability Convention while arbitration is in progress; 2) Whether a contractual waiver precludes recovery for satellite loss;
3) Whether a claimant State may recover lost revenues and refund of the launch
price under the Liability Convention; and 4) Apportionment of liability

Statement of Facts

On May 1, 1998, the Ministry of Industry ("MI") of Parlivia, entered into a launch contract with ISE Enerkru, Ltd. ("ISEE"), a joint venture of International Space Enterprises, Inc. ("ISE") of the Republic of Californium and NPO Enerkru of the Republic of Ukrastan. The contract provided for the launching of MI's satellite, *Environsat,* on Enerkru's *Progyia* launch vehicle. *Progyia* launch vehicles are marketed worldwide by ISEE from its headquarters in the Pleasant Islands.

Parlivia, through MI, had contracted with a local entity to build *Environsat,* a remote sensing satellite to be used for environmental monitoring and for forestry and agricultural applications. Data acquired through the satellite would be used by MI and also would be sold to private entities in Parlivia, as well as to foreign governments.

On April 8, 2000, *Progyia,* with *Environsat* on board, lifted off from its launch pad at the brand new commercial launch site at Cape Kou in Patalia. The two-stage *Progyia* placed *Environsat* in its intended 800 km equatorial orbit.

Due to a thruster malfunction, the *Progyia* second stage remained in an orbit very close to that of *Environsat.* After the initial separation of the *Progyia* second stage from *Environsat* through a spring mechanism (which caused the objects to separate with only a very small distance), ISEE intended to perform 1) a collision avoidance maneuver and 2) a re-orbit assist maneuver. If successful, these maneuvers would have lowered the perigee of the rocket stage to 250 km. The maneuvers were to be accomplished by firing of small thrusters on the *Progyia* second stage, but because of a software error, the thrusters failed to ignite. Neither the launch contract, nor its technical annexes specified how the separation of the *Progyia* second stage would occur.

On July 6, 2000, the *Progyia* second stage exploded due to overpressurization in its propellant tanks caused by the excess propellant remaining after the thruster malfunction. Over one-hundred pieces of debris generated by the explosion were distributed into a variety of orbits, many of which intersected the *Environsat* orbit.

Thirty-five days later, a small fragment of the exploded rocket body hit and completely disabled *Environsat.*

A subsequent failure investigation conducted by a Safety Review Board appointed by ISEE revealed that the software error that prevented the thrusters from firing resulted from a computer coding error made by Dr. Yelkov, an Enerkru computer programmer. Dr. Yelkov had entered an erroneous command code for thruster ignition. The code determined the time of activation of the battery-powered valves which would cause the propellant to flow through the propellant lines and into the combustion chamber and ignite the thrusters. The correct time code was "1.2 x 10^2" seconds, that is, 120 seconds. Instead, the erroneously encoded time was "1.2 x 10^6" seconds, *i.e.*, 1.2 million seconds, or 14 days. By this time, the batteries were dead and the thrusters never fired.

MI had purchased launch and in-orbit insurance through its insurance broker, Will McCoone, Ltd., covering the entire value of the satellite ($90 million) and extending until two years after launch. The insurance underwriters compensated MI under this policy.

MI also had purchased a launch price refund guarantee as part its launch contract with ISEE. MI now claims refund of the launch price in the amount of $50 million from ISEE and its parent ISE. Both ISEE and ISE reject MI's claim for a refund.

A group of insurance underwriters registered in Parlivia known as Space Insurers of South America (SISA), which had paid $10 million of MI's insurance claim, have turned to ISEE and ISE with subrogation claims for their respective insurance payments. They claim ISEE, ISE, and Enerkru acted with negligence and gross negligence in 1) failing to perform the separation maneuvers that would have lowered the orbit of the *Progyia* second stage; and 2) failing to vent or deplete the propellants contained in the rocket stage. ISEE and ISE reject the claim, contending that SISA is precluded under the launch contract between MI and ISEE from bringing the claim.

Both MI's and SISA's claims were submitted to arbitration, since the ISEE-MI contract provided that all disputes thereunder would be settled in this manner. The arbitration proceeding has yet to be concluded.

Concerned that ISEE and ISE would be unable to pay for the damage in a timely fashion even if MI and SISA were to prevail on their respective claims in arbitration, the government of Parlivia asserted claims on behalf of MI and SISA against the governments of Californium, Ukrastan, the Pleasant Islands, and Patalia under the Liability Convention of 1972 for 1) loss of the satellite ($90 million), 2) the launch price ($50 million), and 3) loss of revenues ($20 million). There is no agreement among these four respondent States as to apportionment of potential liability or damages. All four respondent States have rejected Parlivia's claims.

The parties failed to settle the matter through diplomatic channels, as called for by the Liability Convention. Neither party requested the establishment of a Claims Commission under the Liability Convention. To resolve the matter finally, the parties have agreed to refer the case to the International Court of Justice for resolution of the issues stipulated below. There are no issues as to the Court's jurisdiction.

The Court has appointed a Special Master to examine the highly technical issues involved in evaluating fault under the Liability Convention. This Special Master will report to the Court. In the interim, the Court has requested the parties to address the following issues:

Issues Presented Before the ICJ

1) Whether Parlivia may claim under the Liability Convention while the arbitration proceeding is in progress;
2) Whether the ISEE-MI contractual waiver regime precludes Parlivia's recovery of damages for the satellite loss;
3) Whether damages recovered under the Liability Convention may include a) loss of revenues, and b) refund of the launch price (including to what extent the Refund provision in ISEE-MI contract is relevant); and
4) Assuming that the Court finds that ISEE's conduct of launch operations meet the standard of "fault" under the Liability Convention, whether all four respondent States are liable, and how damages to Parlivia should be apportioned among respondent States, if any, found liable under the convention.

Instructions to the Students

1) You should prepare one memorial for the Applicant (Parlivia), and one memorial for the four Respondent States (Californium, *et al*);
2) You should assume that all of the parties to this dispute are parties to all of the relevant international treaties and conventions;
3) You should cite and discuss the relevance of *Martin Marietta v. INTELSAT* (763 F. Supp. 1327 (1991), *aff'd. in part, den. in part,* 991 F. 2d 94 (DC Cir. 1992)) and *Appalachian Insurance Co. v. McDonnell Douglas* (262 Cal Rptr. 716 (1989), copies of which will be provided to the European schools which register for the competition; and
4) You should *not* engage in a discussion of whether ISEE's conduct of launch operations was negligent/culpable (the fault issue). This issue will be addressed by the Court later when it has received a report from the Special Master. The report will not be part of this problem.

Contract between ISE Enerkru, Ltd. ("ISEE") and the Ministry of Industry of Parlivia ("MI") for the Launching of Environsat (Excerpts)

ARTICLE 1 -- DEFINITIONS (Excerpts)

1.1. "Associates" shall mean any individual or entity, governed by public or private law, who shall act, directly or indirectly, on behalf of one party in the fulfillment of the obligations undertaken by such Party in this Contract, for example, but without limitation, the personnel of each of the Parties, their suppliers and contractors, including persons who shall act on behalf of such party upon the fulfillment of its obligations or else during Launch Preparations.
1.2. "Best Efforts" shall mean diligently working in a good workman-like manner as a reasonably prudent Launch Provider.
1.3. "Customer" shall mean MI.
1.7. "Launch" means intentional ignition of the *Progyia* Launch Vehicle.
1.8. "Launch Failure" shall mean the failure of the to accomplish the Launch Mission.
1.9. "Launch Mission" shall mean the launch of the Spacecraft for purposes of enabling said Spacecraft to carry out its operational objectives.
1.10. "Launch Provider" shall mean ISEE.
1.11. "Launch Services" shall mean the services to be provided by Launch Provider under this Contract.
1.12."Launch Vehicle" shall mean the *Progyia* launch vehicle provided by Launch Provider under this Contract.

ARTICLE 2 -- CONTRACTUAL DOCUMENTS

2.1. This Contract shall consist of the following documents, which shall be legally binding upon the Parties:
2.1.1. Terms and Conditions as expressed in Articles 1-30;
2.1.2.Appendix A, Launch Services Technical Specifications;
2.1.3. Appendix B, Customer Technical Commitments; And
2.1.4. Appendix C, Interface Control Document.

ARTICLE 3 -- LAUNCH SERVICES

3.1. Launch Provider shall use its Best Efforts to launch Customer's Spacecraft as specified in APPENDIX A and in accordance with the Launch Mission.

ARTICLE 13 -- REFUND (Excerpts)

13.1. A Refund Guarantee is hereby purchased by MI, the charges of which are included in the Contract Price set forth under ARTICLE 7, Prices for Launch Services.

13.2. In the event of a *Progyia* Launch Failure, Customer shall be entitled to a Refund of the Launch Price.

13.5. The Refund provided for in this Article 13 shall constitute the sole and exclusive remedy available to Customer for any Launch Failure.

ARTICLE 15 -- WAIVER OF CLAIMS (Excerpts)

15.1. Launch Provider hereby waives any and all claims against Customer and against Customer's Associates, directors, officers, servants, agents, contractors, and subcontractors, for any property damage it may sustain and for any bodily injury or property damage sustained by its own employees resulting from Launch Services. This provision applies regardless of whether the claim arises under tort, contract or any other theory of liability.

15.2. Customer hereby waives any and all claims against Launch Provider and against Launch Provider's Associates, directors, officers, servants, agents, contractors, and subcontractors, for any property damage it may sustain and for any bodily injury or property damage sustained by its own employees resulting from Launch Services. This provision applies regardless of whether the claim arises under tort, contract or any other theory of liability.

15.3. Launch Provider and Customer shall each be responsible for and shall release the other Party from liability for any property damage they respectively sustain and for any bodily injury or property damage sustained by its employees resulting from Launch Services. Each party shall purchase the insurance it deems necessary to protect its interests against the risk of damage for which claims are waived and releases are made under this Article 15.

15.6 The reciprocal waivers provided for in this Article 15 shall extend to all indirect and consequential damages . . . .

ARTICLE 16 - THIRD PARTY LIABILITY (Excerpts)

16.1. Launch Provider shall procure and maintain Third Party liability insurance to protect Launch Provider, Customer, the Kingdom of Patalia, the Republic of Ukrastan, the Commonwealth of the Pleasant Islands, the Republic of Californium, and their respective Associates and contractors and Subcontractors arising out of or resulting from Launch Services. Such liability insurance shall name said parties as additional insureds.

ARTICLE 17 -- LIMITATION OF LIABILITY

17.1. Launch Provider's Liability to Customer and its Associates and contractors and subcontractors, whether arising under contract, tort or any other theory of liability, shall not include any loss of use or loss of profit or revenue or any other indirect, special, consequential, or incidental damages. In no event shall Launch Provider's liability to Customer for any claim arising out of a particular Launch exceed the price for Progyia Launch Services as provided for in Article 7, Prices for Launch Services. SUBJECT TO THE REFUND GUARANTEE, LAUNCH PROVIDER HAS NOT MADE NOR DOES MAKE ANY REPRESENTATION OR WARRANTY, WHETHER EXPRESS OR IMPLIED, WITH RESPECT TO THE DESIGN, OPERATION, CONDITION, QUALITY, SUITABILITY OR MERCHANTABILITY, OR FITNESS FOR USE OR FOR A PARTICULAR PURPOSE.

ARTICLE 23 -- DISPUTE SETTLEMENT (Excerpts)

23.1. The Parties shall endeavor to reach an amicable settlement of any dispute or controversy . . . . If such a settlement cannot be reached, the Parties shall submit the dispute or controversy to arbitration . . . .

3. WINNING BRIEFS

A. MEMORIAL FOR PARLIVIA

AGENTS

Bastiaan Coebergh, Joseph Richer

ARGUMENT

I. Parlivia may present a tort claim under the Liability Convention while the contract dispute is in arbitration.

A. The launch services contract between MI and ISEE was fulfilled, and the Liability Convention clearly allows a launching state to submit a claim for adjudication while arbitration is proceeding.

The Applicant is not bound by the contract between ISE Enerku, Ltd. ("ISEE") and the Ministry of Industry of Parlivia ("MI") for the launching of Environsat ("MI- ISEE agreement"). The contract at issue is not a treaty or even an international agreement. Rather, it is a private commercial contract between a government organization and a company.[1] Based on the record, it cannot be said that the parties intended to create obligations in international law.[2] Therefore, the obligations in the contract cannot be imputed to Parlivia.

However, if this Court finds the contract to be an international agreement, Parlivia is not bound by it under the "full powers" doctrine. As a general rule, a person representing a state can bind the state to a treaty if "it appears from the practice of the States concerned or from other circumstances that their intention was to consider that person as representing the State for such purposes."[3] The contract is not in any way an "international agreement having the character [in fact and in law] of a treaty or convention."[4] Even if one would use the term "treaty" in its broadest sense,[5] MI was not an agent with actual or apparent authority[6] to bind Parlivia to this contract. There is no privity of contract between Parlivia and the four respondent states.[7] Therefore, Parlivia is not bound by the MI-ISEE agreement.

Moreover, the contract was fulfilled. ISEE ignited and launched the two-stage *Progyia* launch vehicle with *Environsat* on board. *Progyia* placed the *Environsat* satellite in its intended orbit. Then, the *Progyia* second stage separated from *Environsat* by the use of a spring mechanism. Through these actions, ISEE carried out the "Launch" and completed the "Launch Mission" as defined in article 1 of the contract.[8] The subsequent occurrences, which in the end made *Environsat* useless and incapable of carrying out its intended operational objectives, were not part of the "Launch Mission." Neither the launch contract nor its technical annexes specified how the separation of the *Progyia* second stage would occur. Thus, the contract was obviously not intended to cover occurrences subsequent to the actual separation of *Progyia* from *Environsat*.[9] One could even argue that the launch contract only extended to the intentional ignition.[10] Therefore, ISEE's "Launch Mission" was successfully completed.[11] Accordingly, the contract, including its dispute settlement provisions, does not apply to the issue at hand.

Instead, the Liability Convention[12] is applicable in the case *sub judice*. Until *Progyia* and *Environsat* separated, they obviously formed one "space object" as defined in the Convention.[13] However, after separation, approximately four months passed before *Environsat* was hit by a fragment of the exploded *Progyia*. The definition of "space object" is not static[14] and should be liberally construed "in favor of an innocent victim."[15] Therefore, at the time of the collision, the *Progyia* fragment and *Environsat* constituted two separate "space objects" under the Liability Convention.

Article XI(1) of the Convention advances a "fundamental and sweeping denial of traditional local remedies requirements."[16] Hurwitz remarked in this regard: "The effect of this [exception] is that the process of international claim settlement will be speeded up. This is a positive result in line with the victim orientation of the Convention."[17]

While this exception is to a certain extent qualified by article XI(2), it is certainly broad enough to encompass this situation. Article XI(2) provides that a state cannot present a claim under the Liability Convention when an action has been brought "under another international agreement **which is binding on the States concerned**."[18] As was established above, it does not appear from the record that MI's negotiator had actual or apparent authority to bind Parlivia to this contract, and there is no privity of contract between Parlivia and the Respondent states.[19] Therefore, Parlivia can bring this claim before this Court at this time under article XI(1) of the Liability Convention.

In addition, the Liability Convention's focus on the well-being of the victim and on establishing a swift procedure to make the victims whole should lead to an admission of Parlivia's claim at this time. Article X(1) poses a one year Statute of Limitations, measured from time of occurrence. Parlivia is concerned that ISEE and ISE would be unable to pay for the damage in a timely fashion even if MI and SISA were to prevail in their arbitration claims. Also, if Parlivia would have to wait for the arbitration procedure to conclude, the Liability Convention's Statute of Limitations would almost certainly have run[20] since the arbitration procedure apparently has no tolling effect.

B. General principles and policies of international law indicate that Parlivia should be allowed to proceed with its claim before this Court at this time.

A study of the law of the sea regarding the settlement of disputes is "of specific relevance in our context,"[21] because maritime law has many similarities to space law.[22] Neither the record nor the contract reveal where the arbitration was brought or what procedure is being followed. Under the Law of the Sea Convention,[23] parties can agree "at any time" to adopt a special method for settling their dispute,[24] even after a dispute has arisen and one of the procedures under the Convention has been started. Also, if the procedure chosen by the parties does not lead to a binding decision, a party to the dispute can resort to the institutions under the Law of the Sea Convention to resolve the dispute.[25] The contract at issue does not indicate that the arbitration procedure will lead to a binding decision. Parlivia wants to bring this action under the Liability Convention against four Respondent states which are not parties to the contract. In this situation, the possibility of one state going to an international court against other states exists.[26]

Because the text of the Draft Convention on the Settlement of Space Law Disputes[27] follows "as closely as possible" the approach under the Sea Convention,[28] this Court should adhere to the approach in the Law of the Sea Convention mentioned above. This inescapably leads to the conclusion that Parlivia can bring the action under the Liability Convention at this time before this Court while the arbitration proceeding between the parties to the MI-ISEE agreement is advancing.

C. Even if this Court finds that the launch was not completed and the contract applies, Parlivia may bring its claim under the Liability Convention at this time.

Generally, written arbitration agreements are enforced and broadly interpreted.[29] However, this does not mean that the arbitration clause at issue applies in all instances. First, it appears from the record that the parties did not agree to have their dispute **finally settled** by arbitration but only to **submit** it to arbitration.[30] This already happened, so the parties to the agreement received what they bargained for. Now, the states have agreed to refer the case to this Court. The Respondents have not made their acceptance of this Court's jurisdiction subject to any reservations covering the dispute currently in arbitration. Further, nowhere does it appear that the parties to the contract wanted their disputes to be arbitrated to the exclusion of any other concurrent or consecutive mode of conflict resolution. In such a situation, "[this] Court should not consider a legal dispute as non-justiciable solely because negotiations or other means of settlement are currently in progress or because they have not been exhausted."[31] Therefore, Parlivia's claim under the Liability Convention is admissible before this Court.

The parties to the contract agreed that "**any** dispute or controversy" would be arbitrable.[32] However, it is not clear from the language of the instrument whether this means any dispute **arising under** the contract or any dispute **in connection** with the contract. "Arising hereunder" has been held to indicate a narrow arbitration clause,[33] while "in connection with this Agreement" has been construed to embrace every dispute between the parties having a significant relationship to the contract regardless of the label attached to the dispute.[34] Since the parties did not include the "in connection with" language in the contract, they intended only to cover contractual disputes and not quasi-contractual or tort disputes. Therefore, this Court should consider the tort claims.[35]

The often proffered apparent advantages of the arbitral process on a national level do not apply to the international process.[36] Further, "[e]xperience seems to show that rather than impeding settlement, litigation may serve as a spur to negotiation."[37] Unlike an arbitrator, this Court "can deal as expeditiously with a case as the parties will allow."[38] Moreover, this Court's role would be in danger of becoming highly political and speculative if it had to weigh the consequences of a legal ruling for an eventual settlement.[39] Thus, as a matter of general public policy, it is not desirable to let the arbitration procedure have a staying effect on the proceedings before this Court.

Alternatively, strong public policy considerations dictate that the matter at hand be declared non-arbitrable.[40] Some nations forbid arbitration of "all matters in the realm of public policy."[41] When *Progyia* exploded, it did much more than damage *Environsat*: it brought about significant environmental orbital damage. The explosion generated a large amount of space debris[42] which essentially was dumped in a variety of orbits.[43] Currently, space debris has become a major problem,[44] and any occurrence adding to the problem should be approached with the utmost care as a matter of public policy.[45] Since any existing arbitration institution would be unable to handle this issue, and since it is important that a court give an authoritative decision on the issue, this Court should consider this matter non-arbitrable. Even if this Court finds the contractual issues arbitrable, the tort issues should be declared non-arbitrable due to their different nature.

II. The contractual waiver regime does not preclude Parlivia's recovery of damages for the satellite loss.

A. Since the MI-ISEE contract does not apply to Parlivia's current action against the four Respondent states, the MI-ISEE waiver provisions do not have any restrictive effect on Parlivia's ability to recover its damages for the satellite loss.

As argued above (Part I.B), the collision between the *Progyia* fragment and *Environsat* should be characterized as a collision in space under Article III of the Liability Convention rather than a "Launch Failure" under the MI-ISEE contract. This agreement was fulfilled when *Progyia* separated from *Environsat*. The additional removal of the second stage from Environsat's orbit was ISEE's duty in tort as a reasonable launch provider under the Liability Convention, not a contractual duty.

This Court can take judicial notice of municipal law rules and principles.[46] Therefore, a discussion of decisions of United States courts in cases similar to the one at hand is relevant "as an indication of policy and principles."[47] In Appalachian Insurance[48] and Martin Marietta,[49] which were both decided under the terms of the launch contract, the satellites never reached the intended orbit. In both cases, the boosters from the respective rockets already failed on the way to the satellite's intended orbit.[50] Our case is distinguishable because the rocket did take the satellite to its intended orbit before physically separating from the satellite. A subsequent failure of the rocket boosters to distance the rocket from the satellite rendered the satellite useless. This strongly indicates that after bringing the satellite to its intended orbit and physically separating, the launch mission was over. One could even argue that the launch contract only extended to the intentional ignition and no further.[51]

B. Even if this Court should find that the MI-ISEE agreement controls this situation, the cross waivers contained in that contract do not preclude Parlivia from recovering its damages for the loss of Environsat.

Even if this Court would find that the contract is applicable, the contractual waiver regime is not enforceable against Parlivia. Neither the record nor the contract makes clear whether the parties agreed on what law should control the launch agreement. Thus, it is not readily apparent according to which principles this contract should be interpreted. Several U.S. courts have given guidance to launch contract interpretation by establishing case law precedents with important implications for space activities.[52] The general principles as put forth in these cases[53] are within this Court's purview of judicial notice.[54]

In the MI-SEE agreement, the parties to the contract adopted a contractual waiver regime including waivers, cross waivers and disclaimers of warranties. However, the parties did not intend to exculpate launching states. For waivers to be enforceable in the U.S., "the parties [must] express their intent in clear, plain, and unambiguous language. . . ."[55] The cross-waiver of liability clause in the MI-ISEE agreement is not expressly intended to "flow down" to launching states.[56] Article 15, which deals with waiver of claims, and Article 17, dealing with limitation of liability, nowhere mention or even make reference to any launching state.[57] The parties carefully drafted the waiver provisions and included "[a]ssociates, directors, officers, servants, agents, contractors, and subcontractors" in Article 15 and "[a]ssociates and contractors and subcontractors" in Article 17. If they wanted to cover launching states, they would have included them in this regime. This is even more obvious when one notes that the parties did specifically mention each of the four Respondent states by name in Article 16, dealing with third party liability. This preempts any argument that these states were supposed to be implicitly included in Article 15.

Parlivia can bring a breach of contract claim based on the assertion that ISEE did not use its "Best Efforts to launch [Parlivia's] spacecraft." Under Article 3.1 of the contract, such an action is not possible when the contract clearly and unambiguously bars such a claim.[58] The MI-ISEE contract is not clear and unambiguous on this point. Parlivia could bring its claim for failure of the second stage rocket to remove itself from *Environsat's* orbit rather than for launch failure;[59] Article 13.5 states that MI is entitled to a refund of the launch price as "the sole and exclusive remedy . . . for any Launch Failure." Under Article 1.8, "Launch Failure" means the failure of ISEE to accomplish the "Launch Mission,"[60] which in turn is defined in Article 1.9: "the launch of the Spacecraft for purposes of enabling [*Environsat*] to carry out its operational objectives." The extent of this last provision is unclear. The contract and its appendices obviously do not explicitly cover the stage after separation, but the launch extends that far. The stated purpose is to enable the satellite to carry out its operational objectives, but that does not help us much further since "for purposes of enabling" is a very broad term indeed. Article 13.5 is simply not sufficient to preclude all other claims since the relevant provisions in the contract are ambiguous.

Article 17.1 contains a disclaimer of warranty of merchantability and fitness for purpose, but does not indicate to what this disclaimer applies. Therefore, this provision is unlike the Martin Marietta disclaimer, where a similar clause was followed up by the following passage: "with respect to the [rocket] or associated equipment."[61] A strict rule on disclaimers of such warranties is that they have to be express and conspicuous.[62] In this case, the disclaimer was express and conspicuous as to what was intended to be disclaimed, but neither express nor conspicuous as to what the disclaimer applies to. Therefore, the disclaimer is ambiguous, and this Court should find it unenforceable.

Parlivia can also put forth a negligence claim under the contract. A plaintiff in this context can succeed on its negligence claim only if it can establish a duty in tort distinct from the contractual duties created between the parties.[63] ISEE owed MI a duty in tort, separate and distinct from the duties established by contract, to carry out this separation with due care, and to get the second stage removed from the satellite so as not to form a foreseeable danger to the satellite. Unlike in Martin Marietta and Appalachian Insurance, the satellite in this case was disabled by physical damage rather than being left in the wrong orbit. Based on the tort claim, MI can claim not only economic damages[64] but also the physical damage to the satellite.

In Appalachian Insurance and Martin Marietta, the court rejected a negligence claim because it found no duty of care in tort beyond the obligations specified in the contract. However, the appellate court in Martin Marietta held that even if there would be no negligence claim, a claim for gross negligence would be possible, reasoning that public policy invalidates cross waivers as they apply to gross negligence.[65] "Gross negligence" has been defined as a party's "willful, wanton, reckless, or gross conduct."[66] Therefore, Parlivia can claim its damages based on gross negligence.

Cross-waiver regimes such as the one in the contract have generally been justified on the basis that the private space industry still needs a large degree of protection in order to be able to develop from an "infant" industry into a "mature" industry.[67] As in other fields, "infant" private space industries need protection as long as financial burdens such as litigation and insurance threaten their existence.[68] However, the private space industry has developed in recent years such that it can reasonably be qualified as a "mature" industry: "the pioneering period is clearly coming to an end, and space enterprise seems to flourish."[69] Therefore, the need to protect private space industries such as ISEE is not as great today as it was before. "[I]n the last decade and a half there has been a gradual but steady shifting of the allocation of the risk of loss in commercial space agreements away from the buyers to the manufacturer-sellers of commercial space products and the providers of launch services."[70]

It is appropriate for this Court to reconsider and even to abandon the special protection that has generally been awarded to private space industries, at least in cases involving gross negligence.[71] This Court should recognize that the "risk of loss allocation pendulum" is swinging from the buyer towards the seller and manufacturer of launch services.[72] Thus, this Court, in light of all the foregoing arguments, should allow the Applicant to recover damages for the lost satellite.

Under international principles of justice and equity, Parlivia is entitled to recover for the lost satellite notwithstanding the contractual cross waiver regime. Parlivia has been unjustly disadvantaged by Respondents. Its satellite is completely disabled through Respondents' faulty acts. Therefore, principles of international justice and equity dictate that Parlivia should not be barred by the cross waivers in its quest for relief.

III. Under the tort theory of recovery delineated in the Liability Convention, Parlivia may recover damages for loss of revenues and refund of the launch price.

The international community first reached formal agreement that states should be "internationally liable" for space accidents in the Outer Space Treaty.[73] This concept of international liability was expanded by the Liability Convention, which has been described as "a specialized international tort law on hazards in the space environment."[74] The Liability Convention creates two liability schemes for analyzing space torts. First, if a space object causes damage on earth or to aircraft in flight, absolute (strict) liability applies.[75] Second, if two space objects collide, fault-based liability applies:

> In the event of damage being caused elsewhere than on the surface of the earth to a space object by a space object of another launching State, the latter shall be liable only if the damage is due to its fault or the fault of persons for whom it is responsible.[76]

Fault-based liability could encompass both negligence and intentional torts.

1. Loss of revenues

It is not possible at this time to replace the *Environsat*; therefore, this Court cannot order specific performance or restitution in kind. Substitutionary monetary compensation is the only realistic remedy to make the Applicant whole. In addition to the loss of the satellite, the Applicant must be compensated for lost revenues.

> This Court can substitute monetary compensation for specific restitution. [R]eparation must, as far as possible, wipe out all the consequences of the illegal act and reestablish the situation which would, in all probability, have existed if that act had not been committed. Restitution in kind, or, if that is not possible, payment of a sum corresponding to the value which a restitution in kind would bear; the award, if need be, of damages for loss sustained which would not be covered by restitution in kind or payment in place of it -- such are the principles which should serve to determine the amount of compensation due for an act contrary to international law.[77]

The Liability Convention defines "damage" as "loss of life, personal injury or other impairment of health; or loss of or damage to property."[78] It is not clear from this language that prospective revenue losses or other consequential damages are included in this definition. The U.S. Senate identified this ambiguity with a linkage between consequential damages and a proximate causation requirement.[79]

When the Soviet satellite *Cosmos 954* crashed in Canada, the Canadian government, pursuant to the Liability Convention, claimed damages "undertaken as a consequence of the events giving rise to Canada's claim."[80] Although this case was settled through diplomatic channels, this would seem to establish a customary precedent of interpretation allowing consequential damages under the Convention's tort regime.

Compensation under the Liability Convention should be determined according to international law and general principles of justice and equity[81] rather than national law.[82]

> The Compensation which the launching State shall be liable to pay for damage under this Convention shall be determined in accordance with international law and the principles of justice and equity, in order to provide such reparation in respect of the damage as will restore the person, natural or juridical, State or international organization on whose behalf the claim is presented to the condition which would have existed if the damage had not occurred.[83]

One general principle of justice is the Golden Rule.[84] The United States recognized as much when the space object SKYLAB was deorbiting, threatening to cause ground damage. The U.S. Department of State declared the U.S. would be bound by the Liability

Convention and "principles of simple justice when something you have done causes somebody else damage."[85] Damage compensation thus should make victims whole.

Although the Liability Convention places no limit on liability, equity requires some use of proximate cause[86] to prevent the assignment of infinite liability for every tortious act.[87] International law does not clearly distinguish between direct and indirect damage.[88] While not defined in the Convention, the phrase "international law and the principles of justice and equity" is not meaningless. In international contract law, for example, damages can include lost profits,[89] and reasonable lost profits within the contemplation of the contracting parties.[90]

The Liability Convention's vague language concerning justice and equity allows development in areas of the law "which have not yet crystallized into legal rules."[91] The "evolution of laws and practice applicable to the conduct of space activities and the expansion of this new field of space law"[92] is necessary if the law is to retain its vitality. "In law, we must beware of petrifying the rules of yesterday and thereby halting progress in the name of process. If one consolidates the past and calls it law, he may find himself outlawing the future."[93] The future is now. Application of the Liability Convention to a case where both space objects were launched together, though novel, is essential if the Convention is to remain relevant. This interpretation is consistent with the Convention's pro-victim orientation.[94] One of the purposes of the Liability Convention is to ensure "prompt payment under the terms of this Convention of a full and equitable measure of compensation to victims of such damage."[95] This full compensation provision seems to cover lost profits.[96] Also, according to Professor Christol, the direct damages provision encompasses lost profits.[97] International tribunals have awarded compensation for lost profits for international torts resulting in destruction of property.[98] Indemnification for lost profits is accepted as international law by "the most highly qualified publicists,"[99] and is thus within this Court's scope of judicial notice. "The indemnity should compensate for all damage which follows as a consequence of the unlawful act, including a profit which would have been possible in the ordinary course of events . . . It is not essential that the damage should have already taken place for compensation to be recoverable."[100]

Justice requires that the Applicant be made whole. If not for the negligence of ISEE, the Applicant would have realized US$20 million in revenue. Equity and justice are served when international law protects obligations *erga omnes* (owed to the international community as a whole). Protection of the outer space environment is one such obligation. The space debris problem is fast approaching a crisis.[101] International environmental law is founded on the principle that no state can use its territory to cause injury to another state's territory or property.[102] Judge Manfred Lachs recognized that "[s]pace debris, a byproduct of space activities, seriously endangers all space activities. Parts of space objects, such as payloads, uncontrollable fragments and boosters that continue to travel, may damage newly launched satellites."[103] Judge Lachs, who was one of the framers of the international space law regime,[104] thus foresaw the very fact pattern before this Court today, an uncontrollable booster fragment damaging a newly launched satellite. Although environmental space law is still immature, customary international law imposes obligations on states to protect the environment "beyond the limits of national jurisdiction."[105] This rule of customary law[106] imposes liability on the Respondents for environmental torts in space even beyond the parameters of the Liability Convention.

2. Refund of the launch price

Following the principles of international legal compensation outlined in Factory at Chorzow,[107] the Respondent states are liable for refunding the launch price. Specific restitution would require relaunching another satellite to replace *Environsat*. Any substitutionary monetary compensation must acknowledge this cost. These damages come under the general heading "reasonable costs for the repair of property that has been wrongfully harmed."[108] Replacing *Environsat* without paying for its relaunch would be inadequate. To make the Applicant whole again, an operational satellite must be reorbited. This will cost US$50 million as agreed in the refund clause of the contract.

IV. Under the Liability Convention, all four respondent states are jointly and severally liable. Damages should be equitably divided among the respondents -- proportional to the degree of fault as determined by the special master.

States are generally liable for the activities of their nationals.[109] This Court has held that customary international law imposes an obligation on each state "not to allow knowingly its territory to be used for acts contrary to the rights of other states."[110]

The Outer Space Treaty went further and imposed "international responsibility for national activities in outer space" even when conducted by non-governmental entities.[111] Space activities carried on by non-governmental entities "require authorization and continuing supervision" by the state.[112] The Outer Space Treaty assigns international liability to "[e]ach State Party to the Treaty that launches or procures the launching of an object into outer space . . . and each State Party from whose territory or facility an object is launched."[113] This concept was expanded in the Liability Convention, which imposes liability on the "launching State," defined as a state "which launches or procures the launching of a space object" or a state "from whose territory or facility a space object is launched."[114] Private entities, such as ISEE, can thus incur state liability under the Convention[115] for torts involving their space objects.[116]

Joint and Several Liability

Under the Liability Convention's fault-based liability regime for collisions between space objects, joint and several liability applies against joint participants, including states that allow tortious space launches from their territory.[117] The joint participants are treated as joint tortfeasors and are subject to "broad potential liability."[118] If one joint participant compensates the victim, it may seek indemnification from the other joint participants.[119] Because the Parlivian insurance underwriters' group SISA paid US$10 million, Parlivia can invoke Article V to seek indemnification from the Respondents.

Apportionment under the Liability Convention is to be predetermined by the parties.[120] Since that was not done here, the principles of equity, justice and international law espoused in Article XII should be employed. Article IV, although not applicable,[121] indicates the Convention drafters' conception that equitable apportionment be executed in accordance with degree of fault. The Special Master's report on fault should be considered in calculating the apportionment.[122] Other factors to weigh include: Who can best bear the loss?; Where lies the interest of the world community? The apportionment issue is not ultimately salient to the Applicant, who can employ joint and several liability to recover the full amount awarded from any or all of the Respondents.

Californium and Ukrastan

International Space Enterprises, Inc. ("ISE") is incorporated in the Republic of Californium. Under customary international law, Californium can be held responsible for ISE's torts. The Outer Space Treaty explicitly imposes international responsibility on a state for "national activities in outer space,"[123] even if such national activities are carried out by nongovernmental entities. Article VI imposes "ultimate liability for launches by non-governmental or intergovernmental organizations on the launching state or states."[124] Hence, the Outer Space Treaty applies to private companies[125] and "requires a certain minimum licensing and enforced adherence to government-imposed regulations."[126] Californium is a "launching state" under the Convention, because it is internationally responsible for the national activities of ISE, which, through its joint venture and agent ISEE, launched a space object. ISEE was a joint venture owned by ISE and NPO (scientific research and production association) Enerkru ("NPO"). Under the agency doctrine of *respondeat superior*, the master is vicariously liable for its servant's torts;[127] therefore, ISE and NPO are liable for ISEE's torts.

Even without imputing vicarious tort liability, the parent corporations are financially liable for the ostensibly insolvent joint venture. Any argument that ISE and Enerkru should be insulated from liability by their alter ego ISEE would be frivolous. Aside from the specific international legal obligations imposed by the Outer Space Treaty and the Liability Convention, equity, justice, and customary international law all mandate piercing the corporate veil in this context. "Although an independent juridical personality is conferred on a company, this personality does not present itself as an end, but simply as a means to achieve an economic purpose. . . ."[128] Although ISEE seems to have adopted a corporate or entity form ("Ltd.") to gain some degree of limited liability, joint ventures, which share profits, losses and control, generally are treated as partnerships, implying joint liability for debts and torts.[129] Even if ISEE is a limited liability entity under Pleasant Islands municipal law, piercing the corporate veil would be appropriate when "adherence to the fiction of separate existence would sanction fraud or promote injustice."[130] Piercing is even more likely when the victim is an involuntary tort creditor rather than a contract creditor.[131] In this case, ISEE made use of the resources and employees of ISE and NPO; this "failure to maintain arm's length relationships among related entities"[132] mandates piercing.

Similarly, in the transnational context, piercing the corporate veil is appropriate "to avoid fraud, injustice, or circumvention of an important regulatory policy."[133] Preserving the international legal regime embodied in the Liability Convention is surely an important regulatory policy. ISE, and consequently its alter ego ISEE, were under the jurisdiction and control of Californium.[134] Multinational enterprises are not stateless entities subject to no sovereign; such a situation would undermine large parts of international law. Californium is thus indirectly responsible for ISE's international space torts. This indirect state responsibility results from the "international legal obligation to protect foreign States and their nationals, as well as their property, within its jurisdiction, particularly territorial jurisdiction, from injurious acts committed by persons who are not servants or agents of the State acting in their official capacity, acting individually or in groups of any number, from mobs to revolutionaries."[135] Customary international law supports this interpretation.[136] Californium and Ukrastan cannot be allowed to hide behind Pleasant Islands' "flag of convenience." The principal investors in a space project must not be able to evade liability so easily. "States who are merely used for convenience should be disregarded by the world community."[137]

The Republic of Ukrastan and NPO have the same relationship as Californium and ISE; thus, the analysis is the same. Ukrastan is internationally responsible for NPO's space torts. Ukrastan is a "launching state" under the Convention.

Pleasant Islands

The launch provider ISEE is headquartered in the Commonwealth of the Pleasant Islands, thus exposing Pleasant Islands to international liability. The analysis is familiar. Pleasant Islands is internationally responsible for national activities in outer space carried on by ISEE, a nongovernmental entity. Apparently, Pleasant Islands did not exercise adequate due diligence in monitoring the activities of its corporate entities. It owes this duty to the international community *erga omnes*. ISEE launched a space object; therefore, Pleasant Islands is a "launching state" under the Liability Convention.

Patalia

The Kingdom of Patalia is liable as a "launching state" under the Liability Convention.[138] The *Progyia* launch vehicle carrying *Environsat* was launched from a commercial launch site at Cape Kou in Patalia. By allowing this launch from its territory, Patalia assumed potential liability under international law.

The contracting parties ISEE and MI clearly contemplated that the Respondent states would be liable under the Liability Convention. There is no other plausible explanation for insuring the Respondents. The MI-ISEE contract contains a Third Party Liability provision which explicitly names all four Respondent states.[139] Some nations, recognizing their international liability for private actions under the Outer Space Treaty and the Liability Convention, now require such third party liability insurance to insulate them from the Liability Convention's strict liability provisions for ground damage.[140] The Respondents probably required this Third Party Liability contract provision for similar reasons. This international liability was actually foreseen and, thus, foreseeable.

SUBMISSIONS TO THE COURT

For the foregoing reasons, the Government of Parlivia, Applicant, respectfully submits that this Court:

1. DECLARE that Parlivia may present a tort claim under the Liability Convention while the arbitration proceeding between MI, SISA and ISEE is in progress.

2. DECLARE that the contractual waiver regime of the MI-ISEE agreement does not preclude Parlivia's recovery of damages for the satellite loss.

3. DECLARE that Parlivia may recover damages for loss of revenues and refund of the launch price under the tort theory of recovery delineated in the Liability Convention.

4. DECLARE that all four Respondent states are jointly and severally liable under the Liability Convention and that damages should be equitably divided among the Respondents -- proportional to the degree of fault as determined by the special master.

---

[1] "The fact that a contract has international importance because of its nature and magnitude does not result in an exception to the general principle that contracts are subject to domestic law. A private party does not obtain remedies on the international level against a State that has breached the contract. Nor do provisions in the contract for non-national law and arbitration change that principle." O. Schachter, International Law in Theory and Practice 311 (1991).

[2] See K. Widdows, What is an Agreement in International Law?, in The British Yearbook of International Law 117, 148 (1981).

[3] Article 7(1) of the Vienna Convention On the Law of Treaties, U.N. Doc. A/CONF. 39/27 (1969), 63 Am. J. Int'l. L. 875 (1969), 8 I.L.M. 679 (1969).

[4] South West Africa (Eth. v. S. Afr.; Liber. v. S. Afr.), 1962 I.C.J. 319, 330 (Dec. 21).

[5] See British Yearbook of International Law, supra note 2, at 117.

[6] Apparent authority to conclude agreements can bind a state when it is not evident to the other party that the official acting for the state has exceeded its authority. See Legal Status of Eastern Greenland (Den. v. Nor.), 1933 P.C.I.J. (Ser. A/B) No. 53, at 71 (April 5); Free Zones of Upper Savoy and the District of Gex (Fr. v. Switz.), 1932 P.C.I.J. (Ser. A/B) No. 46 (June 7).

[7] See Anglo-Iranian Oil Co. (U.K. v. Iran), 1952 I.C.J. 93, 112 (July 22).

[8] Respectively articles 1.7 and 1.9.

[9] The collision which completely disabled *Environsat* did not occur until more than four months after *Progyia* brought the satellite to its orbit and separated. This even further buttresses the indication that the launch mission was fulfilled.

[10] It is noteworthy that this argument was actually made by the **launch provider**, Martin Marietta, in AT&T v Martin Marietta but this case never went to litigation. See Ph.D. Bostwick, *AT&T v. Martin Marietta*: Further Reallocation of the Risk of Loss in Commercial Space Agreements, 23 J. Space L. 177, 178-181, 183 n.11 (1995).

[11] See article 3.1 of the contract.

[12] Article III of the Convention on International Liability for Damage caused by Space Objects (1972), Nov. 29, 1971/Mar. 29, 1972, 24 U.S.T. 2389, T.I.A.S. No. 762, 961 U.N.T.S. 187.

[13] Article I(d). "[A]ny object that reaches or is intended to reach outer space is a space object in the eyes of international space law." B. Cheng, International Responsibility and Liability for Launch Activities, 20 Air and Space Law. 297, 299 (1995).

[14] See generally S. Gorove, Space Stations - Issues of Liability, Responsibility and Damage, 27 Proc. Colloq. L. Outer Space 251 (1984).

[15] B.A. Hurwitz, State Liability for Outer Space Activities 25 (1992). The Liability Convention has often been referred to as a "victim-oriented" Convention. Staff of Senate Comm. on Aeronautical and Space Sciences, 92d Cong., 2d Sess., Report on Convention on International Liability for Damage Caused by Space Objects, Analysis and Background Data 20 (Comm. Print 1972) [hereinafter Staff Report].

[16] Convention on International Liability for Damage Caused by Space Objects, Letter of Submittal, John N. Irwin II, No. 65-118, at vii (1972).

[17] Hurwitz, supra note 15, at 52 (citations omitted).

[18] Article XI(2) (emphasis added).

[19] Anglo-Iranian Oil Co., 1952 I.C.J. at 112.

[20] "It often takes many months before an arbitral tribunal

is able to function." L.B. Sohn, Settlement of Disputes Arising Out of the Law of the Sea Convention, 12 San Diego L. Rev. 495, 503 (1975).

[21] K.-H. Böckstiegel, Arbitration and Adjudication Regarding Activities in Outer Space, 6 J. Space L. 3, 11 (1978).

[22] Id. See also H. DeSaussure, Maritime and Space Law, Comparisons and Contrasts (An Oceanic View of Space Transport), 9 J. Space L. 93, 103 (1981); G. Gál, Space Law 117-118 (1969).

[23] Convention on the Law of the Sea, U.N. Doc. A/CONF.62/122 (1982). See generally A.O. Adede, The System For Settlement of Disputes Under the United Nations Convention On the Law Of the Sea (1987).

[24] Convention on the Law of the Sea, article 280.

[25] Id., Article 286. See also L.B. Sohn, Peaceful Settlement of Disputes in Ocean Conflicts: Does UNCLOS III Point the Way?, 46 Law & Contemp. Probs., No. 2, 195, 196 (1983).

[26] L.B. Sohn, Audience Response, in The Law of the Sea - Where Now?, 46 Law & Contemp. Probs., No.2, 1, 209-210 (1983).

[27] The first draft of this draft convention is reproduced in K.-H. Böckstiegel, Proposed Draft Convention on the Settlement of Space Law Disputes, 12 J. Space L. 136, 140-162 (1985); H.L. Van Traa-Engelman, Commercial Utilization of Outer Space: Law and Practice 359-383 (1993).

[28] Böckstiegel, supra note 27, at 140; see also K.-H. Böckstiegel, Developing a System of Dispute Settlement Regarding Space Activities, 35 Proc. Colloq. L. Outer Space 27, 32 (1992).

[29] Ambatielos (Greece v. U.K.), 1953 I.C.J. 10, 23 (May 19); see also Interhandel (Switz. v. U.S.), 1959 I.C.J. 6, 29 (March 21); Certain Norwegian Loans (Fr. v. Nor.), 1957 I.C.J. 9, 24-25 (July 6).

[30] Article 23.1 of the contract. The question of what the parties intended to be covered by the arbitration clause "may turn on eye-crossing subtleties in the way the arbitration agreement was drafted." W.W. Park, International Forum Selection 107 n.460 (1995).

[31] O. Schachter, Disputes Involving the Use of Force, in The International Court of Justice at a Crossroads 223, 238 (L.F. Damrosch ed. 1987) [hereinafter Crossroads]. This Court's jurisprudence "makes it clear that [this] Court is inclined to take a broad view of what constitutes a justiciable dispute." D.E. Acevedo, Disputes Under Consideration by the U.N. Security Council or Regional Bodies, in Crossroads, supra, at 242, 263 (1987). See Military and Paramilitary Activities (Nicar. v. U.S.), 1984 I.C.J. 392, 419 (Nov. 26).

[32] Article 23.1 of the contract (emphasis added).

[33] See Th. Oehmke, International Arbitration 77 (1990).

[34] See Park, supra note 30, at 108 n.460.

[35] See W.W. Park, Arbitration of International Contract Disputes, 39 Bus. Law. 1783, 1785 (1984). See also Park, supra note 30, at 107-108.

[36] H.P. De Vries, International Commercial Arbitration: A Contractual Substitute for National Courts, 57 Tul. L. Rev. 42, 61 (1982). See also The Hon. Justice Kerr, International Arbitration v. Litigation, 1980 J. Bus. L. 164-65 (1980); F.J. Higgins et al., Pitfalls in International Commercial Arbitration, 35 Bus. Law. 1035, 1036 (1980).

[37] Schachter, supra note 31, at 237-38.

[38] Sohn, supra note 20, at 503-504.

[39] Id.

[40] As to the development of the non-arbitrability doctrine in the United States, see G.B. Born, International Commercial Arbitration in the United States 322-382 (1994).

[41] Id. at 323. Examples of such sovereigns are: France, Quebec, and Denmark. Id. at 323 n.319.

[42] This case had much more serious environmental consequences than Appalachian Insurance Co. v. McDonnell Douglas, 262 Cal. Rptr. 716 (Cal. Ct. App. 1989), and Martin Marietta Corp. v. INTELSAT, 991 F.2d 94 (4th Cir. 1992), because in those cases, no explosion took place.

[43] Space debris not only consists of fragments of exploded rocket stages or fragmented satellites, but also a wide variety of smaller items. See B.K. Schafer, Solid, Hazardous, and Radioactive Wastes in Outer Space: Present Controls and Suggested Changes, 19 Cal. W. Int'l L.J. 1, 4 (1989). Nothing in the record indicates that ISEE or any of the four Respondent states initiated any type of clean-up action.

[44] By far the most prolific sources of space debris are explosions and break-ups. COSPAR and the International Aeronautical Federation (IAF), Environmental Effects of Space Activities, Annex to Report, at 12, U.N. Doc. A/AC.105/420 (1988). Especially troublesome is the "cascade effect": because new debris is generated in any collision of two objects, the amount of debris constantly expands. Id. Most orbital debris can be found at roughly 900 km. See Schafer, supra note 43, at 3. The *Progyia* explosion occurred at 800 km., polluting this sensitive zone. Therefore, this explosion has a great potential for a cascade effect.

[45] The International Law Association ("ILA") recognized this and adopted the International Instrument on Space Debris. See Current Documents, 23 J. Space L. 112-116 (1995). See also M. Williams, The ILA Finalizes its International Instrument on Space Debris, 23 J. Space L. at 47. Also, the new Restatement specifically addresses environmental problems in the field of outer space. Restatement (Third) of Foreign Relations Law §601 n.6 (1987). See also G.H. Reynolds, International Space Law: Into the Twenty-First Century, 25 Vand. J. Trans'l L. 225, 227 (1992).

[46] Statute of the International Court of Justice, Article 38(1)(c). "International law has recruited, and continues to recruit many of its rules and institutions from private systems of law." 1 Sir G. Fitzmaurice, The Law and Procedure in the International Court of Justice 11 (1986) (quotation omitted).
[47] Sir Fitzmaurice, supra note 46, at 11. See also id. at 18-19.
[48] Appalachian Insurance, 262 Cal. Rptr. at 718-20.
[49] Martin Marietta, 991 F.2d at 95-97.
[50] Martin Marietta, 991 F.2d at 96; Appalachian Insurance, 262 Cal. Rptr. at 719.
[51] See supra note 10 and accompanying text.
[52] K.-H. Böckstiegel, Case Law on Space Activities, in Space Law: Development and Scope 205, 208 (N. Jasentuliyana ed. 1992).
[53] See generally R.V. Pino and F.A. Silane, Civil Liability in Commercial Space Ventures under United States Law, 6 Air and Space Law. 5 (1991).
[54] See supra notes 46-47 and accompanying text.
[55] Pino and Silane, supra note 53, at 6.
[56] Id. at 10-11.
[57] Compare the approach the court in Appalachian Insurance took with the "flow down" provisions in that case, 262 Cal. Rptr. at 721-23. See also P.L. Meredith and G.S. Robinson, Space Law: A Case Study for the Practitioner - Implementing a Telecommunications Satellite Business Concept 276-79 (1992).
[58] Martin Marietta, 991 F.2d at 97.
[59] Id.
[60] There is a drafting error in article 1.8: "the failure of the [] to accomplish the Launch Mission." The parties probably intended that the word "ISEE" be inserted there.
[61] Martin Marietta Corp. v. INTELSAT, 763 F. Supp. 1327, 1332 n.6 (D. Md. 1991). On this decision, see Meredith and Robinson, supra note 57, at 279-86.
[62] See Appalachian Insurance, 262 Cal. Rptr. at 720-725.
[63] Martin Marietta, 763 F. Supp. at 1331; 991 F.2d at 98. See generally Appalachian Insurance, 262 Cal.Rptr. at 737.
[64] See Martin Marietta, 991 F.2d at 98.
[65] Id. at 99-100.
[66] Martin Marietta, 991 F.2d at 100 (citations omitted).
[67] See Martin Marietta, 763 F. Supp. at 1333-34.
[68] Id.
[69] T.L. Masson-Zwaan, The Martin Marietta Case or How to Safeguard Private Commercial Space Activities, 35 Proc. Colloq. L. Outer Space 239, 244 (1992).
[70] Bostwick, supra note 10, at 181.
[71] Id.
[72] Id. at 182.
[73] Multilateral Treaty on Principles Governing the Activities of States in the Exploration and Use of Outer Space, Including the Moon and Other Celestial Bodies, 18 U.S.T. 2410; T.I.A.S. 6347 (1967).

[74] C. Christol, International Liability for Damage Caused by Space Objects, 74 Am. J. Int'l. L. 346, 369 (1980).
[75] "A launching State shall be absolutely liable to pay compensation for damage caused by its space object on the surface of the earth or to aircraft in flight." Article II.
[76] Article III.
[77] Factory at Chorzow (Ger. v. Pol.), 1928 P.C.I.J. (ser. A.) No. 17, at 47 (Sep. 13).
[78] Art. I(a).
[79] Staff Report, supra note 15, at 23.
[80] Canada: Claim Against the Union of Soviet Socialist Republics for Damage Caused by Soviet Cosmos 954, 18 I.L.M. 899, 900 (1979).
[81] Equity in this context should be distinguished from equity in the context of Article 38(2) of the Statute of the International Court of Justice allowing the Court to decide cases *ex aequo et bono* when the parties consent. This refers to a form of Solomonic "gut justice" -- not general principles of international law. See generally Th.M. Franck, Fairness in International Law and Institutions 54-56 (1995).
[82] In the course of negotiating the Liability Convention, the members of the Legal Subcommittee of the United Nations Committee on Peaceful Uses of Outer Space (UNCOPUOS) treated the compensation issue as a conflicts of laws problem. H. Reis, U.S. Discusses "Applicable Law" for Outer Space Claims, 62 Dep't State Bull. 18 (1970).
[83] Article XII.
[84] "And as ye would that men should do to you, do ye also to them likewise." Jesus Christ, Sermon on the Mount, Luke 6:31 (King James). See also Matthew 7:12 (King James). This principle is not limited to Western or Christian ethics. "All of the great religions prescribe obedience to the Golden Rule . . ." 6 Encyclopœdia Britannica 979 (1984); The Confucius Confusion, Economist 40 (Feb. 24, 1996). Universal acceptance could elevate the Golden Rule to the level of *ius cogens* (peremptory norms), "rules from which no derogation is permissible." Oppenheim's Int'l Law § 2 (1992).
[85] 1979 Digest of United States Practice in International Law 1191.
[86] Administrative Decision No. II, (U.S. v. Ger.), Mixed Claims Commission, 1923, [1923-25] Administrative Decisions and Opinions 5, 12-13, 7 U.N.Rep.Int'l Arb.Awards 23, 29-30.
[87] One must not forget, however, that even routine costs in the space industry are very high. The amount in controversy in the case at bar is rather modest. By comparison, in 1995 AT&T filed a US$400 million breach of contract suit against Martin Marietta after another satellite mishap. S. Medintz, AT&T v. Martin Marietta, 1995 Am. Law. 102 (June 1995). Also, it has been estimated that a hypothetical launch mishap at Cape Canaveral, Florida could cause damages in excess of

US$5 billion in 1989 dollars. G.H. Reynolds and R.P. Merges, Outer Space: Problems of Law and Policy 176 (1989).

[88] Reynolds and Merges, supra note 87, at 176.

[89] UNIDROIT Principles Art. 7.4.2(1).

[90] Shufeldt Claim (U.S. v. Guat.), Dep't of State Arb.Ser. No. 3, 851, 877-78, 2 U.N. Rep. Int'l Arb. Awards 1079, 1099 (1930); 3 Whiteman, Digest of International Law 1858-66 (1967).

[91] Maritime Delimitation in the Area Between Greenland and Jan Mayen (Den. v. Nor.), 1993 I.C.J. 38, 234 (June 14).

[92] P. Nesgos and R. Craft, The Emerging Commerce in Space: New National Policy Sets the Tone, 1988 Nat'l L.J. 22 (1988).

[93] Manfred Lachs, President of the International Court of Justice, speech given at the United Nations General Assembly in 1973.

[94] N.C. Goldman, American Space Law: International and Domestic 80 (2d ed. 1996).

[95] Preamble to the Liability Convention.

[96] 8 M. Whiteman, supra note 90, at 887.

[97] Christol, supra note 74, at 359.

[98] Irene Roberts Case (United States v. Venezuela), Ralston, Venezuelan Arbitrations of 1903, 142, 144, 9 U.N.Rep.Int'l Arb.Awards 204, 207-208; 3 Whiteman, supra note 90, at 1840-58 (If the profits are too speculative, the tribunal can award interest instead of lost profits.)

[99] Statute of the International Court of Justice, Article 38(1)(d).

[100] J. De Arechaga, International Law in the Past Third of a Century, 159 R.C.A.D.I. 285-87 (1978-I).

[101] See generally L. Roberts, Addressing the Problem of Orbital Space Debris: Combining International Regulatory and Liability Regimes, 15 B.C. Int'l & Comp. L. Rev. 51, 53-57 (1992).

[102] Trail Smelter Arbitration (U.S. v. Can.), Trail Smelter Arbitral Tribunal, 3 R. Int'l Arbitral Awards 1905 (1941).

[103] M. Lachs, Views from the Bench: Thoughts on Science, Technology and World Law, 86 Am. J. Int'l. L. 673, 695 (1992).

[104] N. Jasentuliyana, The Lawmaking Process in the United Nations, in Space Law: Development and Scope 35 (N. Jasentuliyana ed. 1992).

[105] Restatement (Third) of Foreign Relations Law § 601.

[106] See, e.g., Stockholm Declaration on the Human Environment, 11 I.L.M. 6, 1416 (1976); International Law Association, Report of the 61st Conference 391 (Paris 1984); see generally V.S. Vereshchetin and G.M. Danilenko, Custom as a Source of International Law of Outer Space, 13 J. Space L. 22, 24-31 (1985).

[107] See supra note 77.

[108] Christol, supra note 74, at 359.

[109] "International law imposes a duty upon every state to exercise due diligence to prevent its own subjects, and such foreign subjects as live within its territory, from committing injurious acts against other states." Oppenheim's Int'l Law § 166, at 549 (1992).

[110] Corfu Channel (U.K. and N. Ir. v. Alb.), 1949 I.C.J. 4, 22 (April 9).

[111] Outer Space Treaty, Article VI.

[112] Id.

[113] Id., Article VII.

[114] Liability Convention, Article I.

[115] "The fact that private individuals or entities launched the space object is irrelevant." S. Murphy, Prospective Liability Regimes for the Transboundary Movement of Hazardous Wastes, 88 Am. J. Int'l. L. 24, 59 (1994).

[116] Article I defines space objects to include launch vehicles and booster rockets, so the booster fragment from the *Progyia* launch vehicle comes within the definition of "space object." B. Reijnen, Pollution of Outer Space and International Law, 32 Proc. Colloq. L. Outer Space 130, 135 (1990).

[117] Article V.

[118] Memorandum of Agreement on Satellite Technology Safeguards between the United States of America and the People's Republic of China, 1989 WL 428790; State Dept. No. 89-115, KAV No. 312 (Treaty Signed at Washington, December 17, 1988)

[119] Article V.

[120] Id.

[121] Article IV concerns an orbital collision causing ground damage to a third party and apportionment of liability between the nations responsible for the two space objects.

[122] On the face of things, it appears that NPO Enerkru was the primary bad actor; NPO's computer programmer made the crucial mistake. However, this assessment was made by an internal Safety Review Board which may be protecting ISE. The Special Master's report must be held determinative.

[123] Outer Space Treaty, Article VI.

[124] Reynolds and Merges, supra note 87, at 175.

[125] G. Zhukov and Y. Kolosov, International Space Law 65 (1984).

[126] Dembling and Arons, The Evolution of the Outer Space Treaty, 33 J. Air L. & Com. 419 (1967).

[127] Restatement (Second) of Agency §219 (1958).

[128] Barcelona Traction, Light & Power Co., Ltd. (Belg. v. Spain), 1970 I.C.J. 3, 131- 32 (Feb. 5).

[129] H. Gelb, Personal Corporate Liability: A Guide for Planners, Litigators, and Creditors' Counsel 300-07 (1991).

[130] Id. at 5.

[131] Id. at 13.

[132] Id. at 9.

[133] D. Aronofsky, Piercing the Transnational Corporate

Veil: Trends, Developments, and the Need for Widespread Adoption of Enterprise Analysis, 10 N.C.J. Int'l. L. & Com. Reg. 31, 86 (1985).

[134] The principle of state responsibility derivative of jurisdiction and control is well- established in international law. For example, in the context of deep sea-bed mining, the United States recognizes jurisdiction over and requires licensing for corporations which are controlled by U.S. nationals (either natural or corporate). J. Fawcett, Outer Space: New Challenges to Law and Policy 41 (1984).

[135] Cheng, supra note 13, at 300.

[136] For example, when the private West German company, Orbital Transport und Raketen Aktiengesellschaft (OTRAG), announced plans to launch space objects from Zaire and Libya, several governments protested and warned "that Germany would be liable for any damage caused by such activities." Böckstiegel, supra note 52, at 207.

[137] W. Wirin, Practical Implications of Launching State - Appropriate State Definitions, 37 Proc. Colloq. L. Outer Space (1994).

[138] "A State from whose territory or facility a space object is launched." Article I.

[139] Article 16.1 of the contract.

[140] See, e.g., Commercial Space Launch Act of 1984, 49 U.S.C. §§ 2601-2623 (1990) for an example from the United States of America.

B. MEMORIAL FOR CALIFORNIUM et al.

AGENTS

Anna Markkanen, Satu Heikkilä

ARGUMENT

PART I: PRELIMINARY OBJECTIONS

Before any further proceedings on the merits of the case, the Republic of Californium, the Republic of Ukrastan, the Commonwealth of the Pleasant Islands, and the Kingdom of Patalia (hereafter Californium, *et al.*) wish to raise preliminary objections to the admissibility[1] of Parlivia's claims under the 1972 Convention on International Liability for Damage caused by Space Objects (Liability Convention).

1. The Liability Convention does not apply to the present case

1.1 The Liability Convention Imposes Liability Only for Third Party Damage

The Liability Convention imposes international liability only for third party damage.[2] Interparty liability for damages caused in the relation between parties of a common space endeavor has to be defined *inter partes*.[3] In the present case Parlivia was a party to the joint launching of the *Environsat* satellite on the *Progyia* launch vehicle, and the liability arrangements between the parties have been made in the launch contract concluded between ISE Enerkru, Ltd. (ISEE) and the Ministry of Industry of Parlivia (MI) (ISEE-MI launch contract). Since no innocent third parties are involved in the present case the provisions of the Liability Convention do not apply, and the liabilities shall be determined in accordance with the ISEE-MI launch contract.

1.2 The Damage Was Not Caused by a Space Object

The Liability Convention applies only to damage caused by a space object. However, the term "space object" has not been clearly defined in the Liability Convention. It is only provided that the component parts of the space object as well as its launch vehicle and partsthereof are included in the term "space object".[4] Thus, it is unclear whether space debris is at all covered by the Convention.[5] Nor is there any State practice to clarify the issue at hand.[6]

The meaning of the term being this obscure and ambiguous a recourse may be made to the *travaux préparatoires* of the Convention. [7] In the debate on the space object issue some States indicated a desire to include a broader definition of "component parts" to the Convention including objects intentionally or unintentionally detached, thrown or launched from a spacecraft.[8] However, this definition was not accepted in the text of the Convention - a fact which establishes that the majority of the States did not approve the broad definition, nor support the inclusion of space debris within the definition. In addition, doctrinal commentary on the convention texts and *travaux préparatoires* has demonstrated that fragmentation debris does not fall within the scope of "space object".[9]

Therefore, the small fragment body from the exploded Progyia second stage does not fall within the definition of "space object" under the Liability Convention and the Convention is not applicable.

1.3 Proximate Causation May Not Be Established

As the name of the Convention suggests, before compensation may be recovered under the Liability Convention, the claimant State has to show that it has suffered damage caused by space object. In addition to the "space object" element discussed above, also another condition has to be fulfilled, namely, a proximate causal connection between the damage and the malfunctioning of the space object shall be established.[10] This means that the claimant is required to show that the harm flowed directly or immediatelly from, and *as the probable or natural result of*, the malfunctioning of the space object.[11] No such proximate causal connection exist in the present case. The collision between the small fragment from the exploded rocket body and the Environsat satellite was not a probable and natural result of the malfunctioning of the thrusters of the Progyia launch vehicle.

Hence, the Liability Convention does not apply to the present case, and claims raised under the Convention are inadmissible.

2. Nationals of a launching state may not claim under the Liability Convention

According to Article VII of the Liability Convention, nationals of a launching State cannot seek compensation under the Convention.[12] The definition of a "launching State" in Article I(c) of the Convention provides that also a State which procures the launching of a space object is regarded as a "launching State" of that space object for the purposes of the Convention.[13] It is generally recognized that under the Liability Convention the term "procures" means at least ordering of the launch, *inter alia*, the State who has ordered the launching of its satellite has been regarded as a launching State.[14] In the present case Parlivia, through MI, ordered the launching of its *Environsat* satellite on the *Progyia* launch vehicle, and thus is regarded as a launching State of the *Progyia* launch vehicle. Since the damage was caused by debris generated from the exploded *Progyia* rocket body, Parlivia, as one of the *Progyia*'s launching States, is not entitled to present claims on behalf of its nationals under the Liability Convention.

Hence, as our Honourable Counterparty has no *locus standi* to claim under the Convention the claims presented by Parlivia are inadmissible.

3. Parlivia may not claim under the Liability Convention while arbitration is in progress

In Article XI(1) of the Liability Convention it is expressly stated that a State is not entitled to present a claim under the Convention in respect of the same damage for which a claim is being pursued in the courts or administrative tribunals or agencies of a launching State, or under another international agreement which is binding on the States concerned.

3.1 The Claims Are in Respect of the Same Damage

It is a general principle of diplomatic protection that, when a State is presenting claims on behalf of its nationals, the claim is that of a State, but the subject-matter of the claim is the individual and his property.[15] Parlivia's claims under the Liability Convention are presented on behalf of MI and the Space Insurers of South America (SISA). Both of these Parlivian nationals have earlier submitted claims to arbitration in respect of the damage caused by the debris generated from the exploded *Progyia* second stage. Thus, it is clear that the subject-matter of the claims is same, and that the claims are in respect of the same damage.

*3.2 Arbitration Is a Procedure Which Prevents a State from Presenting Claims under the Liability Convention_*

Even if arbitration is not expressly mentioned in Article XI(2) of the Liability Convention, this does not mean that arbitration would not be included in the procedures which, while in progress, prevent a State from bringing claims under the Convention. This contention may be based on several grounds.

First of all, the arbitration now in progress is a procedure instituted under the ISEE-MI launch contract and governed by the proper law of the launch contract. Since the launch contract is a contract between a State and a private (non-sovereign) party it is based on the municipal law of some country.[16] The primary rule for determining the proper law of the contract is the will of the parties as expressed in the contract. However, if the parties have failed to include such choice of law provision in the contract, the contract shall be subject to the rules of law with which the contract has the closest connection.[17] This applies also to contracts with States[18], at least when the State is acting *jure gestionis,* that is, when the governmental acts relate rather to private or trade activity than to administrative functions.[19] The ISEE-MI launch contract is a purely commercial contract, and thus falls within the category of acts *jure gestionis.* For the present purposes it is not necessary to decide whether the closest connection shall be based on the place of performance[20], that is the place of launch, or on the nationality of the performer[21]. It is sufficient to note that, in any case, the proper law may not be that of the passive party to the contract, that is the Parlivian law.[22] From this it follows that the law governing the contract is necessarily that of one of the Respondent States, and the arbitration under the launch contract is a procedure pursued in an agency instituted within the legal systems of one of the launching States. Therefore, the claims pursued in the arbitration under ISEE-MI launch contract shall be regarded as claims "being pursued in the agencies of the launching State", as required in Article XI(2) of the Liability Convention.

Second, although exhaustion of local remedies is not required under the Liability Convention[23] Article XI(2) provides individuals an opportunity to take the initiative away from their State and choose to exhaust local remedies.[24] Bearing this in mind, analogy may be made to the rules of international law relating to exhaustion of local remedies to establish that the form of the procedure is not relevant in the present case. Generally in international law the exhaustion of local remedies involves using such local procedures as are available to protect interests which correspond *as closely as may be and in practical terms* with the interests involved in a subsequent international claim - the constitutional status of the agency taking the measure concerned is not important.[25] Accordingly, if remedy is obtainable in another tribunal, whether national or international, it is regarded as adequate for the purposes of determining the admissibility of a State claim.[26] When these rules are applied to the present case it is clear that the form of the on-going procedure is not relevant, and arbitration shall be regarded as a procedure preventing Parlivia from presenting claims under the Liability Convention.

Third, in international law double compensation is not accepted. Reparation should not be awarded more than once in respect of the same damage.[27] Accordingly, any proceeding simultaneously in progress in respect of the same damage should be regarded as a procedure preventing a State from claiming under the Convention.

Fourth, it has to be remembered that the intention of the Article is to avoid collisions of jurisdictions. This intention supports the broad interpretation of Article XI(2) of the Convention so that also arbitration shall be included in procedures listed.

Fifth, in addition it should be noted that the ISEE-MI launch contract is a legally binding agreement on Parlivia, and thus the commitment to submit all the disputes araising under the launch contract to the arbitration bars the Government of Parlivia from submitting claims to other tribunals.

Hence, Parlivia's claims under the Liability Convention are inadmissible while the arbitration under the ISEE-MI launch contract is in progress.

PART II: MERITS

Should this Honourable Court, however, find that Parlivia's claims under the Liability Convention are admissible, Californium, *et al.* wish to present the following arguments on the merits of the case.

4. The waiver of claims regime in the ISEE-MI launch contract precludes Parlivia's recovery of satellite loss

*4.1 The Subject-matter of Parlivia's Claims Shall Be Determined in Accordance with the ISEE-MI Launch Contract_*

Under municipal and international law contracts are considered binding between the parties. This is the well established principle of *pacta sunt servanda,* which is regarded as the very basis for all legal relations.[28] The fact that commercial accords between States, or States and private parties, are to be governed by municipal law does not mean that such agreements are invalid.[29] Although Parlivia as a State is not an original party to the contract, it has the legal interest to present claims only on behalf of its nationals.[30] Since responsibility and liability for damage caused by space objects does not arise as a consequence of an act contrary to international law, the State whose nationals have suffered damage does not have any independent legal interest to claim apart from that of its individuals. From this it follows that the subject-matter of Parlivia's claims shall be determined in accordance with the ISEE-MI launch contract, which is a contract legally binding on MI and SISA.

4.2 The Collision Avoidance and Re-orbit Assist Maneuvers Were a Part of the "Launch Services" and Governed by the Waiver of Claims Regime in the ISEE-MI Launch Contract

In interpretation of the ISEE-MI launch contract, a distinction shall be made between two central terms of the contract, namely, "Launch Mission" and "Launch Services". According to the definitions, "Launch Mission" means the launch of the *Environsat* for purposes of the satellite to carry out its operational objectives.[31] This term refers to the actual launch of the *Environsat* satellite, the task which was accomplished when *Environsat* was successfully placed in its intended 800 km equatorial orbit where it was able to carry out its operational objectives.

"Launch Services", on the other hand, is defined as meaning all the services to be provided by ISEE under the contract.[32] Further, in Article 3(1), entitled "Launch Services", it is provided that ISEE shall use its "Best Efforts"[33] to launch *Environsat* in accordance with the "Launch Mission". This Article lays down the limits of launch provider's obligations under the contract. The term "Best Efforts" enables ISEE, as a reasonably prudent launch provider, to choose the most appropriate manner to accomplish the services, as far as the task is carried on in accordance with the "Launch Mission", that is, for the purposes of enabling the *Environsat* satellite to carry out its operational objectives. Since neither the launch contract nor its technical annexes specified how the separation of *Progyia* launch vehicle would occur, the operations relating to the separation were included in the services to be performed in the manner ISEE found most appropriate. All operations performed by ISEE relating to the separation of the launch vehicle to ensure that the *Environsat* could carry out its operational objectives fall within the definition of "Launch Services", including the subsequent collision avoidance and re-orbit assist maneuvers.

According to Article 15 of the launch contract the waiver of claims regime extends to all damage resulting from "Launch Services".[34] When the definitions explained above are borne in mind it is clear that the intended collision avoidance and re-orbit assist maneuvers are included in the "Launch Services" provided under the contract, and hence, governed by the waiver of claims regime in the ISEE-MI launch contract.

Here a reference may be made to Martin Marietta v. INTELSAT[35], a case where the facts of the case resemble those of the present case. Although Martin Marietta v. INTELSAT is a national case, it has a particular significance for space law in general since most operations in space are performed by the USA.[36] This is specially true since jurisprudence has not acquired any significance in space law on public international level.[37]

The facts of the case run as follows. To put it shortly, Martin Marietta had contracted with INTELSAT for the launching of two satellites on Titan III rockets. One of them failed to separate from the launch vehicle when it was supposed to, due to Martin Marietta's wiring mistake. Eventually INTELSAT separated the satellite from the launch vehicle, but the process of doing so made it impossible for the satellite to attain its proper orbit, which resulted in a substantial loss for INTELSAT.[38]

In the launch contract Martin Marietta had contracted to make its "Best Efforts" to furnish "Launch Services" for the purpose of delivering INTELSAT's payload into orbit. The definition of the "Best Efforts" is similar to that in the ISEE-MI launch contract. The waiver of claims was made in respect of damage arising out of or incident to the Launch Services, and it was provided that following any launch under the contract the sole and exclusive remedy of the buyer from Martin Marietta, in the event the mission fails for any reason, shall be a replacement launch.[39] One of the arguments of INTELSAT was that it did not claim for "mission failure", but for failure of separation of the payload and booster, and thus the replacement launch was not the sole and exclusive remedy available.

Before the decision of the Court of Appeals is discussed, it is important to note that the decision is given as an answer to a motion to dismiss, and not made impartially considering the arguments of both the parties, but the claims of the non-moving party (INTELSAT) are construed in the light most favorable to it and its allegations taken as true.[40] Bearing this in mind the finding of the Court of Appeals that "*while, as a matter of common sense, it seem reasonable to label what happened as a "mission failure"...with the parties contract silent on this point* (whether the failure was a "mission failure" or not), *the district court erred in granting Martin Marietta's motion to dismiss*", does not in any way support the view that the failure did not actually fall within the scope of a "mission failure". On the contrary, the implicit message in the judgment is that, even though the contract may not be free of ambiguity, if it was interpreted impartially taking into account the arguments of both the parties, the finding would be that the failure is regarded as a "mission failure". Accordingly, for the present purposes Martin Marietta v. INTELSAT shall be seen as a precedent supporting the Respondent States' opinion that the collision avoidance and re-orbit assist maneuvers are operations within the "Launch Services."

4.3 The Limitation of Liability Provision Does Not in Any Way Affect the Waiver of Claims Regime in the ISEE-MI Launch Contract

In Martin Marietta v. INTELSAT case[41] the Court found that the contract did not prevent INTELSAT from presenting any claims at all since the Court found that the interplay between the three risk allocation provisions was ambiguous.[42] The ambiguity between the relevant articles was due to the fact that both the "waiver of claims" article and the "limitation of liability" article referred to damage resulting from "Launch Services". In ISEE-MI launch contract there is no such ambiguity between the "waiver of claims" provision in Article 15, "refund of launch price" provision in Article 13 and "limitation of liability" provision in Article 17.[43] The distinct nature of Articles 13 and 15 has already been explained above[44]. Article 17 does not in any way affect these Articles. All the three Articles are independent and have their separate scope of application. Article 13 applies in cases of failure to accomplish the "Launch Mission", Article 15 in cases where damage has been suffered as a result of "Launch Services" and Article 17 in cases of claims arising in respect of a particular "Launch"[45]. As an example, Article 17 would apply to the case of ISEE's refusal to go forward. In this situation damage to MI might be possible although it is not a result from the "Launch Services". As stated earlier, the collision avoidance and re-orbit assist maneuvers are services provided under the contract, and thus, outside the scope of Article 17.

Accordingly, Article 17 does not in any way affect the waiver of claims regime in Article 15.

4.4 The Waiver of Claims extends to the insurers of MI

The waiver of claims regime in the ISEE-MI launch contract extends also to claims of the insurers of the Customer. It is a general principle of law that an insurer who indemnifies the person who has suffered damage acquires the insured's rights against the wrong-doer.[46] Subrogation may be regarded as a form of representation and thus the insurer have only the same rights as the insured.

Therefore, a waiver binding on the insured is also binding on the insurer.

4.5 The Contractual Waivers Shall Be Enforced Even in Case of Negligence or Gross Negligence

The interparty waivers of the ISEE-MI launch contract shall be enforced also in cases of negligence or gross negligence. In the "waiver of claims" Article[47] it is stated that "this provision applies regardless of whether the claim araises under tort, contract or any other theory of liability". Pursuant to this provision Parlivia assumed the risk of loss to its property howsoever caused, including negligence and gross negligence and bars any and all recovery by Parlivia for its losses howsoever caused.

Although it is recognized thatthe law of some States does not permit parties to exclude liability for gross negligence, this does not bar the enforcement With respect to the tort liability question it has to be noted that the insurer cannot allege stict liability when the damage is essentially economic in nature. Here again, in lack of international precedents, a reference may be made to an U.S. national case. In the Appalachian Insurance Co. v. McDonnell Douglas Corp. Case[48] the Court of Appeals stated that strict liability in tort is not available as a legal basis in a commercial setting. The Court declared that the underlying purpose of this doctrine "was to provide a remedy for injury to the customers injured by defective products" and that "when a law suit over a product arises in a commercial setting and involves only a business loss...the strict liability theory is not available"...

5. Parlivia may not claim in respect of the satellite loss

5.1 MI Has Already Received Compensation for the Damage

The Government of Parlivia has asserted claims on behalf of MI and SISA against the Governments of Californium, *et al.* claiming $90 million for the loss of the satellite, $50 million for the launch price and $20 million for the loss of revenues. However, MI has already received compensation from the insurance underwriters of the entire value of the satellite ($90 million). Based on two general principles of law, Parlivia may not claim for satellite loss on behalf of MI. *First of all,* in international law double compensation for same damage is not accepted.[49] *Second,* it is a general principle of law that when the insurer has paid in respect of a damage the right to claim compensation from the wrong-doer is transferred to the insurer.[50] Accordingly, Parlivia is not entitled to present claims in respect of the satellite loss on behalf of MI, since MI has already been compensated by the insurance underwriters to whom the right to claim for the damages has been transferred.

5.2 The Insurers May Claim Only If the Loss Is of Sufficiently Abnormal Character

Since the right to present claims in respect of the satellite loss has been transferred to the insurance underwriters, Parlivia may present claims only on behalf the insurers. A rule of customary international law is that States are entitled to present claims only on behalf of their nationals.[51] The right of diplomatic protection of a corporate entity is attributed to the State under the laws of which it is incorporated and in whose territory it has its registered office.[52] SISA is a group of insurance underwriters registered in Parlivia, and thus, Parlivia has the right to present claims on behalf SISA, but only on behalf of SISA, not on behalf of the other insurance underwriters.[53]

However, the right of the insurers to present claims is limited to situations where the loss is of sufficiently abnormal character.[54] This rule is based on the professional character of the insurers. They have been paid premium for taking upon themselves the risk which produced the loss. In normal situations the insurer discounts in advance the economics of its risk.[55] The collision between the satellite and debris may not be regarded as a loss of a sufficiently abnormal character under an insurance policy of launch and in-orbit insurance. It is a well known fact that space debris constitutes one of the greatest risk for space objects.

Thus, Parlivia is not entitled to claim for the satellite loss.

6. Damages recovered under the Liability Convention may not include loss of revenues

*6.1 As the Recoverable Damages Shall Be Determined In Each Case Individually Applying the Principles of Equity and Unjust Enrichment_*

In Liability Convention damage has been defined as loss of or damage to property.[56] In other words, indemnification shall be granted of the whole real damage caused, but only of existing damage, not of a potential one.[57] The wording of the Article does not give any guidance of whether loss of revenues shall be included in the recoverable damages. Thus, a recourse may be made to the *travaux préparatoires* of the Convention to clarify the meaning of the term damage.[58] During the discussions on the subject in the Legal Sub-Committee of the COPUOS the majority of States thought that the question, what exactly is included in the recoverable damages, should be left open to be dealt with as individual cases arose.[59] It has been concluded that this leaves the measure of damage to be "decided in each case by the parties concerned".[60] This allows a reference to be made to the ISEE-MI launch contract, which expressly provides that ISEE's liability shall not in any case include any loss of use or loss of profit or revenue or any other indirect, special, consequential, or incidental damages.[61] This provision clearly shows that the intention of the parties has been to exclude the loss of revenues from the scope of liability.

Further, both the Preamble and Article XII of the Liability Convention refer to the notion of equity in relation to the measurement of the compensation under the Convention.[62] With equity's central concern for fairness and justice, substantial attention has to be given to the circumstance of unjust enrichment.[63] In the present case awarding compensation for loss of revenues under the Liability Convention would serve as a source of profit for Parlivia since the nationals on whose behalf the claims are presented had not been entitled to such compensation in their contractual relationship. Thus, the rule of unjust enrichment prevents Parlivia's recovery of loss of revenues.

6.2 The "Victim Oriented" Interpretation Is Not Applicable to the Present Case

Since it may be anticipated that Parlivia will invoke the "victim oriented" character of the Convention to establish that loss of revenues shall be included in recoverable damages, it has to be noted that this argument does not have any relevance in the present case. The analysis of the "victim orientation" of the convention[64] are founded on the necessity of protecting innocent third parties in a situation where there is a need to balance the danger to an individual against the benefit obtained of the exploration or exploitation of outer space.[65] In this case there is no innocent third parties involved. Both ISEE and MI are sophisticated parties involved in commercial space activities - both obtaining benefit of exploration and exploitation of outer space - and as such well aware of the risks involved.[66] Accordingly, since the "victim oriented" interpretation does not apply to the present case there is no ground for interpreting the term "damage" beyond its intended meaning.

6.3 International Law Does Not Protect Speculative Expectations

As a secondary argument, Californium, *et al.* wish to present that, even if this Court would find that loss of revenues could be recovered under the Liability Convention, international law does not protect speculative expectations. In cases where damages have been awarded for loss of revenues it has been clearly stated that the revenues must have been reasonably foreseeable.[67] In case of data acquired through remote sensing there are too many uncertain links to allow the possible revenues to be defined as reasonably foreseeable. First of all, there is no certainty of whether the data acquired will be of any economic value at all, and secondly, it would be even more uncertain whether the foreign governments would be willing to buy such information.

Hence, loss of revenues shall not be recovered under the Liability Convention.

7. Refund of the launch price may not be included in the recoverable damages

7.1 Refund of the Launch Price May Not Be Included in the Damages Recovered under the Launch Cotract

As stated earlier, the Liability Convention deals only with third party liability. In the present case the interparty liability has been defined in the ISEE-MI launch contract which provides the "Refund of the Launch Price" only in cases of a "Launch Failure", that is, a failure to accomplish the "Launch Mission". As shown above in the present case the "Launch Mission" was successfully accomplished and *Environsat* placed in its intended orbit. Accordingly, Parlivia is not entitled to the contractual refund of the launch price.

7.2 Refund of the Launch Price May Not Be Included in the Damages Recovered under the Liability Convention

7.2.1 Under the Liability Convention the Damages Shall Be Determined as to Re-establish the Condition Prior to the Accident

According to the Liability Convention, the compensation shall be determined as to restore the victim to the condition which would have existed if the damage had not occurred.[68] The condition which would have existed is the condition prior to the collision, *status quo ante*.[69] At the moment prior to the collision *Environsat* had been successfully launched and had functioned for more than three months in its intended equatorial orbit. During that period of time Parlivia had been able to use the satellite for the purposes for which it was intended. Since the actual lauch was successfully accomplished Parlivia had obtained value for the paid launch price when the damage occurred, and the value of the launch price was not lost as a result of the collision. Hence, *restitutio status quo ante* does not allow recovery of the launch price.

7.2.2 The Rules of Equity and Unjust Enrichment Shall Be Applied

Here also what was said above about the principles of equity and unjust enrichment, applies.[70] As stated earlier, MI is not entitled to the contractual "Refund" since the "Launch Mission" was successfully accomplished. Should this Court award Parlivia damages including the refund of the launch price, such compensation would serve as a source of profit for Parlivia by placing it to a situation better than that determined in accordance with the launch contract, and thus, would be against the principle of unjust enrichment.

Furthermore, if the refund of the launch price was included in the damages recovered under the Liability Convention, the compensation would be unequitable also in the sense that the measure of damages would be dependent, not on the real damage suffered, but on the fact who caused the damage. It is clear that the launch price could not be recovered if the damage had been caused by debris from a space object of some other launching State. The purpose of the compensation under the Liability Convention is to compensate the damage suffered by the claimant, not to punish the launching State. It would not be equitable to include the refund of the launch price to the damages recovered only on the basis that the damage was caused by the States who launched the damaged space object.

Hence, refund of the launch price may not be included to damages recovered under the Liability Convention.

8. Only launching states are liable under the Liability Convention

8.1 Liability for Damage by Space Objects is Different from the International Responsibility of States for Space Activities

According to the Outer Space Treaty States are responsible for the national activities in outer space, whether carried out by governmental or non-governmental entities.[71] However the international liability for damage caused by space objects is completelly different from the international responsibility of States for space activities.[72] A state must have jurisdiction and contol over a space object for it to be held internationally responsible for the conduct of the activities of the space object and its personel. To hold a State liable for damage caused by its space object, however, simply requires it to be a launching State.[73]

8.2 Only Parlivia and Patalia May Be Regarded As Launching States Under the Liability Convention

Both Article VII of the Outer Space Treaty and Article I(c) of the Liability Convention provide for four criteria of possible launching States: a State which launches, a State which procures the launch, a State from whose territory the space object is launched, and a State from whose facility the space object is launched. Although activities of private entities have not been mentioned in the liability provisions of the Outer Space Treaty or the Liability Convention there is no doubt that the liability provisions are applicable also to private enterprises[74], but this doess not mean that the liable State would necessarily be the State of nationality of the enterprice. Most authors seem to favour the view that a State has to be at least somehow actively involved by requesting, initiating or at least promoting the launching of a particular space object in order to consider him as having "procured" the launching.[75] This must applie also to the first criterion of a launching State, that is the State which launches the Space object. Accordingly, only Parlivia may be regarded as a State which launched or procured the launching of the space object.

Another State which may be regarded as a launching State under the criteria of Liability Convention and Article VII of the Outer Space Treaty is Patalia as the State from whose territory and facility the launch took place.

Therefore, only Parlivia and Patalia may, as launching States, be liable under the Liability Convention.

9. None of the respondent states is liable to pay compensation in the present case

Assuming that the Court finds that ISEE's conduct of the launch operations meet the standard of fault, the contention of the Respondent States is that none of the four Respondent

States is liable to pay compensation to Parlivia. As stated above the only possible liable States are Parlivia and Patalia. However, in Article III of the Liability Convention it is provided that the launching States are liable to pay compensation only if the damage is due to its fault or the fault of the persons for whom it is responsible. Since neither of the launching States is internationally responsible for the conducts of ISEE no liability under the Liability Convention may be established.

SUBMISSIONS TO THE COURT

On the basis of the evidence and legal argument presented in this Memorial, the Governments of the Republic of Californium, the Republic of Ukrastan, the Commonwealth of the Pleasant Islands and the Kingdom of Patalia respectfully request the Court to adjudge and declare

(1) that the Liability Convention does not apply to the present case;
(2) that Parlivia as a launching State may not present claims under the Liability Convention on behalf of its nationals;
(3) that Parlivia may not present claims under the Liability Convention in respect of the same damage for which a claim is being pursued in arbitration;
(4) that Californium et al. is not liable for damage caused by space debris;
(5) that the waiver of claims regime in the ISEE-MI launch contract precludes Parliviafs recovery of the satellite loss;
(6) that Parlivia lacks the legal interest to claim for satellite loss;
(7) that loss of revenues and the refund of the launch price shall not be included in damages recovered under the Liability Convention;
(8) that only the launching States are liable under theLiability Convention;
(9) that none of the Respondent States is liable to pay compensation in the present case;

The Republic of Californium, the Republic of Ukrastan, the Commonwealth of the Pleasant Islands and the Kingdom of Patalia avail themselves this opportunity to renew to the Honourable Court the assurance of their highest consideration and undertake to promptly comply with the decision and enforce it with all available measures in order to promote justice and peace in international relations.

---

[1] Rules Art. 79; Rosenne 1985 p. 447.

[2] Meredith & Robinson 1993 p. 267.

[3] von der Dunk 1996.

[4] Liability Convention Art. I(d). (Actually, according to the wording of Article I(d) of the Convention it is possible to say that the small fragments from the exploded Progyia launch vehicle are included in the satellite as a space object - an interpretation which makes it possible to say that in the present case the space object caused damage to itself!)

[5] Hobe 1992 p. 197.

[6] Here it has to be noted that although Canada based its Cosmos 954 Legal Claim 1979 (p. 905) on the Liability Convention the Soviet Union never recognized its liability and agreed to pay only as "in full and final settlement of all matters connected with the disintegration" of Cosmos 954. *i.e.* the payment was made *ex gratia*, not as a compensation based on liability under the Liability Convention. See Canada-Soviet Union Protocol on Settlement 1981 p. 689.

[7] Vienna Convention Art 32.

[8] The space object debate as cited in Christol 1984 p. 84.

[9] Baker 1988 p. 213; Wirin 1992 p. 50.

[10] See *e.g.* Bedjaoui 1987 p. 361; Gorove 1983 p. 375; Stamps 1990 p. 154.

[11] Christol 1980 p. 351. In general international law the principle of proximate causality has been stated simply as that of normal consequences. See e.g. the Antippa (the Spyros) Case (1926), where the Greco-German Mixed Arbitral Tribunal stated that "according to principles recognized both by municipal and by international law, the indemnity due from one who has caused injury to another comprises all loss which may be considered as *the normal consequence of the act causing the damage*". (Case as cited in Cheng 1987 pp. 248-249, italics added).

[12] Liability Convention Art. VII: " The provisions of this Convention shall not apply to damage caused by space object of one launching State to; (a) Nationals of that launching State."

[13] Liability Convention Art. I(c): "The term "launching State" means: (i) A State which launches or *procures* the launching of a space object; (ii) A State from whose territory or facility a space object is launched (italics added)."

[14] Böckstiegel 1995 p. 81; Matte 1977 p. 163; Christol 1984 p. 115; Hurwitz 1992 p. 22; Gorove 1982 pp. 119-120; Nesgos 1985 p. 102.

[15] Brownlie 1990 p. 480.

[16] Serbian Loans case 1929 p. 41, where the PCIJ decided that "any contract which is not a contract between States in their capacity as subjects of international law is based on the municipal law of some country." See also Saudi Arabia v. Arabian American Oil Co. (Aramco) case 1958 p.165; Horn 1982 p.12; Van Hecke 1984 p. 54; Sucharitkul 1991 p. 355.

[17] IDI Resolution 1979 pp. 193, 195, Art. 1 and Art. 5: "In the absence of any choice by the parties, the proper law of the contract shall be derived from indications of the closest link."; Note here that, although in the Serbian Loans case 1929 p. 42 it was stated that "if one party to the contract is a State there is a presumption that the applicable law is the State's own", the most recent view is that no such presumption exists. See *e.g.* Van Hecke 1984 p. 54; Bowett 1989 p. 53; Lando 1984 p. 391 (and notes there in): "Most Western courts have considered the fact that a State is a partner to be "an element to be considered but no more."". See *e.g.* Rex v. International Trustee Company for the Protection of Bondholders 1937 (England) p. 557.

[18] Lando 1984 p. 319; Van Hecke 1984 p. 54.

[19] See *e.g.* Shaw 1991 p. 433; Sucharitkul 1991 p. 335.

[20] See Lando 1984 pp. 324-325, 385; Diamond 1986 p. 275.

[21] Lando 1984 p. 319, 385: "The law of one of the parties must be preferred...the party should be chosen whose performance is more complex...the obligations of the party who might be described compendiously as the "seller" are generally more complex..." See also Diamond 1986 p. 273-274: "the doctrine of characteristic performance."

[22] Diamond 1986 p. 274: "The obligation to pay money can never be the performance that is characteristic of the contract."

[23] Liability Convention Art. XI(1).

[24] Hurwitz 1992 p. 52; Christol 1980 p. 358; Diederiks-Verschoor 1981 p. 365; Foster 1972 p. 177; Gorove 1991 p. 234.

[25] Brownlie 1990 pp. 497, 499; Finnish Ships Arbitration 1934 ; Interhandel case (Judgment) 1959 p. 27.

[26] Brownlie 1990 p. 506.

[27] García Amador 1961 p. 43; Chorzów Factory case (Merits) 1928 p.49: the method to assess damages was to be performed in a way to "avoid awarding double damages".

[28] Fitzmaurice 1986 p. 597.

[29] See *e.g.* Shaw 1991 pp. 561-562.

[30] Panevezys-Saldutiskis Railway case 1939 p. 16: "it is the bond of nationality between the State and the individual which alone confers upon the State the right of diplomatic protection."

[31] ISEE-MI launch contract Art. 1(9): "Launch Mission" shall mean the launch of the Spacecraft for purposes of enabling said Spacecraft to carry out its operational objectives.

[32] *Id.* Art. 1(11): "Launch Services" shall mean the services to be provided by Launch Provider under this Contract.

[33] *Id.* Art. 1(2): "Best Efforts" shall mean diligently working in a good workman-like manner as a reasonably prudent Launch Provider.

[34] *Id.* Art 15(2): Customer hereby waives any and all claims against the Launch Provider and against Launch Provider's Associates, directors, officers, servants, agents, contractors, and subcontractors, for any property damage it may sustain and for any bodily injury or property damage sustained by its by its own employees *resulting from Launch Services*. This provision applies regardless of whether the claim arises under tort, contract or any other theory of liability (italics added).

[35] Martin Marietta v. INTELSAT case 1991 and 1992.

[36] Diederiks-Verschoor 1993 p. 145; Masson-Zwaan 1994 p. 273.

[37] Malanczuk 1994 p. 163.

[38] Martin Marietta v. INTELSAT case 1991 p. 1329 and 1992 p. 96.

[39] Martin Marietta v. INTELSAT case 1992 p. 96.

[40] Federal Rule of Civil Procedure 12(b)(6), 28 U.S.C.A. See *id.* p. 97.

[41] Martin Marietta *v.* INTELSAT 1992 pp. 96, 98.

[42] *Id.* p. 98.

[43] ISEE-MI launch contract Art. 17(1): "Launch Provider's Liability to Customer and its Associates and contractors and subcontractors, whether arising under contract, tort or any other theory of liability, shall not include any loss of use or loss of profit or revenue or any other indirect, special, consequential, or incidental damages. In no event shall Launch Provider's liability to Customer *for any claim arising out of a particular Launch* exceed the price for Progyia Launch Services as provided for in Article 7, Prices for Launch Services (italics added)."

[44] See pp. 11-12.

[45] ISEE-MI launch contract Art. I(7): "Launch shall mean the intentional ignition of the *Progyia* Launch Vehicle.

[46] See Brownlie 1990 p. 483, where he cites the Federal Insurance Company claim, ILR 26 (1958, II) p. 316, in which the US Foreign Claims Settlement Commission said: "By virtue of [a]...principle, recognized and applied alike by courts of law and equity...an insurer who indemnifies the person who has suffered loss through another's wrong-doing, thereby acquires...assured's rights against the wrong-doer."; Whiteman 1937 p. 1296; Meron 1974 p. 638.

[47] ISEE-MI launch contract Art. 15(2).

[48] Appalachian Insurance Co. v. McDonnell Douglas Corporation Case, Court of Appeal, Fourth District, August 29,1989.

[49] In the Chorzów Factory case 1928 the PCIJ stated that the method to assess damages was to be performed in a way to "avoid awarding double damages". See also Cheng 1987 p. 236; García Amador 1961 p. 43.

[50] *Supra* note 44.

[51] Panevezys-Saldutiskis Railway case 1939 p. 16: "it is the bond of nationality between the State and the individual which alone confers upon the State the right of diplomatic protection."; Geck 1987 p. 103; de Aréchaga & Tanzi 1991 p. 370.

[52] Nottebohm case 1955 : "It is international law which determines whether a State is entitled to exercise protection and to seize the Court."; Barcelona Traction case 1970 p. 42: "The traditional rule attributes the right of diplomatic protection of a corporate entity to the State under the laws of which it is incorporated and in whose territory it has its registered office. These two criteria have been confirmed by long practice and by numerous international instruments."

[53] The third preliminary objection of Bulgaria in the Aerial Incident case (Preliminary Objections) 1959 p. 133, where the Court found that "[w]hereas the Government of Israel can act in defence of its nationals only; whereas it does not dispute that all or part of the damage in respect of which it seeks compensation was covered by insurance; whereas it provides no evidence of the Israel nationality of the insurers...the Government of Israel has no capacity to submit to the Court claims to a right to be indemnified which has been the subject of assignment or subrogation in favor of insurance companies not of Israel nationality."

[54] O'Connell 1970 p. 1051.

[55] O'Connell 1970 p. 1051.

[56] Liability Convention Art. I(a); The term "damage" means loss of life, personal injury or other impairment of health; or loss of or damage to property of States or of persons, natural or juridical, or property of international intergovernmental organizations.; Diederiks-Verschoor 1981 p. 373.

[57] Graefrath 1984 p. 90.

[58] Vienna Convention Art. 32.

[59] Foster 1972 p. 158 note 65 (statements of the Indian delegate, the Japanese delegate, the UK delegate, and the USA delegate); Christol 1984 p. 96; Meredith & Robinson 1993 p. 270.

[60] Matte 1977, as cited in Christol 1984 p. 96.

[61] ISEE-MI launch contract Art. 17(1).

[62] Liability Convention para 4 of the Preamble: "...full and equitable measure of compensation to the victims of such damage."; Art. XII: "The compensation which the launching State shall be liable to pay shall be determined in accordance with international law and the principles of justice and equity."

[63] Christol 1991 p. 271; Cook case 1927 , where the United States-Mexican General Claims Commission found that the reparation should not cause the claimant unjust enrichment; Fabiani case 1896, where the tribunal stated that damages ought not to be a source of profit for the persons who obtain

them.(cases as cited in García Amador Report 1961 p. 44); Whiteman III 1943 p. 1786; Bernardez 1991 p. 383.

[64] Christol 1980 p. 351; Hurwitz 1992 pp. 9, 14; Forkosch 1982 p. 74.

[65] See Hurwitz 1992 p. 79; Zhukov & Kolosov 1984 p. 105; See also Foster 1972 pp. 154-155, where he notes that"[t]he position of both parties in this situation is equal; in undertaking space activities they must implicitly be understood to have accepted the risks involved. Nor is there any reason to favor one launching State over another."

[66] See *e.g.* van Bogaert 1986 p. 167.

[67] Naulilaa Arbitration case 1928 p. 1029; Alabama claims 1872 p. 889 (as cited in Verzijl 1973 p. 754), where the claim for loss of profits was dismissed by the Tribunal on the following ground: "And whereas prospective earnings cannot properly be made the subject of compensation, inasmuch as they depend in their nature upon future and uncertain contingencies."; García Amador 1984 p. 141; Graefrath 1984 p. 96.

[68] Liability Convention Art. XII: The compensation which the launching State shall be liable to pay for damage under this Convention shall be determined in accordance with international law and the principles of justice and equity, in order to provide such reparation in respect of the damage as will restore the person, natural or juridical, State or international organization on whose behalf the claim is presented to the condition which would have existed if the damage had not occurred.; This provision follows the rule promulgated in the Chorzów Factory case (Merits)1928 p. 47.

[69] Diederiks-Verschoor 1981 p. 359.

[70] See *supra* pp. 17-18.

[71] Outer Space Treaty Art. VI; Christol 1984 p. 89; van Bogaert 1986 p. 44; Lachs 1972 p.122; Matte 1984 p.294; Diederiks-Verschoor 1993 p.22; Zhukov & Kolosov 1984 p. 101; Fawcett 1984 p. 25; Bourély 1991 p. 245; Gorove 1983 p. 377.

[72] Wassenbergh 1993 p. 252.

[73] *Id.* p. 250.

[74] Böckstiegel 1995a p. 81.

[75] Böckstiegel 1995a p. 81.

INTERNATIONAL INSTITUTE OF SPACE LAW
OF THE INTERNATIONAL ASTRONAUTICAL FEDERATION
INSTITUT INTERNATIONAL DE DROIT SPATIAL
DE LA FÉDÉRATION ASTRONAUTIQUE INTERNATIONALE

3-5, RUE MARIO-NIKIS
75015 PARIS - FRANCE

Telex IAF 205917 F
Téléphone : (1) 45.67.42.60
Telefax : (33-1) 42.73.21.20

STATUTES

ARTICLE I

The name of the Institute shall be the International Institute of Space Law of the International Astronautical Federation.

ARTICLE II

The purposes and objectives of the Institute shall include:

(a) The providing of advice to the President of the International Astronautical Federation when requested;
(b) Cooperation with appropriate international organizations and national institutions in the field of space law;
(c) The holding of meetings, colloquia and competitions on juridical and social science aspects of space activities, thereby providing forums for individuals from different legal systems and regions of the world to engage in the free expression and exchange of ideas relevant to space law and policy;
(d) The preparation or commissioning of studies and reports;
(e) The publication of books, proceedings, reports and other papers;
(f) The granting and presentation of awards and certificates;
(g) The conduct of such other activities as may be considered desirable in fostering the development of space law and studies of legal and social science aspects of the exploration and use of outer space.

ARTICLE III

Section 1

Individuals distinguished by their contributions to or of proven interest in the field of space law or other social science aspects related to space activities, may be elected as members of the Institute by the Board of Directors upon an application recommended in each case by a Director, or by three members of the Institute.

Section 2

Corporate bodies and other institutions not already members of the International Astronautical Federation, and actively engaged or otherwise interested in the field of space law or other social science aspects related to space activities, may be elected by the Board of Directors as institutional members of the Institute upon an application recommended in each case by a Director, or by three members of the Institute.

Section 3

Election to membership of the Institute shall be by a majority vote of the Board of Directors in attendance at a regular or special meeting of the Board, or by a majority of affirmative answers of the members of the Board if the vote is held by mail.

ARTICLE IV

Section 1

All members of the Institute shall pay annual membership dues in accordance with the Bye-laws. These dues are expressed in terms of units.

Section 2

The Board of Directors shall establish the value of the unit in which membership dues are expressed. Alterations in the value of the unit shall take effect for each member or institutional member at the end of the period for which the relevant membership dues have been paid.

Section 3

Members of the Institute who are in default of their membership fee shall lose the right to vote in an annual or other meeting. Members of the Institute may be removed from the membership of the Institute by decision of the Board of Directors, if they are in arrears of membership dues for more than two years.

Section 4

On cause shown, the Board of Directors may reduce or remit the membership fee for a particular member.

Section 5

The Board of Directors may remove from membership of the Institute any member whom they judge to have violated the principles of the Statutes. Such decisions shall be taken by a two thirds vote of members of the Board present at the meeting at which the decision is taken.

ARTICLE V

Section 1

An annual meeting of the Institute shall be held each year, and special meetings may also be held, at such times and places as the Board of Directors may determine.

Section 2

The Board of Directors shall submit to each annual meeting a report on the activities of the Institute. The report shall outline the events and accomplishments of the preceding year and put forward the policy and projects of the Institute for the future.

Section 3

The annual meeting shall elect from among the members of the Institute, by a majority vote of the members present, officers and members of the Board of Directors, with due regard to the provisions of Article VI, Sections 2 and 3.

ARTICLE VI

Section 1

The governing body of the Institute is the Board of Directors. The officers of the Institute are the President, the two Vice-Presidents, the Secretary and the Treasurer. The President, Presidents Emeriti, two Vice-Presidents, and twelve other members shall be the voting members of the Board. Any Honorary Directors of the Institute and the Presidents of the International Astronautical Federation and of the International Academy of Astronautics ex officio shall be non-voting members of the Board of Directors.

Section 2

The Institute will seek that the membership of the Board of Directors shall reflect and represent the different regions of the world and different legal systems, due regard being paid especially to those countries in which significant space programmes or considerable efforts to develop space law have been made.

Section 3

The officers and members of the Board of Directors shall be elected for a period of three years, and may be re-elected. Members of the Nomination Committee acting in accordance with the Bye-laws, and members of the Institute when electing officers and other members of the Board, shall take account of the desirability of ensuring both a continuity and an adequate rotation of membership within the Board.

Section 4

In the case of a vacancy occurring in the Board between two annual meetings, the Board of Directors may appoint an acting Director to fill the vacancy until the expiry of the relevant term, subject to the approval of the appointment by the next annual meeting.

Section 5

An outgoing President, who has served in that capacity over several years and has contributed substantially to the development and the activities of the Institute, may be elected for life as a President Emeritus.

Section 6

Persons who have made outstanding contributions to international cooperation in the peaceful uses of outer space, or to the development of space law, as well as officers of the Institute and members of the Board of Directors who have served for several succeeding terms and have contributed substantially to the work of the Institute, may be elected as Honorary Directors. They may attend meetings of the Board of Directors in a consultative capacity, but without a right to vote.

ARTICLE VII

Section 1

The President of the Institute shall guide and supervise the activities of the Institute pursuant to its Statutes and in accordance with its Bye-laws. The President shall represent the Institute in its external relations, including those with the International Astronautical Federation.

Section 2

The Board of Directors shall:

(a) Carry out the purposes and objectives of the Institute as set forth in Article II of these Statutes;
(b) Implement the resolutions and directives adopted at the annual meetings of the Institute;
(c) Create standing committees with appropriate terms of reference and powers for their functions;
(d) Create ad hoc committees and working groups for specific purposes and functions;
(e) Appoint members of the Institute to fill vacancies occurring in the membership of the Board of Directors in accordance with Art. VI (4) of these Statutes;
(f) Supervise the correspondence of the Institute and provide for the safekeeping of the archives thereof;
(g) Establish a secretariat as appropriate, designate its duties and supervise all its activities;
(h) Arrange for meetings and colloquia;
(i) Arrange for the publication of books, proceedings, reports and other papers;
(j) Make recommendations concerning the awarding of medals, certificates and prizes;
(k) Approve budgets and supervise accounts;
(l) Accept donations and legacies, and funds from private sources, and contributions from national and international organizations, governments and agencies;
(m) Approve the annual reports of the President and the Treasurer to be presented at the annual meetings of the Institute, and the annual report of the President to be presented at the plenary meeting of the General Assembly of the Federation.

Section 3

At least eight of the voting members of the Board of Directors present at its meeting, including the President or Acting President shall constitute a quorum. Where in exceptional cases a matter has to be decided by mail, the same number of answers shall be required for a valid decision of the Board if a vote is held by mail.

Section 4

Decisions of the Board of Directors shall be taken, so far as possible, by consensus. Where a decision is taken by vote, Directors may cast their votes by mail or other written means as to any action proposed to be taken by the Board. Except where these Statutes and relative Bye-laws provide otherwise, decisions by vote of the Board shall be valid when taken by a majority of members present, or indicating their view in writing. In the case of a tie, the President shall have a casting as well as a deliberative vote.

Section 5

The ordinary affairs of the Board of Directors and of the Institute shall be conducted in accordance with the Bye-laws of the Institute. These Bye-laws shall be adopted by the Institute at an annual or special meeting by a majority vote of its members present upon a recommendation of the Board of Directors.

Section 6

The membership of standing committees, of ad hoc committees and of working groups, shall be determined by the President in consultation with the Board of Directors.

Section 7

The President, in consultation with the Board shall, by the end of April of each year, appoint the Chairman and members of the Nomination Committee responsible for nominating candidates for election as officers or other Board members whose terms of office are to begin after each annual meeting. The Committee shall be composed of not less than three, but not more than five members. The Report of the Nomination Committee shall be submitted to the President not later than one month before the annual meeting.

ARTICLE VIII

Section 1

These Statutes and Bye-laws shall be adopted at a meeting of the Board of Directors by a two-thirds majority vote of all members of the Board, subject to confirmation of this adoption at the next annual meeting of the Institute by a simple majority of members of the Institute present at that meeting.

Section 2

These Statutes and relative Bye-laws may be amended at any meeting of the Board of Directors by a two-thirds majority vote of all members of the Board, subject to confirmation of the amendment at the next annual meeting of the Institute by a simple majority of members of the Institute present at that meeting. All members of the Institute shall be informed of the intention to present such an amendment for confirmation at least six weeks prior to the next annual meeting.

Section 3

The Institute shall not enact Statutes or Bye-laws or amendments to either which are inconsistent with the provisions of the Constitution of the International Astronautical Federation, or its resolutions pertaining to the Institute.

BYE-LAWS

1. The President of the Institute shall preside at meetings of the Institute and of the Board of Directors. If unable to do so, the President may appoint one of the Vice-Presidents, and, if either of them is unable to do so, another member of the Board, to preside at a particular meeting. If the President is unable so to appoint or has not done so in time, a Vice-President, or if necessary another member of the Board, appointed by a majority of the members of the Board present, shall so preside and have the powers of the President for the purpose.

2. The Board of Directors shall endeavour to take decisions by consensus, but, if necessary, voting in the Board of Directors shall be by a show of hands, the President or Secretary informing the meeting of the views of those not present who have notified their view in writing on a matter. Such written views shall, wherever possible, be treated as votes on the matter under discussion.

3. The Board of Directors shall cause minutes to be kept of its meetings and of all actions taken by the Board. Such minutes shall be deposited with the Secretariat of the International Astronautical Federation and any member of the Institute in good standing may inspect them at any reasonable time.

4. A Nomination Committee, itself appointed by the President in consultation with the Board, shall make recommendations to the annual meeting as to elections to the offices of the Institute and membership of the Board of Directors. A person may be elected to the Board of Directors even though his or her name is not included in the list of recommendations made by the Nomination Committee. The Board and members attending shall be informed of the recommendations of the Nomination Committee which shall be made available at the latest by forty-eight hours prior to the annual meeting. In making its recommendations the Nomination Committee shall have regard to the distinction of the contribution made to space law by

potential nominees, as well as to the provisions of Article VI Sections 2 and 3 of the Statutes of the Institute.

5. The responsibilities of the Secretary of the Institute include:

(a) Maintaining the list of members of the Institute;
(b) Maintaining all necessary records, including financial records;
(c) Making arrangements for meetings of the Board;
(d) Taking the minutes of the meetings of the Board, and the annual and other meetings of the Institute;
(e) Depositing copies of the minutes of the Board with the International Astronautical Federation, and with the approval of the Board, making suitable arrangements for, the custody of the records of the Institute;
(f) In consultation with the Board and with the Secretariat of the International Astronautical Federation, making arrangements for the annual and other meetings of the Institute;
(g) Coordinating the Institute's involvement in the preparation of and making arrangements for any moot court or other competition involving or run by the Institute;
(h) Conducting the routine correspondence of the Institute;
(i) Communicating with members of the Institute, including preparing and seeing to the circulation of the Newsletter.

6. The responsibilities of the Treasurer of the Institute include:

(a) Ingathering membership dues and receiving donations and other monies received for or arising from the work of the Institute;
(b) Operating appropriate bank accounts on behalf of the Institute;
(c) Preparing appropriate budgets for approval by the Board;
(d) Paying bills incurred by the Institute or its officers in the carrying out of the purposes of the Institute from monies held by the Institute.

6. The President of the Institute shall refer an application for membership of the Institute to a membership committee, which he shall appoint, and the Board shall be informed of the report of that committee before it decides on the election of the applicant.

7. The Secretary of the Institute shall be informed in writing of any proposals for the amendment of the Statutes or Bye-laws of the Institute, other than those made by the Board, at least twelve weeks prior to the annual meeting, and any such proposal must be supported in writing by at least twenty individual fully paid-up members of the Institute.

8. The annual membership dues payable by an individual member of the Institute shall be one unit of contribution dues. Honorary Directors, if not otherwise members of the Institute, are exempt from the requirement to pay annual membership dues. Corporate or institutional members of the Institute shall pay three or more units of contribution dues of membership dues a year, the level of contribution being selected by the Institutional member in agreement with the Board of Directors.

9. A corporate or institutional member paying three contribution units per year has the right to nominate up to three representatives to vote in the annual meeting. Each additional contribution unit allows the institutional member to nominate one additional such representative.

10. A member of the Institute remains in good standing in the Institute provided that membership dues are not in arrear, and that a current mailing address has been received by the Secretary.

Author Index